THE SEARCH FOR MEANING IN LIFE

Edited by ROBERT F. DAVIDSON

St. Andrews Presbyterian College

THE SEARCH FOR MEANING IN LIFE

Readings in Philosophy

HOLT, RINEHART AND WINSTON · New York
Chicago · San Francisco

Copyright © 1962 by Holt, Rinehart and Winston, Inc.
All Rights Reserved
Library of Congress Card Number: 62–10491
03-011300-8
Printed in the United States of America

90123 4 98

Preface

In recent years the book of readings has become increasingly popular as an aid in the teaching of philosophy and is gradually replacing the conventional textbook in most college and university courses. There is good reason for this. Teachers of philosophy expect their better students to come to grips with the ideas of the great philosophers at firsthand, to wrestle with the interpretation of human life and the universe accepted by the ablest minds of the present and the past, not simply to commit to memory a second-hand interpretation or be able to associate the names of such men as Plato and Aristotle, Spinoza or Kant, with a particular philosophical label. A good book of selections drawn from the works of distinguished philosophers should potentially provide a more effective device for achieving this aim than does the conventional textbook, whether it be historical in organization or centered around major philosophical problems.

When philosophy is taught in this fashion, however, there have been unfortunate losses as well as some desirable gains. With a few notable exceptions the works of the great philosophers present almost insurmountable difficulty for the beginning student. For every such student who is excited by the new insights he finds in these works, there are at least three or four who conclude that philosophy is largely incomprehensible and in desperation turn to other subjects that are more immediately rewarding. Such a situation is, of course, not merely undesirable; it is inexcusable. The study of philosophy should not be dull or uninteresting; it should be exciting and provocative, the most immediately rewarding course in the college curriculum for any student with the intellectual ability expected of him in college. And this can be just as true of a beginning course based upon a book of readings as of one in which a stimulating textbook is used. Indeed when the teacher has the imagination and capacity to arouse student interest and understanding, a good book of readings should provide the more provocative material—provided, of course, that the selections themselves are meaningful and appealing to the beginning student.

It is a need such as this that the present volume is designed to meet. Most of the recent collections of readings in philosophy, despite the fact that they claim to be for the beginning student, still demand a technical vocabulary, a scholarly background, and an interest in abstract theory far beyond that possessed by such readers. In the present volume a determined effort has been made to find selections that not only present major philosophical ideas but present them in a fashion that the beginning student will find both intelligible and interesting. Consequently some writers appear here who are not usually included in anthologies of this kind. Likewise, the selections from the better known philosophers are from works that can be read with profit by the average student. Most important of all perhaps, the book is organized in such fashion as to bring together points of view that are similar, and to move in general from contemporary and simple statements of a position to more developed interpretations by outstanding philosophers both past and present. Because of this, the material included in each of the major sections should gradually build understanding and insight until, as the reader completes the section as a whole, he should have a sound and comprehensive grasp of the position under consideration.

For much the same reason the various selections and the major divisions in the volume are themselves not mutually exclusive. In each of these a significant approach to philosophy is presented, and developed with enough fullness to enable a beginner to understand it. But its meaning and its relation to other important points of view are in each case developed more fully in succeeding selections. The book is organized also so that the student's introduction to philosophy will be made at a point closest to his own experience and his vital concerns. He is then led gradually to consideration of more difficult and complex problems farther removed from his own immediate interests. But in no case are these interests lost sight of. The final test of the worth of the book must be found in the contribution it makes to the thought and the working philosophy of those who use it.

It is a pleasure to be able to express here my gratitude to those who have helped me in the preparation of this volume. I am especially indebted to my colleagues at the University of Florida who have made many helpful suggestions in the selection and organization of the material included. While those to whom I have turned here for assistance are too numerous to recognize individually, I must mention the assistance given me by Professor Allison Lewis without whose thoughtful suggestions a number of the more stimulating selections would not have found their way into this anthology. I also want to take this opportunity to express my thanks to the many men in other institutions who have used my *Philosophies Men Live By* as a text during the past ten years; from their generous comments and suggestions the organization and contents of this volume have greatly profited. I am much indebted likewise to Duke University for its kindness in making available the facilities of its library and especially to Dr. B. E. Powell, the Duke University librarian, for assistance during the summer of 1960.

R. F. D.

January, 1962
Gainesville, Florida

Contents

3. The Implications of Naturalism — 157

4. The Pilgrimage of the Pragmatist — 235

THE SEARCH FOR MEANING IN LIFE

The Philosopher
in an Age of Crisis:
An Introduction

The fact that we live today in a time of crisis needs no elaboration; evidences are
too apparent on every hand. An age of crisis, however, can well be a creative age.
The development of Western civilization is marked by a number of creative
periods in which there has been fundamental social and political change. The Age
of Pericles in Athens, the Italian Renaissance, the French Revolution with its
Reign of Terror are but more obvious examples; the crisis of our age may well be
another of the great turning points in the history of Western civilization. In our
cold war today the democratic way of life and human freedom as we understand it
are threatened with destruction in a world-wide life-and-death struggle with
militant communism. And the dangers inherent in this conflict are rendered more
formidable by the means of destruction now in the hands of both contestants. In
America we are more keenly aware of the present crisis, of course, because the
United States finds itself in the unexpected and unintended role of world leader in
the defense of Western civilization.

We are confronted, however, not only with a crisis in our civilization, but
with a crisis in human life itself. The basic values of human personality as we
conceive them—man's integrity, his freedom to think and to speak, his worth as an
individual—are being subjected to such increasing restraint that man's very existence as a person is threatened. This is not a crisis that can be solved by further
developments in science or technology; indeed these developments are among the
major causes of the crisis. Nor is it a crisis that can be solved by new political align-
ments or a more realistic or constructive foreign policy. It is an existential crisis, a
crisis that concerns the very meaning of human life itself, and for this reason it is a
crisis in which the philosopher can and should offer significant assistance.[1]

Without some clear sense of meaning and purpose in life, without some firm
commitment to human freedom, to the life of reason, to the worth and dignity of

---

[1] See Adrienne Koch, *Philosophy for a Time of Crisis*, (New York, E. P. Dutton
and Co., 1953), to which the present introduction is much indebted.

the individual, we cannot hope to meet successfully the uncertainty and danger of our day. Philosophy is deeply concerned with just this problem—more so than science, more so than statesmanship or politics, in a different way than art or poetry. The philosopher alone refuses to recognize boundaries which he must not cross in this search for meaning in life; he alone undertakes to cultivate the kind of integration, of synthesis, of perspective that is essential. Only religion is as directly concerned as is philosophy; and for this reason the insights of religion must be given special consideration in any search for life's meaning.

There is at present, and indeed since the time of Plato there has been, a widespread view that philosophy is at best an academic and intellectual pursuit, largely irrelevant to the vital concerns of living. This view has been given added weight in recent years by the increasing preoccupation of a number of American as well as British professional philosophers with logical positivism and with the formal techniques of linguistic analysis. The proper task of philosophy, as they interpret it, lies largely in re-examining and clarifying both ordinary and scientific language, in determining the kind of statements that are "meaningful" from this point of view, and in demonstrating the "meaninglessness" of most previous philosophy.[2] There is also the more traditional and established view of philosophy in its literal meaning, "a love of wisdom," a view that goes back to the great Greek philosophers with whom the philosophical enterprise as an independent professional undertaking originated. Here in Socrates we see the living example and symbol in our Western civilization of the philosopher at his best, of philosophy as a profession of faith and a deep personal commitment to human values. It is to philosophy in this sense that our search for meaning in life must necessarily be directed.

Without any question, the history of philosophy can help illuminate our present predicament. An acquaintance with the thought of the great philosophers should make it possible for us to be more intelligent and more explicit about what we seek and value today. We can learn much from what the great minds of the past have believed about the nature of man and of the world in which he must work out his destiny. Here also we find insights into the nature of the good life and the good society. Truth, of course, does not come to us from the authority of the past; it can be reached only through a searching criticism and testing that must be a continuous contemporary concern. But this we cannot carry out successfully in ignorance of the insights that constitute our intellectual heritage.

If we can learn from the great philosophers of the past, we must learn also— perhaps we must learn more—from those contemporary thinkers who have been wrestling with the problems of our age and seeking, with the help of the best traditions of the past, to meet the needs of men and women in our day. The ablest contemporary philosophers are all aware of the existential situation that we confront. They bring to it an historical perspective superior to any that has existed

---

[2] A more sympathetic view of analytical philosophy is presented in Morton White's essay, "New Horizons in Philosophy," included here in Part IV.

heretofore. Developments in the sciences have given us a greater knowledge of our universe than man has ever had; the study of anthropology and of depth psychology has given us a new understanding of man himself and of the complex forces at work in the total human personality. With such insights as these, our age must fashion its own understanding of human existence and find for itself a meaning in life that can enable thoughtful men and women to meet successfully the crisis we face. In the light of this understanding, perhaps we may be able not only to re-fashion our lives, but also to some extent to help shape the history of our age.

The dimension of the tasks described in the above paragraph is aptly suggested by a recent and striking portrayal of the sort of material with which we have to work. Man, writes one of the most discerning of contemporary philosophers, "as we have come to know him through the efforts of poets and sages, is a complex, burdened, pitiful, and wonderful creature. He may be the paragon of animals, of noble reason and of infinite faculty; in action he may be like an angel and in apprehension like a god; but he is also a petulant thinking reed and a hopeless mess. He is in love with life but also hates it deeply and subtly. He is capable of crime and sin but also has a tyrannical and whimsical conscience that tortures him for trivial misdemeanors as brutally as it punishes him for unpardonable sins. Narcissistic, he hates himself; full of insufferable vanity, he seeks to humiliate himself; the victim of systematic self-deception, he is capable of unsparing self-knowledge. But, above all, in what he wants he is hopelessly confused, vague, half-deceived, inconsistent, and divided. Nothing, I suspect, would give him a worse sense of misery and of guilt than letting him have all that he wants. In any case it would take an Augustine, a Freud, a Dostoievski, a Kierkegaard, and a Shakespeare, aided by a Boas and a Machiavelli, pooling their several talents and techniques, to split open the secret heart of this contemptible lump of living clay and extract its wonderful essence."[3]

The readings in this book bring together significant statements by leading thinkers of the Western World who have sought to appraise the nature of man and the problems of personal and social living, and to frame a philosophy that would clarify the meaning and purpose of human life and contribute to its enrichment. The insights of the great philosophers of the past are set in conjunction with those of abler thinkers of our own day who have been attracted to much the same points of view. Consequently, the major approaches to philosophy as a way of thinking and of living form the framework of the volume, not historical sequence or chronological development. In this way the student is confronted with an authoritative discussion of life's significant alternatives, alternatives with which he himself must sooner or later come to terms. The point of view of the editor cannot but influence both the general organization and the selection of particular materials, but a serious and sustained effort has been made to find appealing and effective

---

[3] Eliseo Vivas, *The Moral Life and the Ethical Life,* (Chicago, Univ. of Chicago Press, Copyright 1950 by the University of Chicago), p. 60.

statements of each position by philosophers who themselves accept and advocate it.

Certain other criteria have also been employed in making these selections. Content, of course, has been a major concern. Each of the philosophers included here has won recognition and prestige the hard way. His is a mind the intelligent and informed student should be acquainted with; he has something of importance to say to men and women in our age. But within this broad framework, the ability to communicate has also been given consideration. Does the author say what he has to say in a way that the intelligent and serious reader who is not a specialist can understand? In so far as possible a nontechnical, concrete, and interesting presentation has been sought in each case. The great philosophers all have something to say about the meaning of human life that we ought to know, but too often only other philosophers can understand what it is. There is no excuse, however, for the student's first impression of philosophy being one of confusion and disappointment in the face of technical terminology that he does not understand or abstract ideas far removed from the issues of living as he knows them in his own experience. A major purpose of this volume is to make the insights of the great philosophers available to the nonspecialist, the thoughtful layman and the beginning student. Enough biographical and historical background has, therefore, been provided to portray the individual men as real and human. Philosophy is not abstract reason incarnate. Where the thought of important figures in the history of philosophy is apt to be too difficult, enough interpretation of the position itself has been given to enable the beginning student to find the selection meaningful.

Finally, a wide range of significant points of view are included so that something like the intellectual landscape as a whole can be seen. The beginning student will meet the major figures in the history of Western philosophy as well as many of the more thoughtful and stimulating among contemporary philosophers. Here then are a distinguished group of men who make philosophy come alive. They present it, not as a scheme of dry and abstract categories, but as a living and informed vision—a positive faith that can well enhance the dignity and the meaning of life for thoughtful men and women in our disturbed and perplexed generation.

The Philosopher and the Human Situation:
Gabriel Marcel

No group of contemporary philosophers is more conscious of the vital importance of the search for meaning in human life than the existentialists. As a matter of fact, it has been this concern more than any other that gave rise to existentialism and made it one of the dominant forces in contemporary thought. Gabriel Marcel is today the most prominent French advocate of Christian existentialism;[4] many in-

---

[4] Not to be confused with the secular or atheistic existentialism with which the thought of Jean-Paul Sartre is so largely identified in France.

deed consider him the most outstanding living exponent of this position. The task of the philosopher, as he describes it much in the spirit of Socrates, is to "illuminate the human situation."

Modern man, Marcel feels, has cut himself off from the grounds of creativity, of freedom and meaning in life. Our technical civilization tends to stifle what is distinctly human in all of us; the disturbing psychological and sociological conditions of our age are the result. Man's deepest spiritual needs are being ignored. The individual tends to appear to himself and to others as merely "an agglomeration of functions." Marcel uses the conductor on a subway to illustrate this point. To others, even to himself, such a man becomes virtually identical with his functions. His existence is almost completely routinized. It is like a timetable. His job, his role as a member of a union, his voting, even his eating and sleeping—all are mapped out for him. An expert on personal relations specifies how much recreation he needs, what kind and at what hours, if he is to function well as a conductor. And when he dies, the company replaces him much as it does any other piece of worn out machinery. His *existence* is empty, meaningless.

How can man confront this kind of human situation, this "being-in-the-world" in a particular time and place with all the limitations it imposes upon him, and make it the starting point for becoming a significant human person? Here, for Marcel, is the essential question upon which the achievement of meaning and significance in human life depends; it is the question to which the philosopher must address himself. The answer for the existentialist cannot be found in the abstract, in a theory of any kind. Philosophical rationalism can be of little help. Only in steady contact wth everyday life, in personal engagement with concrete reality, and ultimately for Marcel, in a personal act of faith, can man find an answer.

Born in Paris in 1889, Marcel lost his mother when he was only four years of age. His father, an official in the French government, was for a time French ambassador at Stockholm and later director of the National Library and Art Galleries in Paris. He was a typical agnostic of that age to whom religion appeared antiquated and riddled with absurd superstitions. Marcel was raised by an aunt who was a Jewess, but whose family had renounced its religious beliefs. She shared his father's agnosticism and he grew up, he says, in an atmosphere of instability and insecurity. The lonely years of his early youth were certainly instrumental in turning him toward the philosophical position that later became Christian existentialism. At the age of eight he wrote his first two plays and thereafter the theatre never lost its fascination for him. In his plays, as in his later philosophical writing, the nature of man and of human existence is his primary concern. Human loneliness, misunderstanding, and disappointed love together with a longing for friendship, understanding, and fidelity find expression with equal force in both his drama and his philosophy.

Although he was an excellent student, Marcel was repelled by the academic life as he knew it in France. Too much importance was attached to grades, creativity was stifled, and the individual was not valued for himself. When he was constantly asked at home about his grades and the prizes he had won, he came to feel that he himself was somehow not appreciated. The methods of instruction used in the classroom likewise repelled him. The appeal of great books was destroyed by minute analysis, he felt, when they should have been made interesting and attractive. Traveling extensively with his father, Marcel visited all the well-known cultural and artistic centers of Europe and familiarized himself with the great German and Anglo-Saxon writers of the present as well as the past. At eighteen he wrote an academic thesis on "The Metaphysical Ideas of Coleridge and Their Relationship to the Philosophy of Schelling" (1908). This thesis enabled him to secure a position teaching philosophy two years later and also introduced him to germinal ideas in existentialism. (Schelling is now generally regarded as the philosopher to whom existentialism in modern philosophy owes its origin.)

Off and on for the next thirty years, Marcel taught philosophy at various schools and colleges in France, but much of his time and effort was devoted to literary research and creative writing. During World War I, he served with the Red Cross and was given the duty of searching for missing persons, a task that involved him deeply in the drama and tragedy of human existence. He was particularly repelled by the callousness with which people became no more than data on a filing card, to be moved back and forth as other information was secured. The shock of World War I also gave new urgency to his philosophy because it made him realize how very precarious were the material and cultural conditions of life that had seemed so secure. He was never happy with the idea of the philosopher as a college professor, confined to the academic life.

Gradually Marcel's mature Christian existentialism took shape in his thinking. His *Metaphysical Journal,* one of his earliest books written in 1914, consists of reflections on particular situations, events, issues. This already indicates clearly the approach he prefers to philosophy. His instinct as a playwright also keeps him close to concrete situations and particular individuals. In 1928, as a member of the French Society of Philosophy, Marcel vigorously defended the validity of religious faith against attacks being made upon it. Not long afterwards he received a letter about this controversy from a prominent French Catholic writer which ended with the question, "Why after all, are you not one of us?" This incident brought home to Marcel with particular forcefulness the whole question of religious commitment and shortly thereafter (in 1929) he became a member of the Catholic Church. He has retained his intellectual independence, however, and regards his work as strictly philosophical. Quite frequently he is critical of the accepted Thomistic theology, and he always gives the impression of pursuing his convictions wherever they may lead, without worrying about whether or not the outcome is in accord with the orthodox position of his church.

In recent years Marcel has achieved marked distinction in contemporary philosophical circles. He has lectured widely throughout Europe, in 1949–1950 delivering the Gifford Lectures in Scotland perhaps the highest distinction for a philosopher in the English-speaking world. These lectures, entitled *The Mystery of Being,* are among his most significant philosophical writings. What Marcel means by "Being" is best seen in his reaction to the whole pattern of contemporary life. Our existence has become basically empty. The need to find meaning in life reflects our need for Being. Where speculative reason fails to find a satisfying answer, the *act of faith* rescues the individual from the anxiety and perplexity of day-to-day living. In the act of faith, man not only accepts and fulfills the destiny prescribed for him by his particular human situation, but in his union with the transcendent source of Being, all the previously meaningless facts are understood "existentially," that is, as meaningful aspects of the significant human person. The whole self is involved in the act of commitment that establishes the reality of the person. Such an act of faith thus marks the beginning both of genuine human personality and of human freedom. Here is found the element of transcendence that takes man beyond the limitations of his own human situation; here man is restored to that unity of being of which he was deprived by scientific rationalism and an industrial society. Marcel says that, as he looks back on it, he now realizes that he was trying in his early philosophy to find an existential core of meaning in religious faith which could not be explained away by psychology and sociology.

It is clear, of course, that Marcel is brought by his religious existentialism into direct conflict with modern scientific thought. The essential limitation of scientific knowledge lies for him in its objectivity. Such knowledge can be cut asunder from the experience of the man who grasped it; it is abstract and publicly verifiable. Anyone else, if properly equipped, would get the same results. For the existential philosopher, however, truth cannot be anonymous; it cannot be separated from the inner struggle and spiritual development of the individual. The whole self must be involved in our search for truth—not the reason only. It is the function of such existential truth to "recall man to himself." For Marcel, the scientific outlook and our contemporary technological culture have made our spiritual illness and poverty more acute. These forces tend to cut man's linkage with the inner and deeper ground of meaning in the universe and thus to heighten the emptiness, frustration, anguish of modern life.

In the selection that follows, taken from a recent work entitled, *Man Against Mass Society,* Marcel describes the task of the philosopher in the contemporary world, as he sees it. While there are obvious reflections here of his own existential point of view, this selection is also a fine statement of the particular responsibility of the philosopher as he faces the dangerous forces at work in contemporary life.

The Philosopher and the Contemporary World*

I

In all ages, there has been a tendency to emphasize the dubious or risky role of the philosopher in relation to society in general. It does very much seem as if the philosopher had not such deep roots in the world as the average man, even if it is no longer possible for him to detach himself from the world in the fashion of a pure contemplative withdrawal to a hermit's solitude.

The other side of the picture is that the world, for its part, either refuses to recognize the importance of the philosopher and treats him as a figure of comedy—or, on the other hand, if it does take a philosopher up, works unwearyingly to distort his message and, if I dare put it so, to degrade his proper nature.

We ought to notice, in the first place, that our idea of what a philosopher is has, if we compare it to the ancient idea of a philosopher, suffered in modern times and above all in contemporary times a real degradation; it has been degraded in the same degree to which the notion of wisdom, of *sophia,* has lost, if not its meaning, at least its original power of inspiring veneration. In the last century, the practising philosopher was in the majority of cases reduced to becoming a mere professor of philosophy; this to the horror and indignation of the most free and lucid spirits of that time, such as Nietzsche and Schopenhauer. The professor of philosophy is too often a specialist in some degree intoxicated by his own specialty, who expounds to his students or sometimes to a rather wider public either his system, if by good luck he has one, or else a kind of blending and distillation of other men's systems, or else, what is certainly less compromising, a history of the systems that have

* Gabriel Marcel, *Man Against Mass Society,* English translation by G. S. Fraser, La Colombe Edition and Henry Regnery Company, Chicago, 1952).

preceded his own. One ought also to add, and this point is more important than on the surface it might appear to be, that in many countries, and more particularly in France, the professor of philosophy is liable literally to succumb under the burden of tasks connected with his post which have no specific connection with philosophy, but which have to do with helping an enormous number of students to prepare for and pass examinations.

Under such conditions, it may be said that even the head of a university department who does genuinely remain a philosopher—who retains, I mean, his power of meditation or, at a deeper level still, what one might call his intellectual viginity—can only succeed in doing so at the price of an effort which is literally heroic, and on condition that he leads an almost ascetic life. But such an asceticism, admirable in itself, inevitably exacts a price. The philosopher runs the risk of cutting himself off, in some sense, from life, and of little by little, without being aware of it, substituting for life a realm of thought which is quite his own, a sort of closed and well cared-for garden whose shrubs and bushes he expertly lops and prunes. It may be agreed that there goes with this intellectual horticulture a certain sense of inner freedom: but is such a freedom really very different from that which has been known and enjoyed by prisoners in actual prisons of iron and stone?

From another point of view, it is obvious that so soon as philosophy is conceived in this fashion, as a neat enclosed terrain, its possibilities of working fruitfully outwards are very musch reduced. The philosopher confines himself to looking after a certain piece of property in which he takes, we may say, delight; but he is in danger in very many cases of considering, if not with hostility, at least with distrust, those whom we are forced to call his competitors. Of course, there are large-hearted exceptions. But the danger is there, and it is not one to be underestimated. And this is the source of that feeling of discomfort and sometimes of actual disquiet with which one finds oneself considering these peasant-proprietors in the philosophical domain, and their type of activity. Nevertheless, we ought at once to add that the philosopher who, in the precisely contrary case, seeks out huge audiences, multiplies his impact by means of the press and the radio, and plays, if I dare to put it so, the part of a little Jack Horner with a finger in every pie, though he avoids the particular kind of shipwreck I have just been dealing with, in compensation runs the risk of betraying, in the most serious fashion, his fundamental vocation. The profound reflections of Plato on the dangers of flattery, of *kolakeia,* have not lost any contemporary point. A philosopher who is so very well known that it is unnecessary to name him here was playing up to this attitude when he said to the journalists who had gathered to receive him on a Swiss airfield, as soon as he got out of his plane: "Gentlemen, God is dead!" That is a very striking example of the kind of flattery, under the mask of provocation, which I have just been speaking of.

I should like to linger for a moment over this ancedote. Let us leave aside the question of what ultimate judgment we ought to bring to bear on Nietzsche's tragic and prophetic affirmation. What is clear is that as soon as Nietzsche's affirmation, "God is dead," is blared forth to journalists, or is put forward as a possible sensational headline, it becomes degraded, not only in the sense of losing, in this new context, all real meaning, but in the sense of becoming an absurd parody of its original self. There is an existential difference between Nietzsche's sigh and this sort of publicity handout, obviously intended to make a cheap sensation: "Gentlemen, I have a piece of news for you. God has been liquidated. Isn't that something?"

But at the same time we must recognize, not without the deepest anguish, that invitations to the philosopher to conduct himself in this degrading fashion are piling up on every side. So soon as the philosopher consents to be taken in charge by publicity agents, by impresarios, he negates his own function and vocation as a philosopher. It is also, of course, quite natural that the philosopher's desire for publicity should manifest itself more and more in the outward guise of a wish to shock. Let us add that, to the thinker who desires above all to oppose *bourgeois* convictions, this wish to shock will appear as a manifestation of the revolutionary spirit. The effort which certain circles have made to revive interest in the unreadable and rightly infamous works of the Marquis de Sade is a case in point. Let us note also, in passing, that the true revolutionary is quite within his rights in reminding us that a certain sort of anti-*bourgeois* literary attitude may itself be merely a *bourgeois* phenomenon.

To round off these considerations, I should notice that there is still another temptation to which, in fact, contemporary philosophers do frequently yield. There is a danger of the philosopher taking his stand, much too hastily, on paper rather than in reality, and most frequently by appending his signature to some manifesto, about matters of which he has only a superficial knowledge, a hearsay knowledge which is in reality mere ignorance. I will take a specific example again here, that of a petition signed by a number of intellectuals who demanded that the United Nations Assembly should provide a seat for the Government of Communist China. They failed to see that the problem was in the first place one of *opportuneness,* and as such not one on which any of the signatories were in a position to pronounce.

One can think of many other examples of the same sort. The error here consists, also, invariably of first postulating certain general principles in a quite abstract fashion and then declaring hastily that in such or such a concrete case these principles imply such and such a definite practical decision. But, leaving aside the fact that it is sometimes not allowable to postulate such principle as valid in all imaginable cases whatsoever, it very often happens that the particular case to which they are being applied is too imperfectly known, in its particularity and concrete connections, for any such inference from the abstract general principle to the particular decision to be allowable. A good example of this is to be found in the extraordinary rashness with which some French intellectuals have been demanding the immediate evacuation of Indo-China. They start from the idea that colonialism is incompatible with the general notion they have formed of the rights of man. But, quite aside from the fact that their idea of colonialism is much too summary and simplified, and from the fact that in some ways a colonizing power can have a beneficial effect on the colonial peoples themselves, the whole problem lay in knowing whether on the one hand such an evacuation was practically possible, and on the other hand, supposing it were practically possible, whether its effect would not be to deliver the colonial peoples themselves over to the terroristic action of armed groups at the service of Soviet imperialism. In a situation of this sort, everything is involved in almost inextricable complexity, and to formulate imperatives dictated by ignorance, and in many cases by political sectarianism, is to betray the inescapable demands of straight thinking.

Thus the very first duty of a philosopher is to have a clear sense of the limits of his own knowledge and to recognize that there are realms in which his lack of competence to make judgments is complete. Or, in other words, we may say that the philosopher should be perpetually on guard against making false claims that are incompatible with his true vocation.

It may be objected that to deny the philosopher the right to take a definite stand on concrete political issues is at bottom a hypocritical way of inviting him not to commit himself, to remain at the level of assertions of general principle. But that is not what I am aiming at. I will take two examples which should make my drift clearer. I should not hesitate to say that in a country in which people are persecuted for racial or religious reasons, it is the philosopher's duty to commit himself utterly, however many risks he may run, by making his protest. Silence in such a case is complicity. But in this case nobody could claim that the persecutor has

a better knowledge of his special subject than the philosopher. It is even the very opposite that is true. The anti-semite is not better informed about the Jews than the man who fights anti-semitism. In fact, what is at issue here is not knowledge at all but ignorant prejudice, which it is the philosopher's duty to attack. We may say that principle intervenes directly here, in all its sublime irreducibility.

Let me take another example: I personally hold that the philosopher, as such, was bound to protest against the way in which the purge was carried out in France after the war, by men who, often unjustly, claimed to incarnate the Resistance, this at a moment when, the war being at an end, the word "Resistance" was losing all real meaning. That it was permissible to set up irregular courts, to allow victims the right to judge their persecutors just *because* of the spirit of vindictiveness that inspired them— all this the philosopher was in duty bound to deny, as forcibly as possible. Here again the principle at stake was glaringly obvious.

But it goes without saying that these two examples which I have just cited have something in common. In both cases, we have to do with fanaticism. For, in fact—and I assert this without a shadow of hesitation—the first duty of the philosopher in our world to-day is to fight against fanaticism *under whatever guise it may appear.*

II

The reasons why I have chosen to speak here of fanaticism are too obvious to be worth going into in detail: fanaticism literally rings us round. I am not thinking only of Stalinist fanaticism. The anti-Stalinist Communists, particularly the Titoists, are without any doubt fanatics also. But that is not the whole story; the Nazism which, according to the most competent observers, is perhaps being revived in Germany and Austria is also a fanaticism: the worst of all of them. And if one is perfectly frank, one must admit that even religions which are genuine in their principles can, if I may put it so, become fanaticized, just as an originally healthy organic tissue can become cancerous.

What are the combined conditions that must be fulfilled if we are to be in a position to say of some man or other, "He is a fanatic"? Or, in more precise language, what is the fanaticizing power, and where does its stronghold lie? One might be inclined, as a first guess, to say that *ideas* as such have the power of making men fanatical; and certainly this is not absolutely off the mark, but it is not the whole truth, either. First of all, it is not every idea that can make men fanatical; it is not enough even for an idea to acquire an obsessive character, an obsessive grip. Think, for instance, of Balthazar Claes in Balzac's *The Quest of the Absolute,* who is obsessed and perhaps crazily so, but is certainly not a fanatic. We might be tempted to say, without any further reflection, that fanaticism is essentially religious; but that again seems to me at once true and false; true from the point of view of a merely objective description of religion, but more deeply false, since at this level all objective description inevitably and essentially distorts the reality to which it is applied, or more precisely because objective description tends to exclude and to make void of significance the distinction between a true religion and a false one. We have to recognize that a true religion cannot have this power of making men fanatical and that, on the contrary, wherever this fanaticizing power does exist, there is a perversion of religion.

But what, then, has enabled us to say that from the point of view of objective description fanaticism is of the order of religious activity or experience? It is the fact that the fanatic cannot be an isolated being, that on the contrary he exists *among* others, and that between these others and himself there is formed what one would be tempted to call a kind of agglutination, though I would rather speak of a unity or identity of harmonic range. This unity—or this identity —is felt as a link which exalts, and the fanaticism of one man is always kept alight by contact with the fanaticism of another. Also, one could say that fanaticism is always

centered upon an over-developed consciousness of "ourselves, the others" as a group.

This, no doubt, is where we ought to bring in the notion of the masses. Just by looking around us we are in a position to say that the masses, *qua* masses, are essentially the stuff of which fanaticism is made. It is relevant here to refer to the thoughts on this subject put forward by Ortega y Gasset in his book, *The Revolt of the Masses.* This Spanish writer calls our attention to the fact that in groups whose character is precisely that of *not* being crowds or masses, the way the feelings and emotions of their members come together is by centering on some desire, some idea or ideal, which in itself excludes the adherence of very great numbers to the group. The mass may, on the contrary, be defined, in so far as it is a psychological datum, as existing at a level below that at which individuals deliberately organize themselves into groups. A given individual belongs to the mass not only when his estimation of himself, good or bad, does not rest on his rightly judging that he has some kind of special qualification, but also when, feeling himself just the same sort of person as everybody else, he does not experience any anxiety because of this feeling but finds it rather reassuring, on the contrary, to feel that he is just as others are. "The characteristic of this world we are living in to-day is that the mediocre soul, knowing itself to be mediocre, has the boldness to assert the rights of mediocrity, and to impose them everywhere. . . . The mass makes a *tabula rasa* of everything that is not like itself, of everything that is excellent, individual, specially qualified, choice. Whoever is not like everybody else, whoever does not think like everybody else, runs the risk of being eliminated."

But we ought to be able to see more clearly just for what reason the mass-man is so easily turned into a fanatic. What I seem to myself to have grasped is this, that such permeability is due to the fact that man, that the individual, in order to belong to the mass, to be a mass-man, has had, as a preliminary, though without having had the least awareness of it, to divest himself of that substantial reality which was linked to his initial individuality or rather to the fact of his belonging to a small actual group. The incredibly sinister role of the press, the cinema, the radio, has consisted in passing that original reality through a pair of flattening rollers to substitute for it a superimposed pattern of ideas and images with no real roots in the deep being of the subject of this experiment. But does it not seem just as if propaganda offered a kind of nourishment to the unconscious hunger felt by beings thus deprived of their own proper reality? Propaganda will thus create a kind of second and entirely factitious nature, but a nature which can only be sustained and kept alive by a passion, by, in fact, precisely the passion of fanaticism. We ought certainly to add here that the basis of this passion is fear, that it implies an unconfessed emotional insecurity that converts itself into an outward aggressiveness. It is by the existence of this secret fear that we can most conveniently explain the refusal, involved in all types of fanaticism, to bring basic assumptions into question; and we shall have to ask ourselves in what the essential nature of this refusal lies. Such an examination of the nature of the fanatic's refusal to discuss his presuppositions is all the more necessary as we are here in a rather badly charted territory, where there is a risk of confusion arising in our minds between fanaticism and faith.

Fanaticism is essentially *opinion;* opinion pushed to paroxysm; with everything that the notion of opinion may imply of blinded ignorance as to its own nature. Let us notice also that, whatever ends the fanatic is aiming at or thinks he is aiming at, even if he wishes to gather men together, he can only in fact separate them; but as his own interests cannot lie in effecting this separation, he is led, as we have seen, to wish to wipe his opponents out. And when he is thinking of these opponents, he takes care to form the most degrading images of them possible— they are "lubricious vipers" or "hyenas and jackals with typewriters"—and the ones that reduce them to most grossly material terms. In fact, he no longer thinks of these oppon-

ents except as material obstacles to be overturned or smashed down. Having abandoned the behaviour of a thinking being, he has lost even the feeblest notion of what a thinking being, outside himself, could be. It is understandable therefore that he should make every effort to deny in advance the rights and qualifications of those whom he wishes to eliminate; and that he should regard all means to this end as fair. We are back here again at the techniques of degradation. It cannot be asserted too strongly or repeated too often that those the Nazis made use of in their camps—techniques for degrading their victims in their own eyes, for making mud and filth of them—and those which Soviet propagandists use to discredit their adversaries, are not essentially different though we should, in fairness, add that sadism, properly so called, is not to be found in the Russian camps. And it is not enough to say even this. We must add that the Soviet propagandists seek to foster in the adversary, through physical and psychological processes not yet known to us in complete detail, a spirit of complicity which will make him prepare and assure his own ruin.

What does seem to me essential is that we should grasp the terrible logic, the logic of death, at work here. Such manifestations are not, though we tend to think so, mere monstrous aberrations. They are nothing but the logical corollaries of fanaticism; they are not a phenomenon, foreign to fanaticism, which has somehow or other been superimposed on it. They derive from the fact that fanaticism is, of its very nature, incompatible with any regard for truth; and as truth itself is not really separable from our regard for it, we need not hesitate to say that the fanatic is the enemy of truth: even if only because he seeks to monopolize truth for his own profit. And this is so at all levels.

But what should have become almost blindingly clear to us over the last few years is that the fates of truth and justice are linked in such a way that it becomes impossible even to distinguish one fate from the other. As the greatest thinkers in the history of mankind have at all times seen—and I am thinking particularly not only of Plato, but also of Spinoza—there can be no justice where there is no respect for truth. Only, when we talk of having a "respect for truth," we do not mean merely that we are going to use high-sounding phrases; we mean that we are going to keep all the channels open, sometimes exceedingly tenuous channels, by which we can hope, I will not say to attain truth, but at least to approach truth.

III

In this context, it seems necessary to me to clarify as much as possible the stand that the philosopher should take; let me say categorically that he ought not, for instance, to transform himself into a prophet. With the genuine prophet, the philosopher cannot help feeling in sympathy, but at the same time this sympathy, one should emphasize, is always of an anguished sort, for the very reason that prophecy is always like lightning, flashing transversely across the hard and twisty paths along which the philosopher must grope his way. This prophetic foreshortening frightens the philosopher just because of the infinite danger of distortion it implies; yet this infinite danger has also something positive and one might say necessary about it. . . . Yet there is also the false prophet, who remains at the level of experience, who bases his prophecies on some science such as biology, economics, sociology. Obviously, such a false prophet may be sincere; yet it is, I think, the duty of the philosopher not to weary in denouncing the illegitimacy of his claims. Such denunciations, of course, ought not to take the form of invective. A philosophy worthy of the name ought to be incapable of descending to the level of the pamphleteer; philosophy should certainly always retain the critical spirit, but any kind of criticism worth calling criticism implies an anxiety to be fair that is profoundly foreign to the pamphleteering spirit. Philosophical activity also presupposes a certain native courage in the philosopher—for the philosophical spirit is bound to see itself slandered, both by the fanatic and by the false prophet, who in the long run always

runs the risk of himself becoming fanaticized.

It follows from all this that the situation of the philosopher as he confronts our contemporary world is almost the most risky and exposed situation one can imagine. I do not merely mean that the philosopher may expect to pay for his rashness in the depths of some Soviet, or other, prison. The danger is also, and perhaps above all, an inner one. It is very hard for the philosopher to-day to resist the temptation to flee. I will not say into the realm of science—for science, where it is truthfully pursued, retains even to-day all its value, all its dignity—but into the realm of some pretended science, such as psychoanalysis for example, a realm where science bursts its bonds and claims to have grasped the keys of spiritual reality. But that is not the only danger: yielding to what a contemporary thinker calls "the nostalgia for being," the philosopher may deviate into mysticism. This is what I would call the higher escapism, but it is escapism all the same.

While gladly recognizing that mysticism can, to all appearances, reach places that are impenetrable to philosophy, the philosopher nevertheless owes it to himself, I think, to maintain, though without undue display of emotion, the necessity of that way of thought, and I would even say of that way of existence, which are his own. For it may be that this specific way of thought and existence is closely linked to the safeguarding of what has traditionally been denoted by the now rather discredited term, "civilization." I have a deep conviction, at least, that the fate of philosophy and that of civilization are directly and intimately linked. Perhaps one might say that between the world of techniques and that of pure spirituality, the mediation of the philosopher is becoming more and more indispensable. Otherwise, there is a danger of the technician's attitude infringing on a domain that ought to remain inviolate: but, on the other hand, through a natural but dangerous reaction, there is a risk of those who pursue the purely spiritual life passing a verdict of condemnation on all techniques, a verdict that perhaps will not and cannot be put into practical effect, but that might, nevertheless, plunge many minds into a state of terrible confusion. There, no doubt, lies the greatest evil of our time. I have said, in the first volume of my Gifford Lectures, *The Mystery of Being,* that we are living in a world which seems to be founded on the refusal to reflect. It is the place of the philosopher, and per-haps his place only, to attack this contemporary confusion, not in a presumptuous way certainly, not with any illusions about what the effect of his attack is likely to be, but with the feeling that here lies a duty which cannot be evaded, a duty from which he cannot withdraw himself without betraying his true mission.

The Role of the Philosopher: Socrates

It is not necessary to turn to our own age for an interpretation of the role of the philosopher in a time of crisis. The classic statement of this was written almost twenty-five hundred years ago by Plato in his famous description of Socrates' trial in Athens in 399 B.C. The occasion that Plato here so dramatically portrays was clearly a time of crisis not only in the life of the philosopher himself but also in the life of the Athenian state. Under such circumstances the meaning of existence was not a matter of abstract speculation but of concrete and immediate concern. As one reads the *Apology,* and understands its setting and the issues at stake, it is not hard to see why Socrates became one of the great moral heroes of mankind, in the thought of the ancient world a kind of secular saint who lived and died for his faith in man and in the supremacy of human reason.

There is no more picturesque figure anywhere in the history of philosophy than Socrates. With great bald head, round face and protruding eyes, thick lips and snub nose, he was far from handsome. But his personal appearance was soon forgotten by those who came under the influence of his personality and his skill in dialectic. Born in Athens about 469 B.C., the son of a stonecutter, Socrates lived his life almost literally in the market place of his native city. His youth was spent in the golden age of Athens, the age of Pericles, when not only her political and economic power was at its height but also when her greatest democratic leader was likewise her greatest patron of the arts. It was an age when the remarkable victory of the Athenian navy over the great armies of the Persian Empire was still being celebrated, when the impressive temples on the Acropolis including the famous Parthenon were being built, when Greek drama reached its highest point under the inspiration of Aeschylus and Sophocles. The pride of the young philosopher in his Athenian citizenship is not surprising nor was it exceptional. His devotion to Athens served as a determining influence in the life of Socrates, quite obviously shaping his view of the role of the philosopher.

Drawn by his skill and insight in argument, his boldness in challenging all pretense and hypocrisy, his marked success in debunking the stuffed shirts of his day, and withal by his humility of spirit, the youth of Athens flocked about Socrates. All the problems of life were illumined in the clear light of reason by this master craftsman who believed so deeply that "the unexamined life is not worthy of a man." But the fearlessness of Socrates in pushing his philosophical mission brought him enemies quite as often as it made disciples. He insisted upon the critical examination of every belief and unhesitatingly unmasked ignorance or pretense wherever they existed. Even the most prominent public figures among his contemporaries were not safe from his searching inquiry. Few people are able to bear without malice the exposure of their own shortcomings; the Athenian leaders at that time were no exception to the general rule. But Socrates went his own way, doing what he believed to be right, and sparing the feelings of no one who appeared to be incompetent. His hold upon his disciples became so great indeed that one can hardly disentangle the simple truth from the product of imagination in the several accounts of this first great philosophical figure that have come down to us.[1]

The task of the philosopher, as Socrates interprets it, is in large measure social in its implications. He is deeply concerned with moral values; but, in accord with the Greek view of his day, Socrates conceived of human nature as essentially social—to live as a human being a man must live as a citizen of the state. For the Greek philosopher personal and social morality are but aspects of a larger whole, and one cannot propose a meaningful way of life for the individual without recognizing its necessary social implications. Yet, as Socrates looked about him at the Athenian democracy of the day, nowhere did he observe more outmoded tradition and custom, more ignorance and uncritical complacency than in political life. The philosopher, he concluded, could not escape his obligation to help in building a better society. With this in mind, Socrates picturesquely interprets his mission as that of the "gadfly of the State," constantly engaged in stinging the sluggish public into an awareness of the issues before it, much as the horsefly stings the sluggish mare into renewed activity. This task he considered his chief duty as an Athenian, but it was also for Socrates fundamentally a religious as well as a political mission. It was a duty imposed upon him by the God who gave to his own deepest moral convictions a more than merely human significance.

Socrates' later life was spent in the tragic days of the Peloponnesian Wars when Athens and Sparta were engaged in the costly struggle that brought the great age of classic Greece to an end. During these years Athens was little more than an armed camp; the dangers, the turmoil, and the hatreds bred by war were apparent on every hand. War is never healthy for democracies, and in this situation the Athenian democracy began to crack under the strain. Money ran short, the standard of living fell, the democratic leaders became more and more militaristic. In an endeavor to recoup their losses, the Athenians organized an expedition to conquer Sicily, the richest island of the Mediterranean. The failure of this somewhat questionable enterprise—owing in part to the poor judgment and mediocrity of the democratic leaders and in part to the misconduct of Alcibiades, a favorite pupil of Socrates—led to the downfall of Athens. In 404 B.C. she capitulated, and an aristocratic regime subject to Sparta replaced the democratic government.

Through all these years, if Plato's accounts can be relied upon, Socrates continued his role as philosophical critic and catalyst, quite unperturbed by the crisis through which the Athenian democracy was passing. Several times he seems to have been saved from prison by fortunate turns in the political events. But when

---

[1] In addition to the so-called Socratic dialogues written by Plato, among which the *Apology, Crito, Euthyphro* and *Meno* are especially important, there are contemporary descriptions of Socrates in the *Memorabilia* of Xenophon and in Aristophanes' comedy, *The Clouds*.

truth—the result of my mission
: I found that the men most in
all but the most foolish; and
less esteemed were really wiser
I will tell you the tale of my
and of the "Herculean" labours,
ll them, which I endured only to
the oracle irrefutable. After the
I went to the poets; tragic, dithy-
d all sorts. And there, I said to
will be instantly detected; now
d out that you are more ignorant
re. Accordingly, I took them some
st elaborate passages in their own
nd asked what was the meaning
-thinking that they would teach
hing. Will you believe me? I am
hamed to confess the truth, but
ay that there is hardly a person
ho would not have talked better
ir poetry than they did themselves.
knew that not by wisdom do poets
etry, but by a sort of genius and
n; they are like diviners or sooth-
ho also say many fine things, but do
erstand the meaning of them. The
peared to me to be much in the same
d I further observed that upon the
of their poetry they believed them-
o be the wisest of men in other things
ch they were not wise. So I departed,
ing myself to be superior to them for
me reason that I was superior to the
ians.

At last I went to the artisans. I was
ous that I knew nothing at all, as I
ay, and I was sure that they knew many
hings; and here I was not mistaken,
hings; and they did know many things of which I
ey did know many things of which I
gnorant, and in this they certainly were
than I was. But I observed that even
good artisans fell into the same error as
poets;—because they were good work-
they thought that they also knew all
of high matters, and this defect in
overshadowed their wisdom; and there-
I asked myself on behalf of the oracle,
ether I would like to be as I was, neither
ing their knowledge nor their ignorance,
like them in both; and I made answer to

myself and to the oracle that I was better off as I was.

This inquisition has led to my having many enemies of the worst and most dangerous kind, and has given occasion also to many calumnies. And I am called wise, for my hearers always imagine that I myself possess the wisdom which I find wanting in others: but the truth is, O men of Athens, that God only is wise; and by his answer he intends to show that the wisdom of men is worth little or nothing; he is not speaking of Socrates, he is only using my name by way of illustration, as if he said, He, O men, is the wisest, who, like Socrates, knows that his wisdom is in truth worth nothing. And so I go about the world, obedient to the god, and search and make enquiry into the wisdom of any one, whether citizen or stranger, who appears to be wise; and if he is not wise, then in vindication of the oracle I show him that he is not wise; and my occupation quite absorbs me, and I have no time to give either to any public matter of interest or to any concern of my own, but I am in utter poverty by reason of my devotion to the god.

There is another thing:—young men of the richer classes, who have not much to do, come about me of their own accord; they like to hear the pretenders examined, and they often imitate me, and proceed to examine others; there are plenty of persons, as they quickly discover, who think that they know something, but really know little or nothing; and then those who are examined by them instead of being angry with themselves are angry with me: This confounded Socrates, they say; this villainous misleader of youth!—and then if somebody asks them, Why, what evil does he practice or teach? they do not know, and cannot tell; but in order that they may not appear to be at a loss, they repeat the ready-made charges which are used against all philosophers about teaching things up in the clouds and unde the earth, and having no gods, and makir the worse appear the better cause; for th do not like to confess that their pretenc knowledge has been detected—which i truth; and as they are numerous and

the democratic government was restored to power in 403 B.C., its leaders were in no mood to put up with the old philosopher who in their opinion was responsible for so much of the criticism to which they had been subjected. Socrates was brought to trial, accused of corrupting the youth of the city and of disbelief in the gods of the state. Anytus, a democratic leader whose son had become a pupil of Socrates and then laughed at his father's outmoded ideas, was spokesman for the prosecution. A slight compromise with conviction might well have brought Socrates freedom; refusal to compromise meant martyrdom. The working philosophy by which a man's life is guided—his sense of meaning and purpose in life—stands out nowhere so dramatically as in a situation such as this. Plato, who was present at the trial, wrote down what happened in prose more moving than poetry. His account in the *Apology* is now a part of the great literature of the ages.

Eventually the jury decreed that the courageous old philosopher should put an end to his life. As an Athenian he was given the privilege of drinking the cup of hemlock rather than submitting to the indignity of an execution. For almost a month, however, Socrates waited in prison since no death sentences were carried out during the voyage of an Athenian ship sent each year at this time to the festival of Apollo at Delos. Meanwhile his friend Crito bribed the jailer and arranged an easy escape; but Socrates, in a discussion made famous by Plato, refused to take advantage of the arrangement, in the end convincing Crito how contrary to his principles this would be.

At length the ship returned from Delos and the next morning Socrates' friends came early to the prison, knowing that he soon must die. In the *Phaedo* Plato describes that last day in unforgettable fashion. Socrates spent it discoursing with his companions on the immortality of the soul, urging them to be of good cheer since no man who had adorned his soul "in her own proper jewels, which are temperance and justice and courage and nobility and truth," had anything to fear from death. As sunset drew near, he bathed, asked his jailer that the cup of poison be brought, asked the gods to prosper his journey from this world to the next, and then without hesitation or fear drank the poison that was given him.

The Apology*

Persons of the Dialogue: Socrates and Meletus

Scene: In the Court

Socrates speaks: How you, O Athenians, have been affected by my accusers, I can-

---

* From the English translation by Benjamin Jowett. (Oxford, The Clarendon Press, third edition, 1892).

not tell; but I know that they almost made me forget who I was—so persuasively did they speak; and yet they have hardly uttered a word of truth. But of the many falsehoods told by them, there was one which quite amazed me;—I mean when they said that you should be upon your guard and not allow yourselves to be deceived by the force of my eloquence. To say this, when they were certain to be detected as soon as I opened my lips and proved myself to be anything but a great speaker, did indeed appear to me most shameless—unless by the force of eloquence they mean the force of truth; for if such is their meaning, I admit that I am eloquent. But in how different a way from theirs! Well, as I was saying, they have scarcely spoken the truth at all; but from me you shall hear the whole truth: not, however, delivered after their manner in a set oration duly ornamented with words and phrases. No, by heaven! but I shall use the words and arguments which occur to me at the moment; for I am confident in the justice of my cause: at my time of life I ought not to be appearing before you, O men of Athens, in the character of a juvenile orator—let no one expect it of me. And I must beg of you to grant me a favour:—If I defend myself in my accustomed manner, and you hear me using the words which I have been in the habit of using in the agora, at the tables of the money-changers, or anywhere else, I would ask you not to be surprised, and not to interrupt me on this account. For I am more than seventy years of age, and appearing now for the first time in a court of law, I am quite a stranger to the language of the place; and therefore I would have you regard me as if I were really a stranger, whom you would excuse if he spoke in his native tongue, and after the fashion of his country:—Am I making an unfair request of you? Never mind the manner, which may or may not be good; but think only of the truth of my words, and give heed to that: let the speaker speak truly and the judge decide justly.

I

And first, I have to reply to the older charges and to my first accusers, and then I will go on to the later ones. For of old I have had many accusers, who have accused me falsely to you during many years; and I am more afraid of them than of Anytus and his associates, who are dangerous, too, in their own way. But far more dangerous are the others, who began when you were

children, and took possession of your minds with their falsehoods, telling of one Socrates, a wise man, who speculated about the heaven above, and searched into the earth beneath, and made the worse appear the better cause. The disseminators of this tale are the accusers whom I dread; for their hearers are apt to fancy that such enquirers do not believe in the existence of the gods. And they are many, and their charges against me are of ancient date, and they were made by them in the days when you were more impressible than you are now—in childhood, or it may have been in youth—and the cause when heard went by default, for there was none to answer.

Well, then, I must make my defence, and endeavour to clear away in a short time, a slander which has lasted a long time. May I succeed, if to succeed be for my good and yours, or likely to avail me in my cause! The task is not an easy one; I quite understand the nature of it. And so leaving the event with God, in obedience to the law I will now make my defence.

I will begin at the beginning, and ask what is the accusation which has given rise to the slander of me, and in fact has encouraged Meletus to prefer this charge against me. Well, what do the slanderers say? They shall be my prosecutors, and I will sum up their words in an affidavit: "Socrates is an evil-doer, and a curious person, who searches into things under the earth and in heaven, and he makes the worse appear the better cause; and he teaches the aforesaid doctrines to others." Such is the nature of the accusation: it is just what you have yourselves seen in the comedy of Aristophanes,* who has introduced a man whom he calls Socrates, going about and saying that he walks in air, and talking a deal of nonsense concerning matters of which I do not pretend to know either much or little—not that I mean to speak disparagingly of any one who is a student of natural philosophy. I should be very sorry if Meletus could bring so grave a charge against me. But the simple truth is, O

* *Clouds,* p. 225ff.

Athenians, that I have nothing to do with physical speculations. Very many of those here present are witnesses to the truth of this, and to them I appeal. Speak then, you who have heard me, and tell your neighbours whether any of you have ever known me to hold forth in few words or in many upon such matters. . . . You hear their answer. And from what they say of this part of the charge you will be able to judge of the truth of the rest.

I dare say, Athenians, that some one among you will reply, "Yes, Socrates, but what is the origin of these accusations which are brought against you; there must have been something strange which you have been doing? All these rumours and this talk about you would never have arisen if you had been like other men: tell us, then, what is the cause of them, for we should be sorry to judge hastily of you." Now I regard this as a fair challenge, and I will endeavour to explain to you the reason why I am called wise and have such an evil fame. Please to attend then. And although some of you may think that I am joking, I declare that I will tell you the entire truth. Men of Athens, this reputation of mine has come because of a certain wisdom which I possess. And here, O men of Athens, I must beg you not to interrupt me, even if I seem to say something extravagant. For the word which I will speak is not mine. I will refer you to a witness who is worthy of credit; that witness shall be the god of Delphi—he will tell you about my wisdom, if I have any, and of what sort it is. You must have known Chaerephon; he was early a friend of mine, and also a friend of yours, for he shared in the recent exile of the people, and returned with you. Well, Chaerephon, as you know, was very impetuous in all his doings, and he went to Delphi and boldly asked the oracle to tell him whether—as I was saying, I must beg you not to interrupt —he asked the oracle to tell him whether any one was wiser than I was, and the Pythian prophetess answered, that there was no man wiser. Chaerephon is dead himself; but his brother, who is in court, will confirm the truth of what I am saying.

tious and energetic, and are drawn up in battle array and have persuasive tongues, they have filled your ears with their loud and inveterate calumnies. And this is the reason why my three accusers, Meletus and Anytus and Lycon, have set upon me; Meletus, who has a quarrel with me on behalf of the poets; Anytus, on behalf of the craftsmen and politicians; Lycon, on behalf of the rhetoricians: and as I said at the beginning, I cannot expect to get rid of such a mass of calumny all in a moment. And this, O men of Athens, is the truth and the whole truth; I have concealed nothing, I have dissembled nothing. And yet, I know that my plainness of speech makes them hate me, and what is their hatred but a proof that I am speaking the truth?—Hence has arisen the prejudice against me; and this is the reason of it, as you will find out either in this or in any future inquiry.

II

I have said enough in my defence against the first class of my accusers; I turn to the second class. They are headed by Meletus, that good man and true lover of his country, as he calls himself. Against these, too, I must try to make a defence:— Let their affidavit be read: it contains something of this kind: It says that Socrates is a doer of evil, who corrupts the youth; and who does not believe in the gods of the state, but has other new divinities of his own. Such is the charge; and now let us examine the particular counts. He says that I am a doer of evil, and corrupt the youth; but I say, O men of Athens, that Meletus is a doer of evil, in that he pretends to be in earnest when he is only in jest, and is so eager to bring men to trial from a pretended zeal and interest about matters in which he really never had the smallest interest. And the truth of this I will endeavour to prove to you.

I should like to know, Meletus, in what I am affirmed to corrupt the young. I suppose you mean, as I infer from your indictment, that I teach them not to acknowledge the gods which the state acknowledges, but some other new divinities or spiritual

agencies in their stead. These are the lessons by which I corrupt the youth, as you say.

Yes, that I say emphatically.

Then, by the gods, Meletus, of whom we are speaking, tell me and the court, in somewhat plainer terms, what you mean! for I do not as yet understand whether you affirm that I teach other men to acknowledge some gods, and therefore that I do believe in gods, and am not an entire atheist—this you do not lay to my charge,—but only you say that they are not the same gods which the city recognizes—the charge is that they are different gods. Or, do you mean that I am an atheist simply, and a teacher of atheism?

I mean the latter—that you are a complete atheist.

What an extraordinary statement! Why do you think so, Meletus? Do you mean that I do not believe in the godhead of the sun or moon, like other men?

I assure you, judges, that he does not: for he says that the sun is stone, and the moon earth.

Friend Meletus, do you think that you are accusing Anaxagoras? You have but a bad opinion of the judges, if you fancy them illiterate to such a degree as not to know that these doctrines are found in the books of Anaxagoras the Clazomenian, which are full of them. And so, forsooth, the youth are said to be taught them by Socrates, when there are not unfrequently exhibitions of them at the theatre* (price of admission one drachma at the most); and they might pay their money, and laugh at Socrates if he pretends to father these extraordinary views. And so, Meletus, you really think that I do not believe in any god?

I swear by Zeus that you believe absolutely in none at all.

Nobody will believe you, Meletus, and I am pretty sure that you do not believe yourself. I cannot help thinking, men of

---

* Probably an allusion to Aristophanes, who caricatured, and to Euripides, who borrowed the notions of Anaxagoras, as well as to other dramatic poets.

Athens, that Meletus is reckless and impudent, and that he has written this indictment in a spirit of mere wantonness and youthful bravado. Has he not compounded a riddle, thinking to try me? He said to himself:— I shall see whether the wise Socrates will discover my facetious contradiction, or whether I shall be able to deceive him and the rest of them. For he certainly does appear to me to contradict himself in the indictment as much as if he said that Socrates is guilty of not believing in the gods, and yet of believing in them—but this is not like a person who is in earnest.

I have said enough in answer to the charge of Meletus: any elaborate defence is unnecessary; but I know only too well how many are the enmities which I have incurred, and this is what will be my destruction if I am destroyed;—not Meletus, nor yet Anytus, but the envy and detraction of the world, which has been the death of many good men, and will probably be the death of many more; there is no danger of my being the last of them.

Some one will say: And are you not ashamed, Socrates, of a course of life which is likely to bring you to an untimely end? To him I may fairly answer: There you are mistaken: a man who is good for anything ought not to calculate the chance of living or dying; he ought only to consider whether in doing anything he is doing right or wrong— acting the part of a good man or of a bad.

Strange, indeed, would be my conduct, O men of Athens, if I who, when I was ordered by the generals whom you chose to command me at Potidaea and Amphipolis and Delium, remained where they placed me, like any other man, facing death—if now, when, as I conceive and imagine, God orders me to fulfil the philosopher's mission of searching into myself and other men, I were to desert my post through fear of death, or any other fear; that would indeed be strange, and I might justly be arraigned in court for denying the existence of the gods, if I disobeyed the oracle because I was afraid of death, fancying that I was wise when I was not wise. For the fear of death is

indeed the pretence of wisdom, and not real wisdom, being a pretence of knowing the unknown; and no one knows whether death, which men in their fear apprehend to be the greatest evil, may not be the greatest good. Is not this ignorance of a disgraceful sort, the ignorance which is the conceit that a man knows what he does not know? And in this respect only I believe myself to differ from men in general, and may perhaps claim to be wiser than they are:—that whereas I know but little of the world below, I do not suppose that I know: but I do know that injustice and disobedience to a better, whether God or man, is evil and dishonourable, and I will never fear or avoid a possible good rather than a certain evil. And therefore if you let me go now, and are not convinced by Anytus, who said that since I had been prosecuted I must be put to death; (or, if not, that I ought never to have been prosecuted at all); and that if I escape now, your sons will all be utterly ruined by listening to my words—if you say to me, Socrates, this time we will not mind Anytus, and you shall be let off, but upon one condition, that you are not to inquire and speculate in this way any more, and that if you are caught doing so again you shall die;—if this was the condition on which you let me go, I should reply: Men of Athens, I honour and love you; but I shall obey God rather than you, and while I have life and strength I shall never cease from the practice and teaching of philosophy, exhorting any one whom I meet and saying to him after my manner: You, my friend,—a citizen of the great and mighty and wise city of Athens,—are you not ashamed of heaping up the greatest amount of money and honour and reputation, and caring so little about wisdom and truth and the greatest improvement of the soul, which you never regard or heed at all? And if the person with whom I am arguing, says: Yes, but I do care; then I do not leave him or let him go at once; but I proceed to interrogate and examine and cross-examine him, and if I think that he has no virtue in him, but only says that he has, I reproach him with undervaluing the greater, and overvaluing the less. And I shall repeat the same words to every one whom I meet, young and old, citizen and alien, but especially to the citizens, inasmuch as they are my brethren. For know that this is the command of God; and I believe that no greater good has ever happened in the state than my service to the God. For I do nothing but go about persuading you all, old and young alike, not to take thought for your persons or your properties, but first and chiefly to care about the greatest improvement of the soul. I tell you that virtue is not given by money, but that from virtue comes money and every other good of man, public as well as private. This is my teaching, and if this is the doctrine which corrupts the youth, I am a mischievous person. But if any one says that this is not my teaching, he is speaking an untruth. Wherefore, O men of Athens, I say to you, do as Anytus bids or not as Anytus bids, and either acquit me or not; but whichever you do, understand that I shall never alter my ways, not even if I have to die many times.

Men of Athens, do not interrupt, but hear me; there was an understanding between us that you should hear me to the end: I have something more to say, at which you may be inclined to cry out; but I believe that to hear me will be good for you, and therefore I beg that you will not cry out. I would have you know, that if you kill such a one as I am, you will injure yourselves more than you will injure me. Nothing will injure me, not Meletus nor yet Anytus—they cannot, for a bad man is not permitted to injure a better than himself. I do not deny that Anytus may, perhaps, kill him, or drive him into exile, or deprive him of civil rights; and he may imagine, and others may imagine, that he is inflicting a great injury upon him: but there I do not agree. For the evil of doing as he is doing—the evil of unjustly taking away the life of another—is greater far.

And now, Athenians, I am not going to argue for my own sake, as you may think, but for yours, that you may not sin against the God by condemning me, who am his gift to you. For if you kill me, you will not easily find a successor to me, who, if I may

use such a ludicrous figure of speech, am a sort of gadfly, given to the state by God; and the state is a great and noble steed who is tardy in his motions owing to his very size, and requires to be stirred into life. I am that gadfly which God has attached to the state, and all day long and in all places am always fastening upon you, arousing and persuading and reproaching you. You will not easily find another like me, and therefore I would advise you to spare me. I dare say that you may feel out of temper (like a person who is suddenly awakened from sleep), and you think that you might easily strike me dead as Anytus advises, and then you would sleep on for the remainder of your lives, unless God in his care of you sent you another gadfly. When I say that I am given to you by God, the proof of my mission is this:—if I had been like other men, I should have not neglected all my own concerns or patiently seen the neglect of them during all these years, and have been doing yours, coming to you individually like a father or elder brother, exhorting you to regard virtue; such conduct, I say, would be unlike human nature. If I had gained anything, or if my exhortations had been paid, there would have been some sense in my doing so; but now, as you will perceive, not even the impudence of my accusers dares to say that I have ever exacted or sought pay of any one; of that they have no witness. And I have a sufficient witness to the truth of what I say—my poverty.

Some one may wonder why I go about in private giving advice and busying myself with the concerns of others, but do not venture to come forward in public and advise the state. I will tell you why. You have heard me speak at sundry times and in divers places of an oracle or sign which comes to me, and is the divinity which Meletus ridicules in the indictment. This sign, which is a kind of voice, first began to come to me when I was a child; it always forbids but never commands me to do anything which I am going to do. This is what deters me from being a politician. And rightly, as I think. For I am certain, O men of Athens, that if I had engaged in politics,

I should have perished long ago, and done no good either to you or to myself. And do not be offended at my telling you the truth: for the truth is, that no man who goes to war with you or any other multitude, honestly striving against the many lawless and unrighteous deeds which are done in a state, will save his life; he who will fight for the right, if he would live even for a brief space, must have a private station and not a public one.

Now do you really imagine that I could have survived all these years, if I had led a public life, supposing that like a good man I had always maintained the right and had made justice, as I ought, the first thing? No indeed, men of Athens, neither I nor any other man. But I have been always the same in all my actions, public as well as private, and never have I yielded any base compliance to those who are slanderously termed my disciples, or to any other. Not that I have any regular disciples. But if any one likes to come and hear me while I am pursuing my mission, whether he be young or old, he is not excluded. Nor do I converse only with those who pay; but any one, whether he be rich or poor, may ask and answer me and listen to my words; and whether he turns out to be a bad man or a good one, neither result can be justly imputed to me; for I never taught or professed to teach him anything. And if any one says that he has ever learned or heard anything from me in private which all the world has not heard, let me tell you that he is lying.

III

Well, Athenians, this and the like of this is all the defence which I have to offer. Yet a word more. Perhaps there may be some one who is offended at me, when he calls to mind how he himself on a similar, or even a less serious occasion, prayed and entreated the judges with many tears, and how he produced his children in court, which was a moving spectacle, together with a host of relations and friends; whereas I, who am probably in danger of my life, will do none of these things. The contrast may occur to his mind, and he may be set against me, and vote in anger because he is displeased at me on this account. Now if there be such a person among you,—mind, I do not say that there is,—to him I may fairly reply: My friend, I am a man, and like other men, a creature of flesh and blood, and not "of wood or stone," as Homer says; and I have a family, yes, and sons, O Athenians, three in number, one almost a man, and two others who are still young; and yet I will not bring any of them hither in order to petition you for an acquittal. And why not? Not from any self-assertion or want of respect for you. Whether I am or am not afraid of death is another question, of which I will not now speak. But, having regard to public opinion, I feel that such conduct would be discreditable to myself, and to you, and to the whole state. One who has reached my years, and who has a name for wisdom, ought not to demean himself. Whether this opinion of me be deserved or not, at any rate the world has decided that Socrates is in some way superior to other men. And if those among you who are said to be superior in wisdom and courage, and any other virtue, demean themselves in this way, how shameful is their conduct! I have seen men of reputation, when they have been condemned, behaving in the strangest manner: they seemed to fancy that they were going to suffer something dreadful if they died, and that they could be immortal if you only allowed them to live; and I think that such are a dishonour to the state, and that any stranger coming in would have said of them that the most eminent men of Athens, to whom the Athenians themselves give honour and command, are no better than women. And I say that these things ought not to be done by those of us who have a reputation; and if they are done, you ought not to permit them; you ought rather to show that you are far more disposed to condemn the man who gets up a doleful scene and makes the city ridiculous, than him who holds his peace.

But, setting aside the question of public opinion, there seems to be something wrong in asking a favour of a judge, and thus procuring an acquittal, instead of informing and convincing him. For his duty is, not to make a present of justice, but to give judgment; and he has sworn that he will judge according to the laws, and not according to his own good pleasure; and we ought not to encourage you, nor should you allow yourselves to be encouraged, in this habit of perjury—there can be no piety in that. Do not then require me to do what I consider dishonourable and impious and wrong, especially now, when I am being tried for impiety on the indictment of Meletus. For if, O men of Athens, by force of persuasion and entreaty I could overpower your oaths, then I should be teaching you to believe that there are no gods, and in defending should simply convict myself of the charge of not believing them. But that is not so—far otherwise. For I do believe that there are gods, and in a sense higher than that in which any of my accusers believe in them. And to you and to God I commit my cause, to be determined by you as is best for you and me.

* * * * * *

[*The jury decides that Socrates is guilty by a vote of 280 to 220; then after some further deliberation sentences him to die.*]

Not much time will be gained, O Athenians, in return for the evil name which you will get from the detractors of the city, who will say that you killed Socrates, a wise man; for they will call me wise, even although I am not wise, when they want to reproach you. If you had waited a little while, your desire would have been fulfilled in the course of nature. For I am far advanced in years, as you may perceive, and not far from death. I am speaking now not to all of you, but only to those who have condemned me to death. And I have another thing to say to them: You think that I was convicted because I had no words of the sort which would have procured my acquittal—I mean, if I had thought fit to leave nothing undone or unsaid. Not so; the deficiency which led

to my conviction was not of words—certainly not. But I had not the boldness or impudence or inclination to address you as you would have liked me to do, weeping and wailing and lamenting, and saying and doing many things which you have been accustomed to hear from others, and which, as I maintain, are unworthy of me. I thought at the time that I ought not to do anything common or mean when in danger: nor do I now repent of the style of my defence; I would rather die having spoken after my manner, than speak in your manner and live. For neither in war nor yet at law ought I or any man to use every way of escaping death. Often in battle there can be no doubt that if a man will throw away his arms, and fall on his knees before his pursuers, he may escape death; and in other dangers there are other ways of escaping death, if a man is willing to say and do anything. The difficulty, my friends, is not to avoid death, but to avoid unrighteousness; for that runs faster than death. I am old and move slowly, and the slower runner has overtaken me, and my accusers are keen and quick, and the faster runner, who is unrighteousness, has overtaken them. And now I depart hence condemned by you to suffer the penalty of death, —they too go their ways condemned by the truth to suffer the penalty of villainy and wrong; and I must abide by my award—let them abide by theirs. I suppose that these things may be regarded as fated,—and I think that they are well.

And now, O men who have condemned me, I would fain prophesy to you; for I am about to die, and in the hour of death men are gifted with prophetic power. And I prophesy to you who are my murderers, that immediately after my departure punishment far heavier than you have inflicted on me will surely await you. Me you have killed because you wanted to escape the accuser, and not to give an account of your lives. But that will not be as you suppose: far otherwise. For I say that there will be more accusers of you than there are now; accusers whom hitherto I have restrained: and as they are younger they will be more inconsiderate with you, and you will be more offended at them. If you think that by killing men you can prevent some one from censuring your evil lives, you are mistaken; that is not a way of escape which is either possible or honourable; the easiest and the noblest way is not to be disabling others, but to be improving yourselves. This is the prophecy which I utter before my departure to the judges who have condemned me.

Friends, who would have acquitted me, I would like also to talk with you about the thing which has come to pass, while the magistrates are busy, and before I go to the place at which I must die. Stay then a little, for we may as well talk with one another while there is time. You are my friends, and I should like to show you the meaning of this event which has happened to me. O my judges—for you I may truly call judges—I should like to tell you of a wonderful circumstance. Hitherto the divine faculty of which the internal oracle is the source has constantly been in the habit of opposing me even about trifles, if I was going to make a slip or error in any matter; and now as you see there has come upon me that which may be thought, and is generally believed to be, the last and worst evil. But the oracle made no sign of opposition, either when I was leaving my house in the morning, or when I was on my way to the court, or while I was speaking, at anything which I was going to say; and yet I have often been stopped in the middle of a speech, but now in nothing I either said or did touching the matter in hand has the oracle opposed me. What do I take to be the explanation of this silence? I will tell you. It is an intimation that what has happened to me is a good, and that those of us who think that death is an evil are in error. For the customary sign would surely have opposed me had I been going to evil and not to good.

Let us reflect in another way, and we shall see that there is great reason to hope that death is a good; for one of two things— either death is a state of nothingness and utter unconsciousness, or, as men say, there is a change and migration of the soul from this world to another. Now if you suppose that there is no consciousness, but a sleep like the sleep of him who is undisturbed even by dreams, death will be an unspeakable gain. For if a person were to select the night in which his sleep was undisturbed even by dreams, and were to compare with this the other days and nights of his life, and then were to tell us how many days and nights he had passed in the course of his life better and more pleasantly than this one, I think that any man, I will not say a private man, but even the great king will not find many such days or nights, when compared with the others. Now if death be of such a nature, I say that to die is gain; for eternity is then only a single night. But if death is the journey to another place, and there, as men say, all the dead abide, what good, O my friends and judges, can be greater than this? What would not a man give if he might converse with Orpheus and Musaeus and Hesiod and Homer? Nay, if this be true, let me die again and again. I myself, too, shall have a wonderful interest in there meeting and conversing with Palamedes, and Ajax the son of Telamon, and any other ancient hero who has suffered death through an unjust judgment; and there will be no small pleasure, as I think, in comparing my own sufferings with theirs. Above all, I shall then be able to continue my search into true and false knowledge; as in this world, so also in the next; and I shall find out who is wise, and who pretends to be wise, and is not. What would not a man give, O judges, to be able to examine the leader of the great Trojan expedition; or Odysseus or Sisyphus, or numberless others, men and women too! What infinite delight would there be in conversing with them and asking them questions! In another world they do not put a man to death for asking questions: assuredly not. For besides being happier than we are, they will be immortal, if what is said is true.

Wherefore, O judges, be of good cheer about death, and know of a certainty, that no evil can happen to a good man, either in life or after death. He and his are not neglected by the gods; nor has my own approaching end happened by mere chance. But I see clearly that the time had arrived when it was better for me to die and be released from trouble; wherefore the oracle gave no sign. For which reason, also, I am not angry with my condemners, or with my accusers; they have done me no harm, although they did not mean to do me any good; and for this I may gently blame them.

Still I have a favour to ask of them. When my sons are grown up, I would ask you, O my friends, to punish them; and I would have you trouble them, as I have troubled you, if they seem to care about riches, or anything, more than about virtue; or if they pretend to be something when they are really nothing,—then reprove them, as I have reproved you, for not caring about that for which they ought to care, and thinking that they are something when they are really nothing. And if you do this, both I and my sons will have received justice at your hands.

The hour of departure has arrived, and we go our ways—I to die, and you to live. Which is better God only knows.

1

Basic Assumptions
of the Hedonist

Our is an age in which men and women desperately want to be happy. There has probably never been a time when this was more widespread and more openly acknowledged as the aim and purpose of human life. It is a rather significant fact, of course, that in the United States we have always accepted this concern with happiness as a basic principle in our democratic society. Life, liberty, and the pursuit of happiness were God-given rights to those who in 1776 formulated in our Declaration of Independence the principles upon which the new American nation was to be formed. Now for the first time in human history millions of people have at their disposal the economic means and the leisure to enjoy what human life on this planet has to offer. In *The Psychology of Happiness,* one of the popular books of the thirties, Walter B. Pitkin describes the situation in the following manner: "We know today that happy living can be attained by at least six or seven people out of every ten. I do not say that any such proportion of people are now living happily. But I do say, without any qualification whatsoever, that in the more highly civilized sections of the United States in this year 1929, all the *external* conditions required for happy living are present, waiting to be used. The one remaining obstacle is psychological."[1]

Paradoxical as it may at first appear, however, we in America today are not only more prosperous and more obviously concerned with happiness than any other nation, but we also seem among the least satisfied with what life has to offer us. We have the greatest abundance of things and the most numerous opportunities for gratifying our desires. Television and radio daily present detailed comment upon the abundance of new and tempting products that we may easily possess: the newest models in automobiles, refrigerators, and cosmetics, not to mention cigarettes, beer, and the like. Popular novels, available at all drug stores and bus, railway, and airplane terminals, also leave the impression that nothing is so desirable or generally enjoyed as love and romance. Yet it takes little insight to recognize that the benefits of modern civilization, which we so highly prize, have

---

[1] Walter B. Pitkin, *The Psychology of Happiness,* (New York, Simon and Schuster, 1929), pp. 1–2 (condensed).

not brought us the happiness that we sought. "The real paradox of our time," writes one thoughtful observer, "is not poverty in plenty but unhappiness in the pursuit of pleasure."[2] Indeed a startling number of men and women today are deeply unhappy, finding escape from the complexities and frustrations of modern life in alcoholism, in mental breakdowns, in self-destruction.

An understanding of happiness is something that everybody initially takes for granted. We may lack an adequate knowledge of science, have poor taste in art or literature, and very limited moral vision, but most of us imagine that we are quite familiar with the requisites of happiness and have little doubt about our capacity to achieve it if we but had the means to do so. Only when life confronts us with frustrations that seem inescapable do we begin to realize our need for greater understanding. Actually, as one writer has pointed out, the nature of happiness is as puzzling as truth, as subtle as beauty, and quite as difficult to attain as virtue. It has been the concern of the ablest philosophers over the centuries and there is still only very limited agreement among them. Today it is to the psychologists and the psychiatrists rather than to the philosophers that men and women are turning for assistance in their pursuit of happiness, and it is they who are publishing most of the popular books and articles on the subject. Only a little reading and reflection is needed, however, to reveal the fact that the ideas found in our current discussions are not new. They have been proposed and examined with care by thoughtful philosophers of the past in their search for the meaning of life, and to this search we now turn our attention.

Major Types of Hedonism

The philosophy that accepts the pursuit of pleasure as the important and lasting concern of human life is called Hedonism (a term derived from the Greek word for pleasure, *hedoné*). The happy life, so the hedonist argues, is a life marked by the enjoyment of the greatest amount of pleasure and marred by the least amount of pain. Pleasure is desired by all men naturally and without reflection; indeed this seems the normal and instinctive good established by nature for mankind. The problem for the philosopher, the hedonist maintains, is not to decide what constitutes the good life. That we all know well enough: it is a life that affords us maximum enjoyment. What we need to know is how to obtain the greatest pleasure and how to avoid the pain that seems woven into the very fabric of living, no matter in what circumstance our lot is cast. This the philosopher must help us to determine if he is to be of genuine assistance.

Hedonism has always been a popular philosophy; able exponents of its tenets are to be found in every age and culture, and there are times when we all feel its

---

[2] R. G. Taylor, *Conditions of Happiness,* (Boston, Houghton, Mifflin Company, 1951), p. 5.

appeal. We shall do well, therefore, to examine carefully its elements of strength and enduring appeal as well as any limitations that it may contain. In the history of Western philosophy three major types of hedonism can be distinguished. Aristippus, a wandering sophist of Cyrene (c. 430–350 B.C.), is perhaps the earliest and most forthright advocate of hedonism. His "Cyrenaic" hedonism puts its emphasis upon an unrestrained and unreflective pursuit of the pleasures of the moment and the pleasures of the senses. In the teaching of Epicurus, cultured Greek philosopher of the ancient world (341–270 B.C.), hedonism finds a more reasoned and acceptable statement as a philosophy of living. Jeremy Benthan and John Stuart Mill, outstanding British social philosophers of the nineteenth century, undertake the difficult task of freeing hedonism from the self-centered outlook that has seriously limited its appeal for many thoughtful individuals. In his version of Utilitarianism, Mill presents a synthesis of hedonism and altruism that sharply distinguishes his philosophy from that of both the Cyrenaics and the Epicureans. There are, to be sure, many modifications and combinations of these three points of view, but these are the basic and important types of hedonism. In the selections included here, each of these three positions is stated in enough detail to enable the reader to understand its major tenets and also to identify the basic assumptions that distinguish the hedonistic philosophy and reveal its essential nature.

Before turning to the thought of Aristippus, Epicurus, Bentham, and Mill, however, we shall look at a contemporary statement of hedonism which suggests the continued appeal of this philosophy for men and women today and shows clearly its meaning and basic assumptions in our age. In his popular volume, *The Importance of Living*, Lin Yutang presents hedonism in such graphic and concrete fashion that one cannot miss its meaning nor escape its appeal. This familiarity with hedonism as a contemporary philosophy should enable us to read with more understanding and interest the classic Cyrenaic, Epicurean, and Utilitarian philosophies.

The Hedonist in Contemporary Life: Lin Yutang

An urbane and cultural Oriental who now makes his home in New York City, Lin Yutang is a distinguished contemporary interpreter of the mind and spirit of China, familiar with the Confucian classics of his own country as well as with the industrial and urban civilization of the United States. *The Importance of Living*, published in 1937, is a readable account of his philosophy, which reflects the outlook of China before the Communist regime. His book is not the work of a professional philosopher but rather that of a thoughtful man who reached his conclusions at first hand from life as he lived it and saw it lived. Hedonism is presented as the natural and desirable philosophy of contemporary life.

Lin Yutang is an interesting figure. In his experience East and West meet in unusual and provocative fashion, and in hedonism he finds a strong bond between the classic philosophy of China and the contemporary American enjoyment of life. Born in Changchow in 1895, the son of a Chinese Christian pastor, Lin graduated from St. Johns College in Shanghai in 1916. After some further study in Germany and at Harvard University in this country, he took the Ph.D. degree at the University of Leipzig in 1923 and taught for some years at the National University in Peking. Devoting himself more and more fully to writing, he soon attained distinction in the field of literature and was recognized as one of the ablest contemporary Chinese authors. In 1948 Lin was made head of the Arts and Letters Division of UNESCO, and shortly thereafter was appointed Chancellor of Nanyang University in Singapore. Here, however, he was forced to devote most of his time and energy to combating the rising tide of communism; after a few years of such activity he resigned from this position in disappointment and frustration, returning to live in New York City.

Author of numerous works in Chinese, Lin Yutang has published twenty-five books in English, among them novels, essays, and anthologies interpreting Chinese life and philosophy. Best known to American readers are *My Country and My People, The Wisdom of China and India,* and *The Importance of Living.* His most recent book, *From Pagan to Christian* (1959), portrays the latest episode in a busy and fruitful career—the development of convictions that led him to become a member of the Madison Avenue Presbyterian Church in New York City. Perhaps it is not unkind, certainly it is not inaccurate, to point out that Lin writes much more persuasively as a hedonist in *The Importance of Loving* than he does as a Christian in *From Pagan to Christian.*

With something of the gentle satire that marks the volume as a whole, Lin Yutang apologizes in his preface to *The Importance of Living* for his lack of philosophical training. As one easily detects from his remarks, no apology in his opinion is really needed.

I am not deep and not well read. If one is too well-read, then one does not know right is right and wrong is wrong. I have not read Locke or Hume or Berkeley, and have not taken a college course in philosophy. Technically speaking, my method and training are all wrong, because I do not read philosophy but only read life at first hand. Thus deprived of academic training in philosophy I am less scared to write a book about it. Everything seems clearer and simpler for it, if that is any compensation in the eyes of orthodox philosophy. I doubt it. I know that there will be complaints that my words are not long enough, that I make things too easy to understand, and finally that I lack cautiousness, that I do not whisper low and trip with mincing steps in the sacred mansions of philosophy, looking properly scared as I ought to do.[3]

---

[3] Lin Yutang, *The Importance of Living,* (New York, The John Day Company, 1937), pp. viii–ix.

The Enjoyment of Living*

1. Approach to Life

In what follows I am presenting the Chinese point of view, because I cannot help myself. I am interested only in presenting a view of life and of things as the best and wisest Chinese minds have seen it and expressed it in their folk wisdom and their literature. It is an idle philosophy born of an idle life, evolved in a different age, I am quite aware. But I cannot help feeling that this view of life is essentially true, and since we are alike under the skin, what touches the human heart in one country touches all.

It is useless for me to say whether my philosophy is valid or not for the Westerner. To understand Western life, one would have to look at it as a Westerner born, with his own temperament, his bodily attitudes and his own set of nerves. I have no doubt that American nerves can stand a good many things that Chinese nerves cannot stand, and vice versa. It is good that it should be so— that we should all be born different. And yet it is all a question of relativity. I am quite sure that amidst the hustle and bustle of American life, there is a great deal of wistfulness, of the divine desire to lie on a plot of grass under tall beautiful trees of an idle afternoon and *just do nothing*. The necessity for such common cries as "Wake up and live" is to me a good sign that a wise portion of American humanity prefers to dream the hours away. Perhaps the American is merely ashamed of the word "loafing" in a world where everybody is doing something, but somehow, as sure as I know he is also an animal, he likes sometimes to have his muscles relaxed, to stretch on the sand, or to lie still with one leg comfortably curled up and one arm placed below his head as his

*Reprinted from *The Importance of Living* by Lin Yutang by permission of The John Day Company, Inc., publisher. Copyright, 1937, by The John Day Co., Inc.

pillow. The only thing I desire to see is that he be honest about it, and that he proclaim to the world that he likes it when he likes it, that it is not when he is working in the office but when he is lying idly on the sand that his soul utters, "Life is beautiful."

The world, I believe, is far too serious, and being far too serious, it has need of a wise and merry philosophy. The philosophy of the Chinese art of living can certainly be called the "gay science," if anything can be called by that phrase used by Nietzsche. After all, only a gay philosophy is profound philosophy; the serious philosophies of the West haven't even begun to understand what life is. To me personally, the only function of philosophy is to teach us to take life more lightly and gayly than the average businessman does, for no businessman who does not retire at fifty, if he can, is in my eyes a philosopher. This is not merely a casual thought, but is a fundamental point of view with me. The world can be made a more peaceful and more reasonable place to live in only when men have imbued themselves in the light gayety of this spirit. The modern man takes life far too seriously, and because he is too serious, the world is full of troubles. We ought, therefore, to take time to examine the origin of that attitude which will make possible a wholehearted enjoyment of this life and a more reasonable, more peaceful and less hot-headed temperament.

2. A Biological View

The most obvious fact which philosophers refuse to see is that we have got a body. Tired of seeing our mortal imperfections and our savage instincts and impulses, sometimes our preachers wish that we were made like angels, and yet we are at a total loss to imagine what the angels' life would be like. We either give the angels a body and a shape like our own—except for a pair of wings—or we don't. It is interesting that the general conception of an angel is still that of a human body with a pair of wings. I sometimes think that it is an advantage even for angels to have a body with the five senses. If I were to be an angel, I should like to have a school-girl complexion, but how am I going to have a school-girl complexion without a skin? I still should like to drink a glass of tomato juice or iced orange juice, but how am I going to appreciate iced orange juice without having thirst? And how am I going to enjoy food, when I am incapable of hunger? How would an angel paint without pigment, sing without the hearing of sounds, smell the fine morning air without a nose? How would he enjoy the immense satisfaction of scratching an itch, if his skin doesn't itch? And what a terrible loss in the capacity for happiness that would be! Either we have to have bodies and have all our bodily wants satisfied, or else we are pure spirits and have no satisfactions at all. All satisfactions imply want.

I sometimes think what a terrible punishment it would be for a ghost or an angel to have no body, to look at a stream of cool water and have no feet to plunge into it and get a delightful cooling sensation from it, to see a dish of Peking or Long Island duck and have no tongue to taste it, to see crumpets and have no teeth to chew them, to see the beloved faces of our dear ones and have no emotions to feel toward them.

Science, if anything, has taught us an increased respect for our body, by deepening a sense of the wonder and mystery of its workings. In the first place, genetically, we begin to understand how we came about, and see that, instead of being made out of clay, we are sitting on the top of the genealogical tree of the animal kingdom. That must be a fine sensation, sufficiently satisfying for any man who is not intoxicated with his own spirit. Not that I believe dinosaurs lived and died millions of years ago *in order that* we today might walk erect with our two legs upon this earth. Without such gratuitous assumptions, biology has not at all destroyed a whit of human dignity, or cast doubt upon the view that we are probably the most splendid animals ever evolved on this earth. So that is quite satisfying for any man who wants to insist on human dignity. In the second place, we are more impressed than ever with the mystery and beauty of the body. The workings of the internal parts of our body and the wonderful correlation between them compel in us a sense of the extreme difficulty with which these correlations are brought about and the extreme simplicity and finality with which they are nevertheless accomplished. Instead of simplifying these internal chemical processes by explaining them, science makes them all the more difficult to explain. These processes are incredibly more difficult than the layman without any knowledge of physiology usually imagines. The great mystery of the universe without is similar in quality to the mystery of the universe within.

I think that, from a biological standpoint, human life almost reads like a poem. It has its own rhythm and beat, its internal cycles of growth and decay. It begins with innocent childhood, followed by awkward adolescence trying awkwardly to adapt itself to mature society, with its young passions and follies, its ideals and ambitions; then it reaches a manhood of intense activities, profiting from experience and learning more about society and human nature; at middle age, there is a slight easing of tension, a mellowing of character like the ripening of fruit or the mellowing of good wine, and the gradual acquiring of a more tolerant, more cynical and at the same time a kindlier view of life; then in the sunset of our life, the endocrine glands decrease their activity, and if we have a true philosophy of old age and have ordered our life pattern according to it, it is for us the age of peace and security and leisure and contentment; finally, life flickers out and one goes into eternal sleep, never to wake up again. One should be able to sense the beauty of this rhythm of life, to appreciate, as we do in grand symphonies, its main theme, its strains of conflict and the final resolution. The movements of these cycles are very much the same in a normal life, but the music must be provided by the individual himself. In some souls, the discordant note becomes harsher and harsher and finally overwhelms or submerges the main melody. Sometimes the discordant note gains so much power that the music can no longer go on, and the individual shoots himself with a pistol or jumps into a river. But that is because his original *leit-motif* has been hopelessly over-shadowed through the lack of a good self-education. Otherwise the normal human life runs to its normal end in a kind of dignified movement and procession. There are sometimes in many of us too many *staccatos* or *impetuosos,* and because the tempo is wrong, the music is not pleasing to the ear; we might have more of the grand rhythm and majestic tempo of the Ganges, flowing slowly and eternally into the sea.

No one can say that a life with childhood, manhood and old age is not a beautiful arrangement; the day has its morning, noon and sunset, and the year has its seasons, and it is good that it is so. There is no good or bad in life, except what is good according to its own season. And if we take this biological view of life and try to live according to the seasons, no one but a conceited fool or an impossible idealist can deny that human life can be lived like a poem.

3. On Being Human

The human mind, you say, is probably the noblest product of the Creation. This is a proposition that most people will admit, particularly when it refers to a mind like Albert Einstein's that can prove curved space by a long mathematical equation, or Edison's that can invent the gramophone and the motion picture, or the minds of other physicists who can measure the rays of an advancing or receding star or deal with the constitution of the unseen atoms, or that of the inventor of natural-color movie cameras. Compared with the aimless, shifting and fumbling curiosity of the monkeys, we must agree that we have a noble, a glorious intellect that can comprehend the universe in which we are born.

The average mind, however, is charming rather than noble. Had the average mind been noble, we should be completely rational beings without sins or weaknesses or misconduct, and what an insipid world that would be! We should be so much less charming as creatures. I am such a humanist that saints without sins don't interest me. But we are charming in our irrationality, our prejudices, bigotry and forgetfulness. Imagine a renowned, proud composer, whom no one could induce to compose an opera for a certain beautiful woman, but who, on hearing that a hated rival composer is thinking of doing it, immediately snatches at the job; or a scientist who in his life has consistently refused to publish his writings in newspapers, but who, on seeing a rival scientist make a slip with one single letter, forgets his own rule and rushes into print. There we have laid our finger upon the singularly *human* quality of the mind. The human mind is charming in its unreasonableness, its inveterate prejudices, and its waywardness and unpredictability. If we haven't learned this truth, we have learned nothing from the century of study of human psychology. In other words, our minds still retain the aimless, fumbling quality of simian intelligence.

The late James Harvey Robinson has tried to show, in *The Mind in the Making,* how our mind gradually evolved from, and is still operating upon, four underlying layers: the animal mind, the savage mind, the childish mind and the traditional civilized mind, and has further shown us the necessity of developing a more critical mind if the present human civilization is to continue. In my scientific moments, I am inclined to agree with him, but in my wiser moments, I doubt the feasibility, or even the desirability, of such a step of general progress. I prefer to have our mind charmingly unreasonable as it is at present. I should hate to see a world in which we are all prefectly rational beings. Do I distrust scientific progress? No, I distrust sainthood. Am I anti-intellectualistic? Perhaps yes; perhaps no. I am merely in love with life, and being in love with life, I distrust the intellect profoundly. Imagine a world in which there are no stories of murder in newspapers, every one is so omniscient that no house ever catches fire, no airplane ever has an accident, no husband deserts his wife, no pastor elopes with a choir girl, no king abdicates his throne for love, no man changes his mind and everyone proceeds to carry out with logical precision a career that he mapped out for himself at the age of ten —good-by to this happy human world! All the excitement and uncertainty of life would be gone. There would be no literature because there would be no sin, no misbehavior, no human weakness, no upsetting passion, no prejudices, no irregularities and, worst of all, no surprises. Human fallibility is the very essence of the color of life, as the upsets are the very color and interest of a steeplechase. Imagine a Doctor Johnson without his bigoted prejudices! If we were all completely rational beings, we should then, instead of growing into perfect wisdom, degenerate into automatons, the human mind serving merely to register certain impulses as unfailingly as a gas meter. That would be inhuman, and anything inhuman is bad.

My readers may suspect that I am trying a desperate defense of human frailties and making virtues of their vices, and yet it is not so. What we gained in correctness of conduct through the development of a completely rational mind, we should lose in the fun and color of life. And nothing is so uninteresting as to spend one's life with a paragon of virtue as a husband or wife. I have no doubt that a society of such perfectly rational beings would be perfectly fitted to survive, and yet I wonder whether survival on such terms is worth having. Have a society that is well-ordered, by all means—but not too well-ordered!

One must never deprecate the capacity of the human mind when dealing with the natural universe or anything except human relationships. Optimistic about the conquests of science, I am less hopeful about the general development of a critical mind in dealing with human affairs, or about mankind

reaching a calm and understanding far above the sway of passions. Mankind as individuals may have reached austere heights, but mankind as social groups are still subject to primitive passions, occasional back-slidings and outcroppings of the savage instincts, and occasional waves of fanaticism and mass hysteria.

How can we remedy the situation? The critical mind is too thin and cold; thinking itself will help little and reason will be of small avail; only the spirit of reasonableness, a sort of warm, glowing, emotional and intuitive thinking, joined with compassion, will insure us against a reversion to our ancestral type. Only the development of our life to bring it into harmony with our instincts can save us. I consider the education of our senses and our emotions rather more important than the education of our ideas.

4. *The Purpose of Life*

The enjoyment of life covers many things the enjoyment of ourselves, of home life, of trees, flowers, clouds, winding rivers and falling cataracts and the myriad things in Nature, and then the enjoyment of poetry, art, contemplation, friendship, conversation, and reading, which are all some form or other of the communion of spirits. There are obvious things like the enjoyment of food, a gay party or family reunion, an outing on a beautiful spring day; and less obvious things like the enjoyment of poetry, art and contemplation. I have found it impossible to call these two classes of enjoyment material and spiritual, first because I do not believe in this distinction, and secondly because I am puzzled whenever I proceed to make this classification. How can I say, when I see a gay picnic party of men and women and old people and children, what part of their pleasures is material and what part spiritual? Is it so easy to draw a distinction between the enjoyment of a sandwich and the enjoyment of the surrounding landscape, which we call poetry? Is it possible to regard the enjoyment of music which we call art, as decidedly a higher type of pleasure than the smoking of a pipe, which we call material? This classification between material and spiritual pleasures is therefore confusing, unintelligible and untrue for me. It proceeds, I suspect, from a false philosophy, sharply dividing the spirit from the flesh, and not supported by a closer direct scrutiny of our real pleasures.

Or have I perhaps assumed too much and begged the question of the proper end of human life? I have always assumed that the end of living is the true enjoyment of it. It is so simply because it is so. I rather hesitate at the word "end" or "purpose." Such an end or purpose of life, consisting in its true enjoyment, is not so much a conscious purpose, as a natural attitude toward human life. The word "purpose" suggests too much contriving and endeavor. The question that faces every man born into this world is not what should be his purpose, which he should set about to achieve, but just what to do with life, a life which is given him for a period of on the average fifty or sixty years? The answer that he should order his life so that he can find the greatest happiness in it is more a practical question, similar to that of how a man should spend his weekend, than a metaphysical proposition as to what is the mystic purpose of his life in the scheme of the universe.

I rather think that philosophers who start out to solve the problem of the purpose of life beg the question by assuming that life must have a purpose. This question, so much pushed to the fore among Western thinkers, is undoubtedly given that importance through the influence of theology. I think we assume too much design and purpose altogether. And the very fact that people try to answer this question and quarrel over it and are puzzled by it serves to show it up as quite vain and uncalled for. Had there been a purpose or design in life, it should not have been so puzzling and vague and difficult to find out.

The question may be divided into two: either that of a divine purpose, which God has set for humanity, or that of a human purpose, a purpose that mankind should set for itself. As far as the first is concerned, I do not propose to enter into the question, be-

cause everything that we think God has in mind necessarily preceeds from our own mind; it is what we imagine to be in God's mind, and it is really difficult for human intelligence to guess at a divine intelligence. What we usually end up with by this sort of reasoning is to make God the color-sergeant of our army and to make Him as chauvinistic as ourselves. I am quite sure the Nazis can't conceive of God without a swastika arm-band.* But the Germans are not the only people who think this way.

As far as the second question is concerned, the point of dispute is not what *is,* but what *should be,* the purpose of human life, and it is therefore a practical, and not a metaphysical question. Into this question of what should be the purpose of human life, every man projects his own conceptions and his own scale of values. It is for this reason that we quarrel over the question, because our scales of values differ from one another. For myself, I am content to be less philosophical and more practical. I should not presume that there must be necessarily a purpose, a meaning of human existence. As Walt Whitman says, "I am sufficient as I am." It is sufficient that I live—and am probably going to live for another few decades—and that human life exists. Viewed that way, the problem becomes amazingly simple and admits of no two answers. What can be the end of human life except the enjoyment of it?

If we must have a view of the universe, let us forget ourselves and not confine it to human life. Let us stretch it a little and include in our view the purpose of the entire creation—the rocks, the trees and the animals. There is a scheme of things (although "scheme" is another word, like "end" and "purpose," which I strongly distrust)—I mean there is a pattern of things in the creation, and we can arrive at some sort of opinion, however lacking in finality, about this entire universe, and then take our place in it. This view of nature and our place in it must be natural, since we are a vital part of it in our life and go back to it when we die.

---

* This was written in 1937 (Ed.).

Astronomy, geology, biology and history all provide pretty good material to help us form a fairly good view if we don't attempt too much and jump at conclusions. It doesn't matter if, in this bigger view of the purpose of the creation, man's place recedes a little in importance. It is enough that he has a place, and by living in harmony with nature around him, he will be able to form a workable and reasonable outlook on human life itself.

5. The Problem of Happiness

All human happiness is biological happiness. That is strictly scientific. At the risk of being misunderstood, I must make it clearer: all human happiness is sensuous happiness. The spiritualists will misunderstand me, I am sure; the spiritualists and materialists must forever misunderstand each other, because they don't talk the same language or mean by the same word different things. Are we, too, in this problem of securing happiness to be deluded by the spiritualists, and admit that true happiness is only happiness of the spirit? Let us admit it at once and immediately proceed to qualify it by saying that the spirit is a condition of the perfect functioning of the endocrine glands. Happiness for me is largely a matter of digestion.

Let us not lose ourselves in the abstract when we talk of happiness, but get down to facts and analyze for ourselves what are the truly happy moments of our life. In this world of ours, happiness is very often negative, the complete absence of sorrow or mortification or bodily ailment. But happiness can also be positive, and then we call it joy. To me, for instance, the truly happy moments are: when I get up in the morning after a night of perfect sleep and sniff the morning air and there is an expansiveness in the lungs, when I feel inclined to inhale deeply and there is a fine sensation of movement around the skin and muscles of the chest, and when, therefore, I am fit for work; or when I hold a pipe in my hand and rest my legs on a chair, and the tobacco burns slowly and evenly; or when I am traveling on a summer day, my throat parched with thirst, and I see a beautiful clear spring, whose very sound makes me happy, and I take off my socks and shoes and dip my feet in the delightful, cool water; or when after a perfect dinner I lounge in an armchair, when there is no one I hate to look at in the company and conversation rambles off at a light pace to an unknown destination, and I am spiritually and physically at peace with the world; or when on a summer afternoon I see black clouds gathering on the horizon and know for certain a July shower is coming in a quarter of an hour, but being ashamed to be seen going out into the rain with an umbrella, I hastily set out to meet the shower halfway across the fields and come home drenched through and through and tell my family that I was simply caught by the rain.

Just as it is impossible for me to say whether I love my children physically or spiritually when I hear their chattering voices or when I see their plump legs, so I am totally unable to distinguish between the joys of the mind and the joys of the flesh. Does anybody ever love a woman spiritually without loving her physically? And is it so easy a matter for a man to analyze and separate the charms of the woman he loves—things like laughter, smiles, a way of tossing one's head, a certain attitude toward things? And after all every girl feels happier when she is well-dressed. There is a soul-uplifting quality about lipstick and rouge and a spiritual calm and poise that comes from the knowledge of being well-dressed, which is real and definite for the girl herself and of which the spiritualist has no inkling of an idea. Being made of this mortal flesh, the partition separating our flesh from our spirit is extremely thin, and the world of spirit, with its finest emotions and greatest appreciations of spiritual beauty, cannot be reached except with our senses. There is no such thing as morality and immorality in the sense of touch, of hearing and vision. There is a great probability that our loss of capacity for enjoying the positive joys of life is largely due to the decreased sensibility of our senses and our lack of full use of them.

Let us take the supposedly higher pleasures of the mind and the spirit, and see to what extent they are vitally connected with our senses, rather than with our intellect. What are those higher spiritual pleasures that we distinguish from those of the lower senses? Are they not parts of the same thing, taking root and ending up in the senses, and inseparable from them? As we go over these higher pleasures of the mind—literature, art, music, religion and philosophy—we see what a minor role the intellect plays in comparison with the senses and feelings. What does a painting do except to give us a landscape or a beautiful face? And what does literature do except to recreate a picture of life, to give us the atmosphere and color, the fragrant smell of the pastures or the stench of city gutters? We all say that a novel approches the standard of true literature in proportion as it gives us real people and real emotions. The book which takes us away from this human life, or merely coldly dissects it, is not literature and the more humanly true a book is, the better literature we consider it. What novel ever appeals to a reader if it contains only a cold analysis, if it fails to give us the salt and tang and flavor of life?

I can see no other reason for the existence of art and poetry and religion except as they tend to restore in us a freshness of vision and a more emotional glamour and more vital sense of life. For as we grow older in life, our senses become gradually benumbed, our emotions become more callous to suffering and injustice and cruelty, and our vision of life is warped by too much preoccupation with cold, trivial realities. Fortunately, we have a few poets and artists who have not lost that sharpened sensibility, that fine emotional response and that freshness of vision, and whose duties are therefore to be our moral conscience, to hold up a mirror to our blunted vision, to tone up our withered nerves. Art should be a satire and a warning against our paralyzed emotions, our devitalized thinking and our denaturalized living. It teaches us unsophistication in a sophisticated

world. It should restore to us health and sanity of living and enable us to recover from the fever and delirium caused by too much mental activity. It should sharpen our senses, re-establish the connection between our reason and our human nature, and assemble the ruined parts of a dislocated life again into a whole, by restoring our original nature. Miserable indeed is a world in which we have knowledge without understanding, criticism without appreciation, beauty without love, truth without passion, righteousness without mercy, and courtesy without a warm heart!

As for philosophy, which is the exercise of the spirit *par excellence,* the danger is even greater that we lose the feeling of life itself. I can understand that such mental delights include the solution of a long mathematical equation, or the perception of a grand order in the universe. This perception of order is probably the purest of all our mental pleasures and yet I would exchange it for a well-prepared meal. In the first place, it is in itself almost a freak, a by-product of our mental occupations, enjoyable because it is gratuitous, but not in any case as imperative for us as other vital processes. That intellectual delight is, after all, similar to the delight of solving a crossword puzzle successfully. In the second place, the philosopher at this moment more often than not is likely to cheat himself, to fall in love with this abstract perfection, and to conceive a greater logical perfection in the world than is really warranted by reality itself. It is as much a false picture of things as when we print a star with five points—a reduction to formula, an artificial stylizing, an over-simplification. So long as we do not overdo it, this delight in perfection is good, but let us remind ourselves that millions of people can be happy without discovering this simple unity of design. We really can afford to live without it.

Only by placing living above thinking can we get away from this heat and the re-breathed air of philosophy and recapture some of the freshness and naturalness of true insight of the child. The philosopher ought to be ashamed that God-made perfection has sometimes become man-made imperfection, ashamed that he wears spectacles, has no appetite, is often distressed in mind and heart, and is entirely unconscious of the fun in life. From this type of philosopher nothing is to be gained, for nothing that he says can be of importance to us. That philosophy alone can be of use to us which joins hands merrily with poetry and establishes for us a truer vision, first of nature and then of human nature.

6. This Earth the Only Heaven

A sad, poetic touch is added to this intense love of life by the realization that this life we have is essentially mortal. Strange to say, this sad awareness of our mortality makes the Chinese scholar's enjoyment of life all the more keen and intense. For if this earthly existence is all we have, we must try the harder to enjoy it while it lasts. A vague hope of immortality detracts from our wholehearted enjoyment of this earthly existence. As Sir Arthur Keith puts it with a typically Chinese feeling, "For if men believe, as I do, that this present earth is the only heaven, they will strive all the more to make heaven of it." Su Tung p'o says, "Life passes like a spring dream without a trace," and that is why he clung to it so fondly and tenaciously. It is this sentiment of our mortal existence that we run across again and again in Chinese literature. It is this feeling of the impermanence of existence and the evanescence of life, this touch of sadness, which overtakes the Chinese poet and scholar always at the moment of his greatest feasting and merrymaking, a sadness that is expressed in the regret that "the moon cannot always be so round and the flowers cannot forever look so fair" when we are watching the full moon in the company of beautiful flowers.

Belief in our mortality, the sense that we are eventually going to crack up and be extinguished like the flame of a candle, I say, is a gloriously fine thing. It makes us sober; it makes us a little sad; and many of us it makes poetic. But above all, it makes it possible for us to make up our mind and arrange to live sensibly, truthfully and always with a sense of our own limitations. It gives peace also, because true peace of mind comes from accepting the worst. Psychologically, I think, it means a release of energy.

Deprived of immortality, the proposition of living becomes a simple proposition. It is this: that we human beings have a limited span of life to live on this earth, rarely more than seventy years, and that therefore we have to arrange our lives so that we may live as happily as we can under a given set of circumstances. Here we are on Confucian ground. There is something mundane, something terribly earth-bound about it, and man proceeds to work with a dogged common sense, very much in the spirit of what George Santayana calls "animal faith." With this animal faith, taking life as it is, we made a shrewd guess, without Darwin's aid, as to our essential kinship with animals. It made us, therefore, cling to life—the life of the senses—on the belief that, as we are all animals, we can be truly happy only when all our normal instincts are satisfied normally. This applies to the enjoyment of life in all its aspects.

This feeling of the reality and spirituality of life is helped by Chinese humanism, in fact by the whole Chinese way of thinking and living. Chinese philosophy may be briefly defined as a preoccupation with the knowledge of life rather than the knowledge of truth. Brushing aside all metaphysical speculations as irrelevant to the business of living, and as pale reflections engendered in our intellect, the Chinese philosophers clutch at life itself and ask themselves the one and only eternal question: "How are we to live?" Philosophy in the Western sense seems to the Chinese eminently idle. In its preoccupation with logic, which concerns itself with the method of arrival at knowledge, and epistemology, which poses the question of the possibility of knowledge, it has forgotten to deal with the knowledge of life itself. That is so much tomfoolery and a kind of frivolity, like wooing and courtship without coming to marriage and the producing of children, which is as bad as having redcoated regiments marching in military parades without going to battle. The German philosophers are the most frivolous of all; they court truth like ardent lovers, but seldom propose to marry her.

7. *The Feminine Design for Living*

The taking of such a simple and natural biological viewpoint implies two conflicts, first, the conflict between individualism and the family, and second, a deeper conflict between the sterile philosophy of the intellect and the warmer philosophy of the instinct. For individualism and worship of the intellect are likely to blind a man to the beauties of home life, and of the two, I think the first is not so wicked as the second. A man believing in individualism and carrying it to its logical consequences can still be a very intelligent being, but a man believing in the cold head as against the warm heart is a fool. For the collectivism of the family as a social unit, there can be substitutes, but for the loss of the mating and paternal-maternal instincts, there can be none.

Woman, who has a deeper biological sense than man, knows this. Subconsciously all Chinese girls dream of the red wedding petticoat and the wedding sedan, and all Western girls dream of the wedding veil and wedding bells. Nature has endowed women with too powerful a maternal instinct for it to be easily put out of the way by an artificial civilization. I have no doubt that nature conceives of woman chiefly as a mother, even more than as a mate, and has endowed her with mental and moral characteristics which are conductive to her role as mother, and which find their true explanation and unity in the maternal instinct—realism, judgment, patience with details, love of the small and helpless, desire to take care of somebody, strong animal love and hatred, great personal and emotional bias and a generally personal outlook on things. Philosophy, therefore, has gone astray when it departs from nature's own conception and tries to make women happy without taking into account this ma-

ternal instinct which is the dominant trait and central explanation of her entire being. Thus with all uneducated and sanely educated women, the maternal instinct is never suppressed, comes to light in childhood and grows stronger and stronger through adolescence to maturity, while with man, the paternal instinct seldom becomes conscious until after thirty-five, or in any case until he has a son or daughter five years old. I do not think that a man of twenty-five ever thinks about becoming a father. He merely falls in love with a girl and accidentally produces a baby and forgets all about it, while his wife's thoughts are occupied with nothing else, until one day in his thirties he suddenly becomes aware that he has a son or daughter whom he can take to the market and parade before his friends, and only then does he begin to feel paternal. Few men of twenty or twenty-five are not *amused* at the idea of their becoming a father, and beyond amusement, there is little thought spent on it, whereas having a baby, even anticipating one, is probably the most serious thing that ever comes to a woman's life and changes her entire being to the point of affecting a transformation of her character and habits. The world becomes a different world for her when a woman becomes an expectant mother. Thenceforth she has no doubt whatever in her mind as to her mission in life or the purpose of her existence. She is wanted. She is needed. And she functions. I have seen the most pampered and petted only daughter of a rich Chinese family growing to heroic stature and losing sleep for months when her child was ill. In nature's scheme, no such paternal instinct is necessary and none is provided for, for man, like the drake or the gander, has little concern over his offspring otherwise than contributing his part. *Women, therefore, suffer most psychologically when this central motive power of their being is not expressed and does not function.* No one need tell me how kind American civilization is to women, when it permits so many nice women to go unmarried through no fault of their own.

After all, we are concerned only with the question: "How to live a happy life?" and no one's life can be happy unless beyond the superficial attainments of the external life, the deeper springs of his or her character are touched and find a normal outlet. Celibacy as an ideal in the form of "personal career" carries with it not only an individualistic, but also a foolishly intellectualistic taint, and is for the latter reason to be condemned. I always suspect the confirmed bachelor or unmarried woman who remains so by choice of being an ineffectual intellectualist, too much engrossed with his or her own external achievements, believing that he or she can, as a human being, find happiness in an effective substitute for the home life, or find an intellectual, artistic or professional interest which is deeply satisfying. . . . I understand that there has been a swing in the right direction away from the feminist ideal among the American college girls of today, that the majority of them are able to look at life sanely enough to say openly that they want to get married. The ideal woman for me is one who loves her cosmetics along with her mathematics, and who is more feminine than feminist. Let them have their cosmetics, and *if they still have energy left,* as Confucius would say, let them play with mathematics also.

It is to be understood that we are talking of the average ideal of the average man and woman. There are distinguished and talented women as there are distinguished and talented men, whose creative ability accounts for the world's real progress. If I ask the average woman to regard marriage as the ideal profession and to bear babies and perhaps also wash dishes, I also ask the average man to forget the arts and just earn the family bread, by cutting hair or shining shoes or catching thieves or tinkering pots or waiting at tables. Since some one has to bear the babies and take care of them and see them safely through measles and raise them to be good and wise citizens, and since men are entirely ineffectual in bearing babies and frightfully awkward in holding and bathing them, naturally I look to the women to do the job. . . . The important point is that the general assumption that home life, with its important and sacred task of raising and influencing the young of the race, is too low for women can hardly be called a sane social attitude, and it is possible only in a culture where woman and the home and motherhood are not sufficiently respected.

The Uninhibited Pursuit of Pleasure: Aristippus and the Cyrenaics

One of the earliest and most forthright presentations of hedonism is that found in the teaching of Aristippus, a native of Cyrene in North Africa who was for a time a disciple of Socrates in Athens. Unfortunately, nothing written by Aristippus has survived. In his *Lives and Opinions of Eminent Philosophers* (written early in the third century A.D.) Diogenes Laertius attributes a number of essays to Aristippus, some of which he says were in circulation then. Actually, Diogenes Laertius' own account is the oldest extant discussion of the philosophy of Aristippus. To provide some acquaintance with an early philosophical work of considerable historical significance, a selection is included from the chapter on Aristippus in *Lives and Opinions of Eminent Philosophers*.

Little is definitely known of the author of this work. Who Laertius was, when he was born, and where he lived are nowhere recorded. His book professes to give an account of the chief Greek thinkers; by some chance it survived whereas the large number of more important works from which he quotes were destroyed. During the Renaissance Diogenes Laertius became famous and was given much more authority than he deserved. As a result early European histories of philosophy were little more than rearrangements of his material. A careful study of *Lives and Opinions of Eminent Philosophers* shows, however, that the author did not write from personal knowledge but was borrowing, copying, and making excerpts from well-known works of his day. How many of the numerous sources he cited Laertius had read himself there is no way to determine. Many of these references may well come from other authors whom he is using. In any case Laertius is a writer of amazing industry and curiosity; he searched widely for his information and it is reasonable to assume that he had read the more famous of the authors whom he quotes. As was customary in his day, he is obviously looking for interesting personal details, anecdotes and witty sayings which in his opinion revealed character and philosophy better than a volume of annals. Actually, the *Lives and Opinions of Eminent Philosophers* belongs to literature rather than to philosophy, but it has a unique value because so little ancient biography of this sort exists. And its importance is in many ways the greater just because there is so little of Laertius himself in it.[1]

Although interest in philosophical questions is not primary with Laertius, when discussing the Cyrenaics, the Cynics, and the Stoics he deals at length with philosophy, and in the chapter on Epicurus we have perhaps the single most important part of his work. In this chapter (Book X) he reproduces Epicurus' letters and numerous fragments from his philosophy verbatim and by doing so saved

---

[1] The Introduction to the English translation of *Lives of Eminent Philosophers* by R. D. Hicks (Cambridge, Harvard University Press, 1925) provides a careful examination of Laertius' work.

these documents for us. On the other hand, Laertius is uncritical and he wrote for an uncritical age. A number of factual errors resulting from his careless handling of materials have been discovered in his work by recent and more careful historians. Thus, while *Lives and Opinions* contains our earliest account of Aristippus' philosophy, it is by no means the most satisfactory. Among the standard histories of philosophy there is none in which the spirit of the Cyrenaic position is so appealingly expressed, and its major tenets so clearly outlined, as in the account by B. A. G. Fuller in his three-volume *History of Greek Philosophy*. A second brief selection on Aristippus is taken, therefore, from this work.

For over twenty-five years B. A. G. Fuller was one of the popular and successful teachers of philosophy in this country. After some years as a young instructor at Harvard and a period in Italy where he did the initial writing of his *History of Greek Philosophy*, he was for seven years (1924–1931) professor of philosophy at the University of Cincinnati. Then while a professor at the University of Southern California from 1933–1946 he became a leading figure in American philosophical circles, writing and lecturing widely until his death in 1951 at the age of seventy-two. Although his two-volume *History of Philosophy* (1942) was a successful college text, nothing Fuller wrote ever surpassed the early *History of Greek Philosophy* from which our selection is taken.

*Aristippus of Cyrene**

I

Aristippus [*c.* 435–350 B.C.] was by birth a citizen of Cyrene and was drawn to Athens by the fame of Socrates. Having come forward as a lecturer or sophist, he was the first of the followers of Socrates to charge fees and to send money to his master. And on one occasion the sum of twenty minae which he had sent was returned to him, Socrates declaring that the supernatural sign would not let him take it; the very offer, in fact, annoyed him. Xenophon† was no friend

to Aristippus; and for this reason he had made Socrates direct against Aristippus the discourse in which he denounces pleasure [*Memorabilia* ii, 1].

He [Aristippus] was capable of adapting himself to place, time and person, and of playing his part appropriately under whatever circumstances. Hence he found more favour than anybody else with Dionysius‡, because he could always turn the situation to good account. He derived pleasure from what was present, and did not toil to procure the enjoyment of something not present. Hence Diogenes** called him the king's poodle.

He is said to have ordered a partridge to be bought at a cost of fifty drachmae, and, when someone censured him, he inquired, "Would not you have given an obol for it?" and, being answered in the affirmative, re-

* Reprinted by permission of the Publishers and the Loeb Classical Library. Translated by R. D. Hicks, Diogenes Laertius: *Lives of Eminent Philosophers* (Cambridge, Mass., Harvard University Press, 1925. Rev. ed. 1938, 1942, 1950), Vol. 1, Bk ii (abridged).

† Xenophon—an admirer and contemporary of Socrates, who wrote one of the famous accounts of his life and teaching (the *Memorabilia*).

‡ Dionysius—wealthy ruler of Syracuse, c. 430–367 B.C.

** Diogenes—one of the early cynics, who disregarded all social conventions.

joined, "Fifty drachmae are no more to me." And when Dionysius gave him his choice of three courtesans, he carried off all three, saying, "Paris†† paid dearly for giving the preference to one out of three." And when he had brought them as far as the porch, he let them go. To such lengths did he go both in choosing and in disdaining. Hence the remark of Strato, or by some accounts of Plato, "You alone are endowed with the gift to flaunt in robes or go in rags."

Being asked what he had gained from philosophy, he replied, "The ability to feel at ease in any society." Being reproached for his extravagance, he said, "If it were wrong to be extravagant, it would not be in vogue at the festivals of the gods." Being once asked what advantage philosophers have, he replied, "Should all laws be repealed, we shall go on living as we do now." When Dionysius inquired what was the reason that philosophers go to rich men's houses, while rich men no longer visit philosophers, his reply was that "the one know what they need while the other do not." When he was reproached by Plato for his extravagance, he inquired, "Do you think Dionysius a good man?" and the reply being in the affirmative, "And yet," said he, "he lives more extravagantly than I do. So that there is nothing to hinder a man living extravagantly and well."

He gave his daughter Arete the very best advice, training her up to despise excess. He was asked by some one in what way his son would be the better for being educated. He replied, "If nothing more than this, at all events, when in the theatre he will not sit down like a stone upon stone." When some one brought his son as a pupil, he asked a fee of 500 drachmae. The father objected, "For that sum I can buy a slave." "Then do so," was the reply, "and you will have two." He said that he did not take money from his friends for his own use, but to teach them upon what objects their money should be spent. When he was reproached for employing a rhetorician to conduct his case, he made

†† Paris—prince of Troy who selected Aphrodite as more beautiful than Hera or Athena.

reply, "Well, if I give a dinner, I hire a cook."

Being once compelled by Dionysius to enunciate some doctrine of philosophy, "It would be ludicrous," he said, "that you should learn from me what to say, and yet instruct me when to say it." At this, they say, Dionysius was offended and made him recline at the end of the table. And Aristippus said, "You must have wished to confer distinction on the last place." To some one who boasted of his diving, "Are you not ashamed," said he, "to brag of that which a dolphin can do?" Being asked on one occasion what is the difference between the wise man and the unwise, "Strip them both," said he, "and send them among strangers and you will know." To one who boasted that he could drink a great deal without getting drunk, his rejoinder was, "And so can a mule."

To one who accused him of living with a courtesan, he put the question, "Why, is there any difference between taking a house in which many people have lived before and taking one in which nobody has ever lived?" The answer being "No," he continued, "Or again, between sailing in a ship in which ten thousand persons have sailed before and in one in which nobody has ever sailed?" "There is no difference." "Then it makes no difference," said he, "whether the woman you live with has lived with many or with nobody." To the accusation, that, although he was a pupil of Socrates, he took fees, his rejoinder was, "Most certainly I do, for Socrates, too, when certain people sent him corn and wine, used to take a little and return all the rest; and he had the foremost men in Athens for his stewards, whereas mine is my slave Eutychides." He enjoyed the favours of Laïs, as Sotion states in the second book of his *Successions of Philosophers*. To those who censured him his defence was, "I have Laïs, not she me; and it is not abstinence from pleasures that is best, but mastery over them without ever being worsted." To one who reproached him with extravagance in catering, he replied, "Wouldn't you have bought this if you could have got it for three obols?" The answer being in the affirmative, "Very well, then," said Aristippus, "I am no longer a lover of pleasure, it is you who are a lover of money."

When his servant was carrying money and found the load too heavy—the story is told by Bion in his *Lectures*—Aristippus cried, "Pour away the greater part, and carry no more than you can manage." Being once on a voyage, as soon as he discovered the vessel to be manned by pirates, he took out his money and began to count it, and then, as if by inadvertence, he let the money fall into the sea, and naturally broke out into lamentation. Another version of the story attributes to him the further remark that it was better for the money to perish on account of Aristippus than for Aristippus to perish on account of the money. Dionysius once asked him what he was come for, and he said it was to impart what he had and obtain what he had not. But some make his answer to have been, "When I needed wisdom, I went to Socrates; now that I am in need of money, I come to you." He used to complain of mankind that in purchasing earthenware they made trial whether it rang true, but had no regular standard by which to judge life. Others attribute this remark to Diogenes.

There have been four men called Aristippus, (1) our present subject, (2) the author of a book about Arcadia, (3) the grandchild by a daughter of the first Aristippus, who was known as his mother's pupil, (4) a philosopher of the New Academy.

The following books by the Cyrenaic philosopher are in circulation: a history of Libya in three Books, sent to Dionysius; one work containing twenty-five dialogues, some written in Attic, some in Doric.

According to Sotion in his second book, and Panaetius, the following treatises are his:

On Education.	Six books of Essays.
On Virtue.	Three books of Oc-
Introduction to Phi-	casional Writings.
losophy.	To Laïs.
Artabazus.	To Porus.
The Ship-wrecked.	To Socrates.
The Exiles.	On Fortune.

II

Those then who adhered to the teaching of Aristippus and were known as Cyrenaics held the following opinions. They laid down that there are two states, pleasure and pain, the former a smooth, the latter a rough motion, and that pleasure does not differ from pleasure nor is one pleasure more pleasant than another. The one state is agreeable and the other repellent to all living things. They also hold that there is a difference between "end" and "happiness." Our end is particular pleasure, whereas happiness is the sum total of all particular pleasures, in which are included both past and future pleasures.

Particular pleasure is desirable for its own sake, whereas happiness is desirable not for its own sake but for the sake of particular pleasures. That pleasure is the end is proved by the fact that from our youth up we are instinctively attracted to it, and, when we obtain it, seek for nothing more, and shun nothing so much as its opposite, pain. Pleasure is good even if it proceed from the most unseemly conduct, as Hippobatus says in his work *On the Sects*. For even if the action be irregular, still, at any rate, the resultant pleasure is desirable for its own sake and is good. The removal of pain, however, which is put forward in Epicurus, seems to them not to be pleasure at all, any more than the absence of pleasure is pain. For both pleasure and pain they hold to consist in motion, whereas absence of pleasure like absence of pain is not motion, since painlessness is the condition of one who is, as it were, asleep. They assert that some people may fail to choose pleasure because their minds are perverted; not all mental pleasures and pains, however, are derived from bodily counterparts. For instance, we take disinterested delight in the prosperity of our country which is as real as our delight in our own prosperity. Nor again do they admit that pleasure is derived from the memory or expectation of good, which was a doctrine of Epicurus. For they assert that the movement affecting the mind is exhausted in course of time. Again they hold that pleasure is not derived from sight or from hearing alone. At all events, we listen with pleasure to imitation of mourning, while the reality causes pain. They gave the names of absence of pleasure and absence of pain to the intermediate conditions. However, they insist that bodily pleasures are far better than mental pleasures, and bodily pains far worse than mental pains, and that this is the reason why offenders are punished with the former. For they assumed pain to be more repellent, pleasure more congenial. For these reasons they paid more attention to the body than to the mind. Hence, although pleasure is in itself desirable, yet they hold that the things which are productive of certain pleasures are often of a painful nature, the very opposite of pleasure; so that to accumulate the pleasures which are productive of happiness appears to them a most irksome business.

They do not accept the doctrine that every wise man lives pleasantly and every fool painfully, but regard it as true for the most part only. It is sufficient even if we enjoy but each single pleasure as it comes. They say that prudence is a good, though desirable not in itself but on account of its consequences; that we make friends from interested motives, just as we cherish any part of the body so long as we have it; that some of the virtues are found even in the foolish; that bodily training contributes to the acquisition of virtue; that the sage will not give way to envy or love or superstition, since these weaknesses are due to mere empty opinion; he will, however, feel pain and fear, these being natural affections; and that wealth too is productive of pleasure, though not desirable for its own sake.

They also held that nothing is just or honourable or base by nature, but only by convention and custom. Nevertheless the good man will be deterred from wrong-doing by the penalties imposed and the prejudices that it would arouse. Further that the wise man really exists. They allow progress to be attainable in philosophy as well as in other matters. They maintain that the pain of one man exceeds that of another, and that the senses are not always true and trust-worthy.

The Cyrenaics*

I

The Cyrenaic doctrine reflects strikingly the personality and circumstances of its founder. Straight across from the southern-most promontories of Greece the African coast suddenly rises from league on league of sand-bar and shallow waste of shifting dune, and for a space of a hundred and fifty miles thrusts out into the sea a mass of low, dome-shaped mountains. The sea-face of the western mountains was celebrated in ancient times as a veritable garden of the Hesperides. Here the great downs shelved to the Mediterranean in a couple of table-lands, part forest, part open park and grass and rich tillage, furrowed here and there with deep, lush watercourses, and indented at their base with coastal plains of tropical luxuriance. Screened from the hot winds of the desert by the higher crests, and open to the sea-breezes, these northern terraces enjoyed a variety of tempered and equable climates; and from plateau to plateau one passed through every gift of vegetation from tropical groves of date palms to forests of northern oak. So verdant, so lovely, so sudden and gracious in the midst of the melancholy and endless sands, are the terraces of these fair hills, that even to-day they are known to the desert-tribes as Jebal Akdar or the Green Mountain.

* B. A. G. Fuller, *History of Greek Philosophy,* (New York, Henry Holt & Company, 1931), Vol. II, Chap. III, Sec. iv (abridged). Reprinted by permission of the publishers.

Halfway along this smiling coast there is an open bay with good anchorage, sheltered to the east and west by jutting headlands, and backed by a thin strip of plain. Behind, the hills rise sharply, first to a narrow terrace, and then to the broad tableland that caps the range. Here on the edge of the upper plateau, at an elevation of eighteen hundred feet and some ten miles from the Mediterranean, Greek colonists from the island of Thera founded in 631 B.C. the town of Cyrene. And here two hundred years later Aristippus was born.

By that time the original settlement had grown into a rich and splendid city. Its walls and towers, the battlements of its Acropolis, the gleaming marble of its temples and colonnades, floating high in the blue sky above the groves and hanging gardens of the mountain ridge, were a landmark far out to sea. On the shore below, deep in the curve of the bay, lay the busy port of Apollonia, so called by the Cyreneans after the God whose oracle had led them to this promised land. A broad road connected the city with its harbor, down it wound all the varied wealth of the country for export to the ends of the Mediterranean world. The wharves were piled high with jars of wine and olive-oil and honey, and sacks of wheat and baskets of almonds, dates, figs, and truffles, and every sort of fruit and vegetables. Great heaps of ostrich plumes there were, too, and saffron flowers for the making of delicious perfumes, and the rare and celebrated silphium plant, now extinct, and even at that time found nowhere else, whose stalks were used as fodder, and whose resinous gum was in much esteem and demand for medicinal purposes with the physicians of antiquity. Or, it might be that some trader was loading his ship with horses of the famous Cyrenean breed, whose victories in the chariot races at Olympia had been sung more than once by Pindar.

From a people of such easy life and so privileged by nature and by fortune we might expect a certain mellowness and even softness of moral outlook. Nor should we be surprised to hear that by the ancients they were reputed to be pleasure-loving and luxurious.

Certainly Aristippus was by nature both. Born of a wealthy family at the moment when Cyrene was at its best and richest, he fell heir to all the advantages and disadvantages that ease and money bring. He seems to have been a genial, clever, sweet-tempered youth, a "good mixer" with every kind of company, very fond of having a good time, and naturally inclined and able to keep pace with the other rather fast young clubmen about town. But he was also intelligent, ingenious, and resourceful, and, though apparently not a man of great courage, he had a presence of mind and quickness of wit that generally enabled him to do the right thing and give the right answer at a critical moment. And his ability to get on well with all sorts of people developed into considerable skill in getting out of them what he wanted. All in all, if to his adaptability, his intellectual gifts, and his talent for managing men, we add a composure of manner and a strength of mind and will that made him the master rather than the slave of his likes and dislikes, his passions and his prejudices, we may feel that if Aristippus had not become a philosopher he would have made a brilliant diplomat of the old school, and in modern times, at least, would have died an ambassador many times over.

Just when and how he became enamored of philosophy we do not know. But it seems to have been during a visit to the Olympic games that Aristippus' fate was sealed. There, we are told, he heard from a friend a full account of Socrates' personality and teaching, by which he was so ravished that he could scarcely wait to get to Athens and see and hear for himself so delightful and interesting a man. The meeting made of him a confirmed philosopher and one of Socrates' most devoted followers, and he was quickly received into the little circle of the more intimate friends and companions. He was, however, absent in Aegina at the time of the trial, and for some reason did not hasten back, as we should have expected of so close a disciple, to say farewell to his master and stand by him till the last.

After the execution [of Socrates] Aris-

man is the measure of the life that he enjoys most; in other words, of the life that is morally best for him.

The good, [Aristippus] said, is to be found in the pleasure of the moment alone. It has "nothing to do either with the recollection of past enjoyments or with the hope of future ones." The present pleasure is the only pleasure really felt. Past and future pleasures cannot concern us, since the past are no longer in existence and the future have not yet come into being. Had we reminded Aristippus of memory at this point, he would doubtless have replied that remembering a pleasure does not bring it back, and that the images and enjoyments of memory are nothing compared to the vividness of present feelings. And as to the pleasures of anticipation, so far as they are felt, they are present—but how faint they look in comparison with those actually being enjoyed here and now! Moreover, why waste one's time enjoying the prospect of something that, given the unreliability of events, may never occur? Gambling in future pleasures involves too great a risk. To-day should never be sacrificed to the morrow. The truly wise man will make hay while the sun shines, seizing every pleasure as it comes to hand, careless of its origin and past. Nor, in theory at least, ought he to worry too much about consequences, since he cannot know with any certainty what they will be like.

The drift of Aristippus' argument must now be plain. Durability, being an unknown factor, can play no part in determining the goodness of a pleasure. Immediacy and intensity are the only gauges left. Again, since the most available and the most intense pleasures happen generally to be those of the "senses," the pleasures of the senses are better than those, so called, of the mind.

The Rubáiyát of Omar Khayyám

Among classic portrayals of life devoted to the pursuit of pleasure, there are few books comparable to Edward FitzGerald's translation of the *Rubáiyát,* a work originally written by Omar Khayyám, Persian astronomer and poet of the twelfth century. This work was translated in 1859, and for years it was a recognized symbol of revolt against the Victorian morality of nineteenth-century England. Nowhere has Cyrenaic hedonism been expressed with such appeal and poetic beauty as in its familiar lines. Much of the appeal of the *Rubáiyát* is obviously to be found in the haunting imagery of Omar Khayyám and in the poetry of FitzGerald, rather than in the soundness of the Cyrenaic philosophy it reflects. FitzGerald has clothed the hedonism of Aristippus in its most attractive garb, and has likewise stated clearly all its basic assumptions. For this reason a generous selection from the *Rubáiyát* has been included here.

For Omar Khayyám, as for Aristippus, the road to happiness lies in the direct and uninhibited pursuit of pleasure. The pleasures of the moment and the pleasure of the senses are most to be sought, for in them we find immediate and undeniable enjoyment. Life is short, the future uncertain, and the present itself is fast slipping by. He who hesitates may well miss the pleasures that life has to offer, and if he does, he has no one to blame but himself. So, at least, the translator of the *Rubáiyát,* in complete agreement with Aristippus, assures us. This world, the hedonist maintains, is the only one we can count on. It is here that we must find happiness if we are to find it at all. Heaven and Hell are not places to which the soul will go in some future state; they are qualities of experience here and now. Not only is life uncertain and fleeting; our destiny is shaped by a power far greater than our own puny desires and ambitions. Man is but a pawn in the hands of fate, and the individual of no more consequence in the universe than the grains of sand on the seashore. Man has no real freedom, and it is foolish as well as futile to strive against the forces that shape his destiny. God, if God there be, is not troubled by human hopes and fears. In such a world, moreover, there can be no such thing as moral responsibility. The things a man does he has to do, and the God who created him as he is can certainly not blame him for enjoying the pleasures that by nature he is led to desire. Let us then enjoy ourselves while we can, not wasting the precious moments that are ours in fruitless speculation over man's destiny nor in moral condemnation of his natural and inescapable desires.

These are the major tenets advocated in the hedonism of Aristippus and expressed with poetic beauty and without inhibition in the well-known stanzas of the *Rubáiyát.*

The Rubáiyát*

1. Awake! For Morning in the Bowl of Night
   Has Flung the Stone that puts the Stars to Flight:
   And Lo! the Hunter of the East has caught
   The Sultan's Turret in a Noose of Light.

2. Dreaming when Dawn's Left Hand was in the Sky
   I heard a Voice within the Tavern cry,
   "Awake, my Little Ones, and fill the Cup
   Before Life's Liquor in its Cup be dry."

3. And, as the Cock crew, those who stood before
   The Tavern shouted—"Open then the Door!
   "You know how little while we have to stay,
   And, once departed, may return no more."

7. Come, fill the Cup, and in the fire of Spring
   Your Winter-garment of Repentance fling:
   The Bird of Time has but a little way
   To flutter—and the Bird is on the Wing.

8. Whether at Naishapur or Babylon,
   Whether the Cup with sweet or bitter run,
   The Wine of Life keeps oozing drop by drop,
   The Leaves of Life keep falling one by one.

11. With me along the strip of Herbage strown
    That just divides the desert from the sown,
    Where name of Slave and Sultan is forgot—
    And Peace to Mahmud on his golden Throne!

12. A Book of Verses underneath the Bough,
    A Jug of Wine, a Loaf of Bread—and Thou
    Beside me singing in the Wilderness—
    Ah, Wilderness were Paradise enow!

13. Some for the Glories of This World; and some
    Sigh for the Prophet's Paradise to come;
    Ah, take the Cash, and let the Credit go,
    Nor heed the rumble of a distant Drum!

14. Look to the blowing Rose about us—"Lo,
    Laughing," she says, "into the world I blow,
    At once the silken tassel of my Purse
    Tear, and its Treasure on the Garden throw."

15. And those who husbanded the Golden grain,
    And those who flung it to the winds like Rain,

---

* From the English translation by Edward FitzGerald, fourth version, 1879. Stanzas 1 and 2 are from the original version of 1859. Stanzas whose oriental imagery makes them almost unintelligible for the present-day reader have been omitted.

Alike to no such aureate Earth are turn'd
As, buried once, Men want dug up again.

16. The Worldly Hope men set their Hearts upon
Turns Ashes—or it prospers; and anon,
Like Snow upon the Desert's dusty Face,
Lighting a little hour or two—is gone.

17. Think, in this batter'd Caravanserai
Whose Portals are alternate Night and Day,
How Sultan after Sultan with his Pomp
Abode his destined Hour, and went his way.

18. They say the Lion and the Lizard keep
The courts where Jamshyd gloried and drank deep:
And Bahram, that great Hunter—the Wild Ass
Stamps o'er his Head, but cannot break his Sleep.

19. I sometimes think that never blows so red
The Rose as where some buried Caesar bled;
That every Hyacinth the Garden wears
Dropt in her Lap from some once lovely Head.

20. And this reviving Herb whose tender Green
Fledges the River-Lip on which we lean—
Ah, lean upon it lightly! for who knows
From what once lovely Lip it springs unseen!

21. Ah, my Beloved, fill the Cup that clears
To-day of past Regrets and future Fears:
To-morrow!—Why, To-morrow I may be
Myself with Yesterday's Sev'n thousand Years.

22. For some we loved, the loveliest and the best
That from his Vintage rolling Time hath prest,
Have drunk their Cup a Round or two before,
And one by one crept silently to rest.

23. And we, that now make merry in the Room
They left, and Summer dresses in new bloom,
Ourselves must we beneath the Couch of Earth
Descend—ourselves to make a Couch—for whom?

24. Ah, make the most of what we yet may spend,
Before we too into the Dust descend;
Dust into Dust, and under Dust to lie,
Sans Wine, sans Song, sans Singer, and—sans End!

25. Alike for those who for *To-day* prepare,
And those that after some *To-morrow* stare,
A Muezzin from the Tower of Darkness cries,
"Fools! your Reward is neither Here nor There."

26. Why, all the Saints and Sages who discuss'd
Of the Two Worlds so wisely—they are thrust

Like foolish Prophets forth; their Words to Scorn
Are scatter'd, and their Mouths are stopt with Dust.

27. Myself when young did eagerly frequent
Doctor and Saint, and heard great argument
About it and about: but evermore
Came out by the same door where in I went.

28. With them the seed of Wisdom did I sow,
And with mine own hand wrought to make it grow;
And this was all the Harvest that I reap'd—
"I came like Water, and like Wind I go."

29. Into this Universe, and Why not knowing
Nor Whence, like Water willy-nilly flowing;
And out of it, as Wind along the Waste,
I know not Whither, willy-nilly blowing.

31. Up from Earth's Center through the Seventh Gate
I rose, and on the Throne of Saturn sate,
And many a Knot unravel'd by the Road;
But not the Master-knot of Human Fate.

32. There was the Door to which I found no Key;
There was the Veil through which I might not see:
Some little talk awhile of *Me* and *Thee*
There was—and then no more of *Thee* and *Me*.

33. Earth could not answer; nor the Seas that mourn
In flowing Purple, of their Lord forlorn;
Nor rolling Heaven, with all his Signs revealed
And hidden by the sleeve of Night and Morn.

34. Then of the *Thee In Me* who works behind
The Veil, I lifted up my hands to find
A Lamp amid the Darkness; and I heard,
As from Without—"*The Me Within Thee Blind!*"

35. Then to the Lip of this poor earthen Urn
I lean'd, the Secret of my Life to Learn:
And Lip to Lip it murmur'd—"While you live,
"Drink!—for, once dead, you never shall return."

41. Perplext no more with Human or Divine,
To-morrow's tangle to the winds resign,
And lose your fingers in the tresses of
The Cypress-slender Minister of Wine.

42. And if the Wine you drink, the Lip you press,
End in what All begins and ends in—Yes;
Think then you are *To-day* what *Yesterday*
You were—*To-morrow* you shall not be less.

43. So when that Angel of the darker Drink
At last shall find you by the river-brink,

And, offering his Cup, invite your Soul
Forth to your Lips to quaff—you shall not shrink.

44. Why, if the Soul can fling the Dust aside,
And naked on the Air of Heaven ride,
Were't not a Shame—were't not a Shame for him
In this clay carcase crippled to abide?

45. 'Tis but a Tent where takes his one day's rest
A Sultan to the realm of Death addrest;
The Sultan rises, and the dark Ferrash
Strikes, and prepares it for another Guest.

46. And fear not lest Existence closing your
Account, and mine, should know the like no more;
The Eternal Saki from that Bowl has pour'd
Millions of Bubbles like us, and will pour.

47. When You and I behind the Veil are past,
Oh, but the long, long while the World shall last,
Which of our Coming and Departure heeds
As the Sea's self should heed a pebble-cast.

48. A Moment's Halt—a momentary taste
Of *Being* from the Well amid the Waste—
And Lo!—the phantom Caravan has reach'd
The *Nothing* it set out from—Oh, make haste!

54. Waste not your Hour, nor in the vain pursuit
Of This and That endeavor and dispute;
Better be jocund with the fruitful Grape
Than sadden after none, or bitter, Fruit.

55. You know, my Friends, with what a brave Carouse
I made a Second Marriage in my house;
Divorced old barren Reason from my Bed
And took the Daughter of the Vine to Spouse.

56. For "Is" and "Is-not" though with Rule and Line
And "*Up-And-Down*" by Logic I define,
Of all that one should care to fathom, I
Was never deep in anything but—Wine.

58. And lately, by the Tavern Door agape,
Came shining through the Dusk an Angel Shape
Bearing a Vessel on his Shoulder: and
He bid me taste of it; and 'twas—the Grape!

59. The Grape that can with Logic absolute
The Two-and-Seventy jarring Sects confute:
The sovereign Alchemist that in a trice
Life's leaden metal into Gold transmute:

61. Why, be this Juice the growth of God, who dare
Blaspheme the twisted tendril as a Snare?

A Blessing, we should use it, should we not?
And if a Curse—why, then, Who set it there?

62. I must abjure the Balm of Life, I must,
Scared by some After-reckoning ta'en on trust,
Or lured with Hope of some Diviner Drink,
To fill the Cup—when crumbled into Dust!

63. Of threats of Hell and Hopes of Paradise!
One thing at least is certain—This Life flies;
One thing is certain and the rest is Lies;
The Flower that once has blown for ever dies.

64. Strange, is it not? that of the myriads who
Before us pass'd the door of Darkness through,
Not one returns to tell us of the Road,
Which to discover we must travel too.

65. The Revelations of Devout and Learn'd
Who rose before us, and as Prophets burn'd,
Are all but Stories, which, awoke from Sleep
They told their comrades, and to Sleep return'd.

66. I sent my Soul through the Invisible,
Some letter of that After-life to spell:
And by and by my Soul return'd to me,
And answer'd "I Myself am Heav'n and Hell:"

67. Heav'n but the Vision of fulfill'd Desire,
And Hell the Shadow from a Soul on fire,
Cast on the Darkness into which Ourselves,
So late emerged from, shall so soon expire.

68. We are no other than a moving row
Of Magic Shadow-shapes that come and go
Round with the Sun-illumined Lantern held
In Midnight by the Master of the Show;

69. But helpless Pieces of the Game He plays
Upon this Chequer-board of Nights and Days;
Hither and thither moves, and checks, and slays,
And one by one back in the Closet lays.

70. The Ball no question makes of Ayes and Noes,
But Here or There as strikes the Player goes;
And He that toss'd you down into the Field,
He knows about it all—*he* knows—HE knows!

71. The Moving Finger writes; and, having writ,
Moves on: nor all your Piety nor Wit
Shall lure it back to cancel half a Line,
Nor all your Tears wash out a Word of it.

72. And that inverted Bowl they call the Sky,
Whereunder crawling coop'd we live and die,

> Lift not your hands to It for help—for It
> As impotently moves as you or I.

73. With Earth's first Clay They did the Last Man knead,
    And there of the Last Harvest sow'd the Seed:
        And the first Morning of Creation wrote
    What the Last Dawn of Reckoning shall read.

74. *Yesterday* This Day's Madness did prepare;
    To-morrow's Silence, Triumph, or Despair:
        Drink! for you know not whence you came, nor why:
    Drink! for you know not why you go nor where.

77. And this I know: Whether the one True Light
    Kindle to Love, or Wrath-consume me quite,
        One Flash of It within the Tavern caught
    Better than in the Temple lost outright.

78. What! out of senseless Nothing to provoke
    A conscious Something to resent the yoke
        Of unpermitted Pleasure, under pain
    Of Everlasting Penalties, if broke!

79. What! from his helpless Creature be repaid
    Pure Gold for what he lent him dross-allay'd—
        Sue for a Debt he never did contract,
    And cannot answer—Oh the sorry trade!

80. Oh Thou, who didst with pitfall and with gin
    Beset the Road I was to wander in,
        Thou wilt not with Predestined Evil round
    Enmesh, and then impute my Fall to Sin!

81. Oh Thou, who man of baser Earth didst make,
    And ev'n with Paradise devise the Snake:
        For all the Sin wherewith the Face of Man
    Is blacken'd—Man's forgiveness give—and take!

         .   .   .   .

82. As under cover of departing Day
    Slunk hunger-stricken Ramazan away,
        Once more within the Potter's house alone
    I stood, surrounded by the Shapes of Clay.

83. Shapes of all Sorts and Sizes, great and small,
    That stood along the floor and by the wall;
        And some loquacious Vessels were; and some
    Listen'd perhaps, but never talk'd at all.

84. Said one among them—"Surely not in vain
    My substance of the common Earth was ta'en
        And to this Figure molded, to be broke
    Or trampled back to shapeless Earth again."

85. Then said a Second—"Ne'er a peevish Boy
    Would break the Bowl from which he drank in Joy;
        And he that with his hand the Vessel made
    Will surely not in after Wrath destroy."

86. After a momentary silence spake
    Some Vessel of a more ungainly Make;
        "They sneer at me for leaning all awry:
    What! did the Hand then of the Potter shake?"

87. Whereat some one of the loquacious Lot—
    I think a Sufi pipkin—waxing hot—
        "All this of Pot and Potter—Tell me then,
    Who is the Potter, pray, and who the Pot?"

88. "Why," said another, "Some there are who tell
    Of one who threatens he will toss to Hell
        The luckless Pots he marr'd in making—Pish!
    He's a Good Fellow, and 'twill all be well."

89. "Well," murmured one, "Let whoso make or buy,
    My Clay with long Oblivion is gone dry:
        But fill me with the old familiar Juice,
    Methinks I might recover by and by."

. . . .

91. Ah, with the Grape my fading life provide,
    And wash the Body whence the Life has died,
        And lay me, shrouded in the living Leaf,
    By some not unfrequented Garden-side.

93. Indeed the Idols I have loved so long
    Have done my credit in this World much wrong:
        Have drown'd my Glory in a shallow Cup,
    And sold my reputation for a Song.

94. Indeed, indeed, Repentance oft before
    I swore—but was I sober when I swore?
        And then and then came Spring, and Rose-in-hand
    My thread-bare Penitence apieces tore.

95. And much as Wine has play'd the Infidel,
    And robb'd me of my Robe of Honor—Well,
        I wonder often what the Vintners buy
    One half so precious as the stuff they sell.

96. Yet Ah, that Spring should vanish with the Rose!
    That Youth's sweet-scented manuscript should close!
        The Nightingale that in the branches sang,
    Ah whence, and whither flown again, who knows!

97. Would but the Desert of the Fountain yield
    One glimpse—if dimly, yet indeed, reveal'd

To which the fainting Traveler might spring,
As springs the trampled herbage of the field!

98. Would but some wingéd Angel ere too late
Arrest the yet unfolded Roll of Fate,
    And make the stern Recorder otherwise
Enregister, or quite obliterate!

99. Ah Love! could you and I with Him conspire
To grasp this sorry Scheme of Things entire,
    Would not we shatter it to bits—and then
Re-mold it nearer to the Heart's Desire!

. . . .

100. Yon rising Moon that looks for us again—
How oft hereafter will she wax and wane;
    How oft hereafter rising look for us
Through this same Garden—and for one in vain!

101. And when like her, oh Saki, you shall pass
Among the Guests Star-scatter'd on the Grass
    And in your joyous errand reach the spot
Where I made One—turn down an empty Glass!

TAMAN

The Intelligent Hedonist: Epicurus

It was through the teaching of Epicurus (*c.* 341–270 b.c.), a cultured Greek thinker of the ancient world, rather than in the thought of Aristippus and the Cyrenaics, that hedonism became an acceptable and influential philosophy. Our limited knowledge of Epicurus, as well as most of his extant writing, is derived from Diogenes Laertius' *Lives and Opinions of Eminent Philosophers*. Epicurus was born in Samos where his father, an Athenian citizen, had gone as a colonist, and he spent his youth in Asia Minor. Tradition has it that at an early age he assisted his father in conducting an elementary school. When he was about twenty, Epicurus went to Athens to be enrolled as a citizen. Shortly after the death of Alexander the Great in 323 b.c. he returned to Asia Minor to care for his father, and there established himself as a teacher of philosophy. He was eminently successful, rapidly making a name for himself as an able thinker and teacher.

Athens was still the center of intellectual and cultural life. The renown of both Plato and Aristotle continued in the schools that they had founded there earlier in the century. As his fame grew, Epicurus increasingly felt the attraction of this home of philosophy; in 306 b.c., accompanied by a number of his disciples, he moved to Athens where he purchased a garden and opened a school of his own. He soon gathered about him a group of enthusiastic followers, among whom even women and slaves were included. Drawing apart from the political turmoil and the economic unrest which at that time disturbed the ancient world, this group formed a congenial fellowship of kindred spirits.

The Garden of Epicurus became famous in antiquity for its example of goodly living and companionship as well as for its philosophical doctrines. To the members of this closely knit society, Epicurus seems at all times to have been most generous. He rejected the notion of a common purse for the school, a rather widespread practice in such groups, but he did contribute frequently from his own means to meet the common need and was known for his sympathy and reasonableness. Greatly impressed by the wisdom of Epicurus, whom they came to venerate almost as a god, his disciples committed his "golden maxims" to memory verbatim and treated them as the inspired scripture of their philosophical faith. Although always in rather delicate health, Epicurus seems to have borne the infirmities of the flesh calmly and courageously, and not until his seventy-second year did death bring to an end his philosophical reflection and discourse.

Philosophy was for Epicurus a very practical concern—a way of living more than a system of thought. He was thoroughly familiar with the scientific outlook on his age, and derived his general philosophical theory from the atomic materialism of Democritus, a great thinker of the fifth century b.c. Upon this foundation he based the hedonism for which he himself became famous, making large use of Democritus' ideas in supporting his own position. Despite a number of letters and essays dealing with the scientific thought of his day, however, Epicurus exhibits no special keenness of scientific vision. He was in this respect, as Santayana has aptly observed, the Herbert Spencer of antiquity, a sort of encyclopedia of second-hand scientific knowledge. He gathered his scientific facts with an eye fixed not on nature but on the hedonistic ethics for which he was seeking support.

Much of the appeal of the Epicurean hedonism lies in its simplicity and common sense. A letter to one of his disciples, Menoeceus, gives an unusually clear and direct statement of Epicurus' philosophy. A number of his comments on specific topics have also been collected, and from these it is possible to put together his ideas on important issues. It is at once apparent that in the teachings of Epicurus we find a much more restrained and prudent hedonism than that advocated in the bold irresponsibility of the Cyrenaics. Epicureanism, indeed, is more legitimately a *philosophy* of living, a pursuit of pleasure guided by reason rather than by impulse. The Epicurean, not the Cyrenaic, is really the master of his pleasures rather than the slave of his desires. For him intelligence and prudence control emotion and impulse, subjecting momentary passion and desires to a definitely rational ideal and pointing the way to the achievement of happiness through freedom from pain in the body and trouble in the soul. Some of the admonitions of Epicurus to this effect may well astonish those who regard themselves as his disciples. "For myself," he writes a friend, "I can be pleased with bread and water, yet send me a little cheese, that when I want to be extravagant, I may be."

Of all the things that disturb our tranquility of spirit, the most serious for Epicurus is the fear of death. In its attitude toward death one finds perhaps the most revealing insight into his philosophy at its best as well as a clear contrast to the spirit of the Cyrenaic. Despite his dependence upon the scientific materialism of Democritus, Epicurus does not accept the Cyrenaic denial of human freedom. The man of wisdom, in his opinion, will recognize the necessary limitations of scientific determinism and see also the grounds for belief in a limited but basic human freedom.

Every philosophy of life sets up its own cardinal virtues, its own unforgivable sins, its own peculiar moral ideal. If the good life is a life of pleasure, then the good man is he who intelligently orders his life in such fashion as to obtain the greatest amount of pleasure and avoid as much pain as possible. As Robert Louis Stevenson so aptly expressed the Epicurean point of view, "If your morals make you dreary, depend upon it they are wrong." The ideal Epicurean is the man who is wise enough to avoid cheating himself with short-lived pleasures that cost too much, prudent enough to choose simple pleasures that are lasting, and intelligent enough to banish all envy or ambition that troubles his soul. Such a man will live—much as did Epicurus himself—the quiet cultured life of a country gentleman, surrounded by congenial friends, and far removed from the disturbing turmoil of politics or the harassing anxiety of economic strife and competition.

Epicurus to Menoeceus*

Let no one when young delay to study philosophy, nor when he is old grow weary of his study. For no one can come too early or too late to secure the health of his soul. And the man who says that the age for philosophy has either not yet come or has gone by is like the man who says that the age for happiness is not yet come to him, or has passed away. Wherefore both when young and old a man must study philosophy, that as he grows old he may be young in blessings through the grateful recollection of what has been, and that in youth he may be old as well, since he will know no fear of what is to come. We must then meditate on the things that make our happiness, seeing that when that is with us we have all, but when it is absent we do all to win it.

The things which I used unceasingly to commend to you, these do and practise, considering them to be the first principles of the good life. First of all believe that god is a being immortal and blessed, even as the common idea of a god is engraved on men's minds, and do not assign to him anything alien to his immortality or ill-suited to his blessedness: but believe about him everything that can uphold his blessedness and immortality. For gods are, since the knowledge of them is by clear vision. But they are not such as the many believe them to be: for indeed they do not consistently represent them as they believe them to be. And the impious man is not he who denies the gods of the many, but he who attaches to the gods the beliefs of the many. For the statements of the many about the gods are not conceptions derived from sensation, but false suppositions, according to which the greatest misfortunes befall the wicked and the greatest blessings the good by the gift of the gods. For men being accustomed always to their own virtues welcome those like themselves, but regard all that is not of their nature as alien.

Become accustomed to the belief that death is nothing to us. For all good and evil consists in sensation, but death is deprivation of sensation. And therefore a right understanding that death is nothing to us makes the mortality of life enjoyable, not because it adds to it an infinite span of time, but because it takes away the craving for immortality. For there is nothing terrible in life for the man who has truly comprehended that there is nothing terrible in not living. So that the man speaks but idly who says that he fears death not because it will be painful when it comes, but because it is painful in anticipation. For that which gives no trouble when it comes, is but an empty pain in anticipation. So death, the most terrifying of ills, is nothing to us, since so long as we exist death is not with us; but when death comes, then we do not exist. It does not then concern either the living or the dead, since for the former it is not, and the latter are no more.

But the many at one moment shun death as the greatest of evils, at another yearn for it as a respite from the evils in life. But the wise man neither seeks to escape life nor fears the cessation of life, for neither does life offend him nor does the absence of life seem to be any evil. And just as with food he does not seek simply the larger share and nothing else, but rather the most pleasant, so he seeks to enjoy not the longest period of time, but the most pleasant.

And he who counsels the young man to live well, but the old man to make a good end, is foolish, not merely because of the desirability of life, but also because it is the same training which teaches to live well and die well. Yet much worse still is the man who says it is good not to be born, but "once born make haste to pass the gates of Death." For

* *Epicurus: The Extant Remains,* English translation by Cyril Bailey. (London, Oxford University Press, 1926).

if he says this from conviction, why does he not pass away out of life? For it is open to him to do so, if he had firmly made up his mind to this. But if he speaks in jest, his words are idle among men who cannot receive them.

We must then bear in mind that the future is neither ours, nor yet wholly not ours, so that we may not altogether expect it as sure to come, nor abandon hope of it, as if it will certainly not come.

We must consider that of desires some are natural, others vain, and of the natural some are necessary and others merely natural; and of the necessary some are necessary for happiness, others for the repose of the body, and others for very life. The right understanding of these facts enables us to refer all choice and avoidance to the health of the body and the soul's freedom from disturbance, since this is the aim of the life of blessedness. For it is to obtain this end that we always act, namely, to avoid pain and fear. And when this is once secured for us, all the tempest of the soul is dispersed, since the living creature has not to wander as though in search of something that is missing, and to look for some other thing by which he can fulfill the good of the soul and the good of the body. For it is then that we have need of pleasure, when we feel pain owing to the absence of pleasure; but when we do not feel pain, we no longer need pleasure. And for this cause we call pleasure the beginning and end of the blessed life. For we recognize pleasure as the first good innate in us, and from pleasure we begin every act of choice and avoidance, and to pleasure we return again, using the feeling as the standard by which we judge every good.

And since pleasure is the first good and natural to us, for this very reason we do not choose every pleasure, but sometimes we pass over many pleasures, when greater discomfort accrues to us as the result of them: and similarly we think many pains better than pleasures, since a greater pleasure comes to us when we have endured pains for a long time. Every pleasure then because of its natural kinship to us is good, yet not every

pleasure is to be chosen: even as every pain also is an evil, yet not all are always of a nature to be avoided. Yet by a scale of comparison and by consideration of advantages and disadvantages we must form our judgment on all these matters. For the good on certain occasions we treat as bad, and conversely the bad as good.

And again independence of desire we think a great good—not that we may at all times enjoy but a few things, but that, if we do not possess many, we may enjoy the few in the genuine persuasion that those have the sweetest pleasure in luxury who least need it, and that all that is natural is easy to be obtained, but that which is superfluous is hard. And so plain savours bring us a pleasure equal to a luxurious diet, when all the pain due to want is removed; and bread and water produce the highest pleasure, when one who needs them puts them to his lips. To grow accustomed therefore to simple and not luxurious diet gives us health to the full, and makes a man alert for the needful employments of life, and when after long intervals we approach luxuries, disposes us better towards them, and fits us to be fearless of fortune.

When, therefore, we maintain that pleasure is the end, we do not mean the pleasures of profligates and those that consist in sensuality, as is supposed by some who are either ignorant or disagree with us or do not understand, but freedom from pain in the body and from trouble in the mind. For it is not continuous drinking and revellings, nor the satisfaction of lusts, nor the enjoyment of fish and other luxuries of the wealthy table, which produce a pleasant life, but sober reasoning, searching out the motives for all choice and avoidance, and banishing mere opinions, to which are due the greatest disturbance of the spirit.

Of all this the beginning and the greatest good is prudence. Wherefore prudence is a more precious thing even than philosophy: for from prudence are sprung all the other virtues, and it teaches us that it is not possible to live pleasantly without living prudently and honourably and justly, nor, again, to live a life of prudence, honour, and justice without living pleasantly. For the virtues are by nature bound up with the pleasant life, and the pleasant life is inseparable from them. For indeed who, think you, is a better man than he who holds reverent opinions concerning the gods, and is at all times free from fear of death, and has reasoned out the end ordained by nature? He understands that the limit of good things is easy to fulfil and easy to attain, whereas the course of ills is either short in time or slight in pain: he laughs at destiny, whom some have introduced as the mistress of all things. He thinks that with us lies the chief power in determining events, some of which happen by necessity and some by chance, and some are within our control; for while necessity cannot be called to account, he sees that chance is inconstant, but that which is in our control is subject to no master, and to it are naturally attached praise and blame. For, indeed, it were better to follow the myths about the gods than to be-come a slave to the destiny of the natural philosophers: for the former suggests a hope of placating the gods by worship, whereas the latter involves a necessity which knows no placation. As to chance, he does not regard it as a god as most men do (for in a god's acts there is no disorder), nor as an uncertain cause of all things: for he does not believe that good and evil are given by chance to man for the framing of a blessed life, but that opportunities for great good and great evil are afforded by it. He therefore thinks it better to be unfortunate in reasonable action than to prosper in unreason. For it is better in a man's actions that what is well chosen should fail, rather than what is ill chosen should be successful owing to chance.

Meditate therefore on these things and things akin to them night and day by yourself, and with a companion like to yourself, and never shall you be disturbed waking or asleep, but you shall live like a god among men. For a man who lives among immortal blessings is not like to a mortal being.

Principal Doctrines of Epicurus*

I. The blessed and immortal nature knows no trouble itself nor causes trouble to any other, so that it is never constrained by anger or favour. For all such things exist only in the weak.

II. Death is nothing to us: for that which is dissolved is without sensation; and that which lacks sensation is nothing to us.

III. The limit of quantity in pleasures is the removal of all that is painful. Where-ever pleasure is present, as long as it is there, there is neither pain of body nor of mind, nor of both at once.

IV. Pain does not last continuously in the flesh, but the acutest pain is there for a very short time, and even that which just ex-ceeds the pleasure in the flesh does not continue for many days at once. But chronic ill-nesses permit a predominance of pain over pleasure in the flesh.

V. It is not possible to live pleasantly without living prudently and honourably and justly, nor again to live a life of prudence, honour, and justice without living pleasantly. And the man who does not possess the pleasant life, is not living prudently and honourably and justly, and the man who does not possess the virtuous life, cannot possibly live pleasantly.

VI. To secure protection from men anything is a natural good, by which you may be able to attain this end.

VII. Some men wished to become famous and conspicuous, thinking that they would thus win for themselves safety from other men. Wherefore if the life of such men is safe, they have obtained the good which

* Epicurus: The Extant Remains, English translation by Cyril Bailey, (London, Oxford University Press, 1926). Selected items renum-bered consecutively.

nature craves; but if it is not safe, they do not possess that for which they strove at first by the instinct of nature.

VIII. No pleasure is a bad thing in itself: but the means which produce some pleasures bring with them disturbances many times greater than the pleasures.

IX. If every pleasure could be intensified so that it lasted and influenced the whole organism or the most essential parts of our nature, pleasures would never differ from one another.

X. If the things that produce the pleasures of profligates could dispel the fears of the mind about the phenomena of the sky and death and its pains, and also teach the limits of desires and of pains, we should never have cause to blame them: for they would be filling themselves full with pleasures from every source and never have pain of body or mind, which is the evil of life.

XI. If we were not troubled by our suspicions of the phenomena of the sky and about death, fearing that it concerns us, and also by our failure to grasp the limits of pains and desires, we should have no need of natural science.

XII. A man cannot dispel his fear about the most important matters if he does not know what is the nature of the universe but suspects the truth of some mythical story. So that without natural science it is not possible to attain our pleasures unalloyed.

XIII. There is no profit in securing protection in relation to men, if things above and things beneath the earth and indeed all in the boundless universe remain matters of suspicion.

XIV. The most unalloyed source of protection from men, which is secured to some extent by a certain force of expulsion, is in fact the immunity which results from a quiet life and the retirement from the world.

XV. The wealth demanded by nature is both limited and easily procured; that demanded by idle imaginings stretches on to infinity.

XVI. In but few things chance hinders a wise man, but the greatest and most important matters reason has ordained and through-

out the whole period of life does and will ordain.

XVII. The just man is most free from trouble, the unjust most full of trouble.

XVIII. The pleasure in the flesh is not increased, when once the pain due to want is removed, but is only varied: and the limit as regards pleasure in the mind is begotten by the reasoned understanding of these very pleasures and of the emotions akin to them, which used to cause the greatest fear to the mind.

XIX. Infinite time contains no greater pleasure than limited time, if one measures by reason the limits of pleasure.

XX. The flesh perceives the limits of pleasure as unlimited and unlimited time is required to supply it. But the mind, having attained a reasoned understanding of the ultimate good of the flesh and its limits and having dissipated the fears concerning the time to come, supplies us with the complete life, and we have no further need of infinite time: but neither does the mind shun pleasure, nor when circumstances begin to bring about the departure from life, does it approach its end as though it fell short in any way of the best life.

XXI. He who has learned the limits of life knows that that which removes the pain due to want and makes the whole of life complete is easy to obtain; so that there is no need of actions which involve competition.

XXII. We must consider both the real purpose and all the evidence of direct perception, to which we always refer the conclusions of opinion; otherwise, all will be full of doubt and confusion.

XXIII. If you fight against all sensations, you will have no standard by which to judge even those of them which you say are false.

XXIV. If you reject any single sensation and fail to distinguish between the conclusion of opinion as to the appearance awaiting confirmation and that which is actually given by the sensation or feeling, or each intuitive apprehension of the mind, you will confound all other sensations as well with the same groundless opinion, so that you will reject every standard of judgment. And if among the mental images created by your opinion you affirm both that which awaits confirmation and that which does not, you will not escape error, since you will have preserved the whole cause of doubt in every judgment between what is right and what is wrong.

XXV. If on each occasion instead of referring your actions to the end of nature, you turn to some other nearer standard when you are making a choice or an avoidance, your actions will not be consistent with your principles.

XXVI. Of desires, all that do not lead to a sense of pain, if they are not satisfied, are not necessary, but involve a craving which is easily dispelled. when the object is hard to procure or they seem likely to produce harm.

XXVII. Of all the things which wisdom acquires to produce the blessedness of the complete life, far the greatest is the possession of friendship.

XXVIII. The same conviction which has given us confidence that there is nothing terrible that lasts for ever or even for long, has also seen the protection of friendship most fully completed in the limited evils of this life.

XXIX. Among desires some are natural and necessary, some natural but not necessary, and others neither natural nor necessary, but due to idle imagination.

XXX. Wherever in the case of desires which are physical, but do not lead to a sense of pain, if they are not fulfilled, the effort is intense, such pleasures are due to idle imagination, and it is not owing to their own nature that they fail to be dispelled, but owing to the empty imaginings of the man.

XXXI. The justice which arises from nature is a pledge of mutual advantage to restrain men from harming one another and save them from being harmed.

XXXII. For all living things which have not been able to make compacts not to harm one another or be harmed, nothing ever is either just or unjust; and likewise too for all tribes of men which have been unable or unwilling to make compacts not to harm or be harmed.

XXXIII. Justice never is anything in itself, but in the dealings of men with one another in any place whatever and at any time it is a kind of compact not to harm or be harmed.

XXXIV. Injustice is not an evil in itself, but only in consequence of the fear which attaches to the apprehension of being unable to escape those appointed to punish such actions.

XXXV. It is not possible for one who acts in secret contravention of the terms of the compact not to harm or be harmed, to be confident that he will escape detection, even if at present he escapes a thousand times. For up to the time of death it cannot be certain that he will indeed escape.

XXXIX. The man who has best ordered the element of disquiet arising from external circumstances has made those things that he could akin to himself and the rest at least not alien: but with all to which he could not do even this, he has refrained from mixing, and has expelled from his life all which it was of advantage to treat thus.

XL. As many as possess the power to procure complete immunity from their neighbors, these also live most pleasantly with one another, since they have the most certain pledge of security, and after they have enjoyed the fullest intimacy, they do not lament the previous departure of a dead friend, as though he were to be pitied.

The Hedonist as Altruist: Utilitarianism

For many thoughtful men and women the most serious defect of hedonism has been its decided self-interest: an exclusive concern with one's own enjoyment of life, with no apparent interest in the welfare of others except as this makes some contribution to one's own happiness. In somewhat more technical terms, hedonism has generally appeared as essentially egoistic in its outlook on life with little recognition of the fact that a genuine concern for others frequently gives human life its deepest meaning and satisfaction. An able group of British philosophers, known as Utilitarians, undertook to remedy this defect in the thought of Epicurus by introducing an altruistic principle into their essentially hedonistic philosophy.

The utilitarians were outstanding leaders in the nineteenth century movement for social reform in England. They lectured widely, wrote numerous pamphlets and books, edited a serious journal, and organized a new political party, all in order to improve the economic and political conditions of their day. Their concern with the welfare of others was both genuine and practical; for this reason Utilitarianism is often termed *altruistic* hedonism.

Jeremy Bentham (1748–1832) and John Stuart Mill (1806–1873) were the two ablest and most influential exponents of the utilitarian philosophy. Both were child prodigies. They read Latin, Greek, and philosophy when other boys of their age were enjoying fairy tales. Both spent their youth in the company of distinguished scholars and social reformers rather than with young men and women their own age. When only thirteen, Bentham found his religious sensibilities offended and his mind troubled by doubts when he was required to affirm his belief in the Thirty-nine Articles of the Anglican Church before being allowed to matriculate at Oxford University. He did enter Oxford, however, and upon his graduation there proceeded to study law in London. Because of his marked ability, his father had hopes that Jeremy would become a distinguished jurist, but the son neglected the practical side of his profession in order to become an author. Despite this fact, his father continued to support him and found some compensation for his early disappointment when Jeremy's first book, published anonymously not long after its author's twenty-eighth birthday, was immediately ascribed by the public to various eminent writers of the day.

Bentham spent almost his whole life either in London or at his home in the country near by. Like Epicurus, he soon gathered around him a group of devoted friends and admirers who accepted his views almost without question and were eager to help in spreading his philosophy. Although he possessed a genuine concern for social reform, he like many other philosophers was largely a recluse, occupied chiefly in elaborating theories on paper expecting that they would go into effect almost automatically as soon as their logical validity was demonstrated. His close friends looked upon him as a man of profound wisdom and approved almost as a matter of course whatever he proposed. It was a great disappointment to Bentham when he discovered that all men, and especially practical political leaders, were not equally discerning.

In time, however, Bentham and the younger men around him decided to organize a political party in order to achieve lasting political action and social reform. They called themselves the "Philosophical Radicals," worked out a practical political platform, and soon elected to Parliament a number of able spokesmen for their program. The considerable influence which this group exerted during half a century came about in the main not from their numbers but from the exceptional ability and social vision of these exponents of practical utilitarianism. Bentham himself, as a matter of fact, did not call his philosophy by this name. He preferred a somewhat more cumbersome phrase, "the greatest happiness principle." The term Utilitarianism was adopted by John Stuart Mill, first to describe the views of a small literary group among Bentham's disciples and only later, when the name "philosophical Radicals" proved politically inadvisable, to designate the political party and its philosophy. In time Utilitarianism became the accepted name for Bentham's philosophy as well as for Mill's own position.

It was Bentham's hope that he could make ethics as exact and precise as the physical sciences. To this end he sacrificed all literary excellence in his writings and sought rather to achieve the precision and clarity of the lawyer or the physicist. In his famous *hedonistic calculus,* he undertakes the kind of precise formulation that would enable anyone to apply the philosophy of Epicurus with scientific accuracy. It was only as he turned from individual to social morality that Bentham began to modify the traditional Epicureanism but it was here that his chief interest lay. For he was primarily a *legislator* and only secondarily a moralist; his greatest contributions were made in the social sciences and in legal philosophy rather than in ethics.

As a lawmaker Bentham was convinced that good government must promote the greatest happiness of the greatest number, not the interests of the privileged few. Hence it is the function of law to see that a man does consider the welfare of others as well as his own happiness. How is this to be done? Bentham's proposal suggests a shrewd combination of hedonism and altruism. Legislators must pass laws to make sure that men suffer so much pain when they disregard the welfare of others that this will outweigh any pleasure they may derive from an antisocial act. It is to this end that his hedonistic calculus is primarily directed, rather than to provide the basis of a successful moral philosophy for the individual.

John Stuart Mill, Bentham's ablest disciple, is one of the most interesting figures in British philosophy. Hardly anywhere has there been a man whose life was so explicitly shaped to produce a philosopher. In large measure this was the work of his father, James Mill, a recognized leader among the group of younger men gathered around Jeremy Bentham. Mill, in his popular *Autobiography,* has provided a detailed account of the educational experiment undertaken by his father. At three, he began his study of arithmetic and Greek; at eight he took up Latin and was soon reading the great Greek and Latin classics in the original. Later he moved into the field of history; then at twelve he turned to an intensive study of logic, beginning with Aristotle, after which he took up economic and political theory. This exacting educational program, conducted entirely by Mill's father, was designed to make his son a first-rate thinker and the major prophet of utilitarianism. Mill was deliberately shielded from other boys of his own age with whose childish fancies his father had little sympathy. Anything he could find out for himself, he was never told. Even with this kind of training, Mill in later life was no armchair philosopher. He combined his father's interest in practical politics with Bentham's ability to analyze objectively the motives by which human conduct is shaped, and his life was marked by outstanding achievement in a number of fields.

After a brief study of law, which was Bentham's ideal for the well-educated man, Mill took a position with the East India Company where his father also was employed for many years. Despite the large amount of writing that he did, both political and philosophical, Mill retained the position with this company until its dissolution. His first major book, *A System of Logic,* was published in 1843. Generally regarded as his greatest single accomplishment, it ran through many editions and was for years the standard work in the field. The brief essay on *Utilitarianism* is Mill's one direct contribution to ethical theory, but it also became something of a classic among interpretations of hedonism. In an influential work on *The Principles of Political Economy* (1848), Mill undertakes in quite successful fashion to apply the principles of utilitarianism to the field of economic theory. Two widely read essays, *On Liberty* and *Representative Government,* were later combined with the essay on *Utilitarianism* in a small volume that now ranks as one of the classics in the field of political philosophy. During his later life Mill continued to publish numerous essays on current political and social problems, but none so important as those already mentioned. His widely read *Autobiography* was published shortly after his death in 1873; the following year a small volume entitled *Three Essays on Religion* appeared posthumously.

The East India Company was dissolved by the British Parliament in 1858, and Mill retired from business in order to devote himself entirely to writing. But his name was so well known and his influence so extensive that in 1865 he was asked to stand as a candidate for Parliament from Westminster. He agreed to run only if he were not required to make any speeches or to pay others to speak in his behalf; and it was understood also that if elected he would ignore local political interests in order to spend his energy on national problems among which he included women's suffrage. One well-known politician is said to have commented that the Almighty himself could not win office on such conditions but, to Mill's surprise as much as anyone's, he was elected and served with distinction as a member of the House of Commons during the three sessions in which the Reform Bill of 1865 was passed.

It is with some hesitation that one classifies John Stuart Mill as a hedonist, despite the fact that in his essay on *Utilitarianism,* from which a generous selection is here reprinted, he specifically and unequivocally commits himself to the philosophy of Bentham and Epicurus. Within the first fifteen pages of this essay, however, Mill has so modified the hedonism of Bentham that he has with real justification been termed a utilitarian heretic. Almost all that remains of the hedonism he inherited is his commitment to a few basic ideas usually associated with such a philosophy of living. The egoistic view of human nature and conduct, the quantitative calculus of pleasure and pain upon which Bentham puts such store, the appeal to enlightened self-interest—all these Mill discards without hesitation. The philosophy that he adopts is as discerning and appealing as almost any that one can find; its practical results in the social and political life of his day tend to suggest as much. His intellectual ability, the breadth of his sympathy, and his concern to do justice to the facts of life as he saw them, inevitably took Mill beyond the hedonism of Bentham and of Epicurus. If Mill is right, then the orthodox hedonist is wrong, for in his altruistic hedonism a radically different set of basic assumptions replace those adopted by such hedonists as Epicurus, Aristippus, and Lin Yutang.

The Principle of Utility*

I

1. Nature placed mankind under the governance of two sovereign masters, *pain* and *pleasure*. It is for them alone to point out what we ought to do, as well as to determine what we shall do. On the one hand the standard of right and wrong, on the other the chain of causes and effects, are fastened to their throne. They govern us in all we do, in all we say, in all we think: every effort we can make to throw off our subjection, will serve but to demonstrate and confirm it. In words a man may pretend to abjure their empire: but in reality he will remain subject to it all the while. The *principle of utility*[1] recognises this subjection, and assumes it for the foundation of that system, the object of which is to rear the fabric of felicity by the hands of reason and of law.

greatest happiness of all those whose interest is in question, as being the right and proper, and only right and proper and universally desirable, end of human action: of human action in every situation, and in particular in that of a functionary or set of functionaries exercising the power of Government. The word *utility* does not so clearly point to the ideas of *pleasure* and *pain* as the words *happiness* and *felicity* do: nor does it lead us to the consideration of the *number*, of the interests affected; to the *number*, as being the circumstance, which contributes, in the largest proportion, to the formation of the standard here in question; the *standard of right and wrong*, by which alone the propriety of human conduct, in every situation, can with propriety be tried. This want of a sufficiently manifest connexion between the ideas of *happiness* and *pleasure* on the one hand, and the idea of *utility* on the other, I have every now and then found operating, and with but too much efficiency, as a bar to the acceptance, that might otherwise have been given, to this principle. (Note by the Author, July 1822.)

---

* Jeremy Bentham, *An Introduction to Principles of Morals and Legislation* (Oxford, The Clarendon Press, 1907). (First published in 1789; rev. ed., 1823.)

[1] To this denomination has of late been added, or substituted, the *greatest happiness* or *greatest felicity* principle: this for shortness, instead of saying at length *that principle* which states the

Systems which attempt to question it, deal in sounds instead of sense, in caprice instead of reason, in darkness instead of light.

But enough of metaphor and declamation: it is not by such means that moral science is to be improved.

2. By the principle of utility is meant that principle which approves or disapproves of every action whatsoever, according to the tendency which it appears to have to augment or diminish the happiness of the part whose interest is in question: or, what is the same thing in other words, to promote or to oppose that happiness. I say of every action whatsoever; and therefore not only of every action of a private individual, but of every measure of government.

3. By utility is meant that property in any object, whereby it tends to produce benefit, advantage, pleasure, good, or happiness, (all this in the present case comes to the same thing) or (what comes again to the same thing) to prevent the happening of mischief, pain, evil, or unhappiness to the party whose interest is considered: if that party be the community in general, then the happiness of the community: if a particular individual, then the happiness of that individual.

4. The interest of the community is one of the most general expressions that can occur in the phraseology of morals: no wonder that the meaning of it is often lost. When it has a meaning, it is this. The community is a fictitious *body,* composed of the individual persons who are considered as constituting as it were its *members.* The interest of the community then is, what?—the sum of the interests of the several members who compose it.

5. It is in vain to talk of the interest of the community, without understanding what is the interest of the individual. A thing is said to promote the interest, or to be *for* the interest, of an individual, when it tends to add to the sum total of his pleasures: or, what comes to the same thing, to diminish the sum total of his pains.

6. An action then may be said to be conformable to the principle of utility, or, for shortness sake, to utility, (meaning with respect to the community at large) when the tendency it has to augment the happiness of the community is greater than any it has to diminish it.

7. A measure of government (which is but a particular kind of action, performed by a particular person or persons) may be said to be conformable to or dictated by the principle of utility, when in like manner the tendency which it has to augment the happiness of the community is greater than any which it has to diminish it.

8. When an action, or in particular a measure of government, is supposed by a man to be conformable to the principle of utility, it may be convenient, for the purposes of discourse, to imagine a kind of law or dictate, called a law or dictate of utility: and to speak of the action in question, as being conformable to such law or dictate.

9. A man may be said to be a partizan of the principle of utility, when the approbation or disapprobation he annexes to any action, or to any measure, is determined by and proportioned to the tendency which he conceives it to have to augment or to diminish the happiness of the community: or in other words, to its conformity or unconformity to the laws or dictates of utility.

10. Of an action that is conformable to the principle of utility one may always say either that it is one that ought to be done, or at least that it is not one that ought not to be done. One may say also, that it is right it should be done; at least that it is not wrong it should be done: that it is a right action; at least that it is not a wrong action. When thus interpreted, the words *ought,* and *right* and *wrong,* and others of that stamp, have a meaning: when otherwise, they have none.

11. Has the rectitude of this principle been ever formally contested? It should seem that it had, by those who have not known what they have been meaning. Is it susceptible of any direct proof? it should seem not: for that which is used to prove everything else, cannot itself be proved: a chain of proofs must have their commencement somewhere. To give such proof is as impossible as it is needless.

12. Not that there is or ever has been that human creature breathing, however stupid or perverse, who has not on many, perhaps on most occasions of his life, deferred to it. By the natural constitution of the human frame, on most occasions of their lives men in general embrace this principle, without thinking of it: if not for the ordering of their own actions, yet for the trying of their own actions, as well as of those of other men. There have been, at the same time, not many, perhaps, even of the most intelligent, who have been disposed to embrace it purely and without reserve. There are even few who have not taken some occasion or other to quarrel with it, either on account of their not understanding always how to apply it, or on account of some prejudice or other which they were afraid to examine into, or could not bear to part with. For such is the stuff that man is made of: in principle and in practice, in a right track and in a wrong one, the rarest of all human qualities is consistency.

II

Pleasures then, and the avoidance of pains, are the *ends* which the legislator has in view: it behoves him therefore to understand their *value*. Pleasures and pains are the *instruments* he has to work with: it behoves him therefore to understand their force, which is again, in other words, their value.

To a person considered *by himself,* the value of a pleasure or pain considered *by itself,* will be greater or less, according to the four following circumstances:*

---

* These circumstances have since been denominated *elements* or *dimensions* of *value* in a pleasure or a pain.

Not long after the publication of the first edition, the following memoriter verses were framed, in the view of lodging more effectually, in the memory, these points on which the whole fabric of morals and legislation may be seen to rest.

Intense, long, certain, speedy, fruitful, pure—
Such marks in *pleasures* and in *pains* endure.
Such pleasures seek if *private* be thy end:
If it be *public,* wide let them *extend.*

1. Its *intensity.*
2. Its *duration.*
3. Its *certainty* or *uncertainty.*
4. Its *propinquity* or *remoteness.*

These are the circumstances which are to be considered in estimating a pleasure or a pain considered each of them by itself. But when the value of any pleasure or pain is considered for the purpose of estimating the tendency of any *act* by which it is produced, there are two other circumstances to be taken into the account; these are,

5. Its *fecundity,* or the chance it has of being followed by sensations of the *same* kind: that is, pleasures, if it be a pleasure: pains, if it be a pain.

6. Its *purity,* or the chance it has of *not* being followed by sensations of the *opposite* kind: that is, pains, if it be a pleasure: pleasures, if it be a pain.

These two last, however, are in strictness scarcely to be deemed properties of the pleasure or the pain itself; they are not, therefore, in strictness to be taken into the account of the value of that pleasure or that pain. They are in strictness to be deemed properties only of the act, or other event, by which such pleasure or pain has been produced; and accordingly are only to be taken into the account of the tendency of such act or such event.

To a *number* of persons, with reference to each of whom the value of a pleasure or a pain is considered, it will be greater or less, according to seven circumstances: to wit, the six preceding ones; *viz.*

1. Its *intensity*
2. Its *duration.*
3. Its *certainty* or *uncertainty.*
4. Its *propinquity* or *remoteness.*
5. Its *fecundity.*
6. Its *purity.*

And one other; to wit:

7. Its *extent;* that is, the number of persons to whom it *extends;* or (in other words) who are affected by it.

To take an exact account then of the

Such *pains* avoid, whichever by thy view:
If pains *must* come, let them *extend* to few.

general tendency of any act, by which the interests of a community are affected, proceed as follows. Begin with any one person of those whose interests seem most immediately to be affected by it: and take an account,

1. Of the value of each distinguishable *pleasure* which appears to be produced by it in the *first* instance.

2. Of the value of each *pain* which appears to be produced by it in the *first* instance.

3. Of the value of each pleasure which appears to be produced by it *after* the first. This constitutes the *fecundity* of the first *pleasure* and the *impurity* of the first *pain*.

4. Of the value of each *pain* which appears to be produced by it after the first. This constitutes the *fecundity* of the first *pain,* and the *impurity* of the first pleasure.

5. Sum up all the values of all the *pleasures* on the one side, and those of all the pains on the other. The balance, it if be on the side of pleasure, will give the *good* tendency of the act upon the whole, with respect to the interest of that *individual* person; if on the side of pain, the *bad* tendency of it upon the whole.

6. Take an account of the *number* of persons whose interests appear to be concerned; and repeat the above process with respect to each. *Sum up* the numbers expressive of the degrees of *good* tendency, which the act has, with respect to each individual, in regard to whom the tendency of it is *good* upon the whole: do this again with respect to each individual, in regard to whom the tendency of it is *bad* upon the whole. Take the *balance;* which, if on the side of *pleasure,* will give the general good tendency of the act, with respect to the total number or community of individuals concerned; if on the side of pain, the general *evil tendency,* with respect to the same community.

It is not to be expected that this process should be strictly pursued previous to every moral judgment, or to every legislative or judicial operation. It may, however, be always kept in view: and as near as the process actually pursued on these occasions approaches to it, so near will such process approach to the character of an exact one.

The same process is alike applicable to pleasure and pain, in whatever shape they appear: and by whatever denomination they are distinguished: to pleasure, whether it be called *good* (which is properly the cause or instrument of pleasure) or *profit* (which is distant pleasure, or the cause or instrument of distant pleasure,) or *convenience,* or *advantage, benefit, emolument, happiness,* and so forth: to pain, whether it be called *evil,* (which corresponds to *good*) or *mischief,* or *inconvenience,* or *disadvantage,* or *loss,* or *unhappiness,* and so forth.

Nor is this a novel and unwarranted, any more than it is a useless theory. In all this there is nothing but what the practice of mankind, wheresoever they have a clear view of their own interest, is perfectly conformable to. An article of property, an estate in land, for instance, is valuable, on what account? On account of the pleasures of all kinds which it enables a man to produce, and what comes to the same thing the pains of all kinds which it enables him to avert. But the value of such an article of property is universally understood to rise or fall according to the length or shortness of the time which a man has in it: the certainty or uncertainty of its coming into possession: and the nearness or remoteness of the time at which, if at all, it is to come into possession. As to the *intensity* of the pleasures which a man may derive from it, this is never thought of, because it depends upon the use which each particular person may come to make of it; which cannot be estimated till the particular pleasures he may come to derive from it, or the particular pains he may come to exclude by means of it, are brought to view. For the same reason, neither does he think of the fecundity or purity of those pleasures.

Utilitarianism*

I

There are few circumstances among those which make up the present condition of human knowledge, more unlike what might have been expected, or more significant of the backward state in which speculation on the most important subjects still lingers, than the little progress which has been made in the decision of the controversy respecting the criterion of right and wrong. From the dawn of philosophy, the question concerning the *summum bonum,* or, what is the same thing, concerning the foundation of morality, has been accounted the main problem in speculative thought, has occupied the most gifted intellects, and divided them into sects and schools, carrying on a vigorous warfare against one another. And after more than two thousand years the same discussions continue, philosophers are still ranged under the same contending banners, and neither thinkers nor mankind at large seem nearer to being unanimous on the subject, than when the youth Socrates listened to the old Protagoras, and asserted (if Plato's dialogue be grounded on a real conversation) the theory of utilitarianism against the popular morality of the so-called sophist.

On the present occasion, I shall, without further discussion of the other theories, attempt to contribute something towards the understanding and appreciation of the Utilitarian or Happiness theory, and towards such proof as it is susceptible of. It is evident that this cannot be proof in the ordinary and popular meaning of the term. Questions of ultimate ends are not amenable to direct proof. Whatever can be proved to be good, must be so by being shown to be a means to

*John Stuart Mill, *Utilitarianism, Liberty, and Representative Government* (New York, E. P. Dutton & Co., 1910). First published in 1863.

something admitted to be good without proof. The medical art is proved to be good by its conducing to health; but how is it possible to prove that health is good? The art of music is good, for the reason, among others, that it produces pleasure; but what proof is it possible to give that pleasure is good? If, then, it is asserted that there is a comprehensive formula, including all things which are in themselves good, and that whatever else is good, is not so as an end, but as a mean, the formula may be accepted or rejected, but is not a subject of what is commonly understood by proof. We are not, however, to infer that its acceptance or rejection must depend on blind impulse, or arbitrary choice. There is a larger meaning of the word proof, in which this question is as amenable to it as any other of the disputed questions of philosophy. The subject is within the cognisance of the rational faculty; and neither does that faculty deal with it solely in the way of intuition. Considerations may be presented capable of determining the intellect either to give or withhold its assent to the doctrine; and this is equivalent to proof.

We shall examine presently of what nature are these considerations; in what manner they apply to the case, and what rational grounds, therefore, can be given for accepting or rejecting the utilitarian formula. But it is a preliminary condition of rational acceptance or rejection, that the formula should be correctly understood. Before, therefore, I attempt to enter into the philosophical grounds which can be given for assenting to the utilitarian standard, I shall offer some illustrations of the doctrine itself; with the view of showing more clearly what it is, distinguishing it from what it is not, and disposing of such of the practical objections to it as either originate in, or are closely connected with, mistaken interpretations of its meaning. Having thus prepared the ground, I shall afterwards endeavour to throw such light as I can upon the question, considered as one of philosophical theory.

II

The creed which accepts as the foundation of morals, Utility, or the Greatest Happiness Principle, holds that actions are right in proportion as they tend to promote happiness, wrong as they tend to produce the reverse of happiness. By happiness is intended pleasure, and the absence of pain; by unhappiness, pain, and the privation of pleasure. To give a clear view of the moral standard set up by the theory, much more requires to be said; in particular, what things it includes in the ideas of pain and pleasure; and to what extent this is left an open question. But these supplementary explanations do not affect the theory of life on which this theory of morality is grounded—namely, that pleasure, and freedom from pain, are the only things desirable as ends; and that all desirable things (which are as numerous in the utilitarian as in any other scheme) are desirable either for the pleasure inherent in themselves, or as means to the promotion of pleasure and the prevention of pain.

Now, such a theory of life excites in many minds, and among them in some of the most estimable in feeling and purpose, inveterate dislike. To suppose that life has (as they express it) no higher end than pleasure—no better and nobler object of desire and pursuit—they designate as utterly mean and grovelling; as a doctrine worthy only of swine, to whom the followers of Epicurus were, at a very early period, contemptuously likened; and modern holders of the doctrine are occasionally made the subject of equally polite comparisons by its German, French, and English assailants.

When thus attacked, the Epicureans have always answered, that it is not they, but their accusers, who represent human nature in a degrading light; since the accusation supposes human beings to be capable of no pleasures except those of which swine are capable. If this supposition were true, the charge could not be gainsaid, but would then be no longer an imputation; for if the sources of pleasure were precisely the same to human beings and to swine, the rule of life which is good enough for the one would be good enough for the other. The comparison of the Epicurean life to that of beasts is felt as degrading, precisely because a beast's pleasures do not satisfy a human being's conceptions of happiness. Human beings have faculties more elevated than the animal appetites, and when once made conscious of them, do not regard anything as happiness which does not include their gratification. I do not, indeed, consider the Epicureans to have been by any means faultless in drawing out their scheme of consequences from the utilitarian principle. To do this in any sufficient manner, many Stoic, as well as Christian elements require to be included. But there is no known Epicurean theory of life which does not assign to the pleasure of the intellect, of the feelings and imagination, and of the moral sentiments, a much higher value as pleasures than to those of mere sensation. It must be admitted, however, the utilitarian writers in general have placed the superiority of mental over bodily pleasures chiefly in the greater permanency, safety, uncostliness, etc., of the former—that is, in their circumstantial advantages rather than in their intrinsic nature. And on all these points utilitarians have fully proved their case; but they might have taken the other, and, as it may be called, higher ground, with entire consistency. It is quite compatible with the principle of utility to recognize the fact, that some *kinds* of pleasure are more desirable and more valuable than other. It would be absurd that while, in estimating all other things, quality is considered as well as quantity, the estimation of pleasures should be supposed to depend on quantity alone.

If I am asked, what I mean by difference of quality in pleasures, or what makes one pleasure more valuable than another, merely as a pleasure, except its being greater in amount, there is but one possible answer. Of two pleasures, if there be one to which all or almost all who have experience of both give a decided preference, irrespective of any feeling of moral obligation to prefer it, that is the more desirable pleasure. If one of the two is, by those who are competently acquainted with both, placed so far above the other that they prefer it, even though knowing it to be attended with a greater amount of discontent, and would not resign it for any quantity of the other pleasure which their nature is capable of, we are justified in ascribing to the preferred enjoyment a superiority in quality, so far outweighing quantity as to render it, in comparison, of small account.

Now it is an unquestionable fact that those who are equally acquainted with, and equally capable of appreciating and enjoying, both, do give a most marked preference to the manner of existence which employs their higher faculties. Few human creatures would consent to be changed into any of the lower animals, for a promise of the fullest allowance of a beast's pleasures; no intelligent human being would consent to be a fool, no instructed person would be an ignoramus, no person of feeling and conscience would be selfish and base, even though they should be persuaded that the fool, the dunce, or the rascal is better satisfied with his lot than they are with theirs. A being of higher faculties requires more to make him happy, is capable probably of more acute suffering, and certainly accessible to it at more points, than one of an inferior type; but in spite of these liabilities, he can never really wish to sink into what he feels to be a lower grade of existence. We may give what explanation we please of this unwillingness; we may attribute it to pride, a name which is given indiscriminately to some of the most and to some of the least estimable feelings of which mankind are capable; we may refer it to the love of liberty and personal independence, an appeal to which was with the Stoics one of the most effective means for the inculcation of it; to the love of power, or to the love of excitement, both of which do really enter into and contribute to it; but its most appropriate appellation is a sense of dignity, which all human beings possess in one form or other, and in some, though by no means in exact, proportion to their higher faculties, and

which is so essential a part of the happiness of those in whom it is strong, that nothing which conflicts with it could be, otherwise than momentarily, an object of desire to them. Whoever supposes that this preference takes place at a sacrifice of happiness—that the superior being, in anything like equal circumstances, is not happier than the inferior—confounds the two very different ideas, of happiness, and content. It is indisputable that the being whose capacities of enjoyment are low, has the greatest chance of having them fully satisfied; and a highly endowed being will always feel that any happiness which he can look for, as the world is constituted, is imperfect. But he can learn to bear its imperfections, if they are at all bearable; and they will not make him envy the being who is indeed unconscious of the imperfections, but only because he feels not at all the good which those imperfections qualify. It is better to be a human being dissatisfied than a pig satisfied; better to be Socrates dissatisfied than a fool satisfied. And if the fool, or the pig, are of a different opinion, it is because they only know their own side of the question. The other party to the comparison knows both sides.

It may be objected, that many who are capable of the higher pleasures, occasionally, under the influence of temptation, postpone them to the lower. But this is quite compatible with a full appreciation of the intrinsic superiority of the higher. Men often, from infirmity of character, make their election for the nearer good, though they know it to be the less valuable; and this no less when the choice is between two bodily pleasures, than when it is between bodily and mental. They pursue sensual indulgences to the injury of health, though perfectly aware that health is the greater good. It may be further objected, that many who begin with youthful enthusiasm for everything noble, as they advance in years sink into indolence and selfishness. But I do not believe that those who undergo this very common change, voluntarily choose the lower description of pleasures in preference to the higher. I believe that before they devote themselves exclusively to the one, they have already become incapable of the other. Capacity for the nobler feelings is in most natures a very tender plant, easily killed, not only by hostile influences, but by mere want of sustenance; and in the majority of young persons it speedily dies away if the occupations to which their position in life has devoted them, and the society into which it has thrown them, are not favourable to keeping that higher capacity in exercise. Men lose their high aspirations as they lose their intellectual tastes, because they have not time or opportunity for indulging them; and they addict themselves to inferior pleasures, not because they deliberately prefer them, but because they are either the only ones to which they have access, or the only ones which they are any longer capable of enjoying, It may be questioned whether any one who has remained equally susceptible to both classes of pleasures, ever knowingly and calmly preferred the lower; though many, in all ages, have broken down in an ineffectual attempt to combine both.

From this verdict of the only competent judges, I apprehend there can be no appeal. On a question which is the best worth having of two pleasures, or which of two modes of existence is the most grateful to the feelings, apart from its moral attributes and from its consequences, the judgment of those who are qualified by knowledge of both, or, if they differ, that of the majority among them, must be admitted as final. And there needs be the less hesitation to accept this judgment respecting the quality of pleasures, since there is no other tribunal to be referred to even on the question of quantity. What means are there of determining which is the acutest of two pains, or the intensest of two pleasurable sensations, except the general suffrage of those who are familiar with both? Neither pains nor pleasures are homogeneous, and pain is always heterogeneous with pleasure. What is there to decide whether a particular pleasure is worth purchasing at the cost of a particular pain, except the feelings and judgment of the experienced? When, therefore, those feelings and judgment declare the pleasures derived from the higher faculties to be preferable *in kind,* apart from the question of intensity, to those of which the animal nature, disjoined from the higher faculties, is susceptible, they are entitled on this subject to the same regard.

I have dwelt on this point, as being a necessary part of a perfectly just conception of Utility or Happiness, considered as the directive rule of human conduct. But it is by no means an indispensable condition to the acceptance of the utilitarian standard; for that standard is not the agent's own greatest happiness, but the greatest amount of happiness altogether; and if it may possibly be doubted whether a noble character is always the happier for its nobleness, there can be no doubt that it makes other people happier, and that the world in general is immensely a gainer by it. Utilitarianism, therefore, could only attain its end by the general cultivation of nobleness of character, even if each individual were only benefited by the nobleness of others, and his own, so far as happiness is concerned, were a sheer deduction from the benefit. But the bare enunciation of such an absurdity as this last, renders refutation superfluous.

III

According to the Greatest Happiness Principle, as above explained, the ultimate end, with reference to and for the sake of which all other things are desirable (whether we are considering our own good or that of other people), is an existence exempt as far as possible from pain, and as rich as possible in enjoyments, both in point of quantity and quality; the test of quality, and the rule for measuring it against quantity, being the preference felt by those who in their opportunities of experience, to which must be added their habits of self-consciousness and self-observation, are best furnished with the means of comparison. This, being, according to the utilitarian opinion, the end of human action, is necessarily also the standard of morality; which may accordingly be defined, the rules and precepts for human conduct, by the observance of which an existence such as has been described might be, to the greatest extent possible, secured to all mankind; and not to them only, but, so far as the nature of things admits, to the whole sentient creation.

Against this doctrine, however, arises another class of objectors, who say that happiness, in any form, cannot be the rational purpose of human life and action; because, in the first place, it is unattainable: and they contemptuously ask, what right hast thou to be happy? a question which Mr. Carlyle clenches by the addition, What right, a short time ago, hadst thou even *to be?* Next, they say, that men can do *without* happiness; that all noble human beings have felt this, and could not have become noble but by learning the lesson of *Entssagen,* or renunciation; which lesson, thoroughly learnt and submitted to, they affirm to be the beginning and necessary condition of all virtue.

The first of these objections would go to the root of the matter were it well founded; for if no happiness is to be had at all by human beings, the attainment of it cannot be the end of morality or of any rational conduct. Though, even in that case, something might still be said for the utilitarian theory; since utility includes not solely the pursuit of happiness, but the prevention or mitigation of unhappiness; and if the former aim be chimerical, there will be all the greater scope and more imperative need for the latter, so long at least as mankind think fit to live, and do not take refuge in the simultaneous act of suicide recommended under certain conditions by Novalis. When, however, it is thus positively asserted to be impossible that human life should be happy, the assertion, if not something like a verbal quibble, is at least an exaggeration. If by happiness be meant a continuity of highly pleasurable excitement, it is evident enough that this is impossible. A state of exalted pleasure lasts only moments, or in some cases, and with some intermissions, hours or days, and is the occasional brilliant flash of enjoyment, not its permanent and steady flame. Of this the philosophers who have taught that happiness is the end of life were as

fully aware as those who taunt them. The happiness which they meant was not a life of rapture; but moments of such, in an existence made up of few and transitory pains, many and various pleasures, with a decided predominance of the active over the passive, and having as the foundation of the whole, not to expect more from life than it is capable of bestowing. A life thus composed, to those who have been fortunate enough to obtain it, has always appeared worthy of the name of happiness. And such an existence is even now the lot of many, during some considerable portion of their lives. The present wretched education, and wretched social arrangements, are the only real hindrance to its being attainable by almost all.

The objectors perhaps may doubt whether human beings, if taught to consider happiness as the end of life, would be satisfied with such a moderate share of it. But great numbers of mankind have been satisfied with much less. The main constituents of a satisfied life appear to be two, either of which by itself is often found sufficient for the purpose: tranquillity, and excitement. With much tranquillity, many find that they can be content with very little pleasure: with much excitement, many can reconcile themselves to a considerable quantity of pain. There is assuredly no inherent impossibility in enabling even the mass of mankind to unite both; since the two are so far from being incompatible that they are in natural alliance, the prolongation of either being a preparation for, and exciting a wish for, the other. It is only those in whom indolence amounts to a vice, that do not desire excitement after an interval of repose: it is only those in whom the need of excitement is a disease, that feel the tranquillity which follows excitement dull and insipid, instead of pleasurable in direct proportion to the excitement which preceded it. When people who are tolerably fortunate in their outward lot do not find in life sufficient enjoyment to make it valuable to them, the cause generally is caring for nobody but themselves. To those who have neither public nor private affections, the excitements of life are much curtailed, and in any case dwindle in value as the time approaches when all selfish interests must be terminated by death: while those who leave after them objects of personal affection, and especially those who have also cultivated a fellow-feeling with the collective interests of mankind, retain as lively an interest in life on the eve of death as in the vigour of youth and health. Next to selfishness, the principal cause which makes life unsatisfactory is want of mental cultivation. A cultivated mind—I do not mean that of a philosopher, but any mind to which the fountains of knowledge have been opened, and which has been taught, in any tolerable degree, to exercise its faculties—finds sources of inexhaustible interest in all that surrounds it; in the objects of nature, the achievements of art, the imaginations of poetry, the incidents of history, the ways of mankind, past and present, and their prospects in the future. It is possible, indeed, to become indifferent to all this, and that too without having exhausted a thousandth part of it; but only when one has had from the beginning no moral or human interest in these things, and has sought in them only the gratification of curiosity.

Now there is absolutely no reason in the nature of things why an amount of mental culture sufficient to give an intelligent interest in these objects of contemplation, should not be the inheritance of every one born in a civilised country. As little is there an inherent necessity that any human being should be a selfish egotist, devoid of every feeling or care but those which centre in his own miserable individuality. Something far superior to this is sufficiently common even now, to give ample earnest of what the human species may be made. Genuine private affections, and a sincere interest in the public good, are possible, though in unequal degrees, to every rightly brought up human being. In a world in which there is so much to interest, so much to enjoy, and so much also to correct and improve, every one who has this moderate amount of moral and intellectual requisites is capable of an existence

which may be called enviable; and unless such a person, through bad laws, or subjection to the will of others, is denied the liberty to use the sources of happiness within his reach, he will not fail to find this enviable existence, if he escape the positive evils of life, the great sources of physical and mental suffering—such as indigence, disease, and the unkindness, worthlessness, or premature loss of objects of affection. The main stress of the problem lies, therefore, in the contest with these calamities, from which it is a rare good fortune entirely to escape; which, as things now are, cannot be obviated, and often cannot be in any material degree mitigated. Yet no one whose opinion deserves a moment's consideration can doubt that most of the great positive evils of the world are in themselves removable, and will, if human affairs continue to improve, be in the end reduced within narrow limits. Poverty, in any sense implying suffering, may be completely extinguished by the wisdom of society, combined with the good sense and providence of individuals. Even that most intractable of enemies, disease, may be indefinitely reduced in dimensions by good physical and moral education, and proper control of noxious influences; while the progress of science holds out a promise for the future of still more direct conquests over this detestable foe. And every advance in that direction relieves us from some, not only of the changes which cut short our own lives, but, what concerns us still more, which deprive us of those in whom our happiness is wrapt up. As for vicissitudes of fortune, and other disappointments connected with worldly circumstances, these are principally the effect either of gross imprudence, of ill-regulated desires, or of bad or imperfect social institutions. All the grand sources, in short, of human suffering are in a great degree, many of them almost entirely, conquerable by human care and effort; and though their removal is grievously slow—though a long succession of generations will perish in the breach before the conquest is completed, and this world becomes all that, if will and knowledge were not wanting, it might easily be made—yet every mind sufficiently intelligent and generous to bear a part, however small and unconspicuous, in the endeavour, will draw a noble enjoyment from the contest itself, which he would not for any bribe in the form of selfish indulgence consent to be without.

And this leads to the true estimation of what is said by the objectors concerning the possibility, and the obligation, of learning to do without happiness. Unquestionably it is possible to do without happiness; it is done involuntarily by nineteen-twentieths of mankind, even in those parts of our present world which are least deep in barbarism; and it often has to be done voluntarily by the hero or the martyr, for the sake of something which he prizes more than his individual happiness. But this something, what is it, unless the happiness of others, or some of the requisites of happiness? It is noble to be capable of resigning entirely one's own portion of happiness, or chances of it: but, after all, this self-sacrifice must be for some end; and if we are told that its end is not happiness, but virtue, which is better than happiness, I ask, would the sacrifice be made if the hero or martyr did not believe that it would earn for others immunity from similar sacrifices? Would it be made if he thought that his renunciation of happiness for himself would produce no fruit for any of his fellow creatures, but to make their lot like his, and place them also in the condition of persons who have renounced happiness? All honour to those who can abnegate for themselves the personal enjoyment of life, when by such renunciation they contribute worthily to increase the amount of happiness in the world; but he who does it, or professes to do it, for any other purpose, is no more deserving of admiration than the ascetic mounted on his pillar. He may be an inspiriting proof of what men *can* do, but assuredly not an example of what they *should*.

Though it is only in a very imperfect state of the world's arrangements that any one can best serve the happiness of others by the absolute sacrifice of his own, yet so long as the world is in that imperfect state,

I fully acknowledge that the readiness to make a sacrifice is the highest virtue which can be found in man. I will add, that in this condition of the world, paradoxical as the assertion may be, the conscious ability to do without happiness gives the best prospect of realising such happiness as is attainable. For nothing except that consciousness can raise a person above the chances of life, by making him feel that, let fate and fortune do their worst, they have not power to subdue him: which, once felt, frees him from excess of anxiety concerning the evils of life, and enables him, like many a Stoic in the worst times of the Roman Empire, to cultivate in tranquillity the sources of satisfaction accessible to him, without concerning himself about the uncertainty of their duration, any more than about their inevitable end.

Meanwhile, let utilitarians never cease to claim the morality of self devotion as a possession which belongs by as good a right to them, as either to the Stoic or to the Transcendentalist. The utilitarian morality does recognise in human beings the power of sacrificing their own greatest good for the good of others. It only refuses to admit that the sacrifice is itself a good. A sacrifice which does not increase, or tend to increase, the sum total of happiness, it considers as wasted. The only self-renunciation which it applauds, is devotion to the happiness, or to some of the means of happiness, of others; either of mankind collectively, or of individuals within the limits imposed by the collective interests of mankind.

I must again repeat, what the assailants of utilitarianism seldom have the justice to acknowledge, that the happiness which forms the utilitarian standard of what is right in conduct, is not the agent's own happiness, but that of all concerned. As between his own happiness and that of others, utilitarianism requires him to be as strictly impartial as a disinterested and benevolent spectator. In the golden rule of Jesus of Nazareth, we read the complete spirit of the ethics of utility. To do as you would be done by, and to love your neighbour as yourself, constitute the ideal perfection of utilitarian morality. As the means of making the nearest approach to this ideal, utility would enjoin, first, that laws and social arrangements should place the happiness, or (as speaking practically it may be called) the interest, of every individual as nearly as possible in harmony with the interest of the whole; and secondly, that education and opinion, which have so vast a power over human character, should so use that power as to establish in the mind of every individual an indissoluble association between his own happiness and the good of the whole; especially between his own happiness and the practice of such modes of conduct, negative and positive, as regard for the universal happiness prescribes; so that not only he may be unable to conceive the possibility of happiness to himself, consistently with conduct opposed to the general good, but also that a direct impulse to promote the general good may be in every individual one of the habitual motives of action, and the sentiments connected therewith may fill a large and prominent place in every human being's sentient existence. If the impugners of the utilitarian morality represented it to their own minds in this its true character, I know not what recommendation possessed by any other morality they could possibly affirm to be wanting to it; what more beautiful or more exalted developments of human nature any other ethical system can be supposed to foster, or what springs of action, not accessible to the utilitarian, such systems rely on for giving effect to their mandates.

We not uncommonly hear the doctrine of utility inveighed against as a *godless* doctrine. If it be necessary to say anything at all against so mere an assumption, we may say that the question depends upon what idea we have formed of the moral character of the Deity. If it be a true belief that God desires, above all things, the happiness of his creatures, and that this was his purpose in their creation, utility is not only not a godless doctrine, but more profoundly religious than any other. If it be meant that utilitarianism does not recognise the revealed will of God as the supreme law of morals, I answer, that a utilitarian who believes in the perfect goodness and wisdom of God, necessarily believes that whatever God has thought fit to reveal on the subject of morals, must fulfil the requirements of utility in a supreme degree. But others besides utilitarians have been of opinion that the Christian revelation was intended, and is fitted, to inform the hearts and minds of mankind with a spirit which should enable them to find for themselves what is right, and incline them to do it when found, rather than to tell them, except in a very general way, what it is; and that we need a doctrine of ethics, carefully followed out, to *interpret* to us the will of God. Whether this opinion is correct or not, it is superfluous here to discuss; since whatever aid religion, either natural or revealed, can afford to ethical investigation, is open to the utilitarian moralist as to any other. He can use it as the testimony of God to the usefulness or hurtfulness of any given course of action, by as good a right as others can use it for the indication of a transcendental law, having no connection with usefulness or with happiness.

2

Enduring Insights
of the Rationalist

As our examination of hedonism has moved beyond the urbane and sophisticated essays of Lin Yutang to the fundamentally altruistic philosophy of John Stuart Mill, the adequacy of the pursuit of pleasure as an enduring source of meaning and satisfaction in life becomes increasingly open to question. The charm of its simplicity is lost when we begin to feel that it is perhaps too simple. The appeal of its naturalness fades when we suspect that it is perhaps natural for man only at the animal level. Among the critics of hedonism the most forthright and uncompromising are the Rationalists, who propose to develop a philosophy that is more genuinely *human* in outlook and spirit. We are in the world, so the rationalist maintains, not to live pleasantly but to acquit ourselves like men; only by thus acting in accord with our real nature can we hope to find any lasting meaning or purpose in life.

It is the life of reason, these philosophers point out, that is most uniquely human and satisfying, and here alone lies the one dependable avenue to meaning and direction in human life. The insights of the rationalists have had an enduring appeal to intelligent men and women in every age whether they be among the young men of Athens who gathered to hear Socrates insist that the unexamined life is not worthy of a man or among the young men and women of America today who read the popular philosophical essays of Bertrand Russell and discuss the economic and political ideas of Walter Lippmann. Indeed no more persuasive statement of rationalism as a philosophy of living for our age is to be found than that in the pages of Lippmann's *Preface to Morals*. Published in 1929, this book was in part a reaction against the hedonistic spirit of the 1920's in this country. In that age of jazz and bootleg whiskey it was widely asserted that happiness was to be found in a perpetual round of self-indulgence and excess, a Cyrenaic pursuit of pleasure of the most blasé and uninhibited sort. In vigorous opposition to this point of view, Lippmann insisted that a philosophy of living based upon reason rather than upon passion was the only one that could meet the test of experience and common sense.

The central issue that confronts us in seeking some moral meaning and purpose in life, Lippmann feels, is a choice between the pursuit of pleasure and the life of reason. "It is a deep conviction that happiness is possible," he writes, "and all inquiry into the foundations of morals turns ultimately upon whether man can achieve this happiness by pursuing his desires, or whether he must first learn to desire the kind of happiness which is possible." Those who hope to find happiness through the pursuit of pleasure, in Lippmann's opinion, ignore the testimony not merely of their maiden aunts but also of the great teachers of wisdom through the ages. "It is written in many languages and in the idiom of many cultures that if a man is to find happiness, he must reconstruct not merely his world but, first of all, himself."[1]

Rationalism for the Layman: Bertrand Russell

For more than half a century Bertrand Russell has exercised a profound and in many ways remarkable influence over contemporary British and American philosophy. At the age of ninety he is still a controversial figure on the contemporary scene, endorsing moral and social proposals that seem much too radical to many of his younger colleagues. In the field of philosophy itself he has taken an active part in the more important movements that have shaped the direction and outlook of contemporary thought. During his long and distinguished career there have not only been changes in his point of view, but at times inconsistencies, contradictions, and repudiations. His own comment on this is revealing: "I am not myself in any degree ashamed of having changed my opinions. What physicist who was already active in 1900 would dream of boasting that his opinions had not changed during the last half century?"

As a result, Russell is not an easy philosopher to classify; he does not fit readily into any of the conventional categories. But throughout his books, as well as his life, there has run a confidence in human reason as man's best and most dependable source of knowledge and a determination to follow reason as the only reliable guide in dealing with the problems of human conduct. His combination of philosophical distinction with literary excellence makes him an ideal figure to present the enduring insights of rationalism as a practical and appealing way of life for the layman as well as for the professional philosopher.

Born in 1872, into a family long famous in England (his grandfather introduced the great Reform Bill of 1832), Russell was educated at Cambridge University, where he later became a lecturer and fellow. His early work was in the field of mathematics and the philosophy of science. From 1910 to 1913 he cooperated with Alfred North Whitehead at Cambridge in the publication of a monumental contribution to mathematical philosophy, their three-volume *Principia Mathematica*. During the next twenty years he published half a dozen influential books

---

[1] Walter Lippmann, *A Preface to Morals*, (New York, The Macmillan Company, 1929), pp. 151, 153.

of his own that established him as one of the ablest exponents of the scientific point of view in philosophy, but his outspoken opposition to World War I cost Russell his position at Cambridge and for a time he was imprisoned as a pacifist. Because of this and comparable experiences he became increasingly interested in moral problems and in political philosophy. Both his father and his mother were friends and disciples of John Stuart Mill, and both refused to compromise conviction with the conventions accepted by all good Victorians. This heritage was not lost to their son. Bertrand Russell's unconventional ideas, his devotion to the cause of human freedom, and his hatred of tyranny in every form are matters of common knowledge. Soon after World War I he renounced his early pacifism, later supporting the war against the Nazi government in Germany and writing vehement essays attacking Soviet Russia. In the last few years, however, he has become a leader in the worldwide campaign to compel the United States and Russia to destroy all nuclear weapons and renounce nuclear warfare.

One of the most prolific and distinguished writers of contemporary English prose, Russell has published more than fifty influential books covering a wide range of subjects. He writes with such clarity and integrity, even on highly controversial subjects, that his ideas have had wide circulation. In 1950 he became the third philosopher to receive the Nobel Prize for Literature. The prize was awarded, as the citation read, "in recognition of his many-sided and significant authorship, in which he has constantly figured as a defender of humanity and freedom of thought." His *Conquest of Happiness,* published in 1930, presents in vigorous and popular fashion the tolerant rationalism that Russell then found most acceptable as a philosophy of living. The selection included here is from that volume. *Portraits from Memory* (1950) is a brief but entertaining autobiography. Russell's *History of Western Philosophy* (1945) is a readable but frankly biased introduction to philosophy. In a later collection of his essays, entitled *Philosophy for Laymen* (1950), Russell describes in nontechnical language what philosophy tries to do and why he thinks it is important. In *New Hopes for a Changing World* (1951) he suggests his solutions for a number of our more pressing current problems. In 1953 he published a book of short stories called *Satan in the Suburbs.*

The Conquest of Happiness*

I

Perhaps the best introduction to the philosophy which I wish to advocate will be a

* From *The Conquest of Happiness* by Bertrand Russell. By permission of The Liveright Publishing Corporation, New York. Copyright 1958 by Bertrand Russell.

few words of autobiography. I was not born happy. As a child, my favorite hymn was: "Weary of earth and laden with my sin." At the age of five, I reflected that, if I should live to be seventy, I had only endured, so far, a fourteenth part of my whole life, and I felt the long-spread-out boredom ahead of me to be almost unendurable. In adolescence,

I hated life and was continually on the verge of suicide, from which, however, I was restrained by the desire to know more mathematics. Now, on the contrary, I enjoy life; I might almost say that with every year that passes I enjoy it more. This is due partly to having discovered what were the things that I most desired, and having gradually acquired many of these things. Partly it is due to having successfully dismissed certain objects of desire—such as the acquisition of indubitable knowledge about something or other—as essentially unattainable. But very largely it is due to a diminishing preoccupation with myself. Like others who had a Puritan education, I had the habit of meditating on my sins, follies, and shortcomings. I seemed to myself—no doubt justly—a miserable specimen. Gradually I learned to be indifferent to myself and my deficiencies; I came to center my attention increasingly upon external objects: the state of the world, various branches of knowledge, individuals for whom I felt affection. External interests, it is true, bring each its own possibility of pain: the world may be plunged in war, knowledge in some direction may be hard to achieve, friends may die. But pains of these kinds do not destroy the essential quality of life, as do those that spring from disgust with self. And every external interest inspires some activity which, so long as the interest remains alive, is a complete preventive of *ennui*. Interest in oneself, on the contrary, leads to no activity of a progressive kind. It may lead to the keeping of a diary, to getting psychoanalyzed, or perhaps to becoming a monk. But the monk will not be happy until the routine of the monastery has made him forget his own soul. The happiness which he attributes to religion he could have obtained from becoming a crossing-sweeper, provided he were compelled to remain one. External discipline is the only road to happiness for those unfortunates whose self-absorption is too profound to be cured in any other way.

One of the great drawbacks to self-centered passions is that they afford so little variety in life. The man who loves only himself cannot, it is true, be accused of promiscuity in his affections, but he is bound in the end to suffer intolerable boredom from the invariable sameness of the object of his devotion. The man who suffers from a sense of sin is suffering from a particular kind of self-love. In all this vast universe the thing that appears to him of most importance is that he himself should be virtuous. It is a grave defect in certain forms of traditional religion that they have encouraged this particular kind of self-absorption.

The happy man is the man who lives objectively, who has free affections and wide interests, who secures his happiness through these interests and affections and through the fact that they, in turn, make him an object of interest and affection to many others. To be the recipient of affection is a potent cause of happiness, but the man who demands affection is not the man upon whom it is bestowed. The man who receives affection is, speaking broadly, the man who gives it. But it is useless to attempt to give it as a calculation, in the way in which one might lend money at interest, for a calculated affection is not genuine and is not felt to be so by the recipient.

II

Happiness is not, except in very rare cases, something that drops into the mouth, like a ripe fruit, by the mere operation of fortunate circumstances. That is why I have called this book "The Conquest of Happiness." For in a world so full of avoidable and unavoidable misfortunes, of illness and psychological tangles, of struggle and poverty and ill-will, the man or woman who is to be happy must find ways of coping with the multitudinous causes of unhappiness by which each individual is assailed. In some rare cases no great effort may be required. A man of easy good-nature, who inherits an ample fortune and enjoys good health together with simple tastes, may slip through life comfortably and wonder what all the fuss is about; a good-looking woman of an indolent disposition, if she happens to marry a well-to-do husband who demands no exertion from her, and if after marriage she does not mind growing fat, may equally enjoy a certain lazy comfort, provided she has good luck as regards her children. But such cases are exceptional. Most people are not rich; many people are not born good-natured; many people have uneasy passions which make a quiet and well-regulated life seem intolerably boring; health is a blessing which no one can be sure of preserving; marriage is not invariably a source of bliss. For all these reasons, happiness must be, for most men and women, an achievement rather than a gift of the gods, and in this achievement effort, both inward and outward, must play a great part.

Happiness is of two sorts, though, of course, there are intermediate degrees. The two sorts I mean might be distinguished as plain and fancy, or animal and spiritual, or of the heart and of the head. The designation to be chosen among these alternatives depends, of course, upon the thesis to be proved. I am at the moment not concerned to prove any thesis, but merely to describe. Perhaps the simplest way to describe the difference between the two sorts of happiness is to say that one sort is open to any human being, and the other only to those who can read and write. When I was a boy, I knew a man bursting with happiness whose business was digging wells. He was of enormous height and of incredible muscles; he could neither read nor write, and when in the year 1885 he got a vote for Parliament, he learnt for the first time that such an institution existed. His happiness did not depend upon intellectual sources; it was not based upon belief in natural law, or the perfectibility of the species, or any of the other creeds which intellectuals consider necessary to their enjoyment of life. It was based upon physical vigor, a sufficiency of work, and the overcoming of not insuperable obstacles in the shape of rock. The happiness of my gardener is of the same species; he wages a perennial war against rabbits, of which he speaks exactly as Scotland Yard speaks of Bolsheviks; he considers them dark, designing and ferocious, and is of opinion that they can only be met by means of a cun-

ning equal to their own. Like the heroes of Valhalla who spent their day hunting a certain wild boar, which they killed every evening but which miraculously came to life again in the morning, my gardener can slay his enemy one day without any fear that the enemy will have disappeared the next day. Although well over seventy, he works all day and bicycles sixteen hilly miles to and from his work, but the fount of joy is inexhaustible.

But, you will say, these simple delights are not open to superior people like ourselves. The argument, to my mind, is a poor one. Pleasures exactly similar to those of my gardener so far as their emotional content is concerned are open to the most highly educated people. The difference made by education is only in regard to the activities by which these pleasures are to be obtained. Pleasures of achievement demand difficulties such that beforehand success seems doubtful although in the end it is usually achieved. This is perhaps the chief reason why a modest estimate of one's own powers is a source of happiness. The man who underestimates himself is perpetually being surprised by success, whereas the man who overestimates himself is just as often surprised by failure. The former kind of surprise is pleasant, the latter unpleasant. It is therefore wise to be not unduly conceited, though also not too modest to be enterprising.

Of the more highly educated sections of the community, the happiest in the present day are the men of science. Many of the most eminent of them are emotionally simple, and obtain from their work a satisfaction so profound that they can derive pleasure from eating, and even marrying. Artists and literary men consider it *de rigeur* to be unhappy in their marriages, but men of science quite frequently remain capable of old-fashioned domestic bliss. The reason for this is that the higher parts of their intelligence are wholly absorbed by their work and are not allowed to intrude into regions where they have no functions to perform. In their work they are happy because in the modern world science is progressive and powerful, and because its importance is not doubted either by themselves or by laymen. They have therefore no necessity for complex emotions, since the simpler emotions meet with no obstacles. Complexity in emotions is like foam in a river. It is produced by obstacles which break the smoothly flowing current. But so long as the vital energies are unimpeded, they produce no ripple on the surface, and their strength is not evident to the unobservant.

All the conditions of happiness are realized in the life of the man of science. He has an activity which utilizes his abilities to the full, and he achieves results which appear important not only to himself but to the general public, even when it cannot in the smallest degree understand them. In this he is more fortunate than the artist. When the public cannot understand a picture or a poem, they conclude that it is a bad picture or a bad poem. When they cannot understand the theory of relativity they conclude (rightly) that their education has been insufficient. Consequently Einstein is honored while the best painters are (or at least were) left to starve in garrets, and Einstein is happy while the painters are unhappy. Very few men can be genuinely happy in a life involving continual self-assertion against the skepticism of the mass of mankind, unless they can shut themselves up in a coterie and forget the cold outer world. The man of science has no need of a coterie, since he is thought well of by everybody except his colleagues. The artist, on the contrary, is in the painful situation of having to choose between being despised and being despicable. If his powers are of the first order, he must incur one or the other of these misfortunes—the former if he uses his powers, the latter if he does not.

III

Resignation has also its part to play in the conquest of happiness, and it is a part no less essential than that played by effort. The wise man, though he will not sit down under preventable misfortunes, will not waste time and emotion upon such as are unavoid-

able, and even such as are in themselves avoidable he will submit to if the time and labor required to avoid them would interfere with the pursuit of some more important object. Many people get into a fret or a fury over every little thing that goes wrong, and in this way waste a great deal of energy that might be more usefully employed. Even in the pursuit of really important objects, it is unwise to become so deeply involved emotionally that the thought of possible failure becomes a constant menace to peace of mind. Christianity taught submission to the will of God, and even for those who cannot accept this phraseology, there should be something of the same kind pervading all their activities. Efficiency in a practical task is not proportional to the emotion that we put into it; indeed emotion is sometimes an obstacle to efficiency. The attitude required is that of doing one's best while leaving the issue to fate.

Resignation is of two sorts, one rooted in despair, the other in unconquerable hope. The first is bad; the second is good. The man who has suffered such fundamental defeat that he has given up hope of serious achievement may learn the resignation of despair, and, if he does, he will abandon all serious activity; he may camouflage his despair by religious phrases, or by the doctrine that contemplation is the true end of man. But whatever disguise he may adopt to conceal his inward defeat, he will remain essentially useless and fundamentally unhappy. The man whose resignation is based on unconquerable hope acts in quite a different way. Hope which is to be unconquerable must be large and impersonal. Whatever my personal activities, I may be defeated by death, or by certain kinds of diseases; I may be overcome by my enemies; I may find that I have embarked upon an unwise course which cannot lead to success. In a thousand ways the failure of purely personal hopes may be unavoidable, but if personal aims have been part of larger hopes for humanity, there is not the same utter defeat when failure comes. The man of science who desires to make great discoveries himself may fail to do so, or may have to abandon his work owing to a blow on the head, but if he desires profoundly the progress of science and not merely his personal contribution to this object, he will not feel the same despair as would be felt by a man whose research had purely egoistic motives. The man who is working for some much needed reform may find all his efforts sidetracked by a war, and may be forced to realize that what he has worked for will not come about in his lifetime. But he need not on that account sink into complete despair, provided that he is interested in the future of mankind apart from his own participation in it.

The cases we have been considering are those in which resignation is most difficult; there are a number of others in which it is much easier. These are the cases in which only subsidiary purposes suffer a check, while the major purposes of life continue to offer a prospect of success. A man, for example, who is engaged in important work shows a failure in the desirable kind of resignation if he is distracted by matrimonial unhappiness; if his work is really absorbing, he should be able to work as much and as well when his married life is unhappy as when it is happy.

Some people are unable to bear with patience even those minor troubles which make up, if we permit them to do so, a very large part of life. They are furious when they miss a train, transported with rage if their dinner is badly cooked, sunk in despair if the chimney smokes, and vow vengeance against the whole industrial order when their clothes fail to return from the sanitary steam laundry. The energy that such people waste on trivial troubles would be sufficient, if more wisely directed, to make and unmake empires. The wise man fails to observe the dust that the housemaid has not dusted, the potato that the cook has not cooked, and the soot that the sweep has not swept. I do not mean that he takes no steps to remedy these matters, provided he has time to do so, I mean only that he deals with them without emotion. Worry and fret and irritation are emotions which serve no purpose. Those who feel them strongly may say that they are incapable of overcoming them, and I am not sure that they can be overcome by anything short of that fundamental resignation of which we spoke earlier. The same kind of concentration upon large impersonal hopes which enables a man to bear personal failure in his work, or the troubles of an unhappy marriage, will also make it possible for him to be patient when he misses a train or drops his umbrella in the mud. If he is of a fretful disposition, I am not sure that anything less than this will cure him.

Every civilized man or woman has, I suppose, some picture of himself or herself, and is annoyed when anything happens that seems to spoil this picture. The best cure is to have not only one picture, but a whole gallery, and to select the one appropriate to the incident in question. If some of the portraits are a trifle laughable, so much the better; it is not wise to see oneself all day long as a hero of high tragedy. I do not suggest that one should see oneself always as a clown in comedy, for those who do this are even more irritating; a little tact is required in choosing a role appropriate to the situation. Of course, if you can forget yourself and not play a part at all, that is admirable. But if playing a part has become second nature, consider that you act in repertory, and so avoid monotony.

Many active people are of opinion that the slightest grain of resignation, the faintest gleam of humor, would destroy the energy with which they do their work and the determination by which, as they believe, they achieve success. These people, in my opinion, are mistaken. Work that is worth doing can be done even by those who do not deceive themselves either as to its importance or as to the ease with which it can be done. Those who can do their work only when upheld by self-deception had better first take a course in learning to endure the truth before continuing their career, since sooner or later the need of being sustained by myths will cause their work to become harmful instead of beneficial. It is better to do nothing than to do harm. Half the useful work in the world consists of combating the harmful work. A little time spent in learning to appreciate facts is not time wasted, and the work that will be done afterwards is far less likely to be harmful than the work done by those who need a continual inflation of their ego as a stimulant to their energy. A certain kind of resignation is involved in willingness to face the truth about ourselves; this kind, though it may involve pain in the first moments, affords ultimately a protection—indeed the only possible protection—against the disappointments and disillusionments to which the self-deceiver is liable. Nothing is more fatiguing nor, in the long run, more exasperating than the daily effort to believe things which daily become more incredible. To be done with this effort is an indispensable condition of secure and lasting happiness.

It is one of the defects of modern higher education that it has become too much a training in the acquisition of certain kinds of skill, and too little an enlargement of the mind and heart by an impartial survey of the world. You become absorbed, let us say, in a political contest, and work hard for the victory of your own party. So far, so good. But it may happen in the course of the contest that some opportunity of victory presents itself which involves the use of methods calculated to increase hatred, violence and suspicion in the world. For example, you may find that the best road to victory is to insult some foreign nation. If your mental purview is limited to the present, or if you have imbibed the doctrine that what is called efficiency is the only thing that matters, you will adopt such dubious means. Through them you will be victorious in your immediate purpose, while the more distant consequences may be disastrous. If, on the other hand, you have as part of the habitual furniture of your mind the past ages of man, his slow and partial emergence out of barbarism, and the brevity of his total existence in comparison with astronomical epochs—if, I say, such thoughts have molded your habitual feelings, you will realize that the momentary battle upon which you are engaged cannot be of such importance as to risk a backward step towards the darkness out of which we have

been slowly emerging. Nay, more, if you suffer defeat in your immediate objective, you will be sustained by the same sense of its momentariness that made you unwilling to adopt degrading weapons. You will have, beyond your immediate activities, purposes that are distant and slowly unfolding, in which you are not an isolated individual but one of the great army of those who have led mankind towards a civilized existence. If you have attained to this outlook, a certain deep happiness will never leave you, whatever your personal fate may be. Life will become a communion with the great of all ages, and personal death no more than a negligible incident.

If I had the power to organize higher education as I should wish it to be, I should seek to substitute for the old orthodox religions something which is perhaps hardly to be called religion, since it is merely a focusing of attention upon well-ascertained facts. I should seek to make young people vividly aware of the past, vividly realizing that the future of man will in all likelihood be immeasurably longer than his past, profoundly conscious of the minuteness of the planet upon which we live and of the fact that life on this planet is only a temporary incident; and at the same time with these facts which tend to emphasize the insignificance of the individual, I should present quite another set of facts designed to impress upon the mind of the young the greatness of which the individual is capable, and the knowledge that throughout all the depths of stellar space nothing of equal value is known to us. Spinoza long ago wrote of human bondage and human freedom; his form and his language make his thought difficult of access to all students of philosophy, but the essence of what I wish to convey differs little from what he has said.

A man who has once perceived, however temporarily and however briefly, what makes greatness of soul, can no longer be happy if he allows himself to be petty, self-seeking, troubled by trivial misfortunes, dreading what fate may have in store for him. The man capable of greatness of soul will open wide the windows of his mind, letting the winds blow freely upon it from every portion of the universe. He will see himself and life and the world as truly as our human limitations will permit; realizing the brevity and minuteness of human life, he will realize also that in individual minds is concentrated whatever of value the known universe con-tains. And he will see that the man whose mind mirrors the world becomes in a sense as great as the world. In emancipation from the fears that beset the slave of circumstance he will experience a profound joy, and through all the vicissitudes of his outward life he will remain in the depths of his being a happy man.

Early Exponents of Rationalism: The Stoics

The first influential exponents of rationalism as a philosophy of life were the Stoics. Both Socrates and Plato exhibit an unshaken confidence in human reason, but neither of these early Greek philosophers was content with a position that limited itself to the insights of reason. Another group of Greek thinkers, however, the Cynics, found in the stimulating and controversial ideas of Socrates a view of human life that led directly to the rationalism of the Stoics. Antisthenes, the founder of the school, was an Athenian about twenty-five years younger than Socrates. Introduced to philosophy by the Sophists, he learned from them to think of natural law, not human convention, as the proper basis of morals and social life. But Antisthenes soon became an ardent admirer and disciple of Socrates from whom his deepest philosophical insights were derived. He accepted the Socratic principle that reason provides the only sound foundation of morality and the good life, but Socrates' complete lack of interest in the material possessions that so attract most men made an even greater impression upon Antisthenes. When a friend on one occasion poked fun at Socrates because of his frugal circumstances and the absence of pleasure from his life, Socrates is said to have replied: "You, Antiphon, would seem to suggest that happiness consists in luxury and extravagance; I hold a different creed. To have no wants at all is to my mind an attribute of godhead; to have as few wants as possible the nearest approach to godhead."[1]

This Socratic dictum became the cornerstone of the Cynic philosophy. The good life can be found only as man rids himself of all slavery to desire, of all bondage to external circumstances beyond his control. The Cynics, accordingly, rejected all social convention, all the requirements of the civilization of their day, and set out to "live according to nature" so far as humanly possible. Unconcerned both with the material goods of life and with the attitude of their fellowmen, they undertook to master themselves and control their desires in such fashion that nothing outside could disturb them. The spirit of the Cynic is well exemplified in the life of Diogenes, one of Antisthenes' best-known followers. While wandering about Greece in search of an honest man with no other clothing or shelter than a tub, Diogenes noticed a child drinking with its hands and thereupon threw away his cup as a final unnecessary luxury. Or so at least the story goes.

Thoroughgoing individualists themselves, the Cynics carried their contempt for conventional order and decency to lengths that shocked their contemporaries. It is not difficult to see why the word "cynic" has come to denote a contempt for all the accepted conventions of social life. In their independence of mind, their indifference alike to the comforts and the inconveniences of life, their insistence that as the first step in his philosophy a man must master himself, the Cynics afford a good introduction to the enduring insights of the rationalist. Unquestionably, however, they fail to grasp the spirit of the life of reason at its best.

---

[1] Xenophon, *Memorabilia* i. 6.

Zeno (*c.* 335–264 B.C.), the founder of Stoicism,[2] was born in Cyprus when Aristotle's influence in Athens was at its peak. As a young man he spent some time pursuing the commercial activities of his father. Business interests first took him to Athens, but he soon turned to the study of philosophy there and about 300 B.C. established his own school in the *Stoa Poikile* (Painted Porch). He and his followers regularly met for informal philosophical discussions at the *Stoa* and before long were known as Stoics, or "men of the porch." Zeno was a man of marked ability, moral earnestness, and good will. He earned the respect and admiration of his contemporaries, and in time his fame became so great that large crowds of students were drawn to Athens to hear him. Even the tradesmen of the city were pleased at the crowds, and to repay the philosopher who brought them, Athens honored him with a golden crown and a bronze statue—a striking indication of how successful Zeno was in avoiding the difficulties into which a devotion to philosophy led Socrates a little more than a hundred years earlier.

The Stoic school continued under Zeno's direction for about forty years; then at an advanced age he suffered a minor injury which he regarded as an indication of the divine will and accordingly put an end to his own life. Among the group of able disciples whom Zeno gathered about him in Athens, Cleanthes and Chrysippus stand out. Cleanthes' famous *Hymn to Zeus* (included in the selections that follow) is the most important document that has been preserved from the early Stoic writings. (Actually, much of this hymn might easily have been written by Alexander Pope and readily accepted by educated Christians in the century after Newton.)

In the figure of Socrates these early Stoics found their outstanding example of the true philosopher. Socrates' attitude at the time of his trial, his refusal to escape from prison, his calmness in the face of death, and his contention that the man who is guilty of injustice injures himself more than his victims, all illustrated Stoic doctrines. By 150 B.C. the ideas of the Stoics gained great popularity in Rome. There was much in Stoicism that would appeal to the typical Roman during the vigorous days of the Republic, and also much that attracted the abler Roman leaders in the more trying days of the Empire. To the nobler minds of that day Stoicism offered a "welcome refuge from the trivialities and anarchy of the life which surrounded them; and it succeeded in evolving a type of character and belief superior in some respects to anything that the ancient world produced."[3] Such distinguished Roman citizens as Cicero and Cato were numbered among its adherents; Seneca, Epictetus, and Marcus Aurelius, the best-known exponents of the Stoic philosophy, all lived in Rome during the first two centuries of the Christian era.

---

[2] Not to be confused with Zeno, the Eleatic philosopher, who propounded the famous riddle of the tortoise and the hare.

[3] A. K. Rogers, *Student's History of Philosophy* (New York, The Macmillan Company, 1901), p. 137.

In many ways the most significant figure among the Stoic philosophers was Epictetus (A.D. 55–135). He spent much of his life as a Greek slave in the household of a dissolute Roman soldier, but he must have shown signs of unusual intellectual ability for he was permitted to attend lectures by the distinguished philosophers of the day. Shortly after the death of his master, Epictetus was able to obtain his own freedom. Having already gained some renown as a philosopher, he established himself as a teacher in Rome where he continued to live and teach until about A.D. 90. In that year the Emperor Domitian, who had no use for intellectuals, expelled all philosophers from Rome. Epictetus then opened a school at Nicopolis, a town not too far away, and there spent the rest of his life in the company of a group of enthusiastic followers.

Epictetus' early life as a slave at the court of Nero could not have been too happy. The Stoic philosophy to which he was attracted was for him much more than a mere theoretical system. It afforded a way of living adequate to meet the uncertainties in a household ruled by a hard and often irresponsible soldier of fortune. Indeed tradition has it that at one time when his master in a fit of anger was having Epictetus' leg twisted, the young philosopher pointed out to him that under such treatment one's leg would break and, when it did break, his only comment was, "You see, it is as I told you." Whether true or not, the story aptly illustrates one of the major tenets of Stoicism.

Distinguished more as a teacher than as an author, Epictetus wrote nothing that has been preserved. Fortunately, however, one of his disciples copied the master's lectures on philosophy and edited them in eight volumes. Four of these survive, known as the *Discourses of Epictetus*. An especially clear and direct statement of Epictetus' philosophy is contained in the *Manual* or handbook that he prepared for his followers; from this a generous selection is included here.

In the figure of Epictetus one sees Stoicism as the philosophy of a man whom ill fortune has cast in the lot of a slave; in the writings of Seneca and Marcus Aurelius—one a prominent senator, the other an emperor of Rome—there is ample evidence that this philosophy had large appeal as well for those more favored by circumstance. Seneca, who was born at Cordova about 4 B.C. of a wealthy and illustrious Spanish family, had all the material things that are commonly thought to make life agreeable. He had cultured companions, leisure, ample means to satisfy every desire. According to reliable reports, the revenues from his holdings in Brittany alone were worth approximately a million dollars. He was educated for the legal profession in the expectation that he would pursue a political career and rose rapidly in the public life of Rome in A.D. 49, becoming the tutor and counselor of Nero, the young son of the empress. When Nero became emperor in A.D. 54, Seneca's political power and influence reached its zenith but as Nero's true character became apparent and his excesses grew more extreme, Seneca fell increasingly out of favor at court and finally retired to his own private estate. During these years he wrote a number of essays and letters among which "On a

Happy Life," "On Tranquillity," "On the Shortness of Life," and "On Providence," are his best statements of Stoicism. His discussion of the problem of evil in the essay "On Providence," reprinted here in large part, is an especially good example of Stoic doctrine, and it has a very personal meaning for Seneca when seen in the light of his own death in A.D. 66.

The suspicious and vacillating emperor, convinced by rather dubious evidence that Seneca was involved in one of the plots against his life, determined to have his former tutor killed. When Nero's centurion arrived to inform Seneca that he was bidden by the emperor to take his own life, the philosopher without apparent surprise is said to have requested tablets for making his will. This request being denied him, he turned to his friends, and after expressing regret at not being able to reward them as they deserved, remarked: "Never mind, I leave you what is of far more value, the example of a virtuous life."[4] In all fairness one must point out that the pattern of life which Seneca here recommended has not been found so exemplary by his critics. He has been accused of amassing a fortune in Brittany by lending money at such excessive rates of interest that a revolt ensued and likewise of writing a number of almost groveling pleas for restoration to the imperial favor—actions that contrast markedly with his Stoic insistence upon the insignificance of material wealth and indifference to fortune or circumstance. On the other hand, Seneca was held in great favor by the early Church fathers; he was even claimed as a Christian by some and, upon the authority of Saint Jerome, a purported correspondence between Seneca and St. Paul was accepted as genuine until modern times.

If for Seneca there were any unfortunate contrasts between profession and practice, this was not the case with the most illustrious of the Roman Stoics, the Emperor Marcus Aurelius (A.D. 121–180). Early historians consistently ranked Aurelius among the finest individuals not only of the Roman Empire but of any age. "He was certainly the noblest character of his time," writes Barthold Niebuhr, "and I know no other man who combined such unaffected kindness, mildness and humility with such conscientiousness and severity toward himself." Marcus Aurelius while still a youth showed high promise in philosophy as well as in such manly sports as wrestling and boar hunting. His education was definitely not that of the typical prince of his day but more in line with Plato's proposals for the philosopher-king. The most distinguished teachers were his tutors, and at an early age he was exposed to the Stoic philosophy. When only twelve years old he assumed the simple garb of the Stoic disciple and accustomed himself to sleep upon a plank bed. In the first book of his *Meditations,* his debt to these Stoic teachers of his youth is expressed in graphic and interesting fashion.

In 161 A.D. at the age of forty, Aurelius succeeded his foster-father as Emperor of Rome. Almost immediately revolts broke out among the fierce barbarian tribes

---

[4] The description of this scene is given by Tacitus (*Annals* 15.62)

along the borders of the empire, and Aurelius was forced to spend most of his time and energy in restoring order. It was during these military campaigns that his *Meditations* were written, largely as a private diary and with no thought of publication. Their calmness of spirit and insight into human nature reflect the calmness of the emperor's mind, not that of the world in which he lived. In these *Meditations* one finds ample evidence, indeed, that the life of reason can enable a man to master external circumstance, no matter what its nature.

While conducting a campaign against barbarian forces in Germany, Aurelius contracted a contagious malady and died in camp near Vienna in A.D. 180. There was widespread grief among his subjects, and his ashes were carried to Rome where he received the honor of deification. Those who could afford it had his statue or bust placed among their *Dei Penates* (household deities). By no means every philosopher is able to take a place among the saints, but Marcus Aurelius had done much to merit this honor. During his reign as emperor the cardinal ideals of Stoicism—reason, justice, and forbearance—became the principles by which the life of the state was guided. Plato insists that justice will only prevail in the state when philosophers become kings; Marcus Aurelius went far to substantiate the Platonic dictum.

Cleanthes' Hymn to Zeus*

O God most glorious, called by many a name
Nature's great King, through endless years the same;
Omnipotence, who by thy just decree
Controllest all, hail, Zeus, for unto thee
Behoves thy creatures in all lands to call.

We are thy children, we alone, of all
On earth's broad ways that wander to and fro,
Bearing thine image wheresoe'er we go.
Wherefore with songs of praise thy power I will forth show.

Lo! yonder heaven, that round the earth is wheeled,
Follows they guidance, still to thee doth yield
Glad homage; thine unconquerable hand
Such flaming minister, the levin-brand,
Wieldeth, a sword two-edged, whose deathless might
Pulsates through all that Nature brings to light;

Vehicle of the universal Word, that flows
Through all, and in the light celestial glows

---

* Reprinted from *The Stoic and Epicurean Philosophers*, Edited by Whitney J. Oates. Copyright 1940 by Random House, Inc.

Of stars both great and small. O King of Kings
Through ceaseless ages, God, whose purpose brings
To birth, whate'er on land or in the sea
Is wrought, or in high heaven's immensity;
Save what the sinner works infatuate.

Nay, but thou knowest to make crooked straight:
Chaos to thee is order: in thine eyes
The unloved is lovely, who did'st harmonize
Things evil with things good, that there should be
One Word (Reason) through all things everlastingly.

One Word—whose voice alas! the wicked spurn;
Insatiate for the good their spirits yearn:
Yet seeing see not, neither hearing hear
God's universal law, which those revere,
By reason guided, happiness to win.

The rest, unreasoning, diverse shapes of sin
Self-prompted follow: for an idle name
Vainly they wrestle in the lists of fame:
Others inordinately Riches woo.
Or dissolute, the joys of flesh pursue.
Now here, now there they wander, fruitless still,
Forever seeking good and finding ill.

Zeus the all-bountiful, whom darkness shrouds,
Whose lightning lightens in the thunder clouds;
Thy children save from error's deadly sway:
Turn thou the darkness from their souls away:
Vouchsafe that unto knowledge they attain:
For thou by knowledge art made strong to reign
O'er all, and all things rulest righteously.

So by thee honoured, we will honour thee,
Praising they works continually with songs,
As mortals should; nor higher meed belongs
E'en to the gods, than justly to adore
The universal law for evermore.

The Meditations of Marcus Aurelius*

1. From my grandfather I learned good morals and the government of my temper.

2. From the reputation and remembrance of my father, modesty and a manly character.

3. From my mother, piety and beneficence, and abstinence, not only from evil deeds, but even from evil thoughts; and further, simplicity in my way of living, far removed from the habits of the rich.

4. From my great-grandfather, not to have frequented public schools, and to have had good teachers at home, and to know that on such things a man should spend liberally.

5. From my governor, I learned endurance of labour, and to want little, and to work with my own hands, and not to meddle with other people's affairs, and not to be ready to listen to slander.

6. From Diognetus, not to busy myself about trifling things, and not to give credit to what was said by miracle-workers and jugglers about incantations and the driving away of daemons and such things; and not to breed quails for fighting, nor to give myself up passionately to such things; and to endure freedom of speech; and to have become intimate with philosophy; and to have written dialogues in my youth; and to have desired a plank bed and skin, and whatever else of the kind belongs to the Grecian discipline.

7. From Rusticus I received the impression that my character required improvement and discipline; and from him I learned not to be led astray to sophistic emulation, nor to writing on speculative matters, nor to delivering little hortatory orations, nor to showing myself off as a man who practises much discipline, or does benevolent acts in order to make a display; and with respect to those who have offended me by words, or done me wrong, to be easily disposed to be pacified and reconciled, as soon as they have shown a readiness to be reconciled; and to read carefully, and not to be satisfied with a superficial understanding of a book; nor hastily to give my assent to those who talk overmuch; and I am indebted to him for being acquainted with the discourses of Epictetus, which he communicated to me out of his own collection.

8. From Apollonius I learned freedom of will and undeviating steadiness of purpose; and to look to nothing else, not even for a moment, except to reason; and to be always the same, in sharp pains, on the occasion of the loss of a child, and in long illness; and to see clearly in a living example that the same man can be both most resolute and yielding, and not peevish in giving his instruction; and from him I learned how to receive from friends what are esteemed favours, without being either humbled by them or letting them pass unnoticed.

9. From Sextus, a benevolent disposition, and the idea of living conformably to nature; and gravity without affectation, and to look carefully after the interests of friends, and to tolerate ignorant persons, and those who form opinions without consideration.

10. From Alexander the Platonist, not frequently nor without necessity to say to any one, or to write in a letter, that I have no leisure; nor continually to excuse the neglect of duties by alleging urgent occupations.

11. From my brother Severus, to love my kin, and to love truth, and to love justice;

---

* From *The Meditations of Marcus Aurelius*, English translation by George Long. (New York, A. L. Burt Co., 1890.) (Abridged). This selection was written during the campaign against the Quadi in southeast Germany A.D. 174.

and from him I received the idea of a polity in which there is the same law for all, a polity administered with regard to equal rights and equal freedom of speech, and the idea of a kindly government which respects most of all the freedom of the governed; I learned from him also consistency and undeviating steadiness in my regard for philosophy; and a disposition to do good, and to give to others readily, and to cherish good hopes, and to believe that I am loved by my friends; and in him I observed no concealment of his opinions with respect to those whom he condemned, and that his friends had no need to conjecture what he wished or did not wish, but it was quite plain.

12. To the gods I am indebted for having good grandfathers, good parents, a good sister, good teachers, good associates, good kinsmen and friends, nearly everything good. I thank the gods for giving me such a brother, who was able by his moral character to rouse me to vigilance over myself, and who at the same time, pleased me by his respect and affection; that my children have not been stupid nor deformed in body; that

I did not make more proficiency in rhetoric, poetry, and the other studies, in which I should perhaps have been completely engaged, if I had seen that I was making progress in them; that I knew Apollonius, Rusticus, Maximus; that I received clear and frequent impressions about living according to nature, and what kind of a life that is, so that, so far as depended on the gods, and their gifts, and help, and inspirations, nothing hindered me from forthwith living according to nature, though I still fall short of it through my own fault, and through not observing the admonitions of the gods, and, I may almost say, their direct instructions; that, whenever I wished to help any man in his need, or on any other occasion, I was never told that I had not the means of doing it; and that to myself the same necessity never happened, to receive anything from another; and that, when I had an inclination to philosophy, I did not fall into the hands of any sophist, and that I did not waste my time on writers of histories, or in the resolution of syllogisms, for all these things require the help of the gods and fortune.

The Manual of Epictetus*

1

Of all existing things some are in our power, and others are not in our power. In our power are thought, impulse, will to get and will to avoid, and, in a word, everything which is our own doing. Things not in our power include the body, property, reputation, office, and, in a word, everything which is not our own doing. Things in our power are by nature free, unhindered, untram-

melled; things not in our power are weak, servile, subject to hindrance, dependent on others. Remember then that if you imagine that what is naturally slavish is free, and what is naturally another's is your own, you will be hampered, you will mourn, you will be put to confusion, you will blame gods and men; but if you think that only your own belongs to you, and that what is another's is indeed another's, no one will ever put compulsion or hindrance on you, you will blame none, you will accuse none, you will do nothing against your will, no one will harm you, you will have no enemy, for no harm can touch you.

Aiming then at these high matters, you must remember that to attain them requires more than ordinary effort; you will have to give up some things entirely, and put off

---

* This handbook of Epictetus' philosophy contains an excellent summary of his thought. It was probably compiled by Arrian, the disciple upon whose notes *The Discourses of Epictetus* are based. About two-thirds of the *Manual* is reprinted here. English translation by P. E. Matheson. (Oxford, The Clarendon Press, 1916.) Numerical order imposed.

others for the moment. And if you would have these also—office and wealth—it may be that you will fail to get them, just because your desire is set on the former, and you will certainly fail to attain those things which alone bring freedom and happiness.

Make it your study then to confront every harsh impression with the word, "You are but an impression, and not at all what you seem to be." Then test it by those rules that you possess; and first by this—the chief test of all—"Is it concerned with what is in our power or with what is not in our power?" And if it is concerned with what is not in our power, be ready with the answer that it is nothing to you.

2

When anything, from the meanest thing upwards, is attractive or serviceable or an object of affection, remember always to say to yourself, "What is its nature?" If you are fond of a jug, say you are fond of a jug; then you will not be disturbed if it be broken. If you kiss your child or your wife, say to yourself that you are kissing a human being, for then if death strikes it you will not be disturbed.

3

When you are about to take something in hand, remind yourself what manner of thing it is. If you are going to bathe put before your mind what happens in the bath —water pouring over some, others being jostled, some reviling, others stealing; and you will set to work more securely if you say to yourself at once: "I want to bathe, and I want to keep my will in harmony with nature," and so in each thing you do; for in this way, if anything turns up to hinder you in your bathing, you will be ready to say, "I did not want only to bathe, but to keep my will in harmony with nature, and I shall not so keep it, if I lose my temper at what happens."

4

What disturbs men's minds is not events but their judgments on events. For instance, death is nothing dreadful, or else Socrates would have thought it so. No, the only dreadful thing about it is men's judgment that it is dreadful. And so when we are hindered, or disturbed, or distressed, let us never lay the blame on others, but on ourselves, that is, on our own judgments. To accuse others for one's own misfortunes is a sign of want of education; to accuse oneself shows that one's education has begun; to accuse neither oneself nor others shows that one's education is complete.

5

Ask not that events should happen as you will, but let your will be that events should happen as they do, and you shall have peace.

6

It is silly to want your children and your wife and your friends to live for ever, for that means that you want what is not in your control to be in your control, and what is not your own to be yours. In the same way if you want your servant to make no mistakes, you are a fool, for you want vice not to be vice but something different. But if you want not to be disappointed in your will to get, you can attain to that.

Exercise yourself then in what lies in your power. Each man's master is the man who has authority over what he wishes or does not wish, to secure the one or to take away the other. Let him then who wishes to be free not wish for anything or avoid anything that depends on others; or else he is bound to be a slave.

7

Never say of anything, "I lost it," but say, "I gave it back." Has your child died? It was given back. Has your wife died? She was given back. Has your estate been taken from you? Was not this also given back? But you say, "He who took it from me is wicked." What does it matter to you through whom the Giver asked it back? As long as He gives it to you, take care of it, but not as your own; treat it as passers-by treat an inn.

8

Remember that you must behave in life as you would at a banquet. A dish is handed round and comes to you; put out your hand and take it politely. It passes you; do not stop it. It has not reached you; do not be impatient to get it, but wait till your turn comes. Bear yourself thus towards children, wife, office, wealth, and one day you will be worthy to banquet with the gods. But if when they are set before you, you do not take them but despise them, then you shall not only share the gods' banquet, but shall share their rule. For by so doing Diogenes and Heraclitus and men like them were called divine and deserved the name.

9

When you see a man shedding tears in sorrow for a child abroad or dead, or for loss of property, beware that you are not carried away by the impression that it is outward ills that make him miserable. Keep this thought by you: "What distresses him is not the event, for that does not distress another, but his judgment on the event." Therefore do not hesitate to sympathize with him so far as words go, and if it so chance, even to groan with him; but take heed that you do not also groan in your inner being.

10

Remember that you are an actor in a play, and the Playwright chooses the manner of it: if he wants it short, it is short; if long, it is long. If he wants you to act a poor man you must act the part with all your powers; and so if your part be a cripple or a magistrate or a plain man. For your business is to act the character that is given you and act it well; the choice of the cast is Another's.

11

You can be invincible, if you never enter on a contest where victory is not in your power. Beware then that when you see a man raised to honour or great power or high repute you do not let your impression carry you away. For if the reality of good lies in what is in our power, there is no room for envy or jealousy. And you will not wish to be praetor, or prefect or consul, but to be free; and there is but one way to freedom—to despise what is not in our power.

12

It is in our power to discover the will of Nature from those matters on which we have no difference of opinion. For instance, when another man's slave has broken the wine-cup we are very ready to say at once, "Such things must happen." Know then that when your own cup is broken, you ought to behave in the same way as when your neighbour's was broken. Apply the same principle to higher matters. Is another's child or wife dead? Not one of us but would say, "Such is the lot of man"; but when one's own dies, straightway one cries, "Alas! miserable am I." But we ought to remember what our feelings are when we hear it of another.

13

As a mark is not set up for men to miss it, so there is nothing intrinsically evil in the world.

14

If any one trusted your body to the first man he met, you would be indignant, but yet you trust your mind to the chance comer, and allow it to be disturbed and confounded if he revile you; are you not ashamed to do so?

15

For piety towards the gods know that the most important thing is this: to have right opinions about them—that they exist, and that they govern the universe well and justly —and to have set yourself to obey them, and to give way to all that happens, following events with a free will, in the belief that they are fulfilled by the highest mind. For thus you will never blame the gods, nor accuse them of neglecting you. But this you cannot achieve, unless you apply your conception of good and evil to those things only which are in our power, and not to those which are out of our power. For if you apply your notion of good or evil to the latter, then, as soon as you fail to get what you will to get or fail to avoid what you will to avoid, you will be bound to blame and hate those you hold responsible. For every living creature has a natural tendency to avoid and shun what seems harmful and all that causes it, and to pursue and admire what is helpful and all that causes it. It is not possible then for one who thinks he is harmed to take pleasure in what he thinks is the author of the harm, any more than to take pleasure in the harm itself. That is why a father is reviled by his son, when he does not give his son a share of what the son regards as good things; thus Polynices and Eteocles were set at enmity with one another by thinking that a king's throne was a good thing. That is why the farmer, and the sailor, and the merchant, and those who lose wife or children revile the gods. For men's religion is bound up with their interest. Therefore he who makes it his concern rightly to direct his will to get and his will to avoid, is thereby making piety his concern. But it is proper on each occasion to make libation and sacrifice and to offer first-fruits according to the custom of our fathers, with purity and not in slovenly or careless fashion, without meanness and without extravagance.

16

Lay down for yourself from the first a definite stamp and style of conduct, which you will maintain when you are alone and also in the society of men. Be silent for the most part, or, if you speak, say only what is necessary and in a few words. Talk, but rarely, if occasion calls you, but do not talk of ordinary things—of gladiators, or horse-races, or athletes, or of meats or drinks—these are topics that arise everywhere—but above all do not talk about men in blame or compliment or comparison. If you can, turn the conversation of your company by your talk to some fitting subject; but if you should chance to be isolated among strangers, be silent. Do not laugh much, nor at many things, nor without restraint.

Refuse the entertainments of strangers and the vulgar. But if occasion arise to accept them, then strain every nerve to avoid lapsing into the state of the vulgar. For know that, if your comrade have a stain on him, he that associates with him must needs share the stain, even though he be clean in himself.

For your body take just so much as your bare need requires, such as food, drink, clothing, house, servants, but cut down all that tends to luxury and outward show.

In your conversation avoid frequent and disproportionate mention of your own doings or adventures; for other people do not take the same pleasure in hearing what has happened to you as you take in recounting your adventures.

17

When you imagine some pleasure, beware that it does not carry you away, like other imaginations. Wait a while, and give yourself pause. Next remember two things: how long you will enjoy the pleasure, and also how long you will afterwards repent and revile yourself. And set on the other side the joy and self-satisfaction you will feel if you refrain. And if the moment seems come to realize it, take heed that you be not overcome by the winning sweetness and attraction of it; set in the other scale the thought how much better is the consciousness of having vanquished it.

18

When you do a thing because you have determined that it ought to be done, never avoid being seen doing it, even if the opinion of the multitude is going to condemn you. For if your action is wrong, then avoid doing it altogether, but if it is right, why do you fear those who will rebuke you wrongly?

19

If you try to act a part beyond your powers, you not only disgrace yourself in it, but you neglect the part which you could have filled with success.

20

Women from fourteen years upwards are called 'madam' by men. Wherefore, when they see that the only advantage they have got is to be marriageable, they begin to make themselves smart and to set all their hopes on this. We must take pains then to make them understand that they are really honoured for nothing but a modest and decorous life.

21

It is a sign of a dull mind to dwell upon the cares of the body, to prolong exercise, eating, drinking, and other bodily functions. These things are to be done by the way; all your attention must be given to the mind.

22

When a man speaks evil or does evil to you, remember that he does or says it because he thinks it is fitting for him. It is not possible for him to follow what seems good to you, but only what seems good to him, so that, if his opinion is wrong, he suffers, in that he is the victim of deception. In the same way, if a composite judgment which is true is thought to be false, it is not the judgment that suffers, but the man who is deluded about it. If you act on this principle you will be gentle to him who reviles you, saying to yourself on each occasion, "He thought it right."

23

Everything has two handles, one by which you can carry it, the other by which you cannot. If your brother wrongs you, do not take it by that handle, the handle of his wrong, for you cannot carry it by that, but rather by the other handle—that he is a brother, brought up with you, and then you will take it by the handle that you can carry by.

24

On no occasion call yourself a philosopher, nor talk at large of your principles among the multitude, but act on your principles. For instance, at a banquet do not say how one ought to eat, but eat as you ought. Remember that Socrates had so completely got rid of the thought of display that when men came and wanted an introduction to philosophers he took them to be introduced; so patient of neglect was he. And if a discussion arise among the multitude on some principle, keep silent for the most part; for you are in great danger of blurting out some undigested thought. And when some one says to you, "You know nothing," and you do not let it provoke you, then know that you are really on the right road. For sheep do not bring grass to their shepherds and show them how much they have eaten, but they digest their fodder and then produce it in the form of wool and milk. Do the same yourself; instead of displaying your principles to the multitude, show them the results of the principles you have digested.

25

The ignorant man's position and character is this: he never looks to himself for benefit or harm, but to the world outside him. The philosopher's position and character is that he always look to himself for benefit and harm.

The signs of one who is making progress are: he blames none, praises none, complains of none, accuses none, never speaks of himself as if he were somebody, or as if he knew anything. And if any one compliments him he laughs in himself at his compliment; and if one blames him, he makes no defence. He goes about like a convalescent, careful not to disturb his constitution on its road to recovery, until it has got firm hold. He has got rid of the will to get, and his will to avoid is directed no longer to what is beyond our power but only to what is in our power and contrary to nature. In all things he exercises his will without strain. If men regard him as foolish or ignorant he pays no heed. In one word, he keeps watch and guard on himself as his own enemy, lying in wait for him.

26

Whatever principles you put before you, hold fast to them as laws which it will be impious to transgress. But pay no need to what any one says of you; for this is something beyond your own control.

27

How long will you wait to think yourself worthy of the highest and transgress in nothing the clear pronouncement of reason? You have received the precepts which you ought to accept, and you have accepted them. Why then do you still wait for a master, that you may delay the amendment of yourself till he comes? You are a youth no longer, you are now a full-grown man. If now you are careless and indolent and are always putting off, fixing one day after another as the limit when you mean to begin attending to yourself, then, living or dying, you will make no progress but will continue unawares in ignorance. Therefore make up your mind before it is too late to live as one who is mature and proficient, and let all that seems best to you be a law that you cannot transgress. And if you encounter anything troublesome or pleasant or glorious or inglorious, remember that the hour of struggle is come, the Olympic contest is here and you may put off no longer, and that one day and one action determines whether the progress you have achieved is lost or maintained.

This was how Socrates attained perfection, paying heed to nothing but reason, in all that he encountered. And if you are not yet Socrates, yet ought you to live as one who would wish to be a Socrates.

28

The first and most necessary department of philosophy deals with the application of principles; for instance, "not to lie." The second deals with demonstrations; for instance, "How comes it that one ought not to lie?" The third is concerned with establishing and analysing these processes; for instance, "How comes it that this is a demonstration? What is demonstration, what is consequence, what is contradiction, what is true, what is false?" It follows then that the third department is necessary because of the second, and the second because of the first. The first is the most necessary part, and that in which we must rest. But we reverse the order: we occupy ourselves with the third, and make that our whole concern, and the first we completely neglect. Wherefore we lie, but are ready enough with the demonstration that lying is wrong.

29

On every occasion we must have these thoughts at hand,

> Lead me, O Zeus, and lead me, Destiny,
> Whither ordainèd is by your decree.
> I'll follow, doubting not, or if with will
> Recreant I falter, I shall follow still.
> [Cleanthes]

> Who rightly with necessity complies
> In things divine we count him skilled
>   and wise.
> [Euripides]

> Well, Crito, if this be the god's will, so
>   be it.
> [Plato, *Crito*]

> Anytus and Meletus have power to put
>   me to death, but not to harm me.
> [Plato, *Apology*]

On Providence*

I

You have asked me, Lucilius, why it is that many evils befall good men if the world

* From *The Stoic Philosophy of Seneca*, translated by Moses Hadas (New York, Doubleday and Company, Inc., 1958), Dialogue I (abridged). Copyright © 1958 by Moses Hadas. Reprinted by permission of Doubleday and Company, Inc.

is governed by providence. The answer could more conveniently be supplied in an organized treatise in the course of which we would demonstrate that providence rules all things and that god is concerned for our welfare. But since it is your pleasure to pluck one member from the whole and reconcile a single objection without impinging on the problem in its totality I shall acquiesce; the task is not difficult, for it is the gods' cause I shall be pleading.

For our present purpose it is superfluous to point out that so mighty a structure does not persist without some caretaker; that the concourse and dispersal of the heavenly bodies is not an effect of a fortuitous impulse; that whereas what chance sets into motion is without direction and is likely to run into collisions, the course which is guided by the rules of eternal law moves speedily and without running foul and carries with it the multitudes of objects on land and sea and of brilliant lights shining forth according to a fixed plan; that this orderliness is not a property of matter moving at random; and that fortuitous conglomerations cannot arrange their balance so skillfully that the earth, which is heaviest in weight, should abide unmoved and, as spectator, observe the rapid flight of the surrounding sky, how the seas are distilled into the valleys to soften the earth, how huge growths burgeon from tiny seeds. Even those phenomena which seem irregular and anarchic—I mean clouds and rain and the flashes of crashing thunder and flames shot up from riven mountain peaks and the tremors of quaking earth and the other manifestations of the turbulent workings of nature upon earth—even these phenomena do not happen without a plan, though their coming may be unexpected; they have their own causes, as do those phenomena whose incongruous location gives them an aspect of the miraculous, as, for example, hot springs in the midst of the waves or new stretches of island springing up in the vast ocean. Indeed, if a man observe how the shore is laid bare when the sea withdraws into itself and is then flooded again in a short time, he might suppose that it is some blind turbulence which causes the waves at one time to contract with an inward motion and at another to burst forth with a great rush to recover their normal position. In point of fact, their growth is strictly allotted; at the appropriate day and hour they approach in greater volume or less according as they are attracted by the lunar orb, at whose sway the ocean wells up. But such

questions as these must be reserved for their proper occasion, especially since you are merely complaining of providence, not questioning its existence. I shall reconcile you with the gods, who prove best to men who are best. Nature never suffers the good to be harmed by the good; between good men and the gods there subsists a friendship, with virtue as its bond.

Did I say friendship? It is rather a kinship and a close resemblance, for the only difference between the good man and god is in the matter of time. Man is god's disciple and emulator and true progeny, whom the glorious parent, who insists upon virtue, educated very strictly, like a stern father. When you see men who are good and acceptable to the gods toil and sweat and climb laboriously upward, therefore, while the wicked run riot and luxuriate in wantonness, remember that in our sons it is modesty that pleases, whereas pertness pleases us only in home-born slaves; and that our sons we restrain by severe discipline, whereas we encourage the slaves' sauciness. Be sure that god's course is the same. He does not treat the good man like a toy, but tries him, hardens him, and readies him for himself.

II

"Why do many misfortunes fall to the lot of good men?" It is not possible that any evil can befall a good man. Opposites cannot combine. Just as the influx of so many streams and the downpour of so much rain and the flavor of so many mineral springs do not change the tang of the sea or even so much as dilute it, just so the assaults of adversity do not affect the spirit of a stalwart man. He maintains his poise and assimilates all that falls to his lot to his own complexion, for he is more potent than the world without. I do not maintain that he is insensible to externals, but that he overcomes them; unperturbed and serene, he rises to meet every sally. All adversity he regards as exercise. Is not every upstanding man who is intent upon what is right eager for appropriate exertion and ready for service which involves danger? Does not any diligent man regard idleness as a punishment? In the case of athletes, whose concern is for physical strength, we observe that they employ very strong adversaries in their practice bouts and insist that their trainers use all their strength against them. They submit to blows and bruises, and if they cannot find individuals strong enough to match with them, they take on several at once. Without an antagonist prowess fades away. Its true proportions and capacities come to light only when action proves its endurance. You must know that good men should behave similarly; they must not shrink from hardship and difficulty or complain of fate; they should take whatever befalls in good part and turn it to advantage. The thing that matters is not what you bear but how you bear it.

Observe how differently fathers and mothers show their affection. Fathers make their children get up to attend to their tasks betimes; even on holidays they do not suffer them to be idle but drive them to sweat and sometimes to tears. Mothers want to cuddle them in their laps, keep them in the shade, never let them be disappointed or cry or work hard. God's attitude to good men is a father's; his love for them is a manly love. "Let them be harassed by toil and sorrow and loss," says he, "that so they may acquire true strength." Pampered bodies grow sluggish through sloth; not work but movement and their own weight exhausts them. Prosperity unbruised cannot endure a single blow, but a man who has been at constant feud with misfortunes acquires a skin calloused by suffering; he yields to no evil and even if he stumbles carries the fight on upon his knee.

Do you find it strange that god, who so loves good men that he wishes them to attain pre-eminent goodness, should allot them a fortune on which to exercise themselves? I myself do not find it strange that the gods are sometimes moved to enjoy the spectacle of great men wrestling with some disaster. It gives us pleasure, on occasion, when a young man of steadfast courage meets a wild beast's charge with his hunting spear or faces a rushing lion without flinching, and the spectacle is the more pleasing in the degree that the hero is a man of position. Yet those are not achievements to attract the attention of the gods but the childish amusements of human frivolity. But look you upon this spectacle worthy the attention of a god intent upon his own work, look you upon this bout worthy a god—a stalwart man matched with evil fortune, especially when the man takes the initiative. I cannot see, I declare, what fairer spectacle Jupiter could enjoy on earth, if he should wish to direct his attention there, than Cato still standing upright amidst his country's ruins after his party had repeatedly been crushed. "Though all the world has yielded to one man's sway," says he, "though Caesar's legions guard the dry land and his fleets the sea, though his soldiers beset the city gates, yet does Cato possess a way of egress; with a single hand he can open a wide path to freedom. This sword which has remained untainted and guiltless even in civil war shall at last perform a good and noble deed; it shall give Cato the freedom it could not give his country. Take up, my soul, the task you have long studied; deliver yourself from the world of men. Petreius and Juba have already run their race, and each lies slain by the hand of the other. That was a brave and noble compact with fate, but not seemly for my stature; for Cato it is as ignominious to beg death of anyone as it is life."

I am sure the gods looked on with great satisfaction when that man who was so uncompromising in maintaining his own freedom took measures to secure the safety of others and arranged the escape of those who were leaving, when he spent even his last night in study, when he thrust his sword into his hallowed bosom, when he pulled his vitals apart and with his own hand released that holy spirit which was too pure to be defiled by steel. That is why, I should suppose, the wound was badly aimed and ineffectual: for the immortal gods it was not enough to look on Cato but once; he was encored and kept on the stage to exhibit his character in a more demanding role, for it wants a loftier spirit to seek death a second time. How could the gods fail to be pleased when they viewed their charge making his way to freedom by so glorious and memorable a departure? Death hallows men whose mode of dying is praised even by those who dread it.

III

As my discourse proceeds I shall show that what seem to be evils are not actually such. For the present, I will say so much of the eventualities which you style harsh, unfortunate, and detestable: in the first place, they benefit the individuals to whose lot they fall, and, in the second place, they benefit the whole body of mankind, for which the gods are more concerned than they are for individuals; next, good men receive these eventualities willingly, and deserve ill fortune if they do not; further, these things are destined, and befall good men by the same law that makes them good. And finally I shall persuade you never to commiserate a good man; he may be called unhappy, he cannot be unhappy.

Of all these propositions the most difficult, apparently, is the first in the list, that the objects of our dread and horror are actually advantageous to the persons to whose lot they fall. "Is it for the victim's advantage," you object, "to be driven into exile, to be reduced to poverty, to bury wife and children, to be branded with ignominy, to be made a cipher?" If you find it strange that these things are beneficial, you will find it no less strange that certain maladies are treated by surgery and cautery and by hunger and thirst as well. But if you reflect that for the sake of a cure some persons have their bones scraped or removed, their veins pulled out, or members whose presence would be deleterious to the organism as a whole amputated, you will also allow yourself to be convinced that certain misfortunes work to the advantage of those whom they befall—precisely, by Hercules as certain things which are praised and sought after work to the disadvantage of those who delight in them; overeating, drunkenness, and other indulgences, for example, kill through giving pleasure. Among the many magnificent sayings of our friend

Demetrius is the following, which I have just heard; it still rings and reverberates in my ears. "No one is more unhappy, in my judgment," says he, "than a man who has never met with adversity." He has never had the privilege of testing himself. Everything has come easily to him according to his wish; yet the gods' judgment of him has been unfavorable. He was deemed unworthy of ever vanquishing Fortune, which shuns any cowardly antagonist, as if to say, "Why should I take on that kind of opponent? He will lay his arms down at once, and I will not need to use my full strength against him. A threatening gesture will rout him; he cannot face my grim expression. I must look around for someone else with whom to match my strength; I am ashamed to fight a man who is ready to be beaten." A gladiator counts it a disgrace to be matched with an inferior; he knows that a victory devoid of danger is a victory devoid of glory. Fortune follows the same principle: she searches out stalwart adversaries, and passes some by in disdain. It is the upstanding and inflexible that she challenges, for against them she can exert all her force. She tries Mucius by fire, Fabricius by poverty, Rutilius by exile, Regulus by torture, Socrates by poison, Cato by death. Only misfortune can reveal such outstanding models.

Prosperity can come to the vulgar and to the ordinary talents, but to triumph over the disasters and terrors of mortal life is the privilege of the great man. To be lucky always and to pass through life without gnawing of the mind is to be ignorant of the half of nature. You are a great man, but how can I know, if Fortune has never given you a chance to display your prowess? You have entered the Olympic games but have no rival; you gain the crown but not the victory. I felicitate you, not as a brave man, but as one who has obtained a consulship or praetorship; your dignity is enhanced. I can say the same of a good man whom no difficult conjuncture has afforded an occasion for displaying the force of his mind. "I account you unfortunate. You have passed through life without an adversary; no one can know your potentiality, not even you." For self-knowledge, testing is necessary; no one can discover what he can do except by trying. That is why some men have voluntarily exposed themselves to misfortune when it was reluctant, and have sought an opportunity for their prowess, which would otherwise pass into obscurity, to shine forth. Great men, I insist, sometimes rejoice in adversity precisely as brave soldiers rejoice in war. I once heard Triumphus, a gladiator in the days of Caligula, complain of the scarcity of performances. "It was fine in the old days," he said.

Prowess is avid for danger and thinks rather of the goal than of its trials, for these too are part of glory. Soldiers glory in their wounds and gladly vaunt themselves over the blood they were privileged to shed; though those who returned from the fray unhurt may have fought as well, the man who brings back a wound is more respected. To those men he desires shall achieve the highest excellence, god shows his favor whenever he affords them a field for spirited and courageous action, and for this some particular exertion is requisite. You assay a pilot in a storm, a soldier in the battle line. How can I know with what spirit you would confront poverty if you are running over with riches? How can I know with what constancy you will confront disgrace, dishonor, and public contumely if you reach old age amidst acclamations, if you are always attended by an inexpugnable popularity which gravitates in your direction by general inclination? How do I know how serenely you would endure bereavement when all the children you have raised are present to your sight? I have heard you offering condolences to others; I might have glimpsed your true character if you had been consoling yourself, if you had been bidding yourself not to grieve.

Do not, I beseech you, dread the things which the immortal gods apply to our souls like goads; disaster is virtue's opportunity. Those whom an excess of prosperity has rendered sluggish may justly be called unfortunate; a dead calm holds them fast, as it were, on a motionless sea, and whatever befalls them comes as a surprise. Cruelty presses hardest on the inexperienced; the tender neck chafes at the yoke. The recruit pales at the thought of a wound; the veteran can look at his flowing gash with composure, for he knows that he has often won the victory after losing blood. So god hardens and scrutinizes and exercises those he approves and loves; but those he appears to indulge and spare he is only keeping tender for disasters to come. If you suppose that anyone is immune you are mistaken. The man who has long prospered will get his share one day; the man you thought discharged has only been reprieved. Why does god afflict every good man with sickness or grief or other misfortune? Because in the army, too, the most hazardous duties are assigned to the bravest soldiers. It is only the picked men that the general sends to surprise the enemy by a night attack, to reconnoiter the road, or to dislodge a garrison. And no man in such a detachment will say, "The general has treated me badly," but rather, "The general thinks well of me." Similarly, those told off to undergo what cowards and weaklings would weep over should say, "God has judged us fit subjects to try how much human nature can endure."

IV

Consider further that it is to the common interest for the best men to be soldiers, so to speak, and do our service. It is god's purpose, and the sage's as well, to show that what the crowd desires or fears is neither good nor evil; things will evidently be good if god bestows them upon none but good men, and evil if he inflicts them only upon evil men. Blindness would be execrable if no one lost his eyes except the man who deserved to have them gouged out. That is why Appius and Metellus must be deprived of light. Riches are not a good; that is why the pimp Elius must have riches, so that men who sanctify money in temples may see that it is in the brothel also. God can discredit the objects of our concupiscence in no more effective way than by bestowing them upon vile characters and withholding them from the best. "But," you object, "it is unfair for a good man to become invalid or be pierced or fettered while rogues mince about carefree and dainty and in sound health." Why so? Is it not unfair for brave men to take up arms and spend their nights in camp and stand guard before the rampart with bandaged wounds while perverts and professional profligates loll at ease in the city? Why so? Is it not unfair for the noblest of our maidens to be aroused before daylight to perform the Vestal rites while tainted women enjoy sound sleep? The best men are conscripts of toil. Frequently the senate is in session the livelong day while nobodies are taking their pleasure in the sporting field or lurking in some tavern or passing their time with cronies.

The same thing happens in the commonwealth of the world. Good men toil, spend and are spent, and willingly; they are not dragged along by Fortune but follow her and keep in step. If they knew how, they would have outstripped her. Here is another spirited utterance of that stalwart Demetrius which I remember hearing: "This one complaint I can make of you, immortal gods," said he, "you did not make your will known to me sooner, for I would then myself have long ago reached the state to which I am now called. Do you wish to take my children? It was for you I reared them. Do you want some part of my body? Take it; it is no great boon I grant, for soon I shall leave the whole of it. Do you want the breath of my life? Why not? I shall not balk at your taking back what you have given. Whatever you ask you shall obtain from a willing giver. What then is my complaint? I should have preferred to offer rather than to surrender. What need was there for you to take it when I would have handed it to you? But even now you will not really be taking it, for nothing can be wrested from a man if he does not cling to it."

I am not under duress, I do not submit against my will, I am not god's slave but his follower, and the more willingly because I know that all things proceed according to a law that is fixed and eternally valid.

Fate directs us, and the first hour of our birth determines each man's span. Cause is linked with cause, and a long chain of events governs all matters public and private. Everything must therefore be borne with fortitude, because events do not, as we suppose, happen but arrive by appointment. What would make you rejoice and what would make you weep was determined long ago, and though individual lives seem to differ in a wide range, the sum amounts to the same thing: what we receive is perishable and we shall ourselves perish. Why then are we indignant? Why do we complain? It is for this we are born. Nature may use her own bodies as she will; we must be cheerful and steadfast whatever befalls, in the thought that nothing that is ours is lost.

What is the duty of the good man? To offer himself to Fate. It is a great consolation that our rapid course is one with the universe's. Whatever it is that has ordained the mode of our life and the mode of our death has bound the gods, too, by the same necessity. The course that carries human affairs and divine alike is irrevocable. The very founder and ruler of all things has prescribed the fates indeed, but he follows them; he obeys always, he commanded but once. "Yet why was god so unfair in distributing destinies as to allot good men poverty and wounds and painful death?" The artisan cannot transform his material; such is its nature. Certain elements cannot be separated from others; they cohere and are indivisible. Languid constitutions that are prone to sleep or to a wakefulness indistinguishable from sleep are compounded of sluggish elements; it requires more vigorous endowment to produce a man who merits careful study. His path will not be level, he must go uphill and down, he must be wave-tossed and steer his craft through troubled waters, he must maintain his course in the face of Fortune. Much that is hard and rough will befall him, but he will himself soften it and smooth it down. Gold is tried by fire, brave men by misfortune. See how high virtue must mount: you will realize the perils that beset the ascent.

V

"Yet why does god allow evil to happen to good men?" But in fact he does not. From good men he keeps every evil away—sin and crime and wicked thoughts and greedy schemes and blind lust and avarice which covets another's property. The good man himself, god protects and defends; should anyone expect that god will look after the good man's baggage also? Good men release god from this care, for they themselves despise externals. Democritus cast his riches away in the belief that they were a burden to a good mind. Then why should you wonder that god allows a good man to light upon a lot which a good man would sometimes himself choose to light upon? Good men lose their sons: why not, when they sometimes leave their country of their own accord never to return? They are slain: why not, when they sometimes lay hands upon themselves? Why do they suffer certain hardships? To teach others to endure them; they were born to serve as models.

Imagine that god speaks as follows: "What grounds do you have to complain of me, you who have opted for righteousness? Other men I have surrounded with spurious goods, I have beguiled their empty minds, as it were, with a long and deceptive dream. I have adorned them with gold and silver and ivory, but there is nothing good inside. The men you look upon as happy, if you could see not their outward appearance but their inward nature, are wretched, squalid, mean, well groomed on the surface, like their own house walls; that is no solid and genuine happiness but only a veneer, and a thin one. And so, as long as they can keep their feet and give the impression they desire, they glitter and carry it off; but when something happens to set them awry and uncover them, then one can see what a mass of genuine foulness their adventitious glitter concealed. But to you I have given goods that are sure and abiding, goods which are better and greater the more one turns them about and scrutinizes them from every side. To you I have granted scorn of terrors and disdain of passions. You do not shine outwardly because all your goods are turned inward. So does our world scorn what lies without and rejoice in the contemplation of itself. Your whole good I have bestowed within yourselves: your good fortune is not to need good fortune.

"'But,' you object, 'many things which are sad and dreadful and hard to bear do happen.' Because I could not make you evade their assault, I have given your minds armor to withstand them; bear them with fortitude. In this respect you can surpass god: he is exempt from enduring evil, you rise superior to it. Scorn poverty: no one is as poor as he was at birth. Scorn pain: either it will go away or you will. Scorn death: either it finishes you or it transforms you. Scorn Fortune: I have given her no weapon with which to strike your soul. Above all, I have taken pains that nothing should detain you against your will: the way out lies open. If you do not wish to fight you may escape. Of all the things which I deemed necessary for you, therefore, I have made none easier than dying. The soul I have placed on a downgrade, where it is pulled by gravity: only observe and you will see what a short and direct road leads to freedom. I have imposed no such long delays at your egress as at your entry. Otherwise, if a man were as slow in dying as he is in being born, Fortune would have enormous power over you. Let every occasion and every situation teach you how easy it is to renounce Nature and throw her gift in her face. At the very altars and the solemn rites of sacrifice, even as you pray for life, study death. Massive bulls fall by a paltry wound, and the blow of a man's hand fells powerful animals. A thin blade severs the joints of the neck, and when the articulation of head and neck is cut the whole mass collapses. The seat of life is not buried at a great depth and need not be rooted out with steel, the vitals need not be searched out with deep wounds; death is near at hand. For the lethal blow I have appointed no specific spot; whatever way you choose will serve. The process called dying, whereby the soul departs from the body, is so short that its passing is imperceptible. Whether the noose strangles the throat, or water suffocates the breath, or the hard ground which breaks the fall crushes the skull, or fire sucked in blocks respiration—whatever the means, it is swift. Do you not blush at fearing so long a thing that happens so quickly?"

The Rationalism of Descartes

René Descartes, the famous seventeenth-century French philosopher (1596–1650), is responsible in large measure for establishing rationalism as the dominant point of view in the early period of modern European philosophy. More than any other figure in his age, Descartes marks the intellectual transition from the Middle Ages to the modern world. Although well versed in the new sciences, he was not himself a scientist to be ranked with men like Galileo and Newton; rather he was the first man of high philosophical ability whose thought was profoundly altered by the new outlook of modern science and he is usually considered the founder of modern philosophy. In general, Descartes was more impressed with mathematics than with the physical sciences because he found human reason operating with its greatest clarity and precision in mathematics; his one achievement in the field of science that remains of value today is the analytical method in geometry.

What Descartes did accept wholeheartedly from the new science of his day was its confidence in human reason. No philosopher has insisted more clearly and uncompromisingly upon that confidence in human reason, which is the first premise of the rationalist. Upon this foundation Descartes undertook to establish an entirely new system of thought. With remarkable success he set out to make a clear sweep of medieval thought and build the whole edifice of philosophy over again on a new and firm foundation; his philosophy marks a major turning point in the history of thought, as he himself meant it to be.

Descartes writes with a freshness and ease that is too rare among the great philosophers. In his famous *Discourse on Method,* addressed to the intelligent layman, he sets forth in clear and direct fashion a number of the basic convictions that changed the whole course of philosophy and dominated modern thought for at least a century and a half.

One has only to read the works of the great Stoic philosophers, however, to see that in his *Discourse on Method* as well as in his later philosophical writing Descartes is largely clarifying and developing the enduring insights of these early rationalists. He shared their confidence in human reason, but he found in the new physics and astronomy a validation of this confidence that the Stoics did not have, and in mathematics he discovered a guide to the nature of the universe itself which made possible a precision and clarity in human thought that the Stoics did not envision. Thus Descartes was able to build a thoroughly scientific and mechanistic view of the universe to supplant the more religiously oriented approach of the Stoics. But when he goes on to apply reason to the problems of human conduct, his philosophy differs little if any from the Stoic ethical outlook.

In Descartes' life and personality the drama of his age is clearly apparent. Born on the last day of March, 1596, at La Haye in Touraine, he came from one of the older and more prominent families of the region. His father, a counselor to the Parliament of Bordeaux, was determined to give René a good education and sent him as a boy to the Jesuit college at La Fleche where he seems to have received a much better grounding in modern mathematics than he could have found at most of the universities of the time. It was at La Fleche that he began the habit of long periods of meditation from which many of his later insights sprang. But at the age of seventeen he put his books aside, feeling he had squeezed them dry; then, as a young French gentleman should, he took a few lessons in fencing and horsemanship and went to enjoy the great world of Paris.

It did not take long for the delights of the world to lose their charm. Descartes soon cut himself off from his easy-going companions, devoting more time to meditation and also to his friendship with the leading French mathematician of the day, M. Mydorge, a friendship in which he found something that suited him perfectly both in temperament and intellectual bent. To escape his former companions, who still took too much of his time, Descartes surprisingly turned to the career of a soldier and enlisted in the service of Prince Maurice of Orange. His life in the Dutch army seems not to have been marked by too many battles or much discomfort, and he gained a good deal of fame as a mathematician during this period. He fought intermittently for the next twelve years with various armies in Europe; it was while in winter quarters in Bavaria in 1619–1620 that he had the important experience of enlightenment, described in his *Discourse on Method,* that led him to turn to his own reason as the only sound basis for philosophy.

In 1629 Descartes finally gave up the life of a soldier and settled in Holland. There he spent the last twenty years of his life building the reputation and writing the books upon which his place in modern philosophy rests. During the seventeenth century Holland was the one country where genuine freedom of thought was permitted, and many of the outstanding men of that age took refuge there. In going to Holland Descartes no doubt hoped to avoid conflict with the Catholic Church, to which he gave allegiance throughout his life, as well as to escape from the attention of unwanted acquaintances. The *Discourse on Method,* his *Meditations of First Philosophy* that carry further the ideas suggested in the *Discourse,* and his work on *The Principles of Philosophy* that sets forth his scientific theories, were all published during his years in Holland. Among Descartes' many admirers at this time was Queen Christina of Sweden who when not yet twenty conducted a learned correspondence with the celebrated philosopher. His last important work, *The Passions of the Soul,* was written for the young queen. In October 1649 she persuaded Descartes, much against his better judgment, to come to Stockholm, then insisted on his meeting her at five o'clock in the morning to discuss philosophy. Accustomed to working late and rising about noon, Descartes was soon exhausted. Never a robust man, despite his years of military service, he took cold and then became seriously ill with fever. On February 11, 1650, he died in Stockholm after having received the last rites of the Church.

Discourse on Method*

I

Good sense is of all things among men the most equally distributed, for everyone thinks that he is so abundantly provided with it that even those most difficult to please in other ways do not usually want more than they have of this. As it is not likely that everyone is mistaken, this evidence shows that the ability to judge correctly, and to distinguish the true from the false—which is really what is meant by good sense or reason—is the same by nature in all men; and that differences of opinion are not due to differences in intelligence, but merely to the fact that we use different approaches and consider different things. For it is not enough to have a good mind: one must use it well. The greatest minds are capable of the greatest vices as well as of the greatest virtues; and those who walk slowly, can, if they follow the right path, go much farther than those who run rapidly in the wrong direction.

As for myself, I have never supposed that my mind was above the ordinary. On the contrary, I have often wished to have as quick a wit or as clear and distinct an imagination, or as ready and retentive a memory, as another person. And I know of no other qualities which make for a good mind, because as far as reason is concerned, it is the only thing which makes us men and distinguishes us from the animals, and I am therefore satisfied that it is fully present in each one of us. In this I follow the general opinion of philosophers, who say that there are differences in degree only in the *accidental* qualities, and not in the *essential* qualities or natures of individuals of the same species.

But I do not hesitate to claim the good fortune of having stumbled, in my youth, upon certain paths which led me to certain considerations and maxims from which I formed a method of gradually increasing my knowledge and of improving my abilities as much as the mediocrity of my talents and the shortness of my life will permit. For I have already had such results that although in self-judgment I try to lean rather toward undervaluation than to presumption, I cannot escape a feeling of extreme satisfaction with the progress I believe I have already made in the search for truth. And although from the philosophers' viewpoint almost all the activities of men appear to me as vain and useless, yet I conceive such hopes for the future that if some single one of the occupations of men, as men, should be truly good and important, I dare to believe that it is the one I have chosen.

It is always possible that I am wrong, and that I am mistaking a bit of copper and glass for gold and diamonds. I know how subject we are to making false judgments in the things that concern ourselves, and how much we ought to mistrust the judgments of our friends when they are in our own favor. But I should be glad to show in this *Discourse* what are the paths I have taken, and to present a sketch of my life, so that each one can form his own judgment of it. In this way I may learn from the opinions of those who read it, and thus add another to the methods of progress which I am accustomed to use.

So it is not my intention to present a method which everyone ought to follow in order to think well, but only to show how I have made the attempt myself. Those who counsel others must consider themselves superior to those whom they counsel, and if they fall short in the least detail they are to

* Rene Descartes: *Discourse on the Method of Rightly Conducting the Reason,* English translation by Laurence J. Lafluer. New York, 1950, 1956 ("The Library of Liberal Arts" No. 19). Reprinted by permission of the publishers, the Bobbs-Merrill Company, Inc.

blame. I only propose this writing as an autobiography, or, if you prefer, as a story in which you may possibly find some examples of conduct which you might see fit to imitate, as well as several others which you would have no reason to follow. I hope that it will prove useful to some without being harmful to any, and that all will thank me for my frankness.

From my childhood I lived in a world of books, and since I was taught that by their help I could gain a clear and assured knowledge of everything useful in life, I was eager to learn from them. But as soon as I had finished the course of studies which usually admits one to the ranks of the learned, I changed my opinion completely. For I found myself saddled with so many doubts and errors that I seemed to have gained nothing in trying to educate myself unless it was to discover more and more fully how ignorant I was. Nevertheless I had been in one of the most celebrated schools of Europe, where I thought there should be wise men if wise men existed anywhere on earth. I had learned there everything that others learned, and, not satisfied with merely the knowledge that was taught, I had perused as many books as I could find which contained more unusual and recondite knowledge. I also knew the opinions of others about myself, and that I was in no way judged inferior to my fellow students, even though several of them were preparing to become professors. And finally, it did not seem to me that our own times were less flourishing and fertile than were any of the earlier periods. All this led me to conclude that I could judge others by myself, and to decide that there was no philosophy in the world of the kind that I had previously hoped to find.

I esteemed eloquence highly, and loved poetry, but I felt that both were gifts of nature rather than fruits of study. Those who reason most cogently, and work over their thoughts to make them clear and intelligible, are always the most persuasive, even if they speak only a provincial dialect and have never studied rhetoric. Those who have the most agreeable imaginations and can

express their thoughts with most grace and color cannot fail to be the best poets, even if the poetic art is unknown to them.

I was especially pleased with mathematics, because of the certainty and self-evidence of its proofs; but I did not yet see its true usefulness, and thinking that it was good only for the mechanical arts, I was astonished that nothing more noble had been built on so firm and solid a foundation. On the other hand, I compared the ethical writings of the ancient pagans to very superb and magnificent palaces built only on mud and sand: they laud the virtues and make them appear more desirable than anything else in the world; but they give no adequate criterion of virtue, and often what they call by such a name is nothing but apathy, parricide, pride or despair.

I revered our theology, and hoped as much as anyone else to get to heaven, but having learned on great authority that the road was just as open to the most ignorant as to the most learned, and that the truths of revelation which lead thereto are beyond our understanding, I would not have dared to submit them to the weakness of my reasonings. I thought that to succeed in their examination it would be necessary to have some extraordinary assistance from heaven, and to be more than a man.

I will say nothing of philosophy except that it has been studied for many centuries by the most outstanding minds without having produced anything which is not in dispute and consequently doubtful. I did not have enough presumption to hope to succeed better than the others; and when I noticed how many different opinions learned men may hold on the same subject, despite the fact that no more than one of them can ever be right, I resolved to consider almost as false any opinion which was merely plausible.

This is why I gave up my studies entirely as soon as I reached the age when I was no longer under the control of my teachers. I resolved to seek no other knowledge than that which I might find within myself, or perhaps in the great book of nature. I spent the rest of my adolescence traveling, seeing courts and armies, living with people of diverse types and stations of life, acquiring varied experience, testing myself in the episodes which fortune sent me, and above all, thinking about the things around me so that I could derive some profit from them. For it seemed to me that I might find much more of the truth in the cogitations which each man made on things which were important to him, and where he would be the loser if he judged badly, than in the cogitations of a man of letters in his study, concerned with speculations which produce no effect, and which have no consequences to him except perhaps that the farther they are removed from common sense, the more they titillate his vanity, since then he needs so much more wit and skill to make them seem plausible. Besides, I was always eager to learn to distinguish truth from falsehood, so that I could make intelligent decisions about the affairs of this life.

II

I had discovered in college that one cannot imagine anything so strange and unbelievable but that it has been upheld by some philosophers; and in my travels I had found that those who held opinions contrary to ours were neither barbarians nor savages, but that many of them were at least as reasonable as ourselves. I had considered how the same man, with the same capacity for reason, becomes different, as a result of being brought up among Frenchmen or Germans, than he would be if he had been brought up among Chinese or cannibals; and how in our fashions, the thing which pleased us ten years ago and perhaps will please us again ten years in the future, now seems extravagant and ridiculous; and I felt that in all these ways we are much more greatly influenced by custom and example than by any certain knowledge. Faced with this divergence of opinion, I could not accept the testimony of the majority, for I thought it worthless as a proof of anything somewhat difficult to discover, since it is much more likely that a single man will have discovered it than a

whole people. Nor, on the other hand, could I select anyone whose opinions seemed to me to be preferable to those of others, and I was thus constrained to embark on the investigation for myself.

Nevertheless, like a man who walks alone in the darkness, I resolved to go so slowly and circumspectly that if I did not get ahead very rapidly I was at least safe from falling. Also, I did not want to reject all the opinions which had slipped irrationally into my consciousness since birth, until I had first spent enough time planning how to accomplish the task which I was then undertaking, and seeking the true method of obtaining knowledge of everything which my mind was capable of understanding.

Among the branches of philosophy, I had, when younger, studied logic, and among those of mathematics, analytic geometry and algebra; three arts or sciences which should be able to contribute something to my design. But in examining them, I noticed that as far as logic was concerned, its syllogisms and most of its other methods serve rather to explain to another what one already knows . . . than to learn new things. Although it does contain many true and good precepts, they are interspersed among so many others that are harmful or superfluous that it is almost as difficult to separate them as to bring forth a Diana or a Minerva from a block of virgin marble. Then, as far as the analysis of the ancients and the algebra of the moderns is concerned, besides the fact that they deal with abstractions and appear to have no utility, the first is always so limited to the consideration of figures that it cannot exercise the understanding without greatly fatiguing the imagination, and the second is so limited to certain rules and certain numbers that it has become a confused and obscure art which perplexes the mind instead of a science which educates it. In consequence I thought that some other method must be found to combine the advantages of these three and to escape their faults. Finally, just as the multitude of laws frequently furnishes an excuse for vice, and a state is much better governed with a few laws which are strictly adhered to, so I thought that instead of the great number of precepts of which logic is composed, I would have enough with the four following ones, provided that I made a firm and unalterable resolution not to violate them even in a single instance.

The first rule was never to accept anything as true unless I clearly recognized it to be so: that is, carefully to avoid haste and prejudice and to include nothing in my conclusions unless it presented itself so clearly and distinctly to my mind that I had no occasion to doubt it.

The second was to divide each of the difficulties which I encountered into as many parts as possible, and as might be required for an easier solution.

The third was to think in an orderly fashion beginning with the things which were simplest and easiest to understand, and gradually and by degrees reaching toward more complex knowledge, even treating as ordered materials which were not necessarily so.

The last was always to make enumerations so complete, and reviews so general, that I was certain that nothing was omitted.

Those long chains of reasoning, so simple and easy, which enable the geometricians to reach the most difficult demonstrations, had made me wonder whether all things knowable to men might not fall into a similar logical sequence. If so, we need only refrain from accepting as true that which is not true, and carefully follow the order necessary to deduce each one from the others, and there cannot be any propositions so abstruse that we cannot prove them, or so recondite that we cannot discover them. It was not very difficult, either, to decide where we should look for a beginning, for I knew already that one begins with the simplest and easiest to know. Considering that among all those who have previously sought truth in the sciences, mathematicians alone have been able to find some demonstrations, some certain and evident reasons, I had no doubt that I should begin where they did, although I expected no advantage except to accustom my mind to work with truths and not to be satisfied with bad reasoning. In this I trust that I shall not appear too vain, considering that there is only one true solution to a given problem, and whoever finds it knows all that anyone can know about it. Thus, for example, a child who has learned arithmetic and had performed an addition according to the rules may feel certain that as far as that particular sum is concerned, he has found everything that a human mind can discover. For, after all, the method of following the correct order and stating precisely all the circumstances of what we are investigating is the whole of what gives certainty to the rules of arithmetic.

What pleased me most about this method was that it enabled me to reason in all things, if not perfectly, at least as well as was in my power. In addition I felt that in practicing it my mind was gradually becoming accustomed to conceive its objects more clearly and distinctly, and since I had not directed this method to any particular subject matter, I was in hopes of applying it just as usefully to the difficulties of other sciences as I had already to those of algebra. Not that I would dare to undertake to examine at once all the difficulties that presented themselves, for that would have been contrary to the principle of order. But I had observed that all the basic principles of the sciences were taken from philosophy, which itself had no certain ones. It therefore seemed that I should first attempt to establish philosophic principles, and that since this was the most important thing in the world and the place where haste and prejudice were most to be feared, I should not attempt to reach conclusions until I had attained a much more mature age than my then twenty-three years, and had spent much time in preparing for it. This preparation would consist partly in freeing my mind from the false opinions which I had previously acquired, partly in building up a fund of experiences which should serve afterwards as the raw material of my reasoning, and partly in training myself in the method which I had determined upon, so that I should become more and more adept in its use.

III

In planning to rebuild one's house it is not enough to draw up the plans for the new dwelling, tear down the old one, and provide materials and workmen for the task. We must see that we are provided with a comfortable place to stay while the work of rebuilding is going on. Similarly in my own case; while reason obliged me to be irresolute in my beliefs, there was no reason why I should be so in my actions. In order to live as happily as possible during the interval I prepared a provisional code of morality for myself, consisting of three or four maxims which I here set forth.

The first was to obey the laws and customs of my country, constantly retaining the religion in which, by God's grace, I had been brought up since childhood, and in all other matters to follow the most moderate and least excessive opinions to be found in the practices of the more judicious part of the community in which I would live. For I was then about to discard my own opinions in order to reexamine them, and meanwhile could do no better than to follow those of the most reliable judges. While there may be, no doubt, just as reliable persons among the Persians or the Chinese as among ourselves, it seemed more practical to pattern my conduct on that of the society in which I would have to live. Furthermore, it seemed to me that to learn people's true opinions, I should pay attention to their conduct rather than to their words, not only because in our corrupt times there are few who are ready to say all that they believe, but also because many are not aware of their own beliefs, since the mental process of knowing a thing is distinct from, and can occur without, the mental process of knowing that we know it. Among a number of opinions equally widely accepted, I chose only the most moderate, partly because these are always the most convenient in practice and, since excess is usually bad, presumably the best; but also so that I should stray a shorter distance from the true road in case I should make a mistake, than I would in choosing one extreme when it was the other that should have been followed.

My second maxim was to be as firm and determined in my actions as I could be, and not to act on the doubtful decisions, once I had made them, any less resolutely than on the most certain. In this matter I patterned my behavior on that of travelers, who, finding themselves lost in a forest, must not wander about, now turning this way, now that, and still less should remain in one place, but should go as straight as they can in the direction they first select and not change the direction except for the strongest reasons. By this method, even if the direction was chosen at random, they will presumably arrive at some destination, not perhaps where they would like to be, but at least where they will be better off than in the middle of the forest. Similarly, situations in life often permit no delay; and when we cannot determine the course which is certainly best, we must follow the one which is probably best, and when we cannot determine even that, we must nevertheless select one and follow it thereafter as though it were certainly best. If the course selected is not indeed a good one, at least the reasons for selecting it are excellent. This frame of mind freed me also from the repentance and remorse commonly felt by those vacillating individuals who are always seeking as worth while things which they later judge to be bad.

My third maxim was always to seek to conquer myself rather than fortune, to change my ideas rather than the established order, and generally to believe that nothing except our thoughts is wholly under our control, so that after we have done our best in external matters, what remains to be done is absolutely impossible, at least as far as we are concerned. This maxim in itself should suffice to prevent me from desiring in the future anything which I could not acquire, and thus to make me happy. For it is our nature to desire only that which we imagine to be somehow attainable, and if we consider all external benefits equally beyond our reach we will no more regret being unjustly deprived of our birthright than we regret not possessing the kingdoms of China or Mexico. Thus, making a virtue of necessity, we no more desire to be well when we are sick, or to be free when we are in prison, than we now desire bodies as incorruptible as diamonds, or wings to fly like the birds. But I must admit that it takes much practice and frequently repeated meditations to become accustomed to view things in this manner, and I think that this must have been the principal secret of those philosophers of ancient times who were able to rise above fortune, and, despite misfortunes and poverty, to vie with the gods in happiness.

Finally, I planned to make a review of the various occupations possible in this life, in order to choose the best. Without intending to disparage other occupations, I thought I could do no better than to continue in the one I was engaged in, employing my life in improving my mind and increasing as far as I could my knowledge of the truth by following the method that I had outlined for myself. I had experienced such periods of great happiness after I had begun to use this method, that I could hope for no greater or more innocent joys in this life. In discovering day after day truths which seemed fairly important and unknown to other men, I was filled with such satisfaction that other considerations did not affect me. Another reason for my decision was that the three maxims previously considered were based on my plan to continue the search for truth. For as God has given each one of us some ability to distinguish the true from the false, I should not have been content for one instant to rely on the opinions of others if I had not planned to use my own judgment at the proper time; nor could I have followed those opinions with a clear conscience if I had not hoped to take advantage of every opportunity to find better ones, if better ones there were. And finally, I could not have limited my desires, nor been happy, if I were not following a path by which I expected to obtain all the knowledge of which I was capable and all the real values which might be in my power. Besides, since our will neither seeks nor avoids anything except as it is judged good or bad by our

reason, good judgment is sufficient to guarantee good behavior. Judging as best one can therefore implies that one act as well as one can, or in other words, that one will acquire all the virtues and with them all other possible goods. Once we are sure of this, we cannot well fail to be happy.

IV

I do not know whether I ought to touch upon my first meditations here, for they are so metaphysical and out of the ordinary that they might not be interesting to most people. Nevertheless, in order to show whether my fundamental notions are sufficiently sound, I find myself more or less constrained to speak of them. I had noticed for a long time that in practice it is sometimes necessary to follow opinions which we know to be very uncertain, just as though they were indubitable, as I stated before; but inasmuch as I desired to devote myself wholly to the search for truth, I thought that I should take a course precisely contrary, and reject as absolutely false anything of which I could have the least doubt, in order to see whether anything would be left after this procedure which could be called wholly certain. Thus, as our senses deceive us at times, I was ready to suppose that nothing was at all the way our senses represented them to be. As there are men who make mistakes in reasoning even on the simplest topics in geometry, I judged that I was as liable to error as any other, and rejected as false all the reasoning which I had previously accepted as valid demonstration. Finally, as the same precepts which we have when awake may come to us when asleep without their being true, I decided to suppose that nothing that had ever entered my mind was more real than the illusions of my dreams. But I soon noticed that while I thus wished to think everything false, it was necessarily true that I who thought so was something. Since this truth, *I think, therefore I am,* was so firm and assured that all the most extravagant suppositions of the sceptics were unable to shake it, I judged that I could accept it without hesitation as the first principle of the philosophy I was seeking.

I then examined closely what I was, and saw that I could imagine that I had no body, and that there was no world nor any place that I occupied, but that I could not imagine for a moment that I did not exist. On the contrary, from the very fact that I doubted the truth of other things, it followed very evidently and very certainly that I existed. On the ground that, if I had ceased to think while all the rest of what I imagined remained true, I would have had no reason to believe that I had existed, I concluded that I was a substance whose whole essence or nature was only to think, and which, to exist, has no need of space nor of any material thing. Thus it follows that this ego, this soul, by which I am what I am, is entirely distinct from the body and is easier to know than the latter, and that even if the body were not, the soul would not cease to be all that it is.

Next I considered in general what is required of a proposition for it to be true and certain, for since I had just discovered one to be such, I thought I ought also to know of what that certitude consisted. I saw that there was nothing at all in this statement, "I think therefore I am," to assure me that I was saying the truth, unless it was that I saw very clearly that to think one must exist. So I judged that I could accept as a general rule that the things which we conceive very clearly and very distinctly are always true, but that there may well be some difficulty in deciding which are those which we conceive distinctly.

After that I reflected upon the fact that I doubted, and that, in consequence, my spirit was not wholly perfect, for I saw clearly that it was a greater perfection to know than to doubt. I decided to ascertain from what source I had learned to think of something more perfect than myself, and it appeared evidently that it must have been from some nature which was really more perfect. As for my ideas about many other things outside of me, as the sky, earth, light, heat, and thousands of other things, I was not so much

troubled to discover where they came from, because I found nothing in them superior to my own nature. But this could not be the explanation of my idea of a being more perfect than my own. To derive it from nothingness was manifestly impossible, and it is no less repugnant to good sense to assume what is more perfect comes from and depends on the less perfect than it is to assume that something comes from nothing, so that I could not assume that it came from myself. Thus the only hypothesis left was that this idea was put in my mind by a nature that was really more perfect than I was, which had all the perfections that I could imagine, and which was, in a word, God. To this I added that since I knew some perfections which I did not possess, I was not the only being in existence (I will here use freely, if you will pardon me, the terms of the schools), and that it followed of necessity that there was someone else more perfect upon whom I depended and from whom I had acquired all that I possessed. For if I had been alone and independent of anything else, so that I had bestowed upon myself all that limited quantity of value which I shared with the perfect Being, I would have been able to get from myself, in the same way, all the surplus which was lacking, and so would have been myself infinite, eternal, immutable, omniscient, omnipotent, and, in sum, I would possess all the perfections that I could discover in God. For, following the reasoning which I have just explained, to know the nature of God as far as I was capable of it, I had only to consider each quality of which I had an idea, and decide whether it was or was not a perfection to possess it. I would then be certain that none of those which had some imperfection was in Him, but that all the others were. I saw that doubt, inconstancy, sorrow and similar things could not be part of God's nature, since I would be happy to be without them myself. In addition, I had ideas of many sensible and corporeal entities, for although I might suppose that I was dreaming and that all that I saw or imagined was false, I could not at any rate deny that the ideas were truly in my consciousness. Since I had already recognized very clearly that intelligent nature is distinct from corporeal nature, I considered that composition is an evidence of dependency and that dependency is manifestly a defect. From this I judged that it could not be a perfection in God to be composed of these two natures, and that consequently he was not so composed. But if there were in the world bodies, or even intelligences or other natures that were not wholly perfect, their being must depend on God's power in such a way that they could not subsist without him for a single moment.

At this point I wished to seek for other truths, and proposed for consideration the object of the geometricians. This I conceived as a continuous body, or a space infinitely extended in length, breadth, and height or depth; divisible into various parts which can have different shapes and sizes and can be moved in any way: all of which is presumed by geometricians to be true of their object.

I went through some of their simplest demonstrations and noticed that the great certainty which everyone attributes to them is only based on the fact that they appear evident, following the rule just stated. I noticed also that there was nothing at all in them to assure me of the existence of their object; it was clear, for example, that if we posit a triangle, its three angles must be equal to two right angles, but there was nothing in that to assure me that there was a single triangle in the world. When I turned back to my idea of a perfect Being, I found that existence was included in that idea in the same way that the idea of a triangle contains the equality of its angles to two right angles, or that the idea of a sphere includes the equi-distance of all its parts from its center. Perhaps, in fact, the existence of the perfect Being is even more evident. Consequently, it is at least as certain that God, who is this so perfect Being, exists as any theorem of geometry could possibly be.

The Scientific Rationalist: Benedict Spinoza

Benedict Spinoza, an able and discerning exponent of rationalism, ranks among the great figures in the history of modern thought. In the philosophy of Spinoza we find what is perhaps the outstanding effort of the human mind to interpret the meaning of life entirely in rational terms and completely in accord with the conclusions of natural science. Whether dealing with moral conduct or with religious faith, Spinoza sees the scientific view as the only acceptable one. He has developed a thoroughly scientific morality and a completely scientific religion; he will have us make no compromises, no concessions to human hope, frailty, or need. To be good, to be blessed, to be free—these to Spinoza all mean one and the same thing. They are the outcome of a life lived entirely in accord with reason, a life that understands the rational laws at work in the universe, gladly conforms its conduct to them, and thus finds the blessedness all men deeply long to possess.

Those men and women to whom logical consistency and scientific thought are particularly congenial have always found in the philosophy of Spinoza one of the supreme expressions of human reason. In Spinoza's greatest work, the *Ethics,* every aspect of human thought—science, psychology, and religion as well as ethics, metaphysics, and epistemology—are brought together in a closely knit piece of reasoning. This is a book that must certainly be placed with Plato's *Republic* among the greatest single volumes in the literature of philosophy, a book in which the full implications of rationalism are clearly recognized and ruthlessly carried to their logical conclusion.

Among the most impressive characteristics of Spinoza's philosophy are the clarity and depth of his insight. Writing some three hundred years ago, when modern science was in its infancy and when the modern interpretation of religion had not yet been undertaken, he saw clearly what was involved in the scientific interpretation of the universe and of human life in terms of natural law. Only after another two centuries was his position generally adopted by men trained in science, and only even more recently have scientific psychology and sociology come to recognize what Spinoza saw so clearly as essential in the scientific interpretation of human nature and social institutions. It is true that in the last two or three decades our interpretation of the meaning of science has taken a somewhat different turn. This, however, is not because of inadequacies in Spinoza's understanding of Newtonian science, but rather because a revolution in the field of science itself has brought into question much that formerly seemed essential to the very existence of the scientific enterprise.

As one of his biographers has aptly put it, "Spinoza's philosophy was more than a delicate bloom nurtured in the forcing-house of his mind; it was a virile and luxuriant tree rooted in the depths of this soul."[1] The underlying principles of his philosophy are as apparent in the life he lived as they are in the pages of his famous

---

[1] Lewis Browne, *Blessed Spinoza* (New York, Macmillan, 1932), p. 280.

treatise on *Ethics*. Born in Holland in 1632, Baruch Spinoza was the son of a prosperous Jewish merchant in Amsterdam. He was a studious youth with greater taste for the learning of the synagogue than for his father's business and seemed destined for a career as a scholarly Jewish rabbi. But he studied Latin with the Dutch scholar Franciscus van den Ende, a man of wide interests as well as something of a free-thinker, and soon became more absorbed in mastering the new scientific speculation of the seventeenth century than the theology of his religious teachers. During this time Spinoza read widely in philosophy. He knew Socrates, Plato, and Aristotle, but among the ancients he much preferred the great Stoic writers, and above all else he was attracted by the thought of René Descartes, who was then at the height of his influence. This was an age upon which the achievements of the physical sciences were having a profound influence. In the speculation of Copernicus, Kepler, and Galileo, and in the scientific genius of Newton, human reason seemed gradually to be forcing the natural universe to reveal its ways of behavior. Nature's laws proved to be so precise and dependable, so capable of exact mathematical formulation, that with Descartes, Spinoza came to feel that in mathematics human reason expressed her insights most clearly and validly.

As Spinoza was drawn more strongly to the rationalism of Descartes, the religious creed of his fathers proved unequal to the demands made upon it by his growing scientific knowledge and his changing spiritual needs. He began to question the reasonableness of many of his earlier beliefs and soon was accused of accepting heretical doctrines by the elders of the Amsterdam synagogue. Upon refusing to compromise his convictions, Spinoza was formally excommunicated on July 27, 1656, when he was twenty-four years of age. The now famous writ of excommunication is still preserved in the archives of the Amsterdam synagogue.

The young philosopher took the whole experience calmly. It was nothing more than he had expected, he said. Changing his name from Baruch to Benedict (its Latin equivalent), he left his own people and devoted himself completely to work and to study. In a short time Spinoza seems to have become the accepted leader of a small group of intellectuals in Amsterdam interested in the new science and philosophy. In 1663 he published his first book, *The Principles of Cartesian Philosophy,* written originally as the basis of instruction of a young student who was living with him during the three years he spent at Rhynsburg, a village near Leyden. Here Spinoza also wrote his early essay *On the Improvement of the Understanding,* intended like Descartes' *Discourse on Method* to provide a background and introduction to his own rationalistic philosophy. Although never completed, this essay is by far the most revealing and readable introduction to his thought.

In 1664 a strong reaction set in against the liberal policies of Jan de Witt, the head of the Dutch government. The Dutch possessions in North America had been captured by the British, New Amsterdam became New York, the Dutch navy was defeated, and the reactionaries set out to get rid of de Witt, whom they blamed for their losses. Spinoza joined those liberals who rallied at once to de Witt support. Laying aside his more theoretical studies, he wrote a *Treatise on Theology and Politics* in which he vigorously defended the right of each individual to complete freedom of thought, rejected all dictation by either church or state, and insisted that the insights of reason alone provide our final authority in religion and politics as well as in science. Fortunately, the tract was published anonymously. Even in Holland, the most tolerant country in Europe at that time, the unorthodox religious outlook and the liberal spirit of Spinoza's book created quite a furor. The book was almost immediately banned by the church and its sale forbidden by the civil authorities. We now find some three hundred years later that Spinoza's views on both religion and politics are in accord with the democratic ideals of our own day. Indeed, the present conflict between the Communist way of life and our own commitment to the freedom of the individual gives Spinoza's point of view a particular relevance. "Deeds alone should be made the grounds of criminal charges, and speech should be utterly free," he writes. "Every man should be allowed to think what he likes and to say what he thinks; without such freedom there cannot be any peace or true piety."

In 1675, after twelve years of study and writing, Spinoza finished his greatest work, the *Ethics Demonstrated in the Manner of Geometry*. This is not a book to be read for enjoyment but one to be studied page by page, section by section—indeed, almost word by word. For Spinoza's Latin terminology, and his effort to present philosophy in mathematical fashion, must be mastered before the *Ethics* can be understood. Axioms, definitions, theorems, and proofs follow each other in the pages of the *Ethics* in approved Euclidean fashion. Despite the genius and ingenuity of Spinoza, the resulting discussion goes far to prove that philosophy might better use its own methods than those borrowed from science. Too few modern readers attempt to penetrate the obscurity that this geometrizing of ethics produces.

Spinoza for some time made no effort to publish the *Ethics* because of the furor created by his *Treatise on Theology and Politics*. When at length he did think of doing so, a rumor spread to the effect that a book of his was about to appear which endeavored to prove that there was no God. At the advice of friends he decided to await a more favorable time, but such a time did not arrive. When Spinoza died in 1677, the manuscript was still carefully locked in his desk. Fortunately he had made arrangements to have it transmitted to his publisher in Amsterdam. The only instruction he gave was that when the book was published, his name should not appear on it. Its truth, he felt, should be self-evident to the intelligent reader, and he saw no reason to seek further fame or denunciation for himself.

Estimates of Spinoza have varied greatly. In his own day many condemned him unreservedly as an atheist and enemy of religion, but those who then opposed his ideas sought in vain to destroy the dead philosopher. A hundred years later the enduring significance of his rationalism was widely recognized in literary and philosophical circles throughout Europe, and his thought was taken to be so fundamentally religious in spirit that he was described as "God-intoxicated." Two hundred years after his death a statue in his honor was erected in The Hague. To celebrate the three-hundredth anniversary of his birth, philosophers from nations throughout the world gathered in honor of his memory. Selections from his three major works, which give a representative view of his philosophy, are included here.

On the Improvement of The Understanding*

After experience had taught me that all the usual surroundings of social life are vain and futile; seeing that none of the objects of my fears contained in themselves anything either good or bad, except in so far as the mind is affected by them, I finally resolved to inquire whether there might be some real good having power to communicate itself, which would affect the mind singly, to the exclusion of all else; whether, in fact, there might be anything of which the discovery and attainment would enable me to enjoy continuous, supreme, and unending happiness. I say " I *finally* resolved," for at first sight it seemed unwise willingly to lose hold on what was sure for the sake of something then uncertain. I could see the benefits which are acquired through fame and riches, and that I should be obliged to abandon the quest of such objects, if I seriously devoted myself to the search for something different and new. I perceived that if true happiness chanced to be placed in the former I should necessarily miss it; while if, on the other hand, it were not so placed, and I gave them my whole attention, I should equally fail.

I therefore debated whether it would not be possible to arrive at the new principle, or at any rate at a certainty concerning its existence, without changing the conduct and usual plan of my life; with this end in view I made many efforts, but in vain. For the ordinary surroundings of life which are esteemed by men (as their actions testify) to

be the highest good, may be classed under the three heads—Riches, Fame, and the Pleasure of Sense: with these three the mind is so absorbed that it has little power to reflect on any different good. By sensual pleasure the mind is enthralled to the extent of quiescence, as if the supreme good were actually attained, so that it is quite incapable of thinking of any other object: when such pleasure has been gratified it is followed by extreme melancholy, whereby the mind, though not enthralled, is disturbed and dulled.

The pursuit of honors and riches is likewise very absorbing, especially if such objects be sought simply for their own sake, inasmuch as they are then supposed to constitute the highest good. In the case of fame the mind is still more absorbed, for fame is conceived as always good for its own sake, and as the ultimate end to which all actions are directed. Further, the attainment of riches and fame is not followed as in the case of sensual pleasures by repentance, but, the more we acquire, the greater is our delight, and, consequently, the more we are incited to increase both the one and the other; on the other hand, if our hopes happen to be frustrated we are plunged into the deepest sadness. Fame has the further drawback that it compels its votaries to order their lives according to the opinions of their fellowmen, shunning what they usually shun, and seeking what they usually seek.

When I saw that all these ordinary objects of desire would be obstacles in the way of a search for something different and new—nay, that they were so opposed thereto, that either they or it would have to be

---

* Benedict Spinoza, *On The Improvement of the Understanding,* English translation by R. H. M. Elwes (London, 1884).

abandoned, I was forced to inquire which would prove the most useful to me: for, as I say, I seemed to be willingly losing hold on a sure good for the sake of something uncertain. However, after I had reflected on the matter, I came in the first place to the conclusion that by abandoning the ordinary objects of pursuit, and betaking myself to a new quest, I should be leaving a good, uncertain by reason of its own nature, as may be gathered from what has been said, for the sake of a good not uncertain in its nature (for I sought for a fixed good), but only in the possibility of its attainment.

Further reflection convinced me, that if I could really get to the root of the matter, I should be leaving certain evils for a certain good. I thus perceived that I was in a state of great peril, and I compelled myself to seek with all my strength for a remedy, however uncertain it might be; as a sick man struggling with a deadly disease, when he sees that death will surely be upon him unless a remedy be found, is compelled to seek such a remedy with all his strength, inasmuch as his whole hope lies therein. All the objects pursued by the multitude, not only bring no remedy that tends to preserve our being, but even act as hindrances, causing the death not seldom of those who possess them, and always of those who are possessed by them. There are many examples of men who have suffered persecution even to death for the sake of their riches, and of men who in pursuit of wealth have exposed themselves to so many dangers, that they have paid away their life as a penalty for their folly. Examples are no less numerous for men, who have endured the utmost wretchedness for the sake of gaining or preserving their reputation. Lastly, there are innumerable cases of men, who have hastened their death through over-indulgences in sensual pleasure.

All these evils seem to have arisen from the fact, that happiness or unhappiness is made wholly to depend on the quality of the object which we love. When a thing is not loved, no quarrels will arise concerning it— no sadness will be felt if it perishes—no envy if it is possessed by another—no fear,

no hatred, in short no disturbances of the mind. All these arise from the love of what is perishable, such as the objects already mentioned. But love toward a thing eternal and infinite feeds the mind wholly with joy, and is itself unmingled with any sadness, wherefore it is greatly to be desired and sought for with all our strength. Yet it was not at random that I used the words, "If I could go to the root of the matter," for, though what I have urged was perfectly clear to my mind, I could not forthwith lay aside all love of riches, sensual enjoyment, and fame. One thing was evident, namely, that while my mind was employed with these thoughts it turned away from its former objects of desire, and seriously considered the search for a new principle; this state of things was a great comfort to me, for I perceived that the evils were not such as to resist all remedies. Although these intervals were at first rare, and of very short duration, yet afterward, as the true good become more and more discernible to me, they became more frequent and more lasting; especially after I had recognized that the acquisition of wealth, sensual pleasure, or fame, is only a hindrance, so long as they are sought as ends not as means; if they be sought as means they will be under restraint, and, far from being hindrances, will further not a little the end for which they are sought, as I will show in due time.

I will here only briefly state what I mean by true good, and also what is the nature of the highest good. In order that this may be rightly understood, we must bear in mind that the terms good and evil are only applied relatively, so that the same thing may be called both good and bad, according to the relations in view, in the same way as it may be called perfect or imperfect. Nothing regarded in its own nature can be called perfect or imperfect; especially when we are aware that all things which come to pass, come to pass according to the eternal order and fixed laws of nature. However, human weakness cannot attain to this order in its own thoughts, but meanwhile man conceives a human character much more stable than his own, and sees that there is no reason why he should not himself acquire such a character. Thus he is led to seek for means which will bring him to this pitch of perfection, and calls everything which will serve as such means a true good. The chief good is that he should arrive, together with other individuals if possible, at the possession of the aforesaid character. What that character is we shall show in due time, namely, that it is the knowledge of the union existing between the mind and the whole of nature.

This, then, is the end for which I strive, to attain to such a character myself, and to endeavor that many should attain to it with me. In other words, it is part of my happiness to lend a helping hand, that many others may understand even as I do, so that their understanding and desire may entirely agree with my own. In order to bring this about, it is necessary to understand as much of nature as will enable us to attain to the aforesaid character, and also to form a social order such as is most conducive to the attainment of this character by the greatest number with the least difficulty and danger. But, before all things, a means must be devised for improving the understanding and purifying it, as far as may be at the outset, so that it may apprehend things without error, and in the best possible way.

Thus it is apparent to every one that I wish to direct all sciences to one end and aim, so that we may attain to the supreme human perfection which we have named; and, therefore, whatsoever in the sciences does not serve to promote our object will have to be rejected as useless.* To sum up the matter in a word, all our actions and thoughts must be directed to this one end.

---

* This primary, ethical motivation definitely separates Spinoza from Descartes, to whom nothing of this sort is conceivable. [Ed.]

Concerning Miracles*

I

As men are accustomed to call divine the knowledge which transcends human understanding, so also do they style divine, or the work of God, anything of which the cause is not generally known: for the masses think that the power and providence of God are most clearly displayed by events that are extraordinary and contrary to the conception they have formed of Nature, especially if such events bring them any profit or convenience: they think that the clearest possible proof of God's existence is afforded when Nature, as they suppose, breaks her accustomed order, and consequently they believe that those who explain or endeavor to understand phenomena or miracles through their natural causes are doing away with God

and His providence. They suppose, forsooth, that God is inactive so long as Nature works in her accustomed order, and *vice versa,* that the power of Nature and natural causes are idle so long as God is acting: thus they imagine two powers distinct one from the other, the power of God and the power of Nature, though the latter is in a sense determined by God, or (as most people believe now) created by Him. What they mean by either, and what they understand by God and Nature they do not know, except that they imagine the power of God to be like that of some royal potentate, and Nature's power to consist in force and energy.

The masses then style unusual phenomena "miracles," and partly from piety, partly for the sake of opposing the students of science, prefer to remain in ignorance of natural causes, and only to hear of those things which they know least, and consequently admire most. In fact, the common

---

* Benedict Spinoza, *Treatise on Theology and Politics,* English translation by R. H. M. Elwes (London, 1883). Ch. VI (abridged).

people can only adore God, and refer all things to his power by removing natural causes, and conceiving things happening out of their due course, and only admire the power of God when the power of Nature is conceived of as in subjection to it.

This idea seems to have taken its rise among the early Jews who saw the Gentiles round them worshipping visible gods, such as the sun, the moon, the earth, water, air, etc., and in order to inspire the conviction that such divinities were weak and inconstant, or changeable, told how they themselves were under the sway of an invisible God, and narrated their miracles, trying further to show that the God whom they worshipped arranged the whole of nature for their sole benefit. This idea was so pleasing to humanity that men go on to this day imagining miracles, so that they may believe themselves God's favorites and the final cause for which God created and directs all things.

What pretensions will not people in their folly advance! They have no single sound idea concerning either God or Nature, they confounded God's decrees with human decrees, they conceive Nature as so limited that they believe man to be its chief part! I have spent enough space in setting forth these common ideas and prejudices concerning Nature and miracles, but in order to afford a regular demonstration I will show:

1. That Nature cannot be contravened, but that she preserves a fixed and immutable order, and at the same time I will explain what is meant by a miracle.

2. That God's nature and existence, and consequently his providence, cannot be known from miracles, but that they can all be much better perceived from the fixed and immutable order of Nature.

3. That by the decrees and volitions, and consequently the providence of God, Scripture (as I will prove by Scriptural examples) means nothing but Nature's order following necessarily from her eternal laws.

4. Lastly, I will treat of the method of interpreting Scriptural miracles, and the chief points to be noted concerning the narratives of them.

Such are the principal subjects which will be discussed in this chapter, and which will serve, I think, not a little to further the object of this treatise.

II

Our first point is easily proved from what we showed in Chapter V about divine law—namely, that all that God wishes or determines involves eternal necessity and truth, for we demonstrated that God's understanding is identical with his will, and that it is the same thing to say that God wills a thing, as to say that he understands it; hence, as it follows necessarily from the divine nature and perfection that God understands a thing as it is, it follows no less necessarily that he wills it as it is. Now, as nothing is necessarily true save only by divine decree, it is plain that the universal laws of Nature are decrees of God following from the necessity and perfection of the divine nature. Hence, any event happening in Nature which contravened Nature's universal laws, would necessarily also contravene the divine decree, nature, and understanding; or if any one asserted that God acts in contravention to the laws of Nature, he, *ipso facto,* would be compelled to assert that God acted against his own nature—an evident absurdity. One might easily show from the same premises that the power and efficiency of Nature are in themselves the divine power and efficiency, and that the divine power is the very essence of God, but this I will gladly pass over for the present.

Nothing, then, comes to pass in Nature[1] in contravention to her universal laws, nay, everything agrees with them and follows from them, for whatsoever comes to pass, comes to pass by the will and eternal decree of God; that is, as we have just pointed out, whatever comes to pass, comes to pass according to laws and rules which involve eternal necessity and truth; Nature, therefore, always observes laws and rules

---

[1] N. B. I do not mean here by "Nature," merely matter and its modifications, but infinite other things besides matter.

which involve eternal necessity and truth, although they may not all be known to us, and therefore she keeps a fixed and immutable order. Nor is there any sound reason for limiting the power and efficacy of Nature, and asserting that her laws are fit for certain purposes, but not for all; for as the efficacy and power of Nature are the very efficacy and power of God, and as the laws and rules of Nature are the decrees of God, it is in every way to be believed that the power of Nature is infinite, and that her laws are broad enough to embrace everything conceived by the divine intellect. The only alternative is to assert that God has created Nature so weak, and has ordained for her laws so barren, that he is repeatedly compelled to come afresh to her aid if he wishes that she should be preserved, and that things should happen as he desires: a conclusion, in my opinion, very far removed from reason. Further, as nothing happens in Nature which does not follow from her laws, and as her laws embrace everything conceived by the divine intellect, and, lastly, as Nature preserves a fixed and immutable order, it most clearly follows that miracles are only intelligible as in relation to human opinions, and merely mean events of which the natural cause cannot be explained by a reference to any ordinary occurrence, either by us, or at any rate by the writer and narrator of the miracle.

We may, in fact, say that a miracle is an event of which the causes cannot be explained by the natural reason through a reference to ascertained workings of Nature; but since miracles were wrought according to the understanding of the masses, who are wholly ignorant of the workings of Nature, it is certain that the ancients took for a miracle whatever they could not explain by the method adopted by the unlearned in such cases, namely, an appeal to the memory, a recalling of something similar, which is ordinarily regarded without wonder; for most people think they sufficiently understand a thing when they have ceased to wonder at it. The ancients, then, and indeed most men up to the present day, had no other criterion for a miracle; hence we cannot doubt that many things are narrated in Scripture as miracles of which the causes could easily be explained by reference to ascertained workings of Nature. We have hinted as much in Chapter III, in speaking of the sun standing still in the time of Joshua, and going backwards in the time of Ahaz; but we shall soon have more to say on the subject when we come to treat of the interpretation of miracles later on in this chapter.

III

It is now time to pass on to the second point, and show that we cannot gain an understanding of God's essence, existence, or providence by means of miracles, but that these truths are much better perceived through the fixed and immutable order of Nature.

I thus proceed with the demonstration. As God's existence is not self-evident, it must necessarily be inferred from ideas so firmly and incontrovertibly true that no power can be postulated or conceived sufficient to impugn them. They ought certainly so to appear to us when we infer from them God's existence, if we wish to place our conclusion beyond the reach of doubt; for if we could conceive that such ideas could be impugned by any power whatsoever, we should doubt of their truth, we should doubt of our conclusion, namely, of God's existence, and should never be able to be certain of anything. Further, we know that nothing either agrees with or is contrary to Nature, unless it agrees with or is contrary to these primary ideas; wherefore if we would conceive that anything could be done in Nature by any power whatsoever which would be contrary to the laws of Nature, it would also be contrary to our primary ideas, and we should have either to reject it as absurd, or else to cast doubt (as just shown) on our primary ideas, and consequently on the existence of God, and on everything howsoever perceived. Therefore miracles, in the sense of events contrary to the laws of Nature, so far from demonstrating to us the existence of God, would, on the contrary, lead us to doubt it, where, otherwise, we might have been absolutely certain of it, as knowing that Nature follows a fixed and immutable order.

Let us take miracle as meaning that which cannot be explained through natural causes. This may be interpreted in two senses: either as that which has natural causes, but cannot be examined by the human intellect; or as that which has no cause save God and God's will. But as all things which come to pass through natural causes come to pass also solely through the will and power of God, it comes to this: that a miracle, whether it has natural causes or not, is a result which cannot be explained by its cause, that it is a phenomenon which surpasses human understanding; but from such a phenomenon, and certainly from a result surpassing our understanding, we can gain no knowledge. For whatsoever we understand clearly and distinctly should be plain to us either in itself or by means of something else clearly and distinctly understood; wherefore from a miracle or a phenomenon which we cannot understand we gain no knowledge of God's essence, or existence, or indeed anything about God or nature; whereas when we know that all things are ordained and ratified by God, that the operations of Nature follow from the essence of God, and that the laws of Nature are eternal decrees and volitions of God, we must perforce conclude that our knowledge of God and of God's will increases in proportion to our knowledge and clear understanding of Nature, as we see how she depends on her primal cause, and how she works according to eternal law. Wherefore so far as our understanding goes, those phenomena which we clearly and distinctly understand have much better right to be called works of God, and to be referred to the will of God, than those about which we are entirely ignorant, although they appeal powerfully to the imagination, and compel men's admiration.

We may conclude, then, that we cannot gain knowledge of the existence and providence of God by means of miracles, but that we can far better infer them from the fixed and immutable order of Nature. By

miracle I here mean an event which surpasses, or is thought to surpass, human comprehension: for in so far as it is supposed to destroy or interrupt the order of Nature or her laws, it not only can give us no knowledge of God, but, contrariwise, takes away that which we naturally have, and makes us doubt of God and everything else. If therefore anything should come to pass in Nature which does not follow from her laws, it would also be in contravention to the order which God has established in Nature forever through universal natural laws. It would, therefore, be in contravention to God's nature and laws, and, consequently belief in it would throw doubt upon everything, and lead to Atheism.

I think I have now sufficiently established my second point, so that we can again conclude that a miracle, whether in contravention to, or beyond, Nature, is a mere absurdity; and therefore that what is meant in Scripture by a miracle can only be a work of Nature, which surpasses, or is believed to surpass, human comprehension.

IV

I now go on to my third point, and show from Scripture that the decrees and mandates of God, and consequently His providence, are merely the order of Nature—that is, when Scripture describes an event as accomplished by God or God's will, we must understand merely that it was in accordance with the law and order of Nature, not, as most people believe, that Nature had for a season ceased to act, or that her order was temporarily interrupted. But Scripture does not directly teach matters unconnected with its doctrine, wherefore it has no care to explain things by their natural causes, nor to expound matters merely speculative. Wherefore our conclusion must be gathered by inference from those Scriptural narratives which happen to be written more at length and circumstantially than usual. Of these I will cite a few.

In the first book of Samuel (ix. 15, 16), it is related that God revealed to Samuel that He would send Saul to him, yet God did not send Saul to Samuel as people are wont to send one man to another. His "sending" was merely the ordinary course of Nature. Saul was looking for the asses he had lost, and was meditating a return home without them, when, at the suggestion of his servant, he went to the Prophet Samuel, to learn from him where he might find them. From no part of the narrative does it appear that Saul had any command from God to visit Samuel beyond this natural motive.

In Psalm civ. 4, wind and fire are called the angels and ministers of God, and various other passages of the same sort are found in Scripture, clearly showing that the decree, commandment, fiat, and word of God are merely expressions for the action and order of nature.

Thus it is plain that all the events narrated in Scripture came to pass naturally, and are referred directly to God because Scripture, as we have shown, does not aim at explaining things by their natural causes, but only at narrating what appeals to the popular imagination, and doing so in the manner best calculated to excite wonder, and consequently to impress the minds of the masses with devotion. If, therefore, events are found in the Bible which we cannot refer to their causes, nay, which seem entirely to contradict the order of nature, we must not come to a stand, but assuredly believe that whatever did really happen happened naturally. This view is confirmed by the fact that in the case of every miracle there were many attendant circumstances, though these were not always related, especially where the narrative was of a poetic character.

For instance, in order to infect the Egyptians with blains, it was necessary that Moses should scatter ashes in the air (Exod. ix. 10); the locusts also came upon the land of Egypt by a command of God in accordance with nature, namely, by an east wind blowing for a whole day and night; and they departed by a very strong west wind (Exod. x. 14, 19). By a similar Divine mandate the sea opened a way for the Jews (Exod. xiv. 21), namely, by an east wind which blew very strongly all night.

Wherefore we may believe that, although the circumstances attending miracles are not related always or in full detail, yet a miracle was never performed without them. This is confirmed by Exodus xiv. 27, where it is simply stated that "Moses stretched forth his hand, and the waters of the sea returned to their strength in the morning," no mention being made of a wind; but in the song of Moses (Exod. xv. 10) we read, "Thou didst blow with Thy wind (*i.e.* a very strong wind), and the sea covered them." Thus the attendant circumstance is omitted in the history, and the miracle is thereby enhanced.

We may then be absolutely certain that every event which is truly described in Scripture necessarily happened, like everything else, according to natural laws; and if anything is there set down which can be proved in set terms to contravene the order of Nature, or not be deducible therefrom, we must believe it to have been foisted into the sacred writings by irreligious hands; for whatsoever is contrary to Nature is also contrary to reason, and whatsoever is contrary to reason is absurd, and, *ipso facto,* to be rejected.

Scripture makes the general assertion in several passages that nature's course is fixed and unchangeable. (In Ps. cxlviii. 6, for instance, and Jer. xxxi. 35.) The wise man also (in Eccles. i. 10) distinctly teaches that "there is nothing new under the sun," and (in verses 11, 12), illustrating the same idea, he adds that although something occasionally happens which seems new, it is not really new, but "hath been already of old time, which was before us, whereof there is no remembrance, neither shall there be any remembrance of things that are to come with those that come after." Again (in chap. iii. 11), he says, "God hath made everything beautiful in his time," and immediately afterwards adds, "I know that whatsoever God doeth, it shall be for ever; nothing can be put to it, nor anything taken from it."

Now all these texts teach most distinctly that Nature preserves a fixed and unchangeable order and that God in all ages known and unknown has been the same; further, that the laws of Nature are so perfect that nothing can be added thereto nor taken therefrom; and, lastly, that miracles only appear as something new because of man's ignorance.

Such is the express teaching of Scripture. Nowhere does Scripture assert that anything happens which contradicts, or cannot follow from the laws of Nature; and therefore we should not attribute to it such a doctrine.

Concerning God*

Definitions

I. By that which is *self-caused,* I mean that of which the essence involves existence, or that of which the nature is only conceivable as existent.

II. A thing is called *finite* when it can be limited by another thing of the same nature; for instance, a body is called finite, because we always conceive another greater body. So, also, a thought is limited by another thought, but a body is not limited by thought, nor a thought by body.

III. By *substance,* I mean that which is in itself, and is conceived through itself: in other words, that of which a conception can be formed independently of any other conception.

IV. By *attribute,* I mean that which the intellect perceives as constituting the essence of substance.

V. By *mode,* I mean the modifications of substance, or that which exists in, and is perceived through, something other than itself.

VI. By *God,* I mean a being absolutely infinite—that is, a substance consisting in infinite attributes, of which each expresses eternal and infinite essentiality.

VII. That thing is called *free,* which exists solely by the necessity of its own nature, and of which the action is determined by itself alone. On the other hand, that thing is necessary, or rather compelled, which is determined by something external to itself

to a fixed and definite method of existence or action.

VIII. By *eternity,* I mean existence itself, in so far as it is conceived necessarily to follow solely from the definition of that which is eternal.

Explanation.—Existence of this kind is conceived as an eternal truth, like the essence of a thing, and, therefore, cannot be explained by means of duration or time, though duration may be conceived without a beginning or end.

* * * * *

God acts solely by the laws of his own nature, and is not compelled by anyone.

It follows: (1) That there can be no cause which, either extrinsically or intrinsically, besides the perfection of his own nature, moves God to act. (2) That God is the sole free cause. For God alone exists by the sole necessity of his nature and acts by the sole necessity of his nature, wherefore God is the sole free cause.

Others think that God is a free cause, because he can, as they think, bring it about, that those things which we have said follow from his nature—that is, which are in his power, should not come to pass, or should not be produced by him. But this is the same as if they said, that God could bring it about, that it should not follow from the nature of a triangle, that its three interior angles should not be equal to two right angles; of that from a given cause no effect should follow, which is absurd.

Moreover, I will show below, that neither intellect nor will pertain to God's nature. I know that there are many who

---

* Benedict Spinoza, *The Ethics Demonstrated in the Manner of Geometry* (*Ethica Ordine Geometrico Demonstrata*), English trans. by R. H. M. Elwes (London, 1884), from Parts I and II.

think that they can show, that supreme intellect and free will do pertain to God's nature; for they say they know of nothing more perfect, which they can attribute to God, than that which is the highest perfection in ourselves. Further, although they conceive God as actually supremely intelligent, they yet do not believe, that he can bring into existence everything which he actually understands, for they think that they would thus destroy God's power. If, they contend, God had created everything which is in his intellect, he would not be able to create anything more, and this, they think, would clash with God's omnipotence; therefore, they prefer to assert that God is indifferent to all things, and that he creates nothing except that, which he has decided, by some absolute exercise of will, to create. However, I think I have shown sufficiently clearly that from God's supreme power, or infinite nature, all things have necessarily flowed or always follow from the same necessity and in the same way as from the nature of a triangle it follows from eternity and for eternity, that its three interior angles are equal to two right angles.

Further (to say a word here concerning the intellect and the will which we attribute to God), if intellect and will pertain to the eternal essence of God, we must take these words in some significations quite different from those they usually bear. For intellect and will, which should constitute the essence of God, would perforce be as far apart as the poles from the human intellect and will, in fact, would have nothing in common with them but the name; there would be about as much correspondence between the two as there is between the Dog, the heavenly constellation, and a dog, an animal that barks. This I will prove as follows. If intellect belongs to the divine nature, it cannot be in nature, as ours is generally thought to be, either after or simultaneous with the things understood, inasmuch as God is prior to all things by reason of his causality. On the contrary, the truth and formal essence of things is as it is, because it exists as such in the intellect of God.

Wherefore the intellect of God, in so far as it is conceived to constitute God's essence, is, in reality, the cause of things, both of their essence and of their existence. This seems to have been recognized by those who have asserted, that God's intellect, God's will, and God's power, are one and the same. As, therefore, God's intellect is the sole cause of things, namely, both of their essence and existence, it must necessarily differ from them in respect to its essence, and in respect to its existence. For a cause differs from a thing it causes, precisely in the quality which the latter gains from the former.

Now the intellect of God is the cause of both the essence and the existence of our intellect; therefore, the intellect of God in so far as it is conceived to constitute the divine essence, differs from our intellect both in respect to essence and in respect to existence, nor can it in anywise agree therewith save in name, as we said before. The reasoning would be identical in the case of the will, as anyone can easily see.

Note.—Before going any further, I wish here to explain, what we should understand by nature viewed as active (*natura naturans*), and nature viewed as passive (*natura naturata*). I say to explain, or rather call attention to it, for I think that, from what has been said, it is sufficiently clear, that by nature viewed as active we should understand that which is in itself, and is conceived through itself, or those attributes of substance which express eternal and infinite essence, in other words God, in so far as he is considered as a free cause.

By nature viewed as passive (*natura naturata*), I understand all that which follows from the necessity of the nature of God, or of any of the attributes of God, that is, all the modes of the attributes of God, in so far as they are considered as things which are in God, and which without God cannot exist or be conceived.

Appendix

I have now explained the nature and properties of God. I have shown that he necessarily exists, that he is one: that he is, and acts solely by the necessity of his own nature; that he is the free cause of all things, and how he is so; that all things are in God, and so depend on him, that without him they could neither exist nor be conceived; lastly, that all things are predetermined by God, not through his free will or absolute fiat, but from the very nature of God or infinite power. I have further, where occasion offered, taken care to remove the prejudices, which might impede the comprehension of my demonstrations. Yet there still remain not a few misconceptions which may prove very grave hindrances to the understanding of the connection of things, as I have explained it above. I have therefore thought it worth while to bring these misconceptions before the bar of reason.

All such opinions spring from the notion commonly entertained, that all things in nature act as men themselves act, namely, with an end in view. It is accepted as certain, that God himself directs all things to a definite goal (for it is said that God made all things for man, and man that he might worship him). I will, therefore, consider this opinion, asking first, why it obtains general credence, and why all men are naturally so prone to adopt it? secondly, I will point out its falsity; and, lastly, I will show how it has given rise to prejudices about good and bad, right and wrong, praise and blame, order and confusion, beauty and ugliness, and the like.

This is not the place to deduce these misconceptions from the nature of the human mind: it will be sufficient here, if I assume as a starting point, what ought to be universally admitted, namely, that all men are born ignorant of the causes of things, that all have the desire to seek for what is useful to them, and that they are conscious of such desire. Herefrom it follows, first, that men think themselves free inasmuch as they are conscious of their wishes and desires, and never even dream, in their ignorance, of the causes which have disposed them so to wish and desire.

Secondly, that men do all things for an end, namely, for that which is useful to them, which they seek. Thus it comes to pass that they only look for a knowledge of the final causes of events; when these are learned, they are content and have no further doubt. If they cannot learn such causes from external sources, they are compelled to turn to themselves, considering what end would have induced them personally to bring about the given event, and thus they necessarily judge other natures by their own. Further, as they find in themselves and outside themselves many means which assist them not a little in their search for what is useful, for instance, eyes for seeing, teeth for chewing, herbs and animals for yielding food, the sun for giving light, the sea for breeding fish, &c., they come to look on the whole of nature as a means for obtaining such conveniences. Now as they are aware, that they found these conveniences and did not make them, they think they have cause for believing, that some other being has made them for their use. As they look upon things as means, they cannot believe them to be self-created; but, judging from the means which they are accustomed to prepare for themselves, they are bound to believe in some ruler or rulers of the universe endowed with human freedom, who have arranged and adapted everything for human use. They are bound to estimate the nature of such rulers (having no information on the subject) in accordance with their own nature, and therefore they assert that the gods ordained everything for the use of man, in order to bind man to themselves and obtain from him the highest honour.

It also follows that everyone thought out for himself, according to his abilities, a different way of worshipping God, so that God might love him more than his fellows, and direct the whole course of nature for the satisfaction of his blind cupidity and insatiable avarice. Thus prejudice developed into superstitition, and took deep root in the human mind; and for this reason everyone strove most zealously to understand and explain the final causes of things; but in their endeavour to show that nature does nothing in vain, *i.e.,* nothing which is useless to man, they only seem to have demonstrated that nature, the gods, and men are all alike mad. Consider, I pray you, the result: among the many helps of nature they were bound to find some hindrances, such as storms, earthquakes, diseases, &c.: so they declared that such things happen, because the gods are angry at some wrong done them by men, or at some fault committed in their worship. Experience day by day protested and showed by infinite examples, that good and evil fortunes fall to the lot of pious and impious alike; still they would not abandon their inveterate prejudice, for it was more easy for them to class such contradictions among other unknown things of whose use they were ignorant, and thus to retain their actual and innate condition of ignorance, than to destroy the whole fabric of their reasoning and start afresh. They therefore laid down as an axiom, that God's judgments far transcend human understanding. Such a doctrine might well have sufficed to conceal the truth from the human race for all eternity, if mathematics had not furnished another standard of verity in considering solely the essence and properties of figures without regard to their final causes.

Many argue in this way: If all things follow necessarily from the absolutely perfect nature of God, why are there so many imperfections in nature? such, for instance, as things corrupt to the point of putridity, loathsome deformity, confusion, evil, sin, &c. But these reasoners are, as I have said, easily confuted, for the perfection of things is to be reckoned only from their own nature and power; things are not more or less perfect, according as they delight or offend human senses, or according as they are serviceable or repugnant to mankind. To those who ask why God did not so create all men, that they should be governed only by reason, I give no answer but this: because matter was not lacking to him for the creation of every degree of perfection from highest to lowest; or, more strictly, because the laws of his nature are so vast, as to suffice for the production of everything conceivable by an infinite intelligence.

Such are the misconceptions I have undertaken to note; if there are any more of the same sort, everyone may easily dissipate them for himself with the aid of a little reflection.

The Life of Reason*

I

Most persons who have written about the emotions and human conduct seem to discuss, not the natural things which follow the common laws of nature, but things which are outside her. They seem indeed to consider man in nature as a kingdom within a kingdom. For they believe that man disturbs rather than follows her order; that he is altogether self-determined. They then proceed to attribute the cause of human weakness and changeableness, not to the common power of nature, but to some vice of human nature, which they therefore bewail, laugh at, mock, or, as is more generally the case, detest; whilst he who knows how to revile most eloquently or subtilely the weakness of the mind is looked upon as a seer.

To such as these it will doubtless seem a marvellous thing for me to endeavour to treat by a geometrical method the vices and follies of men, and to desire by a sure method to demonstrate those things which these peo-

---

* Benedict Spinoza, *The Ethics, Demonstrated in the Manner of Geometry,* English translation by W. H. White and A. M. Stirling (London, Oxford University Press, 1927), from Parts III, IV, V. Throughout the more familiar term "emotion" has been substituted for "affect." (Ed.).

ple cry out against as being opposed to reason, or as being vanities, absurdities, and monstrosities. The following is my reason for so doing. Nothing happens in nature which can be attributed to any vice of nature, for she is always the same and everywhere one. Her virtue is the same, and her power of acting; that is to say, her laws and rules, according to which all things are and are changed from form to form, are everywhere and always the same; so that there must also be one and the same method of understanding the nature of all things whatsoever, that is to say, by the universal laws and rules of nature.

The emotions, therefore, of hatred, anger, envy, considered in themselves, follow from the same necessity and virtue of nature as other individual things; they have therefore certain causes through which they are to be understood, and certain properties which are just as worthy of being known as the properties of any other thing in the contemplation alone of which we delight. I shall, therefore, pursue the same method in considering the nature and strength of the emotions and the power of the mind over them which I pursued in our previous discussion of God and the mind, and I shall consider human actions and appetites just as if I were considering lines, planes, or bodies.

This will be better understood from what has been said [above], that is to say, that the mind and the body are one and the same thing, conceived at one time under the attribute of thought, and at another under that of extension. For this reason, the order or concatenation of things is one, whether nature be conceived under this or under that attribute, and consequently the order of the actions and passions of our body is coincident in nature with the order of the actions and passions of the mind.

Although these things are so, and no ground for doubting remains, I scarcely believe, nevertheless, that, without a proof derived from experience, men will be induced calmly to weigh what has been said, so firmly are they persuaded that, solely at the bidding of the mind, the body moves or rests, and

does a number of things which depend upon the will of the mind alone, and upon the power of thought. For what the body can do no one has hitherto determined, that is to say, experience has taught no one hitherto what the body, without being determined by the mind, can do and what it cannot do from the laws of nature alone, in so far as nature is considered merely as corporeal. For no one as yet has understood the structure of the body so accurately as to be able to explain all its functions, not to mention the fact that many things are observed in brutes which far surpass human sagacity, and that sleepwalkers in their sleep do very many things which they dare not do when awake; all this showing that the body itself can do many things from the laws of its own nature alone at which the mind belonging to that body is amazed.

So that it follows that when men say that this or that action of the body springs from the mind which has command over the body, they do not know what they say, and they do nothing but confess with pretentious words that they know nothing about the cause of the action, and see nothing in it to wonder at. They say it is in their experience that the mind alone has power both to speak and be silent, and to do many other things which they therefore think to be dependent on a decree of the mind. But I ask them if experience does not also teach that if the body be sluggish the mind at the same time is not fit for thinking? When the body is asleep, the mind slumbers with it, and has not the power to think, as it has when the body is awake. . . . Thus the infant believes that it is by free will that it seeks the breast; the angry boy believes that by free will he wishes vengeance; the timid man thinks it is with free will he seeks flight; the drunkard believes that by a free command of his mind he speaks the things which when sober he wishes he had left unsaid. Thus the madman, the chatterer, the boy, and others of the same kind, all believe that they speak by a free command of the mind, whilst, in truth, they have no power to restrain the impulse which they have to speak, so that experience itself, no less than reason, clearly teaches that men believe themselves to be free simply because they are conscious of their own actions but know nothing of the causes by which they are determined; it teaches, too, that the decrees of the mind are nothing but the appetites themselves, which differ, therefore, according to the different temper of the body.

All this plainly shows that the decision of the mind, the appetite, and a determined condition of the body are coincident in nature, or rather that they are one and the same thing, which, when it is considered under the attribute of thought and manifested by that, is called a decision, and when it is considered under the attribute of extension and is deduced from the laws of motion and rest, is called a determined condition.

* * * * *

With regard to good and evil, these terms indicate nothing positive in things considered in themselves, nor are they anything else than modes of thought, or notions which we form from the comparison of one thing with another. For one and the same thing may at the same time be both good and evil or indifferent. Music, for example, is good to a melancholy person, bad to one mourning, while to a deaf man it is neither good nor bad. But although these things are so, we must retain these words. For since we desire to form for ourselves an idea of man upon which we may look as a model of human nature, it will be of service to us to retain these expressions in the sense I have mentioned. By *good,* therefore, I understand in the following pages everything which we are certain is a means by which we may approach nearer and nearer to the model of human nature we set before us. By *evil,* on the contrary, I understand everything which we are certain hinders us from reaching that model. Again, I shall call men more or less perfect or imperfect in so far as they approach more or less nearly to this same model. For it is to be carefully observed, that when I say

that an individual passes from a less to a greater perfection and *vice versa,* I do not understand that from one essence or form he is changed into another (for a horse, for instance, would be as much destroyed if it were changed into a man as if it were changed into an insect), but rather we conceive that his power of action, in so far as it is understood by his own nature, is increased or diminished. Finally, by perfection generally, I understand as I have said, reality; that is to say, the essence of any object in so far as it exists and acts in a certain manner, no regard being paid to its duration. For no individual thing can be said to be more perfect because for a longer time it has persevered in existence; inasmuch as the duration of things cannot be determined by their essence, the essence of things involving no fixed or determined period of existence; any object, whether it be more or less perfect, always being able to persevere in existence with the same force as that with which it commenced existence. All things, therefore, are equal in this respect.

II

Since reason demands nothing which is opposed to nature, it demands, therefore, that every person should love himself, should seek his own profit—what is truly profitable to him—should desire everything that really leads man to greater perfection, and absolutely that every one should endeavour, as far as in him lies, to preserve his own being. This is all true as necessarily as that the whole is greater than its part.

Again, since virtue means nothing but acting according to the laws of our own nature, and since no one endeavours to preserve his being except in accordance with the laws of his own nature, it follows: *Firstly,* That the foundation of virtue is that endeavour itself to preserve our own being, and that happiness consists in this— that a man can preserve his own being. *Secondly,* It follows that virtue is to be desired for its own sake, nor is there anything more excellent or more useful to us than virtue, for the sake of which virtue ought to be desired. *Thirdly,* It follows that all persons who kill themselves are impotent in mind, and have been thoroughly overcome by external causes opposed to their nature.

* * * * *

My observations concerning the right way of life have not been arranged so that they could be seen at a glance, but have been demonstrated as I could more easily deduce one from another. I have determined, therefore, here to collect them, and reduce them under principal heads.*

1. All our efforts or desires follow from the necessity of our nature in such a manner that they can be understood either through it alone as their proximate cause, or in so far as we are a part of nature, which part cannot be adequately conceived through itself and without the other individuals.

2. The desires which follow from our nature in such a manner that they can be understood through it alone, are those which are related to the mind, in so far as it is conceived to consist of adequate ideas. The remaining desires are not related to the mind, except in so far as it conceives things inadequately; [their] power and increase cannot be determined by human power, but by the power of objects which are without us. The first kind of desires, therefore, are properly called actions, but the latter passions; for the first always indicate our power, and the latter, on the contrary, indicate our impotence and imperfect knowledge.

3. It is therefore most profitable to us in life to make perfect the intellect or reason as far as possible, and in this one thing consists the highest happiness or blessedness of man; for blessedness is nothing but the peace of mind which springs from the intuitive knowledge of God, and to perfect the intellect is nothing but to understand God, together with the attributes and actions of God, which flow from the necessity of His nature. The final aim, therefore, of a man is guided by reason, that is to say, the chief

desire by which he strives to govern all his other desires, is that by which he is led adequately to conceive himself and all things which can be conceived by his intelligence.

4. There is no rational life therefore, without intelligence, and things are good only in so far as they assist man to enjoy that life of the mind which is determined by intelligence. Those things alone, on the other hand, we call evil which hinder man from perfecting his reason and enjoying a rational life.

5. But because all those things of which man is the efficient cause are necessarily good, it follows that no evil can happen to man except from external causes, that is to say, except in so far as he is a part of the whole of nature, whose laws human nature is compelled to obey—compelled also to accommodate himself to this whole of nature in almost an infinite number of ways.

6. It is impossible that a man should not be a part of nature and follow her common order; but if he be placed amongst individuals who agree with his nature, his power of action will by that very fact be assisted and supported. But if, on the contrary, he be placed amongst individuals who do not in the least agree with his nature, he will scarcely be able without great change on his part to accommodate himself to them.

7. Nothing, therefore, can agree better with the nature of any object than other individuals of the same kind, and so (see 6) there is nothing more profitable to man for the preservation of his being and the enjoyment of a rational life than a man who is guided by reason. Again, since there is no single thing we know which is more excellent than a man who is guided by reason, it follows that there is nothing by which a person can better show how much skill and talent he possesses than by so educating men that at last they will live under the direct authority of reason.

8. In so far as men are carried away by envy or any emotion of hatred towards one another, so far are they contrary to one another, and consequently so much the more are they to be feared, as they have more power than other individuals of nature.

---

* The points listed by Spinoza have been considerably shortened. [Ed.].

9. Minds, nevertheless, are not conquered by arms, but by love and generosity.

10. Above all things is it profitable to men to form communities and to unite themselves to one another by bonds which may make all of them as one man; and absolutely, it is profitable for them to do whatever may tend to strengthen their friendships.

11. Although, therefore, men generally determine everything by their pleasure, many more advantages than disadvantages arise from their common union. It is better, therefore, to endure with equanimity the injuries inflicted by them, and to apply our minds to those things which subserve concord and the establishment of friendship.

The man who has properly understood that everything follows from the necessity of the divine nature, and comes to pass according to the eternal laws and rules of nature, will in truth discover nothing which is worthy of hatred, laughter, or contempt, nor will he pity any one, but, so far as human virtue is able, he will endeavour to *do well,* as we say, and to *rejoice.* We must add also, that a man who is easily touched by the emotion of pity, and is moved by the misery or tears of another, often does something of which he afterward repents, both because from an emotion we do nothing which we certainly know to be good, and also because we are so easily deceived by false tears. But this I say expressly of the man who lives according to the guidance of reason. For he who is moved neither by reason nor pity to be of any service to others is properly called inhuman; for he seems to be unlike a man.*

12. But human power is very limited, and is infinitely surpassed by the power of external causes, so that we do not possess an absolute power to adapt to our service the things which are without us. Nevertheless we shall bear with equanimity those things which happen to us contrary to what a consideration of our own profit demands, if we are conscious that we have performed our

---

* This paragraph is not in the order of the original. There it is a part of Book IV, Prop. L. [Ed.]

duty, that the power we have could not reach so far as to enable us to avoid those things, and that we are a part of the whole of nature, whose order we follow. If we clearly and distinctly understand this, the part of us which is determined by intelligence, that is to say, the better part of us, will be entirely satisfied therewith, and in that satisfaction will endeavour to persevere; for, in so far as we understand, we cannot desire anything excepting what is necessary, nor absolutely, can we be satisfied with anything but the truth. Therefore in so far as we understand these things properly will the efforts of the better part of us agree with the order of the whole of nature.

III

It remains for me now to show what service to our own lives a knowledge of this doctrine is. This we shall easily understand from the remarks which follow. Notice—

1. It is of service in so far as it teaches us that we do everything by the will of God alone, and that we are partakers of the divine nature in proportion as our actions become more and more perfect and we more and more understand God. This doctrine, therefore, besides giving repose in every way to the soul, has also this advantage, that it teaches us in what our highest happiness or blessedness consists, namely, in the knowledge of God alone, by which we are drawn to do those things only which love and piety persuade. Hence we clearly see how greatly those stray from the true estimation of virtue who expect to be distinguished by God with the highest rewards for virtue and the noblest actions as if for the completest servitude, just as if virtue itself and the service of God were not happiness itself and the highest liberty.

2. It is of service to us in so far as it teaches us how we ought to behave with regard to the things of fortune, or those which are not in our power, that is to say, which do not follow from our own nature; for it teaches us with equal mind to wait for and bear each form of fortune, because we know that all things follow from the eternal

decree of God, according to that same necessity by which it follows from the essence of a triangle that its three angles are equal to two right angles.

3. This doctrine contributes to the welfare of our social existence, since it teaches us to hate no one, to despise no one, to mock no one, to be angry with no one, and to envy no one. It teaches every one, moreover, to be content with his own, and to be helpful to his neighbour, not from any womanish pity, from partiality, or superstition, but by the guidance of reason alone, according to the demand of time and circumstance.

4. This doctrine contributes not a little to the advantage of common society, in so far as it teaches us by what means citizens are to be governed and led; not in order that they may be slaves, but that they may freely do those things which are best.

IV

I have finished everything I wished to explain concerning the power of the mind over the emotions and concerning its liberty. From what has been said we see what is the strength of the wise man, and how much he surpasses the ignorant who is driven forward by lust alone. For the ignorant man is not only agitated by external causes in many ways, and never enjoys true peace of soul, but lives also ignorant, as it were, both of God and of things, and as soon as he ceases to suffer ceases also to be. On the other hand, the wise man, in so far as he is considered as such, is scarcely ever moved in his mind, but, being conscious by a certain eternal necessity of himself, of God, and of things, never ceases to be, and always enjoys true peace of soul. If the way which, as I have shown, leads hither seems very difficult, it can nevertheless be found. It must indeed be difficult since it is so seldom discovered; for if salvation lay ready to hand and could be discovered without great labor, how could it be possible that it should be neglected almost by everybody? But all excellent things are as difficult as they are rare.

The Rationalist As Idealist: Plato

In the history of philosophy no figure is so definitely identified with idealism as Plato, and in no single book is there so popular and influential a statement of a man's philosophy as in Plato's *Republic*. Spinoza's *Ethics* is one of the great books in philosophy, but it is not a book that attracts the ordinary reader. Even for the student of philosophy it is not an easy book to read. In the *Republic,* on the other hand, there is not only the same remarkable synthesis of all the major concerns of philosophy, but one also finds philosophy presented in such casual and appealing fashion that almost without realizing it he is considering the most basic problems of ethics, epistemology, and metaphysics or dealing with aspects of psychology, sociology, and government that have baffled the experts for centuries. No work in philosophy has exerted greater influence upon human thought than Plato's *Republic,* and with the possible exception of Aristotle, no other philosopher has had a comparable influence.

It is true that in our own day there have been many attacks upon Plato, both political and philosophical. His obvious preference for aristocracy and his unhesitating condemnation of democractic theory and practices are not popular. His skillful advocacy of idealism, his insistence that rationalism is the only philosophy that can make any sense of human experience—such convictions do not endear him to an age in which empiricism and positivism of various sorts are widely accepted. But in the philosophy of Plato our age still finds one of the most influential statements of idealism from the point of view of the rationalist and also a most penetrating criticism of democracy by a philosopher who sees in an aristocracy of intellect the only sure path to good government.

Today a philosopher is generally a specialist in a field of thought distinct from the various sciences, but this was not the case for Plato. For him philosophy was the study of reality in all its aspects, an insight into the whole of truth; even more, philosophy was a way of life, a serious and satisfying search for meaning in human experience. Far from being a mere indulgence of intellectual curiosity, it was the endeavor to fashion one's life intelligently in the broad setting of the universe itself. Philosophy thus calls on the resources of the entire personality. The philosopher must possess not only keenness of intellect, but courage to face the truth, moral integrity, and greatness of spirit. Plato found in Socrates the embodiment of the ideal philosopher, and his whole life was changed by his close association with Socrates.

Plato was born in Athens in 427 B.C. Pericles, the great Athenian democratic leader, had been dead two years, and the dreary Peloponnesian war with Sparta had just begun. Athens itself at this time was little more than an armed camp. Plato grew to manhood amid the dangers, the turmoil, and the hatred bred by war. Under this strain the Athenian democracy began to lose both vision and vitality; its leaders did little but quarrel and compromise. Plato, a member of one of the most distinguished families of the city, came to regard democracy as only another name for mediocrity and corruption. Experience did not change his mind.

There is good reason to believe that, until Socrates was put to death in 399 B.C., Plato's chief interests and ambitions were political. But the tragic death of Socrates at the hands of his peers in Athens had a powerful effect upon his ablest disciple. It left Plato thoroughly skeptical of democracy as he knew it; and it led him to the continued search for a society in which the rule of the wisest and the best might replace the rule of the masses, which seemed to him to condemn democracy to mediocrity. After some twelve years of travel following Socrates' death, Plato returned to Athens in 387 B.C. to open his own school of philosophy. Its name, the Academy, was derived from the suburb northwest of Athens in which it was located. This school became the center of the intellectual world of that day, and during forty years as head of the Academy, Plato established himself as the outstanding figure in Western philosophy. After a life devoted largely to scholarly endeavor, in the company of the ablest men of his day, he died in 346 B.C. in his eighty-first year. For another nine hundred years the Academy continued its existence until in A.D. 529 its funds were embezzled by Justinian. Undoubtedly one of the major factors in the remarkable preservation of Plato's philosophical works was this long life of the school he founded.

During his early years at the Academy Plato produced the more popular books that are still widely known and read: the *Apology,* the *Crito,* and the *Euthyphro* (the early Socratic dialogues); then the *Republic,* the *Symposium,* the *Phaedo* and the *Meno.* In these works there is a strong emphasis upon the separation of the world of "ideas" and the world of sense experience, the world of universals and the world of concrete, individual things. In the works of his more mature years, however, Plato begins to show more interest in the necessary connection between the two worlds and to revise somewhat his earlier treatment of the physical and material as only a hindrance to the spiritual. These later treatises are less popular, more dialectical and technical in character; they are also increasingly religious in tone. The *Theaetetus, Parmenides, Sophist, Statesman, Philibus, Timaeus* and *The Laws* belong here.

While no aspect of his thought is unrelated to his position as a whole, it is not difficult to divide Plato's philosophy into two large sections—his theory of reality and his theory of life, his metaphysics and his ethics. And whichever of these one considers, it is easy to see there the essential union of rationalism and idealism. Plato is most famous perhaps for his so-called "theory of ideas"—this is the focal point in his philosophy toward which all problems converge and from which all solutions arise. But the term "ideas" is a misleading one; its connotation is much too subjectivistic. Plato's idealism rests upon a theory of universals. It is at once apparent, Plato points out, that man lives in two worlds—a world of sense experience, of particular things, of change and opinion, and a world of rational thought, of general principles, of permanence. And, he goes on to argue, knowledge and understanding are to be found not in the particular thing but only in the universal. Indeed the particular things are *real* only insofar as they participate in the universals.

To the ordinary reader Plato's point of view seems at first just backwards One has the instinctive feeling that Plato has taken the real thing and explained it by the idea. Universals like mankind and goodness and beauty seem to be only generalizations, names for groups of things or experiences which they describe. But a closer look does provide support for Plato. Take the work of the scientist for example. Is a geologist interested in the particular rocks that he collects, or is he seeking something that he finds in them all? When studying each individual rock, he is actually trying to find out something about rocks in general, something universal about rocks. It is not the particular facts of immediate experience that concern him, but something that reason discovers or recognizes in all the particular objects. So also in a number of specific events, the astronomer or physicist seeks a general principle—a law that explains them all. For Plato, the laws that the scientist finds and formulates are the universals that give meaning to the particular experiences. Such universals are neither mental nor physical. They do not depend for their reality upon being thought; yet they are abstract and changeless, not concrete or material. These universals are not "ideas" in the usual sense, nor are they "things." They belong for Plato to a new category of reality, which in the usual translations is called "the world of ideas" but which must be understood in the more adequate fashion suggested above.

Now Plato like all rationalists was greatly attracted by mathematics. Mathematical knowledge, he felt, was indispensible for the philosopher. Above the Academy that he founded in Athens there is reputed to have been the admonition: "Let no one who is ignorant of mathematics enter here." For the mathematician more than any other scientist seems directly concerned with those rational principles that are enduring—those that we must grasp in order to understand the physical and material things in our experience, rational principles that alone lead us to truth and to reality. As Spinoza so frequently points out, given any triangle, the sum of its angles must equal two right angles. Indeed, this is one of the things that makes it a triangle—the very essence of triangularity—something more real and enduring than any particular triangle. So for Plato as for Spinoza, to be rational whether in science, in mathematics, or in philosophy, means to move away from the particulars to the universals, from sense experience to "idea," from the changing or temporal to the enduring.

Plato, moreover, finds this to be just as true of the moral life and of our experience of art as it is of mathematics and science. We respect and admire the prophet or the statesman as contrasted with the politician or advocate of expediency because the former look to universal principles, to enduring ideals, while the latter are concerned only with immediate results or particular interests. Moral insight rests upon the vision of ideals that are never quite realized in actual life, but which somehow give meaning and purpose to the changing and conflicting daily conduct of men and women. The great prophet points men to religious principles by which our actual achievements are to be measured and as a rule found wanting. The Sophists in the age of Socrates and Plato, like the relativists of every age, argued that moral standards are only social conventions, the interests of the more powerful projected into law and accepted social behavior. Plato, like Socrates, is forthright in his denunciation of such a doctrine. Accept it and the real meaning of what is good and right has been destroyed.

In several places one finds Plato presenting this philosophy in popular fashion. His "Allegory of the Cave" in the seventh book of the *Republic* is one of the most famous. The theory of the divided line, which almost immediately precedes it, provides a less poetic and more carefully organized statement. In a well-known passage in the *Meno* Plato has Socrates show by his discussion with a slave boy that rational insight is a possession of the human mind, in some sense it is inborn—or to use Kant's term, *a priori* (prior to all experience). There is nothing in experience that can explain man's ability to grasp the universal and use it to give meaning to life and understanding to science. This is the kernel of Plato's rationalism, namely that there is a nonempirical element in all knowledge which is supplied by the human mind. And upon this he builds his "idealism": his conviction that the real world is the world of universals, a world of rational order, of moral principle, of esthetic form—a world from which our ordinary world of sense experience, of social behavior, of individual striving receives its meaning, its purpose, its very being or *reality*.

Brief selections cannot do justice to the range and complexity of Plato's thought. This is especially true of the *Republic,* a work of such essential unity that no single selection is satisfactory. Fortunately, however, even the beginning student can read all but the more technical of Plato's dialogues with interest and profit and these works are now easily available in inexpensive editions. It is hoped that the selections which follow will stimulate the kind of interest in Plato that will lead the serious student first to the *Republic* and then to other of the Platonic dialogues. The *Phaedo* contains what is perhaps the clearest statement of Plato's early idealism; included here with the "Allegory of the Cave" is a generous selection from the *Phaedo*.

The Allegory of the Cave*

Socrates Speaks:

And now, I said, let me show in a parable how far our nature is enlightened or unenlightened: Imagine mankind living in an underground cave, which has a mouth open towards the light and reaching all along the cave. Here they have been from their childhood, and have their legs and necks chained so that they cannot move, and can only see before them, being prevented by the chains from turning round their heads. Above and behind them a fire is blazing at a distance, and between the fire and the prisoners there is a raised walk, and you will see, if you look, a low wall built along the walk, like the screen which marionette players have in front of them, over which they show the puppets.

I see, [Glaucon replied].

And see, I said, men are passing along the wall carrying all sorts of vessels, and statues and figures of animals made of wood and stone and various materials, which appear over the wall. Some of them are talking, others silent.

You have shown me a strange image, and they are strange prisoners.

Like ourselves, I replied; and they see only their own shadows, or the shadows of one another, which the fire throws on the opposite wall of the cave?

True, he said; how could they see anything but the shadows if they were never allowed to move their heads?

And of the objects which are being carried in like manner they would only see the shadows?

Yes, he said.

And if they were able to converse with one another, would they not suppose that they were naming what was actually before them?

Very true.

And suppose further that the prison had an echo which came from the other side, would they not be sure to fancy when one of the passers-by spoke that the voice which they heard came from the passing shadow?

Without question.

To them, I said, the truth would be literally nothing but the shadows of the images.

That is certain.

And now look again, and see what will naturally follow if the prisoners are released and disabused of their error. At first, when any of them is liberated and compelled suddenly to stand up and turn his neck round and walk and look towards the light, he will suffer sharp pains; the glare will distress him, and he will be unable to see the realities of which in his former state he had seen the shadows; and then conceive some one saying to him, that what he saw before was an illusion, but that now, when he is approaching nearer to being and his eye is turned towards more real existence, he has a clearer vision—what will be his reply? And you may further imagine that his instructor is pointing to the objects as they pass and requiring him to name them,—will he not be perplexed? Will he not fancy that the shadows which he formerly saw are truer than the objects which are now shown to him?

Far truer.

And if he is compelled to look straight at the light, will he not have a pain in his eyes which will make him turn away to take refuge in the objects of vision which he can see, and which he will conceive to be in reality clearer than the things which are now being shown to him?

True.

And suppose once more, that he is reluctantly dragged up a steep and rugged ascent, and held fast until he is forced into the

---

*Plato, *The Republic,* Book VII. The Benjamin Jowett translation (Oxford, The Clarendon Press, 3rd edition, 1892, with slight revision.)

presence of the sun himself, is he not likely to be pained and irritated? When he approaches the light his eyes will be dazzled, and he will not be able to see anything at all of what are now called realities.

Not all in a moment.

He will have to grow accustomed to the sight of the upper world. And first he will see the shadows best, next the reflections of men and other objects in the water, and then the objects themselves; then he will gaze upon the light of the moon and the stars and the spangled heaven; and he will see the sky and the stars by night better than the sun or the light of the sun by day?

Certainly.

Last of all he will be able to see the sun, and not mere reflections of it in the water, but he will see it in his own proper place, and not in another; and he will contemplate it as it is.

Certainly.

He will then proceed to argue that this is what gives the season and the years, and is the guardian of all that is in the visible world, and in a certain way the cause of all things which he and his fellows have been accustomed to behold?

Clearly, he said, he would first see the sun and then reason about it.

And when he remembered his old habitation, and the wisdom of the cave and his fellow-prisoners, do you not suppose that he would felicitate himself on the change, and pity them?

Certainly, he would.

And if they were in the habit of conferring honours among themselves on those who were quickest to observe the passing shadows and to remark which of them went before, and which followed after, and which were together; and who were therefore best able to draw conclusions as to the future, do you think that he would care for such honours and glories, or envy the possessors of them? Would he not say with Homer,

"Better to be the poor servant of a poor master,"

and to endure anything, rather than think as they do and live after their manner?

Yes, he said, I think that he would rather suffer anything than entertain these false notions and live in this miserable manner.

Imagine once more, I said, such a one coming suddenly out of the sun to be replaced in his old situation; would he not be certain to have his eyes full of darkness?

To be sure, he said.

And if there were a contest, and he had to compete in measuring the shadows with the prisoners who had never moved out of the cave, while his sight was still weak, and before his eyes had become steady (and the time which would be needed to acquire this new habit of sight might be very considerable) would he not be ridiculous? Men would say of him that up he went and down he came without his eyes; and that it was better not even to think of ascending; and if any one tried to loose another and lead him up to the light, let them only catch the offender, and they would put him to death.

No question.

This entire allegory, I said, you may now append, dear Glaucon, to the previous argument; the prison-house is the world of sight, the light of the fire is the sun, and you will not misapprehend me if you interpret the journey upwards to be the ascent of the soul into the intellectual world according to my poor belief, which, at your desire, I have expressed—whether rightly or wrongly God knows. But, whether true or false, my opinion is that in the world of knowledge the idea of good appears last of all, and is seen only with an effort; and, when seen, is also inferred to be the universal author of all things beautiful and right, parent of light and of the lord of light in this visible world, and the immediate source of reason and truth in the intellectual; and that this is the power upon which he who would act rationally either in public or private life must have his eye fixed.

I agree, he said, as far as I am able to understand you.

Moreover, I said, you must not wonder that those who attain to this beatific vision are unwilling to descend to human affairs; for their souls are ever hastening into the upper world where they desire to dwell; which desire of theirs is very natural, if our allegory may be trusted.

Yes, very natural.

And is there anything surprising in one who passes from divine contemplations to the evil state of man, behaving himself in a ridiculous manner; if, while his eyes are blinking and before he has become accustomed to the surrounding darkness, he is compelled to fight in courts of law, or in other places, about the images or the shadows of images of justice, and is endeavouring to meet the conceptions of those who have never yet seen absolute justice?

Anything but surprising.

Any one who has common sense will remember that the bewilderments of the eyes are of two kinds, and arise from two causes, either from coming out of the light or from going into the light, which is true of the mind's eye, quite as much as of the bodily eye; and he who remembers this when he sees any one whose vision is perplexed and weak, will not be too ready to laugh; he will first ask whether that soul of man has come out of the brighter life, and is unable to see because unaccustomed to the dark, or having turned from darkness to the day is dazzled by excess of light. And he will count the one happy in his condition and state of being, and he will pity the other; or, if he have a mind to laugh at the soul which comes from below into the light, there will be more reason in this than in the laugh which greets him who returns from above out of the light into the cave.

That is a very just distinction.

But then, if I am right, certain professors of education must be wrong when they say that they can put a knowledge into the soul which was not there before, like sight into blind eyes.

They undoubtedly say this.

Whereas, our argument shows that the power and capacity of learning exists in the soul already; and that just as the eye was unable to turn from darkness to light without the whole body, so too the instrument of knowledge can only by the movement of the whole soul be turned from the world of becoming into that of being, and learn by degrees to endure the sight of being, and of the brightest and best of being, or in other words, of the good.

The Wisdom of the True Philosopher*

Persons of the Dialogue

PHAEDO, the narrator of the dialogue, one of the group of Socrates' friends who spent the last day in prison with him discussing the immortality of the soul.
SOCRATES
SIMMIAS and CEBES, friends of Socrates who take part in the discussion included here.

ECHECRATES, to whom the scene is described.
Scene: the Prison of Socrates
Time: 399 B.C.

I

Socrates speaks:

What shall we say of the actual acquirement of knowledge?—is the body, if invited to share in the enquiry, a hinderer or a helper? I mean to say, have sight and hearing any truth in them? Are they not, as the poets are always telling us, inaccurate witnesses? and yet, if even they are inaccurate and in-

---

* Plato, *Phaedo*. The Benjamin Jowett translation. (Oxford, The Clarendon Press, 3rd edition, 1892.)

distinct, what is to be said of the other senses? —for you will allow that they are the best of them?

Certainly, [Simmias] replied.

Then when does the soul attain truth? —for in attempting to consider anything in company with the body she is obviously deceived.

True.

Then must not true existence be revealed to her in thought, if at all?

Yes.

And thought is best when the mind is gathered into herself and none of these things trouble her—neither sounds nor sights nor pain nor any pleasure,—when she takes leave of the body, and has as little as possible to do with it, when she has no bodily sense or desire, but is aspiring after true being?

Certainly.

And in this the philosopher dishonours the body; his soul runs away from his body and desires to be alone and by herself?

That is true.

Well, but there is another thing, Simmias. Is there or is there not an absolute justice?

Assuredly there is.

And an absolute beauty and absolute good.

Of course.

But did you ever behold any of them with your eyes?

Certainly not.

Or did you ever reach them with any other bodily sense?—and I speak not of these alone, but of absolute greatness, and health, and strength, and of the essence or true nature of everything. Has the reality of them ever been perceived by you through the bodily organs? or rather, is not the nearest approach to the knowledge of their several natures made by him who so orders his intellectual vision as to have the most exact conception of the essence of each thing which he considers.

Certainly.

And he attains to the purest knowledge of them who goes to each with the mind alone, not introducing or intruding in the act of thought, sight or any other sense together with reason, but with the very light of the mind in her own clearness searches into the very truth of each; he who has got rid, as far as he can, of eyes and ears and, so to speak, of the whole body, these being in his opinion distracting elements which when they infect the soul hinder her from acquiring truth and knowledge—who, if not he, is likely to attain to the knowledge of true being?

What you say has a wonderful truth in it, Socrates, replied Simmias.

And when real philosophers consider all these things, will they not be led to make a reflection which they will express in words something like the following? "Have we not found," they will say, "a path of thought which seems to bring us and our arguments to the conclusion, that while we are in the body, and while the soul is infected with the evils of the body, our desire will not be satisfied, and our desire is of the truth? For the body is a source of endless trouble to us by reason of the mere requirement of food; and is liable also to diseases which overtake and impede us in the search after true being: it fills us full of loves, and lusts, and fears, and fancies of all kinds, and endless foolery, and in fact, as men say, takes away from us the power of thinking at all. Whence come wars, and fightings, and factions? whence but from the body and the lusts of the body? Wars are occasioned by the love of money, and money has to be acquired for the sake and service of the body; and by reason of all these impediments we have no time to give to philosophy; and, last and worst of all, even if we are at leisure and betake ourselves to some speculation, the body is always breaking in upon us, causing turmoil and confusion in our enquiries, and so amazing us that we are prevented from seeing the truth. It has been proved to us by experience that if we would have pure knowledge of anything we must be quit of the body—the soul in herself must behold things in themselves; and then we shall attain the wisdom which we desire, and of which we say that we are lovers; not while we live, but after death; for if while in company with the body, the soul cannot have pure knowledge, one of two things follows—either knowledge is not to be attained at all, or, if at all, after death. For then, and not till then, the soul will be parted from the body and exist in herself alone. In this present life, I reckon that we make the nearest approach to knowledge when we have the least possible intercourse or communion with the body, and are not surfeited with the bodily nature, but keep ourselves pure until the hour when God himself is pleased to release us. And thus having got rid of the foolishness of the body we shall be pure and hold converse with the pure, and know of ourselves the clear light everywhere, which is no other than the light of truth. For the impure are not permitted to approach the pure." These are the sort of words, Simmias, which the true lovers of knowledge cannot help saying to one another, and thinking. You would agree; would you not?

Undoubtedly, Socrates.

But, O my friend, if this be true, there is great reason to hope that, going whither I go, when I have come to the end of my journey, I shall attain that which has been the pursuit of my life. And therefore I go on my way rejoicing, and not I only, but every other man who believes that his mind has been made ready and that he is in a manner purified.

II

Cebes added: Your favourite doctrine, Socrates, that knowledge is simply recollection, if true, also necessarily implies a previous time in which we have learned that which we now recollect. But this would be impossible unless our soul had been in some place before existing in the form of man; here then is another proof of the soul's immortality.

But tell me, Cebes, said Simmias, interposing, what arguments are urged in favour of this doctrine of recollection. I am not very sure at the moment that I remember them.

One excellent proof, said Cebes, is afforded by questions. If you put a question to a person in a right way, he will give a true answer of himself, but how could he do this

unless there were knowledge and right reason already in him? And this is most clearly shown when he is taken to a diagram or to anything of that sort.

But if, said Socrates, you are still incredulous, Simmias, I would ask you whether you may not agree with me when you look at the matter in another way;—I mean, if you are still incredulous as to whether knowledge is recollection?

Incredulous I am not, said Simmias; but I want to have this doctrine of recollection brought to my own recollection, and, from what Cebes has said, I am beginning to recollect and be convinced; but I should still like to hear what you were going to say.

This is what I would say, he replied:— We should agree, if I am not mistaken, that what a man recollects he must have known at some previous time.

Very true.

And what is the nature of this knowledge or recollection? I mean to ask, Whether a person who, having seen or heard or in any way perceived anything knows not only that, but has a conception of something else which is the subject, not of the same but of some other kind of knowledge, may not be fairly said to recollect that of which he has the conception?

What do you mean?

I mean what I may illustrate by the following instance:—The knowledge of a lyre is not the same as the knowledge of a man?

True.

And yet what is the feeling of lovers when they recognize a lyre, or a garment, or anything else which the beloved has been in the habit of using? Do they not, from knowing the lyre, form in the mind's eye an image of the youth to whom the lyre belongs? And this is recollection; in like manner any one who sees Simmias may remember Cebes; and there are endless examples of the same thing.

Endless, indeed, replied Simmias.

And recollection is most commonly a process of recovering that which has been already forgotten through time and inattention.

Very true, he said.

Well; and may you not also from seeing the picture of a horse or a lyre remember a man? and from the picture of Simmias you may be led to remember Cebes.

True.

Or you may also be led to the recollection of Simmias himself?

Quite so.

And in all these cases, the recollection may be derived from things either like or unlike?

It may be.

And when the recollection is derived from like things, then another consideration is sure to arise, which is—whether the likeness in any degree falls short or not of that which is recollected?

Very true, he said.

And shall we proceed a step further, and affirm that there is such a thing as equality, not of one piece of wood or stone with another, but that, over and above this, there is absolute equality? Shall we say so?

Say so, yes, replied Simmias, and swear to it, with all the confidence in life.

And do we know the nature of this absolute essence?

To be sure, he said.

And whence did we obtain our knowledge? Did we not see equalities of material things, such as pieces of wood and stones, and gather from them the idea of an equality which is different from them? For you will acknowledge that there is a difference. Or look at the matter in another way:—Do not the same pieces of wood or stone appear at one time equal, and at another time unequal?

That is certain.

But are real equals ever unequal? Or is the idea of equality the same as of inequality?

Impossible, Socrates.

Then these (so-called) equals are not the idea of equality?

I should say, clearly not, Socrates.

And yet, from these equals, although differing from the idea of equality, you conceived and attained that idea?

Very true, he said.

Which might be like, or might be unlike them?

Yes.

But that makes no difference. Whenever from seeing one thing you conceived another, whether like or unlike, there must surely have been an act of recollection?

Very true.

But what would you say of equal portions of wood and stone, or other material equals? and what is the impression produced by them? Are they equals in the same sense in which absolute equality is equal? Or do they fall short of this perfect equality in a measure?

Yes, he said, in a very great measure too.

And must we not allow, that when I or any one, looking at any object, observes that the thing which he sees aims at being some other thing, but falls short of, and cannot be, that other thing, but is inferior, he who makes this observation must have had a previous knowledge of that to which the other, although similar, was inferior?

Certainly.

And has not this been our own case in the matter of equals and of absolute equality?

Precisely.

Then we must have known equality previously to the time when we first saw the material equals, and reflected that all these apparent equals strive to attain absolute equality, but fall short of it?

Very true.

And we recognize also that this absolute equality has only been known, and can only be known, through the medium of sight or touch, or of some other of the senses, which are all alike in this respect?

Yes, Socrates, as far as the argument is concerned, one of them is the same as the other.

From the senses then is derived the knowledge that all sensible things aim at an absolute equality of which they fall short?

Yes.

Then before we began to see or hear or perceive in any way, we must have had a knowledge of absolute equality, or we could not have referred to that standard the equals which are derived from the senses?—for to that they all aspire, and of that they fall short.

No other inference can be drawn from the previous statements.

And did we not see and hear and have the use of our other senses as soon as we were born?

Certainly.

Then we must have acquired the knowledge of equality at some previous time?

Yes.

That is to say, before we were born, I suppose?

True.

And if we acquired this knowledge before we were born, and were born having the use of it, then we also knew before we were born and at the instant of birth not only the equal or the greater or the less, but all other ideas; for we are not speaking only of equality, but of beauty, goodness, justice, holiness, and of all which we stamp with the name of essence in the dialectical process, both when we ask and when we answer questions. Of all this we may certainly affirm that we acquired the knowledge before birth?

We may.

But if, after having acquired, we have not forgotten what in each case we acquired, then we must always have come into life having knowledge, and shall always continue to know as long as life lasts—for knowing is the acquiring and retaining knowledge and not forgetting. Is not forgetting, Simmias, just the losing of knowledge?

Quite true, Socrates.

But if the knowledge which we acquired before birth was lost by us at birth, and if afterwards by the use of the senses we recovered what we previously knew, will not the process which we call learning be a recovering of the knowledge which is natural to us, and may not this be rightly termed recollection?

Very true.

So much is clear—that when we perceive something, either by the help of sight, or some other sense, from that perception we are able to obtain a notion of some other thing like or unlike which is associated with it but has been forgotten. Whence, as I was saying, one of two alternatives follows:—either we had this knowledge at birth, and continued to know through life; or, after birth, those who are said to learn only remember, and learning is simply recollection.

Yes, that is quite true, Socrates.

And which alternative, Simmias, do you prefer? Had we the knowledge at our birth, or did we recollect the things which we knew previously to our birth?

I cannot decide at the moment.

At any rate you can decide whether he who has knowledge will or will not be able to render an account of his knowledge? What do you say?

Certainly, he will.

But do you think that every man is able to give an account of these very matters about which we are speaking?

Would that they could, Socrates, but I rather fear that to-morrow, at this time, there will no longer be any one alive who is able to give an account of them such as ought to be given.

Then you are not of opinion, Simmias, that all men know these things?

Certainly not.

They are in process of recollecting that which they learned before?

Certainly.

But when did our souls acquire this knowledge?—not since we were born as men?

Certainly not.

And therefore, previously?

Yes.

Then, Simmias, our souls must also have existed without bodies before they were in the form of man, and must have had intelligence.

Unless indeed you suppose, Socrates, that these notions are given us at the very moment of birth; for this is the only time which remains.

Yes, my friend, but if so, when do we lose them? for they are not in us when we are born—that is admitted. Do we lose them at the moment of receiving them, or, if not, at what other time?

No, Socrates, I perceive that I was unconsciously talking nonsense.

Then may we not say, Simmias, that if, as we are always repeating, there is an absolute beauty, and goodness, and an absolute essence of all things; and if to this, which is now discovered to have existed in our former state, we refer all our sensations, and with this compare them, finding these ideas to be pre-existent and our inborn possession—then our souls must have had a prior existence, but if not, there would be no force in the argument? There is the same proof that these ideas must have existed before we were born, as that our souls existed before we were born; and if not the ideas, then not the souls.

Yes, Socrates; I am convinced that there is precisely the same necessity for the one as for the other; and the argument retreats successfully to the position that the existence of the soul before birth cannot be separated from the existence of the essence of which you speak. For there is nothing which to my mind is so patent as that beauty, goodness, and the other notions of which you were just now speaking, have a most real and absolute existence; and I am satisfied with the proof.

III

Then, now let us return to the previous discussion. Is that idea or essence, which in the dialectical process we define as essence or true existence—whether essence of equality, beauty, or anything else—are these essences, I say, liable at times to some degree of change? Or are they each of them always what they are, having the same simple self-existent and unchanging forms, not admitting of variation at all, or in any way, or at any time?

They must be always the same, Socrates, replied Cebes.

And what would you say of the many beautiful things—whether men or horses or garments or any other things which are named by the same names and may be called equal or beautiful—are they all unchanging and the same always, or quite the reverse? May they not rather be described as almost always changing and hardly ever the same, either with themselves or with one another?

The latter, replied Cebes; they are always in a state of change.

And these you can touch and see and perceive with the senses, but the unchanging things you can only perceive with the mind —they are invisible and are not seen?

That is very true, he said.

Well, then, added Socrates, let us suppose that there are two sorts of existences— one seen, the other unseen.

Let us suppose them.

The seen is the changing, and the unseen is the unchanging?

That may also be supposed.

And, further, is not one part of us body, another part soul?

To be sure.

And to which class is the body more alike and akin?

Clearly to the seen—no one can doubt that.

And is the soul seen or not seen?

Not by man, Socrates.

And what we mean by "seen" and "not seen" is that which is or is not visible to the eye of man?

Yes, to the eye of man.

And is the soul seen or not seen?

Not seen.

Unseen then?

Yes.

Then the soul is more like to the unseen, and the body to the seen?

That follows necessarily, Socrates.

And were we not saying long ago that the soul when using the body as an instrument of perception, that is to say, when using the sense of sight or hearing or some other sense (for the meaning of perceiving through the body is perceiving through the senses)— were we not saying that the soul too is then dragged by the body into the region of the changeable, and wanders and is confused; the world spins round her, and she is like a drunkard, when she touches change?

Very true.

But when returning into herself she reflects, then she passes into the other world, the region of purity, and eternity, and immortality, and unchangeableness, which are her kindred, and with them she ever lives, when she is by herself and is not let or hindered; then she ceases from her erring ways, and being in communion with the unchanging is unchanging. And this state of the soul is called wisdom?

That is well and truly said, Socrates, he replied.

And to which class is the soul more nearly alike and akin, as far as may be inferred from this argument, as well as from the preceding one?

I think, Socrates, that, in the opinion of every one who follows the argument, the soul will be infinitely more like the unchangeable—even the most stupid person will not deny that.

And the body is more like the changing?

Yes.

Yet once more consider the matter in another light: When the soul and the body are united, then nature orders the soul to rule and govern, and the body to obey and serve. Now, which of these two functions is akin to the divine? and which to the mortal? Does not the divine appear to you to be that which naturally orders and rules, and the mortal to be that which is subject and servant?

True.

And which does the soul resemble?

The soul resembles the divine, and the body the mortal—there can be no doubt of that, Socrates.

Then reflect, Cebes: of all which has been said is not this the conclusion?—that the soul is in the very likeness of the divine, and immortal, and intellectual, and uniform, and indissoluble, and unchangeable; and that the body is in the very likeness of the human,

and mortal, and unintellectual, and multiform, and dissoluble, and changeable. Can this, my dear Cebes, be denied?

It cannot.

But if it be true, then is not the body liable to speedy dissolution? and is not the soul almost or altogether indissoluble?

Certainly.

And do you further observe, that after a man is dead, the body, or visible part of him, which is lying in the visible world, and is called a corpse, and would naturally be dissolved and decomposed and dissipated, is not dissolved or decomposed at once, but may remain for some time, nay, even for a long time, if the constitution be sound at the time of death, and the season of the year favourable? For the body when shrunk and embalmed, as the manner is in Egypt, may remain almost entire through infinite ages; and even in decay, there are still some portions, such as the bones and ligaments, which are practically indestructible:—Do you agree?

Yes.

And is it likely that the soul, which is invisible, in passing to the place of the true Hades, which like her is invisible, and pure, and noble, and on her way to the good and wise God, whither, if God will, my soul is also soon to go,—that the soul, I repeat, if this be her nature and origin, will be blown away and destroyed immediately on quitting the body, as the many say? That can never be, my dear Simmias and Cebes. The truth rather is, that the soul which is pure at departing and draws after her no bodily taint, having never voluntarily during life had connection with the body, which she is ever avoiding, herself gathered into herself;— and making such abstraction her perpetual study—which means that she has been a true disciple of philosophy; and therefore has in fact been always engaged in the practice of dying? For is not philosophy the study of death?—

Certainly—

That soul, I say, herself invisible, departs to the invisible world—to the divine and immortal and rational; thither arriving, she is secure of bliss and is released from the error and folly of men, their fears and wild passions and all other human ills, forever dwells, as they say of the initiated, in company with the gods. Is not this true, Cebes?

Yes, said Cebes, beyond a doubt.

But the soul which has been polluted, and is impure at the time of her departure, and is the companion and servant of the body always, and is in love with and fascinated by the body and by the desires and pleasures of the body, until she is led to believe that the truth only exists in a bodily form, which a man may touch and see and taste, and use for the purposes of his lusts,—the soul, I mean, accustomed to hate and fear and avoid the intellectual principle, which to the bodily eye is dark and invisible, and can be attained only by philosophy;—do you suppose that such a soul will depart pure and unalloyed?

Impossible, he replied.

She is held fast by the corporeal, which the continual association and constant care of the body have wrought into her nature.

Very true.

And this corporeal element, my friend, is heavy and weighty and earthy, and is that element of sight by which a soul is depressed and dragged down again into the visible world, because she is afraid of the invisible and of the world below—prowling about tombs and sepulchres, near which, as they tell us, are seen certain ghostly apparitions of souls which have not departed pure, but are cloyed with sight and therefore visible.

That is very likely, Socrates.

Yes, that is very likely, Cebes; and these must be the souls, not of the good, but of the evil, which are compelled to wander about such places in payment of the penalty of their former evil way of life; and they continue to wander until through the craving after the corporeal which never leaves them they are imprisoned finally in another body. And they may be supposed to find their prisons in the same natures which they have had in their former lives.

What natures do you mean, Socrates?

What I mean is that men who have followed after gluttony, and wantonness, and drunkenness, and have had no thought of avoiding them, would pass into asses and animals of that sort. What do you think?

I think such an opinion to be exceedingly probable.

And those who have chosen the portion of injustice and tyranny, and violence, will pass into wolves, or into hawks and kites;—whither else can we suppose them to go?

Yes, said Cebes; with such natures, beyond question.

And there is no difficulty, he said, in assigning to all of them places answering to their several natures and propensities?

There is not, he said.

Some are happier than others; and the happiest both in themselves and in the place to which they go are those who have practised the civil and social virtues which are called temperance and justice, and are acquired by habit and attention without philosophy of mind.

Why are they the happiest?

Because they may be expected to pass into some gentle and social kind which is like their own, such as bees or wasps or ants, or back again into the form of man, and just and moderate men may be supposed to spring from them.

Very likely.

No one who has not studied philosophy and who is not entirely pure at the time of his departure is allowed to enter the company of the Gods, but the lover of knowledge only. And this is the reason, Simmias and Cebes, why the true votaries of philosophy abstain from all fleshly lusts, and hold out against them and refuse to give themselves up to them,—not because they fear poverty or the ruin of their families, like the lovers of money, and the world in general; nor like the lovers of power and honour, because they dread the dishonour or disgrace of evil deeds.

No, Socrates, that would not become them, said Cebes.

No, indeed, he replied; and therefore they who have any care of their own souls, and do not merely live molding and fashioning the body, say farewell to all this; they will not walk in the ways of the blind: and when philosophy offers them purification and release from evil, they feel that they ought not to resist her influence, and whither she leads, they turn and follow.

What do you mean, Socrates?

I will tell you, he said. The lovers of knowledge are conscious that the soul was simply fastened and glued to the body—until philosophy received her, she could only view real existence through the bars of a prison, not in and through herself; she was wallowing in the mire of every sort of ignorance, and by reason of lust had become the principal accomplice in her own captivity. This was her original state; and then, as I was saying, and as the loves of knowledge are well aware, philosophy, seeing how terrible was her confinement, of which she was herself the cause, received and gently comforted her and sought to release her, pointing out that the eye and the ear and the other senses are full of deception, and persuading her to retire from them, and abstain from all the necessary use of them, and be gathered up and collected into herself, bidding her trust in herself and her own pure apprehension of pure existence, and to mistrust whatever comes to her through other channels and is subject to variation; for such things are visible and tangible, but what she sees in her own nature is intelligible and invisible. And the soul of the true philosopher thinks that she ought not to resist this deliverance, and therefore abstains from pleasures and desires and pains and fears, as far as she is able; reflecting that when a man has great joys or sorrows or fears or desires, he suffers from them, not merely the sort of evil which might be anticipated—as, for example, the loss of his health or property which he has sacrificed to his lusts—but an evil greater far, which is the greatest and worst of all evils, and one of which he never thinks.

What is it, Socrates? said Cebes.

The evil is that when the feeling of pleasure or pain is most intense, every soul of man imagines the objects of this intense feeling to be then plainest and truest; but this is not so, they are really the things of sight.

Very true.

And is not this the state in which the soul is most enthralled by the body?

How so?

Why, because each pleasure and pain is a sort of nail which nails and rivets the soul to the body, until she becomes like the body, and believes that to be true which the body affirms to be true; and from agreeing with the body and having the same delights she is obliged to have the same habits and haunts, and is not likely ever to be pure at her departure to the world below, but is always infected by the body; and so she sinks into another body and there germinates and grows, and has therefore no part in the communion of the divine and pure and simple.

Most true, Socrates, answered Cebes.

And this, Cebes, is the reason why the true lovers of knowledge are temperate and brave; and not for the reason which the world gives.

Certainly not.

Certainly not! The soul of a philosopher will reason in quite another way; she will not ask philosophy to release her in order that when released she may deliver herself up again to the thraldom of pleasures and pains, doing a work only to be outdone again, weaving instead of unweaving, her Penelope's web. But she will calm passion, and follow reason, and dwell in the contemplation of her, beholding the true and divine (which is not matter of opinion), and thence deriving nourishment. Thus she seeks to live while she lives, and after death she hopes to go to her own kindred and to that which is like her, and to be freed from human ills. Never fear, Simmias and Cebes, that a soul which has been thus nurtured and has had these pursuits, will at her departure from the body be scattered and blown away by the winds and be nowhere and nothing.

When Socrates had done speaking, there was silence for a considerable time; he himself appeared to be meditating, as most of us were, on what had been said.

3

The Implications
of Naturalism

Until recently the major figures in contemporary American thought accepted Naturalism in some form. There were notable exceptions, but naturalism was the dominant point of view. In large measure this was an indication of the lasting impact upon American philosophy of the thought of John Dewey; no single individual did so much to make naturalism convincing and almost inescapable for the intellectually self-respecting. At least three other outstanding philosophers, George Santayana, Frederick Woodbridge, and Morris Cohen, should be mentioned with Dewey as influential American exponents of naturalism. In the development of contemporary naturalism in this country these four men were the pioneers. In 1935 John Herman Randall, Jr., Dewey's younger associate, declared that in this country we had returned finally from the long odyssey of modern philosophy, with many a wound and many a deep scar, to the naturalism of Greek thought. Out of this modern soul searching there had come, in Randall's words, "an Aristotelianism extended and deepened, more Aristotelian than Aristotle himself"—what in the philosophical jargon of the day is known as "empirical naturalism."[1]

The initial selection in this section might readily be taken from any of half a dozen well-known contemporary American philosophers. Max Otto, long a distinguished professor at the University of Wisconsin, has written frequently and persuasively in support of the naturalistic point of view. A generation ago, in both *Things and Ideals* (published in 1924) and *Natural Laws and Human Hopes* (in 1927), Otto was the recognized spokesman of philosophical naturalism in this country. In more recent years Sidney Hook, of New York University, has perhaps replaced Otto as the most vocal and vigorous American champion of naturalism. At Columbia University a number of able men have also carried on the tradition of Dewey and Woodbridge, modifying and developing their philosophy at various points, but remaining true to the naturalism that lies at its heart. Among these men John Herman Randall, Jr., is certainly one of the better known and respected, but no other advocate of naturalism has presented this philosophy with the charm

---

[1] "Historical Naturalism," in H. M. Kallen and Sidney Hook, eds., *American Philosophy Today and Tomorrow*, (1935).

and poetic vision of Irwin Edman, another of the Columbia University group. Hence, to present the appeal of naturalism to the contemporary mind, we include here a selection from Irwin Edman's *Four Ways of Philosophy*.

The Vision of Contemporary Naturalism:
Irwin Edman

Born in New York City in 1896 only a few blocks from Columbia University, Irwin Edman spent almost all of his life at Columbia. He graduated there in 1917 and there in 1920 he was awarded his Ph.D. degree. For the next fifteen years he worked his way from instructor to full professor in the department of philosophy, and by that time had become one of the distinguished members of the Columbia University faculty. Despite this unbroken allegiance to Columbia, Edman's experience of persons and places was extensive and varied. He traveled extensively and lectured widely. His Beecher Lectures at Amherst College in 1936 formed the substance of the *Four Ways of Philosophy*. In 1939 he was visiting lecturer at the University of California, in 1944 at Harvard, in 1945 in Brazil; he was invited also to lecture at Oxford University in England and at the Sorbonne in France. Wherever he went, he took with him a gift for friendship, and for understanding the place, the culture, and the spirit of the people.

Edman's influence at Columbia was remarkable, and his untimely death in 1954 was a major loss not only to Columbia but to American philosophy in general. "He was a radiantly effective teacher, who taught as much by the contagion of his personality, its warmth and balance and wit, as by the lucidity and sympathy he brought to the statement of a philosophical position. In his classroom and in his books, to paraphrase a remark he once made about Plato, nothing was explained, but somehow everything was made clear and enhanced. He did not seem to expound a philosophy. He seemed to enact it, to move to its rhythms and live with its moods . . . probably no teacher in the two-hundred-year history of Columbia drew more affection to himself from his students; and no professor of philosophy in recent years has succeeded quite so well in domesticating the idea of philosophy on the American scene, in transmitting to a wide public the themes of philosophy, its idiom and its fever. He made it plain that the impulse to philosophy exists in most of us, and that it can be denied only with difficulty and at great risk."[2]

The title of Edman's most popular work, *Philosopher's Holiday*, suggests just the right spirit to describe its author himself. Throughout his daily life as a

---

[2] From *The Uses of Philosophy*, Copyright © 1955 by Charles Frankel, Introduction, pp. 1–2, 4. Reprinted by permission of Simon and Schuster, Inc. The comments made here about Irwin Edman are much indebted to this introduction by Professor Frankel (Ed.).

teacher of philosophy as well as when traveling at home and abroad, he always enjoyed himself as if on a holiday. For him life was never merely routine, dull, or monotonous. With a matter-of-fact appreciation of what was possible and impossible, he combined a longing for things beyond the world of the senses; in the temporal he could not help hearing echoes of the eternal. "While he did not believe a word that Plato said, Plato was his favorite philosopher." This sense of the double character of human experience, the real and the ideal, the scientific and the poetic, marked Edman's life as well as his philosophy. He was always ready to face facts without self-deception, but he looked also for what they represented, for the suggestion they gave of the ideal. This helps explain the central place in his philosophy that he gave to the arts; for him art was not a separate aspect of human life but a quality that all life should have when lived fully and harmoniously.

Edman's work in philosophy, especially in the interpretation of philosophy in more popular and literary fashion, has an unusual extent and variety. While still an undergraduate, he published light verse in the old *New York World*. His doctoral dissertation, *Human Traits and Their Social Significance,* published in 1920 just three years after his graduation, had the unique distinction of having been adopted immediately as a text for the Contemporary Civilization course in Columbia College. *Richard Kane Looks at Life,* written a few years later and dealing with the adventures of a young college graduate in search of a philosophy of life, is done to an extent in the form of a novel. *Four Ways of Philosophy* (1937) is his most sustained book in philosophy and the fullest statement of his own philosophical position. *Philosopher's Holiday,* published the next year, is a humorous memoir of men, places, and ideas that he found appealing; *Philosopher's Quest* is a later book in the same vein on the major themes of philosophy. The selection included here from *Four Ways of Philosophy* provides a thoughtful introduction to the kind of naturalism to which Edman gave his own allegiance and which he saw underlying a sound philosophy for our age. Its insight and clarity in dealing with the implications of naturalism is especially impressive, and its historical perspective paves the way for better understanding the poetry of Lucretius, the influential philosophy of Aristotle, and the empirical naturalism of Dewey.

Philosophy as Nature Understood*

I

A certain rough and ready naturalism has always been imposed upon men, what-

ever they may say in their books—a recognition of nature in the characteristic traits of the environment with which they have to deal, in the habits and impulses of their own bodies and in the practical necessities imposed upon them by things and by their impulses toward and their need for things. The facts

* Irwin Edman, *Four Ways of Philosophy,* (New York, Henry Holt and Company, Inc., 1947). Part IV shortened.

of food and of hunger and the relation between them have made men naturalists in practice long before they made theories about nature, and long after their theories have fairly expressed or flagrantly contradicted nature. However fantastic the mythologies that poets and soothsayers may have passed off as truth, men have early learned to be realistic in dealing with fire and food and hunger, with their means of sustenance and with their desires. The arts of agriculture preceded theories about the gods of the soil and of fertility, and continued, often in contradiction to those theories or along with them when these did arise. Nature was and continues to be saluted and respected in fact, whatever dialectic devices be developed to explain it away. The recurrence of the seasons, the cycle of births and of deaths, the habits of animals, the growth of plants, the ways of men in love and hate, in peace and war, have all impressed men with a primitive urgency, and first and last have compelled some honesty, precision and common sense in dealing with them. Common sense has been a persistent philosophy in all ages, although it has not always been the most fashionable, or the most articulate or the officially acknowledged one.

Theory, in the Greek language, is identical with vision, and somewhere about the sixth century B.C. in the Greek islands of Asia Minor, there seemed to have been sufficient leisure and sufficient speculative interest to generate on the part of a number of thinkers (whom, from their few written remains, students have come to think of as thinking in fragments) attempts to think the fragments of their experience into a consistent and single whole. For it very early occurred to thinkers, as it very early occurs to any reflective person, that, whatever be the confusion and chaos or miscellany of things, we are after all living in *one* universe, and that if we could penetrate surfaces sufficiently, all the variety of things might be found to be variations of one substance, changes effected somehow in one fundamental and essentially changeless stuff. It is natural enough to assume, as did the early cosmologists of the Greek Mediterranean world, some *matter* of which all things are somehow transformations.

The earliest philosopher known to us —and only just known—is Thales, who, legend has it, gazing upon all the things spread before his eyes, said that all was water. That familiar fluid element seemed ubiquitous enough, and it seemed easy to believe that all things were in some way or other freezings or compressions or vaporizings of it. There were other guesses: that of Anaximenes, who imagined that all things were air; that of Anaximander, who thought they were made out of something he called the Boundless or Infinite; that of Empedocles (celebrated in Matthew Arnold's poem for his suicide on Mount Aetna), who asserted that all things were combinations of earth, air, fire and water. We smile a little at these guesses and wonder how the so much bruited Greek genuis could arrive at hypotheses so childish. Yet the nature of the intention rather than the substance of the guess is important. These early Greek thinkers were making one of the most audacious and fruitful leaps of human imagination. They were the first to realize that all substance might be variations of one substance, and hit at once upon the fact that where there is change, so patent in our experience, those changes might be changes of one material. They hit upon the central idea of Substance, and, in thinking of all things as forms of one stuff, hit at the same time upon the general principles of persistence amid transformation.

But the guess at a single substance was not enough to be intellectually satisfying. For it left unanswered the question, Why the transformation? Why should air or water become the myriad forms of life and plants and animals, of cabbages and kings? Why should there be cycles of recurrence? Why should there be an *order* in change itself? Nor did a single element or a single combination of elements seem enough to explain the incredible variety of appearances which the underlying substance seemed to have, or *how* these appearances arose.

The genius of Democritus, whose wisdom was immortalized and extended by Lucretius, tried by a simple and intelligible system of thought to account for both the changing and the permanent. His conception of mechanism is, in one form or another, still the technique if not the ideal of most naturalistic philosophies. One may say he divided Being into little particles of being, neutral atoms, the ultimate elements of the universe. Colorless, of various sizes and forms, they constituted the irreducible permanent substance of things. All the variety of things consisted in combinations of atoms, but the combinations were according to regular though blind motions. The world was rendered intelligible in terms of "constant parts and constant laws."

The Democritean physics seems simple, almost simple-minded now, but the analytic ideal of mechanism was revived in modern times with the rise of Newtonian science and in the thought of Descartes in philosophy. Nature was conceived as a great machine, though for various reasons, including the theological, Descartes himself felt it necessary to exclude the soul of man from that mathematically calculable system. The laws of physics, earthly and celestial (for the line between things below and above the moon was rendered obsolete by Copernican astronomy), made it seem that everything on earth and indeed in the whole solar sytsem happened according to mathematically definable regularities, another name for mechanical laws. By the eighteenth century this had become so favorite a way of conceiving the universe that one French philosopher, La Mettrie, could write a book, immensely popular in the salons, called *Man a Machine,* which attempted to show that all the operations of human emotion and thought as well as all the physiological activities of the human body could be explained in terms of the laws of mechanical motion. Deists could say that the perfect machine of nature had been set in motion by God (as "natural reason" clearly revealed) or that the very conception of so perfect a machine implied an intelligent designer. A universal mechanical system could be used as an argument that that order was itself God. Spinoza said just that, and said

that the true love of God was the intellectual understanding of the order of nature. Or the notion of the blind regularity of nature could be used as an argument against the presence within it of anything like a general purpose or a general directing mind.

By the nineteenth century the sway of mechanical law was extended to the field of physiology and psychology, until by the twentieth century there arose psychologies, still fashionable, which could insist that all human behavior, that of a poet writing a sonnet or a thinker arriving at his conclusions, could be completely and exhaustively described and explained in purely mechanical terms.

II

The cogency of naturalism as a point of view has been lately called into question. Both the stuff of nature, matter, and the billiard-ball physics of nineteenth century mechanism have been called into question in the fields of the sciences themselves. Matter has dissolved into centers of force or foci of energy; matter itself is simply known by what it does; in itself it is, as Herbert Spencer said, the unknowable. The scientist turns out to be dealing with the relation of events; he never deals immediately with any gross palpable stuff called matter. The simple atoms of Democritus seem absurd to the modern biochemist. The sciences of life have moreover emphasized the habits of growth, the "tropes" of development in nature, in which an inert and dead matter, made up of static, inert and lifeless atoms, seems irrelevant. There seem, furthermore, to be elements in life and in mind not reducible to matter in motion. The phenomena of purpose, for instance, and the total reaction of an organism are not analyzable in terms of mechanical physics. The new physics itself, moreover, has reduced the whole conception of mechanism to that of a convenient system of "pointer readings." The world that the physicist used to think of as basically real turns out to be simply the "world" of laboratory measurements and mathematical deductions, marvelously fertile in practical use, and fascinating to the intellectual virtuoso. But it is hardly nature itself in its absoluteness. No, the mechanical description of nature has no more right to call itself nature than a ticket of admission has a right to call itself the concert or a key to call itself a door. The identification of the reality of nature with the description of it in mechanical terms has certainly become suspect. "Nature is no system but that to which all our systems refer."

But all this is far from being tantamount to saying that the naturalistic point of view has broken down. For the faith of the philosophical (not biological) naturalist is simply that there is something substantial, not our own invention, not to be wholly described by our descriptions or any descriptions of it, with which we must deal. It holds further there are no breaks in the order of events; everything that happens has consequences, and to learn to discern those causes and consequences is to understand nature.

For the naturalist the conception of philosophy simply as nature understood has been fortified rather than undermined by the growth of the biological sciences and the biological point of view toward experience and knowledge. The existence of an order of nature is confirmed not by a theory of physics, nor for that matter by a theory of biology, but by the fact that human beings, in their unsophisticated and in their sophisticated experience, find themselves in a world marked by the presence of an obdurate but flexible something, that for want of a better word we may call matter. They find also that the world in which they live has its nature disclosed by the traits which individuals in their isolation and in their lives together find experience itself to have.

It is, of course, easy to say that a philosophy is based on experience without indicating what one means by that. Experience has a pleasant matter-of-fact sound, as when a politician says he is not talking in vague generalities but in terms of "hard realities and long, bitter experience." In philosophy, however, even in the so-called empirical tradition, experience has been a quite sophisticated term, different in character from what the ordinary man means by it. For, as the reader

of the chapter on Idealism will recall, once you reduce experience to what the senses reveal, you have no ground for assuming that things as they are are in any way like what they appear on the evidence and through the agencies of the senses to be.

When a contemporary thinker like John Dewey refers to the term experience he means practically something much closer to what the common man means by it, and theoretically something that takes its meaning from the biological rather than the logical approach to knowledge. Practically speaking, to have experience of anything means to know what one may expect from it, to know what to count on, what may be done with it, what its possibilities are. To have had experience with persons and with things is not to have had acquaintance with some static image of them. It is to have some fairly secure and verified anticipations of what under given circumstances they will do or what may be done to them. The reason the term "theoretical" is so often used as a term of dispraise in politics and affairs is that men substitute sentimental images or dialectical stereotypes for a "working knowledge" of what will specifically happen under certain given conditions, or what under given conditions may be accomplished.

Now when it is said that the traits of experience disclose nature, several things are meant. The first is that experience *überhaupt* is simply the name for all kinds of *experiences*. Secondly, all kinds of experience show certain common traits. These are the traits which characterize the behavior of men, the traits which characterize and determine what they do, feel, suffer, think and believe. They are traits of all possible experiences because they are traits of the nature with which men must deal and of which their own nature is a derivation. Thirdly, the most subtilized and refined forms of scientific inquiry and technical control start with the kind of experiences common to all men in their ordinary pursuits and perplexities. Fourthly, the methods of science and of philosophy are simply refinements upon, disciplined forms of, that method of exploration and hypothesis, guess and verification and testing, which we all practice in finding our way to a house never before visited, which the artist practices in his work, the statesman when he plans, the cook when he prepares a dinner. "Lyell revolutionized geology by perceiving that the sort of thing that can be experienced now in the operations of fire, water, pressure, is the sort of thing by which the earth took on its present structural forms."[1] Darwin began with the pigeons, cattle and plants of breeders and gardeners. And the most highly elaborate methods of reflection of an Einstein are tested in "crude, primary experience." Experience, so far from being a term to denote "intellectual acquaintance," is merely the generalized name for all that men do and suffer.

On the theoretical side, the conception of "experience" and of the nature which critical and circumspect experience discloses stems from the approach to both that biology since Darwin has afforded. It is difficult now to think of the problem of philosophical truth as that of a static and bodiless mind, disinterestedly mirroring a timeless and changeless universe. For man is shown to be an animal living precariously, with the help of an exploring intelligence, in a process of events itself a mixture of stability and change. The world in which man lives and of which he is a part is, like himself, changing, a process of growth, Nature, far from being like a machine, is like an organism, like a plant or animal, and man is one among its flora and fauna. He happens to be so complicated an organic creature that he can think, that is, experimentally explore, imagine consequences and verify them. The world is not a thing but a process: thinking is not a static contemplation but a process of experimental control, a process central and directive, but itself a process among the other processes of nature.

The naturalism of the eighteenth and nineteenth centuries seems now almost a form of rationalism. It was dominated by the idea of mathematics. The naturalism of the twentieth, however, much as it may use the language of mathematics, is dominated in both its description of the world and its description of the thinker by biology. And above all the thinker and the world are no longer to be regarded as separated, but as phases of a common process which is substance or matter. Nature is experienced, but it is in general what it is experienced as, and the bearer or agent of that experience is one with the processes of that nature whose possibilities he explores and of whose qualities he is aware.

Common experience is, furthermore, filled with meanings and suggestions. One thing *stands* for another. The cloud portends rain; the fever indicates illness; the footprints suggest a man. Out of these suggestions generated by perception arise all the possibilities of disciplined thought. But unless nature were a field of possibilities, of possible growths, these inferences would be misleading (as, uncritically taken—*e.g.,* a mirage seen in a desert—they often are). Thinking is possible because it occurs in a thinkable world. Experience constantly tempts us with a house to build or build over, a view to clear, a business to be developed, a book to be written, a marriage to be arranged. It could not do so unless nature were full of potentialities, some of which may be furthered by exploration and thought. Such explorations are fruitful because of the stabilities recognized among changes, and the fact that a choice may be made of the changes to be furthered by the stabilities used.

Experience, again, is filled with sharing and communication. This is so in no small part because we live naturally in a world where sharing and communication are traits of human nature, itself one of the processes of the natural world. Experience is pregnant with dreams to the imagination, and imagination itself is a natural trait of human nature. Experience is what it is because existence is what it is. There is no radical, there could be no fundamental dichotomy between the two.

---

[1] John Dewey, *Experience and Nature,* p. 3a.

III

The whole view of the relation of nature and experience profoundly modifies the moral consequences and the esthetic and spiritual overtones to the naturalistic point of view. Naturalism in the nineteenth century and earlier left many of those intellectually convinced of its truth morally at sea, spiritually in despair, and esthetically in a minor key. For the picture of nature given in the mathematico-physical "structure" of it left not only much to be desired, but made desire and the objects of desire themselves seem to be illusions. The "world of nature," in terms of the Newtonian and Cartesian world scheme, of matter in motion, left out precisely those qualities which in human experience are most precious. It left out God and robbed man of comfortable providential illusions. It made man a trivial and tremulous cloud of stardust in infinite astronomical space. It rendered fantastic any alleged meaning of the universe, and made it impossible to explain all events (of which earthly events were a very small portion) in terms of the salvation of man. Moreover it did something far worse. It made love and all other values unreal. For all that was real was only the movement of particles of matter in blind regularities in the infinite spaces of the solar system. All color, quality and value were removed from the "scientifically" real universe. Nature was an alien world, unduly foreign to everything that men held beautiful or good. God was a myth or an unnecessary or confused hypothesis. Moral values were a farce in an unmoral cosmic machine; even the colors, so familiar in experience, the green of the grass, the blue of the sky, the tastes and odors of food were subjective and "secondary" qualities.

From the time of Epicurus down, therefore, naturalism has repeatedly had about it a kind of sunset glow, as well as a nostalgia for a world that might have been, and by all moral and human standards should have been, different. Men, however realistic they might be in practice, had for centuries nourished and comforted themselves on the supernatural. The martyr thinks of the flame of God's love even while the physical flames flicker around his tortured feet. Job trusts in God though God afflicts and seems about to slay him. For the supernatural picture gives a compensatory ideal world in which the brusque crudities and cruelties of this one will be forgotten or adjusted. The naturalistic world-view seemed (and still does seem) cold to those brought up on the warm comfort of providential myths. Everything precious and individual has seemed shadowy compared with the "realities" of the bare mathematico-physical universe. The water, sparkling in the sun, cool to the touch, refreshing to the parched throat, is H_2O. The most cherished and irreplaceable person is simply one among millions of biochemical objects, a body among other bodies.

All human aspirations, all apparent meaning in the universe, seemed to be rendered nugatory by the vast meaninglessness of the "blind march of matter on its relentless way." Everything that seemed distinctively human—hope and faith and charity, spiritual ends and esthetic raptures, the colors of the sea and the sky, and the complexion of one's friends—threatened to vanish in the scientific picture of the world. Man was an accident, an incident, a casualty, helpless and hopeless, in the relentless movement of matter in motion. It was not one against the gods, but against nature. The latter seemed by a conspiracy of indifference to be the enemy of man, or his ironic destroyer, not even aware of the values of what it was destroying.

Consciousness in a world thus conceived is a blind brief flicker between two oblivions, that before birth, and that after death. For there can be no immortality if the soul is simply a fortuitous combination of atoms destined like all other such combinations to dissolution. The most that can be hoped for is to crowd those fated few moments with pleasure, to escape during that short interlude of consciousness from pain. A timid temperance or an occasional orgy of intense pleasure is the most that life can provide in a meaningless world. The gross can find their pleasures in the grosser intensities of the senses, in food and drink and sex. The refined Epicurean can find them in those subtleties of the senses which are fulfilled in works of art, in those finesses of emotion which are gratified in friendship and in affection, or for rare minds in the spectacle, ironic in its amusement, multiform, miscellaneous, evenescent, and recurrent, of nature itself. Even the fact that things recur in nature, that death is replaced by birth, can afford only a subject for laughter. For a cycle of this sort is meaningless, and the new flower is doomed to perish quite like the old. One can hardly think of a philosophy of pleasure that is not crossed with the sense of its transiency, its precariousness, its emptiness. Those who gather the flowers die almost as soon as the flowers they have gathered, and it is only a faint consolation to know that another lover will be born to find another creature, passing and perishing, whom he may embrace.

Now, as we shall see presently, the division between man and nature is made more absolute in such a picture than it actually is. All man's achievements are in a large sense nature's too. It needs also to be pointed out that much of the sadness in the presence of the mechanistic picture of the world is a piece of romantic impertinence on the part of those who have it. Human beings tend to be babies bursting into tears because the whole cosmos is not paying them concentrated attention and is not arranged to set up their egos. It is well to remember that the mathematico-mechanistic evolutionary picture of the world had its impact on imaginations nurtured on romantic poetry and on a religious tradition which pictured the whole history of the cosmos as the romantic story of man's salvation through the grace of God who had specially created him.

But to call romantic the despair induced by nineteenth century naturalism is not sufficient to close the matter. There is a deeper issue involved than merely a sulkiness arising from the disillusioning recognition that we are born into a world which was not made for us but in which we must willy-nilly grow. The poetic, the sensitive, the morally serious are Platonists at heart. It has hurt them deeply to realize that the True, the Good and the Beautiful are simply illusions, the shadows of desire cast upon the walls of that Heartbreak House which is the universe mechanistically conceived. It is depressing to have to face the apparent fact that Platonism itself is a dream of eternal things by a creature whose very birth is a sentence to extinction. There is for all their solemnities, a pathetic incapacity in men to take themselves or their moral standards seriously unless somebody else does, unless ultimately it can be proved that the cosmos takes them seriously. What men call good they have wished to see inscribed on the tablets of eternity as good, and as constituting the substance of reality itself.

IV

The naturalistic faith as above described is not so much a conception as the expression of a faith that animates most human practice and must always to some degree have animated it, or human life would long ago have come to an end. Whatever they say theoretically, men do recognize a something not themselves with which they must reckon. They do in action acknowledge that in some way their own nature is a phase of that larger nature which generates all the processes of things with which they must deal. Men act with respect to a future which they cannot do more than assume and a past which they cannot do more than remember. On the basis of their memories and hopes and anticipations, of their pleasures and pains, they credit themselves with being selves. They may bring all the canny ingenuity of a David Hume to prove that there is no *necessity* in causal relations; fire *must* not burn nor poison kill, but it has repeatedly in the history of the race been found well to act as if they did. For men have discovered that, whatever the books of the metaphysician say, given things behave in given ways. Men act as if, given the same conditions, the same consequences would occur. Scientific procedure is simply an elaborate technique, developed out of the natural guessing of men, for studying the uniformities of things, the *practical* universality of cause and effect. This order men call the order of nature, and the following of it as studiously and honestly as possible may be called nature understood.

Men have also felt nature so understood to be one, and man one with nature. The most airy theory of the soul has not quite blinded even those who held it to the obvious ways in which the soul or the "psyche" is the sum total, the entelechy, the summary expression of the body's activities. The soul bears the same relation to the body that the flame does to the candle, that seeing does to the eye. The same substance that flowers into corn or into roses blossoms into man, and in him into imagination, thinking, feeling and thought. The same vitality that generates mastodons, breeds poets and poetry. The symphonies of Beethoven are just as natural as flowers or snakes. The picture of man over against nature is a contradiction in terms. Man is one of the forms and habits of nature. The notion that man's highest ideals are somehow pathetic oppositions to nature neglects the important fact that those ideals are themselves generated in the imagination and mind of a creature to whom thinking and imagination are themselves natural. And if one means that there is nothing in any other part or phase of nature that exhibits such ideals or gives them sustenance, even here one must pause before so declaring. For gregariousness and sympathy are present in the animal kingdom and the highest vision of a just society has its roots partly in these traits. Nor would it follow, if man alone generated such values as we call specifically human, that nature is their enemy or that nature gives them no support. The impulses that sustain these values and the materials which make it possible for some of them to come to fruition are in exactly the same world; man's preferences and standards originate where everything else does, in the universal, fertile flux of natural processes.

One of the reasons that thinkers deeply concerned with "morality" look askance at a naturalistic point of view is that nearly everything that the classical tradition has identified with morals has supernatural sources. Morality has been a pendant to religion, and religion has in its metaphysical basis been transcendental and other-worldly. Morality has connoted obligation, and the imperious demands of obligation display a quality that seems hardly explicable by an analysis of physical origin or social pressure. The voice of duty has seemed too stern to be anything other or less than the voice of God.

Those who take their morals seriously feel that on a purely naturalistic basis morals become simply frivolous or worse. Very early in the European tradition it was considered accurate enough to speak of the Epicurean moral ideal as the Epicurean sty. What else than sensual excitement can those hold as good who claim that the soul is merely the function of the body, perception and thought a chemistry of the nerves and brain? What indeed do they mean by goodness at all who have no standard by which anything alleged to be good can be finally and fundamentally measured? The quarrel is an extremely grave one. It raises the fundamental issue as to whether, unless there is such a thing as value woven into the very texture of the universe, there can be such a thing as good or value at all. The naturalist in philosophy says that there can be, and we must examine why.

The good, as Aristotle pointed out long ago, must be the good for some creature; a value must be valuable to somebody. The good that moralists speak of is obviously the good for man, and unless one is merely making a solemn hypocritical face about it (or unless one has a theological ax to grind) the good is generally acknowledged to consist in human happiness. When the promise of a future life is to say the least problematic, happiness in *this* world is clearly meant. But to understand what happiness for man consists in, one must examine realistically the capacities human beings have, the desires they exhibit, and the conditions of their possible satisfaction. Happiness would, at least at first blush, seem to consist in the fulfillment of desire and the exercise of capacity. That indeed is where most human beings would place it; not in the fulfillment of one desire or capacity, but in the harmonious satisfaction of them all, in so far as that is possible.

There are probably few who will deny that the simple goods of life are what they are, that these constitute the fulfillment of honestly acknowledged human desires. There are few likewise who will be prepared to deny that a good in excess may become an evil. Food is a good, but gorging is an evil; sexual enjoyment is a good, but nymphomania is a disease. Impulses, themselves innocent enough in the tempered context of a life, turn into evils when they make men their slaves. Spinoza believed that understanding would free men from the "bondage" of passions, tense, narrow and destructive, which destroyed their powers and prevented life-giving union, wide and deep, with the movement of nature itself. Such a union was for him the greatest of passions, the *amor dei intellectualis,* but this passion alone gave at once power and peace. Modern psychiatrists who try to teach us to know ourselves honestly and live in consonance with reality are, in other terms, speaking Spinoza's doctrine. They are teaching joy through the power and peace which come through understanding.

The failure of Epicureanism, ancient or modern, lies not in the elements of happiness it notes, but in its analysis of their operation. A realistic theory of the good tries to find a framework in the natural processes of which life is one. It can hardly neglect the pleasures of the senses, of love and friendship, of the arts and, for those capable of it, of thought— the most exigent and the most rewarding of the arts, both in the power and the vistas it gives. But the conception of life as the passive reception of pleasures seems fantastic to those who have come to realize that man is an animal, and life a natural process. Pleasures are not things but phases of activity, the echoes of good functioning in good feeling. Happiness is the name for that architectonic good feeling present when the whole of a man, not simply one capacity or impulse, is functioning well. the moral ideal of the naturalist may be fitly compared to that of an orchestra which might wish to sound well entire, to function well *as an orchestra.* The soul of an orchestra is not something that enters into it from the outside, like a brownie in a fairy tale. Its soul and spirit are what it does, the functioning of all the instruments in it. If that complex had awareness as the human organism does, that awareness of playing well would be its happiness. Happiness is, as Aristotle insisted, a living and a doing well; it is the functioning of a whole life, not one aspect of it; it is the realization of a human nature, complex, various and whole.

V

There seem to the writer several grounds for suspecting that naturalism, if not the last word in philosophy (where there are no last words), is the implicit or unspoken word in all philosophies. In their theories, however contradictory of the naturalistic assumptions, other philosophers by implication as well as in their daily lives recognize those aspects of nature to which the mechanist and the materialist constantly call attention. Whatever philosophers say and whatever they say they are talking about, it turns out to be the same world of processes living, fertile, perilous and promising. It is only in their talk that they differ, and the naturalist differs from others only in insisting that when he talks philosophically he wishes to keep his mind as well as his rhetoric on the world in which he lives when he is not talking, or not talking philosophy.

That the talk of philosophers should differ is for exactly the same reason that speech of poets differs. For philosophy has mistaken its function in arrogating to itself the notion that it is either a transcript of reality or a specific program for life. It is a lyric but a lyric whose theme happens to be nature and destiny. It may seem odd to call philosophy a lyric, its language is often so prosaic and so dull. And even where its theme is poetic, as are, spectacularly, those of the mystics and metaphysicians, it might seem more like an epic poem, the saga of things, than the lyric of a private consciousness. Philosophy is lyric in the sense that any view of the world is a commentary by a private spirit on the public domain of nature. It is epic poetry when as in Vergil it tries to celebrate not its own tears but the tears of things. There might be some poet arising who could see the sweep and grandeur, the pathos and distances of the cosmos, and see it all in one comprehensive and sustained act of vision, for which a language at once elevated and exact would be the vehicle. There might be a poet to do for a modern naturalistic version of nature what Lucretius did for the ancient. He would borrow his language, his materials and his point of view from the scientist. He would borrow his heart from no one, but its utterance, candid and liberated, would be that of the liberated spirit of men everywhere.

Philosophy conceived as a wide and disciplined poetry, celebrating man's origins, his vicissitudes and his objects of love, would clarify the question of progress in philosophy. There has not been progress in poetry either. Each poet is original, but living in the world of men and nature, he deals freshly with ancient themes, love and death and destiny. The case in philosophy is similar: other questions concerning philosophy would also be clarified if it were thus conceived. Philosophers have yearned to make a transcript of reality and speak eternal truths. They have longed to provide the philosopher's stone and cure all human evils. Not the philosopher's stone but the philosopher's vision is his contribution; his technique and his logic are simply the discipline that makes that vision ordered and responsible. Plato declared the philosopher to be the spectator of all time and all existence. But the philosopher is always a mortal creature at a given place and juncture of time. His whole vocation is that of expressing with all the ardor, clarity and coherence that are in him, from whatever miscellaneous sources they come, his perspective upon time and existence. In so doing he will be giving expression to what by not too grand a hyperbole may be called eternal—both the forms disclosed by the spirit of man, and the spirit of man itself, perpetually reincarnate. In so far as he does this, his words, while the race lives, will be immortal.

The Poet of Nature: Lucretius

In his famous *De Rerum Natura* Lucretius, Roman poet of the first century B.C. combines a remarkably contemporary statement of scientific naturalism with a strong condemnation of the fears and superstitions of religion as he saw them in the Roman world of his own day. So far as the knowledge of that day would allow him to be, Lucretius was as completely and consistently scientific in his outlook on life and as naturalistic in his philosophy as any of our contemporary thinkers. As Santayana suggests in his *Three Philosophical Poets,* if we take nature to mean the great system of causes that brings all things into existence, "it may be said that Lucretius, more than any other man, is the poet of nature." The whole of the universe, Lucretius sees as made up of atoms in various forms of combination. These atoms are solid, indestructible, invisible, and of many sizes and shapes. Hard substances are composed of rough atoms, liquids of round, smooth ones. The only reality is the changing world of matter, the stuff from which the world and all that is in it is made. Beyond space (the void) and atoms, and the laws in accord with which the atoms move, no other principles of explanation are needed. Nothing else exists or ever can exist.

Lucretius' poem shows a marked hatred of conventional superstitions, a commitment to scientific method and accuracy of observation, a profound sense of the beauty of nature and its works, and complete confidence in natural law and in cause and effect. These are attitudes that have great appeal today; we must be careful, however, not to treat Lucretius as a contemporary figure. Each age deals with its own problems in their own peculiar setting, and Lucretius should be seen as an unusually intelligent and gifted Epicurean of the last century B.C. The Republican regime in Rome was breaking down and with it the system of morals and religion upon which it rested. To the more thoughtful of that age, philosophy professed to place man above the conflicts and superstitions of religion; it offered what religion failed to provide, a guide to moral conduct and a source of peace and tranquility. Stoicism appealed to the more religious; among those inclined to a matter-of-fact scientific outlook the doctrines of Epicurus had a stronger influence. Epicurus himself is best known for the hedonism that he so strongly advocated, but Lucretius was particularly attracted by the naturalistic philosophy of Democritus upon which the ethical theory of Epicurus rests. Lucretius is a hedonist, to be sure, and, especially in one long and famous passage on love in his poem, he clearly follows Epicurus in putting the satisfactions that come to friends with common intellectual interests above the constant anguish and unrest that the passion of love engenders. In several highly laudatory passages Lucretius also gives credit to Epicurus for the general point of view that his own poem expresses, but the naturalistic philosophy that he builds upon the thought of Epicurus and Democritus is quite genuinely his own.

In the science of *De Rerum Natura* one may, of course, point to many crude, and for us childish, ideas. Modern atomic physics has gone a long way beyond Lucretius. But it is far better to remember how extraordinary is the insight and how exciting the philosophical imagination of this early Roman poet. Without any of the scientific equipment with which the modern scientist works and in spite of his relatively primitive concept of scientific method, he was able to present the vision of naturalism in a great poem that has endured as one of the major works of literature and philosophy in our Western culture. The praise of Lucretius by one of his recent translators, Dr. Alban D. Winspear, Headmaster, North Shore College, Vancouver, Canada, while perhaps a bit enthusiastic, is certainly impressive:

> For majesty of theme and subject matter, for sustained eloquence of exposition, for acuteness of philosophical insight and argumentation, for poetical imagery and musical cadence, and for the sheer enthusiasm of scientific passion, the Greeks produced nothing to rival Lucretius. Indeed I am not sure that, as regards these qualities, Lucretius is not the greatest poet that ever lived.[1]

Of his own translation of *De Rerum Natura,* from which our selection is taken, Winspear writes:

> I have worked this translation of Lucretius into English verse with one good reason in mind—I wanted my favorite poet to be read. Lucretius has a great deal to say to the ordinary man in this generation, and in the current translations his message does not always get across.

About Lucretius himself surprisingly little is known although a few things can readily be inferred from the poem itself. It is the picture of an educated and aristocratic Roman, familiar with the luxurious palaces and country houses, the ostentation and vulgarity, and the inevitable boredom that accompanied the life of the wealthy in the first century B.C. It was clearly in this atmosphere that Lucretius grew up. The best conjecture places his birth about 95 B.C. and his death at 55 B.C. By 54 B.C. both Cicero and his brother had read *De Rerum Natura* and written to each other about it. Lucretius' friendship with Memmius, a Roman patrician whose identity is not too certain, suggests also that he came of a family of good standing in Rome. Beyond this there are only the conjectures of the curious in later ages.[2]

Lucretius' version of naturalism in *De Rerum Natura* is striking enough to merit more than mere historical interest. As he portrays it, the universe as a whole, and in particular the earth and everything that is a part of it, have come to be what it is by a process of natural selection. From the motion of atoms throughout infinite time an infinite variety of combinations have been produced; those alone

---

[1] A. D. Winspear, *The Roman Poet of Science Lucretius: De Rerum Natura* (New York, The Harbor Press, 1956), Introduction, pp. xiii; vii.

[2] Cf. Cyril Bailey, *Lucretius on the Nature of Things* (London, Oxford University Press, 1920), Introduction, pp. 8–9.

persist that are fit to survive. Life and consciousness are the result of atomic combination and development of an exceptionally noble kind; animals and men like everything else are to be explained in terms of this process. Human civilization with its social, moral, and religious institutions has been the result of the same process. Not only our world but many more like it have doubtless been produced in this fashion. In such naturalistic terms Lucretius explains all animal and vegetable life, the origin of man, the ways of primitive society, the way in which family life and the mutual care of children began to modify man's early savage tendencies, and the gradual development of his own relatively advanced civilization. His account of the rise of civilization is especially interesting. As wealth and luxury increased, there came inevitably the rebellion of the poor and revolution. To help control the clash of the rich and the poor, laws and magistrates were devised and social institutions as we know them are the result.

The methods by which Lucretius endeavors to support these conclusions are essentially the same as those of the scientist today. He reasons from the known and the observable to the unknown. All the familiar details of daily life, as well as all the mysteries of the cosmos, are interpreted as the result of a cause-and-effect sequence that we can verify every day by the evidence of our own senses. With regard to conscious life, his conclusions are surprisingly similar to the latest scientific and naturalistic philosophy. All conscious life comes into existence with the body, and disappears with its dissolution. In this connection Lucretius sharply attacks the theory of special creation. Neither man nor the universe is the miraculous creation of any deity or deities; there is no transcendent design or purpose in the nature of things but all things are the result of natural laws at work. If any deities exist, they emerge from the nature of things just as man does and have no concern with human conduct. For man himself, this life is all there is, and he must make the most that he can of it with the intelligence and understanding that he possesses.

Life would be tolerable enough and often quite happy, were it not for one thing, the universal dread, not so much of death but of the future that awaits us after death. It is for this fear of what the gods may do to us that religion in Lucretius' opinion is so greatly to be blamed, and from such fear a scientific philosophy alone is able to free us. In his opposition to the religion of his day Lucretius expresses his deepest emotion and finds occasion for some of his most moving poetry. Here also is the key to his view of how it is best for men to live. The intelligent man will not live as most men do, in a constant struggle for power and wealth. Avarice, ambition, lust bring no lasting satisfaction; the only happiness is found not in excess but in moderation. Insecurity and fear of death are the things that destroy man's enjoyment of life. For the attainment of tranquility of spirit, Lucretius believes that the study of nature and nature's laws affords the greatest promise. From such a study can come a satisfying emotional and intellectual acceptance of universal law operative everywhere in the universe, by which all things are governed with order, regularity, and consistency. In this understanding alone lies the peace man seeks—a view that is clearly reminiscent of Spinoza's *amor dei intellectualis*.

On the Nature of Things*

I

Invocation to Venus

Mother of Aeneas' clan, of man and gods delight,
Since thou alone are Nature's queen,
Without thy help can nothing come to shining shores of light,
Nothing is gay without thee, nothing lovable,
I want thy help in writing verse
The verse I try to write for Memmius, my friend.
(Hast thou not willed that he excel at every time, in every thing?)
So, goddess, give eternal beauty to my words;
Grant me that while I write
Fierce war on land and sea may sleep and rest.
For thou alone canst grant to mortal man
Peace and its blessings,
Since Mars, in arms all-powerful, rules the fierce works of war,
Thy lover, Mars, who often sinks upon thy breast
Completely overcome by love's eternal wound.
And so, in thy embrace,
His shapely head pillowed upon thy breast,
He gazes on thee, feeds his eager eyes with love,
His whole soul hangs upon thy lips.
Do thou, Divine, embracing him reclined, with holy frame,
Pour out sweet whispered words, O goddess famed,
And beg the quiet of peace for Roman folk.†
I cannot carry out this task of mine with mind at peace
At such a crisis of my country's fate,
Nor could my Memmius betray his stock,
Or heedless be and fail his country's safety.
And so I pray for peace.
For all the gods enjoy eternal life in everlasting peace

---

* *The Roman Poet of Science Lucretius: De Rerum Natura*. English verse by Alban D. Winspear. (New York, S. A. Russell—The Harbor Press. Copyright © 1956 by A. D. Winspear.) Selected passages.

† Santayana makes the apt suggestion that Venus and Mars are for Lucretius but mythological symbols for the Love and Strife that the Greek philosopher Empedocles took to be fundamental forces in the universe: "The Mars and Venus of Lucretius are not moral forces, incompatible with the mechanism of the atoms; they are this mechanism itself insofar as it now produces and now destroys life." (*Three Philosophical Poets*, p. 40)

Far, far away from all the troubles of our world.
Free from danger, free from grief, strong through their strength alone
The godhead needs us not,
Nor is it won by our deserts nor moved by wrath.

The Poet begs his Friend, Memmius, to be attentive

Now for the rest lend me attentive ears
And turn a piercing mind not burdened down with cares
To true philosophy.
I would not have these gifts of mine
Set out for you with constant, faithful zeal,
Disdained before they're understood.
For I propose to tell
The highest laws of heaven and the gods,
Reveal the primal stuff of things
And show how from this primaeval atom stuff
Creative nature forms all things, and grows and nurtures them;
To which again
This same creative nature breaks them up and sends them back.
And this in our account we call
Matter, creative stuff of things or seeds of things,
Or primal bodies, some might say,
Because from these as elementary principles
Emerge all things that are.

II

The Joy and Peace that comes from Philosophy

O Sweet it is when on the mighty sea,
The wind stirs up great billows,
One's own foot firm on steady earth,
To watch another's troubles.
Not that we find delight in others' strugglings,
But that it's sweet to look on ills
From which oneself escapes.
Sweet, too, to look
When cavalcades of war contend upon the plain,
And one is safe, oneself.
But far surpassing everything in bliss it is
To occupy the high, serene, embattled eminence,
The ivory tower,
Whose muniments are thought and high philosophy,
The wisdom of the wise.
Here you look down and see, like tiny ants,
Men scurry to and fro, wandering here and there
Seeking to find the hidden path of life,
Well-spent, well-ordered.
You see them battle with their wits,

Pit lineage 'gainst lineage,
Working day and night with sinews and with mind,
To gain the crown of wealth, the pride of power.
Men's wretched minds, men's blinded hearts!
In darkness deep, in peril sore,
This little life of ours is passed.

How can you doubt that freedom from external things
Is sovereign gift of reason?
Is not all life in darkness spent?
Like tiny boys who tremble in the dark
And think that anything may come,
We, also, tremble in the light,
And shrink from things that, in themselves, are no more terrible
Than what boys fear in dreams and fancy sure to be.
And so this darkened terror of the mind
Must be dispelled
Not by the rays of sun, the gleaming shafts of day,
But by nature's laws, by looking in her face.

What Movement of the Atom Stuff made Things
And broke them down again when made

Come now, I will unfold and tell
What movement of the atom stuff made things
And broke them down again when made,
And what compulsion's brought to bear on them,
And what velocity's assigned to them,
To fall through mighty void.
You lend attentive ears.
We surely know,
That matter does not cling close packed.
We see a thing grow small in lapse of time
And flow away as in a stream
When age removes it from our eyes;
And yet the sum of things remains the same.
The reason is
That bodies moving from a thing diminish what they left
Augment the thing to which they come.
The one grows old, the other waxes strong.
Yet even with the new they don't remain eternally.
And so the sum of things is ever new
And all things mortal live by give and take.
The generations wax, the generations wane;
In time's brief span all living things are changed,
Like runners in a race pass on life's torch.
Now if you think
That atom stuff can stand quite still
And standing still create new movements in the world of things

You're very wrong.
For since the atoms wander through the void
They either move by their own weight
Or else from impulse of the other atoms striking them.
For in their motion atom forms have often met and clashed
And so they leap apart—this way and that.
Nor is this wonderful,
For atoms are of stuff most hard with solid weight,
And nothing can withstand them in the rear.
The more you contemplate the atoms tossing here and there
The more you'll bring to mind
There is no bottom to the whole vast universe
No place for atom stream to rest,
Since space is limitless and stretches far on every side.
All this I've shown in many words
And proved with reasoning acute.
Since this is true
No rest is there for atoms moving through the mighty void,
But rather harassed as they are with motion endless and diverse
Some, when they clash, leap apart in mighty intervals
Others a small way only from the blow.
And when the unity of atom forms is close
When atoms only leap a little way apart
(Because entangled by their own close-locking shapes)
These constitute the hardy roots of rock,
The savage bulk of iron and other things like that.
But of the rest which wander through the mighty void
A few leap far apart and leave great space between.
Now these create thin air, and shining light of sun.
But many wander through unending space
And have no chance
To meet and link themselves with other atom forms,
Or unify their moves with theirs.
Of these lone atoms, just as I've said
An image and a likeness ever turns
And presses on our eyes.

The Conservation of Matter and Motion

The total stock of matter was not in days of old more dense,
Nor looser packed with greater intervals
Than now it is.
For nothing ever comes to join the total stock
Nor leaves,
To lessen or increase its store.
The atoms through the ages past
Moved as now they do;
And even so they'll move eternally.
And what before was wont to come to be
Will come to be again by laws the same;

Exist and grow, be strong and flourishing
So far as Nature's laws permit.
No force can change the sum of things.
There's nothing left beyond the boundaries of the universe
To which the atoms might escape,
Nor whence a force might rise and burst into the world,
To alter all the motions of the universe and change its basic laws.

Everything in the Universe is made of Atoms and Space. There cannot be a third principle

The whole of Nature is of two things built,
Atoms and void.
The void in which the atom forms are placed
In which they move, hither and yon.
The universal sense of eyes and ears declare to men
Bodies exist.
Unless our faith in sense is grounded sure and strong,
Beyond the sense there's not a single principle
To which we can appeal to prove a thought about the hidden things.
By reason's sheer unaided power,
Nothing could we prove by reasoning of the mind.
Were there not room and empty space
The space which we call void
No bodies ever, anywhere could find a place
Nor could they move at all in various ways.
And this I've proved to you a little while ago.
Besides these two first principles,
There could not be a third constituent in the eternal scheme of things
Severed alike from body and from void.
For whatever is, must, of necessity,
Be something in itself.
And if it can be touched, however small and light the touch,
It swells the sum of things by increase small or great,
Provided only that it *is* at all.
If it's beyond the reach of touch
It has no power to stop another thing from passing through,
Right through itself and passing on its way.
It then must be what we've described
As empty space or void.
Again whate'er exists
Must either act on things, be acted on,
Or else allow action, reaction somewhere in its frame.
Unless it's bodily, no thing can act, be acted on, or space afford
For action and reaction; unless it's empty space or void.
And so apart from void and bodies there can never be
A third constituent in the scheme of things.
Nothing to move our sense at any time
Or let itself be grasped by reasoning of the mind.

A Doctrine New and Wonderful is struggling to penetrate your ears

And now please turn your mind to true philosophy.
A doctrine new and wonderful is struggling to penetrate your ears,
A novel face of things to show itself.
For even the easiest truth must find it hard at first to win belief,
And nothing is so great and marvellous,
But bit by bit men fail to hold the thing in awe.
The bright clear colour of the sky, and all its holds,
The stars that wander here and there,
The moon and shining sun with glorious light
Suppose that human kind could see all this afresh, anew.
If unexpectedly this pageant of the universe
Were placed before their eyes
What story could be told more marvellous than this
To what could human kind be less inclined to lend
Prior belief?
This is my view:—
There's nothing could compare in wonder with a novel sight like this.

And yet,
Sated and weary with the wonted sight
There's no one now who'll deign an upward glance,
Or gaze upon the shining temples of the sky.
So you,
Not struck with empty terror of the new
Spit not the glorious good of reason from your mind;
Rather with eager thought and judgment keen,
Weigh everything.
If you find it true then raise your hands and yield;
But if you find it false, prepare yourself to fight.
The human mind seeks truth.
Since space is infinite beyond the ramparts of the universe
It needs to know what lies afar in this infinity,
As far as human thought can penerate,
As far as free assault of mind can range unchecked.
Now first I claim our search has shown;—
In all directions, everywhere,
On every side, above, below, through all the universe,
That space is infinite.
This I have shown; the truth of this must scream aloud,
The darkness of the deep abyss, shine clear.

There are Many Worlds

Now here is something we must not think probable
Since space is infinite on every side,
Since atoms numberless throughout the mighty universe
Fly here and there, by motion everlasting e'er impelled,

That this one world of ours, this earth and sky
Alone were brought to birth.
We cannot cherish this belief—
Beyond the confines of the world we know,
Nature does nothing.
Particularly as the world we know
Was made by Nature thus;—
The atoms of their own accord
Jostled from time to time by chance,
In random fashion, clashed, and blindly, heedlessly
And oft in vain,
Until at last were unions suddenly achieved
To be the starting points of mighty things,
Of earth and sea and sky, of every living thing.
And so I say again, again you must confess
That somewhere in the universe
Are other meetings of the atom stuff resembling this of ours;
And these the ether holds in greedy grip.
For when the atom stuff is there,
And space in which the atom stuff can move,
And neither thing nor cause to bring delay,
The process of creation must go on; things must be made.
Now as it is,
If atom stocks are inexhaustible,
Greater than power of living things to count,
If Nature's same creative power were present too
To throw the atoms into unions—exactly as united now,
Why then confess you must
That other worlds exist in other regions of the sky,
And different tribes of men, kinds of wild beasts.

And if you learn this lesson well and cling to it
Why then you'll see
Nature in freedom now, her tyrant lords dethroned
Accomplish everything by her own spontaneous activity,
Without the help of gods.

III

In Praise of Epicurus, "the Teacher whom he held Divine"

Into thick darkness came of old bright light.
You do I follow, you, who brought the light
To show us what is good and bad in human life,
You do I follow, glory of the Grecian race,
And in your footsteps firmly plant my own.
Not that I want to rival you; affection makes me want to imitate.
How can a swallow vie with swans
Or kids with little tottering limbs
On race track vie with mighty practiced horse?
You are the father of my mind, discoverer of Nature.

From your books, O seer renowned,
You give a father's precepts in philosophy.
As bees in blooming meadows suck each flower,
So we your golden words repeatedly
We feed on them and find them golden,
Worthy of eternal life.
Soon as your thought, born of a godlike mind,
Began to thunder forth on Nature's laws,
Then all terrors from our spirit flee;
The ramparts of the world are torn apart.
I see the atoms' pageant streaming through the void.
The power of godhead is revealed,
The quiet untroubled haunts of deity,
Which are not shaken by the wanton winds,
Nor lashed from cloud with rain.
No snow falls white nor frost assails;
Cloudless the air that covers them, and heaven bounteously smiles,
While sky is bathed in light.
Nature supplies them all they need for tranquil life
And nothing ever mars "their sacred everlasting calm."
Guided by you we never catch a glimpse of Hell's recess.
Earth cannot block our vision. We can see
Whate'er goes on in space beneath our feet.
And so, thinking your thoughts
And with your guidance mastering science
A kind of godlike pleasure comes on me,
Pleasure and horror mixed,
Because your power of mind
Has left the works of Nature naked to my view.

"Now I must Tear up by the Roots and cast away that Fear of Death"

Now since I have discoursed on atoms and have shown
What kind they are, how different in shape,
And how, self-moved, they ever fly,
In motion everlasting e'er impelled,
And how from atoms every object can be made,
Now I must tear up by the roots and cast away
That fear of death,
That fear that sullies mortal life from end to end
And pours the murk of death on everything,
Leaves no man's pleasure pure and unalloyed.
For though men often say disease and infamy
More dreadful are than deepest depths of hell;
And though they hold that soul is blood or wind
(Whichever theory they are clinging to),
And so they claim they need not our philosophy,
Yourself can judge that this is done for pomp and arrogance
Rather than deep belief.

For these same men,
Exiled from country, banished from human sight,
Black with the blackest crimes, gnawed by a hundred cares,
Live all the same.
Wherever wretchedness and anguish places them,
They worship all the same,
Butcher their sleek black bulls and give their offerings
To guardian spirits of the dead.
Their troubles turn their mind to creed and cult.
And so it's good to watch men in adversity,
By mounting dangers pressed.
At times like these
Men pour their deepest thoughts from depth of breast.
The mask is torn away, the face remains.
Then too, the lust for power and place and wealth,
Motives which make men pass the bounds of law,
And join in crime and struggle night and day
With all their might to scale the heights of wealth,
These wounds of life are too much nurtured by the fear of death.
Like tiny boys who tremble in the dark
And think that anything may come,
We also tremble in the light and shrink from things
That in themselves are no more terrible
Than what boys fear in dreams and fancy sure to be.
And so this darkened terror of the mind must be dispelled
Not by the rays of sun or gleaming shafts of day,
But by Nature's laws, by looking in her face.

Death then is Nothing, affects us not at all, Since Mind is made of Mortal Stuff

Death then is nothing, affects us not at all,
Since soul is held to be of mortal stuff.
And just as in the past we knew no ill
When Punic hosts from all sides rushed to war,
When all the earth beneath the lofty shores of sky,
Trembled in dreadful battle,
And men could doubt which side was doomed for fall
And loss of empire on land and sea alike;
So, when we're dead,
When soul and body out of which we're formed, one entity,
Are torn apart in death,
Nothing can touch our sense at all or move our consciousness
(For we shall not be alive to know).

From this we learn there's naught to fear in death;
That once a man is dead he cannot be in misery,
That there's no difference if he never had been born,
When death immortal once has snatched away our mortal life.

So when you see a man lament
That after death his body rots away,
Is licked by flame or torn by teeth of beasts,
This you must know;
His words do not ring true,
Some hidden goad is lurking in his heart,
Even while his verbal creed denies
The fact of consciousness in death.
He does not (here's my view)
Follow his verbal creed nor ground thereof.
He does not fully tear his roots from life and throw himself away.
He unconsciously assumes a part of him remains.
For when a man, while still alive,
Pictures his body after death,
Imagines birds and beasts are gnawing at the corpse,
Indulges in self-pity,
His thought has failed to free his sense from that poor corpse,
Confounds it with himself and thinks the body "he."
And so he groans that he was born a mortal man,
And does not see that in real death there'll be no second self,
To live and mourn the dead and stand in lamentations,
While the self outstretched is torn or burned.

Why do you weep and groan at death?
If life was good for you
And all its joys have not drained off,
Like water poured in cracked receptacle,
And left untasted,
Why do you not, like guest at feast of life,
Slip peacefully away, with mind serene, poor fool,
Grasp quiet and nothingness?
But if your pleasures all have slipped away and life is burdensome,
Why add some more which in its turn will slip away
And never give you zest?
Should you rather not make an end to life and toil?

Does that seem sad, does that seem grim?
It seems to me more tranquil far,
Than any kind of sleep.

If the Whim takes hold of us to think of any Thing Straightway our Mind reflects on the same Thing

In these investigations, many questions we must ask and many things explain,
To meet our deep desire to find the truth.
And first we ask how this can be—
That if the whim takes hold of us to think of any thing,
Straightway our mind reflects on that same thing.
Does Nature for our whim create them all,

Prepare them for our mood?
(Though here and now, at this same time and place,
The folks around have minds on other things?)
And since the images are very rare and fine
The mind cannot with clarity descry them all,
Except the one it strains to see.
The others pass away
All but the one the mind's prepared to see.
The mind prepares itself and hopes to see
The several images in natural consequence.
And just because the mind prepares itself,
The images arrive in this same consequence.
This too you must have seen:
When eyes begin to see things that are fine
They strain themselves, prepare.
Nor without this can eyes perceive the finer things with clarity.
And even when the object of our vision's plain to see,
You must have noticed this:—
Unless you turn your mind to them,
It's just as though the thing were far away,
And all the time were never there.
Why wonder then if mind misses all else,
Except those things which eager attentiveness
Compels the mind to see.
Then to, the human race
Often will base a broad belief on tiny bits of evidence
And so wrap ourselves in snares of self-deceit.

Avoid, I beg You, Teleology

With all my heart I long that you should shun this fault of reasoning.
Through prudent fear and foresight in advance
This blunder miss:—
Don't ever think that eyes were made
In order that the human race might have the power to see.
Don't ever think that thighs or legs, based on the feet
Were made to bend that man might take long steps.
Don't ever think that forearms, joined to upper hands and arms
Were given us as servants either side
That we might do the things that serve our life.
Ideas like these which men proclaim are false in reasoning,
Abysmally confound effect with cause.
Nothing at all was brought to be in all our human frame
In order that the human race might use it;
What is brought to be creates its use.
Vision existed not at all
Before the light of eyes was brought to be;
Nor did men learn to pray in words before the tongue was brought to be.
The tongue arrived much before speech;
Ears before sound was heard;

And all the human limbs I think
Were there before their use.
And so I think they have not come to be because of us.

The Abode of the Gods

This, too, it cannot be that you believe
That holy places of the gods exist
In some remote abode of this great universe.
The nature of the gods is very fine
And from the grasp of human sense
Far, far, removed;
Nay scarcely to be grasped by power of human mind.
Now since the godhead is thus far below
The touch or blow of human hands,
It cannot touch whatever we find touchable.
(Nothing can touch which cannot in its turn be touched.)
Thus the abodes and seats of mighty gods
Cannot resemble ours.
They're rather rare and fine as gods themselves are fine.
All this I'll later prove with bounteous floods of argument.
And then to say that for the sake of man
The will of god brought forth the glorious universe,
And therefore man should praise this glorious work of god,
All worthy of all praise;
Hold that creation always was and always will endure;
To think it impious ever to shake in its eternal haunts
Assail with human arguments or overwhelm it utterly
What once for endless time
Was by the ancient wisdom of the deity
Established for the human race;
To think all this, pile up a mountainous argument,
Is foolishness, my friend.
What profit could our gratitude ensure to blessed and immortal gods,
That they attempt a favour for the sake of man?
Or after all the previous ages of tranquillity
What novelty could prompt a god to change his mode of life?
For only those can long for fundamental change,
To whom the old was not endurable.
For these immortal ones
Who never felt the pang of pain throughout the past,
Who lived a lovely life,
How could desire for basic change enkindle these?

This is Not Holiness

This is not holiness, before the sight of men,
Day after day to crawl up to a stone
(The ritual veil on head)
And never miss an altar;

Nor prostrate lie before the shrines of gods with outstretched palms
Nor slaughter hecatomb on hecatomb,*
Nor weave a litany of vow on vow.
No. Holiness is this: to contemplate with mind serene the whole.

---

* Sacrifice of a hundred oxen.

From Naturalism Toward Idealism: Aristotle

For sheer intellectual achievement, Aristotle stands with Plato, unequaled in the ancient world and perhaps not surpassed in the modern. Those who study his works in their entirety never cease to wonder at the range and power of his insight. It is easy to understand why Aristotle so overawed his readers for nearly two thousand years and led them to accept his word as the final authority on almost every conceivable subject. In all his far-reaching speculation, however, reason and experience are his sole authorities. His complete objectivity, his exactness, and his incisiveness stand among the best examples of scientific writing, but the vision and the poetic charm of Plato are not to be found in Aristotle's philosophy. Bertrand Russell has described Aristotle's work in typical fashion: "He is the first [philosopher] to write like a professor: his treatises are systematic, his discussions are divided into heads, he is a professional teacher, not an inspired prophet. His work is critical, careful, pedestrian, without any trace of Bacchic enthusiasm."[1]

Aristotle was born about 384 B.C. at Stagira, a town in Macedonia some two hundred miles north of Athens, where his father Nicomachus was a prominent physician. Soon after the boy's birth Nicomachus became court physician to the king of Macedonia and the family moved to Pella, the Macedonian capital. Little more is known of Aristotle's youth until when about eighteen he appeared in Athens to study at Plato's Academy. He was soon recognized as one of the ablest and most promising of the group gathered about Plato and remained at the academy until Plato's death in 347 B.C. Without any question Aristotle hoped to succeed Plato as head of the Academy but in time tension developed between the old master and his brilliant pupil, and upon Plato's death his nephew Speusippus, a man much less able than Aristotle, was selected as head of the Academy.

Under these circumstances Aristotle was happy to accept an invitation from Hermias, a former friend and colleague, to visit Assos in Asia Minor where Hermias had established himself as a benevolent dictator. Here Aristotle spent three or four pleasant years, beginning some lectures of his own in philosophy, gathering about him a group of disciples, and also marrying Pythias, the niece and adopted daughter of his benefactor. His reputation spread and Philip of Macedonia, whom he had probably known as a boy when his father was court physician in Pella, invited Aristotle to become the tutor of his son, Alexander. After some hesitation Aristotle decided to accept the offer. No doubt Plato's emphasis upon the idea of the philosopher king helped him reach this decision, but there is little indication that Aristotle exerted any lasting influence upon the young prince. When Philip was assassinated at the wedding of one of his daughters a few years later, Alexander became ruler of Macedonia and very soon established an empire quite

---

[1] *A History of Western Philosophy,* (New York, Simon & Schuster Inc., Copyright 1945 by Bertrand Russell), p. 161.

different in character from the political ideal favored by Aristotle in his well-known work on *Politics*.

In 334 B.C., just thirteen years after leaving Plato's Academy, Aristotle returned to Athens. Now fifty years old and the acknowledged leader of the former Platonists who had drifted away from the Academy, he was ready to establish a rival school of his own. For this purpose he rented some buildings—as an alien he could not buy them—in a park northeast of Athens dedicated to Apollo Lyceus. The school soon became known as the Lyceum, and the group were nicknamed the Peripatetic philosophers because of Aristotle's practice of walking about in the park as he discussed philosophy informally with his followers each morning. The afternoons, however, seem to have been devoted to more formal lectures on rhetoric and oratory given to larger audiences. There is a record that the Lyceum also contained a chapel dedicated to the Muses and a colonnade to house a display of maps.

Upon the death of Alexander in 323 B.C. the Athenians rebelled against their Macedonian rulers. Aristotle, even though he had refrained from active participation in local politics, was associated with the Macedonian party in Athens and was at once attacked. Remembering the fate of Socrates, he decided to depart from the city before it was too late, not wishing, he said "to give the Athenians the chance to sin a second time against philosophy." Turning the direction of the Lyceum over to Theophrastus, one of his more able associates, he retired to his country estate a safe distance away. In ill health when he retired, he died at his estate the following summer (322 B.C.) at the age of sixty-two.

Aristotle's approach to philosophy in general and his major disagreement with Plato in particular can best be understood in terms of the divergent scientific outlook of the two men. Plato, as we have seen, was attracted primarily by mathematics. As a mathematician, he thought in terms of laws and principles that are rational and universal; two plus two has always equaled four and always will. The laws of gravity are not something we see but something we discern by reason. Reality, as the mathematician conceives it, is rational, unchanging, and eternal. Aristotle, on the other hand, was deeply influenced by the natural sciences, especially biology, and he was impressed, first of all by change and development. To be alive, a thing must grow, change, mature. But Aristotle also recognized the necessity of patient observation, collection of factual information, and careful analysis if one hoped to gain valid knowledge. Hence, it was not the universal but the particular, the concrete, and the specific that demanded attention. The fundamental difference in philosophical outlook and spirit between Plato and Aristotle rests upon the fact that Plato saw the world through the eyes of a mathematician, whereas Aristotle saw life and reality largely as the biologist sees it. Thus, where Plato ranks among the ablest and most distinguished of the rationalists, Aristotle became one of the most influential exponents of naturalism.

The naturalism of Aristotle is apparent in every aspect of his thought. As a biologist, he conducted an extensive and painstaking investigation of some five hundred or more kinds of animals, describing the results of this study in half a dozen important works which gave birth to the scientific study of zoology.[2] The process of growth and development he recognized as by far the most important thing about life; and as life developed, it progressed steadily in complexity and in power. It is also possible, Aristotle saw, to correlate the growth of intelligence with complexity of structure and mobility of form. The surprising thing is that with all this data before him he did not arrive at a theory of biological evolution. His failure to do so was due in some measure no doubt to the influence upon him of Plato's theory of forms, for in the species Aristotle thought he discovered a form or pattern as fixed and immutable as those described by Plato.

When he moved from biology to psychology, Aristotle remained true to his naturalistic point of view. He rejects completely the dualism of Plato which would separate the soul from the body, and insists instead that body and soul, like form and matter, are two inseparable elements in a single reality. "The soul," he writes, "is the determining principle of the living body," "the essential and enduring character of a body possessing the capacity of life." Aristotle, moreover, finds an essential similarity between life at the lower vegetable and animal levels and life at the more complex and developed human level. It is just as meaningful to speak of the animal soul or the vegetable soul as of the human soul. For the "soul," as interpreted by Aristotle, is the entire vital principle of any living organism, the inner form that guides the life and development of the whole—or, to use his own term, its *entelechy*. Man's rational capacity, to be sure, distinguishes the human soul from that of the animal as in similar fashion the animal's ability to feel sensations and move about distinguishes the animal from the vegetable soul. But in each case the "soul" functions to give direction and purpose to the life of the organism. While this concept of "entelechy" clearly reflects the naturalism of Aristotle, one discovers here a naturalism in which the spirit of idealism is also present. "Nature, like mind," Aristotle writes, "always acts for a purpose, and this purpose is its end. In animals the soul is such an end (*telos*). That it should be so is according to nature, for every part of a living body is an organ of the soul. Evidently then all such parts are for the sake of the soul, which is their natural end."[3]

The moral philosophy of Aristotle, like his study of biology and psychology, is empirical and practical and thoroughly naturalistic in spirit. But here too one finds a clear synthesis of naturalism and idealism. As Aristotle interprets morals, there is no conflict between the natural and the ideal in human life; the moral ideal is not something artificial or arbitrary, to be imposed upon an individual at heart antagonistic to it. Excellence of all kinds, whether intellectual or moral, has its roots in nature. "We are just, temperate, courageous, and the like from our very birth," Aristotle writes; "natural moral states exist even in children and lower ani-

---

[2] Chief among these are his *Historia Animalium, De Partibus Animalium,* and *De Generatione Animalium.*

[3] *De Anima,* II, 1, 4.

mals. . . . It is neither by nature nor in defiance of nature that virtues arise in us. Nature gives us the capacity, and that capacity is perfected by habit."[4] For Aristotle, as Santayana has so well pointed out, "every ideal has a natural basis, and everything natural has an ideal development."

What then is the good life? It is, Aristotle affirms with frank simplicity, the happy life. The purpose of ethics is not to make men good against their wills, but to make them happy in accord with their deepest natural desires; and happiness can only be achieved as the potentialities of human nature are discovered and given opportunity for full development. The happy man is the man who is most fully and completely himself. Only in his metaphysics, culminating in the idea of God, does Aristotle find it necessary to move perhaps beyond the limits of naturalism for a final and adequate explanation of the universe as a whole; but even here he carries the naturalistic point of view as far as he feels it can be consistently and convincingly employed.

Some twenty major works of Aristotle have been preserved. Comments by early writers indicate that this is but a small part of the entire body of writing that he did, but even so almost every major field of scientific and philosophical thought is covered in these works. His books on biology and psychology have already been mentioned; those on physics and astronomy were almost as important. His six books on logic, later known as the *Organon* or "instruments of thought," became the established textbook in this field for almost two thousand years. But his works on ethics, metaphysics, and esthetics were even more significant. *The Nicomachean Ethics* (named for his son, Nicomachus, who edited it), the *Politics,* the *Poetics,* and the *Metaphysics* are still standard works not only for those interested in the history of thought, but for all who are genuinely concerned with basic issues in these fields.

---

[4] *Nicomachean Ethics,* VI, 13; II, 1.

The Ethics of Aristotle*

Book One

I

Aristotle begins, in a way characteristic of his method, with a generalization which, if accepted, will lead to a more exact account of his subject. It is a generalization which is fundamental to his philosophy and in his own mind there is no doubt about the truth of it.

It is thought that every activity, artistic or scientific, in fact every deliberate action or pursuit, has for its object the attainment of some good. We may therefore assent to the view which has been expressed that "the

---

* Aristotle, *The Nicomachean Ethics,* English translation by J. A. K. Thomson (London, Allen and Unwin, 1953). Book I, chapter subtitles shortened.

good" is "that at which all things aim."[1] Since modes of action involving the practiced hand and the instructed brain are numerous, the number of their ends is proportionately large. For instance, the end of medical science is health; of military science, victory; of economic science, wealth. All skills of that kind which come under a single "faculty"—a skill in making bridles or any other part of a horse's gear come under the faculty or art of horsemanship, while horsemanship itself and every branch of military practice comes under the art of war, and in like manner other arts and techniques are subordinate to yet others —in all these the ends of the master arts are to be preferred to those of the subordinate skills, for it is the former that provide the motive for pursuing the latter.

II

Ethics, a Branch of Politics

Now if there is an end which as moral agents we seek for its own sake, and which is the cause of our seeking all the other ends— if we are not to go on choosing one act for the sake of another, thus landing ourselves in an infinite progression with the result that desire will be frustrated and ineffectual—it is clear that this must be the good, that is, the absolutely good. May we not then argue from this that a knowledge of the good is a great advantage to us in the conduct of our lives? Are we not more likely to hit the mark if we have a target? If this be true, we must do our best to get at least a rough idea of what the good really is, and which of the sciences, pure or applied, is concerned with the business of achieving it.

Now most people would regard the good as the end pursued by that study which has the most authority and control over the rest. Need I say that this is the science of poli-

---

[1] It is of course obvious that to a certain extent they do not all aim at the same thing, for in some cases the end will be an activity, in others the product which goes beyond the actual activity. In the arts which aim at results of this kind the results or products are intrinsically superior to the activities.

tics? It is political science that prescribes what subjects are to be taught in states, which of these the different sections of the population are to learn, and up to what point. We see also that the faculties which obtain most regard come under this science; for example, the art of war, the management of property, the ability to state a case. Since, therefore, politics makes use of the other practical sciences, and lays it down besides what we must do and what we must not do, its end must include theirs. And that end, in politics as well as in ethics, can only be the good for man. For even if the good of the community coincides with that of the individual, the good of the community is clearly a greater and more perfect good both to get and to keep. This is not to deny that the good of the individual is worth while. But what is good for a nation or a city has a higher, a diviner quality.

Such being the matters we seek to investigate, the investigation may fairly be represented as the study of politics.

III

Politics not an Exact Science

In studying this subject we must be content if we attain as high a degree of certainty as the matter of it admits. The same accuracy or finish is not to be looked for in all discussions any more than in all the productions of the studio and the workshop. The question of the morally fine and the just—for this is what political science attempts to answer—admits of so much divergence and variation of opinion that it is widely believed that morality is a convention and not part of the nature of things. We find a similar fluctuation of opinion about the character of the good. The reason for this is that quite often good things have hurtful consequences. There are instances of men who have been ruined by their money or killed by their courage. Such being the nature of our subject and such our way of arguing in our discussions of it, we must be satisfied with a rough outline of the truth, and for the same reason we must be content with broad conclusions. Indeed we must preserve this attitude when it comes to a more detailed statement of the views that are held. It is a mark of the educated man and a proof of his culture that in every subject he looks for only so much precision as its nature permits. For example, it is absurd to demand logical demonstrations from a professional speaker; we might as well accept mere probabilities from a mathematician.

Every man is a good judge of what he understands: in special subjects the specialist, over the whole field of knowledge the man of general culture. This is the reason why political science is not a proper study for the young. The young man is not versed in the practical business of life from which politics draws its premises and its data. He is, besides, swayed by his feelings, with the result that he will make no headway and derive no benefit from a study the end of which is not *knowing* but *doing*. It makes no difference whether the immaturity is in age or in character. The defect is not due to lack of years but to living the kind of life which is a succession of unrelated emotional experiences. To one who is like that, knowledge is as unprofitable as it is to the morally unstable. On the other hand, for those whose desires and actions have a rational basis a knowledge of these principles of morals must be of great advantage.

IV
Happiness, the Supreme Good

To resume. Since every activity involving some acquired skill or some moral decision aims at some good, what do we take to be the end of politics—what is the supreme good attainable in our actions? Well, so far as the name goes there is pretty general agreement. "It is happiness," say both intellectuals and the unsophisticated, meaning by "happiness" living well or faring well. But when it comes to saying in what happiness consists, opinions differ, and the account given by the generality of mankind is not at all like that given by the philosophers. The masses take it to be something plain and tangible, like pleasure or money or social standing. Some maintain that it is one of these, some that it is another, and the same man will change his opinion about it more than once. When he has caught an illness he will say that it is health, and when he is hard up he will say that it is money. Conscious that they are out of their depths in such discussions, most people are impressed by anyone who pontificates and says something that is over their heads. Now it would no doubt be a waste of time to examine all these opinions; enough if we consider those which are most in evidence or have something to be said for them. Among these we shall have to discuss the view held by some that, over and above particular goods like those I have just mentioned, there is another which is good in itself and the cause of whatever goodness there is in all these others.

V
Views on Happiness

There is a general assumption that the manner of a man's life is a clue to what he on reflection regards as the good—in other words, happiness. Persons of low tastes (always in the majority) hold that it is pleasure. Accordingly they ask for nothing better than the sort of life which consists in having a good time. (I have in mind the three well-known types of life—that just mentioned, that of the man of affairs, and the contemplative life.) The utter vulgarity of the herd of men comes out in their preference for the sort of existence a cow leads. Their view would hardly get a respectful hearing, were it not that those who occupy great positions sympathize with a monster of sensuality like Sardanapalus. This gentleman, however, and the man of affairs identify the good with honour, which may fairly be described as the end which men pursue in political or public life. Yet honour is surely too superficial a thing to be the good we are seeking. Honour depends more on those who confer than on him who receives it, and we cannot but feel that the good is something personal and almost inseparable from its possessor. Again why do men seek honour? Surely in order to confirm the favourable opinion they have formed of themselves. It is at all events by intelligent men who know them personally that they seek to be honoured. And for what? For their moral qualities. The inference is clear; public men prefer virtue to honour. It might therefore seem reasonable to suppose that virtue rather than honour is the end pursued in the life of the public servant. But clearly even virtue cannot be quite the end. It is possible, most people think, to possess virtue while you are asleep, to possess it without acting under its influence during any portion of one's life. Besides, the virtuous man may meet with the most atrocious luck or ill-treatment; and nobody, who was not arguing for argument's sake, would maintain that a man with an existence of that sort was "happy."[2] The third type is the "contemplative," and this we shall discuss later.

As for the life of the business man, it does not give him much freedom of action. Besides, wealth obviously is not the good we seek, for the sole purpose it serves is to provide the means of getting something else. So far as that goes, the ends we have already mentioned would have a better title to be considered the good, for they are desired on their own account. But in fact even their claim must be disallowed. We may say that they have furnished the ground for many arguments, and leave the matter at that.

VI
Plato's Theory Examined

But we can hardly avoid examining the problem raised by the concept of a universal good. One approaches it with reluctance because the theory of "forms" was brought into philosophy by friends of mine. Yet surely it is the better, or rather the unavoidable, course above all for philosophers to defend the truth even at the cost of our most intimate feelings, since, though both are dear, it would be wrong to put friendship before the truth.

Those who introduced the theory of forms did not suppose that there existed forms of *groups* of things in which one of the things is thought of as prior in nature to an-

[2] I am absolved from a more detailed discussion of this point by the full treatment it has received in current literature.

other. This accounts for their not attempting to construct a form of "number" as distinct from particular numbers. Now a thing may be called good in three ways; in itself, in some quality it has, in some relation it bears to something else. But the essence of a thing —what it is in itself—is by its very nature prior to any relation it may have, such a relation being an offshoot or "accident" of it. Therefore there cannot be one form embracing *both* the absolutely *and* the relatively good.

Again, the word "good" is used in as many senses as the word "is." We may describe a person or a thing—God, for instance, or the reasoning faculty—as good in the sense of absolutely good. Or we may speak of things as good when we are thinking of their qualities or special excellences. Or we may use the word in connexion with the quantity of something, when we mean that there is a right amount of it; or in connexion with its relation to something else, as when we say that it is "useful," meaning good as means to an end; or in connexion with its occurrence in time, describing it as "the right moment," or in connexion with its position in space, as "a good place to live in." And so on. Using technical language we may predicate "good" in the categories of (a) substance, (b) quality, (c) quantity, (d) relation, (e) time, (f) space. Clearly then "good" is not something that can be said in one and the same sense of everything called "good." For then it could not be said in all these *different* senses, but only in one.

Again, things of which there is a single form must be things of which there is a single science. Consequently there should be (if the view we are discussing is right) a single science dealing with *all* good things. But what do we find? An indefinite number of sciences dealing with the goods coming under even one of the heads we have mentioned. Take "the right moment." The right moment in war is studied under military science, the right moment in sickness under the science of medicine. Similarly the right quantity in diet is considered by medicine, in bodily exercise by physical training.

Next, what do they mean by "the thing as it really is?" The question deserves some answer. For in their own terminology "man as he really is" is just another way of saying "man." In this respect, then, there will be no difference between them—they are both "man." But, if we are allowed to argue on these lines, we shall find no difference either between the really good and the good, in so far as both are good. Nor will the really good be any more good by being "eternal." You might as well say that a white thing which lasts a long time is whiter than one which lasts only a day.

To the arguments we have been using the objection may present itself that the champions of the forms did not mean their words to apply to *every* good. What they meant (it may be argued) was this. Those things, and those things only, which are pursued and desired on their own account are good. They are good as belonging to one species, while things tending in any way to produce or conserve them, or to check their opposites, are good in a different way, namely as means of achieving them. Clearly then there would be two kinds of "goods"—things good in themselves and things good as means to these. Let us take them separately. Consider first the things that are good in themselves. Are they called "good" because they come under a single form? Then what sort of things are the good in themselves? Are they all those things—intelligence, for example, or sight or certain pleasures and honours—that are sought entirely on their own merits? For these are things which, even if we pursue them with some remoter object in view, might be classified as things good in themselves. Or is there nothing good in itself except the form of the good? That would leave the class empty of content. If on the other hand things of the kind I have mentioned do form a class of things good in themselves, it will follow that the same notion of good will be as clearly recognizable in them as the same notion of whiteness presents itself to us in snow and in white lead. But when it comes to honour and sagacity and pleasure, the notions we have of them in respect of their goodness

are different and distinguishable. Therefore "good" is not a general term corresponding to a single form. How then does it happen that these different things are all called "good"? It can hardly be a mere coincidence. Various answers suggest themselves. All goods may derive from a single good, or all may contribute to form a single good. Or perhaps the answer may be expressed in an equation "As sight is good in the body, so is rationality in the mind." We could frame a series of such equations. But perhaps it is better to drop the discussion of that point here, since a full examination of it is more suited to another branch of philosophy.

And we must follow the same course in dealing with the form of the good. For, even if the good which is predicated of a number of different things exists only in one element common to them all, or has a separate existence of its own, clearly it cannot be realized in action or acquired by man. Yet it is just a good of that kind that is the subject of our present inquiry. The thought may indeed suggest itself that a knowledge of the absolute good may be desirable as a means of attaining to those goods which a man may acquire and realize in practice. Might we not use it as a pattern to guide us in acquiring a better knowledge of the things that are good "for us" and, so knowing, obtaining them? The argument has a certain plausibility, but it manifestly does not accord with the procedure followed by the sciences. For all these aim at some *particular* good and seek to fill up the gaps in their knowledge of how to attain *it*. They do not think it any business of theirs to learn the nature of the *absolute* good. Now it will take some persuading to make us believe that all the matters of technique do not possess, or even make an effort to possess, this knowledge, if it be so powerful an aid to them as is pretended. And there is another puzzle. What advantage in his art will a weaver or a joiner get from a knowledge of the absolute good? Or how shall a doctor or a general who has had a vision of Very Form become thereby a better doctor or general? As a matter of fact it does not appear that the doctor makes a study even of health in the abstract. What he studies is the health of the human subject or rather of a particular patient. For it is on such a patient that he exercises his skill. . . .

VII
Functional Definition of the Highest Good

From this digression, we may return to the good which is the object of our search. What is it? The question must be asked because good seems to vary with the art of pursuit in which it appears. It is one thing in medicine and another in strategy, and so in the other branches of human skill. We must inquire, then, what is the good which is the end common to all of them. Shall we say it is that for the sake of which everything else is done? In medicine this is health, in military science victory, in architecture a building, and so on—different ends in different arts; every consciously directed activity has an end for the sake of which everything that it does is done. This end may be described as its good. Consequently, if there be some one thing which is the end of all things consciously done, this will be the final good; or, if there be more than one end, then it will be all of these. Thus the ground on which our argument proceeds is shifted, but the conclusion arrived at is the same.

I must try, however, to make my meaning clearer.

In our actions we aim at more ends than cne—that seems to be certain—but, since we choose some (wealth, for example, or flutes and tools or instruments generally) as means to something else, it is clear that not all of them are ends in the full sense of the word, whereas the good, that is the supreme good, is surely such an end. Assuming then that there is some one thing which alone is an end beyond which there are no further ends, we may call *that* the good of which we are in search. If there be more than one such final end, the good will be that end which has the highest degree of finality than one pursued with an eye to something else. A corollary to that is that a thing which is never chosen as a means to some remoter object has a higher degree of finality than things which are chosen both as ends in themselves and as means to such ends. We may conclude, then, that something which is always chosen for its own sake and never for the sake of something else is without qualification as a final end.

Now happiness more than anything else appears to be just such an end, for we always choose it for its own sake and never for the sake of some other thing. It is different with honour, pleasure, intelligence, and good qualities generally. We choose them indeed for their own sake in the sense that we should be glad to have them irrespective of any advantage which might accrue from them. But we also choose them for the sake of our happiness in the belief that they will be instrumental in promoting that. On the other hand nobody chooses happiness as a means of achieving them or anything else whatsoever than just happiness.

The same conclusion would seem to follow from another consideration. It is a generally accepted view that the final good is self-sufficient. By "self-sufficient" is meant not what is sufficient for oneself living the life of a solitary but includes parents, wife and children, friends and fellow-citizens in general. For man is a social animal. A self-sufficient thing, then, we take to be one which on its own footing tends to make life desirable and lacking in nothing. And we regard happiness as such a thing. Add to this that we regard it as the most desirable of all things without having it counted in with some other desirable thing. For, if such an addition were possible, clearly we should regard it as more desirable when even the smallest advantage was added to it. For the result would be an increase in the number of advantages, and the larger sum of advantages is preferable to the smaller.

Happiness, then, the end to which all our conscious acts are directed, is found to be something final and self-sufficient.

But no doubt people will say, "To call happiness the highest good is a truism. We want a more distinct account of what it is."

We might arrive at this if we could grasp what is meant by the "function" of a human being. If we take a flutist or a sculptor or any craftsman—in fact any class of men at all who have some special job or profession—we find that his special talent and excellence comes out in that job, and this is his function. The same thing will be true of man simply as man—that is of course if "man" does have a function. But is it likely that joiners and shoemakers have certain functions or specialized activities, while man as such has none but has been left by Nature a functionless being? Seeing that eye and hand and foot and every one of our members has some obvious function, must we not believe that in like manner a human being has a function over and above these particular functions? Then what exactly is it? The mere act of living is not peculiar to man—we find it even in the vegetable kingdom—and what we are looking for is something peculiar to him. We must therefore exclude from our definition the life that manifests itself in mere nurture and growth. A step higher should come the life that is confined to experiencing sensations. But that we see is shared by horses, cows, and the brute creation as a whole. We are left, then, with a life concerning which we can make two statements. First, it belongs to the rational part of man. Secondly, it finds expression in actions. The rational part may be either active or passive: passive in so far as it follows the dictates of reason, active in so far as it possesses and exercises the power of reasoning. A similar distinction can be drawn within the rational life; that is to say, the reasonable element in it may be active or passive. Let us take it that what we are concerned with here is the reasoning power in action, for it will be generally allowed that when we speak of "reasoning" we really mean *exercising* our reasoning faculties. (This seems the more correct use of the word.) Now let us assume for a moment the truth of the following propositions. (a) The function of a man is the exercise of his noncorporeal faculties or "soul" in accordance with, or at least not divorced from, a rational principle. (b) The function of an individual

and of a *good* individual in the same class— a harp player, for example, and a good harp player, and so through the classes—is generically the same, except that we must add superiority in accomplishment to the function, the function of the harp player being merely to play on the harp, while the function of the good harp player is to play on it well. (c) The function of man is a certain form of life, namely an activity of the soul exercised in combination with a rational principle or reasonable ground of action. (d) The function of a good man is to exert such activity well. (e) A function is performed well when performed in accordance with the excellence proper to it.—If these assumptions are granted, we conclude that the good for man is "an activity of soul in accordance with goodness" or (on the supposition that there may be more than one form of goodness) "in accordance with the best and most complete form of goodness."

There is another condition of happiness; it cannot be achieved in less than a complete lifetime. One swallow does not make a summer; neither does one fine day. And one day, or indeed any brief period of felicity, does not make a man entirely and perfectly happy.

VIII
Virtue and Pleasure

Now our definition of happiness as an activity in accordance with virtue is in agreement with that of those who say it *is* virtue so far as such an activity *involves* virtue. But of course it makes a great difference whether we think of the highest good as consisting in the possession or in the exercise of virtue. It is possible for a disposition to goodness to exist in a man without anything coming of it; he might be asleep or in some other way have ceased to exercise his function as a man. But that is not possible with the activity in our definition. For in "doing well" the happy man will of necessity *do*. Just as at the Olympic games it is not the best-looking or the strongest men present who are crowned with victory but competitors—the successful competitors—so in the arena of human life the honours and rewards fall to those who show their good qualities in action.

Observe, moreover, that the life of the actively good is inherently pleasant. Pleasure is a psychological experience, and every man finds that pleasant for which he has a liking —"fond of" so-and-so is the expression people use. For example, a horse is a source of pleasure to a man who is fond of horses, a show to a man who is fond of sight-seeing. In the same way just actions are a source of pleasure to a man who likes to see justice done, and good actions in general to one who likes goodness. Now the mass of men do not follow any consistent plan in the pursuit of their pleasures, because their pleasures are not inherently pleasurable. But men of more elevated tastes and sentiments find pleasure in things which are in their own nature pleasant, for instance virtuous actions, which are pleasant in themselves and not merely to such men. So their life does not need to have pleasure fastened about it like a necklace, but possesses it as a part of itself. We may go further and assert that there is no good man who does not find pleasure in noble deeds. Nobody would admit that a man is just, unless he takes pleasure in just actions; or liberal, unless he takes pleasure in acts of liberality; and so with the other virtues. Grant this, and you must grant that virtuous actions are a source of pleasure in themselves. And surely they are also both good and noble, and that always in the highest degree, if we are to accept, as accept we must, the judgment of the good man about them, he judging in the way I have described. Thus, happiness is the best, the noblest, the most delightful thing in the world, and in it meet all those qualities which are separately enumerated in the inscription upon the temple at Delos:

> Justice is loveliest, and health is best
> And sweetest to obtain is heart's desire.

All these good qualities inhere in the activities of the virtuous soul, and it is these, or the best of them, which we say constitute happiness.

For all that those are clearly right who, as I remarked, maintain the necessity to a happy life of an addition in the form of material goods. It is difficult, if not impossible, to engage in noble enterprises without money to spend on them; many can only be performed through friends, or wealth, or political influence. There are also certain advantages, such as the possession of honoured ancestors or children, or personal beauty, the absence of which takes the bloom from our felicity. For you cannot quite regard a man as happy if he be very ugly to look at, or of humble origin, or alone in the world and childless, or—what is probably worse—with children or friends who have not a single good quality or whose virtues died with them. Well, as I said, happiness seems to require a modicum of external prosperity.

IX
*Friendship and Happiness**

Another debatable point concerning the happy man is this. Will friends be necessary to his happiness or not? It is commonly said that the happy, being sufficient to themselves, have no need of friends. All the blessings of life are theirs already; so, having all resources within themselves, they are not in need of anything else, whereas a friend, being an alter ego, is only there to supply what one cannot supply for oneself. Hence that line in the Orestes of Euripides:

> When Fortune smiles on us, what need
> of friends?

Yet it seems a strange thing that in the process of attributing every blessing to the happy man we should not assign him friends, who are thought to be the greatest of all external advantages. Besides, if it is more like a friend to confer than to receive benefits, and doing good to others is an activity which especially belongs to virtue and the virtuous man, and if it is better to do a kindness to a friend than to a stranger, the good man will have need of friends as objects of his active benevolence.

---

* This chapter is from Book IX (Ed.).

Hence a second question. Does one need friends more in prosperity than in adversity? There is a case for either of these alternatives. The unfortunate need people who will be kind to them; the prosperous need people to be kind to.

Surely also there is something strange in representing the man of perfect blessedness as a solitary or a recluse. Nobody would deliberately choose to have all the good things in the world, if there was a condition that he was to have them all by himself. Man is a social animal, and the need for company is in his blood. Therefore the happy man must have company, for he has everything that is naturally good, and it will not be denied that it is better to associate with friends than with strangers, with men of virtue than with the ordinary run of persons. We conclude then that the happy man needs friends.

As I said at the outset, happiness is an *activity*. Now an activity is demonstrably something that is in the course of doing, not something that has already come into existence as a material object. Suppose then that the following statements are true, as they evidently are. (a) Happiness consists in living and acting. (b) The activity of a good man is good and, being good, intrinsically pleasant. (c) The consciousness that a thing is one's own is pleasant. (d) We are better able to study our neighbors than ourselves, and their actions than our own. (e) Good men derive pleasure from the actions of other good men, their friends, inasmuch as such actions possess the quality of being good and the quality of being their own or as good as their own, both naturally pleasant qualities. If these five propositions are true, it follows that the perfectly happy man will have need of virtuous friends. For he elects to give his mind to the contemplation of actions that are good and his own, and the actions of a good man who is his friend may be so described. Besides, we all assume that the hapy man ought to enjoy life. Now the solitary man has a hard time of it. It is not easy to keep up a continuous activity by oneself; in the company of others and in relation to others it is not so difficult. Consequently the activity of the good man, which is pleasurable in itself, will be less discontinuous if he has friends about him. And this will help him to enjoy without intermission that pleasurable feeling which should be part of the happy man's existence.[3]

---

[3] Note that a good man, just because he is good, takes pleasure in virtuous actions and is disgusted with those which spring from wickedness in much the same way as a musician likes good music and is irritated by bad.

Romantic Naturalism: Rousseau

Jean Jacques Rousseau has a place today among the outstanding literary and philosophical figures of France, although for almost a century critics outside France were perplexed by his strange genius. Certainly no other writer of his time has exercised an influence such as his. The romantic movement in arts and letters owes as much or more to Rousseau than to any other man; the German romantics, and Goethe himself, all felt his influence; the poetry of Wordsworth reflects his ideas in line after line. In his *Confessions* Rousseau set the fashion for a new introspective approach that has permeated much of the best-known literature of our own century; in *Émile* he outlined an educational theory that marked a complete break with traditional practice and anticipated the philosophy of John Dewey. In political theory Rousseau's influence has been equally significant, his work in this field providing a transition from the outlook of the Middle Ages to our modern philosophy of the democratic state. His *Social Contract* easily ranks as the central document of the French Revolution, but his influence was not limited, of course, to the Revolution in France. Along with the thought of John Locke, his ideas are clearly evident in the political theory of Thomas Jefferson and the founding fathers of our American republic. In the opinion of G. D. H. Cole, Rousseau's *Social Contract* is a work of permanent insight and truth, to be classed among the world's greatest books on political philosophy.[1]

Perhaps the most extraordinary fact about Rousseau is that fame and even genius came to him almost despite himself. He was born in Geneva in 1712 and spent his youth in indolent, fickle, and lazy fashion, with no intellectual or social ambition. He aspired apparently to nothing beyond the passing pleasures of a mediocre existence and seemed to have no other interests than a sensual taste for romantic adventure. When only sixteen he ran away from home, during the next ten years wandering from one French city to another in circumstances which reflected no credit upon his character or ability.

Thereafter for much of his life he was supported by French women of means and social position to whom he was genuinely devoted in his own curious fashion. For some years as a young man he had a place in the household of Madame de Warren near Paris, and it was here, as a matter of fact, that his literary education really began. Under the stimulus of Madame de Warren's friendship he formed a taste for reading and, for a brief period of time, he read widely and with growing interest. Rousseau writes that during the pleasant summers that he spent at her country estate near Chambery (1738–1740) he tasted happiness pure and complete. But his deepest education did not come from the books he read; his real master was nature. To nature he was passionately devoted from childhood, and he felt that

---

[1] Jean Jacques Rousseau, *The Social Contract*, English translation and introduction by G. D. H. Cole (London, J. M. Dent and Sons, Ltd., 1913), p. viii.

burning love of nature which became so important in the work of the celebrated English romantic poets a century later.

For the first thirty-seven years of his life Rousseau gave little indication of any real ability, then suddenly without warning he was inspired and seemingly infused with genius. In 1749 he saw the announcement of a prize offered by the Academy of Dijon for the best essay on the question: "Has the progress of the arts and sciences tended to the purification or to the corruption of morality?" With his imagination fired for the first time by this idea, Rousseau composed a violent attack on the evil effects of civilization that won the prize and brought him almost immediate fame in French literary circles. His *Discourse on the Moral Effects of the Arts and Sciences* was at once vigorously attacked, however, by outraged philosophers and theologians, even indeed by the King of Poland. In the attempt to defend himself and develop his ideas, Rousseau produced within the next twelve years the influential works that have given him so important a place in modern thought.

These twelve years, 1750 to 1762, are the creative and significant years in his life. During the last six of them he was a guest in the household of Madame d'Épinay at the Hermitage in the forest of Montmorency. He took up his abode there on April 9, 1756, and in typical fashion later wrote: "It was on that day that I began to live." While at the Hermitage Rousseau completed his three greatest books, the *New Heloise, Émile,* and the *Social Contract.* These books brought to a climax the controversy he had stirred up and brought down on him the public condemnation that forced him to leave the Hermitage and end his life in loneliness and unhappiness. After 1762, his writing was all controversial, stirred by the violence that greeted *Émile* in particular. His final work, *The Reveries of a Solitary Walker,* was begun in 1776 and left incomplete at his death in 1778. His *Confessions* were published several years after his death.

Rousseau's early *Discourse on the Moral Effects of the Arts and Sciences* is not in itself of great importance, but in this essay he does vigorously advocate the naturalism that is central in all his later thought. The misery and immorality of modern civilization is traced to man's departure from his "natural" state and already there is clearly in his mind an ideal concept of "nature" that provides the key to the development of his philosophy as a whole. Five years later, in 1755, this basic concept is more clearly developed in a second work, his *Discourse on the Origin and Foundation of Inequality Among Men.* Half this essay is taken up with an imaginary description of the state of nature as Rousseau conceived it, and here his "noble savage" is born—man in the state of nature without the corruption, vice, and antagonism that Rousseau attributes to the forces of civilization. Rousseau declares explicitly that he does not suppose that this state of nature ever existed, but the Discourse gives his picture of the "natural man," of man's inherent human qualities stripped of all the sham and pretense that civilization forces upon him. This essay also contains his famous explanation of the source of most—if not all—of the evils of modern society:

The first man who, having enclosed a piece of ground, bethought himself of saying, *this is mine,* and found people simple enough to believe him, was the real founder of civil society. From how many crimes, wars and murders, from how many horrors and misfortunes might not any one have saved mankind, by pulling up the stakes, or filling up the ditch, and crying to his fellows, "Beware of listening to this imposter; you are undone if you once forget that the fruits of the earth belong to us all, and the earth itself to nobody."

The heart of Rousseau's naturalism lies in his concept of man's natural goodness; a fundamental contrast between the "state of nature" and the "state of society" runs through all his philosophy. Evil, he maintains, is not a part of man's nature but is introduced from without. The burden of guilt is thus conveniently shifted to society. Instead of the old Stoic and Christian dualism between good and evil in the human heart, a new dualism is set up between an artificial, corrupt society on the one hand, and "nature," or human nature, that is essentially good, on the other. What we must have in Rousseau's opinion are laws to regulate our social and economic life so as to prevent poverty, exploitation, slums, and unemployment, and thus make it possible for men and women to be the kind of people they naturally are and want to be. Rousseau is close here, of course, to much social thought of our own day, by no means all Marxist in outlook.

In his attack on social convention and hypocrisy Rousseau consistently finds beauty in the soul of anyone who is condemned by conventional social morality. The courtesan rehabilitated by love, a figure that enjoyed great literary popularity during the past century, goes back directly to Rousseau. If it can only be shown that a person is sympathetic, devoted to others, ready to sacrifice himself for the one he loves, we can pardon his sins of unrestraint, his lack of common honesty and decency. As Rousseau writes of Madame de Warren, "her conduct was reprehensible but her heart was pure." The chief sins fostered by society are hypocrisy, pretense, self-righteousness, the exploitation of the weak by the strong. The next step is inevitable: a crusade against the class that exploits and oppresses other classes and forces them into moral transgression. France in the mid-eighteenth century was ripe for such a doctrine, and the French Revolution found in Rousseau its greatest and most inspiring philosopher.

In *Émile* Rousseau was father of a revolution of a different sort, a revolution in educational philosophy and practice that has found its fullest expression in the work of John Dewey and the Progressive Education Movement on our own American scene. Three of Rousseau's basic ideas are given clear and persuasive expression in *Émile*. First, his doctrine of *the natural man:* What nature produces in man is good and right, but nature is more than desire and passion. Conscience and reason are the better part of human nature, designed to control and direct desire. The instincts of self-preservation (self-love) and sympathy (mutual-aid) are basic in man's nature for Rousseau. These instincts are prior to reason, just as goodness in man precedes morality.

Second, Rousseau's doctrine of *the natural education:* To return to nature does not mean to return to savagery; it means to provide for the full development of the inherent capacities of human nature. We are free and happy only as we develop naturally and are kept from the inhibitions, conventions, and hypocrisies that society would force upon the growing child. Education, religion, and government are the three great social institutions that guide the destiny of mankind and reform in all three is essential if the full development of man's natural capacities in the best society is to be achieved. *Émile,* although written as a detailed account of the ideal education for a youth turned over to Rousseau's care, is not intended as a practical manual so much as the broad outline of a philosophy and a system.

Third, *the natural religion:* Discarding both science and rational skepticism as well as the dogmatism of the established churches (whether Catholic or Protestant), Rousseau turns to conscience as the real source of religious faith. The moral sense is natural and common to all mankind, he argues; putting our faith in conscience, we are led naturally to belief in God. The world of nature outside and above us confirms the convictions of our moral nature inside. This picture of natural religion and of the general philosophy it entails is best stated by Rousseau in his famous "Creed of a Savoyard Priest," a part of which is reprinted in the selection included here.

The naturalism of Rousseau is quite obviously not that of Lucretius nor Irwin Edman. Neither is it the naturalism of John Dewey, even though it does show much similarity to Dewey's philosophy of education. Scientific naturalism, whether that of Dewey or of Lucretius, is essentially analytical, placing its confidence in intelligence and in scientific method, in reason rather than in emotion. Rousseau, on the other hand, is hostile to the intellectual, to logical analysis, and to scientific thought. As Irving Babbit points out, "Rosseau is the first of the great anti-intellectualists."[2] He assails skepticism in the name of instinct and emotion, his romantic philosophy providing a quite different dimension of naturalism in which moral conviction and religious faith play a much greater role than do scientific knowledge and the objective pursuit of truth.

[2] *Rousseau and Romanticism* (Boston, Houghton Mifflin Company, 1919), p. 166.

The Creed of A Savoyard Priest*

I

My child, do not look to me for learned speeches or profound arguments. I am no

* From the book *Émile; Or Education* by Jean Jacques Rousseau, translated by Barbara Foxley. Everyman's Library Edition (1911). Reprinted by permission of E. P. Dutton and Co., Inc.

great philosopher, nor do I desire to be one. I have, however, a certain amount of common-sense and a constant devotion to truth. I have no wish to argue with you nor even to convince you; it is enough for me to show you, in all simplicity of heart, what I really think. Consult your own heart while I speak; that is all I ask. If I am mistaken, I am honestly mistaken, and therefore my error will not be counted as a crime; if you, too, are honestly mistaken, there is no great harm done. If I am right, we are both endowed with reason, we have both the same motive for listening to the voice of reason. Why should not you think as I do?

By birth I was a peasant and poor; to till the ground was my portion; but my parents thought it a finer thing that I should learn to get my living as a priest and they found means to send me to college. I am quite sure that neither my parents nor I had any idea of seeking after what was good, useful, or true; we only sought what was wanted to get me ordained. I learned what was taught me, I said what I was told to say, I promised all that was required, and I became a priest. But I soon discovered that when I promised not to be a man, I had promised more than I could perform.

Conscience, they tell us, is the creature of prejudice, but I know from experience that conscience persists in following the order of nature in spite of all the laws of man. In vain is this or that forbidden; remorse makes her voice heard but feebly when what we do is permitted by well-ordered nature, and still more when we are doing her bidding. My good youth, nature has not yet appealed to your senses; you may long remain in this happy state when her voice is the voice of innocence. Remember that to anticipate her teaching is to offend more deeply against her than to resist her teaching; you must first learn to resist, that you may know when to yield without wrong-doing.

From my youth up I had reverenced the married state as the first and most sacred institution of nature. Having renounced the right to marry I was resolved not to profane the sanctity of marriage; for in spite of my education and reading I had always led a simple and regular life, and my mind had preserved the innocence of its natural instincts; these instincts had not been obscured by worldly wisdom, while my poverty kept me remote from the temptations dictated by the sophistry of vice.

This very resolution proved my ruin. My respect for marriage led to the discovery of my misconduct. I was arrested, suspended, and dismissed; I was the victim of my scruples rather than of my incontinence, and I had reason to believe, from the reproaches which accompanied my disgrace, that one can often escape punishment by being guilty of a worse fault.

A thoughtful mind soon learns from such experiences. I found my former ideas of justice, honesty, and every duty of man overturned by these painful events, and day by day I was losing my hold on one or another of the opinions I had accepted. What was left was not enough to form a body of ideas which could stand alone and I felt that the evidence on which my principles rested was being weakened; at last I knew not what to think, and I came to the same conclusion as yourself, but with this difference My lack of faith was the slow growth of manhood, attained with great difficulty and all the harder to uproot.

I was in that state of doubt and uncertainty which Descartes considers essential to the search for truth. It is a state which cannot continue, it is disquieting and painful; only vicious tendencies and an idle heart can keep us in that state. My heart was not so corrupt as to delight in it, and there is nothing which so maintains the habit of thinking as being better pleased with oneself than with one's lot.

I pondered, therefore, on the sad fate of mortals, adrift upon this sea of human opinions, without compass or rudder, and abandoned to their stormy passions with no guide but an inexperienced pilot who does not know whence he comes or whither he is going. I said to myself, "I love truth, I seek her, and cannot find her. Show me truth and I will hold her fast; why does she hide her face from the eager heart that would fain worship her?"

Although I have often experienced worse sufferings, I have never led a life so uniformly distressing as this period of unrest and anxiety, when I wandered incessantly from one doubt to another, gaining nothing from my prolonged meditations but uncertainty, darkness, and contradiction with regard to the source of my being and the rule of my duties.

I cannot understand how any one can be a sceptic sincerely and on principle. Either such philosophers do not exist or they are the most miserable of men. Doubt with regard to what we ought to know is a condition too violent for the human mind; it cannot long be endured; in spite of itself the mind decides one way or another, and it prefers to be deceived rather than to believe nothing.

I consulted the philosophers, I searched their books and examined their various theories; I found them all alike proud, assertive, dogmatic, professing, even in their so-called scepticism, to know everything, proving nothing, scoffing at each other. This last trait, which was common to all of them, struck me as the only point in which they were right. Braggarts in attack, they are weaklings in defence. Weigh their arguments, they are all destructive; count their voices, every one speaks for himself; they are only agreed in arguing with each other. I could find no way out of my uncertainty by listening to them.

I suppose this prodigious diversity of opinion is caused, in the first place, by the weakness of the human intellect; and, in the second, by pride. We have no means of measuring this vast machine, we are unable to calculate its workings; we know neither its guiding principles nor its final purpose; we do not know ourselves, we know neither our nature nor the spirit that moves us; we scarcely know whether man is one or many; we are surrounded by impenetrable mysteries. These mysteries are beyond the region of sense, we think we can penetrate them by the light of reason, but we fall back on our imagination. Through this imagined world each forces a way for himself which he holds to be right; none can tell whether his path will lead him to the goal. Yet we long to know and understand it all. The one thing we do not know is the limit of the knowable. We prefer to trust to chance and to believe what is not true, rather than to own that not one of us can see what really is. A fragment of some vast whole whose bounds are beyond our gaze, a fragment abandoned by its Crea-

tor to our foolish quarrels, we are vain enough to want to determine the nature of that whole and our own relations with regard to it.

If the philosophers were in a position to declare the truth, which of them would care to do so? Every one of them knows that his own system rests on no surer foundations than the rest, but he maintains it because it is his own. There is not one of them who, if he chanced to discover the difference between truth and falsehood, would not prefer his own lie to the truth which another had discovered. Where is the philosopher who would not deceive the whole world for his own glory? If he can rise above the crowd, if he can excel his rivals, what more does he want? Among believers he is an atheist; among atheists he would be a believer.

II

The first thing I learned from these considerations was to restrict my inquiries to what directly concerned myself, to rest in profound ignorance of everything else, and not even to trouble myself to doubt anything beyond what I required to know.

I also realised that the philosophers, far from ridding me of any vain doubts, only multiplied the doubts that tormented me and failed to remove any one of them. So I chose another guide and said, "Let me follow the Inner Light; it will not lead me so far astray as others have done, or if it does it will be my own fault, and I shall not go so far wrong if I follow my own illusions as if I trusted to their deceits."

Bearing thus within my heart the love of truth as my only philosophy and as my only method a clear and simple rule which dispensed with the need for vain and subtle arguments, I returned with the help of this rule to the examination of such knowledge as concerned myself; I was resolved to admit as self-evident all that I could not honestly refuse to believe, and to admit as true all that seemed to follow directly from this; all the rest I determined to leave undecided, neither accepting nor rejecting it, nor yet troubling myself to clear up difficulties which did not lead to any practical ends.

But who am I? What right have I to decide? What is it that determines my judgments? If they are inevitable, if they are the results of the impressions I receive, I am wasting my strength in such inquiries; they would be made or not without any interference of mine. I must therefore first turn my eyes upon myself to acquaint myself with the instrument I desire to use, and to discover how far it is reliable.

I exist, and I have senses through which I receive impressions. This is the first truth that strikes me and I am forced to accept it. Have I any independent knowledge of my existence, or am I only aware of it through my sensations? This is my first difficulty, and so far I cannot solve it. For I continually experience sensations, either directly or indirectly through memory, so how can I know if the feeling of *self* is something beyond these sensations or if it can exist independently of them?

My sensations take place in myself, for they make me aware of my own existence; but their cause is outside me, for they affect me whether I have any reason for them or not, and they are produced or destroyed independently of me. So I clearly perceive that my sensation, which is within me, and its cause or its object, which is outside me, are different things.

Thus, not only do I exist, but other entities exist also, that is to say, the objects of my sensations; and even if these objects are merely ideas, still these ideas are not me.

But everything outside myself, everything which acts upon my senses, I call matter, and all the particles of matter which I suppose to be united into separate entities I call bodies. Thus all the disputes of the idealists and the realists have no meaning for me; their distinctions between the appearance and the reality of bodies are wholly fanciful.

I am now as convinced of the existence of the universe as of my own. I next consider the objects of my sensations, and I find that I have the power of comparing them, so I perceive that I am endowed with an active force of which I was not previously aware.

To perceive is to feel; to compare is to judge; to judge and to feel are not the same. Through sensation objects present themselves to me separately and singly as they are in nature; by comparing them I rearrange them. I shift them so to speak, I place one upon another to decide whether they are alike or different, or more generally to find out their relations. To my mind, the distinctive faculty of an active or intelligent being is the power of understanding the word "is." I seek in vain in the merely sensitive entity that intelligent force which compares and judges; I can find no trace of it in its nature. This passive entity will be aware of each object separately, it will even be aware of the whole formed by the two together, but having no power to place them side by side it can never compare them, it can never form a judgment with regard to them.

This power of my mind which brings my sensations together and compares them may be called by any name; let it be called attention, meditation, reflection, or what you will; it is still true that it is in me and not in things, that it is I alone who produce it, though I only produce it when I receive an impression from things. Though I am compelled to feel or not to feel, I am free to examine more or less what I feel.

Being now, so to speak, sure of myself, I begin to look at things outside myself, and I behold myself with a sort of shudder flung at random into this vast universe, plunged as it were into the vast number of entities, knowing nothing of what they are in themselves or in relation to me. I study them, I observe them; and the first object which suggests itself for comparison with them is myself.

All that I perceive through the senses is matter, and I deduce all the essential properties of matter from the sensible qualities which make me perceive it, qualities which are inseparable from it. I see it sometimes in motion, sometimes at rest; hence I infer that neither motion nor rest is essential to it, but motion, being an action, is the result of a cause of which rest is only the absence. When, therefore, there is nothing acting upon matter, it does not move, and for the very reason that rest and motion are indifferent to it, its natural state is a state of rest.

Yet this visible universe consists of matter, matter diffused and dead, matter which has none of the cohesion, the organisation, the common feeling of the parts of a living body, for it is certain that we who are parts have no consciousness of the whole. This same universe is in motion, and in its movements, ordered, uniform, and subject to fixed laws; it has none of that freedom which appears in the spontaneous movements of men and animals. So the world is not some huge animal which moves of its own accord; its movements are therefore due to some external cause, a cause which I cannot perceive, but the inner voice makes this cause so apparent to me that I cannot watch the course of the sun without imagining a force which drives it, and when the earth revolves I think I see the hand that sets it in motion.

If I must accept general laws whose essential relation to matter is unperceived by me, how much further have I got? These laws, not being real things, not being substances, have therefore some other basis unknown to me. Experiment and observation have acquainted us with the laws of motion; these laws determine the results without showing their causes; they are quite inadequate to explain the system of the world and the course of the universe. With the help of dice Descartes made heaven and earth; but he could not set his dice in motion, nor start the action of his centrifugal force without the help of rotation. Newton discovered the law of gravitation; but gravitation alone would soon reduce the universe to a motionless mass; he was compelled to add a projectile force to account for the elliptical course of the celestial bodies; let Newton show us the hand that launched the planets in the tangent of their orbits.

III

The first causes of motion are not to be found in matter; matter receives and transmits motion, but does not produce it. The more I observe the action and reaction of the forces of nature playing on one another, the more I see that we must always go back from one effect to another, till we arrive at a first cause in some will; for to assume an infinite succession of causes is to assume that there is no first cause. In a word, no motion which is not caused by another motion can take place, except by a spontaneous voluntary action; inanimate bodies have no action but motion, and there is no real action without will. This is my first principle. I believe, therefore, that there is a will which sets the universe in motion and gives life to nature. This is my first dogma, or the first article of my creed.

How does a will produce a physical and corporeal action? I cannot tell, but I perceive that it does so in myself; I will to do something and I do it; I will to move my body and it moves, but if an inanimate body, when at rest, should begin to move itself, the thing is incomprehensible and without precedent. The will is known to me in its action, not in its nature. I know this will as a cause of motion, but to conceive of matter as producing motion is clearly to conceive of an effect without a cause, which is not to conceive at all.

If matter in motion points me to a will, matter in motion according to fixed laws points me to an intelligence; that is the second article of my creed. To act, to compare, to choose, are the operations of an active, thinking being; so this being exists. Where do you find him existing, you will say? Not merely in the revolving heavens, nor in the sun which gives us light, not in myself alone, but in the sheep that grazes, the bird that flies, the stone that falls, and the leaf blown by the wind.

I judge of the order of the world, although I know nothing of its purpose, for to judge of this order it is enough for me to compare the parts one with another, to study their co-operation, their relations, and to observe their united action. I know not why the universe exists, but I see continually how it is changed; I never fail to perceive the close connection by which the entities of which it consists lend their aid to one another. I am like a man who sees the mechanism, though he does not know the use of the instrument and has never seen its face. I do not know what this is for, says he, but I see that each part of it is fitted to the rest, I admire the workman in the details of his work, and I am quite certain that all these wheels only work together in this fashion for some common end which I cannot perceive.

Let us compare the special ends, the means, the ordered relations of every kind, then let us listen to the inner voice of feeling; what healthy mind can reject its evidence? Unless the eyes are blinded by prejudices, can they fail to see that the visible order of the universe proclaims a supreme intelligence? What sophisms must be brought together before we fail to understand the harmony of existence and the wonderful cooperation of every part for the maintenance of the rest? Say what you will of combinations and probabilities; what do you gain by reducing me to silence if you cannot gain my consent? And how can you rob me of the spontaneous feeling which, in spite of myself, continually gives you the lie? If organised bodies had come together fortuitously in all sorts of ways before assuming settled forms, if stomachs are made without mouths, feet without heads, hands without arms, imperfect organs of every kind which died because they could not preserve their life, why do none of these imperfect attempts now meet our eyes; why has nature at length prescribed laws to herself which she did not at first recognise? I must not be surprised if that which is possible should happen, and if the improbability of the event is compensated for by the number of the attempts. I grant this: yet if any one told me that printed characters scattered broadcast had produced the *Aeneid* all complete, I would not condescend to take a single step to verify this falsehood. You will tell me I am forgetting the multitude of attempts. But how many such attempts must I assume to bring the combination within the bounds of probability? For my own part the only possible assumption is that the chances are infinity to one that the product is not the work of chance. In addi-

tion to this, chance combinations yield nothing but products of the same nature as the elements combined, so that life and organization will not be produced by a flow of atoms, and a chemist when making his compounds will never give them a thought and feeling in his crucible.

What absurd assumptions are required to deduce all this harmony from the blind mechanism of matter set in motion by chance! In vain do those who deny the unity of intention manifested in the relations of all the parts of this great whole, in vain do they conceal their nonsense under abstractions, coordinations, general principles, symbolic expressions; whatever they do I find it impossible to conceive of a system of entities so firmly ordered unless I believe in an intelligence that orders them. It is not in my power to believe that passive and dead matter can have brought forth living and feeling beings, that blind chance has brought forth intelligent beings, that that which does not think has brought forth thinking beings.

I believe, therefore, that the world is governed by a wise and powerful will; I see it or rather I feel it, and it is a great thing to know this. But has this same world always existed, or has it been created? Is there one source of all things? Are there two or many? What is their nature? I know not; and what concern is it of mine? When these things become of importance to me I will try to learn them; till then I abjure these idle speculations, which may trouble my peace, but cannot affect my conduct nor be comprehended by my reason.

Recollect that I am not preaching my own opinion but explaining it. Whether matter is eternal or created, whether its origin is passive or not, it is still certain that the whole is one, and that it proclaims a single intelligence; for I see nothing that is not part of the same ordered system, nothing which does not co-operate to the same end, namely the conservation of all within the established order. This being who wills and can perform his will, this being active through his own power, this being, whoever he may be, who moves the universe and orders all things, is what I call God. To this name I add the ideas of intelligence, power, will, which I have brought together, and that of kindness which is their necessary consequence; but for all this I know no more of the being to which I ascribe them. He hides himself alike from my senses and my understanding; the more I think of him, the more perplexed I am; I know full well that he exists, and that he exists of himself alone; I know that my existence depends on his, and that everything I know depends upon him also. I see God everywhere in his works; I feel him within myself; I behold him all around me; but if I try to ponder him himself, if I try to find out where he is, what he is, what is his substance, he escapes me and my troubled spirit finds nothing.

IV

While I meditated upon man's nature, I seemed to discover two distinct principles in it; one of them raised him to the study of the eternal truths, to the love of justice, and of true morality, to the regions of the world of thought, which the wise delight to contemplate; the other led him downwards to himself, made him the slave of his senses, of the passions which are their instruments, and thus opposed everything suggested to him by the former principle. When I felt myself carried away, distracted by these conflicting motives, I said, No; man is not one; I will and I will not; I feel myself at once a slave and a free man; I perceive what is right, I love it, and I do what is wrong; I am active when I listen to the voice of reason; I am passive when I am carried away by my passions; and when I yield, my worst suffering is the knowledge that I might have resisted.

I know very well in myself when I have done what I wanted and when I have merely given way to my passions. I have always the power to will, but not always the strength to do what I will. When I yield to temptation, I surrender myself to the action of external objects. When I blame myself for this weakness, I listen to my own will alone; I am a slave in my vices, a free man in my remorse; the feeling of freedom is never effaced in me but when I myself do wrong, and when I at length prevent the voice of the soul from protesting against the authority of the body.

No doubt I am not free not to desire my own welfare. I am not free to desire my own hurt; but my freedom consists in this very thing, that I can will what is for my own good, or what I esteem as such, without any external compulsion. Does it follow that I am not my own master because I cannot be other than myself?

The motive power of all action is the will of a free creature; we can go no farther. It is not the word freedom that is meaningless, but the word necessity, To suppose some action which is not the effect of an active motive power is indeed to suppose effects without cause, to reason in a vicious circle. Either there is no original impulse, or every original impulse has no antecedent cause, and there is no will properly so-called without freedom. Man is therefore free to act, and as such he is animated by an immaterial substance; that is the third article of my creed. From these three you will easily deduce the rest, so that I need not enumerate them.

If man is at once active and free, he acts of his own accord; what he does freely is no part of the system marked out by Providence and it canot be imputed to Providence. Providence does not will the evil that man does when he misuses the freedom given to him; neither does Providence prevent him from doing it, either because the wrong done by so feeble a creature is as nothing in its eyes, or because it could not prevent it without doing a greater wrong and degrading his nature. Providence has made him free that he may choose the good and refuse the evil. It has made him capable of this choice if he uses rightly the faculties bestowed upon him, but it has so strictly limited his powers that the misuse of his freedom cannot disturb the general order. The evil that man does reacts upon himself without affecting the system of the world, without preventing the preservation of the human species in spite of itself. To complain that God does not prevent us from doing wrong is to complain because he has made man of so excellent a nature, that he has endowed his actions with that morality by which they are ennobled, that he has made virtue man's birthright. Supreme happiness consists in self-content; that we may gain this self-content we are placed upon this earth and endowed with freedom, we are tempted by our passions and restrained by conscience. What more could divine power itself have done on our behalf? Could it have made our nature a contradiction, and have given the prize of well-doing to one who was incapable of evil? To prevent a man from wickedness, should Providence have restricted him to instinct and made him a fool? Not so, O God of my soul, I will never reproach thee that thou has created me in thine own image, that I may be free and good and happy like my Maker!

O Man! seek no further for the author of evil; thou art he. There is no evil but the evil you do or the evil you suffer, and both come from yourself. Evil in general can only spring from disorder, and in the order of the world I find a never-failing system. Evil in particular cases exists only in the mind of those who experience it; and this feeling is not the gift of nature, but the work of man himself. Pain has little power over those who, having thought little, look neither before nor after. Take away our fatal progress, take away our faults and our vices, take away man's handiwork, and all is well.

V

Having thus deduced from the perception of objects of sense and from my inner consciousness, which leads me to judge of causes by my native reason, the principal truths which I require to know, I must now seek such principles of conduct as I can draw from them, and such rules as I must lay down for my guidance in the fulfilment of my destiny in this world, according to the purpose of my Maker. Still following the same method, I do not derive these rules from the principles of the higher philosophy. I find them in the depths of my heart, traced by nature in characters which nothing can efface. I need only consult myself with re-

gard to what I wish to do; what I feel to be right is right, what I feel to be wrong is wrong; conscience is the best casuist; and it is only when we haggle with conscience that we have recourse to the subtleties of argument. Our first duty is towards ourself; yet how often does the voice of others tell us that in seeking our good at the expense of others we are doing ill? We think we are following the guidance of nature, and we are resisting it; we listen to what she says to our senses, and we neglect what she says to our heart; the active being obeys, the passive commands. Conscience is the voice of the soul; the passions are the voice of the body. Is it strange that these voices often contradict each other? And then to which should we give heed? Too often does reason deceive us; we have only too good a right to doubt her; but conscience never deceives us; she is the true guide of man; it is to the soul what instinct is to the body; he who obeys his conscience is following nature and he need not fear that he will go astray. This is a matter of great importance, continued my benefactor, seeing that I was about to interrupt him; let me stop awhile to explain it more fully.

The morality of our actions consists entirely in the judgments we ourselves form with regard to them. If good is good, it must be good in the depth of our heart as well as in our actions; and the first reward of justice is the consciousness that we are acting justly. If moral goodness is in accordance with our nature, man can only be healthy in mind and body when he is good. If it is not so, and if man is by nature evil, he cannot cease to be evil without corrupting his nature, and goodness in him is a crime against nature. If he is made to do harm to his fellow-creatures, as the wolf is made to devour his prey, a humane man would be as depraved a creature as a pitiful wolf; and virtue alone would cause remorse.

There are many bad men in this world, but there are few of these dead souls, alive only to self-interest, and insensible to all that is right and good. We only delight in injustice so long as it is to our own advantage; in every other case we wish the innocent to be protected. If we see some act of violence or injustice in town or country, our hearts are at once stirred to their depths by an instinctive anger and wrath, which bids us go to the help of the oppressed; but we are restrained by a stronger duty, and the law deprives us of our right to protect the innocent. On the other hand, if some deed of mercy or generosity meets our eye, what reverence and love does it inspire! Do we not say to ourselves, "I should like to have done that myself"? We do not hate the wicked merely because of the harm they do to ourselves, but because they are wicked. Not only do we wish to be happy ourselves, we wish others to be happy too, and if this happiness does not interfere with our own happiness, it increases it. In conclusion, whether we will or not, we pity the unfortunate; when we see their suffering we suffer too. Even the most depraved are not wholly without this instinct, and it often leads them to self-contradiction. The highwayman who robs the traveller, clothes the nakedness of the poor; the fiercest murderer supports a fainting man.

Men speak of the voice of remorse, the secret punishment of hidden crimes, by which such are often brought to light. Alas! who does not know its unwelcome voice? We speak from experience, and we would gladly stifle this imperious feeling which causes us such agony. Let us obey the call of nature; we shall see that her yoke is easy and that when we give heed to her voice we find a joy in the answer of a good conscience. The wicked fears and flees from her; he delights to escape from himself; his anxious eyes look around him for some object of diversion; without bitter satire and rude mockery he would always be sorrowful; his scornful laugh is his one pleasure. Not so the just man, who finds his peace within himself; there is joy not malice in his laughter, a joy which springs from his own heart; he is as cheerful alone as in company, his satisfaction does not depend on those who approach him; it includes them.

There is therefore at the bottom of our hearts an innate principle of justice and virtue, by which, in spite of our maxims, we judge our own actions or those of others to be good or evil; and it is this principle that I call conscience.

It is no part of my scheme to enter at present into metaphysical discussions which neither you nor I can understand, discussions which really lead nowhere. I have told you already that I do not wish to philosophize with you, but to help you to consult your own heart. If all the philosophers in the world should prove that I am wrong, and you feel that I am right, that is all I ask.

To exist is to feel; our feeling is undoubtedly earlier than our intelligence, and we had feelings before we had ideas. Whatever may be the cause of our being, it has provided for our preservation by giving us feelings suited to our nature; and no one can deny that these at least are innate. These feelings, so far as the individual is concerned, are self-love, fear, pain, the dread of death, the desire for comfort. Again, if, as it is impossible to doubt, man is by nature sociable, or at least fitted to become sociable, he can only be so by means of other innate feelings, relative to his kind; for if only physical well-being were considered, men would certainly be scattered rather than brought together. But the motive power of conscience is derived from the moral system formed through this twofold relation to himself and to his fellow-men. To know good is not to love it; this knowledge is not innate in man; but as soon as his reason leads him to perceive it, his conscience impels him to love it; it is this feeling which is innate.

Conscience! Conscience! Divine instinct, immortal voice from heaven; sure guide for a creature ignorant and finite indeed, yet intelligent and free; infallible judge of good and evil, making man like to God! In thee consists the excellence of man's nature and the morality of his actions; apart from thee, I find nothing in myself to raise me above the beasts—nothing but the sad privilege of wandering from one error to another, by the help of an unbridled understanding and a reason which knows no principle.

Thank heaven we have now got rid of all that alarming show of philosophy; we may be men without being scholars; now that we need not spend our life in the study of morality, we have found a less costly and surer guide through this vast labyrinth of human thought. But it is not enough to be aware that there is such a guide; we must know her and follow her. If she speaks to all hearts, how is it that so few give heed to her voice? She speaks to us in the language of nature, and everything leads us to forget that tongue. Conscience is timid, she loves peace and retirement; she is startled by noise and numbers; the prejudices from which she is said to arise are her worst enemies. She flees before them or she is silent; their noisy voices drown her words, so that she cannot get a hearing; fanaticism dares to counterfeit her voice and to inspire crimes in her name. She is discouraged by ill-treatment; she no longer speaks to us, no longer answers to our call; when she has been scorned so long, it is as hard to recall her as it was to banish her.

There is an age when the heart is still free, but eager, unquiet, greedy of a happiness which is still unknown, a happiness which it seeks in curiosity and doubt; deceived by the senses it settles at length upon the empty show of happiness and thinks it has found it where it is not. In my own case these illusions endured for a long time. Alas! too late did I become aware of them, and I have not succeeded in overcoming them altogether; they will last as long as this mortal body from which they arise. If they lead me astray, I am at least no longer deceived by them; I know them for what they are, and even when I give way to them, I despise myself; far from regarding them as the goal of my happiness, I behold in them an obstacle to it.

In my well-founded self-distrust the only thing that I ask of God, or rather expect from his justice, is to correct my error if I go astray, if that error is dangerous to me. To be honest I need not think myself infallible; my opinions, which seem to me true, may be so many lies; for what man is there who does not cling to his own beliefs; and how many men are agreed in everything? The illusion which deceives me may indeed have its sources in myself, but it is God alone who can remove it. I have done all I can to attain to truth; but its source is beyond my reach; is it my fault if my strength fails me and I can go no further; it is for Truth to draw near to me.

Disillusioned Naturalism: W. T. Stace

The philosophy of Rousseau is not a typical expression of naturalism, either before or after his own time. As modern scientific thought more and more completely dominated the outlook of naturalistic philosophy during the late nineteenth and early twentieth centuries, a strong vein of pessimism about human nature and the future of human civilization began to appear. The classic statement of this point of view is found in Bertrand Russell's famous essay, "A Free Man's Worship," published in 1909. Russell here portrays with customary insight and clarity an aspect of naturalism that should not be overlooked, and one which recently has been restated in more contemporary and popular fashion in an essay by Walter T Stace, entitled "Man Against Darkness."

Stace, who was born in London in 1886, was educated in Trinity College in Dublin, and then for some twenty years served in the British Civil Service in Ceylon. At various times he held such positions there as magistrate, judge, and finally mayor of Colombo, positions which brought him into contact with aspects of human life and human nature seldom met by the typical academic philosopher. But, in the British tradition of men like John Stuart Mill and Herbert Spencer, Stace did not let the pressure of everyday affairs turn his attention from philosophy. While in the Civil Service he wrote several books on philosophical subjects, and in 1932 he was appointed a member of the faculty at Princeton University. During his twenty years at Princeton his philosophical interests and publications covered a wide range. *The Concept of Morals* in 1936, *The Destiny of Western Man* in 1942, *Time and Eternity* and *Religion and the Modern Mind* in 1952, are among the better known of his works. In these books one finds a fuller statement of his philosophy, with some modification of the view of man and the universe expressed in the more popular essay, "Man Against Darkness," which is reprinted here.

After retiring from the faculty of Princeton University some years ago, Stace continued his work in philosophy with characteristic British intellectual vigor. A recent study of *Mysticism and Philosophy,* published in 1961, carries further his analysis of religious experience and the light that this casts upon human nature and upon the nature of the universe by which man's ultimate destiny is shaped.

*Man against Darkness**

I

The Catholic bishops of America recently issued a statement in which they said that the chaotic and bewildered state of the modern world is due to man's loss of faith, his abandonment of God and religion. For my part I believe in no religion at all. Yet I entirely agree with the bishops. It is no doubt an oversimplification to speak of *the* cause of so complex a state of affairs as the tortured condition of the world today. Its causes

* W. T. Stace, "Man Against Darkness," *The Atlantic Monthly* (September 1948), pp. 53–58. Copyright by The Atlantic Monthly Co., Boston, Mass. Reprinted by permission of the author.

are doubtless multitudinous. Yet allowing for some element of oversimplification, I say that the bishops' assertion is substantially true.

M. Jean-Paul Sartre, the French existentialist philosopher, labels himself an atheist. Yet his views seem to me plainly to support the statement of the bishops. So long as there was believed to be a God in the sky, he says, men could regard him as the source of their moral ideals. The universe, created and governed by a fatherly God, was a friendly habitation for man. We could be sure that, however great the evil in the world, good in the end would triumph and the forces of evil would be routed. With the disappearance of God from the sky all this has changed. Our own ideals, therefore, must proceed only from our own minds; they are our own inventions. Thus the world which surrounds us is nothing but an immense spiritual emptiness. It is a dead universe. We do not live in a universe which is on the side of our values. It is completely indifferent to them.

Years ago Mr. Bertrand Russell, in his essay *A Free Man's Worship,* said much the same thing:

Such in outline, but even more purposeless, more void of meaning, is the world which Science presents for our belief. Amid such a world, if anywhere, our ideals henceforward must find a home. . . . Blind to good and evil, reckless of destruction, omnipotent matter rolls on its relentless way; for man, condemned today to lose his dearest, tomorrow himself to pass through the gate of darkness, it remains only to cherish, ere yet the blow falls, the lofty thoughts that ennoble his little day; . . . to worship at the shrine his own hands have built; . . . to sustain alone, a weary but unyielding Atlas, the world that his own ideals have fashioned despite the trampling march of unconscious power.

It is true that Mr. Russell's personal attitude to the disappearance of religion is quite different from either that of M. Sartre or the bishops or myself. The bishops think it a calamity. So do I. M. Sartre finds it "very distressing." And he berates as shallow the attitude of those who think that without God the world can go on just the same as before, as if nothing had happened. This creates for mankind, he thinks, a terrible crisis. And in this I agree with him. Mr. Russell, on the other hand, seems to believe that religion has done more harm than good in the world, and that its disappearance will be a blessing. But his picture of the world, and of the modern mind, is the same as that of M. Sartre. He stresses the *purposelessness* of the universe, the facts that man's ideals are his own creations, that the universe outside him in no way supports them, that man is alone and friendless in the world.

Mr. Russell notes that it is science which has produced this situation. There is no doubt that this is correct. But the way in which it has come about is not generally understood. There is a popular belief that some particular scientific discoveries or theories, such as the Darwinian theory of evolution or the views of geologists about the age of the earth, or a series of such discoveries, have done the damage. It would be foolish to deny that these discoveries have had a great effect in undermining religious dogmas. But this account does not at all go to the root of the matter. Religion can probably outlive any scientific discoveries which could be made. It can accommodate itself to them. The root cause of the decay of faith has not been any particular discovery of science, but rather the general spirit of science and certain basic assumptions upon which modern science, from the seventeenth century onwards, has proceeded.

II

It was Galileo and Newton—notwithstanding that Newton himself was a deeply religious man—who destroyed the old comfortable picture of a friendly universe governed by spiritual values. And this was effected, not by Newton's discovery of the law of gravitation nor by any of Galileo's brilliant investigations, but by the general picture of the world which these men and others of their time made the basis of science, not only of their own day, but of all succeeding generations down to the present. That is why the century immediately following Newton, the eighteenth century, was notoriously an age of religious skepticism. Skepticism did not have to wait for the discoveries of Darwin and the geologists in the nineteenth century. It flooded the world immediately after the age of the rise of science.

Neither the Copernican hypothesis nor any of Newton's or Galileo's particular discoveries were the real causes. Religious faith might well have accommodated itself to the new astronomy. The real turning point between the medieval age of faith and the modern age of unfaith came when the scientists of the seventeenth century turned their backs upon what used to be called "final causes." The final cause of a thing or event meant the purpose which it was supposed to serve in the universe, its cosmic purpose. What lay back of this was the presupposition that there is a cosmic order or plan and that everything which exists could in the last analysis be explained in terms of its place in this cosmic plan, that is, in terms of its purpose.

Plato and Aristotle believed this, and so did the whole medieval Christian world. For instance, if it were true that the sun and the moon were created and exist for the purpose of giving light to man, then this fact would explain why the sun and the moon exist. We might not be able to discover the purpose of everything, but everything must have a purpose. Belief in final causes thus amounted to a belief that the world is governed by purposes, presumably the purposes of some overruling mind. This belief was not the invention of Christianity. It was basic to the whole of Western civilization, whether in the ancient pagan world or in Christendom, from the time of Socrates to the rise of science in the seventeenth century.

The founders of modern science—for instance, Galileo, Kepler, and Newton—were mostly pious men who did not doubt God's purposes. Nevertheless they took the revolutionary step of consciously and deliberately expelling the idea of purpose as controlling nature from their new science of nature.

They did this on the ground that inquiry into purposes is useless for what science aims at; namely the prediction and control of events. To predict an eclipse, what you have to know is not its purpose but its causes. Hence science from the seventeenth century onwards became exclusively an inquiry into causes. The conception of purpose in the world was ignored and frowned on. This, though silent and almost unnoticed, was the greatest revolution in human history, far outweighing in importance any of the political revolutions whose thunder was reverberated through the world.

For it came about in this way that for the past three hundred years there has been growing up in men's minds, dominated as they are by science, a new imaginative picture of the world. The world, according to this new picture, is purposeless, senseless, meaningless. Nature is nothing but matter in motion. The motions of matter are governed, not by any purpose, but by blind forces and laws. Nature on this view, says Whitehead—to whose writings I am indebted in this part of my paper, is "merely the hurrying of material, endlessly, meaninglessly." You can draw a sharp line across the history of Europe dividing it into two epochs of very unequal length. The line passes through the lifetime of Galileo. European man before Galileo—whether ancient pagan or more recent Christian—thought of the world as controlled by plan and purpose. After Galileo European man thinks of it as utterly purposeless. This is the great revolution of which I spoke.

It is this which has killed religion. Religion could survive the discoveries that the sun, not the earth, is the center; that men are descended from simian ancestors; that the earth is hundreds of millions of years old. These discoveries may render out of date some of the details of older theological dogmas, may force their restatement in new intellectual frameworks. But they do not touch the essence of the religious vision itself, which is the faith that there is plan and purpose in the world, that the world is a moral order, that in the end all things are for the best. This faith may express itself through many different intellectual dogmas, those of Christianity, of Hinduism, of Islam. All and any of these intellectual dogmas may be destroyed without destroying the essential religious spirit. But that spirit cannot survive destruction of belief in a plan and purpose of the world, for that is the very heart of it. Religion can get on with any sort of astronomy, geology, biology, physics. But it cannot get on with a purposeless and meaningless universe.

If the scheme of things is purposeless and meaningless, then the life of man is purposeless and meaningless too. Everything is futile, all effort is in the end worthless. A man may, of course, still pursue disconnected ends, money, fame, art, science, and may gain pleasure from them. But his life is hollow at the center. Hence the dissatisfied, disillusioned, restless, spirit of modern man.

The picture of a meaningless world, and a meaningless human life is, I think, the basic theme of much modern art and literature. Certainly it is the basic theme of modern philosophy. According to the most characteristic philosophies of the modern period from Hume in the eighteenth century to the so-called positivists of today, the world is just what it is, and that is the end of all inquiry. There is no reason for its being what it is. Everything might just as well have been quite different, and there would have been no reason for that either. When you have stated what things are, what things the world contains, there is nothing more which could be said, even by an omniscient being. To ask any question about *why* things are thus, or what purpose their being so serves, is to ask a senseless question, because they serve no purpose at all. For instance, there is for modern philosophy no such thing as the ancient problem of evil. For this once famous question presupposes that pain and misery, though they seem so inexplicable and irrational to us, must ultimately subserve some rational purpose, must have their places in the cosmic plan. But this is nonsense. There is no such overruling rationality in the universe. Belief in the ultimate irrationality of everything is the quintessence of what is called the modern mind.

It is true that, parallel with these philosophies which are typical of the modern mind, preaching the meaninglessness of the world, there has run a line of idealistic philosophies whose contention is that the world is after all spiritual in nature and that moral ideals and values are inherent in its structure. But most of these idealisms were simply philosophical expressions of romanticism, which was itself no more than an unsuccessful counterattack of the religious against the scientific view of things. They perished, along with romanticism in literature and art, about the beginning of the present century, though of course they still have a few adherents.

At the bottom these idealistic systems of thought were rationalizations of man's wishful thinking. They were born of the refusal of men to admit the cosmic darkness. They were comforting illusions within the warm glow of which the more tender-minded intellectuals sought to shelter themselves from the icy winds of the universe. They lasted a little while. But they are shattered now and we return once more to the vision of a purposeless world.

III

Along with the ruin of the religious vision there went the ruin of moral principles and indeed of all values. If there is a cosmic purpose, if there is in the nature of things a drive towards goodness, then our moral systems will derive their validity from this. But if our moral rules do not proceed from something outside us in the nature of the universe—whether we say it is God or simply the universe itself—then they must be our own inventions. Thus it came to be believed that moral rules must be merely an expression of our own likes and dislikes. But likes and dislikes are notoriously variable. What pleases one man, people, or culture displeases another. Therefore morals are wholly relative.

This obvious conclusion from the idea of a purposeless world made its appearance in Europe immediately after the rise of science, for instance in the philosophy of Hobbes. Hobbes saw at once that if there is no purpose in the world there are no values either. "Good and evil," he writes, "are names that signify our appetites and aversions; which in different tempers, customs, and doctrines of men are different. . . . Every man calleth that which pleaseth him, good; and that which displeaseth him, evil."

This doctrine of the relativity of morals, though it has recently received an impetus from the studies of anthropologists, was thus really implicit in the whole scientific mentality. It is disastrous for morals because it destroys their entire traditional foundation. That is why philosophers who see the danger signals, from the time at least of Kant, have been trying to give morals a new foundation, that is, a secular or nonreligious foundation. This attempt may very well be intellectually successful. Such a foundation, independent of the religious view of the world, might well be found, but the question is whether it can ever be a *practical* success, that is, whether apart from its logical validity and its influence with intellectuals, it can ever replace among the masses of men the lost religious foundation. On that question hangs perhaps the future of civilization. But meanwhile disaster is overtaking us.

The widespread belief in "ethical relativity" among philosophers, psychologists, ethnologists, and sociologists is the theoretical counterpart of the repudiation of principle which we see all around us, especially in international affairs, the field in which morals have always had the weakest foothold. No one any longer effectively believes in moral principles except as the private prejudices either of individual men or of nations or cultures. This is the inevitable consequence of the doctrine of ethical relativity, which in turn is the inevitable consequence of believing in a purposeless world.

Another characteristic of our spiritual state is loss of belief in the freedom of the will. This also is a fruit of the scientific spirit, though not of any particular scientific discovery. Science has been built up on the basis of determinism, which is the belief that every event is completely determined by a chain of causes and is therefore theoretically predictable beforehand. It is true that recent physics seems to challenge this. But so far as its practical consequences are concerned, the damage has long ago been done. A man's actions, it was argued, are as much events in the natural world as is an eclipse of the sun. It follows that men's actions are as theoretically predictable as an eclipse. But if it is certain now that John Smith will murder Joseph Jones at 2:15 P.M. on January 1, 1963, what possible meaning can it have to say that when that time comes John Smith will be *free* to choose whether he will commit the murder or not? And if he is not free, how can he be held responsible?

It is true that the whole of this argument can be shown by a competent philosopher to be a tissue of fallacies—or at least I claim that it can. But the point is that the analysis required to show this is much too subtle to be understood by the average entirely unphilosophical man. Because of this, the argument against free will is generally swallowed whole by the unphilosophical. Hence the thought that man is not free, that he is the helpless plaything of forces over which he has no control, has deeply penetrated the modern mind. We hear of economic determinism, cultural determinism, historical determinism. We are not responsible for what we do because our glands control us, or because we are the products of environment or heredity. Not moral self-control, but the doctor, the psychiatrist, the educationist, must save us from doing evil. Pills and injections in the future are to do what Christ and the prophets have failed to do. Of course I do not mean to deny that doctors and educationists can and must help. And I do not mean in any way to belittle their efforts. But I do wish to draw attention to the weakening of moral controls, the greater or less repudiation of personal responsibility which, in the popular thinking of the day, result from these tendencies of thought.

IV

What, then, is to be done? Where are we to look for salvation from the evils of our time? All the remedies I have seen suggested so far are, in my opinion, useless. Let us look at some of them.

Philosophers and intellectuals generally can, I believe, genuinely do something to help. But it is extremely little. What philosophers can do is to show that neither the relativity of morals nor the denial of free will really follows from the grounds which have been supposed to support them. They can also try to discover a genuine secular basis for morals to replace the religious basis which has disappeared. Some of us are trying to do these things. But in the first place philosophers unfortunately are not agreed about these matters, and their disputes are utterly confusing to the non-philosophers. And in the second place their influence is practically negligible because their analyses necessarily take place on a level on which the masses are totally unable to follow them.

The bishops, of course, propose as remedy a return to belief in God and in the doctrines of the Christian religion. Others think that a new religion is what is needed. Those who make these proposals fail to realize that the crisis in man's spiritual condition is something unique in history for which there is no sort of analogy in the past. They are thinking perhaps of the collapse of the ancient Greek and Roman religions. The vacuum then created was easily filled by Christianity, and it might have been filled by Mithraism if Christianity had not appeared. By analogy they think that Christianity might now be replaced by a new religion, or even that Christianity itself, if revivified, might bring back health to men's lives.

But I believe that there is no analogy at all between our present state and that of the European peoples at the time of the fall of paganism. Men had at that time lost their belief only in particular dogmas, particular embodiments of the religious view of the world. It had no doubt become incredible that Zeus and the other gods were living on the top of Mount Olympus. You could go to the top and find no trace of them. But the imaginative picture of a world governed by purpose, a world driving towards the good—which is the inner spirit of religion—had at that time received no serious shock. It had merely to re-embody itself in new dogmas, those of Christianity or some other religion. Religion itself was not dead in the world, only a particular form of it.

But now the situation is quite different. It is not merely that particular dogmas, like that of the virgin birth, are unacceptable to the modern mind. That is true, but it constitutes a very superficial diagnosis of the present situation of religion. Modern skepticism is of a wholly different order from that of the intellectuals of the ancient world. It has attacked and destroyed not merely the outward forms of the religious spirit, its particularized dogmas, but the very essence of that spirit itself, belief in a meaningful and purposeful world. For the founding of a new religion a new Jesus Christ or Buddha would have to appear, in itself a most unlikely event and one for which in any case we cannot afford to sit and wait. But even if a new prophet and a new religion did appear, we may predict that they would fail in the modern world. No one for long would believe in them, for modern men have lost the vision, basic to all religion, of an ordered plan and purpose of the world. They have before their minds the picture of a purposeless universe, and such a world-picture must be fatal to any religion at all, not merely to Christianity.

We must not be misled by occasional appearances of a revival of the religious spirit. Men, we are told, in their disgust and disillusionment at the emptiness of their lives, are turning once more to religion, or are searching for a new message. It may be so. We must expect such wistful yearnings of the spirit. We must expect men to wish back again the light that is gone, and to try to bring it back. But however they may wish and try, the light will not shine again—not at least in the civilization to which we belong.

Another remedy commonly proposed is that we should turn to science itself, or the scientific spirit, for our salvation. Mr. Russell and Professor Dewey both make this proposal, though in somewhat different ways. Professor Dewey seems to believe that discoveries in sociology, the application of scientific method to social and political problems, will rescue us. This seems to me to be utterly naive. It is not likely that science, which is basically the cause of our spiritual troubles, is likely also to produce the cure for them. Also it lies in the nature of science that, though it can teach us the best means for achieving our ends, it can never tell us what ends to pursue. It cannot give us any ideals. And our trouble is about ideals and ends, not about the means for reaching them.

V

No civilization can live without ideals, or to put it in another way, without a firm faith in moral ideas. Our ideals and moral ideas have in the past been rooted in religion. But the religious basis of our ideals has been undermined, and the superstructure of ideals is plainly tottering. None of the commonly suggested remedies on examination seems likely to succeed. It would therefore look as if the early death of our civilization were inevitable.

Of course we know that it is perfectly possible for individual men, very highly educated men, philosophers, scientists, intellectuals in general, to live moral lives without any religious convictions. But the question is whether a whole civilization, a whole family of people, composed almost entirely of relatively uneducated men and women, can do this.

It follows, of course, that if we could make the vast majority of men as highly educated as the very few are now, we might save the situation. And we are already moving slowly in that direction through the techniques of mass education. But the critical question seems to concern the time-lag. Perhaps in a few hundred years most of the population will, at the present rate, be sufficiently highly educated and civilized to combine high ideals with an absence of religion. But long before we reach any such stage, the collapse of our civilization may have come about. How are we to live through the intervening period?

I am sure that the first thing we have to do is to face the truth, however bleak it may be, and then next we have to learn to live with it. Let me say a word about each of these two points. What I am urging as regards the first is complete honesty. Those who wish to resurrect Christian dogmas are not, of course, consciously dishonest. But they have that kind of unconscious dishonesty which consists in lulling oneself with opiates and dreams. Those who talk of a new religion are merely hoping for a new opiate. Both alike refuse to face the truth that there is, in the universe outside man, no spirituality, no regard for values, no friend in the sky, no help or comfort for man of any sort. To be perfectly honest in the admission of this fact, not to seek shelter in new or old illusions, not to indulge in wishful dreams about this matter, this is the first thing we shall have to do.

I do not urge this course out of any special regard for the sanctity of truth in the abstract. It is not self-evident to me that truth is the supreme value to which all else must be sacrificed. Might not the discoverer of a truth which would be fatal to mankind be justified in suppressing it, even in teaching men a falsehood? Is truth more valuable than goodness and beauty and happiness? To think so is to invent yet another absolute, another religious delusion in which Truth with a capital T is substituted for God. The reason why we must now boldly and honestly face the truth that the universe is non-spiritual and indifferent to goodness, beauty, happiness, or truth is not that it would be wicked to suppress it, but simply that it is too late to do so, so that in the end we cannot do anything else but face it. Yet we stand on the brink, dreading the icy plunge. We need courage. We need honesty.

Now about the other point, the necessity of learning to live with the truth. This means learning to live virtuously and happily, or at least contentedly, without illusions.

And this is going to be extremely difficult because what we have now begun dimly to perceive is that human life in the past, or at least human happiness, has almost wholly depended upon illusions. It has been said that man lives by truth, and that the truth will make us free. Nearly the opposite seems to me to be the case. Mankind has managed to live only by means of lies, and the truth may very well destroy us. If one were a Bergsonian one might believe that nature deliberately puts illusions into our souls in order to induce us to go on living.

The illusions by which men have lived seem to be of two kinds. First, there is what one may perhaps call the Great Illusion—I mean the religious illusion that the universe is moral and good, that it follows a wise and noble plan, that it is gradually generating some supreme value, that goodness is bound to triumph in it. Secondly, there is a whole host of minor illusions on which human happiness nourishes itself. How much of human happiness notoriously comes from the illusions of the lover about his beloved? Then again we work and strive because of the illusions connected with fame, glory, power, or money. Banners of all kinds, flags, emblems, insignia, ceremonials, and rituals are invariably symbols of some illusion or other. The British Empire, the connection between mother country and dominions, is partly kept going by illusions surrounding the notion of kingship. Or think of the vast amount of human happiness which is derived from the illusion of supposing that if some nonsense syllable, such as "sir" or "count" or "lord" is pronounced in conjunction with our names, we belong to a superior order of people.

There is plenty of evidence that human happiness is almost wholly based upon illusions of one kind or another. But the scientific spirit, or the spirit of truth, is the enemy of human happiness. That is why it is going to be so difficult to live with the truth.

There is no reason why we should have to give up the host of minor illusions which render life supportable. There is no reason why the lover should be scientific about the loved one. Even the illusions of fame and glory may persist. But without the Great Illusion, the illusion of a good, kindly, and purposeful universe, we shall *have* to learn to live. And to ask this is really no more than to ask that we become genuinely civilized beings and not merely sham civilized beings.

I can best explain the difference by a reminiscence. I remember a fellow student in my college days, an ardent Christian, who told me that if he did not believe in a future life, in heaven and hell, he would rape, murder, steal, and be a drunkard. That is what I call being a sham civilized being. On the other hand, not only could a Huxley, a John Stuart Mill, a David Hume, live great and fine lives without any religion, but a great many others of us, quite obscure persons, can at least live decent lives without it.

To be genuinely civilized means to be able to walk straightly and to live honorably without the props and crutches of one or another of the childish dreams which have so far supported men. That such a life is likely to be ecstatically happy, I will not claim. But that it can be lived in quiet content, accepting resignedly what cannot be helped, not expecting the impossible, and thankful for small mercies, this I would maintain. That it will be difficult for men in general to learn this lesson I do not deny. But that it will be impossible I would not admit since so many have learned it already.

Man has not yet grown up. He is not adult. Like a child he cries for the moon and lives in a world of fantasies. And the race as a whole has perhaps reached the great crisis of its life. Can it grow up as a race in the same sense as individual men grow up? Can man put away childish things and adolescent dreams? Can he grasp the real world as it actually is, stark and bleak, without its romantic or religious halo, and still retain his ideals, striving for great ends and noble achievements? If he can, all may yet be well. If he cannot, he will probably sink back into the savagery and brutality from which he came, taking a humble place once more among the lower animals.

From Naturalism to Humanism: John Dewey

Those who reject naturalism usually condemn it for not giving proper importance to human ideals and values, values that are essential for any enduring meaning or purpose in life. Also, naturalism has often pictured the forces at work in nature as in direct conflict with man's highest moral and spiritual aspirations. This was especially true of naturalistic philosophy in the decades following Darwin's *Origin of Species* (1859), when Thomas Henry Huxley became the symbol for such a conflict between nature "red in tooth and claw" and a human society based upon good will, cooperation, and mutual understanding. A generation ago Bertrand Russell in "A Free Man's Worship" gave classic statement to much the same sort of philosophy; more recently W. T. Stace in the essay "Man Against Darkness," reprinted above, forcefully restates Russell's position for a popular audience.

More than any other philosopher of our day John Dewey has sought to refute this image of man and nature in fundamental conflict. In the spirit of Aristotle, he has sought to bridge the gap between naturalism and humanism. Human nature can only be understood, Dewey insists, when man is seen as an integral part of the larger natural universe through which he came into existence and in accord with which his ideals and values must be fashioned.

> In truth, experience knows no distinction between human concerns and a purely mechanical world. Man's home is in nature; his purposes and aims are dependent for execution upon natural conditions. Separated from such conditions they become empty dreams and idle indulgences of fancy. This philosophy is vouched for by the doctrine of biological development which shows that man is continuous with nature, not an alien entering her processes from without.[1]

Dewey, who was born in Vermont in 1859, was educated at the University of Vermont and at Johns Hopkins University. After teaching for ten years at the University of Michigan, he became head of the philosophy department at the newly established University of Chicago in 1894. It was here that he first developed and put into practice the educational philosophy with which his name has become so closely associated. At Chicago he also gathered together an able group of men in psychology and philosophy who brought distinction to the new university. In 1905 Dewey joined the faculty of Columbia University. For more than forty-five years he was associated with Columbia, first as professor of philosophy, then as head of the department, and finally as a distinguished professor emeritus.

His years at Columbia were remarkably productive, both in scholarship and in the active support of causes that promised to promote the democratic ideals to which he was deeply committed. His long support of the women's suffrage movement grew out of his belief that the full enfranchisement of women was a neces-

---

[1] John Dewey, *Democracy and Education.* (New York, The Macmillan Co., 1916) p. 333.

sary part of political democracy. For a number of years he was chairman of the League for Independent Political Action. He helped organize the Teachers Guild, affiliated with the American Federation of Labor, and he was active in founding the American Association of University Professors and served as its first president.

Trips to China, Japan, and Russia strengthened the social emphasis in Dewey's philosophy. His lectures at the University of Tokyo in 1919, entitled *Reconstruction in Philosophy,* provide one of the best statements of his general position. What he found in China so interested him that he remained for two years instead of one, watching the world's oldest culture struggling to meet new social conditions. He was impressed especially by the important part being played by education and by university students in modernizing China, freeing it from Japanese control and reforming the government along more genuinely democratic lines. These experiences in China rekindled Dewey's own intellectual and social enthusiasm; upon his return to the United States he wrote and spoke frequently urging a more enlightened American policy in the Far East.

In 1928 Dewey spent a short time in the Soviet Union. Here, too, he was impressed by the enthusiasm of the men and women engaged in building a new and better world for themselves and their countrymen; but the sympathy Dewey expressed for the Soviet experiment led him to be branded as a radical and a communist by the conservative press in this country. The increasing regimentation of the schools under the Stalin regime, however, and the use of education as a tool of the dictatorship greatly disappointed Dewey. He gradually became convinced that by its very nature violent revolution and dictatorship cannot produce a desirable social order, no matter what set of leaders is in power. A careful study of the Stalin-Trotsky feud finally disillusioned him completely. He became as unalterably opposed to revolutionary communism as to fascism and was in turn called a reactionary by the left-wing press.

The importance of these experiences becomes clear when we recognize that Dewey's philosophy as a whole is social in intent and direction. For Dewey social philosophy is not a separate area or division of philosophy but rather the goal and culmination of all philosophical thought. It is the function of philosophy, he writes, "to free men's minds from bias and prejudice and to enlarge their perceptions of the world about them." Philosophy should clarify men's "ideas as to the social and moral strifes of their own day," and "become so far as is humanly possible an organ for dealing with these conflicts."[2] With this in mind Dewey consistently works out the social and political implications of his thought in each area with which he deals.

The range, the influence, and the enduring significance of Dewey's achievement have been widely acclaimed. Like Aristotle, whose naturalism he seeks to make more consistent, Dewey has written extensively in almost every field and

---

[2] John Dewey, *Reconstruction in Philosophy* (New York, Henry Holt and Company, Inc., 1920), p. 20.

illuminated all areas with which he dealt. A bibliography of his published work which fills sixty-five pages and includes twenty-nine major books together with innumerable articles, essays and reviews, is included as an Appendix to the volume on *The Philosophy of John Dewey* in the Library of Living Philosophy. To this the interested student is referred.

In almost every aspect of Dewey's philosophy,[3] the intimate relationship between naturalism and humanism is of fundamental importance. His treatment of morals is a good example. All our moral values are for Dewey based directly upon natural desires of the human organism and can be understood only in this context. His position like that of Aristotle is directly opposed to a philosophy that separates moral conduct from ordinary natural desires; and Dewey is anxious to show that an empirical naturalism can understand and promote human values far more effectively than the traditional moral philosophy he rejects. In almost every statement of his philosophy he includes some discussion of this point. His popular book on *Democracy and Education* (1916) concludes with a chapter entitled "Theory of Morals." With Edgar Tufts he published a widely used college text on *Ethics* (in 1908) in which this naturalistic interpretation is developed in detail. However, in *Human Nature and Conduct* (1922) and *Reconstruction in Philosophy* (1920) Dewey's position is stated most clearly and directly, and selections from these two volumes are included here.

It is helpful to distinguish Dewey's position from earlier naturalistic philosophies that are derived more directly from the physical sciences and the scientific view of the universe as a whole. The initial selection, from *The Influence of Darwin on Philosophy* (1910), indicates the Darwinian and biological basis upon which Dewey's naturalism rests. This Darwinian approach not only leads Dewey to naturalism, but also quite easily to humanism as well in his moral philosophy, and again makes clear the similarity of his approach to that of Aristotle. Dewey's naturalism in morals exhibits indeed a basic agreement with the thought of Socrates: Before we can be good, we must know what we are doing. Intelligence is the one enduring virtue. The need in morals, as in the natural sciences, is for specific methods of inquiry to clarify particular situations and problems. An empirical and inductive logic is as essential, therefore, in the field of ethics as in every other branch of philosophy, and this Dewey undertakes to provide.[4]

---

[3] A further discussion of Dewey's philosophy will be found in the next section on pages 265–271.

[4] In this connection one should also note the very different approach to morals that is found in the romantic naturalism of Rousseau or the radical naturalism of Nietzsche. There the morals of impulse, of passion, of race, and of aristocratic tradition are emphasized; for Dewey it is a morality based upon intelligence and supported by experience to which naturalistic humanism points.

The Influence of Darwin on Philosophy*

I

That the publication of the "Origin of Species" marked an epoch in the development of the natural sciences is well known to the layman. That the combination of the very words *origin* and *species* embodied an intellectual revolt and introduced a new intellectual temper is easily overlooked by the expert. The conceptions that had reigned in the philosophy of nature and knowledge for two thousand years, the conceptions that had become the familiar furniture of the mind, rested on the assumption of the superiority of the fixed and final; they rested upon treating change and origin as signs of defect and unreality. In laying hands upon the sacred ark of absolute permanency, in treating the forms that had been regarded as types of fixity and perfection as originating and passing away, the "Origin of Species" introduced a mode of thinking that in the end was bound to transform the logic of knowledge, and hence the treatment of morals, politics, and religion.

No wonder, then, that the publication of Darwin's book, a half century ago, precipitated a crisis. The true nature of the controversy is easily concealed from us, however, by the theological clamor that attended it. The vivid and popular features of the anti-Darwinian row tended to leave the impression that the issue was between science on one side and theology on the other. Such was not the case—the issue lay primarily within science itself, as Darwin himself early recognized. The theological outcry he discounted from the start, hardly noticing it save as it bore upon the "feelings of his female relatives." But for two decades before final publication he contemplated the possibility of being put down by his scientific peers as a fool or as crazy; and he set, as the measure of his success, the degree in which he should affect

* John Dewey, *The Influence of Darwin on Philosophy,* (New York, Henry Holt & Co., 1910), Essay I (shortened).

three men of science: Lyell in geology, Hooker in botany, and Huxley in zoology.

Religious considerations lent fervor to the controversy, but they did not provoke it. Intellectually, religious emotions are not creative but conservative. They attach themselves readily to the current view of the world and consecrate it. They steep and dye intellectual fabrics in the seething vat of emotions; they do not form their warp and woof. There is not, I think, an instance of any large idea about the world being independently generated by religion. Although the ideas that rose up like armed men against Darwinism owed their intensity to religious associations, their origin and meaning are to be sought in science and philosophy, not in religion.

II

Darwin was not, of course, the first to question the classic philosophy of nature and of knowledge. The beginnings of the revolution are in the physical science of the sixteenth and seventeenth centuries. When Galileo said: "It is my opinion that the earth is very noble and admirable by reason of so many and so different alterations and generations which are incessantly made therein," he expressed the changed temper that was coming over the world; the transfer of interest from the permanent to the changing. When Descartes said: "The nature of physical things is much more easily conceived when they are beheld coming gradually into existence, than when they are only considered as produced at once in a finished and perfect state," the modern world became self-conscious of the logic that was henceforth to control it, the logic of which Darwin's "Origin of Species" is the latest scientific achievement. Without the methods of Copernicus, Kepler, Galileo, and their successors in astronomy, physics, and chemistry, Darwin would have been helpless in the organic sciences. But prior to Darwin the impact of the new scientific method upon life, mind, and politics, had been arrested, because between these ideal or moral interests and the inorganic world intervened the kingdom of plants and animals. The gates of the garden of life were barred to the new ideas; and only through this garden was there access to mind and politics. The influence of Darwin upon philosophy resides in his having conquered the phenomena of life for the principle of transition, and thereby freed the new logic for application to mind and morals and life. When he said of species what Galileo had said of the earth, *e pur se muove,* he emancipated, once for all, genetic and experimental ideas as an organon of asking questions and looking for explanations.

The exact bearings upon philosophy of the new logical outlook are, of course, as yet, uncertain and inchoate. We live in the twilight of intellectual transition. One must add the rashness of the prophet to the stubbornness of the partisan to venture a systematic exposition of the influence upon philosophy of the Darwinian method. At best, we can but inquire as to its general bearing—the effect upon mental temper and complexion, upon that body of half-conscious, half-instinctive intellectual aversions and preferences which determine, after all, our more deliberate intellectual enterprises. In this vague inquiry there happens to exist as a kind of touchstone a problem of long historic currency that has also been much discussed in Darwinian literature. I refer to the old problem of design *versus* chance, mind *versus* matter, as the causal explanation, first or final, of things.

The classic notion of species carried with it the idea of purpose. In all living forms, a specific type is present directing the earlier stages of growth to the realization of its own perfection. Since this purposive regulative principle is not visible to the senses, it follows that it must be an ideal or rational force. Since, however, the perfect form is gradually approximated through the sensible changes, it also follows that in and through a sensible realm a rational force is working out its own ultimate manifestation. These inferences were extended to nature: (a) She does nothing in vain; but all for an ulterior purpose. (b) Within natural sensible events there is therefore contained a spiritual causal force, which as spiritual escapes perception, but is apprehended by an enlightened reason. (c) The manifestation of this principle brings about a subordination of matter and sense to its own realization, and this ultimate fulfilment is the goal of nature and of man. The design argument thus operated in two directions. Purposefulness accounted for the intelligibility of nature and the possibility of science, while the absolute or cosmic character of this purposefulness gave sanction and worth to the moral and religious endeavors of man. Science was underpinned and morals authorized by one and the same principle, and their mutual agreement was eternally guaranteed.

The Darwinian principle of natural selection cut straight under this philosophy. If all organic adaptations are due simply to constant variation and the elimination of those variations which are harmful in the struggle for existence that is brought about by excessive reproduction, there is no call for a prior intelligent causal force to plan and preordain them. Hostile critics charged Darwin with materialism and with making chance the cause of the universe.

III

When Henry Sedgwick casually remarked in a letter that as he grew older his interest in what or who made the world was altered into interest in what kind of a world it is anyway, his voicing of a common experience of our own day illustrates also the nature of that intellectual transformation effected by the Darwinian logic. Interest shifts from the wholesale essence back of special changes to the question of how special changes serve and defeat concrete purposes; shifts from an intelligence that shaped things once for all to the particular intelligences which things are even now shaping; shifts from an ultimate goal of good to the direct increments of justice and happiness that intelligent administration of existent conditions may beget and that present carelessness or stupidity will destroy or forego.

The habit of derogating from present meanings and uses prevents our looking the facts of experience in the face; it prevents serious acknowledgment of the evils they present and serious concern with the goods they promise but do not as yet fulfil. It turns thought to the business of finding a wholesale transcendent remedy for the one and guarantee for the other. One is reminded of the way many moralists and theologians greeted Herbert Spencer's recognition of an unknowable energy from which welled up the phenomenal physical processes without and the conscious operations within. Merely because Spencer labeled his unknowable energy "God," this faded piece of metaphysical goods was greeted as an important and grateful concession to the reality of the spiritual realm. Were it not for the deep hold of the habit of seeking justification of ideal values in the remote and transcendent, surely this reference of them to an unknowable absolute would be despised in comparison with the demonstration of experience that knowable energies are daily generating about us precious values.

The displacing of this wholesale type of philosophy will doubtless not arrive by sheer logical disproof, but rather by growing recognition of its futility. Were it a thousand times true that opium produces sleep because of its dormitive energy, yet the inducing of sleep in the tired, and the recovery to waking life of the poisoned, would not be thereby one least step forwarded. And were it a thousand times dialectically demonstrated that life as a whole is regulated by a transcendent principle to a final inclusive goal, none the less truth and error, health and disease, good and evil,

hope and fear in the concrete, would remain just what and where they now are. To improve our education, to ameliorate our manners, to advance our politics, we must have recourse to specific conditions of generation.

Finally, the new logic introduces responsibility into the intellectual life. To idealize and rationalize the universe at large is after all a confession of inability to master the courses of things that specifically concern us. As long as mankind suffered from this impotency, it naturally shifted a burden of responsibility that it could not carry over to the more competent shoulders of the transcendent cause. But if insight into specific conditions of value and into specific consequences of ideas is possible, philosophy must in time become a method of locating and interpreting the more serious of the conflicts that occur in life, and a method of projecting ways for dealing with them: a method of moral and political diagnosis and prognosis.

The claim to formulate *a priori* the legislative constitution of the universe is by its nature a claim that may lead to elaborate dialectic developments. But it is also one that removes these very conclusions from subjection to experimental test, for, by definition, these results make no differences in the detailed course of events. But a philosophy that humbles its pretensions to the work of projecting hypotheses for the education and conduct of mind, individual and social, is thereby subjected to test by the way in which the ideas it propounds work out in practice. In having modesty forced upon it, philosophy also acquires responsibility.

Morals and Scientific Knowledge*

I

"Give a dog a bad name and hang him." Human nature has been the dog of professional moralists, and consequences ac-

---

*John Dewey, *Human Nature and Conduct*, (New York, Henry Holt & Co., 1922), Introduction and Part IV, Sec. III (shortened).

cord with the proverb. Man's nature has been regarded with suspicion, with fear, with sour looks, sometimes with enthusiasm for its possibilities but only when these were placed in contrast with its actualities. It has appeared to be so evilly disposed that the business of morality was to prune and curb it; it would be thought better of if it could be replaced by something else. It has been supposed that morality would be quite superfluous were it not for the inherent weakness, bordering on depravity, of human nature. Some writers with a more genial conception have attributed the current blackening to theologians who have thought to honor the divine by disparaging the human. Theologians have doubtless taken a gloomier view of man than have pagans and secularists. But this explanation doesn't take us far. For after all these theologians are themselves human, and they would have been without influence if the human audience had not somehow responded to them.

Morality is largely concerned with controlling human nature. When we are attempting to control anything, we are acutely aware of what resists us. Everybody knows that good children are those who make as little trouble as possible for their elders, and since most of them cause a good deal of annoyance, they must be naughty by nature. Generally speaking, good people have been those who did what they were told to do, and lack of eager compliance is a sign of something wrong in their nature. So moralists were led, perhaps, to think of human nature as evil because of its reluctance to yield to control, its rebelliousness under the yoke. But this explanation only raises another question. Why did morality set up rules so foreign to human nature? The ends it insisted upon, the regulations it imposed, were after all outgrowths of human nature. Why then was human nature so averse to them? Moreover rules can be obeyed and ideals realized only as they appeal to something in human nature and awaken in it an active response. Moral principles that exalt themselves by degrading human nature are in effect committing suicide.

Lack of understanding of human nature is the primary cause of disregard for it. Lack of insight always ends in despising or else unreasoned admiration. When men had no scientific knowledge of physical nature, they either passively submitted to it or sought to control it magically. What cannot be understood cannot be managed intelligently. It has to be forced into subjection from without.

Our science of human nature in comparison with physical sciences is rudimentary, and morals which are concerned with the health, efficiency and happiness of a development of human nature are correspondingly elementary. These pages are a discussion of some phases of the ethical change involved in positive respect for human nature when the latter is associated with scientific knowledge. We may anticipate the general nature of this change through considering the evils which have resulted from severing morals from the actualities of human physiology and psychology.

There is a pathology of goodness as well as of evil; that is, of that sort of goodness which is nurtured by this separation. The badness of good people, for the most part recorded only in fiction, is the revenge taken by human nature for the injuries heaped upon it in the name of morality. In the first place, morals cut off from positive roots in man's nature is bound to be mainly negative. Practical emphasis falls upon avoidance, escape of evil, upon not doing things, observing prohibitions. Negative morals assume as many forms as there are types of temperament subject to it. Its commonest form is the protective coloration of a neutral respectability, an insipidity of character. For one man who thanks God that he is not as other men there are a thousand to offer thanks that they are as other men, sufficiently as others are to escape attention. Absence of social blame is the usual mark of goodness for it shows that evil has been avoided. Blame is most readily averted by being so much like everybody else that one passes unnoticed. Conventional morality is a drab morality, in which the only fatal thing is to be conspicuous. If there be flavor left in it, then some natural traits have somehow escaped being subdued. To be so good as to attract notice is to be priggish, too good for this world. The same psychology that brands the convicted criminal as forever a social outcast makes it the part of a gentleman not to obtrude virtues noticeably upon others.

There are always ruder forceful natures who cannot tame themselves to the required level of colorless conformity. To them conventional morality appears as an organized futility; though they are usually unconscious of their own attitude since they are heartily in favor of morality for the mass as making it easier to manage them. Their only standard is success, putting things over, getting things done. Being good is to them practically synonymous with ineffectuality; and accomplishment, achievement, is its own justification. They know by experience that much is forgiven to those who succeed, and they leave goodness to the stupid, to those whom they qualify as boobs. Their gregarious nature finds sufficient outlet in the conspicuous tribute they pay to all established institutions as guardians of ideal interests, and in their denunciations of all who openly defy conventionalized ideals. Or they discover that they are the chosen agents of a higher morality and walk subject to specially ordained laws. Hypocrisy in the sense of a deliberate covering up of a will to evil by loud-voiced protestations of virtue is one of the rarest of occurrences. But the combination in the same person of an intensely executive nature with a love of popular approval is bound, in the face of conventional morality, to produce what the critical term hypocrisy.

Another reaction to the separation of morals from human nature is a romantic glorification of natural impulse as something superior to all moral claims. There are those who lack the persistent force of the executive will to break through conventions and to use them for their own purposes, but who unite sensitiveness with intensity of desire. Fastening upon the conventional element in morality, they hold that all morality is a conventionality hampering to the development of individuality. Although appetites are the commonest things in human nature, the least distinctive or individualized, they identify unrestraint in satisfaction of appetite with free realization of individuality. They treat subjection to passion as a manifestation of freedom in the degree in which it shocks the bourgeois. The urgent need for a transvaluation of morals is caricatured by the notion that an avoidance of the avoidances of conventional morals constitutes positive achievement. While

the executive type keeps its eyes on actual conditions so as to manipulate them, this school abrogates objective intelligence in behalf of sentiment, and withdraws into little coteries of emancipated souls.

II

If we turn from concrete effects upon character to theoretical issues, we single out the discussion regarding freedom of will as typical of the consequences that come from separating morals from human nature. Men are wearied with bootless discussion, and anxious to dismiss it as a metaphysical subtlety. But nevertheless it contains within itself the most practical of all moral questions, the nature of freedom and the means of its achieving. The separation of morals from human nature leads to a separation of human nature in its moral aspects from the rest of nature, and from ordinary social habits and endeavors which are found in business, civic life, the run of companionships and recreations. These things are thought of at most as places where moral notions need to be applied, not as places where moral ideas are to be studied and moral energies generated. In short, the severance of morals from human nature ends by driving morals inwards from the public open out-of-doors air and light of day into the obscurities and privacies of an inner life. The significance of the traditional discussion of free will is that it reflects precisely a separation of moral activity from nature and the public life of men.

One has to turn from moral theories to the general human struggle for political, economic and religious liberty, for freedom of thought, speech, assemblage and creed, to find significant reality in the conception of freedom of will. Then one finds himself out of the stiflingly close atmosphere of an inner consciousness and in the open-air world. The cost of confining moral freedom to an inner region is the almost complete severance of ethics from politics and economics. The former is regarded as summed up in edifying exhortations, and the latter as connected with arts of expediency separated from larger issues of good.

In short, there are two schools of social reform. One bases itself upon the notion of a morality which springs from an inner freedom, something mysteriously cooped up within personality. It asserts that the only way to change institutions is for men to purify their own hearts, and that when this has been accomplished, change of institutions will follow of itself. The other school denies the existence of any such inner power, and in so doing conceives that it has denied all moral freedom. It says that men are made what they are by the forces of the environment, that human nature is purely malleable, and that till institutions are changed, nothing can be done. Clearly this leaves the outcome as hopeless as does an appeal to an inner rectitude and benevolence. For it provides no leverage for change of environment. It throws us back upon accident, usually disguised as a necessary law of history or evolution, and trusts to some violent change, symbolized by civil war, to usher in an abrupt millennium. There is an alternative to being penned in between these two theories. We can recognize that all conduct is *interaction* between elements of human nature and the environment, natural and social. Then we shall see that progress proceeds in two ways, and that freedom is found in that kind of interaction which maintains an environment in which human desire and choice count for something. There are in truth forces in man as well as without him. While they are infinitely frail in comparison with exterior forces, yet they may have the support of a foreseeing and contriving intelligence. When we look at the problem as one of an adjustment to be intelligently attained, the issue shifts from within personality to an engineering issue, the establishment of arts of education and social guidance.

It is not pretended that a moral theory based upon realities of human nature and a study of the specific connections of these realities with those of physical science would do away with moral struggle and defeat. It would not make the moral life as simple a matter as wending one's way along a well-lighted boulevard. All action is an invasion of the future, of the unknown. Conflict and uncertainty are ultimate traits. But morals based upon concern with facts and deriving guidance from knowledge of them would at least locate the points of effective endeavor and would focus available resources upon them. It would put an end to the impossible attempt to live in two unrelated worlds. It would destroy fixed distinction between the human and the physical, as well as that between the moral and the industrial and political. A morals based on study of human nature instead of upon disregard for it would find the facts of man continuous with those of the rest of nature and would thereby ally ethics with physics and biology. It would find the nature and activities of one person coterminous with those of other human beings, and therefore link ethics with the study of history, sociology, law and economics.

Such a morals would not automatically solve moral problems, nor resolve perplexities. But it would enable us to state problems in such forms that action could be courageously and intelligently directed to their solution. It would not assure us against failure, but it would render failure a source of instruction. It would not protect us against the future emergence of equally serious moral difficulties, but it would enable us to approach the always recurring troubles with a fund of growing knowledge which would add significant values to our conduct even when we overtly failed—as we should continue to do. Until the integrity of morals with human nature and of both with the environment is recognized, we shall be deprived of the aid of past experience to cope with the most acute and deep problems of life. Accurate and extensive knowledge will continue to operate only in dealing with purely technical problems. The intelligent acknowledgment of the continuity of nature, man and society will alone secure a growth of morals which will be serious without being fanatical, aspiring without sentimentality, adapted to reality without conventionality, sensible without taking the form of calculation of profits, idealistic without being romantic.

III

The place of natural fact and law in morals brings us to the problem of freedom. We are told that seriously to import empirical facts into morals is equivalent to an abrogation of freedom. Facts and laws mean necessity we are told. The way to freedom is to turn our back upon them and take flight to a separate ideal realm. Even if the flight could be successfully accomplished, the efficacy of the prescription may be doubted. For we need freedom in and among actual events, not apart from them. It is hoped therefore that there remains an alternative; that the road to freedom may be found in that knowledge of facts which enables us to employ them in connection with desires and aims. A physician or engineer is free in his thought and his action in the degree in which he knows what he deals with. Possibly we find here the key to any freedom.

What men have esteemed and fought for in the name of liberty is varied and complex—but certainly it has never been a metaphysical freedom of will. It seems to contain three elements of importance, though on their face not all of them are directly compatible with one another. (i) It includes efficiency in action, ability to carry out plans, the absence of cramping and thwarting obstacles. (ii) It also includes capacity to vary plans, to change the course of action, to experience novelties. And again (iii) it signifies the power of desire and choice to be factors in events.

Few men would purchase even a high amount of efficient action along definite lines at the price of monotony, or if success in action were bought by all abandonment of personal preference. They would probably feel that a more precious freedom was possessed in a life of ill-assured objective achievement that contained undertaking of risks, adventuring in new fields, a pitting of personal choice against the odds of events, and a mixture of success and failures, provided choice had a career. The slave is a man who executes the wish of others, one doomed to act along lines predetermined to regularity. Those who have defined freedom as ability to act have

unconsciously assumed that this ability is exercised in accord with desire, and that its operation introduces the agent into fields previously unexplored. Hence the conception of freedom as involving three factors.

Intelligence is the key to freedom in act. We are likely to be able to go ahead prosperously in the degree in which we have consulted conditions and formed a plan which enlists their consenting cooperation. The gratuitous help of unforeseen circumstance we cannot afford to despise. Luck, bad if not good, will always be with us. But it has a way of favoring the intelligent and showing its back to the stupid. And the gifts of fortune when they come are fleeting except when they are made taut by intelligent adaption of conditions. In neutral and adverse circumstances, study and foresight are the only roads to unimpeded action.

Choice is an element in freedom and there can be no choice without unrealized and precarious possibilities. It is this demand for genuine contingency which is caricatured in the orthodox doctrine of a freedom of indifference, a power to choose this way or that apart from any habit or impulse, without even a desire on the part of will to show off. Such an indetermination of choice is not desired by the lover of either reason or excitement. The theory of arbitrary free choice represents indeterminateness of conditions grasped in a vague and lazy fashion and hardened into a desirable attribute of will. Under the title of freedom men prize such uncertainty of conditions as give deliberation and choice an opportunity. But uncertainty of volition which is more than a reflection of uncertainty of conditions is the mark of a person who has acquired imbecility of character through permanent weakening of his springs of action.

Whether or not indeterminateness, uncertainty, actually exists in the world is a difficult question. It is easier to think of the world as fixed, settled once for all, and man as accumulating all the uncertainty there is in his will and all the doubt there is in his intellect. The rise of natural science has facilitated this dualistic partitioning, making nature wholly fixed and mind wholly open and empty. Fortunately for us we do not have to settle the question. A hypothetical answer is enough. *If* the world is already done and done for, if its character is entirely achieved so that its behavior is like that of a man lost in routine, then the only freedom for which man can hope is one of efficiency in overt action. But *if* change is genuine, if accounts are still in process of making, and if objective uncertainty is the stimulus to reflection, then variation in action, novelty and experiment, have a true meaning. In any case the question is an objective one. It concerns not man in isolation from the world but man in his connection with it. A world that is at points and times indeterminate enough to call out deliberation and to give play to choice to shape its future is a world in which will is free, not because it is inherently vacillating and unstable, but because deliberation and choice are determining and stabilizing factors.

Upon an empirical view, uncertainty, doubt, hesitation, contingency and novelty, genuine change which is not mere disguised repetition, are facts. Only deductive reasoning from certain fixed premises creates a bias in favor of complete determination and finality. To say that these things exist only in human experience not in the world, and exist there only because of our "finitude" is dangerously like paying ourselves with words. Empirically the life of man seems in these respects as in others to express a culmination of facts in nature. To admit ignorance and uncertainty in man while denying them to nature involves a curious dualism. Variability, initiative, innovation, departure from routine, experimentation are empirically the manifestation of a genuine nisus in things. At all events it is these things that are precious to us under the name of freedom. It is their elimination from the life of a slave which makes his life servile, intolerable to the freeman who has once been on his own, no matter what his animal comfort and security. A free man would rather take his chance in an open world than be guaranteed in a closed world.

These considerations give point to the third factor in love of freedom: the desire to have desire count as a factor, a force. Even if will chooses unaccountably, even if it be a capricious impulse, it does not follow that there are real alternatives, genuine possibilities, open in the future. What we want is possibilities open in the *world* not in the will, except as will or deliberate activity reflects the world. To foresee future objective alternatives and to be able by deliberation to choose one of them and thereby weight its chances in the struggle for future existence, measures our freedom. It is assumed sometimes that if it can be shown that deliberation determines choice and deliberation is determined by character and conditions, there is no freedom. This is like saying that because a flower comes from root and stem it cannot bear fruit. The question is not what are the antecedents of deliberation and choice, but what are their consequences. What do they do that is distinctive? The answer is that they give us all the control of future possibilities which is open to us. And this control is the crux of our freedom. Without it, we are pushed from behind. With it we walk in the light.

The doctrine that knowledge, intelligence rather than will, constitutes freedom is not new. It has been preached by moralists of many a school. All rationalists have identified freedom with action emancipated by insight into truth. But insight into necessity has by them been substituted for foresight of possibilities. Tolstoy for example expressed the idea of Spinoza and Hegel when he said that the ox is a slave as long as he refuses to recognize the yoke and chafes under it, while if he identifies himself with its necessity and draws willingly instead of rebelliously, he is free. But as long as the yoke is a yoke it is impossible that voluntary identification with it should occur. Conscious submission is then either fatalistic submissiveness or cowardice. The ox accepts in fact not the yoke but the stall and the hay to which the yoke is a necessary incident. But if the ox foresees the consequences of the use of the yoke, if he anticipates the possibility of harvest, and identifies himself not with the yoke but with the realization of its possibilities, he acts freely, voluntarily. He hasn't accepted a necessity as unavoidable; he has welcomed a possibility as a desirability.

Perception of necessary law plays, indeed, a part. But no amount of insight into necessity brings with it, as such, anything but a consciousness of necessity. Freedom is the "truth of necessity" only when we use one "necessity" to alter another. When we use the law to foresee consequences and to consider how they may be averted or secured, then freedom begins. Employing knowledge of law to enforce desire in execution gives power to the engineer. Employing knowledge of law in order to submit to it without further action

constitutes fatalism, no matter how it be dressed up. Thus we recur to our main contention. Morality depends upon events, not upon commands and ideals alien to nature. But intelligence treats events as moving, as fraught with possibilities, not as ended, final. In forecasting their possibilities, the distinction between better and worse arises. Human desire and ability cooperates with this or that natural force according as this or that eventuality is judged better. We do not use the present to control the future. We use the foresight of the future to refine and expand present activity. In this use of desire, deliberation and choice, freedom is actualized.

*Reconstruction in Morals**

I

Moral goods and ends exist only when something has to be done. The fact that something has to be done proves that there are deficiencies, evils in the existent situation. This ill is just the specific ill that it is. It never is an exact duplicate of anything else. Consequently the good of the situation has to be discovered, projected and attained on the basis of the exact defect and trouble to be rectified. It cannot intelligently be injected into the situation from without. Yet it is the part of wisdom to compare different cases, to gather together the ills from which humanity suffers, and to generalize the corresponding goods into classes. Health, wealth, industry, temperance, amiability, courtesy, learning, esthetic capacity, initiative, courage, patience, enterprise, thoroughness and a multitude of other generalized ends are acknowledged as goods. But the *value* of this systematization is intellectual or analytic. Classifications *suggest* possible traits to be on the lookout for in studying a particular case; they suggest methods of action to be tried in removing the inferred causes of ill. They are tools of in-

---

* John Dewey, *Reconstruction in Philosophy*, (New York, Henry Holt & Co., 1920), Ch. VII (shortened).

sight; their value is in promoting an individualized response in the individual situation.

Morals is not a catalogue of acts nor a set of rules to be applied like drugstore prescriptions or cook-book recipes. The need in morals is for specific methods of inquiry and of contrivance: Methods of inquiry to locate difficulties and evils; methods of contrivance to form plans to be used as working hypotheses in dealing with them. And the pragmatic import of the logic of individualized situations, each having its own irreplaceable good and principle, is to transfer the attention of theory from preoccupation with general conceptions to the problem of developing effective methods of inquiry.

Two ethical consequences of great moment should be remarked. The belief in fixed values has bred a division of ends into intrinsic and instrumental, of those that are really worth while in themselves and those that are of importance only as means to intrinsic goods. Indeed, it is often thought to be the very beginning of wisdom, of moral discrimination, to make this distinction. Dialectically, the distinction is interesting and seems harmless. But carried into practice it has an import that is tragic. Historically, it has been the source and justification of a hard and fast difference between ideal goods one one side and material goods on the other. At present those who would be liberal conceive intrinsic goods as esthetic in nature rather than as exclusively religious or as intellectually contemplative. But the effect is the same. So-called intrinsic goods, whether religious or esthetic, are divorced from those interests of daily life which because of their constancy and urgency form the preoccupation of the great mass. Aristotle used this distinction to declare that slaves and the working class though they are necessary *for* the state—the commonweal—are not constituents *of* it. That which is regarded as *merely* instrumental must approach drudgery; it cannot command either intellectual, artistic or moral attention and respect. Anything becomes *unworthy* whenever it is thought of as intrinsically lacking worth. So men of "ideal" interests have chosen for the most part the way of neglect and escape. The urgency and pressure of "lower" ends have been covered up by polite conventions. Or, they have been relegated to a baser class of mortals in order that the few might be free to attend to the goods that are really or intrinsically worth while. This withdrawal, in the name of higher ends, has left, for mankind at large and especially for energetic "practical" people the lower activities in complete command.

No one can possibly estimate how much of the obnoxious materialism and brutality of our economic life is due to the fact that economic ends have been regarded as *merely* instrumental. When they are recognized to be as intrinsic and final in their place as any others, then it will be seen that they are capable of idealization, and that if life is to be worth while, they must acquire ideal and intrinsic value. Esthetic, religious and other "ideal" ends are now thin and meagre or else idle and luxurious because of the separation from "instrumental" or economic ends. Only in connection with the latter can they be woven into the texture of daily life and made substantial and pervasive. The vanity and irresponsibility of values that are merely final and not also in turn means to the enrichment of other occupations of life ought to be obvious. But now the doctrine of "higher" ends gives aid, comfort and support to

every socially isolated and socially irresponsible scholar, specialist, esthete and religionist. It protects the vanity and irresponsibility of his calling from observation by others and by himself. The moral deficiency of the calling is transformed into a cause of admiration and gratulation.

The other generic change lies in doing away once for all with the traditional distinction between moral goods, like the virtues, and natural goods like health, economic security, art, science and the like. The point of view under discussion is not the only one which has deplored this rigid distinction and endeavored to abolish it. Some schools have even gone so far as to regard moral excellencies, qualities of character as of value only because they promote natural goods. But the experimental logic when carried into morals makes every quality that is judged to be good according as it contributes to amelioration of existing ills. And in so doing, it enforces the moral meaning of natural science. When all is said and done in criticism of present social deficiencies, one may well wonder whether the root difficulty does not lie in the separation of natural and moral science. When physics, chemistry, biology, medicine, contribute to the detection of concrete human woes and to the development of plans for remedying them and relieving the human estate, they become moral; they become part of the apparatus of moral inquiry or science. The latter then loses its peculiar flavor of the didactic and pedantic; its ultra-moralistic and hortatory tone. It loses its thinness and shrillness as well as its vagueness. It gains agencies that are efficacious. But the gain is not confined to the side of moral science. Natural science loses its divorce from humanity; it becomes itself humanistic in quality. It is something to be pursued not in a technical and specialized way for what is called truth for its own sake, but with the sense of its social bearing, its intellectual indispensableness. It is technical only in the sense that it provides the technique of social and moral engineering.

When the consciousness of science is fully impregnated with the consciousness of human value, the greatest dualism which now weighs humanity down, the split between the material, the mechanical, the scientific and the moral and ideal will be destroyed. Human forces that now waver because of this division will be unified and reinforced. As long as ends are not thought of as individualized according to specific needs and opportunities, the mind will be content with abstractions, and the adequate stimulus to the moral or social use of natural science and historical data will be lacking. But when attention is concentrated upon the diversified concretes, recourse to all intellectual materials needed to clear up the special cases will be imperative. At the same time that morals are made to focus in intelligence, things intellectual are moralized. The vexatious and wasteful conflict between naturalism and humanism is terminated.

II

These general considerations may be amplified. First: Inquiry, discovery take the same place in morals that they have come to occupy in sciences of nature. Validation, demonstration become experimental, a matter of consequences. Reason, always an honorific term in ethics, becomes actualized in the methods by which the needs and conditions, the obstacles and resources, of situations are scrutinized in detail, and intelligent plans of improvement are worked out. Remote and abstract generalities promote jumping at conclusions, "anticipations of nature." Bad consequences are then deplored as due to natural perversity and untoward fate. But shifting the issue to analysis of a specific situation makes inquiry obligatory and alert observation of consequences imperative. No past decision nor old principle can ever be wholly relied upon to justify a course of action. No amount of pains taken in forming a purpose in a definite case is final; the consequences of its adoption must be carefully noted, and a purpose held only as a working hypothesis until results confirm its rightness. Mistakes are no longer either mere unavoidable accidents to be mourned or moral sins to be expiated and forgiven. They are lessons in wrong methods of using intelligence and instructions as to a

better course in the future. They are indications of the need of revision, development, readjustment. Ends grow, standards of judgment are improved. Man is under just as much obligation to develop his most advanced standards and ideals as to use conscientiously those which he already possesses. Moral life is protected from falling into formalism and rigid repetition. It is rendered flexible, vital, growing.

In the second place, every case where moral action is required becomes of equal moral importance and urgency with every other. If the need and deficiencies of a specific situation indicate improvement of health as the end and good, then for that situation health is the ultimate and supreme good. It is no means to something else. It is a final and intrinsic value. The same thing is true of improvement of economic status, of making a living, of attending to business and family— all of the things which under the sanction of fixed ends have been rendered of secondary and merely instrumental value, and so relatively base and unimportant. Anything that in a given situation is an end and good at all is of equal worth, rank and dignity with every other good of any other situation, and deserves the same intelligent attention.

We note thirdly the effect in destroying the roots of Phariseeism. We are so accustomed to thinking of this as deliberate hypocrisy that we overlook its intellectual premises. The conception which looks for the end of action within the circumstances of the actual situation will not have the same measure of judgment for all cases. When one factor of the situation is a person of trained mind and large resources, more will be expected than with a person of backward mind and uncultured experience. The absurdity of applying the same standard of moral judgment to savage peoples that is used with civilized will be apparent. No individual or group will be judged by whether they come up to or fall short of some fixed result, but by the direction in which they are moving. The bad man is the man who no matter how good he *has* been is beginning to deteriorate, to grow less good. The good man is the man who no matter how morally unworthy he *has* been is moving to become better. Such a conception makes one severe in judging himself and humane in judging others. It excludes that arrogance which always accompanies judgment based on degree of approximation to fixed ends.

In the fourth place, the process of growth, of improvement and progress, rather than the static outcome and result, becomes the significant thing. Not health as an end once and for all, but the needed improvement in health—a continual process—is the end and good. The end is no longer a terminus or limit to be reached. It is the active process of transforming the existent situation. Not perfection as a final goal, but the ever-enduring process of perfecting, maturing, refining is the aim in living. Honesty, industry, temperance, justice, like health, wealth and learning, are not goods to be possessed as they would be if they expressed fixed ends to be attained. They are directions of change in the quality of experience. Growth itself is the only moral "end."

Although the bearing of this idea upon the problem of evil and the controversy between optimism and pessimism is too vast to be here discussed, it may be worth while to touch upon it superficially. The problem of evil ceases to be a theological and metaphysical one, and is perceived to be the practical problem of reducing, alleviating, as far as may be removing, the evils of life. Philosophy is no longer under obligation to find ingenious methods for proving that evils are only apparent, not real, or to elaborate schemes for explaining them away or, worse yet, for justifying them. It assumes another obligation:— That of contributing in however humble a way to methods that will assist us in discovering the causes of humanity's ills. Pessimism is a paralyzing doctrine. In declaring that the world is evil wholesale, it makes futile all efforts to discover the remediable causes of specific evils and thereby destroys at the root every attempt to make the world better and happier. Wholesale optimism, which has been the consequence of the attempt to explain evil away, is, however, equally an incubus.

After all, the optimism that says that the world is already the best possible of all worlds might be regarded as the most cynical of pessimisms. If this is the best possible, what would a world which was fundamentally bad be like? Meliorism is the belief that the specific conditions which exist at one moment, be they comparatively bad or comparatively good, in any event may be bettered. It encourages intelligence to study the positive means of good and the obstructions to their realization, and to put forth endeavor for the improvement of conditions. It arouses confidence and a reasonable hopefulness as optimism does not. For the latter in declaring that good is already realized in ultimate reality tends to make us gloss over the evils that concretely exist. It becomes too readily the creed of those who live at ease, in comfort, of those who have been successful in obtaining this world's rewards. Too readily optimism makes the men who hold it callous and blind to the sufferings of the less fortunate, or ready to find the cause of troubles of others in their personal viciousness. It thus co-operates with pessimism, in spite of the extreme nominal differences between the two, in benumbing sympathetic insight and intelligent effort in reform. It beckons men away from the world of relativity and change into the calm of the absolute and eternal.

The import of many of these changes in moral attitude focusses in the idea of happiness. Happiness has often been made the object of the moralists' contempt. Yet the most ascetic moralist has usually restored the idea of happiness under some other name, such as bliss. Goodness without happiness, valor and virtue without satisfaction, ends without conscious enjoyment—these things are as intolerable practically as they are self-contradictory in conception. Happiness is not, however, a bare possession; it is not a fixed attainment. Such a happiness is either the unworthy selfishness which moralists have so bitterly condemned, or it is, even if labelled bliss, an insipid tedium, a millennium of ease in relief from all struggle and labor. It could satisfy only the most delicate of molly-coddles.

Happiness is found only in success; but success means succeeding, getting forward, moving in advance. It is an active process, not a passive outcome. Accordingly it includes the overcoming of obstacles, the elimination of sources of defect and ill.

Government, business, art, religion, all social institutions have a meaning, a purpose. That purpose is to set free and to develop the capacities of human individuals without respect to race, sex, class or economic status. And this is all one with saying that the test of their value is the extent to which they educate every individual into the full stature of his possibility. Democracy has many meanings, but if it has a moral meaning, it is found in resolving that the supreme test of all political institutions and industrial arrangements shall be the contribution they make to the all-around growth of every member of society.

4

The Pilgrimage
of the Pragmatist

The Pragmatism of the twentieth century is largely an American philosophy. Its ablest exponents, William James, Charles S. Peirce, and John Dewey, were all Americans, and for two or three decades during the first half of the century pragmatism was easily the most influential movement in American thought. While essentially American in spirit and point of view, the pragmatism of James did, nevertheless, give clear and forceful expression to the spirit of the age in which he lived. The broad evolutionary and anti-intellectual forces at work in the late nineteenth century touched James' sympathies and shaped his thinking as directly as they did that of such men as Henri Bergson in France or Friedrich Nietzsche in Germany. James' ability to express the spirit of the age with such insight and feeling gained for him a world reputation and influence such as few American philosophers before or since his day have been able to achieve. James was the first American to be recognized as comparable in ability and stature to the ablest philosophers of Great Britain, France, and Germany. He was the first American to develop a philosophical position that attracted enthusiastic disciples throughout Europe and took its place as one of the important systems of thought in the Western world.

In recent years Charles S. Peirce, a friend and contemporary of James at Harvard University, has also been widely hailed as one of the outstanding figures in American philosophy. James was among the few men who recognized Peirce's philosophical stature at the time, and looked to him as the actual author of the pragmatic philosophy of which James himself became the best-known and most influential advocate. But in interpreting pragmatism James wrote and spoke with the directness and appeal of the popular lecturer, while the thought of Peirce exhibits the scholarly detachment and the formidable technical vocabulary of the research scientist. As a result, it was James who became one of Harvard's influential professors, much sought after as a popular speaker as well as a lecturer to university audiences, while Peirce to whom James owed so much, was almost completely neglected even in university circles until many years after both men were dead.

The pragmatic philosophy of James and Peirce was carried one step further by John Dewey and together these three men stand as the great American empiricists of our age. Their influence is clearly to be seen not only in the development of American philosophy, but also in the reaction and criticism their ideas stirred up in European philosophical circles.[1] More recently the growing appeal of logical positivism and of analytical philosophy, in Europe as well as America, has focused attention upon certain aspects of the thought of Dewey and Peirce which make quite clear a fundamental difference in spirit between the meaning of pragmatism to James and that given it by the other two men most responsible for its development. It is in general this spiritual pilgrimage of American pragmatism that the selections included here illustrate.

Pragmatism as a Philosophy to Live By: William James

James was born in New York City in 1842. He spent his early years in school or travel abroad; then when about twenty he enrolled at Harvard University, and for the next forty-six years he was intimately connected with that institution. The evolutionary theories of Darwin and Herbert Spencer were just beginning to influence the thinking of the universities, and James was soon caught up in these controversies. His interest in experimental physiology and psychology led him to study medicine at Harvard and later to spend a winter at the University of Berlin. Upon returning to Harvard he took his degree in medicine, and in 1872 was appointed instructor in physiology there. Gradually but surely he began working his way from physiology through psychology to philosophy.

In 1890 James published an influential two-volume work on *The Principles of Psychology,* and in 1897, when he was fifty-five, his first book in philosophy, *The Will to Believe and Other Essays in Popular Philosophy.* Several years later he was invited to deliver the Gifford Lectures in Edinburgh (a signal distinction among philosophers), and in 1902 these lectures were published under the title *Varieties of Religious Experience.* Like his earlier work on psychology, this book also has had a wide and lasting influence. In a series of lectures which he gave at Harvard in 1906, James for the first time drew together his ideas into a well-organized philosophical position. These lectures, published the next year under the title, *Pragmatism,* were read and discussed widely. James himself was greatly heartened by the reception given his book. "I shouldn't be surprised," he wrote his brother Henry, "if ten years hence it would be rated as 'epoch making.'" And his prophecy proved to be right. Actually, however, James was never successful in developing a thoroughly consistent systematic philosophy. He died in 1910 with this task incomplete. Probably it was an impossible one. The breadth of his sympathy,

---

[1] In England F. C. S. Schiller was the ablest exponent at Oxford University of an essentially pragmatic philosophy, and in Florence a small but vigorous Italian "pragmatist" movement flourished for a while. Neither of these had any widespread or permanent impact upon European philosophy.

his eagerness to do justice to the richness and concreteness of experience, his commitment to change, development, and freedom was such as to make any logical system unacceptable. On his desk when he died lay a paper upon which he had written his last work in philosophy—a revealing and characteristic comment: "There is no conclusion. What has concluded that we might conclude regarding it? There are no fortunes to be told and there is no advice to be given. Farewell."

For James philosophy was always a very practical concern. It was a program for action rather than a matter of abstract speculation; a faith that gives life meaning and purpose, never a detached or dispassionate search for some "metaphysical" truth unrelated to the important issues of everyday life. He quotes with approval the statement of G. K. Chesterton: "There are some people, and I am one of them, who think that the most important and the most practical thing about a man is his view of the universe. We think that for a landlady considering a lodger it is important to know his income, but still more important to know his philosophy." And James made it clear that unless a philosophy of life would work, it could not hope to hold the allegiance of men and women in our age. He wanted a philosophy concerned directly with human experience, with the present rather than the past, with progress and concrete results not theory or speculation. He wanted to give to philosophy something of the practical temper of scientific method without the abstraction and detachment of scientific theory.

As a consequence of this approach, a moral earnestness permeates James' philosophical thinking. The major issues that we face in life arise from the continuing conflict between good and evil, he feels, and he is eager to discover a moral ideal that we can not only *believe in* but also put into practice. He has a strong distaste for anything superficial, mediocre, or decadent. The only thing that makes life worth living is a "real fight," actual risks, the determination to choose the course one believes to be right, and the courage to fight for one's convictions. In his famous essay, *The Moral Equivalent of War*, published in 1910, James argued that the trouble with the typical American way of life was its easy acceptance of mediocrity, its dullness, and its failure to meet squarely the moral issues of the day. A more determined struggle with the forces of evil in this world was necessary, in his opinion, to recapture something of the courage and heroism, the sacrifice and devotion, that have made men praise war through the ages. Men from all walks of life were attracted by James' frank contention that the horrors of war, as bad as they are, "are a cheap price to pay for our rescue from a world of clerks and school teachers, of co-education, associated charities and feminism. No scorn, no hardness, no valor any more. Fie upon such a cattle-yard of a planet."

James was always a vigorous exponent of the *contemporary*, committed to the good life here and now. There is much to be done *today* to make the world a better place in which to live, and to this the philosopher should direct his attention. His reaction to travel in Europe well illustrates James' point of view. A brief visit was enough. "Italy is a very delightful place to dip into but no more," he wrote his sister from Rome. "The weight of the past world here is fatal—one ends by becoming its mere parasite instead of its equivalent. The ancients did things by doing the business of their own day, not by gaping at their grandfather's tombs,—and a normal man today will do likewise."

No essay of James' created more controversy in philosophical circles than that which gave its name to his famous book, *The Will to Believe*. He adopts here a view that is clearly of great importance in the development of his own version of pragmatism. Our deepest convictions, he points out, directly reflect our own needs, desires, and past experiences. Such forces as these are much more basic in shaping our beliefs than is rational reflection. Most of us do not believe in Buddhism, for example, but we probably would had we grown up in certain parts of the Orient instead of in America. We do not believe in communism, but we might if we now lived in Russia. "If one should assume that pure reason is what settles our opinions, he would fly in the teeth of the facts," James writes. "As a rule we disbelieve all facts and theories for which we have no use."

Two markedly divergent attitudes toward belief are possible. On the one hand, we can determine not to believe anything unless we have sufficient evidence to make it completely certain. This is the position of science, and James is emphatic in insisting that the scientist, who is dealing with the world of nature and can wait as long as necessary before making a decision, should accept only those beliefs for which he can find such convincing evidence. But many decisions, he points out, must be made without this kind of evidence. A judge, for example, must decide whether a man is guilty or not in the light of the evidence at hand. He simply cannot postpone the matter for another six or eight months as can the scientist who may have to wait years before making up his mind. Moreover, most of the important decisions we have to make in life are decisions that must be made in the light of the evidence at hand, and in many of these decisions it is clear that what we believe actually helps determine the outcome. In circumstances such as these, especially in our moral and religious decisions, "the will to believe" has for James an important function.

"If you believe well of your fellow men, you may well help create the good you believe in." This was a favorite maxim for James, and he practiced as well as preached it. "There are, then, cases where a fact cannot come at all unless a preliminary faith in its coming exists," he writes, "and when faith in the fact can help create the fact, that would be an insane logic which should say that faith running ahead of scientific evidence is the 'lowest kind of immorality' into which a thinking being can fall. Yet such is the logic by which our scientific absolutists pretend to regulate their lives."[1]

It is here that religion at its best has an important contribution to make to one's philosophy. James had no patience with religion that was merely conventional

---

[1] William James, *The Will to Believe and Other Essays in Popular Philosophy*, (New York, Longmans, Green and Company, Inc., 1896), p. 251.

and superficial; in a lively analysis of his experiences at the well-known Assembly Grounds on Lake Chautauqua, he attacks this kind of religion with his accustomed directness and vigor. However, in the essay entitled "Is Life Worth Living?" (which is included here), he describes the positive contribution that religious faith can make to effective living—a contribution that for him is essential and one that science by its very nature cannot be expected to provide.

Is Life Worth Living?*

When Mr. Mallock's book with this title appeared some fifteen years ago, the jocose answer that "it depends on the *liver*" had great currency in the newspapers. The answer which I propose to give tonight cannot be jocose. In the words of one of Shakespeare's prologues,—

> I come no more to make you laugh, things now,
> that bear a weighty and a serious brow,
> Sad, high, and working, full of state and woe,—

must be my theme. In the deepest heart of all of us there is a corner in which the ultimate mystery of things works sadly; and I know not what such an association as yours intends, nor what you ask of those whom you invite to address you, unless it be to lead you from the surface-glamour of existence, and for an hour at least to make you heedless to the buzzing and jigging and vibration of small interests and excitements that form the tissue of our ordinary consciousness. Without further explanation or apology, then, I ask you to join me in turning an attention, commonly too unwilling, to the profounder bass-note of life. Let us search the lonely depths for an hour together, and see what answers in the

last folds and recesses of things our question may find.

I

To come immediately to the heart of my theme, what I propose is to imagine ourselves reasoning with a fellow-mortal who is on such terms with life that the only comfort left is to brood on the assurance, "You may end it when you will." What reasons can we plead that may render such a brother willing to take up the burden again? Ordinary Christians, reasoning with would-be suicides, have little to offer them beyond the usual negative, "Thou shalt not." God alone is master of life and death, they say, and it is a blasphemous act to anticipate his absolving hand. But can *we* find nothing richer or more positive than this, no reflections to urge whereby the suicide may actually see, and in all sad seriousness feel, that in spite of adverse appearances even for him life is still worth living? There are suicides and suicides (in the United States about three thousand of them every year),* and I must frankly confess that with perhaps the majority of these my suggestions are impotent to deal. Where suicide is the result of insanity or sudden frenzied impulse, reflection is impotent to arrest its headway; and cases like these belong to the ultimate mystery of evil, concerning which I can only offer considerations tending toward religious patience at the end of this hour. My task, let me say now, is practically narrow, and my words are to deal only with that metaphysical *tedium vitae* which is peculiar to reflecting men. Most

* An address by William James to the Harvard Young Men's Christian Association, published in the *International Journal of Ethics* for October, 1895. Reprinted from William James, *The Will to Believe and Other Essays in Popular Philosophy,* (New York, Longmans, Green and Company, Inc., 1896). (Shortened.)

* In 1895.

of you are devoted, for good or ill to the reflective life. Many of you are students of philosophy, and have already felt in your own persons the scepticism and unreality that too much grubbing in the abstract roots of things will breed. This is, indeed, one of the regular fruits of the over-studious career. Too much questioning and too little active responsibility lead, almost as often as too much sensualism does, to the edge of the slope, at the bottom of which lie pessimism and the nightmare or suicidal view of life. But to the diseases which reflection breeds, still further reflection can oppose effective remedies; and it is of the melancholy and *Weltschmerz* bred of reflection that I now proceed to speak.

Let me say, immediately, that my final appeal is to nothing more recondite that religious faith. So far as my argument is to be destructive, it will consist in nothing more than the sweeping away of certain views that often keep the springs of religious faith compressed; and so far as it is to be constructive, it will consist in holding up to the light of day certain considerations calculated to let loose these springs in a normal, natural way. Pessimism is essentially a religious disease. In the form of it to which you are most liable, it consists in nothing but a religious demand to which there comes no normal religious reply.

That is why I call pessimism an essentially religious disease. The nightmare view of life has plenty of organic sources; but its great reflective source has at all times been the contradiction between the phenomena of nature and the craving of the heart to believe that behind nature there is a spirit whose expression nature is. What philosophers call "natural theology" has been one way of appeasing this craving; that poetry of nature in which our English literature is so rich has been another way. Now, suppose a mind whose imagination is pent in and who take its facts "hard"; suppose it, moreover, to feel strongly the craving for communion [with the total soul of things] and yet to realize how desperately difficult it is to construe the scientific order of nature either theologically or poetically—and what result *can* there be but inner discord and contradiction? Now,

this inner discord (merely as discord) can be relieved in either of two ways: The longing to read the facts religiously may cease, and leave the bare facts by themselves; or, supplementary facts may be discovered or believed in, which permit the religious reading to go on. These two ways of relief are the two stages of recovery, the two levels of escape from pessimism, which the sequel will, I trust, make more clear.

II

And now, in turning to what religion may have to say to the question, I come to what is the soul of my discourse. Religion has meant many things in human history; but when from now onward I use the word I mean to use it in the supernaturalist sense, as declaring that the so-called order of nature, which constitutes this world's experience, is only one portion of the total universe, and that there stretches beyond this visible world an unseen world of which we now know nothing positive, but in its relation to which the true significance of our present mundane life consists. A man's religious faith (whatever more special items of doctrine it may involve) means for me essentially his faith in the existence of an unseen order of some kind in which the riddles of the natural order may be found explained. In the more developed religions the natural world has always been regarded as the mere scaffolding or vestibule of a truer, more external world, and affirmed to be a sphere of education, trial, or redemption. In these religions, one must in some fashion die to the natural life before one can enter into life eternal. The notion that this physical world of wind and water, where the sun rises and the moon sets, is absolutely and ultimately the divinely aimed-at and established thing, is one which we find only in very early religions, such as that of the most primitive Jews. It is this natural religion (primitive still, in spite of the fact that poets and men of science whose good-will exceeds their perspicacity keep publishing it in new editions tuned to our contemporary ears) that, as I said a while ago, has suffered definitive bankruptcy in the opinion of a circle of persons, among whom I must count myself, and who are growing more numerous every day. For such persons the physical order of nature, taken simply as science knows it, cannot be held to reveal any one harmonious spiritual intent. It is mere *weather,* as Chauncey Wright called it, doing and undoing without end.

Now I wish to make you feel, if I can in the short remainder of this hour, that we have a right to believe the physical order to be only a partial order; that we have a right to supplement it by an unseen spiritual order which we assume on trust, if only thereby life may seem to us better worth living again. But as such a trust will seem to some of you sadly mystical and execrably unscientific, I must first say a word or two to weaken the veto which you may consider that science opposes to our act.

There is included in human nature an ingrained naturalism and materialism of mind which can only admit facts that are actually tangible. Of this sort of mind the entity called "science" is the idol. Fondness for the word "scientist" is one of the notes by which you may know its votaries; and its short way of killing any opinion that it disbelieves in is to call it "unscientific." It must be granted that there is no slight excuse for this. Science has made such glorious leaps in the last three hundred years, and extended our knowledge of nature so enormously both in general and in detail; men of science, moreover, have as a class displayed such admirable virtues, that it is no wonder if the worshippers of science lose their head. In this very University, accordingly, I have heard more than one teacher say that all the fundamental conceptions of truth have already been found by science, and that the future has only the details of the picture to fill in. But the slightest reflection on the real conditions will suffice to show how barbaric such notions are. They show such a lack of scientific imagination, that it is hard to see how one who is actively advancing any part of science can make a mistake so crude. Think how many absolutely new scientific conceptions have arisen in our own generation, how many new problems

have been formulated that were never thought of before, and then cast an eye upon the brevity of science's career. It began with Galileo, not three hundred years ago. Four thinkers since Galileo, each informing his successor of what discoveries his own lifetime had been achieved, might have passed the torch of science into our hands as we sit here in this room. Indeed, for the matter of that, an audience much smaller than the present one, an audience of some five or six score people, if each person in it could speak for his own generation, would carry us away to the black unknown of the human species, to days without a document or monument to tell their tale. Is it credible that such a mushroom knowledge, such a growth overnight as this, can represent more than the minutest glimpse of what the universe will really prove to be when adequately understood? No! our science is a drop, our ignorance a sea. Whatever else be certain, this at least is certain—that the world of our present natural knowledge is enveloped in a larger world of some sort of whose residual properties we at present can frame no positive idea.

Agnostic positivism, of course, admits this principle theoretically in the most cordial terms, but insists that we must not turn it to any practical use. We have no right, this doctrine tells us, to dream dreams, or suppose anything about the unseen part of the universe, merely because to do so may be for what we are pleased to call our highest interests. We must always wait for sensible evidence for our beliefs; and where such evidence is inaccessible we must frame no hypotheses whatever. Of course this is a safe enough position *in abstracto.* If a thinker had no stake in the unknown, no vital needs, to live or languish according to what the unseen world contained, a philosophic neutrality and refusal to believe either one way or the other would be his wisest cue. But, unfortunately, neutrality is not only inwardly difficult, it is also outwardly unrealizable, where our relations to an alternative are practical and vital. This is because, as the psychologists tell us, belief and doubt are living attitudes, and involve conduct on our part. Our only way, for example, of doubting, or refusing to believe, that a certain thing is, is continuing to act as if it were *not*. If, for instance, I refuse to believe that the room is getting cold, I leave the windows open and light no fire just as if it still were warm. If I doubt that you are worthy of my confidence, I keep you uninformed of all my secrets just as if you were unworthy of the same. If I doubt the need of insuring my house, I leave it uninsured as much as if I believed there were no need. And so if I must not believe that the world is divine, I can only express that refusal by declining ever to act distinctively as if it were so, which can only mean acting on certain critical occasions as if it were not so, or in an irreligious way. There are, you see, inevitable occasions in life when inaction is a kind of action, and must count as action, and when not to be for is to be practically against; and in all such cases strict and consistent neutrality is an unattainable thing.

And, after all, is not this duty of neutrality where only our inner interests would lead us to believe, the most ridiculous of commands? Is it not sheer dogmatic folly to say that our inner interests can have no real connection with the forces that the hidden world may contain? In other cases divinations based on inner interests have proved prophetic enough. Take science itself! Without an imperious inner demand on our part for ideal logical and mathematical harmonies, we should never have attained to proving that such harmonies lie hidden between all the chinks and interstices of the crude natural world. Hardly a law has been established in science, hardly a fact ascertained, which was not first sought after, often with sweat and blood, to gratify an inner need. Whence such needs come from we do not know: we find them in us, and biological psychology so far only classes them with Darwin's "accidental variations." But the inner need of believing that this world of nature is a sign of something more spiritual and eternal than itself is just as strong and authoritative in those who feel it, as the inner need of uniform laws of causation ever can be in a professionally scientific head. The toil of many generations has

proved the latter need prophetic. Why *may* not the former one be prophetic, too? And if needs of ours outrun the visible universe, why *may* not that be a sign that an invisible universe is there? What, in short, has authority to debar us from trusting our religious demands? Science as such assuredly has no authority, for she can only say what is, not what is not; and the agnostic "thou shalt not believe without coercive sensible evidence" is simply an expression (free to any one to make) of private personal appetite for evidence of a certain peculiar kind.

Now, when I speak of trusting our religious demands, just what do I mean by "trusting"? Is the word to carry with it licence to define in detail an invisible world, and to anathematize and excommunicate those whose trust is different? Certainly not! Our faculties of belief were not primarily given us to make orthodoxies and heresies withal; they were given us to live by. And to trust our religious demands means first of all to live in the light of them and to act as if the invisible world which they suggest were real. It is a fact of human nature, that men can live and die by the help of a sort of faith that goes without a single dogma or definition. The bare assurance that this natural order is not ultimate but a mere sign or vision, the external staging of a many-storied universe, in which spiritual forces have the last word and are eternal,—this bare assurance is to such men enough to make life seem worth living in spite of every contrary presumption suggested by its circumstances on the natural plane. Destroy this inner assurance, however, vague as it is, and all the light and radiance of existence is extinguished for these persons at a stroke. Often enough the wild-eyed look at life—the suicidal mood—will then set in.

And now the application comes directly home to you and me. Probably to almost every one of us here the most adverse life would seem well worth living, if we only could be *certain* that our bravery and patience with it were terminating and eventuating and bearing fruit somewhere in an unseen spiritual world. But granting we are not certain, does it then follow that a bare trust in such a world is a fool's paradise and lubberland, or rather that it is a living attitude in which we are free to indulge? Well, we are free to trust at our own risks anything that is not impossible, and that can bring analogies to bear in its behalf. That the world of physics is probably not absolute, all the converging multitude of arguments that make in favor of idealism tend to prove; and that our whole physical life may lie soaking in a spiritual atmosphere, a dimension of being that we at present have no organ for apprehending, is vividly suggested to us by the analogy of the life of our domestic animals. Our dogs, for example, are in our human life but not of it. They witness hourly the outward body of events whose inner meaning cannot, by any possible operation, be revealed to their intelligence,—events in which they themselves often play the cardinal part. My terrier bites a teasing boy, for example, and the father demands the damages. The dog may be present at every step of the negotiations, and see the money paid, without an inkling of what it all means, without a suspicion that it has anything to do with *him;* and he never *can* know in his natural dog's life. Or take another case which used greatly to impress me in my medical-student days. Consider a poor dog whom they are vivisecting in a laboratory. He lies strapped on a board and shrieking at his executioners, and to his own dark consciousness is literally in a sort of hell. He cannot see a single redeeming ray in the whole business; and yet all these diabolical-seeming events are often controlled by human intentions with which, if his poor benighted mind could only be made to catch a glimpse of them, all that is heroic in him would religiously acquiesce. Healing truth, relief to future sufferings of beast and man, are to be bought by them. It may be genuinely a process of redemption. Lying on his back on the board there he may be performing a function incalculably higher than any that prosperous canine life admits of; and yet, of the whole performance, this function is the one portion that must remain absolutely beyond his ken.

Now turn from this to the life of man. In the dog's life we see the world invisible to him because we live in both worlds. In human life, although we only see our world, and his within it, yet encompassing both these worlds a still wider world may be there, as unseen by us as our world is by him; and to believe in that world *may* be the most essential function that our lives in this world have to perform. But "may be! may be!" one now hears the positivist contemptuously exclaim; "what use can a scientific life have for maybes?" Well, I reply, the "scientific" life itself has much to do with maybes, and human life at large has everything to do with them. So far as man stands for anything, and is productive or originative at all, his entire vital function may be said to have to deal with maybes. Not a victory is gained, not a deed of faithfulness or courage is done, except upon a maybe; not a service, not a sally of generosity, not a scientific exploration or experiment or textbook, that may not be a mistake. It is only by risking our persons from one hour to another that we live at all. And often enough our faith beforehand in an uncertified result is the only thing that makes the result come true. Suppose, for instance, that you are climbing a mountain, and have worked yourself into a position from which the only escape is by a terrible leap. Have faith that you can successfully make it, and your feet are nerved to its accomplishment. But mistrust yourself, and think of all the sweet things you have heard the scientists say of *maybes,* and you will hesitate so long that, at last, all unstrung and trembling, and launching yourself in a moment of despair, you roll in the abyss. In such a case (and it belongs to an enormous class), the part of wisdom as well as of courage is to *believe what is in the line of your needs,* for only by such belief is the need fulfilled. Refuse to believe, and you shall indeed be right, for you shall irretrievably perish. But believe and again you shall be right, for you shall save yourself. You make one or the other of two possible universes true by your trust or mistrust, both universes having been only *maybes,* in this particular, before you contributed your act.

Now, it appears to me that the question whether life is worth living is subject to conditions logically much like these. It does, indeed, depend on you *the liver*. If you surrender to the nightmare view and crown the evil edifice by your own suicide, you have indeed made a picture totally black. Pessimism, completed by your act, is true beyond a doubt, so far as your world goes. Your mistrust of life has removed whatever worth your own enduring existence might have given to it; and now, throughout the whole sphere of possible influence of that existence, the mistrust has proved itself to have had divining power. But suppose, on the other hand, that instead of giving way to the nightmare view you cling to it that this world is not the *ultimatum*. Suppose you find yourself a very wellspring, as Wordsworth says, of—

> Zeal, and the virtue to exist by faith
> As soldiers live by courage; as, by strength
> Of heart, the sailor fights with roaring seas.

Suppose, however thickly evils crowd upon you, that your unconquerable subjectivity proves to be their match, and that you find a more wonderful joy than any passive pleasure can bring in trusting ever in the larger whole. Have you not now made life worth living on these terms? What sort of a thing would life really be, with your qualities ready for a tussle with it, if it only brought fair weather and gave these higher faculties of yours no scope? Please remember that optimism and pessimism are definitions of the world, and that our own reactions on the world, small as they are in bulk, are integral parts of the whole thing, and necessarily help to determine the definition. They may even be the decisive elements in determining the definition. A large mass can have its unstable equilibrium overturned by the addition of a feather's weight; a long phrase may have its sense reversed by the addition of the three letters n-o-t. This life is worth living, we can say, *since it is what we make it, from the moral point of view;* and we are determined to make it from that point of view so far as we have anything to do with it, a success.

Now, in this description of faiths that verify themselves I have assumed that our faith in an invisible order is what inspires those efforts and that patience which make this visible order good for moral men. Our faith in the seen world's goodness (goodness now meaning fitness for successful moral and religious life) has verified itself by leaning on our faith in the unseen world. But will our faith in the unseen world similarly verify itself? Who knows?

Once more it is a case of *maybe;* and once more *maybes* are the essence of the situation. I confess that I do not see why the very existence of an invisible world may not in part depend on the personal response which any one of us may make to the religious appeal. God himself, in short, may draw vital strength and increase of very being from our fidelity. For my own part, I do not know what the sweat and blood and tragedy of this life mean, if they mean anything short of this. If this life be not a real fight, in which something is eternally gained for the universe by success, it is no better than a game of private theatricals from which one may withdraw at will. But it *feels* like a real fight,—as if there were something really wild in the universe which we, with all our idealities and faithfulnesses, are needed to redeem; and first of all to redeem our own hearts from atheisms and fears. For such a half-wild, half-saved universe our nature is adapted. The deepest thing in our nature is this *Binnenleben* (as a German doctor lately has called it), this dumb region of the heart in which we dwell alone with our willingnesses and unwillingnesses, our faiths and fears. As through the cracks and crannies of caverns those waters exude from the earth's bosom which then form the fountainheads of springs, so in these crepuscular depths of personality the sources of all our outer deeds and decisions take their rise. Here is our deepest organ of communication with the nature of things; and compared with these concrete movements of our soul all abstract statements and scientific arguments—the veto, for example, which the strict positivist pronounces upon our faith—sound to us like mere chatterings of the teeth. For here possibilities, not finished facts, are the realities with which we have actively to deal; and to quote my friend William Salter, of the Philadelphia Ethical Society, "as the essence of courage is to stake one's life on a possibility, so the essence of faith is to believe that the possibility exists."

These, then, are my last words to you: Be not afraid of life. Believe that life is worth living, and your belief will help create the fact. The "scientific proof" that you are right may not be clear before the day of judgment (or some stage of being which that expression may serve to symbolize) is reached. But the faithful fighters of this hour, or the beings that then and there will represent them, may then turn to the faint-hearted, who here decline to go on, with words like those with which Henry IV greeted the tardy Crillon after a great victory had been gained: "Hang yourself, brave Crillon! we fought at Arques, and you were not there."

What Pragmatism Means*

Some years ago, being with a camping party in the mountains, I returned from a solitary ramble to find every one engaged in a ferocious metaphysical dispute. The *corpus* of the dispute was a squirrel—a live squirrel supposed to be clinging to one side of a tree-trunk; while over against the tree's opposite side a human being was imagined to stand. This human witness tries to get sight of the squirrel by moving rapidly around the tree, but no matter how fast he goes, the squirrel moves as fast in the opposite direction, and always keeps the tree between himself and the man, so that never a glimpse of him is caught. The resultant metaphysical problem now is this: *Does the man go round the squirrel or not?* He goes round the tree, sure enough, and the squirrel is on the tree; but does he go round the squirrel? In the unlimited leisure of the wilderness, discussion had been worn threadbare. Every one has taken sides, and was obstinate; and the numbers on both sides were even. Each side, when I appeared therefore appealed to me to make it a majority. Mindful of the scholastic adage that whenever you meet a contradiction you must make a distinction, I immediately sought and found one, as follows: "Which party is right," I said, "depends on what you *practically mean* by 'going round' the squirrel. If you mean passing from the north of him to the east, then to the south, then to the west, and then to the north of him again, obviously the man does go round him, for he occupies these successive positions. But if on the contrary you mean being first in front of him, then on the right of him, then behind him, then on his left, and finally in front again, it is quite as obvious that the man fails to go round him, for by the compensating movements the squirrel makes, he keeps his belly turned toward the man all the time, and his back turned away. Make the distinction, and there is no occasion for any farther dispute. You are both right and both wrong according as you conceive the verb—'to go round' in one practical fashion or the other."

Although one or two of the hotter disputants called my speech a shuffling evasion, saying they wanted no quibbling or scholastic hair-splitting, but meant just plain honest English "round," the majority seemed to think that the distinction had assuaged the dispute.

I

I tell this trivial anecdote because it is a peculiarly simple example of what I wish now to speak of as *the pragmatic method.* The pragmatic method is primarily a method of settling metaphysical disputes that other-

* William James, *Pragmatism,* (New York, Longmans, Green and Co., Copyright © 1907 by William James) Lecture II. Reprinted by permission of Paul R. Reynolds and Son, 599 Fifth Avenue, New York 17, N.Y.

wise might be interminable. Is the world one or many?—fated or free?—material or spiritual?—here are notions either of which may or may not hold good of the world; and disputes over such notions are unending. The pragmatic method in such cases is to try to interpret each notion by tracing its respective practical consequences. What difference would it practically make to any one if this notion rather than that notion were true? If no practical difference whatever can be traced, then the alternatives mean practically the same thing and all dispute is idle. Whenever a dispute is serious, we ought to be able to show some practical difference that must follow from one side or the other's being right.

A glance at the history of the idea will show you still better what pragmatism means. The term is derived from the same Greek word πρᾶγμα meaning action, from which our words "practice" and "practical" come. It was first introduced into philosophy by Mr. Charles Peirce in 1878. In a article entitled "How to Make our Ideas Clear," in *Popular Science Monthly* for January of that year, Mr. Peirce, after pointing out that our beliefs are really rules for action, said that, to develop a thought's meaning, we need only determine what conduct it is fitted to produce: that conduct is for us its sole significance. And the tangible fact at the root of all our thought-distinctions, however subtle, is that there is no one of them so fine as to consist in anything but a possible difference of practice. To attain perfect clearness in our thoughts of an object, then, we need only consider what conceivable effects of a practical kind the object may involve—what sensations we are to expect from it, and what reactions we must prepare. Our conception of these effects, whether immediate or remote, is then for us the whole of our conception of the object, so far as that conception has positive significance at all.

This is the principle of Peirce, the principle of pragmatism. It lay entirely unnoticed by any one for twenty years, until I, in an address before Professor Howison's philosophical union at the University of California, brought it forward again and made a special application of it to religion. By that date

(1898) the times seemed ripe for its reception. The word "pragmatism" spread, and at present it fairly spots the pages of the philosophic journals. On all hands we find the "pragmatic movement" spoken of, sometimes with respect, sometimes with contumely, seldom with clear understanding. It is evident that the term applies itself conveniently to a number of tendencies that hitherto have lacked a collective name, and that it has "come to stay."

I found a few years ago that Ostwald, the illustrious Leipzig chemist, had been making perfectly distinct use of the principle of pragmatism in his lecture on the philosophy of science, though he had not called it by that name. "All realities influence our practice," he wrote me, "and that influence is their meaning for us. I am accustomed to put questions to my classes in this way: In what respects would the world be different if this alternative or that were true? If I can find nothing that would become different, then the alternative has no sense."

It is astonishing to see how many philosophical disputes collapse into insignificance the moment you subject them to this simple test of tracing a concrete consequence. There can *be* no difference anywhere that doesn't *make* a difference elsewhere—no difference in abstract truth that doesn't express itself in a difference in concrete fact and in conduct consequent upon that fact, imposed on somebody, somehow, some where, and some when. The whole function of philosophy ought to be to find out what definite difference it will make to you and me, at definite instants of our life, if this world-formula or that world-formula be the true one.

There is absolutely nothing new in the pragmatic method. Socrates was an adept at it. Aristotle used it methodically. Locke, Berkeley, and Hume made momentous contributions to truth by its means. Shadworth Hodgson keeps insisting that realities are only what they are "known as." But these forerunners of pragmatism used it in fragments; they were a prelude only. Not until in our time has it generalized itself, become conscious of a universal mission, pretended to a conquering destiny. I believe in that destiny, and I hope I may end by inspiring you with my belief.

Pragmatism represents a perfectly familiar attitude in philosophy, the empiricist attitude, but it represents it, as it seems to me, both in a more radical and in a less objectionable form than it has ever yet assumed. A pragmatist turns his back resolutely and once for all upon a lot of inveterate habits dear to professional philosophers. He turns away from abstraction and insufficiency, from verbal solution, from bad *a priori* reasons, from fixed principles, closed system, and pretended absolutes and origins. He turns toward concreteness and adequacy, towards facts, towards action and towards power. That means the empiricist temper regnant and the rationalist temper sincerely given up. It means the open air and possibilities of nature, as against dogma, artificiality, and the pretence of finality in truth.

At the same time, it does not stand for any special results. It is a method only. But the general triumph of that method would mean an enormous change in what I called in my last lecture the "temperament" of philosophy. Teachers of the ultra-rationalistic type would be frozen out, much as the courtier type is frozen out in republics, as the ultra-montane type of priest is frozen out in protestant lands. Science and metaphysics would come much nearer together, would in fact work absolutely hand in hand.

You know how men have always hankered after unlawful magic, and you know what a great part in magic *words* have always played. If you have his name, or the formula of incantation that binds him, you can control the spirit, genie, afrite, or whatever the power may be. Solomon knew the names of all the spirits, and having their names, he held them subject to his will. So the universe has always appeared to the natural mind as a kind of enigma, of which the key must be sought in the shape of some illuminating or power-bringing word or name. That word names the universe's *principle,* and to possess it is after a fashion to possess the universe itself. "God," "Matter," "Reason," "the Absolute," "Energy," are so many solving names.

You can rest when you have them. You are at the end of your metaphysical quest.

But if you follow the pragmatic method, you cannot look on any such word as closing your quest. You must bring out of each word its practical cash-value, set it at work within the stream of your experience. It appears less as a solution, then, than as a program for more work, and more particularly as an indication of the ways in which existing realities may be *changed. Theories thus become instruments, not answers to enigmas, in which we can rest.* We don't lie back upon them, we move forward, and, on occasion, make nature over again by their aid. Pragmatism unstiffens all our theories, limbers them up and sets each one at work.

All these, you see, are *anti-intellectualist* tendencies. Against rationalism as a pretension and a method pragmatism is fully armed and militant, but, at the outset, at least, it stands for no particular results. It has no dogmas, and no doctrines save its method. As the young Italian pragmatist Papini has well said, it lies in the midst of our theories, like a corridor in a hotel. Innumerable chambers open out of it. In one you may find a man writing an atheistic volume; in the next some one on his knees praying for faith and strength; in a third a chemist investigating a body's properties. In a fourth a system of idealist metaphysics is being excogitated; in a fifth the impossibility of metaphysics is being shown. But they all own the corridor and all must pass through it if they want a practicable way of getting into or out of their respective rooms.

No particular results then, so far, but only an attitude of orientation, is what the pragmatic method means. *The attitude of looking away from first things, principles, "categories," supposed necessities; and of looking towards last things, fruits, consequences, facts.*

II

So much for the pragmatic method! You may say that I have been praising it rather than explaining it to you, but I shall presently explain it abundantly enough by showing how it works on some familiar problems. Meanwhile, the word pragmatism has come to be used in a still wider sense, as meaning also a certain theory of truth. I mean to give a whole lecture to the statement of that theory, after first paving the way, so I can be very brief now. But brevity is hard to follow, so I ask for your redoubled attention for a quarter of an hour.

One of the most successfully cultivated branches of philosophy in our time is what is called inductive logic, the study of the conditions under which our sciences have evolved. Writers on this subject have begun to show a singular unanimity as to what the laws of nature and elements of fact mean, when formulated by mathematicians, physicists, and chemists. When the first mathematical, logical, and natural uniformities, the first *laws,* were discovered, men were so carried away by the clearness, beauty and simplification that resulted that they believed themselves to have deciphered authentically the eternal thoughts of the Almighty. His mind also thundered and reverberated in syllogisms. He also thought in conic sections, squares and roots and ratios, and geometrized like Euclid. He made Kepler's laws for the planets to follow; he made velocity increase proportionally to the time in falling bodies; he made the law of the sines for light to obey when refracted; he established the classes, orders, families and genera of plants and animals, and fixed the distances between them. He thought the archetypes of all things, and devised their variations; and when we rediscover any one of these his wondrous institutions, we seize his mind in its very literal intention.

But as the sciences have developed farther, the notion has gained ground that most, perhaps all, of our laws are only approximations. The laws themselves, moreover, have grown so numerous that there is no counting them; and so many rival formulations are proposed in all the branches of science that investigators have become accustomed to the notion that no theory is absolutely a transcript of reality, but that any one of them may from some point of view be useful. Their great use is to summarize old facts and to lead to new ones. They are only a man-made language, a conceptual shorthand, as someone calls them, in which we write our reports of nature; and languages, as is well known, tolerate much choice of expression and many dialects.

Riding now on the front of this wave of scientific logic Messrs. Schiller and Dewey appear with their pragmatistic acount of what truth everywhere signifies. Everywhere, these teachers say, "truth" in our ideas and beliefs means the same thing that it means in science. It means, they say, nothing but this, that *ideas (which themselves are but parts of our experience) become true just in so far as they help us to get into satisfactory relation with other parts of our experience,* to summarize them and get about among them by conceptual short-cuts instead of following the interminable succession of particular phenomena. Any idea upon which we can ride, so to speak; any idea that will carry us prosperously from any one part of our experience to any other part, linking things satisfactorily, working securely, simplifying, saving labor; is true for just so much, true in so far forth, true *instrumentally.* This is the "instrumental" view of truth taught so successfully at Chicago, the view that truth in our ideas means their power to "work," promulgated so brilliantly at Oxford.

Messrs. Dewey, Schiller and their allies, in reaching this general conception of all truth, have only followed the example of geologists, biologists and philologists. In the establishment of these other sciences, the successful stroke was always to take some simple process actually observable in operation—as denudation by weather, say, or variation from parental type, or change of dialect by incorporation of new words and pronunciations —and then to generalize it, making it apply to all times, and produce great results by summating its effect through the ages.

The observable process which Schiller and Dewey particularly singled out for generalization is the familiar one by which any individual settles into new opinions. The process here is always the same. The individual has a stock of old opinions already, but he meets a new experience that puts them to a strain Somebody contradicts them; or in a reflective moment he discovers that they contradict each other; or he hears of facts with which they are incompatible; or desires arise in him which they cease to satisfy. The result is an inward trouble to which his mind till then had been a stranger, and from which he seeks to escape by modifying his previous mass of opinions. He saves as much of it as he can, for in this matter of belief we are all extreme conservatives. So he tries to change first this opinion, and then that (for they resist change very variously), until at last some new idea comes up which he can graft upon the ancient stock with a minimum of disturbance of the latter, some idea that mediates between the stock and the new experience and runs them into one another most felicitously and expediently.

This new idea is then adopted as the true one. It preserves the older stock of truths with a minimum of modification, stretching them just enough to make them admit the novelty but conceiving that in ways as familiar as the case leaves possible. An *outrée* explanation, violating all our preconceptions, would never pass for a true account of a novelty. We should scratch round industriously till we found something less eccentric. The most violent revolutions in an individual's beliefs leave most of his old order standing. Time and space, cause and effect, nature and history, and one's own biography remain untouched. New truth is always a go-between, a smoother-over of transitions. It marries old opinion to new fact so as ever to show a minimum of jolt, a maximum of continuity. We hold a theory true just in proportion to its success in solving this "problem of maxima and minima." But success in solving this problem is eminently a matter of approximation. We say this theory solves it on the whole more satisfactorily than that theory; but that means more satisfactorily to ourselves, and individuals will emphasize their points of satisfaction differently. To a certain degree, therefore, everything here is plastic.

The point I now urge you to observe particularly is the part played by the older truths. Failure to take account of it is the source of much of the unjust criticism levelled against pragmatism. Their influence is absolutely controlling. Loyalty to them is the first principle—in most cases it is the only principle; for by far the most usual way of handling phenomena so novel that they would make for a serious rearrangement of our preconception is to ignore them altogether, or to abuse those who bear witness for them.

You doubtless wish examples of this process of truth's growth, and the only trouble is their superabundance. The simplest case of new truth is of course the mere numerical addition of new kinds of facts, or of new single facts of old kinds, to our experience—an addition that involves no alteration in the old beliefs. Day follows day, and its contents are simply added. The new contents themselves are not true, they simply come and are. Truth is what we say about them, and when we say that they have come, truth is satisfied by the plain additive formula.

But often the day's contents oblige a rearrangement. If I should now utter piercing shrieks and act like a maniac on this platform, it would make many of you revise your ideas as to the probable worth of my philosophy. "Radium" came the other day as part of the day's content, and seemed for a moment to contradict our ideas of the whole order of nature, that order having come to be identified with what is called the conservation of energy. The mere sight of radium paying heat away indefinitely out of its own pocket seemed to violate that conservation. What to think? If the radiations from it were nothing but an escape of unsuspected "potential" energy, pre-existent inside of the atoms, the principle of conservation would be saved. The discovery of "helium" as the radiation's outcome, opened a way to this belief. So Ramsay's view is generally held to be true, because, although it extends our old ideas of energy, it causes a minimum of alternation in their nature.

I need not multiply instances. A new opinion counts as "true" just in proportion as it gratifies the individual's desire to assimilate the novel in his experience to his beliefs in stock. It must both lean on old truth and grasp new fact; and its success (as I said a moment ago) in doing this, is a matter for the individual's appreciation. When old truth grows, then, by new truth's addition, it is for subjective reasons. We are in the process and obey the reasons. That new idea is truest which performs most felicitously its function of satisfying our double urgency. It makes itself true, gets itself classed as true, by the way it works; grafting itself then upon the ancient body of truth, which thus grows much as a tree grows by the activity of a new layer of cambium.

Now Dewey and Schiller proceed to generalize this observation and to apply it to the most ancient parts of truth. They also once were plastic. They also were called true for human reasons. They also mediated between still earlier truths and what in those days were novel observations. Purely objective truth, truth in whose establishment the function of giving human satisfaction in marrying previous parts of experience with newer parts played no role whatever, is nowhere to be found. The reasons why we call things true is the reason why they are true, for "to be true" means only to perform this marriage-function.

The trail of the human serpent is thus over everything. Truth independent; truth that we *find* merely; truth no longer malleable to human need; truth incorrigible, in a word; such truth exists indeed superabundantly—or is supposed to exist by rationalistically minded thinkers; but then it means only the dead heart of the living tree, and its being there means only that truth also has its paleontology, and its "prescription," and may grow stiff with years of veteran service and petrified in men's regard by sheer antiquity. But how plastic even the oldest truths nevertheless really are has been vividly shown in our day by the transformation of logical and mathematical ideas, a transformation which seems even to be invading physics. The an-

cient formulas are reinterpreted as special expressions of much wider principles, principles that our ancestors never got a glimpse of in their present shape and formulation.

Our account of truth is an account of truths in the plural, of processes of leading, realized *in rebus,* and having only this quality in common, that they *pay*. They pay by guiding us into or towards some part of a system that dips at numerous points into sense-precepts, which we may copy mentally or not, but with which at any rate we are now in the kind of commerce vaguely designated as verification. Truth for us is simply a collective name for verification-processes, just as health, wealth, strength, etc., are names for other processes connected with life, and also pursued because it pays to pursue them. Truth is *made,* just as health, wealth and strength are made, in the course of experience. Experience, as we know, has ways of *boiling over,* and making us correct our present formulas.

The "absolutely" true, meaning what no farther experience will ever alter, is that ideal vanishing-point towards which we imagine that all our temporary truth will some day converge. It runs on all fours with the perfectly wise man, and with the absolutely complete experience; and, if these ideals are ever realized, they will all be realized together. Meanwhile we have to live to-day by what truth we can get to-day, and be ready to-morrow to call it falsehood. Ptolemaic astronomy, euclidean space, aristotelian logic, scholastic metaphysics, were expedient for centuries, but human experience has boiled over those limits, and we now call these things only relatively true, or true within those borders of experience. "Absolutely" they are false; for we know that those limits were casual, and might have been transcended by past theorists just as they are by present thinkers.

The Scientist as Pragmatist: Charles Sanders Peirce

Not until a decade or two after his death in 1914 were the intellectual stature and achievements of Charles Sanders Peirce given due recognition. Today Peirce is ranked among the ablest and most influential American philosophers, but his contemporaries, except for a select few, had little regard for his philosophical approach. In the years since his death admiring editors have published eight volumes of his *Collected Papers* and scholars throughout the world now realize that in Peirce the United States produced a philosopher comparable in depth and range of intellectual insight with the ablest contemporary figures.

An original thinker, Peirce began almost a century ago to formulate theories that have become quite influential in scientific circles and today are widely accepted. His discussion of the theory of probability, for example, anticipated the present scientific outlook. In the field of symbolic logic and its relation to the foundations of mathematics, he was also one of the great pioneers. Much of contemporary semantics and analytical philosophy is a direct continuation of Peirce's work in the analysis and meaning of signs and symbols in both everyday and scientific language. In the 1930's the logical positivists, now the most influential advocates of a thoroughly scientific philosophy, hailed him as the great forerunner of their point of view. A generation earlier William James borrowed from Peirce the basic ideas of pragmatism, which James then made the most popular philosophy in the country. But in none of these fields was Peirce himself able to command any immediate recognition.

Born in Cambridge, Massachusetts, in 1839, Peirce was the son of a distinguished mathematician who encouraged his early interest in science and also, if the stories are reliable, planted in his mind a growing skepticism with regard to the accepted philosophies of the day. Peirce was educated at Harvard, where he moved in a small circle of intellectually gifted friends. There he grew accustomed to careful and stimulating discussions of the controversies provoked by the growing prestige of science and by the "positivism" of Auguste Comte, who maintained that the sciences alone provide reliable knowledge and lead to social progress.

After graduating from Harvard in 1859, and taking a master's degree in chemistry, Peirce was employed as a physicist and astronomer in the United States Geodetic Survey for a number of years. For a brief period (1879–1884) he was an instructor in logic at the Johns Hopkins University, the first graduate school in the United States, but his courses were not popular with the students. After five years of lecturing to no more than a dozen students in any of his classes, he was not reappointed. Such distinguished men as John Dewey, Josiah Royce, and Thorstein Veblen were among the students who received Ph.D. degrees in philosophy at Johns Hopkins while Peirce was there, but Dewey later remarked that he did not appreciate Peirce's work in logic for another twenty years. When Peirce moved back to Boston, William James tried unsuccessfully to persuade President Eliot to allow him to lecture at Harvard. Eliot's refusal is not hard to understand. Not only were Peirce's lectures lacking in appeal to university audiences but by now his personal life had also become quite involved. He had divorced his first wife, a New England woman, to marry a French girl; he was constantly in acrimonious controversy with his associates, always in debt and hounded by his creditors. The last twenty-five years of his life Peirce spent near Boston, pursuing his studies and writing under most adverse circumstances. When he died, there was not even enough money for a decent burial, and his widow was forced to sell all his manuscripts for $500 to Harvard.

Peirce is not an easy philosopher to read or understand. He was an original and independent thinker, pioneering in logical analysis and scientific philosophy with no desire to please a popular audience or to conform to accepted ideas. To clarify his meaning, he found it necessary to invent many new technical terms, usually derived from Greek roots; consequently, his vocabulary is often remote from ordinary language. Pragmatism is one of the very few of his new terms that came to be widely used.

As a young man Peirce undertook to analyze, as thoroughly as any one could, the basic logic and structure of the sciences before committing himself to a philosophical point of view. In an appealing little essay, entitled "Concerning the Author" (included here in part), he describes something of his early experience. It is from this standpoint—the meaning of scientific thought in its bearing on human conduct—that his pragmatism may best be approached.

The pragmatism of William James is better known than that of Peirce largely because James wrote with more emotional appeal and literary skill. However, Peirce is much more analytical and precise than James in the presentation of his thought; his philosophy rests upon a more careful logical analysis and an uncompromising commitment to scientific method, and he avoids entirely the psychological approach that made the thought of James so appealing and popular. Peirce also distinguishes more sharply and more clearly than James between the subjective meaning of our beliefs and their objective implication, and is thus able to escape some of the more serious dilemmas which weaken the pragmatism of James. He insists, that is, upon a careful distinction between the *meaning* of an idea in our own experience and its *truth*. The *meaning* of any idea, like the hardness of diamonds, is to be found in the total conceivable consequences that the idea has on our conduct. The meaning of a diamond's hardness is found in part, for example, in using it to drill through most rocks. (Peirce first developed this point in some detail in his now famous article, "How to Make Our Ideas Clear," in the *Popular Science Monthly,* January 1878.) But the *truth* that we discover by observing how our experience conforms to the predicted behavior of the diamond is for Peirce something independent of anyone's idea of hardness. In the end he explicitly disclaims the philosophy that James developed in his name and calls his own position *pragmaticism* to distinguish it from James' more psychological and subjective version of pragmatism.

The heart of Peirce's thought, as a recent interpreter points out, lies in the supreme value of honest, persevering inquiry by men who share a common desire to learn and a common commitment to the discovery of truth through the use of scientific method. He had great faith in the power of logical thought to liberate men from moral confusion, provided that they were willing to devote themselves to arduous inquiry and to subordinate their own interests to verifiable knowledge. Coupled with this faith, moreover, there is for Peirce a profound sense of the fallibility of his own thought and that of all other individuals, a fallibility that must be constantly acknowledged and guarded against.[1]

---

[1] See Philip Wiener, *Values in a Universe of Chance* (Garden City, N.Y., Doubleday & Co., Inc., 1958), Intro. pp. x-xi.

Concerning the Author[*]

The reader has a right to know how the author's opinions were formed. Not, of course, that he is expected to accept any conclusions which are not borne out by argument. But in discussions of extreme difficulty, like these, when good judgment is a factor, and pure ratiocination is not everything, it is prudent to take every element into consideration. From the moment when I could think at all, until now, about forty years, I have been diligently and incessantly occupied with the study of methods of inquiry, both those which have been and are pursued and those which ought to be pursued. For ten years before this study began, I had been in training in the chemical laboratory. I was thoroughly grounded not only in all that was then known of physics and chemistry, but also in the way in which those who were successfully advancing knowledge proceeded. I have paid the most attention to the methods of the most exact sciences, have intimately communed with some of the greatest minds of our times in physical science, and have myself made positive contributions—none of them of any very great importance, perhaps—in mathe-

matics, gravitation, optics, chemistry, astronomy, etc. I am saturated, through and through, with the spirit of the physical sciences. I have been a great student of logic, having read everything of any importance on the subject, devoting a great deal of time to medieval thought, without neglecting the works of the Greeks, the English, the Germans, the French, etc., and have produced systems of my own both in deductive and inductive logic. In metaphysics my training has been less systematic; yet I have read and deeply pondered upon all the main systems, never being satisfied until I was able to think about them as their own advocates thought.

The first strictly philosophical books that I read were of the classical German schools; and I became so deeply imbued with many of their ways of thinking that I have never been able to disabuse myself of them. Yet my attitude was always that of a dweller in a laboratory, eager only to learn what I did not yet know, and not that of philosophers bred in theological seminaries, whose ruling impulse is to teach what they hold to be infallibly true. I devoted two hours a day to the study of Kant's *Critic of the Pure Reason* for more than three years until I almost knew the whole book by heart, and had crit-

---

[*] From Justus Buchler, *The Philosophy of Peirce: Selected Writings,* (London, Routledge & Kegan Paul, Ltd., 1940.)

ically examined every section of it. For about two years, I had long and almost daily discussions with Chauncey Wright, one of the most acute of the followers of J. S. Mill.

Thus, in brief, my philosophy may be described as the attempt of a physicist to make such conjecture as to the constitution of the universe as the methods of science may permit, with the aid of all that has been done by previous philosophers. I shall support my propositions by such arguments as I can. Demonstrative proof is not to be thought of. The demonstrations of the metaphysicians are all moonshine. The best that can be done is to supply a hypothesis, not devoid of all likelihood, in the general line of growth of scientific ideas, and capable of being verified or refuted by future observers.

Though infallibility in scientific matters seems to me irresistibly comical, I should be in a sad way if I could not retain a high respect for those who lay claim to it, for they comprise the greater part of the people who have any conversation at all. When I say they lay claim to it, I mean they assume the functions of it quite naturally and unconsciously. The full meaning of the adage *Humanum est errare,* they have never waked up to. In those sciences of measurement which are the least subject to error—metrology, geodesy, and metrical astronomy—no man of self-respect ever now states his result, without affixing to it its probable error; and if this practice is not followed in other sciences it is because in those the probable errors are too vast to be estimated.

Only once, as far as I remember, in all my lifetime have I experienced the pleasure of praise—not for what it might bring but in itself. That pleasure was beatific; and the praise that conferred it was meant for blame. It was when a critic said of me that I did not seem to be *absolutely sure of my own conclusions.* Never, if I can help it, shall that critic's eye ever rest on what I am now writing; for I owe a great pleasure to him; and, such was his evident animus, that should he find that out, I fear the fires of hell would be fed with new fuel in his breast.

The development of my ideas has been the industry of thirty years. I did not know as I ever should get to publish them, their ripening seemed so slow. But the harvest time has come, at last, and to me that harvest seems a wild one, but of course it is not I who have to pass judgment. It is not quite you, either, individual reader; it is experience and history.

For years in the course of this ripening process, I used for myself to collect my ideas under the designation *fallibilism;* and indeed the first step toward finding out is to acknowledge you do not satisfactorily know already; so that no blight can so surely arrest all intellectual growth as the blight of cocksureness; and ninety-nine out of every hundred good heads are reduced to impotence by that malady—of whose inroads they are most strangely unaware!

Indeed, out of a contrite fallibilism, combined with a high faith in the reality of knowledge, and an intense desire to find things out, all my philosophy has always seemed to me to grow.

The Fixation of Belief *

I

Few persons care to study logic, because everybody conceives himself to be proficient enough in the art of reasoning already. But I

---

* This essay by Peirce appeared originally in the November 1877 issue of *Popular Science Monthly,* pp. 1–15.

observe that this satisfaction is limited to one's own ratiocination, and does not extend to that of other men.

We come to the full possession of our power of drawing inferences the last of all our faculties, for it is not so much a natural gift as a long and difficult art. The history of its practice would make a grand subject for a book. The medieval schoolman, following the Romans, made logic the earliest of a boy's studies after grammar, as being very easy. So it was as they understood it. Its fundamental principle according to them, was that all knowledge rests on either authority or reason; but that whatever is deduced by reason depends ultimately on a premise derived from authority. Accordingly, as soon as a boy was perfect in the syllogistic procedure, his intellectual kit of tools was held to be complete.

To Roger Bacon, that remarkable mind who in the middle of the thirteenth century was almost a scientific man, the schoolmen's conception of reasoning appeared only an obstacle to truth. He saw that experience alone teaches anything—a proposition which to us seems easy to understand, because a distinct conception of experience has been handed down to us from former generations; which to him also seemed perfectly clear, because its difficulties had not yet unfolded themselves. Of all kinds of experience, the best, he thought, was interior illumination, which teaches many things about nature which the external senses could never discover, such as the transubstantiation of bread.

Four centuries later, the more celebrated Bacon, in the first book of his *Novum Organum,* gave his clear account of experience as something which must be opened to verification and re-examination. But, superior as Lord Bacon's conception is to earlier notions, a modern reader who is not in awe of his grandiloquence is chiefly struck by the inadequacy of his view of scientific procedure. That we have only to make some crude experiments, to draw up briefs of the results in certain blank forms, to go through these by rule, checking off everything disproved and setting down the alternatives, and that thus in a few years physical science would be finished up—what an idea! "He wrote on science like a Lord Chancellor," indeed, as Harvey, a genuine man of science, said.

The early scientists, Copernicus, Tycho Brahe, Kepler, Galileo, Harvey, and Gilbert, had methods more like those of their modern brethren. Kepler undertook to draw a curve through the places of Mars;[1] and his greatest service to science was in impressing on men's minds that this was the thing to be done if they wished to improve astronomy; that they were not to content themselves with inquiring whether one system of epicycles was better than another but that they were to sit down by the figures and find out what the curve, in truth, was. He accomplished this by his incomparable energy and courage, blundering along in the most inconceivable way (to us), from one irrational hypothesis to another, until, after trying twenty-two of these, he fell, by the mere exhaustion of his invention, upon the orbit which a mind well furnished with the weapons of modern logic would have tried almost at the outset.

In the same way, every work of science great enough to be remembered for a few generations affords some exemplification of the defective state of the art of reasoning of the time when it was written; and each chief step in science has been a lesson in logic. It was so when Lavoisier and his contemporaries took up the study of chemistry. The old chemist's maxim had been *lege, lege, lege, labora, ora, et relege.* Lavoisier's method was not to read and pray, not to dream that some long and complicated chemical process would have a certain effect, to put it into practice with dull patience, after its inevitable failure to dream that with some modification it would have another result, and to end by publishing the last dream as a fact: his way was to carry his mind into his laboratory, and to make of his alembics and cucurbits instruments of thought, giving a new conception of reasoning as something which was to be done with one's eyes open, by manipulating real things instead of words and fancies.

The Darwinian controversy is, in large part, a question of logic. Mr. Darwin proposed to apply the statistical method to biology. The same thing has been done in a widely different branch of science, the theory of gases. Though unable to say what the movement of any particular molecule of gas

---

[1] Not quite so, but as nearly as can be told in words.

would be on a certain hypothesis regarding the constitution of this class of bodies, Clausius and Maxwell were yet able, by the application of the doctrine of probabilities, to predict that in the long run such and such a proportion of the molecules would, under given circumstances, acquire such and such velocities; that there would take place, every second, such and such a number of collisions, etc.; and from these propositions they were able to deduce certain properties of gases, especially in regard to their heat-relations. In like manner, Darwin, while unable to say what the operation of variation and natural selection in every individual case will be, demonstrates that in the long run they will adapt animals to their circumstances. Whether or not existing animal forms are due to such action, or what position the theory ought to take, forms the subject of a discussion in which questions of fact and questions of logic are curiously interlaced.

II

The object of reasoning is to find out, from the consideration of what we already know, something else which we do not know. Consequently, reasoning is good if it be such as to give a true conclusion from true premises, and not otherwise. Thus, the question of validity is purely one of fact and not of thinking. A being the premises and B being the conclusion, the question is, whether these facts are really so related that if A is B is. If so, the inference is valid; if not, not. It is not in the least the question whether, when the premises are accepted by the mind, we feel an impulse to accept the conclusion also. It is true that we do generally reason correctly by nature. But that is an accident; the true conclusion would remain true if we had no impulse to accept it; and the false one would remain false, though we could not resist the tendency to believe in it.

We are doubtless, in the main logical animals, but we are not perfectly so. Most of us, for example, are naturally more sanguine and hopeful than logic would justify. We seem to be so constituted that in the absence of any facts to go upon we are happy and self-satisfied; so that the effect of experience is continually to counteract our hopes and aspirations. Yet a lifetime of the application of this corrective does not usually eradicate sanguine disposition. Where hope is unchecked by any experience, it is likely that our optimism is extravagant. Logicality in regard to practical matters is the most useful quality an animal can possess, and might, therefore, result from the action of natural selection; but outside of these it is probably of more advantage to the animal to have his mind filled with pleasing and encouraging visions, independently of their truth; and thus, upon unpractical subjects, natural selection might occasion a fallacious tendency of thought.

That which determines us, from given premises, to draw one inference rather than another is some habit of mind, whether it be constitutional or acquired. The habit is good or otherwise, according as it produces true conclusions from true premises or not; and an inference is regarded as valid or not, without reference to the truth or falsity of its conclusion specially, but acording as the habit which determines it is such as to produce true conclusions in general or not. The particular habit of mind which governs this or that inference may be formulated in a proposition whose truth depends on the validity of the inferences which the habit determines; and such a formula is called a *guiding principle* of inference. Suppose, for example, that we observe that a rotating disk of copper quickly comes to rest when placed between the poles of a magnet, and we infer that this will happen with every disk of copper. The guiding principle is that what is true of one piece of copper is true of another. Such a guiding principle with regard to copper would be much safer than with regard to many other substances—brass, for example.

A book might be written to signalize all the most important of these guiding principles of reasoning. It would probably be, we must confess, of no service to a person whose thought is directed wholly to practical subjects, and whose activity moves along thoroughly beaten paths. The problems which present themselves to such a mind are matters of routine which he has learned once for all to handle in learning his business. But let a man venture into an unfamiliar field, or where his results are not continually checked by experience, and all history shows that the most masculine intellect will ofttimes lose his orientation and waste his efforts in directions which bring him no nearer to his goal, or even carry him entirely astray. He is like a ship on the open sea, with no one on board who understands the rules of navigation. And in such a case some general study of the guiding principles of reasoning would be sure to be found useful.

The subject could hardly be treated, however, without being first limited; since almost any fact may serve as a guiding principle. But it so happens that there exists a division among facts, such that in one class are all those which are absolutely essential as guiding principles, while in the other are all those which have any other interest as objects of research. This division is between those which are necessarily taken for granted in asking whether a certain conclusion follows from certain premises, and those which are not implied in that question. A moment's thought will show that a variety of facts are already assumed when the logical question is first asked. It is implied, for instance, that there are such states of mind as doubt and belief—that a passage from one to the other is possible, the object of thought remaining the same, and that this transition is subject to some rules which all minds are alike bound by. As these are facts which we must already know before we can have any clear conception of reasoning at all, it cannot be supposed to be any longer of much interest to inquire into their truth or falsity. On the other hand, it is easy to believe that those rules of reasoning which are deduced from the very idea of the process are the ones which are the most essential; and, indeed, that so long as it conforms to these it will, at least, not lead to false conclusions from true premises. In point of fact, the importance of what may be deduced from the assumptions involved in the logical question turns out to be greater than might be supposed, and this for reasons which it is difficult to exhibit at the outset. The only one which I shall here mention is that conceptions which are really products of logical reflections, without being readily seen to be so, mingle with our ordinary thoughts, and are frequently the causes of great confusion. This is the case, for example, with the conception of quality. A quality as such is never an object of observation. We can see that a thing is blue or green, but the quality of being blue and the quality of being green are not things which we see; they are products of logical reflections. The truth is that common sense, or thought as it first emerges above the level of the narrowly practical, is deeply imbued with that bad logical quality to which the epithet *metaphysical* is commonly applied; and nothing can clear it up but a severe course of logic.

III

We generally know when we wish to ask a question and when we wish to pronounce a judgment, for there is a dissimilarity between the sensation of doubting and that of believing.

But this is not all which distinguishes doubt from belief. There is a practical difference. Our beliefs guide our desires and shape our actions. The Assassins, or followers of the Old Man of the Mountain, used to rush into death at his least command, because they believed that obedience to him would insure everlasting felicity. Had they doubted this, they would not have acted as they did. So it is with every belief, according to its degree. The feeling of believing is a more or less sure indication of there being established in our nature some habit which will determine our actions. Doubt never has such an effect.

Nor must we overlook a third point of difference. Doubt is an uneasy and dissatisfied state from which we struggle to free ourselves and pass into the state of belief, while the latter is a calm and satisfactory state which we do not wish to avoid, or to change to a belief in anything else. On the contrary, we cling tenaciously, not merely to believing, but to believing just what we do believe.

Thus, both doubt and belief have positive effects upon us, though very different ones. Belief does not make us act at once, but puts us into such a condition that we shall behave in a certain way, when the occasion arises. Doubt has not the least effect of this sort, but stimulates us to action until it is destroyed. This reminds us of the irritation of a nerve and the reflex action produced thereby; while for the analogue of belief, in the nervous system, we must look to what are called nervous associations—for example, to that habit of the nerves in consequence of which the smell of a peach will make the mouth water.

IV

The irritation of doubt causes a struggle to attain a state of belief. I shall term this struggle *inquiry,* though it must be admitted that this is sometimes not a very apt designation.

The irritation of doubt is the only immediate motive for the struggle to attain belief. It is certainly best for us that our beliefs should be such as may truly guide our actions so as to satisfy our desires; and this reflection will make us reject any belief which does not seem to have been so formed as to insure this result. But it will only do so by creating a doubt in the place of that belief. With the doubt, therefore, the struggle begins, and with the cessation of doubt it ends. Hence, the sole object of inquiry is the settlement of opinion. We may fancy that this is not enough for us, and that we seek not merely an opinion, but a true opinion. But put this fancy to the test, and it proves groundless; for as soon as a firm belief is reached we are entirely satisfied, whether the belief be false or true. And it is clear that nothing out of the sphere of our knowledge can be our object, for nothing which does not affect the mind can be a motive for a mental effort. The most that can be maintained is that we seek for a belief that we shall *think* to be true. But we think each one of our beliefs to be true, and, indeed, it is mere tautology to say so.

That the settlement of opinion is the sole end of inquiry is a very important proposition. It sweeps away, at once, various vague

and erroneous conceptions of proof. A few of these may be noticed here.

1. Some philosophers have imagined that to start an inquiry it was only necessary to utter a question or set it down on paper, and have even recommended us to begin our studies with questioning everything! But the mere putting of a proposition into the interrogative form does not stimulate the mind to any struggle after belief. There must be a real and living doubt, and without all this, discussion is idle.

2. It is a very common idea that a demonstration must rest on some ultimate and absolutely indubitable propositions. These, according to one school, are first principles of a general nature; according to another, are first sensations. But, in point of fact, an inquiry, to have that completely satisfactory result called demonstration, has only to start with propositions perfectly free from all actual doubt. If the premises are not in fact doubted at all, they cannot be more satisfactory than they are.

3. Some people seem to love to argue a point after all the world is fully convinced of it. But no further advance can be made. When doubt ceases mental action of the subject comes to an end; and, if it did go on, it would be without a purpose, except that of self-criticism.

V

If the settlement of opinion is the sole object of inquiry, and if belief is of the nature of a habit, why should we not attain the desired end, by taking any answer to a question which we may fancy, and constantly reiterating it to ourselves, dwelling on all which may conduct to that belief, and learning to turn with contempt and hatred from anything which might disturb it? This simple and direct method is really pursued by many men. I remember once being entreated not to read a certain newspaper lest it might change my opinion upon free-trade. "Lest I might be entrapped by its fallacies and misstatements" was the form of expression. "You are not," my friend said, "a special student of political economy. You might, therefore, easily be deceived by fallacious arguments upon the subject. You might, then, if you read this paper, be led to believe in protection. But you admit that free-trade is the true doctrine; and you do not wish to believe what is not true." I have often known this system to be deliberately adopted. Still oftener, the instinctive dislike of an undecided state of mind, exaggerated into a vague dread of doubt, makes men cling spasmodically to the views they already take. The man feels that if he only holds to his belief without wavering, it will be entirely satisfactory. Nor can it be denied that a steady and immovable faith yields great peace of mind. It may, indeed, give rise to inconveniences, as if a man should resolutely continue to believe that fire would not burn him, or that he would be eternally damned if he received his *ingesta* otherwise than through a stomach-pump. But then the man who adopts this method will not allow that its inconveniences are greater than its advantages. He will say, "I hold steadfastly to the truth and the truth is always wholesome." And in many cases it may very well be that the pleasure he derives from his calm faith overbalances any inconveniences resulting from its deceptive character. Thus, if it be true that death is annihilation, then the man who believes that he will certainly go straight to heaven when he dies, provided he have fulfilled certain simple observances in this life, has a cheap pleasure which will not be followed by the least disappointment. A similar consideration seems to have weight with many persons in religious topics, for we frequently hear it said, "Oh, I could not believe so-and-so, because I should be wretched if I did." When an ostrich buries its head in the sand as danger approaches, it very likely takes the happiest course. It hides the danger, and then calmly says there is no danger; and if it feels perfectly sure there is none, why should it raise its head to see? A man may go through life, systematically keeping out of view all that might cause a change in his opinions, and if he only succeeds—basing his method, as he does, on two fundamental psychological laws—I do not see what can be said against his doing so. It would be an egotistical impertinence to object that his procedure is irrational, for that only amounts to saying that his method of settling belief is not ours. He does not propose to himself to be rational, and indeed, will often talk with scorn of man's weak and illusive reason. So let him think as he pleases.

But this method of fixing belief, which may be called the method of tenacity, will be unable to hold its ground in practice. The social impulse is against it. The man who adopts it will find that other men think differently from him, and it will be apt to occur to him in some saner moment that their opinions are quite as good as his own, and this will shake his confidence in his belief. This conception, that another man's thought or sentiment may be equivalent to one's own, is a distinctly new step, and a highly important one. It arises from an impulse too strong in man to be suppressed, without danger of destroying the human species. Unless we make ourselves hermits, we shall necessarily influence each other's opinions; so that the problem becomes how to fix belief, not in the individual merely, but in the community.

Let the will of the state act, then, instead of that of the individual. Let an institution be created which shall have for its object to keep correct doctrines before the attention of the people, to reiterate them perpetually, and to teach them to the young; having at the same time power to prevent contrary doctrines from being taught, advocated, or expressed. Let all possible causes of a change of mind be removed from men's apprehensions. Let them be kept ignorant, lest they should learn of some reason to think otherwise than they do. Let their passions be enlisted, so that they may regard private and unusual opinions with hatred and horror. Then, let all men who reject the established belief be terrified into silence. Let the people turn out and tar-and-feather such men, or let inquisitions be made into the manner of thinking of suspected persons, and, when they are found guilty of forbidden beliefs, let them be subjected to some signal punishment. When complete agreement could not otherwise be reached, a general massacre of all who have not thought in a certain way has proved a very effective means of settling opinion in a country. If the power to do this be wanted, let a list of opinions be drawn up, to which no man of the least independence of thought can assent, and let the faithful be required to accept all these propositions, in order to segregate them as radically as possible from the influence of the rest of the world.

This method has, from the earliest times, been one of the chief means of upholding correct theological and political doctrines, and of preserving their universal or catholic character. In Rome, especially, it has been practiced from the days of Numa Pompilius to those of Pius Nonus. This is the most perfect example in history; but wherever there is a priesthood—and no religion has been without one—this method has been more or less made use of. Wherever there is aristocracy, or a guild, or any association of a class of men whose interests depend or are supposed to depend on certain propositions, there will be inevitably found some traces of this natural product of social feeling. Cruelties always accompany this system; and when it is consistently carried out, they become atrocities of the most horrible kind in the eyes of any rational man. Nor should this occasion surprise, for the officer of a society does not feel justified in surrendering the interests of that society for the sake of mercy, as he might his own private interests. It is natural, therefore, that sympathy and fellowship should thus produce a most ruthless power.

In judging this method of fixing belief, which may be called the method of authority, we must, in the first place, allow its immeasurable mental and moral superiority to the method of tenacity. Its success is proportionally greater; and in fact it has over and over again worked the most majestic results. The mere structures of stone which it has caused to be put together—in Siam, for example, in Egypt, and in Europe—have many of them a sublimity hardly more than rivaled by the greatest works of nature. And, except the geological epochs, there are no periods of time so vast as those which are measured by some of these organized faiths. If we scrutinize the matter closely, we shall find that there has not been one of their creeds which has remained always the same; yet the change is so slow as to be imperceptible during one person's life, so that individual belief remains sensibly fixed. For the most of mankind, then, there is perhaps no better method than this. If it is their highest impulse to be intellectual slaves, then slaves they ought to remain.

But no institution can undertake to regulate opinions upon every subject. Only the most important ones can be attended to, and on the rest men's minds must be left to the action of natural causes. This imperfection will be no source of weakness so long as men are in such a state of culture that one opinion does not influence another—that is, so long as they cannot put two and two together. But in the most priest-ridden states some individuals will be found who are raised above that condition. These men possess a wider sort of social feeling; they see that men in other countries and in other ages have held to very different doctrines from those which they themselves have been brought up to believe; and they cannot help seeing that it is the mere accident of their having been taught as they have, and of their having been surrounded with the manners and associations they have, that has caused them to believe as they do and not far differently. And their candor cannot resist the reflection that there is no reason to rate their own views at a higher value than those of other nations and other centuries; and this gives rise to doubts in their minds.

They will further perceive that such doubts as these must exist in their minds with reference to every belief which seems to be determined by the caprice either of themselves or of those who originated the popular opinions. The willful adherence to a belief, and the arbitrary forcing of it upon others, must, therefore, both be given up and a new method of settling opinions must be adopted, which shall not only produce an impulse to believe, but shall also decide what proposition it is which is to be believed. Let the action of natural preferences be unimpeded, then, and under their influence let men conversing together and regarding matters in different lights, gradually develop beliefs in harmony with natural causes. This method resembles that by which conceptions of art have been brought to maturity. The most perfect example of it is to be found in the history of metaphysical philosophy. Systems of this sort have not usually rested upon observed facts, at least not in any great degree. They have been chiefly adopted because their fundamental propositions seemed "agreeable to reason." This is an apt expression; it does not mean that which agrees with experience, but that which we find ourselves inclined to believe. Plato, for example, finds it agreeable to reason that the distances of the celestial spheres from one another should be proportional to the different lengths of strings which produce harmonious chords. Many philosophers have been led to their main conclusions by considerations like this; but this is the lowest and least developed form which the method takes, for it is clear that another man might find Kepler's [earlier] theory, that the celestial spheres are proportional to the inscribed and circumscribed spheres of the different regular solids, more agreeable to *his* reason. But the shock of opinions will soon lead men to rest on preferences of a far more universal nature. Take, for example, the doctrine that man only acts selfishly—that is, from the consideration that acting in one way will afford him more pleasure than acting in another. This rests on no fact in the world, but it has had a wide acceptance as being the only reasonable theory.

This method is far more intellectual and respectable from the point of view of reason than either of the others which we have noticed. But its failure has been the most manifest. It makes of inquiry something similar to the development of taste; but taste, unfortunately, is always more or less a matter of fashion, and accordingly, metaphysicians have never come to any fixed agreement, but the pendulum has swung backward and forward between a more material and a more spiritual philosophy, from the earliest times to the latest. And so from this, which has been called the *a priori* method, we are driven, in

Lord Bacon's phrase, to a true induction. We have examined into this *a priori* method as something which promised to deliver our opinions from their accidental and capricious element. But development, while it is a process which eliminates the effect of some casual circumstances, only magnifies that of others. This method, therefore, does not differ in a very essential way from that of authority. The government may not have lifted its finger to influence my convictions; I may have been left outwardly quite free to choose, we will say, between monogamy and polygamy, and appealing to my conscience only, I may have concluded that the latter practice is in itself licentious. But when I come to see that the chief obstacle to the spread of Christianity among a people of as high culture as the Hindoos has been a conviction of the immorality of our way of treating women, I cannot help seeing that, though governments do not interfere, sentiments in their development will be very greatly determined by accidental causes. Now, there are some people, among whom I must suppose that my reader is to be found, who, when they see that any belief of theirs is determined by any circumstance extraneous to the facts, will from that moment not merely admit in words that that belief is doubtful, but will experience a real doubt of it, so that it ceases in some degree at least to be a belief.

To satisfy our doubts, therefore, it is necessary that a method should be found by which our beliefs may be caused by nothing human, but by some external permanency—by something upon which our thinking has no effect. Some mystics imagine that they have such a method in a private inspiration from on high. But that is only a form of the method of tenacity, in which the conception of truth as something public is not yet developed. Our external permanency would not be external, in our sense, if it was restricted in its influence to one individual. It must be something which affects, or might affect, every man. And, though these affections are necessarily as various as are individual conditions, yet the method must be such that the ultimate conclusion of every man shall be the same, or would be the same if inquiry were sufficiently persisted in. Such is the method of science. Its fundamental hypothesis, restated in more familiar language, is this: There are real things, whose characters are entirely independent of our opinions about them; those realities affect our senses according to regular laws, and, though our sensations are as different as our relations to the objects, yet, by taking advantage of the laws of perception, we can ascertain by reasoning how things really are, and any man, if he have sufficient experience and reason enough about it, will be led to the one true conclusion. The new conception here involved is that of reality. It may be asked how I know that there are any realities. If this hypothesis is the sole support of my method of inquiry, my method of inquiry must not be used to support my hypothesis. The reply is this: (1) If investigation cannot be regarded as proving that there are real things, it at least does not lead to a contrary conclusion; but the method and the conception on which it is based remain ever in harmony. No doubts of the method, therefore, necessarily arise from its practice, as is the case with all the others. (2) The feeling which gives rise to any method of fixing belief is a dissatisfaction at two repugnant propositions. But here already is a vague concession that there is some *one* thing to which a proposition should conform. Nobody, therefore, can really doubt that there are realities, or, if he did, doubt would not be a source of dissatisfaction. The hypothesis, therefore, is one which every mind admits. So that the social impulse does not cause men to doubt it. (3) Everybody uses the scientific method about a great many things, and only ceases to use it when he does not know how to apply it. (4) Experience of the method has not led us to doubt it, but, on the contrary, scientific investigation has had the most wonderful triumphs in the way of settling opinion. These afford the explanation of my not doubting the method or the hypothesis which it supposes; and not having any doubt, nor believing that anybody else whom I could influence has, it would be the merest babble for me to say more about it. If there be anybody with a living doubt upon the subject, let him consider it.

To describe the method of scientific investigation is the object of this series of papers. At present I have only room to notice some points of contrast between it and other methods of fixing belief.

This is the only one of the four methods which presents any distinction of a right and a wrong way. If I adopt the method of tenacity and shut myself out from all influences, whatever I think necessary to doing this is necessary according to that method. So with the method of authority; the state may try to put down heresy by means which, from a scientific point of view, seems very ill-calculated to accomplish its purposes; but the only test on that method is what the state thinks, so that it cannot pursue the method wrongly. So with the *a priori* method. The very essence of it is to think as one is inclined to think. All metaphysicians will be sure to do that, however they may be inclined to judge each other to be perversely wrong. The Hegelian system recognizes every natural tendency of thought as logical, although it is certain to be abolished by counter-tendencies. Hegel thinks there is a regular system in the succession of these tendencies, in consequence of which, after drifting one way and the other for a long time, opinion will at last go right. And it is true that metaphysicians get the right ideas at last; one may be sure that whatever scientific investigation has put out of doubt will presently receive *a priori* demonstration on the part of the metaphysicians.

It is not to be supposed that the first three methods of settling opinion present no advantage whatever over the scientific method. On the contrary, each has some peculiar convenience of its own. The *a prior* method is distinguished for its comfortable conclusions. It is the nature of the process to adopt whatever belief we are inclined to, and there are certain flatteries to one's vanities which we all believe by nature, until we are awakened from our pleasing dream by rough facts. The method of authority will always govern the mass of mankind; and those who wield the various forms of organized force in the state will never be convinced that dangerous reasoning ought not to be suppressed in some way. If liberty of speech is to be untrammeled from the grosser forms of constraint, then uniformity of opinion will be secured by a moral terrorism to which the respectability of society will give its thorough approval. Following the method of authority is the path of peace. Certain non-conformities are permitted; certain others (considered unsafe) are forbidden. These are different in different countries and in different ages; but, wherever you are, let it be known that you seriously hold a tabooed belief, and you may be perfectly sure of being treated with a cruelty no less brutal but more refined than hunting you like a wolf. Thus, the greatest intellectual benefactors of mankind have never dared, and dare not now, to utter the whole of their thought; and thus a shade of *prima facie* doubt is cast upon every proposition which is considered essential to the security of society. Singuarly enough, the persecution does not all come from without; but a man torments himself and is oftentimes most distressed at finding himself believing propositions which he has been brought up to regard with aversion. The peaceful and sympathetic man will, therefore, find it hard to resist the temptation to submit his opinions to authority. But most of all I admire the method of tenacity for its strength, simplicity, and directness. Men who pursue it are distinguished for their decision of character, which becomes very easy with such a mental rule. They do not waste time in trying to make up their minds to what they want, but, fastening like lightning upon whatever alternative comes first, they hold to it to the end, whatever happens, without an instant's irresolution. This is one of the splendid qualities which generally accompany brilliant, unlasting success. It is impossible not to envy the man who can dismiss reason, although we know how it must turn out at last.

Such are the advantages which the other methods of settling opinions have over scientific investigation. A man should consider well of them; and then he should consider that, after all, he wishes his opinions to coincide with the fact, that there is no reason why the results of those first three methods should do so. To bring about this effect is the prerogative of the method of science. Upon such considerations he has to make his choice —a choice which is far more than the adoption of any intellectual opinion, which is one of the ruling decisions of his life, to which when once made he is bound to adhere. The force of habit will sometimes cause a man to hold on to old beliefs after he is in a condition to see that they have no sound basis. But reflection upon the state of the case will overcome these habits, and he ought to allow reflection full weight. People sometimes shrink from doing this, having an idea that beliefs are wholesome which they cannot help feeling rest on nothing. But let such persons suppose an analogous though different case from their own. Let them ask themselves what they would say to a reformed Mussulman who should hesitate to give up his old notions in regard to the relations of the sexes; or to a reformed Catholic who should still shrink from the Bible. Would they not say that these persons ought to consider the matter fully, and clearly understand the new doctrine, and then ought to embrace it in its entirety? But, above all, let it be considered that what is more wholesome than any particular belief is integrity of belief; and that to avoid looking into the support of any belief from a fear that it may turn out rotten is quite as immoral as it is disadvantageous. The person who confesses that there is such a thing as truth, which is distinguished from falsehood simply by this, that if acted on it should, on full consideration, carry us to the point we aim at and not astray, and then, though convinced of this, dares not know the truth and seeks to avoid it, is in a sorry state of mind, indeed.

Yes, the other methods do have their merits: a clear logical conscience does cost something—just as any virtue, just as all that we cherish, costs us dear. But, we should not desire it to be otherwise. The genius of a man's logical method should be loved and reverenced as his bride, whom he has chosen from all the world. He need not condemn the others; on the contrary, he may honor them deeply, and in doing so he only honors her the more. But she is the one that he has chosen, and he knows that he was right in making that choice. And having made it, he will work and fight for her, and will not complain that there are blows to take, hoping that there may be as many and as hard to give, and will strive to be the worthy knight and champion of her from the blaze of whose splendors he draws his inspiration and his courage.

The Pragmatist as Instrumentalist: John Dewey

Although more directly influenced by William James than by Peirce in the formulation of his thought, John Dewey[1] is closer to the "scientific" pragmatism of Peirce than he is to James' more popular version of pragmatism. Actually Dewey preferred the term "instrumentalism" to describe what he calls "the logical version of pragmatism," and thus to distinguish his position from that of James. Dewey was profoundly impressed by the Darwinian point of view, with which he became familiar as a college student, and his entire philosophy—in particular his approach to logic—was shaped by the theory of evolution. Human intelligence he sees as a direct outcome of the evolutionary process. The mind developed as the biological organism sought to adjust itself more successfully to its environment; man began to think in order to survive and to improve his life. When seen in its biological context, thinking is a kind of *activity* as natural to the human animal as breathing or eating—but it is also an activity that can profoundly modify all other activities, in particular, the habits implanted by custom and the impulses of immediate desire.

One of Dewey's earliest and most popular discussions of thinking as a practical and functional activity is his volume, *How We Think*. Published originally in 1910, it was reprinted a number of times, widely read, and finally rewritten and brought up to date in 1933. This book did much to help establish the fact that thinking is essentially a problem-solving activity. Men do not in their natural state begin to think when they have no troubles to cope with, no difficulties to overcome, Dewey points out. A life of ease, or of completely successful effort, would actually be a thoughtless life. It is because of difficulties or obstructions in our way that we are forced to pause and to think reflectively in order to move ahead again. Thus thinking begins in what Dewey calls a *forked-road* situation—that is to say, a situation that presents a dilemma and offers alternatives between which we must choose. Reflection is aimed at the discovery of facts that will enable us to make the necessary choice. "The function of thought is therefore, to transform a situation in which there is obscurity, doubt, conflict, disturbance of some sort, into a situation that is clear, coherent, settled, harmonious."[2]

As a practical activity, thinking then has something to do and the success of our ideas can always be checked by the results they achieve. One does not understand the nature of an idea, Dewey argues, until he recognizes that ideas are actually instruments by which we accomplish certain desired results. They are the tools used to enable us to do something, to do something better, more intelligently, more successfully, than we could do it by simple instinct or impulse. "Ideas are not genuine ideas," he writes, "unless they are tools with which to search for material to solve a problem. An idea, logically speaking, is not a faded perception of an

---

[1] A brief biographical background for Dewey is provided in the preceding section, pages 218–220.

[2] John Dewey, *How We Think* (New York, D. C. Health and Company, 1933), p. 100.

object, nor is it a compound of a number of sensations. A savage might be able to form an image of poles and wires. But unless the savage knew something about telegraphy, he would have no idea, or at least no correct idea, of the poles and wires. The fact is that an idea, intellectually, cannot be defined by its structure, but only by its function and use. It is an idea because of what it *does* in clearing up a perplexity, or in harmonizing what is otherwise fragmentary, not because of its physical make-up."[3]

His biological point of view leads Dewey also to the conviction that the fundamental meaning and purpose of human life is found in growth, and growth demands a constant alertness to the concrete facts of experience, indeed a constant reshaping and remaking of experience. For the enemy of life is rigidity, blind resistence to change. Here then lies the chief function of intelligence in Dewey's social philosophy. Intelligence must be sharply critical of the rigidities in all our social institutions, of all outmoded practices in government, in economics, in morals, if growth for the society and for the individuals who compose it is to be possible.

Human intelligence functions best, of course, where there is a free interplay among individuals, where life is varied and uninhibited by social or political authoritarianism. Dewey is led, therefore, to a vigorous opposition to all those forces that tend to limit the freedom of thought and expression so essential for the spirit of inquiry, and also to a deep commitment to the democratic way of life. He takes his place in the long tradition of able philosophers from Socrates to John Stuart Mill who have championed the cause of freedom, and becomes in a peculiar sense the philosopher of American democracy. Democracy in America, as Dewey sees it, is a society relatively free from the rigidities of the older European cultures and a society dedicated to the use of contemporary scientific thought and technique in the remaking of a continent and a way of life; it is a society committed to the free exploration of human experience in order to realize all the possibilities for individual growth. For this reason Dewey championed every cause that enlarged man's freedom, and he attacked every authoritarian effort to limit this freedom. He became in a real sense the voice of the *liberal* movement in this country for a generation and was identified with all the causes associated with this movement, both political and economic.

---

[3] *Ibid,* pp. 133, 136.

Reconstruction in Logic*

I

Men have been thinking for ages. They have observed, inferred, and reasoned in all

---

* John Dewey, *Reconstruction in Philosophy,* (New York, Henry Holt & Co., 1920) Ch. VI (shortened).

sorts of ways and to all kinds of results. Anthropology, the study of the origin of myth, legend and cult; linguistics and grammar; rhetoric and former logical compositions all tell us how men have thought and what have been the purposes and consequences of different kinds of thinking. Psychology, experimental and pathological, makes important contributions to our knowledge of how thinking goes on and to what effect. Especially does the record of the growth of the various sciences afford instruction in those concrete ways of inquiry and testing which have led men astray and which have proved efficacious. Each science from mathematics to history exhibits typical fallacious methods and typical efficacious methods in special subject-matters. Logical theory has thus a large, almost inexhaustible field of empirical study.

Logic is a matter of profound human importance precisely because it is empirically founded and experimentally applied. So considered, the problem of logical theory is none other than the problem of the possibility of the development and employment of intelligent method in inquiries concerned with deliberate reconstruction of experience. And it is only saying again in more specific form what has been said in general form to add that while such logic has been developed in respect to mathematics and physical science, intelligent method, logic, is still far to seek in moral and political affairs.

Assuming, accordingly, this idea of logic without argument, let us proceed to discuss some of its chief features. First, light is thrown by the origin of thinking upon a logic which shall be a method of intelligent guidance of experience. In line with what has already been said about experience being a matter primarily of behavior, a sensori-motor matter, is the fact that thinking takes its departure from specific conflicts in experience that occasion perplexity and trouble. Men do not, in their natural estate, think when they have no troubles to cope with, no difficulties to overcome. A life of ease, of success without effort, would be a thoughtless life, and so also would a life of ready omnipotence. Beings who think are beings whose life is so hemmed in and constricted that they cannot directly carry through a course of action to victorious consummation. Men also do not tend to think when their action, when they are amid difficulties, is dictated to them by authority. Soldiers have difficulties and restrictions in plenty, but *qua* soldiers (as Aristotle would

say) they are not notorious for being thinkers. Thinking is done for them, higher up. The same is too true of most workingmen under present economic conditions. Difficulties occasion thinking only when thinking is the imperative or urgent way out, only when it is the indicated road to a solution. Wherever external authority reigns, thinking is suspected and obnoxious.

The first distinguishing characteristic of thinking then is facing the facts—inquiry, minute and extensive scrutinizing, observation. Nothing has done greater harm to the successful conduct of the enterprise of thinking (and to the logics which reflect and formulate the undertaking) than the habit of treating observation as something outside of and prior to thinking, and thinking as something which can go on in the head without including observation of new facts as part of itself. It creates a class of "thinkers" who are remote from practice and hence from testing their thought by application—a socially superior and irresponsible class. This is the condition causing the tragic division of theory and practice, and leading to an unreasonable exaltation of theory on one side and an unreasonable contempt for it on the other. It confirms current practice in its hard brutalities and dead routines just because it has transferred thinking and theory to a separate and nobler region. Thus has the idealist conspired with the materialist to keep actual life impoverished and inequitable.

The isolation of thinking from confrontation with facts encourages that kind of observation which merely accumulates brute facts, which occupies itself laboriously with mere details, but never inquires into their meaning and consequences—a safe occupation, for it never contemplates any use to be made of the observed facts in determining a plan for changing the situation. Thinking which is a method of reconstructing experience treats observation of facts, on the other hand, as the indispensable step of defining the problem, of locating the trouble, of forcing home a definite, instead of a merely vague emotional, sense of what the difficulty is and where it lies. It is not aimless, random, miscellaneous, but purposeful, specific and limited by the character of the trouble undergone. The purpose is so to clarify the disturbed and confused situation that reasonable ways of dealing with it may be suggested. When the scientific man appears to observe aimlessly, it is merely that he is so in love with problems as sources and guides of inquiry, that he is striving to turn up a problem where none appears on the surface: he is, as we say, hunting for trouble because of the satisfaction to be had in coping with it.

Specific and wide observation of concrete fact always, then, corresponds not only with a sense of a problem or difficulty, but with some vague sense of the meaning of the difficulty, that is, of what it imports or signifies in subsequent experience. It is a kind of anticipation or prediction of what is coming. We speak, very truly, of impending trouble, and in observing the signs of what the trouble is, we are at the same time expecting, forecasting—in short, framing an idea, becoming aware of meaning. When the trouble is not only impending but completely actual and present, we are overwhelmed. We do not think, but give way to depression. The kind of trouble that occasions thinking is that which is incomplete and developing, and where what is found already in existence can be employed as a sign from which to infer what is likely to come. When we intelligently observe, we are, as we say apprehensive, as well as apprehending. We are on the alert for something still to come. Curiosity, inquiry, investigation, are directed quite as truly into what is going to happen next as into what has happened. An intelligent interest in the latter is an interest in getting evidence, indications, symptoms for inferring the former. Observation is diagnosis and diagnosis implies an interest in anticipation and preparation. It makes ready in advance an attitude of response so that we shall not be caught unawares.

That which is not already in existence, that which is only anticipated and inferred, cannot be observed. It does not have the status of fact, of something given, a datum, but of a meaning, an idea. So far as ideas are

not fancies, framed by emotionalized memory for escape and refuge, they are precisely anticipations of something still to come aroused by looking into the facts of a developing situation. The blacksmith watches his iron, its color and texture, to get evidence of what it is getting ready to pass into; the physician observes his patient to detect symptoms of change in some definite direction; the scientific man keeps his attention upon his laboratory material to get a clue as to what will happen under certain conditions. The very fact that observation is not an end in itself but a search for evidence and signs shows that along with observation goes inference, anticipatory forecast—in short an idea, thought or conception.

In a more technical context, it would be worth while to see what light this logical correspondence of observed fact and projected idea or meaning throws upon certain traditional philosophical problems and puzzles, including that of subject and predicate in judgment, object and subject in knowledge, "real" and "ideal" generally. But at this time, we must confine ourselves to pointing out that this view of the correlative origin and function of observed fact and projected idea in experience, commits us to some very important consequences concerning the nature of ideas, meanings, conceptions, or whatever word may be employed to denote the specifically *mental* function. Because they are suggestions of something that may happen or eventuate, they are (as we saw in the case of ideals generally) platforms of response to what is going on. The man who detects that the cause of his difficulty is an automobile bearing down upon him is not guaranteed safety; he may have made his observation-forecast too late. But if his anticipation-perception comes in season, he has the basis for doing something which will avert threatening disaster. Because he foresees an impending result, he may do something that will lead to the situation eventuating in some other way. All intelligent thinking means an increment of freedom in action—an emancipation from chance and fatality. "Thought" represents the suggestion of a way of response that is different from that which would have been followed if intelligent observation had not effected an inference as to the future.

Now a method of action, a mode of response, intended to produce a certain result —that is, to enable the blacksmith to give a certain form to his hot iron, the physician to treat the patient so as to facilitate recovery, the scientific experimenter to draw a conclusion which will apply to other cases,—is by the nature of the case tentative, uncertain till tested by its results. The significance of this fact for the theory of truth will be discussed below. Here it is enough to note that notions, theories, systems, no matter how elaborate and self-consistent they are, must be regarded as hypotheses. They are to be accepted as bases of actions which test them, not as finalities. To perceive this fact is to abolish rigid dogmas from the world. It is to recognize that conceptions, theories and systems of thought are always open to development through use. It is to enforce the lesson that we must be on the lookout quite as much for indications to alter them as for opportunities to assert them. They are tools. As in the case of all tools, their value resides not in themselves but in their capacity to work shown in the consequences of their use.

Nevertheless, inquiry is free only when the interest in knowing is so developed that thinking carries with it something worth while for itself, something having its own esthetic and moral interest. Just because knowing is not self-enclosed and final but is instrumental to reconstruction of situations, there is always danger that it will be subordinated to maintaining some preconceived purpose or prejudice. Then reflection ceases to be complete; it falls short. Being precommitted to arriving at some special result, it is not sincere. It is one thing to say that all knowing has an end beyond itself, and another thing, a thing of a contrary kind, to say that an act of knowing has a particular end which it is bound, in advance, to reach. Much less is it true that the instrumental nature of thinking means that it exists for the sake of attaining some private, one-sided advantage upon which one has set one's heart.

Any limitation whatever of the end means limitation in the thinking process itself. It signifies that it does not attain its full growth and movement, but is cramped, impeded, interfered with. The only situation in which knowing is fully stimulated is one in which the end is developed in the process of inquiry and testing.

II

Little time is left to speak of the account of the nature of truth given by the experimental and functional type of logic. This is less to be regretted because this account is completely a corollary from the nature of thinking and ideas. If the view held as to the latter is understood, the conception of truth follows as a matter of course. If it be not understood, any attempt to present the theory of truth is bound to be confusing, and the theory itself to seem arbitrary and absurd. If ideas, meanings, conceptions, notions, theories, systems are instrumental to an active reorganization of the given environment, to a removal of some specific trouble and perplexity, then the test of their validity and value lies in accomplishing this work. If they succeed in their office, they are reliable, sound, valid, good, true. If they fail to clear up confusion, to eliminate defects, if they increase confusion, uncertainty and evil when they are acted upon, then are they false. Confirmation, corroboration, verification lie in works, consequences. Handsome is that handsome does. By their fruits shall ye know them. That which guides us truly is true—demonstrated capacity for such guidance is precisely what is meant by truth. The adverb "truly" is more fundamental than either the adjective, true, or the noun, truth. An adverb expresses a way, a mode of acting. Now an idea or conception is a claim or injunction or plan to act in a certain way as the way to arrive at the clearing up of a specific situation. When the claim or pretension or plan is acted upon it guides us truly or falsely; it leads us to our end or away from it. Its active, dynamic function is the all-important thing about it, and in the quality of activity induced by it lies all its truth and falsity. The hypothesis that works is the true one; and truth is an abstract noun applied to the collection of cases, actual, foreseen, and desired, that receive confirmation in their works and consequences.

So wholly does the worth of this conception of truth depend upon the correctness of the prior account of thinking that it is more profitable to consider why the conception gives offence than to expound it on its own account. Part of the reason why it has been found so obnoxious is doubtless its novelty and defects in its statement. Too often, for example, when truth has been thought of as satisfaction, it has been thought of as merely emotional satisfaction, a private comfort, a meeting of purely personal need. But the satisfaction in question means a satisfaction of the needs and conditions of the problem out of which the idea, the purpose and method of action, arises. It includes public and objective conditions. It is not to be manipulated by whim or personal idiosyncrasy. Again when truth is defined as utility, it is often thought to mean utility for some purely personal end, some profit upon which a particular individual has set his heart. So repulsive is a conception of truth which makes it a mere tool of private ambition and aggrandizement, that the wonder is that critics have attributed such a notion to sane men. As a matter of fact, truth as utility means service in making just that contribution to reorganization in experience that the idea or theory claims to be able to make. The usefulness of a road is not measured by the degree in which it lends itself to the purposes of a highwayman. It is measured by whether it actually functions as a road, as a means of easy and effective public transportation and communication. And so with the serviceableness of an idea or hypothesis as a measure of its truth.

Turning from such rather superficial misunderstandings, we find, I think, the chief obstacle to the reception of this notion of truth is an inheritance from the classic tradition that has become so deeply engrained in men's minds. In just the degree in which existence is divided into two realms, a higher one of perfect being and a lower one of seeming, phenomenal, deficient reality, truth and

falsity are thought of as fixed, ready-made static properties of things themselves. Supreme Reality is true Being, inferior and imperfect Reality is false Being. It makes claims to Reality which it cannot substantiate. It is deceitful, fraudulent, inherently unworthy of trust and belief. Beliefs are false not because they mislead us; they are not mistaken ways of thinking. They are false because they admit and adhere to false existences or subsistences. Other notions are true because they do have to do with true Being —with full and ultimate Reality. Such a notion lies at the back of the head of every one who has, in however an indirect way, been a recipient of the ancient and medieval tradition. This view is radically challenged by the pragmatic conception of truth, and the impossibility of reconciliation or compromise is, I think, the cause of the shock occasioned by the newer theory.

This contrast, however, constitutes the importance of the new theory as well as the unconscious obstruction to its acceptance. The older conception worked out practically to identify truth with authoritative dogma. A society that chiefly esteems order, that finds growth painful and change disturbing, inevitably seeks for a fixed body of superior truths upon which it may depend. It looks backward, to something already in existence, for the source and sanction of truth. It falls back upon what is antecedent, prior, original, *a priori,* for assurance. The thought of looking ahead, toward eventual results, toward consequences, creates uneasiness and fear. It disturbs the sense of rest that is attached to the ideas of fixed Truth already in existence. It puts a heavy burden of responsibility upon us for search, unremitting observation, scrupulous development of hypotheses and thorough-going testing. In physical matters men have slowly grown accustomed in all specific beliefs to identifying the true with the verified. But they still hesitate to recognize the implication of this identification and to derive the definition of truth from it. For while it is nominally agreed upon as a commonplace that definitions ought to spring from concrete and specific cases rather than be invented in the empty air and imposed upon particulars, there is a strange unwillingness to act upon the maxim in defining truth. To generalize the recognition that the true means the verified and means nothing else places upon men the responsibility for surrendering political and moral dogmas, and subjecting to the test of consequences their most cherished prejudices. Such a change involves a great change in the seat of authority and the methods of decision in society.

The Age of Analysis: Morton White

In his recent survey of the philosophy of the twentieth century, Morton White
impressed enough by the importance of the philosophers whose primary concern is
with logical or linguistic analysis to entitle this volume, *The Age of Analysis*. The
school of American pragmatists (Peirce, James, and Dewey) he sees as standing
between the more traditional approach to philosophy as the search for values in
human life and in the universe (the attempt to fashion a sound over-all world-
view) and the more recent tendency to see philosophy as essentially a matter of
linguistic or logical analysis. Pragmatism, he suggests, is a mediating movement
in philosophy which aspires to a total systematic view of reality without losing
sight of the primary importance of scientific method and logical analysis.[1]

In the historical development of pragmatism, Peirce can be seen as the pragmatic philosopher of science, James as the pragmatic philosopher of religion, and
Dewey as the pragmatic philosopher of morals. In a quite striking fashion the
concern of much philosophy in America has now returned to the work of Peirce
and carried further ideas of his in which neither James or Dewey were directly
interested. The important work of Peirce in logic and his contributions to semantics and to the philosophy of language bring pragmatism into close contact with
logical and linguistics analysis. They make it clear that "the age of analysis" is in
many ways a direct continuation of aspects of the pragmatism of Peirce which
were not developed in the philosophy of James or Dewey. As White puts it, Dewey
and James managed for a time to blunt the point and edge of scientific and logical
analysis, and so soften the blow directed at traditional philosophy by the work of
Peirce.

While it is true that the "analytic movement" finds its historical impetus in
the later thought of Bertrand Russell, in Wittgenstein, and in Carnap, rather than
in Peirce, it is equally true that his own version of pragmatism pointed clearly in
this direction, more directly indeed than to those ideas which had immediate appeal to James and Dewey. Russell's defense of the analytic approach, in a discussion
of "The Philosophy of Logical Analysis," might easily have been written by Peirce
himself:

> In the welter of conflicting fanaticisms, one of the few unifying forces is
> scientific truthfulness, by which I mean the habit of basing our beliefs upon ob-
> servations and inferences as impersonal, and as much divested of local and
> temperamental bias, as is possible for human beings. To have insisted upon the
> introduction of this virtue into philosophy, and to have invented a powerful
> method by which it can be rendered fruitful, are the chief merits of the phil-
> osophical school of which I am a member. The habit of careful veracity acquired
> in the practice of this philosophical method can be extended to the whole sphere

---

[1] Morton White, *The Age of Analysis* (New York, New American Library, 1955), p.
19.

of human activity, producing, wherever it exists, a lessening of fanaticism with an increasing capacity of sympathy and mutual understanding. In abandoning a part of its dogmatic pretensions, philosophy does not cease to suggest and inspire a way of life."[2]

Morton White was born in New York City in 1917. He studied philosophy at Columbia University when John Dewey's influence was still strong; in 1942 he received his Ph.D. at Columbia and the following year published his first book, *The Origin of Dewey's Instrumentalism*. After teaching at Columbia University and the University of Pennsylvania, White joined the faculty at Harvard in 1948 and later served as chairman of the department of philosophy. In 1953 he was a visiting member of the Institute for Advanced Study at Princeton. In addition to *The Age of Analysis,* which appeared in 1955, he published a volume on *Social Thought in America* in 1942 and one entitled *Toward Reunion in Philosophy* in 1956. The essay reprinted here, "New Horizons in Philosophy," first appeared in the more popular *Saturday Evening Post* series of articles discussing important contemporary ideas and movements.

---

[2] Bertrand Russell, *The History of Western Philosophy* (New York, Simon and Schuster, 1945) p. 836.

New Horizons in Philosophy*

I

The most arresting and most distinctive feature of philosophy in the English-speaking world today is concentration on linguistic and logical analysis. While *dialectical materialism* is the official philosophy of the Soviet bloc, and Western Europe continues to be strongly affected by existentialism, Britain and the United States are primarily the homes of what is called analytic or linguistic philosophy. Analytic philosophers are neither sponsored nor controlled by any government or political party, and they do not appeal to the Bohemian or the beatnik. They invite both *Marxist* and *existentialist* scorn because they spurn the pretentiousness and murk of much traditional philosophy. For good reasons analytic philosophy has never become

the favorite subject of the bistro or the espresso café, and it needs no proof of its seriousness. It respects the values of the reasonable man rather than those of the irrational man, though it fully recognizes the existence of irrationality.

Analytic philosophy begins with an awareness of the fact that philosophy is not a rival of science and that it cannot provide us with another way of studying the world with which the scientist deals. When in the nineteenth century natural science grew so highly specialized, it became evident that nobody could encompass the whole of knowledge. And so the drift of philosophy was away from encyclopedism, away from thinking that the philosopher was a superscientist, a universal genius, a know-it-all.

Not only did it become evident that universal knowledge was humanly impossible, but it was seen how grotesque it was to think that one could construct a system in

---

* Morton White, "New Horizons in Philosophy," *The Saturday Evening Post,* September 17, 1960. Reprinted by permission of the author.

which all our knowledge could be derived from a few philosophical principles, as the geometrical theorems of Euclid are deduced from his axioms. It was this mistake which resulted in the illusion that philosophers could dominate all knowledge through the command of a few pivotal truths. This may be called the metaphysical illusion, the product of a vast inflation of the powers and prospects of metaphysics, one of the oldest and most mysterious branches of philosophy.

According to tradition, *metaphysics* is the most fundamental of all disciplines. The first part of the word "metaphysics" is derived from the Greek *meta,* meaning "beyond," so that the subject was conceived as that which went beyond the problems of physics. Physicists, some metaphysicians said, deal with material things, biologists with living things, mathematicians with numbers, points and lines. But the metaphysician cuts a much wider swath; indeed he takes the whole cloth as his province, for he studies being as such. Not any particular being or limited class of beings, but just plain being, since the traditional metaphysician is the spectator of all time and eternity.

It took philosophers a long time to realize that the number of interesting things that one can say about all things in one fell swoop is very limited. When you lump together such different items as kings, cabbages, bits of sealing wax, number, thoughts and electrons in order to say what they all have in common, you are likely to discover that what they have in common is the fact that they exist. You lapse into emptiness through the effort to become supremely general.

Having reached this dour conclusion about the most central of philosophical disciplines, some philosophers asked themselves just what was left for them to do. If all of existence could be parceled out to different scientists who worked so effectively by specializing, and if the philosopher was unable to supply any significant first principles which could neatly order the tangled forest of modern science and information, what was the philosopher's function in the intellectual world? Once philosophy was everything. Now it threatened to become nothing.

Fortunately the story of philosophy did not end here. There were some who did not desert the battered, beleaguered ship. They knew that there were nonmetaphysical questions of large import which had always been asked by philosophers and which had to be asked more relentlessly than ever in an age of scientific specialization. One of these questions—short, but powerful—was "What do you mean?" The patron saint of philosophy, Socrates, had spent most of his time asking it, often to the discomfort of those with whom he conversed in Plato's *Dialogues* and to the immense delight of centuries of readers who watched Socrates puncture humbug and ironically examine ideas which could not stand the test of honest logical criticism. The question "What do you mean?" could be directed even at scientists. It was the tiny candle which had flickered since antiquity, which had never gone out even in philosophy's darkest days. It was used to light a philosophical bonfire by a generation of thinkers at the turn of the century—Ernst Mach, the Austrian philosopher-physicist who influenced Einstein; *Bertrand Russell* and G. E. Moore in England; *Charles Peirce* and *William James* in the United States. They sparked the various new explosive movements of the twentieth century—*pragmatism* in the United States, logical positivism in Austria, and the Cambridge School of analysis, so called in honor of the English university where it first flourished.*

No matter how far scientific specialization went it left the possibility of asking Socrates' question. In fact, the more the scientists specialized, the more their preoccupation with description, experiment, observation and prediction robbed them of the time and energy needed for the clarification of their fundamental concepts. Physicists before Einstein had failed to be sufficiently clear about the notions of space and time, and biologists were not always prepared to give comprehensible answers to the question, "What is

---

* Italics inserted. Ed.

life?" Even mathematicians were foggy about the idea of number and had fallen into serious paradoxes. Here, then, was an opportunity for philosophers to co-operate with scientists in an effort to elucidate the basic concepts of special sciences, instead of pretending that the philosopher possessed a mysterious key to all scientific doors. The revival of the Socratic question "What do you mean?" as applied to the words of the scientist, thus preserved for the philosopher a central, if not regal, position. He was no longer a surveyor of everything, but rather a careful student of language who at this stage of the analytic movement tended to concentrate on the terms of natural science and mathematics. The most brilliant monument to this pre-World War I era in philosophy was the three-volumed *Principia Mathematica* of Russell and Whitehead.

After the First World War the harvest of this intellectual activity was reaped by younger philosophers who described themselves as logical positivists. Philosophy, they said in going beyond Russell and Whitehead, was nothing but the philosophy of science. And philosophy of science, as someone put it, was philosophy enough. A story was told of a philosopher of the old school who came into the office of his department during the '30's and overheard two of his younger colleagues arguing about the meaning of a physical theory. The disputants grew more and more intense, and just after one shouted, "What do you mean by saying that space is curved?" the other yelled, "What do you mean by saying it's not?" The first, not to be outdone, then produced that classic in philosophical oneupmanship "What do you mean by 'mean'?" At this point the old professor could not contain himself and spoke up for his own generation as he interrupted the conversation to say, "Good morning, gentlemen. If that means anything to you."

The professor's greeting pointed a moral. It revealed a grave limitation in the conception of meaning itself. For the logical positivist a meaningful utterance was simply one that could be verified or falsified. And verifiability and falsifiability, it was said, were

limited to scientific statements. Small wonder that a greeting like "Good morning" was said to be meaningless. But much more than "Good morning" was at stake. For by these same narrow standards, poetry and ethics, in addition to metaphysics, were all nonsense.

At this point in its history analytic philosophy was at its furthest from the humanistic tradition. The verifiability theory of meaning was to the positivist in the 1930's what the guillotine was to the French Revolution, and like the guillotine it destroyed indiscriminately. It was one thing to attack metaphysics, another to say that every poetic or moral utterance was meaningless. And it did not help to add that moral and poetic language had what was called "emotive meaning," or the capacity to stimulate emotions. That was often a polite way of sweeping much of human language under the rug, to put it where the positivist could conveniently avoid it, indeed walk all over it while he puzzled about the meaning of space, time and number.

It soon became evident that the question "What do you mean?" had been conceived too narrowly. It tended to direct the philosopher's attention only to language in which knowledge was communicated. Under Plato's influence philosophers had identified the meaning of a term with an abstract concept, thinking of the word on the page as expressing a cloudy entity in Plato's realm of ideas. And therefore they tended to think that only declarative sentences, such as "Socrates is a man," had meaning as they conceived it. On this theory the command "Socrates, come here!" was strictly nonsensical. And so was the exclamation "Great Socrates!" because obviously it was hard to suppose that there were some weird resident of Plato's real world called "Great Socrateshood" which could serve as the meaning of the exclamation.

Partly because of these consequences and other more technical difficulties, and partly because of the intellectual mood created by the aftermath of the war, the influence of logical positivism waned perceptibly in the '40s. Unfortunately, however the phrase "logical positivist" continued as an epithet which was wrongly applied to anyone with the faintest interest in the philosophy of language. For that reason an entirely different attitude in analytic philosophy has been hidden from public view. It is dominated by the idea that the philosopher should ask of utterances and writings not what their Platonic meaning is, but rather what their use is. This attitude is usually identified with the late Ludwig Wittgenstein, who was the leading philosophical figure at Cambridge University after the days of Russell and Moore, and who influences contemporary philosophy mainly through his posthumous writings and through his loyal disciples.

As is so often the case in the history of ideas, a simple suggestion, undoubtedly present in the minds of many others who had failed to stress it sufficiently or to carry it out as brilliantly as Wittgenstein did, caught on among a great number of English and American philosophers after the Second World War. I am not a follower of Wittgenstein, and I regard a good deal of what he has said as dubious. But in the history of recent philosophy he is a liberating force. Once he said plainly and insistently that the main subject matter of the philosopher was the behavior of human beings trying to communicate with one another, a whole new world seemed to open up to the analytic philosopher, the many-sided world of language in all of its employments. Not just the language of scientific assertion and proof, for man does not communicate by assertion and proof alone. He greets, exclaims, exhorts, commands, judges, describes, promises and does many other things with words. And all of these linguistic activities have now become fair game for the philosopher who has abandoned the Platonic version of the question "What do you mean?"

II

What should the analytic philosopher do, now that he has been shown these new horizons, now that he has been freed from the restrictive idea that he is merely a logician of natural science? In the remainder of this article I should like to formulate and illustrate my own answer to this vital question.

Philosophers have an unprecedented opportunity to clarify the language which men use in the writing of history, in morality, law, religion, politics and education, to take the most challenging examples. And so I label my viewpoint "institutionalism" in order to suggest that one of the primary tasks of philosophy is to analyze, compare and contrast language as it is used for purposes of communication within these different institutions. While communicating in these situations, men use language in a variety of intertwined ways which express their beliefs, hopes, their needs and their values; and one job of the philosopher is to draw an intellectual map, to provide a coherent picture of the interconnections between these different modes of speech, feeling and thought.

Language is a cultural instrument, and it must be seen in its cultural setting. Those who fail to view it in this way and who instead regard it as a collection of dead sentences fall into two related errors. One may be called formalism and the other essentialism. Formalism is the tendency to view language as if it were an inscription on a scroll or a monument rather than as the living, complex, subtle tool that it is. Essentialism is the idea that the philosopher can look at these dead words and, without attention to their use, summarize the essence of complex forms of communication. Philosophers given to such oversimplification have said that religion is merely a belief in God. Law has been defined as the command of the sovereign. History has been glibly summarized as the effort to report what actually happened in the past. Questions in each of these areas have been separated sharply from questions of morality. The icy hand of overabstraction guides the writing of those philosophers who think that merely by examining the forms of the words, they can characterize the essence of religion, history or law. Their most common assumption is that by looking at any kind of language one can always single out those statements in it which are factual, objective and descriptive, and separate them sharply from statements of value. And this assumption, I think, is a mistake, notably when it is applied uniformly to the writings of historians and the language of lawyers. It is often the result of a failure to study the actual processes of law and historical writing, a failure which is encouraged by the formalism and essentialism of which I have spoken.

Of course, I do not wish to deny that sometimes we can make a distinction between statements of fact and evaluations in a given context. For example, two men can agree that someone has told a lie and yet judge his lying differently. In such cases our conclusion about the lying may be reported in a conjunction of a factual statement and a moral statement "Jones lied, and it was wrong of him to do so." Here another person is logically free to agree with the first or factual part of the conjunctive statement, while he denies the second if his moral viewpoint is different from ours. But a careful study of communication, especially in history and law, brings to light a kind of blended or hybrid language which defies any effort to decompose it into factual and moral parts that may be accepted or rejected independently. There are, I believe, uses of language which are simultaneously descriptive and evaluative, and which cannot be broken down into the assertion of a factual statement and an evaluative statement which may be judged separately. The person who speaks or writes in this way is doing two inseparable things at once, stating a matter of fact and evaluating, and therefore his audience must take or leave his speech as a whole. To acknowledge this possibility is to abandon certain conventional modes of classifying language which have dominated the history of philosophy.

My contention is that this hybrid kind of language is most commonly found in an institutional setting. It is too large, sprawling and complex for textbooks of logic, for they are too often dominated by a passion for neatness and an interest in classifying isolated statements. Therefore, in order to illustrate and clarify what I have in mind, I shall turn to a basic problem in the philosophy of

history and another in the philosophy of law. History is an institution insofar as no civilized society can live without some image of its past. And no one can deny the pervasiveness of legal institutions.

One of the historian's concerns is to report particular facts, and another is to present a connected picture of the past. The first expresses itself in simple declarative statements, such as "Caesar crossed the Rubicon," and the second in lengthy sequential narratives about the life of some person or the development of a society or a nation. And narrative is not usually studied by formal logicians. It is one thing to report the simple fact that Caesar crossed the Rubicon, but it is another to present Caesar's biography or the history of Rome. By holding fast to this distinction between statement and narration one can see a profoundly important distinction between two ways in which value judgments operate in history. When the historian is assessing the evidence for individual statements of fact, his value judgments—whether on political or religious matters—are properly distinguished from his factual conclusions. But when he is forming his narrative, the historian is often unable to separate these two parts of his thinking. To show this let us consider some illustrations that are closer to home than Julius Caesar.

Historian Charles Beard once argued that President Franklin D. Roosevelt had planned to bring the United States into World War II soon after its beginning, had deceived the people into electing him for a third time by promising that he would keep us out of war, and had "maneuvered" Japan into attacking us at Pearl Harbor. Other historians have tried to refute these assertions by citing fresh evidence, by suggesting that he deliberately neglected available evidence which did not fit in with his beliefs. I am not interested here in the historical details. But I do want to point out that the issue was simply whether Roosevelt did plan, deceive and maneuver in the manner alleged, and that in principle this can be settled in an objective way. We should not excuse anyone who would distort the facts. And no reference to the differing political values of historians should lead us to say that two contradictory views of Roosevelt's behavior are logically admissible, that because Beard and his critics operated with different value schemes, their contradictory views were equally valid from their different points of view. Either Roosevelt did or did not do the things attributed to him, and double talk should be ruthlessly excluded.

The situation changes dramatically, however, when we are asked to choose between two general narrative histories of the United States. Here we are not faced with a short question about one man's actions at a certain time. And here our values do play a part in determining which of two general histories we should write or prefer. Take, for example, the difference between general histories of the United States which take the Federalist point of view and those which are Jeffersonian in their slant.

Prof. Samuel Eliot Morison points out that sixty years ago it was difficult to find a general history of the United States that did not, as he puts it, "present the Federalist-Whig-Republican point of view, or express a very dim view of all Democratic leaders except Grover Cleveland." But by the middle of this century the fashion had changed and it was then equally difficult to find a good general history of the country "that did not follow the Jefferson-Jackson-Roosevelt line." Morison says that he was converted to the latter as a young man when he discovered in his first researches on New England Federalism that "the 'wise and good and rich' whom Fisher Ames thought should rule the nation were stupid, narrow-minded and local in their outlook." But isn't it clear that Morison's conclusion presupposed values which some other historian might not share? And is it not clear, therefore, that the historian who tells a story following a "line" is engaged in an undecomposable blend of description and evaluation?

Something similar is true of the history of philosophy. The historian of philosophy does not expound the views of any and all human beings who have philosophized. Consciously or unconsciously he adopts standards of philosophical excellence by which he judges who is to be admitted into his history. Doctrinal agreement with the historian is not the standard, but his history incorporates a judgment of importance and interest which rests on values that another historian of philosophy might easily reject. Any Catholic reader of histories of philosophy which skip lightly over the medieval period will understand what I mean.

When a historian believes that a certain political tradition is superior to another, he tends to see the history of the country as a development of that tradition. And when we see that history in terms of another tradition, we are no more in a position to say he speaks falsely than we would be if he and we were to see certain trick figures in psychology books differently. The reader may have seen the illustration that can at one moment be seen as a rabbit's head and at another as a duck's.

Well, the historian who tells the story of the United States in Jeffersonian terms because he admires that tradition is a little like the man who always sees the duck-rabbit as a duck because he likes ducks more than rabbits. And we who evaluate his history are likely to praise it in the degree to which he sees the past as we see it in the light of our values. I think that opposing narrative historians sometimes confront each other as rabbit-loving rabbit seers confront duck-loving duck seers.

Some historians are loath to admit this because they view the problem absolutistically. They think of the general historian of the United States as confronted with an "actuality" whose main line is either Federalist or Jeffersonian and not both. They tend to assimilate the logic of narrative history to the logic of historical statement, and to hold that general historian of the United States who is preparing to write his book is faced with just as objective an "either-or" as the historian who is trying to decide whether Caesar crossed the Rubicon. They argue that the Jeffersonian line or the Federalist line is the line which the main stream of American life has followed, and they refuse to allow that anything as ambiguous as the duck-rabbit turns up in their subject. But can they define the notion of a main stream in a completely objective manner? Can it be explained so as to make it possible for historians to converge on it in anything like the way in which scientific students of rivers locate their main streams? I doubt that it can, even though I am willing to grant that no one has said the last or even the next-to-last philosophical word on this subject. Until those words are spoken, historians should admit that one man's duck might be another's rabbit.

The historians must grant that in some parts of his work he engages in a blend of fact finding and evaluation, and that when he pretends in such cases to be recording merely what happened, he is not being accurate about the nature of his enterprise. Moreover, it is impossible to see what could be meant by saying that we can treat the narrative as a conjunction of factual statements and value judgments so that the reader can distinguish them and test them independently. It makes no sense to ask us to remove the Jeffersonian slant from a Jeffersonian history in order to see whether the remainder is factually true. And this is because the value orientation does not figure detachably in the narrative as it figures in the conjunction "Jones lied, and it was wrong of him to do so." The value orientation pervades or colors the narrative and he who would call the narrative a good one must be sympathetic to this coloring and orientation. He must therefore judge the history as a whole, simultaneously guided by the evidence and his values.

History is not the only mode of discourse in which the language of value and the language of fact are not related conjunctively. The law presents us with a similar kind of complexity. Take the case of a statute forbidding the entry of a vehicle into a public park. One might be tempted to say that whether anything is a vehicle is a question of fact, settled by purely empirical means and having nothing to do with the values of those who are trying to find out whether it is a vehicle. One dictionary at hand says, "VE-

HICLE: That in or on which a person or thing may be carried." But suppose that the statute had been enacted before the existence of roller skates. And suppose that a case were to come up in which it was necessary to decide whether a pair of roller skates was a vehicle. Surely the judge might hesitate before saying with a straight face that because a pair of roller skates is something "on which a person or thing is or may be carried" it should be excluded from a park by the statute.

When the judge reaches one of these puzzling examples, he might be moved to ask two questions. He might ask what the enactors of the statue would have said if roller skates had existed when they enacted the statute. This is a straightforward factual question of a kind that can rarely be answered with confidence. But even if it could be, its answer would not be decisive in all cases like this. The judge might more sensibly ask what social good or evil would be brought about by regarding a pair of roller skates as a vehicle and hence keeping it out of a public park. And this is a straightforward value question, the answer to which can play a vital part in the judge's effort to answer the question, "Are roller skates vehicles?" It shows that in the process of answering what is on the linguistic surface a question of fact, the judge can advert to his own values, to his own ideas of what is good for the community.

What shall we call this hyphenated process of looking-at-the-roller-skates-and-deciding - whether - it - is - good - to - call - them - vehicles? We may not have a simple name for it, but it is surely a mode of linguistic activity. It is not logically analyzable into two activities which may be judged independently, like walking and talking. It is not analogous to the combination of separable processes that leads us to the conjunctive conclusion, "Jones lied, and it was wrong of him to do so." If the judge in the roller-skate case were asked what he was doing, he might fairly reply, "Trying to decide whether roller skates are vehicles." And if asked to introspect further and to break down the activity into two separate processes, one of which was merely looking and another merely evaluating, he might be unable to do so.

What general significance should be attached to the existence of these hybrid processes in historical and legal thinking? First of all they show that when we turn to language in a complex cultural setting—the telling of stories and the settling of legal disputes are basic to most civilizations—we find uses of language that cannot be adequately understood if we remain prisoners of an exclusive and exhaustive dichotomy of language into the factual and the evaluative. Some linguistic activities are in a sense both. Reflecting on such modes of thinking and language makes the philosopher aware of a certain narrowness in the traditional philosophical classification of language. The case of the narrative shows that there are modes of discourse which go beyond the simple, isolated statements treated by logicians who work with science and mathematics as their models. The philosopher of language who looks at law and history discovers modes of speech which require new philosophical categories.

This is not all. The philosopher who moves in this direction comes to see that the philosophy of language is not a dreary grammatical exercise. For once he begins to think about modes of discourse in a cultural setting, he will come to see that there are many others which transcend the word and the statement. The religious believer finds it impossible to characterize his religion merely by reference to a few propositions that he accepts. For religion is an organic unity of theological belief, moral attitude, emotional reaction to liturgy, view of human nature, and much more.

Those who accept the same religion agree on many issues of value and fact which cannot always be separated.

The philosopher who tries to understand the use of religious language will meet in even more complicated form the sort of thing encountered in our discussion of history and law. He will find himself more and more concerned with the description and the evaluation of blends of thinking, feeling and doing. In short, with ways of life. And by dealing with ways of life he will come closer to the concerns of the ordinary man. The philosopher who begins by recognizing that a narrative is more than a mere conjuction of factual and evaluative statements, or who sees that some linguistic activities of lawyers fall under hybrid categories not usually acknowledged by philosophers, will soon see a whole new world of language opening up before his eyes. Philosophy of science is not philosophy enough. The philosopher must broaden his vision to civilization itself.

Such a philosophical student of human institutions need not be a mere reporter of linguistic behavior. He can also stimulate new ways of thinking and speaking. But the philosophic institutionalist should emulate the good and effective legislator who studies the customs of his land before he draws up new statutes. If the philosopher conceives of his function in this broad and generous way, he will help restore philosophy to its deserved central place in the intellectual world. Not through empty speculation about "being as such," but through a deeper understanding of man gained from a study of his ways of communicating with his fellow men.

5

The Faith of the Theist

It is in the field of religion, rather than philosophy, that man's highest ideals and aspirations have always found their most direct and clearest expression. For a faith to give life meaning and direction, and to sustain them in time of need, men and women in every age have looked to religion and to the church. In man's search today for an answer to the age-old question concerning the meaning of human life, a question made increasingly urgent by the present crisis in our civilization, a renewed interest in the traditional Christian faith is again apparent. For this reason among others, the relation between philosophy and religion in general, and of philosophy to faith in particular, is a matter of increasing importance and concern. The selections in the present section undertake to explore with some care the faith of the Theist in the light of problems raised in preceding selections.

It is essential, of course, for our purposes that this discussion of religious faith be carried on by men of recognized intellectual stature as well as unquestioned sincerity and religious insight. The readings are selected from the writing of men who rank among the ablest thinkers of the past and present, men whose influence has been felt in the field of philosophy as well as religion.

Faith and Philosophy: Étienne Gilson

Among contemporary religious leaders writing in the field of philosophy, there are few as outstanding as Étienne Gilson, distinguished medieval scholar who was the founder and for many years director of the Institute of Medieval Studies at the University of Toronto. Gilson was born in Paris in 1884 and was educated at the Sorbonne, receiving his doctorate there in 1913 with a dissertation on Descartes. During World War I he spent three years in a German prison where he devoted his time largely to the study of St. Bonaventure and the Russian language. In 1919 he became a member of the faculty at the University of Strasbourg and in 1921 professor of the History of Philosophy at the Sorbonne. During the next ten years he achieved world-wide acclaim as the most distinguished medieval scholar of our day. In 1929 Gilson established the Institute of Medieval Studies at Toronto; shortly thereafter (1932) he inaugurated the first chair of the History of Medieval Philosophy at the College of France in Paris. Fifteen years later he was received into that small but august body, the French Academy, thus at sixty-three taking his place among the French immortals.

His Gifford Lectures at Aberdeen in 1932, on the *Spirit of Medieval Philosophy,* established Gilson's reputation in the English-speaking world. The *Unity of Philosophical Experience* (in 1937), *Reason and Revelation in the Middle Ages* (1938), and *Christianity and Philosophy* (1939) are also important philosophical works. No contemporary thinker is better acquainted with the traditional Christian philosophy; among some thirty-five books, written by Gilson over a period of fifty years, there are several studies of St. Thomas Aquinas, several also of St. Augustine, a volume on the philosophy of St. Bonaventure, two studies of Descartes, a book on the mysticism of Saint Bernard, one on Dante the philosopher, and one on Duns Scotus. Commenting upon the work of Professor Gilson, one of his younger colleagues at Toronto writes: "Gilson the scholar has come to stand for three things in the contemporary world: a humble and tenacious pursuit of truth, a zealous and ever fierce defense of intellectual freedom, and an enormous erudition."[1]

Our initial selection is taken from a series of lectures, entitled *God and Philosophy,* given at Indiana University in 1941. In these lectures Gilson examines the philosophical foundation of the faith of the theist, and also deals at some length with the relation of religious faith to contemporary scientific thought. The point of view that he adopts, known as "the teleological argument for God," is based upon the evidence of purpose found in the ongoing processes of the universe. This is a position directly related to the thought of Thomas Aquinas, accepted by Aquinas from Aristotle, and restated here in interesting and appealing fashion by Gilson.

By way of introduction to *God and Philosophy* Gilson writes: "The following lectures rest on the assumption that truth can be found, even in metaphysics. ... I would like to think that, after reading them, some among my readers will at least understand the meaning of their own words, when they say that the existence of God cannot be demonstrated. The philosopher who has made me clearly realize the implications of this problem is Saint Thomas Aquinas. I am as fond of my own intellectual freedom as any one else, but I want to be free to agree with somebody when I think that what he says is right."[2] The study of medieval philosophy and of the Schoolmen "has wholly convinced me," Gilson continues, "not at all that to philosophize consists in repeating what they said, but rather that no philosophical progress will ever be possible unless we first learn to know what they knew."[3] Philosophy today is in such chaotic condition, such confusion and uncertainty, not because of any lack of philosophical ability among contemporary thinkers, but simply "from the fact that we have lost our way because we have lost the knowl-

---

[1] A. C. Pegis, Ed., *A Gilson Reader,* (Garden City, N.Y., Doubleday & Co., Inc., 1957) p. 7.

[2] *God and Philosophy,* (New Haven, Yale University Press, 1941) pp. xv-xvi (condensed).

[3] *Ibid,* p. xiv.

edge of some fundamental principles which, since they are true, are the only ones on which, today as well as in Plato's day, any philosophical knowledge worthy of the name can possibly be established."[4]

[4] *Ibid*, p. xv.

God and Contemporary Science[*]

I

Quite apart from any philosophical demonstration of the existence of God, there is such a thing as a spontaneous natural theology. A quasi-instinctive tendency, observable in most men, seems to invite them to wonder from time to time if, after all, there is not such an unseen being as the one we call God. The current objection that such a feeling is but a survival in us of primitive myths, or of our own early religious education, is not a very strong one. Primitive myths do not account for the human belief in the existence of the Divinity; obviously, it is the reverse which is true. Early religious education is no sufficient explanation for the questions which sometimes arise in the minds of men concerning the reality or unreality of God. The natural invitations to apply his mind to the problem come to man from quite different sources. These are the very selfsame sources which once gave rise not only to Greek mythology but to all mythologies. God spontaneously offers himself to most of us, more as a confusedly felt presence than as an answer to any problem, when we find ourselves confronted with the vastness of the ocean, the still purity of mountains, or the mysterious life of a midsummer starry sky. Far from being social in essence, these fleeting temptations to think of God usually visit us in our moments of solitude. But there is no more solitary solitude than that of a man in deep sorrow or confronted with the tragic perspective of his own impending end. "One dies alone," Pascal says. That is perhaps the reason why so many men

finally meet God waiting for them on the threshold of death.

What do such feelings prove? Absolutely nothing. They are not proofs but facts, the very facts which give philosophers occasion to ask themselves precise questions concerning the possible existence of God. Just as such personal experiences precede any attempt to prove that there is a God, they survive our failures to prove it. It may even appear to be true that, out of its own nature, the human mind is equally unable both to prove the existence of any God and "to escape its deep-seated instinct to personify its intellectual conceptions." Whether we make it the result of spontaneous judgment of reason, with Thomas Aquinas; or an innate idea, with Descartes; or an intellectual intuition, with Malebranche; or an idea born of the unifying power of human reason, with Kant; or a phantasm of human imagination, with Thomas Henry Huxley, this common notion of God is there as a practically universal fact whose speculative value may well be disputed, but whose existence cannot be denied. The only problem is for us to determine the truth value of this notion.

At first sight, the shortest way to test it seems to judge it from the point of view of scientific knowledge. But the shortest way might not be the safest one. This method rests upon the assumption that nothing can be rationally known unless it be scientifically known, which is far from being an evident proposition. The simple truth may be that while human reason remains one and the same in dealing with different orders of problems, it nevertheless must approach these various orders of problems in as many different ways. Whatever our final answer to the prob-

[*] Étienne Gilson, *God and Philosophy,* New Haven, Yale University Press, 1941. Ch. IV (shortened).

lem of God may be, we all agree that God is not an empirically observable fact. Mystical experience itself is both unspeakable and intransmissible; hence, it cannot become an objective experience. If, speaking in the order of pure natural knowledge, the proposition "God exists" makes any sense at all, it must be for its rational value as a philosophical answer to a metaphysical question.

When a man falls to wondering whether there is such a being as God, he is not conscious of raising a scientific problem, or hoping to give it a scientific solution. Scientific problems are all related to the knowledge of *what* given things actually are. An ideal scientific explanation of the world would be an exhaustive rational explanation of *what* the world actually is; but *why* nature exists is not a scientific problem, because its answer is not susceptible of empirical verification. The notion of God, on the contrary, always appears to us in history as an answer to some existential problem, that is, as the *why* of a certain existence. The Greek gods were constantly invoked in order to account for various "happenings" in the history of men as well as in that of things. A religious interpretation of nature never worries about what things are—that is a problem for scientists—but it is very much concerned with the questions why things happen to be precisely what they are, and why they happen to be at all. The Jewish-Christian God to whom we are introduced by the Bible is there at once posited as the ultimate explanation for the very existence of man, for the present condition of man upon earth, for all the successive events that make up the history of the Jewish people as well as for these momentous events: the Incarnation of Christ and the Redemption of man by Grace. Whatever their ultimate value, these are existential answers to existential questions. As such, they cannot possibly be transposed into terms of science, but only into terms of an existential metaphysics.

II

In 1930, in his Rede Lecture delivered before the University of Cambridge, Sir James Jeans decided to deal with philosophical prob-

lems in the light of contemporary science. The upshot was his most popular book: *The Mysterious Universe*. Now, if the universe of science is mysterious, what is not? We do not need science to tell us that the universe is indeed mysterious. Men have known that since the very beginning of the human race. The true and proper function of science is, on the contrary, to make as much of the universe as possible grow less and less mysterious to us. Science does it, and she does it magnificently. Any sixteen-year-old boy, in any one of our schools, knows more today about the physical structure of the world than Thomas Aquinas, Aristotle, or Plato ever did. He can give rational explanations of phenomena which once appeared to the greatest minds as puzzling mysteries. The universe of science *qua* science exactly consists of that part of the total universe from which, owing to human reason, mysteries have been removed.

How is it, then, that a scientist can feel well founded in calling this universe a "mysterious universe"? Is it because the very progress of science brings him face to face with phenomena that are more and more difficult to observe and whose laws are more and more difficult to formulate? But the unknown is not necessarily a mystery; and science naturally proceeds upon the assumption that it is not, because it is at least knowable, even though we do not yet know it. The true reason why this universe appears to some scientists as mysterious is that, mistaking existential, that is, metaphysical, questions for scientific ones, they ask science to answer them. Naturally, they get no answers. Then they are puzzled, and they say that the universe is mysterious.

The scientific cosmogony of Sir James Jeans himself exhibits an instructive collection of such perplexities. His starting point is the actual existence of innumerable stars "wandering about space" at such enormous distances from one another "that it is an event of almost unimaginable rarity for a star to come anywhere near to another star." Yet, we must "believe" that "some two thousand million years ago, this rare event took place, and that a second star, wandering blindly through space," happened to come so near the sun that it raised a huge tidal wave on its surface. This mountainous wave finally exploded, and its fragments, still "circulating around their parent sun . . . are the planets, great and small, of which our earth is one." These ejected fragments of the sun gradually cooled; "in course of time, we know not how, when, or why, one of these cooling fragments gave birth to life." Hence, the emergence of a stream of life which has culminated in man. In a universe where empty space is deadly cold and most of the matter deadly hot, the emergence of life was highly improbable. Nevertheless, "into such a universe we have stumbled, if not exactly by mistake, at least as the result of what may properly be described as an accident." Such is, Sir James Jeans concludes, "the surprising manner in which, so far as science can at present inform us, we came into being."

That all this is very mysterious everybody will agree, but the question then arises: Is this science? Even if we take them, as their author evidently does, for so many "provisional hypotheses," can we consider such hypotheses as being, in any sense of the word, scientific? Is it scientific to explain the existence of man by a series of accidents, each of which is more improbable than the other one? The truth of the case simply is that on the problem of the existence of man modern astronomy has strictly nothing to say. And the same conclusion holds good if, to modern astronomy, we add modern physics. When, after describing the physical world of Einstein, Heisenberg, Dirac, Lemaître, and Louis de Broglie, he at last takes a dive into what, this time at least, he knows to be "the deep waters" of metaphysics, what conclusion does Sir James Jeans ultimately reach? That although many scientists prefer the notion of a "cyclic universe, the more orthodox scientific view" is that this universe owes its present form to a "creation" and that "its creation must have been an act of thought." Granted. But what have these answers to do with Einstein, Heisenberg, and the justly famous galaxy of modern physicists? "Modern scientific theory," Jeans adds, "compels us to think of

the creator as working outside time and space, which are part of his creation, just as the artist is outside his canvas." Why should modern theory compel us to say what has already been said, not only by Saint Augustine, whom our scientist quotes, but by any and every one of countless Christian theologians who knew no other world than that of Ptolemy? Clearly enough, the philosophical answer of Sir James Jeans to the problem of the world order has absolutely nothing to do with modern science. And no wonder, since it has absolutely nothing to do with any scientific knowledge at all.

If we consider it more closely, the initial question asked by Jeans had taken him at once not only into deep waters but, scientifically speaking, out of soundings. To ask the question why, out of an infinity of possible combinations of physico-chemical elements, there has arisen the living and thinking being we call man is to seek the cause why such a complex of physical energies as man actually is, or exists. In other words, it is to inquire into the possible causes for the *existence* of living and thinking organisms upon earth. The hypothesis that living substances may tomorrow be produced by biochemists in their laboratories is irrelevant to the question. If a chemist ever succeeds in turning out living cells, or some elementary sorts of organisms, nothing will be easier for him than to say why such organisms exist. His answer will be: I made them. Our own question is not at all: Are living and thinking beings made up of nothing else than physical elements? It rather is: Supposing they ultimately consist of nothing else, how can we account for the *existence* of the very order of molecules which produces what we call life, and thought?

Scientifically speaking, such problems do not make sense. If there were no living and thinking beings, there would be no science. Hence there would be no questions. Even the scientific universe of inorganic matter is a structural universe; as to the world of organic matter, it everywhere exhibits coördination, adaptation, functions. When asked why there are such organized beings, scientists answer: Chance. Now anybody may fluke a brilliant stroke at billiards; but when a billiard player makes a run of a hundred, to say that he fluked it is to offer a rather weak explanation. Some scientists know this so well that they substitute for the notion of chance the notion of mechanical laws, which is its very reverse. But when they come to explaining how these mechanical laws have given rise to living organized beings, they are driven back to chance as to the last reason it is possible to quote. In other words, the only scientific reasons why our billiard player makes a run of a hundred are that he cannot play billiards and that all the chances are against it.

III

If scientists, speaking as scientists, have no intelligible answer to this problem, why are some of them so keen on talking nonsense about it? The reason is simple, and this time we can be sure that chance has nothing to do with their obstinacy. They prefer to say anything rather than to ascribe existence to God on the ground that a purpose exists in the universe. Now there is some justification for their attitude. Just as science can play havoc with metaphysics, metaphysics can play havoc with science. Coming before science in the past, it has often done so to the point of preventing its rise and of blocking its development. For centuries final causes have been mistaken for scientific explanations by so many generations of philosophers that today many scientists still consider the fear of final causes as the beginning of scientific wisdom. Science is thus making metaphysics suffer for its centuries-long meddling in matters of physics and biology.

In both cases, however, the real victim of this epistemological strife is one and the same: the human mind. Nobody denies that living organisms appear as though they had been designed, or intended, to fulfill the various functions related to life. Everybody agrees that this appearance may be but an illusion. We would be bound to hold it for an illusion if science could account for the rise of life by its usual explanations of mechanical type,

where nothing more is involved than the relations of observable phenomena according to the geometrical properties of space and the physical laws of motion. What is most remarkable, on the contrary, is that many scientists obstinately maintain the illusory character of this appearance though they freely acknowledge their failure to imagine any scientific explanation for the organic constitution of living beings. As soon as modern physics had reached the structural problems raised by molecular physics, it found itself confronted with such difficulties. Yet scientists much preferred to introduce into physics the nonmechanical notions of discontinuity and indeterminacy rather than resort to anything like design.

By accepting design, or purposiveness, as a possible principle of explanation, a scientist would introduce into his system of laws a ring wholly heterogeneous with the rest of the chain. He would intertwine the metaphysical causes for the existence of organisms with the physical causes which he must assign to both their structure and their functioning. Still worse, he might feel tempted to mistake the existential causes of living organisms for their efficient and physical causes, thus coming back to the good old times when fishes had fins because they had been made to swim. Now it may well be true that fishes have been made to swim, but when we know it we know just as much about fishes as we know about airplanes when we know that they are made to fly. If they had not been made to fly, there would be no airplanes, since to be flying-machines is their very definition; but it takes us at least two sciences, aerodynamics and mechanics, in order to know how they do fly. A final cause has posited an existence whose science alone can posit the laws.

If the only intelligible way to explain the existence of organized bodies is to admit that there is design, purposiveness, at their origin, then let us admit it, if not as scientists, at least as metaphysicians. And since the notions of design and of purpose are for us inseparable from the notion of thought, to posit the existence of a thought as cause of the purposiveness of organized bodies is also to posit an end of all ends, or an ultimate end, that is, God.

It goes without saying that this is the very consequence which the adversaries of final causes intend to deny. "Purpose," Julian Huxley says, "is a psychological term; and to ascribe purpose to a process merely because its results are somewhat similar to those of a true purposeful process is completely unjustified, and a mere projection of our own ideas into the economy of nature." This is most certainly what we do, but why should we not do so? We do not need to *project* our own ideas into the economy of nature; they belong there in their own right. Our own ideas are in the economy of nature because we ourselves are in it. Any and every one of the things which a man does intelligently is done with a purpose and to a certain end which is the final cause why he does it. Whatever a worker, an engineer, an industrialist, a writer, or an artist makes is but the actualization, by intelligently selected means, of a certain end. There is no known example of a self-made machine spontaneously arising in virtue of the mechanical laws of matter. Through man, who is part and parcel of nature, purposiveness most certainly is part and parcel of nature. In what sense then is it arbitrary, knowing from within that where there is organization there always is a purpose, to conclude that there is a purpose wherever there is organization? I fully understand a scientist who turns down such an inference as wholly non-scientific. I also understand a scientist who tells me that, as a scientist, he has no business to draw any inference as to the possible cause why organized bodies actually exist. But I wholly fail to see in what sense my inference, if I choose to draw it, is "a common fallacy."

Why should there be a fallacy in inferring that there is purpose in the universe on the ground of biological progress? Because, Julian Huxley answers, this "can be shown to be as natural and inevitable a product of the struggle for existence as is adaptation, and to be no more mysterious than, for instance, the increase in effectiveness both of armour-piercing projectile and armour-plate during the last century." Does Julian Huxley suggest that steel plates have spontaneously grown thicker as shells were growing heavier during the last century? In other words, does he maintain that purposiveness is as wholly absent from human industry as it is from the rest of the world? Or does he perhaps maintain that the rest of the world is as full of purposiveness as human industry obviously is? In the name of science he maintains both, namely, that adaptations in organisms are no more mysterious where there is no purposiveness to account for them, than is adaptation in human industry where purposiveness everywhere accounts for it. That adaptations due to a purpose*less* struggle for life are no more mysterious than adaptations due to a purpose*ful* struggle—whether this proposition is "a common fallacy," I do not know, but it certainly seems to be a fallacy. It is the fallacy of a scientist who, because he does not know how to face metaphysical problems, obstinately refuses their correct metaphysical answers.

IV

A world which has lost the Christian God cannot but resemble a world which had not yet found him. Just like the world of Thales and of Plato, our own modern world is "full of gods." There are blind Evolution, clearsighted Orthogenesis, benevolent Progress, and others which it is more advisable not to mention by name. Why unnecessarily hurt the feelings of men who, today, render them a cult? It is however important for us to realize that mankind is doomed to live more and more under the spell of a new scientific, social, and political mythology, unless we resolutely exorcise these befuddled notions whose influence on modern life is becoming appalling. Millions of men are starving and bleeding to death because two or three of these pseudoscientific or pseudosocial deified abstractions are now at war. For when gods fight among themselves, men have to die. Could we not make an effort to realize that evolution is to be largely what we will make it to be? That Progress is not an automatically self-achieving law but something to be patiently achieved by the will of men? That

Equality is not an actually given fact but an ideal to be progressively approached by means of justice? That Democracy is not the leading goddess of some societies but a magnificent promise to be fulfilled by all through their obstinate will for friendship, if they are strong enough to make it last for generations after generations?

I think we could, but a good deal of clear thinking should come first, and this is where, in spite of its proverbial helplessness, philosophy might be of some help. The trouble with so many of our contemporaries is not that they are agnostics but rather that they are misguided theologians. Real agnostics are exceedingly rare, and they harm nobody but themselves. Just as they have no God, these have no gods. Much more common, unfortunately, are those pseudo-agnostics who, because they combine scientific knowledge and social generosity with a complete lack of philosophical culture, substitute dangerous mythologies for the natural theology which they do not even understand.

The problem of final causes is perhaps the problem most commonly discussed by these modern agnostics. As such, it particularly recommended itself to our attention. It is nevertheless only one among the many aspects of the highest of all metaphysical problems, that of Being. Beyond the question: Why are there organized beings? lies this deeper one: Why is there something rather than nothing? Here again, I fully understand a scientist who refuses to ask it. He is welcome to tell me that the question does not make sense. Scientifically speaking, it does not. Metaphysically speaking, however, it does. Science can account for many things in the world; it may some day account for all that which the world of phenomena actually is. But why anything at all is, or exists, science knows not, precisely because it cannot even ask the question.

To this supreme question, the only conceivable answer is that each and every particular existing thing, depends for its existence upon a pure Act of existence. In order to be the ultimate answer to all existential prob-

lems, this supreme cause has to be absolute existence. Being absolute, such a cause is self-sufficient; if it creates, its creative act must be free. Since it creates not only being but order, it must be something which at least eminently contains the only principle of order known to us in experience, namely, thought. Now an absolute, self-subsisting, and knowing cause is not an It but a He. In short, the first cause is the One in whom the cause of both nature and history coincide, a philosophical God who can also be the God of a religion.[1]

To go one step further would be to match the mistake of some agnostics with a similar one. The failure of too many metaphysicians to distinguish between philosophy and religion has proved no less harmful to natural theology than have the encroachments of pseudometaphysical science. Metaphysics posits God as a pure Act of existence, but it does not provide us with any concept of His

---

[1] Dr. A. H. Compton is an interesting instance of those many scientists who do not seem to be aware of crossing any border lines when they pass from science to philosophy and from philosophy to religion. To them the "hypothesis God" is just one more of those "working hypotheses" which a scientist provisorily accepts as true in spite of the fact that none of them can be proved. Hence the consequence that "faith in God may be a thoroughly scientific attitude, even though we may be unable to establish the correctness of our belief." (*The Religion of a Scientist*, p. 13.) This is a regrettable confusion of language. It is true that the principle of the conservation of energy and the notion of evolution are hypotheses; but they are *scientific* hypotheses because, according as we accept or reject them, our scientific interpretation of observable facts is bound to become different. The existence or non-existence of God, on the contrary, is a proposition whose negation or affirmation determines no change whatever in the structure of our scientific explanation of the world and is wholly independent of the contents of science as such. Supposing, for instance, there be design in the world, the existence of God cannot be posited as a *scientific* explanation for the presence of design in the world; it is a *metaphysical* one; consequently, God has not to be posited as a *scientific probability* but as a *metaphysical necessity*.

essence. We know that He is; we do not comprehend Him. Simple-minded metaphysicians have unwillingly led agnostics to believe that the God of natural theology was the "watchmaker" of Voltaire, or the "carpenter" of cheap apologetics. First of all, no watch has ever been made by any watchmaker; "watchmakers" as such simply do not exist; watches are made by men who know how to make watches. Similarly, to posit God as the supreme cause of that which is, is to know that He is He who can create, because He is "He who is"; but this tells us still less concerning what absolute existence can be than any piece of carpentry tells us about the man who made it. Being men, we can affirm God only on anthropomorphic grounds, but this does not oblige us to posit Him as an anthropomorphic God. As Saint Thomas Aquinas says:

> The verb *to be* is used in two different ways: in a first one, it signifies the act of existing (*actu essendi*); in the second one it signifies the composition of those propositions which the soul invents by joining a predicate with a subject. Taking *to be* in the first way, we cannot know the "to be" of God (*esse Dei*), no more than we know His essence. We know it in the second way only. For, indeed, we know that the proposition we are forming about God, when we say: God is, is a true proposition, and we know this from His effects.

If such be the God of natural theology, true metaphysics does not culminate in a concept, be it that of Thought, of Good, of One, or of Substance. It does not even culminate in an essence, be it that of Being itself. Its last word is not *ens,* but *esse;* not *being,* but *is.* The ultimate effort of true metaphysics is to posit an Act by an act, that is, to posit by an act of judging the supreme Act of existing whose very essence, because it is to be, passes human understanding. Where a man's metaphysics comes to an end, his religion begins. But the only path which can lead him to the point where the true religion begins must of necessity lead him beyond the contemplation of essences, up to the very mystery of existence. This path is not very hard to find, but few are those who dare follow it to the end. Seduced as they are by the intelligible beauty of science, many men lose all taste for metaphysics and religion. A few others, absorbed in the contemplation of some supreme cause, become aware that metaphysics and religion should ultimately meet, but they cannot tell how or where; hence they separate religion from philosophy, or else they renounce religion for philosophy, if they do not, like Pascal, renounce philosophy for religion. Why should not we keep truth, and keep it whole? It can be done. But only those can do it who realize that He Who is the God of the philosophers is HE WHO IS, the God of Abraham, of Isaac, and of Jacob.

Faith and Reason: St. Augustine

Augustine is a man who cannot be ignored in any adequate account of Western civilization. He lived at that point in history when all the major forces of the ancient world had come together into a cultural amalgam. The Roman Empire was near the end of its existence, and its civilization was destined soon to disintegrate. Greek culture had been consolidated into the life of Rome in the two centuries before the Christian era and in the age of Augustus had reached a high state of development; the Christian tradition with its basic Hebraic foundation by A.D. 350 held a place of influence and prominence in the Empire. This was the world of the mid-fourth century A.D. None of Augustine's contemporaries was more keenly aware than he of the challenge in that situation, nor did anyone produce a more significant and influential response. Augustine's impressive answer to the end of an age is found in his last great work, *The City of God* (A.D. 413–426); his mature life was devoted to interpreting the Christian faith in such fashion as to meet the moral and spiritual need of his day.

Few men in history have exerted so much influence. Augustine gave a definitive stamp to Roman Catholic theology and until the thirteenth century his ideas dominated the thinking of the Catholic Church. Equally significant, the Protestant reformers, Wyclif, Luther, and Calvin, all believed that they were returning to Augustine when they broke with the Catholic Church. As a philosopher, Augustine likewise stimulated the intellectual development of Western civilization and provided insights of enduring significance. In refuting the skeptics of his own day, he anticipated Descartes' famous *Cogito, ergo sum,* asking in the spirit of Descartes: "How can one doubt that he lives and thinks? For if he doubts, he lives and thinks." He discussed the nature of time with an insight and subtlety that reminds one of Immanuel Kant. He stated clearly the essential principle of idealistic philosophy, that since matter is known only through mind, we cannot logically reduce mind to matter. He was the ablest psychologist in the ancient world. His *Confessions* (*c.* A.D. 400) belong to the classics of world literature; his observation and description of human motives and human nature in this work make him an important source for contemporary depth psychology and existential philosophy. Most important of all, perhaps, he reinterpreted the philosophy of Plato in essentially Christian terms and established this as the orthodox Christian philosophy for a thousand years. Mystics followed his example in seeking a vision of God, while countless ordinary men and women found their faith renewed and strengthened by the humility and tenderness of his prayers.

Born in Tagasto, a small town in North Africa just west of Carthage, in A.D. 354, Augustine as a boy lived the normal life of the son of a family of modest circumstances in a small Roman provincial community. His mother, Monica, was a devout Christian and throughout her life worked constantly to bring her son into the Catholic Church. At seventeen as a student in rhetoric in nearby Carthage,

Augustine entered with gusto into all phases of the life of that dissolute city, called by some the cesspool of Africa. Nonetheless, he was soon recognized as one of the promising young men of the day. Even as a youth he was fascinated by Plato, and he did not cease to be a Platonist when he later became a Christian. When only twenty, he embarked upon his career as a teacher, became closely associated with the Platonic *New Academy* in Rome, and gradually worked out the Neo-Platonism that so deeply marked his later Christian thought.

In 384 Augustine moved to Milan where an important new influence came into his life in the person of Saint Ambrose, the great Bishop of Milan. The bishop's sermons deeply moved him, and finally in 386, after a period of intense inner conflict, he decided to become a Christian. In the summer of that year he had the decisive spiritual experience in the gardens of St. Ambrose that enabled him to throw off the pride, ambition, and sensuality that had hitherto prevented his acceptance of Christianity. Shortly after his baptism he returned to Rome with a few close friends and from Rome he went back to North Africa where within a year he was made auxiliary Bishop of Hippo and then succeeded Valenius as bishop. The next thirty-four years, until his death in 430, were years of incredible activity and achievement. Not only did he have heavy responsibilities as an administrator of the diocese, but also he was an indefatigable preacher and letter_writer. At the same time he devoted himself to careful study and exegesis of the Scriptures and wrote voluminously. In some two hundred and thirty treatises he spoke his mind on almost every problem of theology and philosophy. Among the ninety-three of these that he himself judged important, several such as *The Confessions, On The Trinity,* and *The City of God,* stand out as masterpieces in the Christian literature of all ages.

Plato was the most important philosopher to whom Augustine was attracted. Marked similarities in temperament and in attitude can be found between the two, and upon a Platonic basis Augustine built his own Christian philosophy. As his later writing becomes more and more distinctly Christian and theological in its character, his Platonic views are less clearly discernible, but the relationship is, nevertheless, always evident. In his early works, however, one of Augustine's most characteristic habits is to use quotations from the Scriptures to show how the ideas of Plato are expressed in them, and during these years he also did several dialogues in the spirit of Plato that are of particular interest. One of his first Christian writings, *Against the Academics,* is a delightful Platonic dialogue, done while he was in Rome soon after his conversion. Likewise his work *On Free Will,* completed about the time he became Bishop of Hippo (in 396) is largely in dialogue form. Among the more significant of his earlier works, this dialogue contains the clearest and fullest statement of Augustine's Neo-Platonism. His approach to philosophy is the approach through reason, and religious faith itself is for him clearly a position to which reason can and does give solid foundation.

It is not easy to find a suitable brief selection from Augustine. His thought is no longer as contemporary in spirit as that of Plato to whom he was so deeply indebted nor as that of the Stoic philosophers whom he also regarded rather highly. Since for some thousand years, however, he was recognized spokesman for the Christian faith and is still today so significant a figure, there is good reason to examine the philosophical basis upon which his Christian view of the meaning of life rested. The selection included here is Augustine's famous argument for belief in God found in the treatise *On Free Will.* In his later writing Augustine mentions this treatise often and evidently had a high opinion of it, frequently recommending it as a desirable book to be read by other thoughtful Christians. Since it is more philosophical than theological, it is not usually found among his religious works reprinted today.

On the Existence of God*

A dialogue based upon discussions between Augustine and Evodius, a young friend of his who later became bishop of Uzala.

Augustine: You remember the position we adopted at the beginning of our former discussion. We cannot deny that believing and knowing are different things, and that in matters of great importance, pertaining to divinity, we must first believe before we seek to know. Otherwise the words of the prophet would be vain, where he says: "Except ye believe ye shall not understand" (Isa. 7:9 LXX). Our Lord himself, both in his words and by his deeds, exhorted those whom he called to salvation first of all to believe. And no one is fit to find God, who does not first believe what he will afterwards learn to know. Wherefore, in obedience to the precepts of the Lord, let us press on in our inquiry. What we seek at his bidding we shall find, as far as that can be done in this life, and by people such as we are.

Let us discuss these three questions, if you please, and in this order. First, how it is manifest that God exists. Secondly, whether all good things, in so far as they are good, are from him. Lastly, whether free will is to

* From *Augustine: Earlier Writings.* Tr. J. H. S. Burleigh. Published 1953, The Westminster Press. By permission.

be counted among the good things. When these questions have been answered it will, I think, be evident whether free will has been rightly given to man. First, then, to begin with what is most obvious, I ask you: "Do you exist?" Are you perhaps afraid to be deceived by that question? But if you did not exist it would be impossible for you to be deceived.

Evodius: Proceed to your other questions.

Aug.: Since it is manifest that you exist and that you could not know it unless you were living, it is also manifest that you live. You know these two things are absolutely true.

Ev.: I do.

Aug.: Therefore this third fact is likewise manifest, namely, that you have intelligence.

Ev.: Clearly.

Aug.: Of these three things which is most excellent?

Ev.: Intelligence.

Aug.: Why do you think so?

Ev.: To exist, to live and to know are three things. A stone exists but does not live. An animal lives but has not intelligence. But he who has intelligence most certainly both exists and lives. Hence I do not hesitate to judge that that is more excellent, which has all these qualities, than that in which one or both of them is absent. That which lives, thereby exists, but it does not follow that it has also intelligence. That is a life like that of an animal. That which exists does not necessarily have either life or intelligence. Dead bodies must be said to exist but cannot be said to live. Much less can that which has not life have intelligence.

Aug.: We gather, therefore, that of these three things a dead body lacks two, an animal one, and man none.

Ev.: That is true.

Aug.: And of these three things that is most excellent which man has along with the other two, that is intelligence. Having that, it follows that he has both being and life.

Ev.: I am sure of that.

I

Aug.: Now consider carefully, and tell me whether anything can be found which all reasoning beings can see in common, each with his own mind and reason; something which is present for all to see but which is not transformed like food and drink for the use of those for whom it is present; something which remains complete and unchanged, whether they see it or do not see it. Do you perhaps think there is nothing of that kind?

Ev.: Indeed, I see many such, but it will be sufficient to mention one. The science of numbers is there for all reasoning persons, so that all calculators may try to learn it, each with his own reason and intelligence. One can do it easily, another with difficulty, another cannot do it at all. But the science itself remains the same for everybody who can learn it, nor is it converted into something consumed like food by him who learns it. If anyone makes a mistake in numbers, the science itself is not at fault. It remains true and entire. The error of the poor arithmetician is all the greater, the less he knows of the science.

Aug.: Quite right. I see you are not untaught in these matters, and so have quickly found a reply. But suppose someone said that numbers make their impression on our minds not in their own right but rather as images of visible things, springing from our contacts by bodily sense with corporeal objects, what would you reply?

Ev.: I could never agree to that. Even if I did perceive numbers with the bodily senses I could not in the same way perceive their divisions and relations. By referring to these mental operations I show anyone to be wrong in his counting who gives a wrong answer when he adds or subtracts. Moreover, all that I contact with a bodily sense, such as this sky and this earth and whatever I perceive to be in them, I do not know how long it will last. But seven and three make ten not only now but always. In no circumstances have seven and three ever made anything else than ten, and they never will. So I maintain that the unchanging science of numbers is common to me and to every reasoning being.

Aug.: I do not deny that your reply is certainly most true. But you will easily see that numbers are not conveyed to us by our bodily senses if you consider that the value of every number is calculated according to the number of times it contains the number one. For example, twice one is called two; thrice one is called three; ten times one is called ten, and every number receives its name and its value according to the number of times it contains the number one. Whoever thinks with exactitude of unity will certainly discover that it cannot be perceived by the senses. Whatever comes into contact with a bodily sense is proved to be not one but many, for it is corporeal and therefore has innumerable parts. I am not going to speak of parts so minute as to be almost unrealizable; but, however small the object may be, it has at least a right-hand part and a left-hand part, an upper and a lower part, a further and a nearer part, one part at the end and another at the middle. We must admit that these parts exist in any body however small, and accordingly we must agree that no corporeal object is a true and absolute unity. And yet all these parts could not be counted unless we had some notion of unity. When I am seeking unity in the corporeal realm and am at the same time certain that I have not found it, nevertheless I know what I am seeking and failing to find, and I know that I cannot find it, or rather that it does not exist among corporeal things. When I know that no body is a unity, I know what unity is. If I did not know what unity is, I could not count the plurality of parts in a body. However I have come to know unity, I have not learned it from the bodily senses, for by them I can know only corporeal objects, and none of them, as we have proved, is a true unity. Moreover, if we do not perceive unity with any bodily sense, neither do we perceive any number of the kind at any rate which we discern with the intellect.

By many such evidences all disputants to whom God has given ability and who are not clouded by obstinacy, are driven to admit that the science of numbers does not pertain to bodily sense, but stands sure and unchangeable, the common possession of all reasoning beings. Many other things might occur to one that belong to thinkers as their common and, as it were, public property, things which each beholder sees with his own mind and reason, and which abide inviolate and unchangeable. But I am glad that the science of numbers most readily occurred to you when you had to answer my question. For it is not in vain that the holy books conjoin number and wisdom, where it is written, "I turned and [inclined] my heart to know and consider and seek wisdom and number" (Eccl. 7:25).

Now, I ask, what are we to think of wisdom itself? Do you think that individual men have wisdoms of their own? Or is there one wisdom common to all, so that a man is wiser the more he participates in it?

Ev.: I do not yet know what you mean by wisdom. I observe that men judge variously of what deeds or words are wise. Soldiers think they are acting wisely in following their profession. Those who despise military service and give all their care and labour to agriculture think themselves wise. Those who leave all these things aside or reject all such temporal concerns and devote all their zeal to the search for truth, how they can know themselves and God, judge that this is the chief task of wisdom. Those who are unwilling to give themselves to the life of leisure for the purpose of seeking and contemplating truth, but prefer to accept laborious care and duties in the service of their fellows and to take part in justly ruling and governing human affairs, they too think themselves to be wise. Moreover, those who do both of these things, who live partly in the contemplation of truth and partly in laborious duties, which they think they owe to human society, those think they hold the palm of wisdom. I do not mention the sects innumerable, of which there is none which does not put its own members above all others and claim that they alone are wise. Since we are now carrying on this discussion on the understanding that we are not to state what we merely believe but what we clearly understand, I can make no answer to your question, unless in addition to believing I also know by contemplation and reason what wisdom is.

Aug.: Surely you do not suppose that wisdom is anything but the truth in which the chief good is beheld and possessed? All those people whom you have mentioned as following diverse pursuits seek good and shun evil, but they follow different pursuits because they differ as to what they think to be good. Whoever seeks that which ought not to be sought, even though he would not seek it unless it seemed to him to be good, is nevertheless in error. There can be no error when nothing is sought, or when that is sought which ought to be sought. In so far as all men seek the happy life they do not err. But in so far as anyone does not keep to the way that leads to the happy life, even though he professes to desire only to reach happiness, he is in error. Error arises when we follow something which does not lead to that which we wish to reach. The more a man errs in his way of life, the less is he wise, the further he is from the truth in which the chief good is beheld and possessed. Everyone is happy who attains the chief good, which indisputably is the end which we all desire. Just as it is universally agreed that we wish to be happy, it is similarly agreed that we wish to be wise, because no one is happy without wisdom. For no one is happy except by the possession of the chief good which is beheld and possessed in the truth which we call wisdom. Before we are happy the notion of happiness is stamped upon our minds; that is why we know and can say confidently without any hesitation that we want to be happy. Likewise, even before we are wise we have the notion of wisdom stamped upon our minds. For that reason each of us, if asked whether he wants to be wise, will, without any groping in the dark, answer that, of course, he does.

Perhaps we are now agreed as to what wisdom is. You may not be able to express it in words, but if you had no notion in your mind of what it is you would not know that you want to be wise, and that you ought to want to be wise. That, I am sure you will not deny. Suppose, then, that we are agreed as to what wisdom is, please tell me whether you think that wisdom too, like the science of numbers, is common to all reasoning beings. Or, seeing that there are as many minds as there are men, and I cannot observe anything that goes on in your mind, nor you what goes on in mine, do you suppose that there are as many wisdoms as there can be wise men?

Ev.: If the chief good is one for all men, the truth in which it is seen and possessed, that is, wisdom, must be one and common to all.

Aug.: Have you any doubt that the chief good, whatever it may be, is one for all men?

Ev.: I certainly have, because I see that different men rejoice in different things as if they were their chief good.

Aug.: I wish there were no more doubt about the nature of the chief good than there is about the fact that without it, whatever it may be, no one can become happy. But that is a big question and demands a long discourse, so let us suppose that there are just as many "chief goods" as there are different things sought by different people under the impression that they are "chief goods." Surely it does not follow that wisdom is not one and common to all because the good things which men see in it and choose are manifold and diverse? If you think it does, you might as well doubt whether the light of the sun is one

light because there are many diverse things which we see by means of it. Of these each one chooses at will something to enjoy looking at. One man likes to behold a high mountain and rejoices to look at it. Another prefers the plain, another a hollow valley, or green woods, or the wavy expanse of the sea. Some one may like all these or some of them whose united beauty contributes to the pleasure of looking at them. The things which men see by the light of the sun and choose for enjoyment are many and various, but the light is one in which each man sees what he enjoys looking at. So, although there are many diverse good things from among which each may choose what he likes, and seeing and possessing it and enjoying it, may rightly and truly constitute it his own chief good, nevertheless it may be that the light of wisdom in which these things can be seen and possessed is one light common to all wise men.

Ev.: I admit it may be so, and that there is nothing to prevent there being one wisdom common to all, though there are many various chief goods. But I should like to know whether it is so. To admit that something may be is not exactly the same as to admit that it is.

Aug.: Meantime we have established that there is such a thing as wisdom, but we have not yet determined whether it is one and common to all, or whether individual wise men have their particular wisdoms just as they have their particular souls or minds.

Ev.: That is so.

Aug.: We hold it as settled that there is such a thing as wisdom, or at least that there are wise men, and also that all men want to be happy. But where do we see this? For I have no doubt at all that you see this and that it is true. Do you see this truth in such a way that I cannot know it unless you tell me what you think? Or could I see this truth, just as you understand it, even if you did not tell me?

Ev.: I do not doubt that you too could see it even if I did not want you to.

Aug.: Is not one truth which we both see with our different minds common to both of us?

Ev.: Clearly.

Aug.: Again, I believe you do not deny that men should strive after wisdom. You admit that that is true?

Ev.: I have no doubt about that.

Aug.: Here is another truth which is one and common to all who know it, though each one sees it with his own mind and not with mine or yours or any other man's. Can we deny that, since what is seen can be seen in common by all who see it?

Ev.: We cannot deny it.

Aug.: Again, take such propositions as these: Man ought to live justly; the worse ought to be subjected to the better; like is to be compared with like; each man should be given his due. Don't you admit that these statements are absolutely true and stable, to be shared by you and me and all who see them?

Ev.: I agree.

Aug.: The same would be true of these statements: The incorrupt is better than the corrupt, the eternal than the temporal, the inviolable than the violable?

Ev.: Undeniably.

Aug.: Could anyone claim truths of that kind as his own private truths, seeing they are unchangeably present for all to contemplate who have the capacity to contemplate them?

Ev.: No one could claim any one of them as his own, for not only are they true but they are equally common property to all.

Aug.: And again, who denies that the soul ought to be turned from corruption and converted to incorruption, in other words not corruption but incorruption ought to be loved? Who, confessing that that is true, does not also understand that it is unchangeably true and can be understood in common by all minds which have the capacity to understand it?

Ev.: Most true.

Aug.: Will anyone doubt that a life which no adversity can drive from a certain and honourable opinion is better than one which is easily broken and overwhelmed by temporal disadvantages?

Ev.: Who can doubt it?

Aug.: I shall ask no more questions of that kind. It is sufficient that you see as I do that these rules and guiding lights of the virtues, as we may call them, are true and unchangeable, and singly or all together they stand open for the common contemplation of those who have the capacity to behold them, each with his own mind and reason. This you admit is quite certain. But I do ask whether you think these truths belong to wisdom. For I am sure you think that he who has acquired wisdom is wise.

Ev.: I most certainly do.

Aug.: Could the man who lives justly so live unless he saw how to apply the principles of subordinating the inferior to the superior, joining like to like, and giving to each his due?

Ev.: He could not.

Aug.: Would you deny that he who sees this sees wisely?

Ev.: I would not.

Aug.: Does not he who lives prudently choose incorruption and perceive that it is preferable to corruption?

Ev.: Clearly.

Aug.: If he makes what no one doubts is the right choice as to the goal towards which he should direct his mind, can it be denied that he has made a wise choice?

Ev.: I could not deny it.

Aug.: When he directs his mind to what he has wisely chosen, again he does it wisely?

Ev.: Most certainly.

Aug.: And if by no terrors or penalties can he be driven from what he has wisely chosen and towards which he has wsiely directed his mind, again there is no doubt that he acts wisely?

Ev.: There is no doubt.

Aug.: It is therefore abundantly evident that these rules and guiding lights of virtue, as we have called them, belong to wisdom. The more a man uses them in living his life, and the more closely he follows them, the more wisely does he live and act. Everything that is wisely done cannot rightly be said to be done apart from wisdom.

Ev.: That is perfectly true.

Aug.: Just as the rules of numbers are true and unchangeable, and the science of numbers is unchangeably available for all who can learn it, and is common to them all, so the rules of wisdom are true and unchangeable. When you were asked about them one by one you replied that they were true and evident and open to the common contemplation of all who have the capacity to examine them.

Ev.: I cannot doubt it. But I should very much like to know whether wisdom and numbers are contained within one class of things. You mentioned that they were linked together in the Holy Scriptures. Or is one of them derived from the other or contained within the other? For example, is number derived from wisdom or is it contained in wisdom? I should not dare to suggest that wisdom is derived from number or is contained in it. For I know many arithmeticians or accountants, or whatever they are to be called, who count perfectly and indeed marvellously, but somehow very few of them have wisdom, perhaps none. So wisdom strikes me as being far more worthy of respect than arithmetic.

Aug.: You mention a matter which has often made me wonder, too. When I consider in my mind the unchangeable science of numbers and the recondite sanctuary or region, or whatever other name we are to give to the realm and abode of numbers, I find myself far removed from the corporeal sphere. I find possibly some vague idea but no words adequate to express it, and so in order to say something I return wearily to these numbers which are set before our eyes and call them by their wonted names. The same thing happens when I am thinking as carefully and intently as I can about wisdom. And so I greatly marvel that though wisdom and number are alike in being mysteriously and certainly true, and are linked together by the testimony of Scripture which I have quoted, I say I marvel greatly that number is so contemptible to the majority of men, while wisdom is precious. To be sure it may be because they are one and the same thing. On the other hand it is also written in Scripture of Wisdom that "she reaches from one end of the world to the other with full strength and ordereth things graciously" (Wisdom 8:I). Perhaps it is called number from its potency to reach with strength from end to end, and is properly called wisdom because it graciously ordereth all things. For both are functions of wisdom alone.

II

Aug.: Though it cannot be made crystal-clear to us whether number is part of wisdom or is derived from wisdom or vice versa, or whether both names can be shown to designate one thing, it is at least evident that both are true and unchangeably true.

Accordingly, you will never deny that there is an unchangeable truth which contains everything that is unchangeably true. You will never be able to say that it belongs particularly to you or to me or to any man, for it is available and offers itself to be shared by all who discern things immutably true, as if it were some strange mysterious and yet public light. Who would say that what is available to be shared by all reasoning and intelligent persons can be the private property of any of them? You remember, I dare say, our recent discussion about the bodily senses. Those things with which we both make contact by means of our eyes or ears, colours and sounds which you and I see or hear together, do not belong to our actual eyes or ears, but are common to both of us so that we may alike perceive them. So you would never say that those things which you and I behold in common, each with his own mind, belong to the actual mind of either of us. You would not say that what the eyes of two persons see belongs to the eyes of one or the other of them. It is a third thing towards which both direct their regard.

Ev.: That is most clear and true.

Aug.: Do you, then, think that this truth of which we have already spoken so much and in which we behold so many things, is more excellent than our minds, or equal to our minds, or inferior? If it were inferior we should not use it as a standard of judgment, but should rather pass judgment on it, as we do on bodies which are inferior to our minds. For of them we often say not only that it *is* so or is not so, but that it *ought to be* so or not so. Similarly with our minds we know not only that it *is* thus or thus, but often also that it *ought to be* thus or thus. We judge of bodies when we say this is not so white as it ought to be, or not so square, and so on. Of minds we say this one is not so capable as it ought to be, or it is not gentle enough or eager enough, according to our moral standard. All these judgments we make according to those inward rules of truth, which we discern in common. But no man passes any judgment on these rules. One may say the eternal *is* superior to the temporal, or seven and three *are* ten, but no one says these things *ought to be* so. Knowing simply that they are so one does not examine them with a view to their correction but rejoices to have discovered them. If, then, truth were the equal of our minds, it too would be mutable. Our minds sometimes see more sometimes less, and so confess their mutability. But truth abiding steadfast in itself neither advances when we see more, nor falls short when we see less. Abiding whole and uncorrupt it rejoices with its light those who turn to it, and punishes with blindness those who turn from it. We pass judgment on our minds in accordance with truth as our standard, while we cannot in any way pass judgment on truth. For we say of our mind it understands less than it ought, or it understands exactly as it ought; and a mind approaches the proper standard of intelligence as it is brought nearer to unchangeable truth, and becomes able to cleave to it. Hence if truth is neither inferior to nor equal to our mind it must be superior and more excellent.

I promised, if you remember, to show you something superior to the human mind and reason. There it is, truth itself. Embrace it if you can. Enjoy it. Delight in the Lord and he will grant you the petitions of your heart. What do you ask for more than to be happy? And what is more happy than to enjoy unshakable, unchangeable truth which is excellent above all things? Men exclaim that they are happy when with throats parched with heat they find a fountain flowing with pure water, or being hungry, find a copious meal all ready prepared, and shall we deny that we are happy when truth is our meat and drink? We are wont to hear the voices of people proclaiming that they are happy if they lie among roses or other flowers and enjoy scented ointments, and shall we hesitate to call ourselves happy when we are inspired by truth? Many place happiness in music, vocal and instrumental, flutes and strings. When they are without music, they consider themselves unhappy; when they have it, they are transported with joy. Shall we, when the harmonious and creative silence of truth steals, so to speak, noiselessly over our minds, seek the happy life elsewhere, and fail to enjoy that which is ours now and securely. Men delight in the sheen of gold and silver, gems and colours. They delight in the brightness, and pleasantness of visible light as it appears in fire or in the sun, moon and stars. When no trouble or want comes to rob them of that pleasure they think themselves happy, and therefore wish to live forever. Shall we fear to place the happy life in the light of truth?

Nay, since the chief good is recognized to be truth and is possessed when truth is possessed, and truth is wisdom, in wisdom let us discern the chief good and possess it and enjoy it. He is happy indeed who enjoys the chief good. Truth points out all the things that are truly good, and intelligent men, according to their capacity, choose one or more of them in order to enjoy them. People, for example, find pleasure in looking at some object which they are glad to behold in the light of the sun. Those among them who are endowed with strong healthy eyes love to look at nothing better than at the sun itself, which sheds its light upon the other things which delight weaker eyes. So a strong and vigorous mental vision may behold many true and changeless things with certain reason, but directs its regard to the truth itself whereby all things are made clear, and, cleaving to the truth and forgetting, as it were, all other things, it enjoys them all together in the truth. Whatever is pleasant in other true things is pleasant also in truth itself.

But no one is secure in the possession of goods which he can lose against his will. Truth and wisdom no one can lose unwillingly. From them there can be no spatial separation. What is called separation from truth and wisdom is a perverse will which loves lower things. No one wills anything involuntarily. Here is something which we can all enjoy equally and in common. Here there is no straitness, no deficiency. She receives all her lovers, being grudging to none, shared by all in common but chaste to each. None says to another: "Stand back that I too may approach," or "Remove your hand that I too may touch." All cleave to the same wisdom. All are brought into contact with it. Nothing is consumed as in the case of food, and you cannot drink so as to prevent me from drinking too. From that common store you can convert nothing into your private possession. What you take remains unharmed for me to take also. I do not have to wait for you to breathe out what you have breathed in that I may then breathe it in. Nothing ever belongs to one man or to any group of men as a private possession. The whole is common to all at one and the same time.

Truth, therefore, is less like the things we touch or taste or smell, and more like the things we hear and see. For every word is heard as a whole by all who hear it and by each one at the same time. And every sight offered to the eyes is exactly the same for all who see it, and is seen by all at the same time. But though there is similarity there is also a great difference. [Truth] does not pass with time or change with locality. It is not interrupted by night or shut off by shadow, and is not subject to the bodily senses. To all who turn to it from the whole world, and love it, it is close at hand, everlasting, bound to no particular spot, never deficient. Externally it suggests, internally it teaches. All who

behold it, it changes for the better, and by none is it changed for the worse. No one judges it, and no one without it judges aright. Hence it is evident beyond a doubt that wisdom is better than our minds, for by it alone they are made individually wise, and are made judges, not of it, but by it of all other things whatever.

You admitted for your part that if I could show you something superior to our minds you would confess that it was God, provided nothing existed that was higher still. I accepted your admission and said it would be sufficient if I demonstrated that. If there is anything more excellent than wisdom, doubtless it, rather, is God. But if there is nothing more excellent, then truth itself is God. Whether there is or is not such a higher thing, you cannot deny that God exists, and this was the question set for our discussion. If you are influenced by what we have received in faith from the holy discipline of Christ, that there is the Father of Wisdom, remember that we also received in faith that there is one equal to the eternal Father, namely Wisdom who is begotten of him. Hence there should be no further question, but we should accept it with unshakable faith. God exists and is the truest and fullest being. This I suppose we hold with undoubting faith. Now we attain it with a certain if tenuous form of knowledge. This is sufficient for the question in hand, so that we can go on to explain other pertinent questions; unless you have any opposition to offer.

Ev.: I accept what you have said with incredible and inexpressible joy, and I declare it to be absolutely certain. I declare it in my mind where I hope to be heard by the truth itself, and where I hope to cleave to truth. For I confess that it is not only good, but the chief good and the beatific good.

The Moral Imperative and Religious Faith: Immanuel Kant

During the seventeenth and eighteenth centuries many thoughtful Christians hoped to derive substantial support for religion from the findings of science. The deists strongly advocated such an approach, and Deism eventually became the dominant point of view among the intellectuals of the Age of Reason. Spinoza, whose insight into the implications of modern science probably surpassed that of any of his contemporaries, went so far as to interpret religion almost wholly in scientific terms, and in doing so felt that he had provided for religion a sound rational foundation. Most of those who attacked the pantheism of Spinoza, or the views of the deists, reflected only the conventional religious outlook of their time, but there was one philosopher at least whose basic disagreement with Spinoza drew its inspiration from an original and much more significant insight into the nature of religion. This was Immanuel Kant (1724–1804).

Small, quiet, and unassuming, no one would have chosen Immanuel Kant as the author of a revolution in philosophical thought. Yet from his ideas there came a new point of view that for more than a hundred years shaped the development of modern philosophy in Germany, in England, and in the United States. Even today there are those who find in his philosophy insights into the nature of scientific thought more penetrating than any elsewhere available. Born in Königsberg, a city in East Prussia, in 1724, Kant spent almost all his long life in this city and died there in 1804. His father was a poor saddlemaker, and young Immanuel was the fourth of nine children. Both Kant's parents were deeply religious, being members of a German Pietest congregation much like the Puritans of New England in its moral and religious spirit. Although he later reacted against the narrowness and dogmatism of the religion of his youth, Kant never ceased to feel the effect of this early moral and religious instruction.

At sixteen he entered the University of Königsberg, and he was connected with this small undistinguished university for most of his life. He spent several years as a private tutor with families in East Prussia—about the only way in which a poor scholar like himself could earn a living; but he saved his money, continued to read widely in science and philosophy, and returned to the university as soon as he could complete work for his Ph.D. He then remained as a lecturer, giving courses in mathematics, physics, and anthropology as well as in logic, metaphysics, and ethics. His lectures were popular, and his writing soon made him the most distinguished man on the faculty, but the university was so poor that for fifteen years he was not promoted. Finally, at forty-four he was made professor of logic and metaphysics, a post he held until he retired thirty years later.

The things that made a difference in Kant's life were not the external events —these to him were unimportant. The important things were the influences upon his thought, three of which stand out most prominently: (1) his introduction to

Newton and the spirit of modern science when he was still a student at the university; (2) his first reading of Rousseau's *Émile* when he was about forty (the only time that Kant missed his regular afternoon walk, so the story goes, was the day he became so absorbed in reading *Émile* that he completely forgot everything else); and (3) his contact with British empiricism and the philosophy of David Hume, at about this same time, which woke him "from his dogmatic slumber," Kant says, and caused him to modify drastically the rationalistic metaphysics that he had until then accepted without serious question.

Kant's early work, inspired in large part by his reading of Newton, was almost all in the field of science. By the time that he had completed his doctorate he had written essays discussing the age of the earth, the earth's rotation about its axis, and, interestingly enough, the nature of the atom. His most important early achievement, however, was a volume published in 1755, entitled *The General Natural History and Theory of the Heavens*. With surprising imagination and insight, Kant here suggests that all the planets have been or will be inhabited, and proposes a nebular hypothesis to account for their origin which, as developed later by Laplace with greater scientific precision, became for almost two centuries the accepted scientific position. More important than these particular hypotheses is the clear insight into the nature of scientific thought that this volume reveals. Kant stands with Spinoza at the beginning of the modern age, recognizing clearly significant implications of modern science long before these had been spelled out by the psychologist and sociologist as well as the physicist for all to understand. And more uncompromisingly than Spinoza Kant faces the central problem of modern philosophy: how can the thorough-going mechanical view of the universe to which modern science is committed be reconciled with the belief in human freedom and responsibility that is essential for any genuine moral conviction and meaning in life.

The initial, and in many ways the most famous, volume of Kant's philosophy is his *Critique of Pure Reason,* published in 1781 after he had worked on it for eleven years. This book is really a philosophy of science. What he hoped to accomplish, Kant states, is a sort of "Copernican revolution" in the field of philosophy. The old rationalism had run into a blind alley, he felt, and nothing more could be done until philosophy was given a new start in a new direction. Philosophers like Spinoza had assumed too uncritically that human reason in itself gives us valid knowledge about the physical world. Actually, we are not in a position to deal with the world outside us, Kant maintains, until we know how the mind itself works. We must understand ourselves before we can understand the nature of the universe or God. Kant sets out, therefore, to provide a comprehensive analysis (*Critique*) of human reason.

The first reaction to his *Critique of Pure Reason* was a sort of dazed incomprehension. Many felt that Kant had destroyed science, not saved it as he proposed to do. Others said it was a dangerous book; this man doubts everything. Almost everyone complained of Kant's obscurity and his almost incomprehensible terminology—and ever since his book was published, critics have disagreed with each other as to what he meant. Gradually, however, the German universities introduced a study of the *Critique;* soon it became prescribed reading for all students of philosophy, and by the early nineteenth century it was generally recognized that no one could hope to understand philosophy until he had mastered Kant.

Kant's careful study of the methods and findings of modern science convinced him that by its very nature science must treat human behavior, like the behavior of the universe, as completely determined; cause and effect must apply everywhere with equal rigidity. "If it were possible to have so profound an insight into a man's mental character as to know all its motives and likewise all the external occasions that can influence them, we could calculate a man's conduct for the future with as great certainty as a lunar or solar eclipse," Kant writes in discussing the scientific point of view.[1] Science can find no place for God, for human freedom, or for belief in immortality without violating the very principles upon which it is established.

In Kant's opinion, therefore, it is a mistake to try to use science as a foundation for religious faith. Such an attempt can only lead to contradictions or place us in uncertainty; arguments on one side will be, at best, just as inconclusive as those on the other. It is impossible to argue an atheist into believing in God; but neither can you destroy the faith of a deeply religious person by argument based on science. For scientific knowledge deals only with the world of sense experience, Kant maintains. It is a rational interpretation of the nature of the physical universe, not of man's moral or spiritual life. The only sound basis for religious faith is to be found not in science but in man's moral experience, his sense of duty, of obligation to do what he sees to be right. What we can show in Kant's opinion is that religious faith is *morally* necessary. That is, in order to make sense of the moral life, and of the categorical imperative of duty, we *must* believe in God, in freedom, and perhaps in immortality. These beliefs, Kant insists, are matters of faith, not of verifiable knowledge, as religion has always rightly maintained. The proper thing for the churches to do then, is not to marshal rational or scientific argument in support of a belief in God or immortality but rather to deepen a man's moral insight and conviction. Once he becomes fully and inescapably aware of the moral imperative, of duty as a vital part of his own experience, he will find faith in God and in human freedom a rational necessity.

Surprisingly enough it was Rousseau who suggested the approach to moral conviction and religious faith upon which Kant built his own philosophy. No two men seem less alike than Kant and Rousseau—one, careful, meticulous, and respectable, the other brilliant but wayward. In the philosophy of Rousseau, however, Kant found a new appreciation of the worth of ordinary men and women, people like his own parents, and Rousseau's view of religion, as well as his view of human

---

[1] Immanuel Kant, *Critique of Practical Reason,* translated by L. W. Beck, (Chicago, University of Chicago Press, Copyright 1949 by the University of Chicago) p. 204.

nature, made a lasting impression on Kant. Just as he himself was coming to see clearly that religion could not be based upon a scientific philosophy, he found Rousseau pointing to conscience rather than reason or science as the true source and justification of religious faith. When Kant somewhat later came to write his own philosophy of religion, he adopted the views of Rousseau and carried them much further than Rousseau himself was ever able to go.

The *Fundamental Principles of the Metaphysic of Morals* and the *Critique of Practical Reason,* works from which our selections are taken, contain Kant's analysis of moral experience and his new approach to religious faith. Finally in two later books, the *Critique of Judgment* and *Religion Within the Limits of Reason Alone,* Kant completed his study of the human mind with an examination of esthetic and religious experience. It had taken him twenty-five years and five impressive closely-reasoned volumes to state the "critical philosophy" to his own satisfaction but his place among the great philosophers of all time was now secure. When the volume on religion was published in 1793, Kant was sixty-nine. His energy was exhausted, and his life work was done. He did publish a monograph on *Everlasting Peace* the following year, which is still read and contains a remarkable anticipation of the principles upon which the League of Nations was organized, but shortly thereafter he retired from his professorship at Königsberg. Gradually his mind began to fail, and finally as he was approaching eighty, the distinguished old philosopher died as quietly and peacefully as he had lived.

The Nature of Morality*

I

Moral Laws are not Empirical

We may call all philosophy *empirical,* so far as it is based on grounds of experience: on the other hand, that which derives its doctrines from *a priori* principles alone we may call *pure* philosophy. When the latter is merely formal, it is *logic;* if it is restricted to definite objects of the understanding, it is *metaphysic.*

In this way there arises the idea of a twofold metaphysic—a *metaphysic of nature* and a *metaphysic of morals.* Physics will thus have an empirical and also a rational part. It

* Immanuel Kant, *Fundamental Principles of the Metaphysic of Morals,* English trans. by T. K. Abbott (New York, Longmans, Green and Company, Inc., 1909). (Subtitles added).

is the same with Ethics; but here the empirical part might have the special name of *practical anthropology,* the name *morality* being appropriated to the rational part.

As my concern here is with moral philosophy, I limit the question suggested to this: Whether it is not of the utmost necessity to construct a pure moral philosophy, perfectly cleared of everything which is only empirical, and which belongs to anthropology? For that such a philosophy must be possible is evident from the common idea of duty and of the moral laws. Everyone must admit that if a law is to have moral force, i.e., to be the basis of an obligation, it must carry with it absolute necessity; that, for example, the precept, "Thou shalt not lie," is not valid for men alone, as if other rational beings had no need to observe it; and so with all the other moral laws properly so called; that, therefore, the basis of obligation must not be sought in the nature of man, or in the circumstances in the world in which he is placed, but *a priori* simply in the conceptions of pure reason; and although any other precept which is founded on principles of mere experience may be in certain respects universal, yet in as far as it rests even in the least degree on an empirical basis, perhaps only as to a motive, such a precept, while it may be a practical rule, can never be called a moral law.

A Good Will the Only Thing Good in Itself

Nothing can posssibly be conceived in the world, or even out of it, which can be called good without qualification, except a Good Will. Intelligence, wit, judgment, and the other talents of the mind, however they may be named, or courage, resolution, perseverance, as qualities of temperament, are undoubtedly good and desirable in many respects; but these gifts of nature may also become extremely bad and mischievous if the will which is to make use of them and which, therefore, constitutes what is called *character,* is not good. It is the same with the *gifts of fortune.* Power, riches, honour, even health, and the general well-being and contentment with one's condition which is called happiness, inspire pride, and often presumption, if there is not a good will to correct the influence of these on the mind, and with this also to rectify the whole principle of acting, and adapt it to its end. The sight of a being who is not adorned with a single feature of a pure and good will, enjoying unbroken prosperity, can never give pleasure to an impartial rational spectator. Thus a good will appears to constitute the indispensable condition even of being worthy of happiness.

There are even some qualities which are of service to this good will itself, and may facilitate its action, yet which have no intrinsic unconditional value, but always presuppose a good will, and this qualifies the esteem that we justly have for them, and does not permit us to regard them as absolutely good. Moderation in the affections and passions, self-control, and calm deliberation are not only good in many respects, but even seem to constitute part of the intrinsic worth of the person; but they are far from deserving to be called good without qualification, although they have been so unconditionally praised by the ancients. For without the principles of a good will they may become extremely bad; and the coolness of a villain not only makes him far more dangerous, but also directly makes him more abominable in our eyes than he would have been without it.

A good will is good not because of what it performs or effects, not by its aptness for the attainment of some proposed end, but simply by virtue of the volition, that is, it is good in itself, and considered by itself is to be esteemed much higher than all that can be brought about by it in favour of any inclination, nay, even of the sum total of all inclinations. Even if it should happen that, owing to special disfavour of fortune, or the niggardly provision of a step-motherly nature, this will should wholly lack power to accomplish its purpose, if with its greatest efforts it should yet achieve nothing, and there should remain only the good will (not, to be sure, a mere wish, but the summoning of all means in our power), then, like a jewel, it would still shine by its own light, as a thing which has its whole value in itself. Its usefulness or fruitlessness can neither add to nor take away anything from this value. It would be, as it were, only the setting to enable us to handle it the more conveniently in common commerce, or to attract to it the attention of those who are not yet connoissuers, but not to recommend it to true connoisseurs, or to determine its value.

There is, however, something so strange in this idea of the absolute value of the mere will, in which no account is taken of its utility, that notwithstanding the thorough assent of even common reason to the idea, yet a suspicion must arise that it may perhaps really be the product of mere high-flown fancy, and that we may have misunderstood the purpose of nature in assigning reason as the governor of our will. Therefore we will examine this idea from this point of view.

In the physical constitution of an organized being, that is, a being adapted suitably to the purposes of life, we assume it as a fundamental principle that no organ for any purpose will be found but what is also the fittest and best adapted for that purpose. Now in a being which has reason and a will, if the proper object of nature were its conservation, its welfare, in a word, its happiness, then nature would have hit upon a very bad arrangement in selecting the reason of the creature to carry out this purpose. For all the actions which the creature has to perform with a view to this purpose, and the whole rule of its conduct, would be far more surely prescribed to it by instinct, and that end would have been attained thereby much more certainly than it ever can be by reason. Should reason have been communicated to this favoured creature over and above, it must only have served it to contemplate the happy constitution of its nature, to admire it, to congratulate itself thereon, and to feel thankful for it to the beneficent cause, but not that it should subject its desires to that weak and delusive guidance, and meddle bunglingly with the purpose of nature. In a word, nature would have taken care that reason should not break forth into practical exercise, nor have the presumption, with its weak insight, to think out for itself the plan of happiness, and of the means of attaining it. Nature would not only have taken on herself the choice of the ends, but also of the means, and with wise foresight would have entrusted both to instinct.

And, in fact, we find that the more a cultivated reason applies itself with deliberate purpose to the enjoyment of life and happiness, so much the more does the man fail of true satisfaction. And from this circumstance there arises in many, if they are candid enough to confess it, a certain degree of misology, that is, hatred of reason, especially in the case of those who are most experienced in the use of it, because after calculating all the advantages they derive, I do not say from the invention of all the arts of common lux-ury, but even from the sciences (which seem to them to be after all only a luxury of the understanding), they find that they have, in fact, only brought more trouble on their shoulders, rather than gained in happiness; and they end up envying, rather than despising, the more common stamp of men who keep closer to the guidance of mere instinct, and do not allow their reason much influence on their conduct. And this we must admit, that the judgment of those who would very much lower the lofty eulogies of the advantages which reason gives us in regard to the happiness and satisfaction of life, or who would even reduce them below zero, is by no means morose or ungrateful to the goodness with which the world is governed, but that there lies at the root of these judgments the idea that our existence has a different and far nobler end, for which, and not for happiness, reason is properly intended, and which must, therefore, be regarded as the supreme condition to which the private ends of man must, for the most part, be postponed.

For as reason is not competent to guide the will with certainty in regard to its objects and the satisfaction of all our wants (which it to some extent even multiplies), this being an end to which an implanted instinct would have led with much greater certainty; and since, nevertheless, reason is imparted to us as a practical faculty, i.e., as one which is to have influence on the will, therefore, admitting that nature generally in the distribution of her capacities has adapted the means to the end, its true destination must be to produce a will, not merely good as a means to something else, but good in itself, for which reason was absolutely necessary. This will then, though not indeed the sole and complete good, must be the supreme good and the condition of every other, even of the desire of happiness. Under these circumstances, there is nothing inconsistent with the wisdom of nature in the fact that the cultivation of the reason, which is requisite for the first and unconditional purpose, does in many ways interfere, at least in this life, with the attainment of the second, which is always conditional, namely, happiness. Nay, it may even reduce it to nothing, without nature thereby failing of her purpose. For reason recognizes the establishment of a good will as its highest practical destination, and in attaining this purpose is capable only of a satisfaction of its own proper kind, namely, that from the attainment of an end, which end again is determined by reason only, notwithstanding that this may involve many a disappointment to the ends of inclination.

Duty the Only Motive of Moral Worth

We have then to develop the notion of a will which deserves to be highly esteemed for itself, and is good without a view to anything further, a notion which exists already in the sound natural understanding, requiring rather to be cleared up than to be taught, and which in estimating the value of our actions always takes the first place, and constitutes the condition of all the rest. In order to do this, we will take the notion of duty, which includes that of a good will, although implying certain subjective restrictions and hindrances. These, however, far from concealing it, or rendering it unrecognizable, rather bring it out by contrast, and make it shine forth so much the brighter.

I omit here all actions which are already recognized as inconsistent with duty, although they may be useful for this or that purpose, for with these the question whether they are done from duty cannot arise at all, since they even conflict with it. It is much harder to make this distinction when the action accords with duty, and the subject has besides a direct inclination to it. For example, it is always a matter of duty that a dealer should not overcharge an inexperienced purchaser; and wherever there is much commerce the prudent tradesman does not overcharge, but keeps a fixed price for everyone, so that a child buys of him as well as any other. Men are thus honestly served; but this is not enough to make us believe that the tradesman has so acted from duty and from principles of honesty: his own advantage required it; it is out of the question in this case to suppose that he might besides have a direct inclination in favour of the buyers, so that, as it were, from love he should give no advantage to one over another. Accordingly the action was done neither from duty nor from direct inclination, but merely with a selfish view.

On the other hand, it is a duty to maintain one's life; and, in addition, everyone has also a direct inclination to do so. But on this account the often anxious care which most men take for it has no intrinsic worth, and their maxim has no moral import. They preserve their life *as duty requires,* no doubt, but not *because duty requires.* On the other hand, if adversity and hopeless sorrow have completely taken away the relish for life; if the unfortunate one, strong in mind, indignant at his fate rather than desponding or dejected, wishes for death, and yet preserves his life without loving it—not from inclination or fear, but from duty—then his maxim has a moral worth.

It is in this manner, undoubtedly, that we are to understand those passages of Scripture also in which we are commanded to love our neighbor, even our enemy. For love, as an affection, cannot be commanded, but beneficence for duty's sake may; even though we are not impelled to it by any inclination—nay, are even repelled by a natural and unconquerable aversion. This is *practical* love, and not *pathological*—a love which is seated in the will, and not in the propensions of sense—in principles of action and not of tender sympathy; and it is this love alone which can be commanded.

The second[1] proposition is: That an action done from duty derives its moral worth, not from the purpose which is to be attained by it, but from the maxim by which it is determined, and therefore does not depend on the realization of the object of the action, but merely on the principle of volition by which the action has taken place, without regard to any object of desire. It is clear from what precedes that the purposes

---

[1] [The first proposition was that to have moral worth an action must be done from duty. Tr.'s note.]

which we may have in view in our actions, or their effects regarded as ends and springs of the will, cannot give to actions any unconditional or moral worth. In what, then, can their worth lie, if it is not to consist in the will and in reference to its expected effect? It cannot lie anywhere but in the principle of the will without regard to the ends which can be attained by the action. For the will stands between its *a priori* principle, which is formal, and its *a posteriori* spring, which is material, as between two roads, and as it must be determined by something, it follows that it must be determined by the formal principle of volition when an action is done from duty, in which case every material principle has been withdrawn from it.

The third proposition, which is a consequence of the two preceding, I would express thus: Duty is the necessity of acting from respect for the law. I may have inclination for an object as the effect of my proposed action, but I cannot have respect for it, just for this reason, that it is an effect and not an energy of will. Similarly, I cannot have respect for inclination, whether my own or another's; I can at most, if my own, approve it; if another's, sometimes even love it; i.e., look on it as favourable to my own interest. It is only what is connected with my will as a principle, by no means as an effect—what does not subserve my inclination, but overpowers it, or at least in case of choice excludes it from its calculation—in other words, simply the law of itself, which can be an object of respect, and hence a command. Now an action done from duty must wholly exclude the influence of inclination, and with it every object of the will, so that nothing remains which can determine the will except objectively the law, and subjectively pure respect for this practical law, and consequently the maxim that I should follow this law even to the thwarting of all my inclinations.

Thus the moral worth of an action does not lie in the effect expected from it, nor in any principle of action which requires to borrow its motive from this expected effect. For all these effects—agreeableness of one's condition, and even the promotion of the hap-piness of others—could have been also brought about by other causes, so that for this there would have been no need of the will of a rational being; whereas it is in this alone that the supreme and unconditional good can be found. The pre-eminent good which we call moral can therefore consist in nothing else than the conception of law in itself, which certainly is only possible in a rational being, in so far as this conception, and not the expected effect, determines the will. This is a good which is already present in the person who acts accordingly, and we have not to wait for it to appear first in the result.

But what sort of law can that be, the conception of which must determine the will, even without paying any regard to the effect expected from it, in order that this will may be called good absolutely and without qualification? As I have deprived the will of every impulse which could arise to it from obedience to any law, there remains nothing but the universal conformity of its actions to law in general, which alone is to serve the will as a principle, i.e., *I am never to act otherwise than so that I could also will that my maxim should become a universal law.* Here, now, it is the simple conformity to law in general, without assuming any particular law applicable to certain actions, that serves the will as its principle, and must so serve it, if duty is not to be a vain delusion and a chimerical notion. The common reason of men in its practical judgments perfectly coincides with this, and always has in view the principle here suggested. Let the question be, for example: May I when in distress make a promise with the intention not to keep it? I really distinguish here between the two significations which the question may have: Whether it is prudent, or whether it is right, to make a false promise? The former may undoubtedly often be the case. I see clearly indeed that it is not enough to extricate myself from a present difficulty by means of this subterfuge, but it must be well considered whether there may not hereafter spring from this lie much greater inconvenience than that from which I now free myself, and as, with all my supposed cunning, the consequences cannot be so easily foreseen but that credit once lost may be much more injurious to me than any mischief which I seek to avoid at present, it should be considered whether it would not be more prudent to act herein according to a universal maxim, and to make it a habit to promise nothing except with the intention of keeping it. But it is soon clear to me that such a maxim will still only be based on the fear of consequences. Now it is a wholly different thing to be truthful from duty, and to be so from apprehension of injurious consequences. In the first case, the very notion of the action already implies a law for me; in the second case, I must first look about elsewhere to see what results may be combined with it which would affect myself. For to deviate from the principle of duty is beyond all doubt wicked; but to be unfaithful to my maxim of prudence may often be very advantageous to me, although to abide by it is certainly safer. The shortest way, however, and an unerring one, to discover the answer to this question whether a lying promise is consistent with duty, is to ask myself, Should I be content that my maxim (to extricate myself from difficulty by a false promise) should hold good as a universal law, for myself as well as for others? and should I be able to say to myself, "Every one may make a deceitful promise when he finds himself in a difficulty from which he cannot otherwise extricate himself"? Then I presently become aware that while I can will the lie, I can by no means will that lying should be a universal law. For with such a law there would be no promises at all, since it would be in vain to allege my intention in regard to my future actions to those who would not believe this allegation, or if they overhastily did so, would pay me back in my own coin. Hence, my maxim, as soon as it should be made a univeral law, would necessarily destroy itself.

I do not, therefore, need any far-reaching penetration to discern what I have to do in order that my will may be morally good. Inexperienced in the course of the world, incapable of being prepared for all its contingencies, I only ask myself: Canst thou also will that thy maxim should be a universal law? If not, then it must be rejected, and that not because of a disadvantage accruing from it to myself or even to others, but because it cannot enter as a principle into a possible universal legislation, and reason extorts from me immediate respect for such legislation. I do not indeed as yet discern on what this respect is based (this the philosopher may inquire), but at least I understand this, that it is an estimation of the worth which far outweighs all worth of what is recommended by inclination, and that the necessity of acting from pure respect for the practical law is what constitutes duty, to which every other motive must give place, because it is the condition of a will being good in itself, and the worth of such a will is above everything.

Morality Within the Reach of All Men

Thus, then, without quitting the moral knowledge of common human reason, we have arrived at its principle. And although, no doubt, common men do not conceive it in such an abstract and universal form, yet they always have it really before their eyes, and use it as the standard of their decision. Here it would be easy to show how, with this compass in hand, men are well able to distinguish, in every case that occurs, what is good, what bad, conformably to duty or inconsistent with it, if, without in the least teaching them anything new, we only, like Socrates, direct their attention to the principle they themselves employ; and that, therefore, we do not need science and philosophy to know what we should do to be honest and good, yea, even wise and virtuous. Indeed, we might well have conjectured beforehand that the knowledge of what every man is bound to do, and therefore also to know, would be within the reach of every man, even the commonest. Here we cannot forbear admiration when we see how great an advantage the practical judgment has over the theoretical in the common understanding of men. In the latter, if common reason ventures to depart from the laws of experience, and from the perceptions of the senses, it falls into mere inconceivabilities and self-contradictions, at least into a chaos of uncertainty, obscurity, and instability. But in the practical sphere it is just when the common understanding excludes all sensible springs from practical laws that its power of judgment begins to show itself to advantage. Would it not therefore be wiser in moral concerns to acquiesce in the judgment of common reason, or at most only to call in philosophy for the purpose of rendering the system of morals more complete and intelligible, and its rules more convenient for use (especially for disputation), but not so as to draw off the common understanding from its happy simplicity, or to bring it by means of philosophy into a new path of inquiry and instruction?

II

The Categorical Imperative of Duty

Everything in nature works according to laws. Rational beings alone have the faculty of acting according to the conception of laws, that is according to principles, i.e., have a *will*.

The conception of an objective principle, in so far as it is obligatory for a will, is called a command (of reason), and the formula of the command is called an Imperative.

Now all *imperatives* command either *hypothetically* or *categorically*. The former represent the practical necessity of a possible action as means to something else that is willed (or at least which one might possibly will). The categorical imperative would be that which represented an action as necessary of itself without reference to another end, i.e., as objectively necessary. If now the action is good only as a means to something else, then the imperative is hypothetical; if it is conceived as good in itself and consequently as being necessarily the principle of a will which of itself conforms to reason, then it is categorical.

There is but one categorical imperative, namely, this: *Act only on that maxim*

whereby thou canst at the same time will that it should become a universal law.

Since the universality of the law according to which effects are produced constitutes what is properly called nature in the most general sense (as to form), that is, the existence of things so far as it is determined by general laws, the imperative of duty may be expressed thus: *Act as if the maxim of thy action were to become by thy will a universal law of nature.*

We will now enumerate a few duties, adopting the usual division of them into duties to ourselves and to others, and into perfect and imperfect duties.

1. A man reduced to despair by a series of misfortunes feels wearied of life, but is still so far in possession of his reason that he can ask himself whether it would not be contrary to his duty to himself to take his own life. Now he inquires whether the maxim of his action could become a universal law of nature. His maxim is: From self-love I adopt it as a principle to shorten my life when its longer duration is likely to bring more evil than satisfaction. It is asked then simply whether this principle founded on self-love can become a universal law of nature. Now we see at once that a system of nature of which it should be a law to destroy life by means of the very feeling whose special nature it is to impel to the improvement of life would contradict itself, and therefore could not exist as a system of nature; hence that maxim cannot possibly exist as a universal law of nature, and consequently would be wholly inconsistent with the supreme principle of all duty.

2. Another finds himself forced by necessity to borrow money. He knows that he will not be able to repay it, but sees also that nothing will be lent to him, unless he promises stoutly to repay it in a definite time. He desires to make this promise, but he has still so much conscience as to ask himself: Is it not unlawful and inconsistent with duty to get out of a difficulty in this way? Suppose, however, that he resolves to do so, then the maxim of his action would be expressed thus: When I think myself in want of money, I

will borrow money and promise to repay it, although I know that I never can do so. Now this principle of self-love or of one's own advantage may perhaps be consistent with my whole future welfare; but the question now is, Is it right? I change then the suggestion of self-love into a universal law, and state the question thus: How would it be if my maxim were a universal law? Then I see at once that it could never hold as a universal law of nature, but would necessarily contradict itself. For supposing it to be a universal law that everyone when he thinks himself in a difficulty should be able to promise whatever he pleases, with the purpose of not keeping his promise, the promise itself would become impossible, as well as the end that one might have in it, since no one would consider that anything was promised to him, but would ridicule all such statements as vain pretences.

3. A third finds in himself a talent which with the help of some culture might make him a useful man in many respects. But he finds himself in comfortable circumstances, and prefers to indulge in pleasure rather than to take pains in enlarging and improving his happy natural capacities. He asks, however, whether his maxim of neglect of his natural gifts, besides agreeing with his inclination to indulgence, agrees also with what is called duty. He sees then that a system of nature could indeed subsist with such a universal law although men (like the South Sea islanders) should let their talents rest, and resolve to devote their lives merely to idleness, amusement, and propagation of their species—in a word, to enjoyment; but he cannot possibly will that this should be a universal law of nature, or be implanted in us as such by a natural instinct. For, as a rational being, he necessarily wills that his faculties be developed, since they serve him, and have been given him, for all sorts of possible purposes.

4. A fourth, who is in prosperity, while he sees that others have to contend with wretchedness and that he could help them, thinks: What concern is it of mine? Let everyone be as happy as Heaven pleases, or as he can make himself; I will take nothing from him nor even envy him, only I do not wish to contribute anything to his welfare or to his assistance in distress! Now no doubt if such a mode of thinking were a universal law, the human race might very well subsist, and doubtless even better than in a state in which everyone talks of sympathy and good will, or even takes care occasionally to put it into practice, but, on the other side, also cheats when he can, betrays the rights of men, or otherwise violates them. But although it is possible that a universal law of nature might exist in accordance with that maxim, it is impossible to will that such a principle should have the universal validity of a law of nature. For a will which resolved this would contradict itself, inasmuch as many cases might occur in which one would have need of the love and sympathy of others, and in which, by such a law of nature, sprung from his own will, he would deprive himself of all hope of the aid he desires.

These are a few of the many actual duties, or at least what we regard as such, which obviously fall into two classes on the one principle that we have laid down. We must be able to will that a maxim of our action should be a universal law. This is the canon of the moral appreciation of the action generally. Some actions are of such a character that their maxim cannot without contradiction be ever conceived as a universal law of nature, far from it being possible that we should will that it should be so. In others this intrinsic impossibility is not found, but still it is impossible to will that their maxim should be raised to the universality of a law of nature, since such a will would contradict itself. It is easily seen that the former violate strict or rigorous (inflexible) duty; the latter only laxer (meritorious) duty. Thus it has been completely shown by these examples how all duties depend as regards the nature of the obligation (not the object of the action) on the same principle.

Human Personality an End in Itself

Supposing that there were something whose existence has in itself an absolute worth, something which, being an end in itself, could be a source of definite laws, then in this and this alone would lie the source of a possible categorical imperative, i.e., a practical law.

Now I say: man and generally any rational being exists as an end in himself, not merely as a means to be arbitrarily used by this or that will, but in all his actions, whether they concern himself or other rational beings, must be always regarded at the same time as an end. All objects of the inclinations have only a conditional worth; for if the inclinations and the wants founded on them did not exist, then their object would be without value. But the inclinations themselves being sources of want are so far from having an absolute worth for which they should be desired, that, on the contrary, it must be the universal wish of every rational being to be wholly free from them. Thus the worth of any object which is to be acquired by our action is always conditional. Beings whose existence depends not on our will but on nature's, have nevertheless, if they are rational beings, only a relative value as means, and are therefore called things; rational beings, on the contrary, are called persons, because their very nature points them out as ends in themselves, that is as something which must not be used merely as means, and so far therefore restricts freedom of action (and is an object of respect). These, therefore, are not merely subjective ends whose existence has a worth for us as an effect of our action, but objective ends, that is things whose existence is an end in itself: an end moreover for which no other can be substituted, which they should subserve merely as means, for otherwise nothing whatever would possess absolute worth; but if all worth were conditioned and therefore contingent, then there would be no supreme practical principle of reason whatever.

If then there is a supreme practical principle or, in respect of the human will, a categorical imperative, it must be one which, being drawn from the conception of that which is necessarily an end for everyone because it is an end in itself, constitutes an ob-

jective principle of will, and can therefore serve as a universal practical law. The foundation of this principle is: *rational nature exists as an end in itself.* Man necessarily conceives his own existence as being so: so far then this is a subjective principle of human actions. But every other rational being regards its existence similarly, just on the same rational principle that holds for me: so that it is at the same time an objective principle, from which as a supreme practical law all laws of the will must be capable of being deduced. Accordingly the practical imperative will be as follows: *So act as to treat humanity, whether in thine own person, or in that of any other, in every case as an end withal, never as means only.* We will now inquire whether this can be practically carried out.

To abide by the previous examples:

Firstly, under the head of necessary duty to oneself: He who contemplates suicide should ask himself whether his action can be consistent with the idea of humanity as an end in itself. If he destroys himself in order to escape from painful circumstances, he uses a person merely as a mean to maintain a tolerant condition up to the end of life. But a man is not a thing, that is to say, something which can be used merely as means, but must in all his actions be always considered as an end in himself. I cannot, therefore, dispose in any way of a man in my own person so as to mutilate him, to damage or kill him.

Secondly, as regards necessary duties, or those of strict obligation, towards others; he who is thinking of making a lying promise to others will see at once that he would be using another man merely as a means, without the latter containing at the same time the end in himself. For he whom I propose by such a promise to use for my own purposes cannot possibly assent to my mode of acting towards him, and therefore cannot himself contain the end of this action. This violation of the principle of humanity in other men is more obvious if we take in examples of attacks on the freedom and property of others. For then it is clear that he who transgresses the rights of men intends to use the person of others merely as means, without considering that as rational beings they ought always to be esteemed also as ends, that is, as beings who must be capable of containing in themselves the end of the very same action.

Man Lives in Two Worlds

Duty! Thou sublime and mighty name that does embrace nothing charming or insinuating, but requirest submission, and yet seekest not to move the will by threatening aught that would arouse natural aversion or terror, but merely holdest forth a law which of itself finds entrance into the mind, and yet gains reluctant reverence (though not always obedience), a law before which all inclinations are dumb, even though they secretly counter-work it; what origin is there worthy of thee, and where is to be found the root of thy noble descent which proudly rejects all kindred with the inclinations; a root to be derived from which is the indispensable conditions of the only worth which men can give themselves.

It can be nothing less than a power which elevates man above himself (as a part of the world of sense), a power which connects him with an order of things that only the understanding can conceive, with a world which at the same time commands the whole sensible world, and with it the empirically determinable existence of man in time, as well as the sum-total of all ends (which totality alone suits such unconditional practical laws as the moral). This power is nothing but *personality,* that is, freedom and independence of the mechanism of nature, yet, regarded also as a faculty of a being which is subject to special laws, namely, pure practical laws given by its own reason; so that the person as belonging to the sensible world is subject to his own personality as belonging to the intelligible [supersensible] world. It is, then, not to be wondered at that man, as belonging to both worlds, must regard his own nature in reference to its second and highest characteristic only with reverence, and its laws with the highest respect.

On this origin are founded many expressions which designate the worth of objects according to moral ideas. The moral law is holy (inviolable). Man is indeed unholy enough; but he must regard humanity in his own person as holy. In all creation everything one chooses, and over which one has any power, may be used merely as means; man alone, and with him every rational creature, is an end in himself. By virtue of the autonomy of his freedom he is the subject of the moral law, which is holy. Just for this reason every will, even every person's own individual will, in relation to itself, is restricted to the condition of agreement with the autonomy of the rational being, that is to say, that it is not to be subject to any purpose which cannot accord with a law which might arise from the will of the passive subject himself; the latter is, therefore, never to be employed merely as means, but as itself also concurrently, an end. We justly attribute this condition even to the Divine will, with regard to the rational beings in the world, which are His creatures since it rests on their personality, by which alone they are ends in themselves.

This respect-inspiring idea of personality which sets before our eyes the sublimity of our nature (in its highest aspect), while at the same time it shows us the want of accord of our conduct with it, and thereby strikes down self-conceit, is even natural to the commonest reason, and easily observed. Has not every even moderately honourable man sometimes found that, where by an otherwise inoffensive lie he might either have withdrawn himself from an upleasant business, or even have procured some advantage for a loved and well-deserving friend, he has avoided it solely lest he should despise himself secretly in his own eyes? When an upright man is in the greatest distress, which he might have avoided if he could only have disregarded duty, is he not sustained by the consciousness that he has maintained humanity in its proper dignity in his own person and honoured it, that he has no reason to be ashamed of himself in his own sight, or to dread the inward glance of self-examination?

This consolation is not happiness, it is not even the smallest part of it, for no one would wish to have occasion for it, or would perhaps even desire a life in such circumstances. But he lives, and he cannot endure that he should be in his own eyes unworthy of life. This inward peace is therefore merely negative as regards what can make life pleasant; it is, in fact, only the escaping the danger of sinking in personal worth, after everything else that is valuable has been lost. It is the effect of a respect for something quite different from life, something in comparison and contrast with which life with all its enjoyment has no value. He still lives only because it is his duty, not because he finds anything pleasant in life.

Such is the nature of the true motive of pure practical reason; it is no other than the pure moral law itself, inasmuch as it makes us conscious of the sublimity of our own supersensible existence, and subjectively produces respect for their higher nature in men who are also conscious of their sensible existence and of the consequent dependence of their pathologically very susceptible nature.

Now with this motive may be combined so many charms and satisfactions of life, that even on this account alone the most prudent choice of a rational Epicurean reflecting on the greatest advantage of life would declare itself on the side of moral conduct, and it may even be advisable to join this prospect of a cheerful enjoyment of life with that supreme motive which is already sufficient in itself; but only as a counterpoise to the attractions which vice does not fail to exhibit on the opposite side, and not so as, even in the smallest degree, to place in this the proper moving power when duty is in question. For that would be just the same as to wish to taint the purity of the moral disposition in its source. The majesty of duty has nothing to do with enjoyment of life; it has its special law and its special tribunal, and though the two should be never so well shaken together to be given well mixed, like medicine, to the sick soul, yet they will soon separate of themselves; and if they do not, the former will not act; and although physical life might gain somewhat in force, the moral life would fade away irrecoverably.

Moral Conviction and Religious Faith*

The Problem of Human Freedom

The will is a kind of causality, belonging to living beings in so far as they are rational, and freedom would be this property of such causality that it can be efficient, independent of foreign causes determining it; just as physical necessity is the property that the causality of all irrational beings has of being determined to activity by the influence of foreign causes.

The preceding definition of freedom is negative, and therefore unfruitful for the discovery of its essence; but it leads to a positive

* Immanuel Kant, *Fundamental Principles of the Metaphysic of Morals,* Part III, and *Critique of Practical Reason,* trans. by T. K. Abbott (New York, Longmans, Green and Company, Inc., 1909). (Subtitles added.)

conception which is so much the more full and fruitful. Since the conception of causality involves that of laws, according to which, by something that we call cause, something else, namely, the effect, must be produced; hence, although freedom is not a property of the will depending on physical laws, yet it is not for that reason lawless; on the contrary, it must be a causality acting accordingly to immutable laws, but of a peculiar kind; otherwise a free will would be an absurdity. What else then can freedom of the will be but autonomy, that is the property of the will to be a law to itself? But the proposition: The will is in every action a law to itself, only expresses the principle, to act on no other maxim than that which can also have as an object itself as a universal law. Now this is precisely the formula of the categorical imperative and is the principle of morality, so that a free will and a will subject to moral laws are one and the same.

It is not enough to predicate freedom of our own will, from whatever reason, if we have not sufficient grounds for predicating the same of all rational beings. For as morality serves as a law for us only because we are rational beings, it must also hold for all rational beings; and as it must be deduced simply from the property of freedom, it must be shown that freedom also is a property of all rational beings. It is not enough, then, to prove it from certain supposed experiences of human nature (which indeed is quite impossible, and it can only be shown *a priori*), but we must show that it belongs to the activity of all rational beings endowed with a will. Now I say every being that cannot act except under the idea of freedom is just for that reason in a practical point of view really free, that is to say, all laws which are inseparably connected with freedom have the same force for him as if his will had been shown to be free in itself by a proof theoretically conclusive. Now I affirm that we must attribute to every rational being which has a will that it has also the idea of freedom and acts entirely under this idea. For in such a being we conceive a reason that is practical, that is, has causality in reference to its objects. Now we cannot possibly conceive a reason consciously receiving a bias from any other quarter with respect to its judgments, for then the subject would ascribe the determination of its judgment not to its own reason, but to an impulse. It must regard itself as the author of its principles independent of foreign influences. Consequently as practical reason or as the will of a rational being it must regard itself as free, that is to say, the will of such a being cannot be a will of its own except under the idea of freedom. This idea must therefore in a practical point of view be ascribed to every rational being.

Every rational being reckons himself *qua* intelligence as belonging to the world of understanding, and it is simply as an efficient cause belonging to that world that he calls his causality a will. On the other side he is also conscious of himself as a part of the world of sense in which his actions which are mere appearances [phenomena] of that causality, are displayed; we cannot, however, discern how they are possible from this causality which we do not know; but instead of that, these actions as belonging to the sensible world must be viewed as determined by other phenomena, namely, desires and inclinations. If therefore I were only a member of the world of understanding, then all my actions would perfectly conform to the principle of autonomy of the pure will; if I were only a part of the world of sense, they would necessarily be assumed to conform wholly to the natural law of desires and inclinations, in other words, to the heteronomy of nature. (The former would rest on morality as the supreme principle, the latter on happiness.) Since, however, *the world of understanding contains the foundation of the world of sense, and consequently of its laws also,* and accordingly gives the law to my will (which belongs wholly to the world of understanding) directly, and must be conceived as doing so, it follows that, although on the one side I must regard myself as a being belonging to the world of sense, yet on the other side I must recognize myself as subject as [a rational being] to the law of the world of understanding, i.e., to reason, which contains this law in the idea of freedom, and therefore as subject to the autonomy of the will: consequently I must regard the laws of the world of understanding as imperatives for me, and the actions which conform to them as duties.

The Summum Bonum

It has been shown that virtue (as worthiness to be happy) is the supreme condition of all that can appear to us desirable, and consequently of all our pursuit of happiness, and is therefore the supreme good. But it does not follow that it is the whole and perfect good as the object of the desires of rational finite beings; for this requires happiness also, and that not merely in the partial eyes of the person who makes himself an end, but even in the judgment of an impartial reason, which regards persons in general as ends in themselves. For to need happiness, to deserve it, and yet at the same time not to participate in it, cannot be consistent with the perfect volition of a rational being possessed at the same time of all power, if, for the sake of experiment, we conceive such a being. Now inasmuch as virtue and happiness together constitute the possession of the *summum bonum* in a person, and the distribution of happiness in exact proportion to morality (which is the worth of the person, and his worthiness to be happy) constitutes the *summum bonum* of a possible world; hence this *summum bonum* expresses the whole, the perfect good, in which, however, virtue as the condition is always the supreme good, since it has no condition above it; whereas happiness, while it is pleasant to the possessor of it, is not of itself absolutely and in all respects good, but always presupposes morally right behaviour as its condition.

Now it is clear that the maxims of virtue and those of private happiness are quite heterogeneous and although they belong to one *summum bonum* which together they make possible, yet they are so far from coinciding that they restrict and check one another very much in the same subject. Thus the question, *How is the summum bonum practically possible?* still remains an unsolved problem, notwithstanding all the *attempts at coalition* that have hitherto been made.

Belief in Immortality

The realization of the *summum bonum* in the world is the necessary object of a will determinable by the moral law. But in this will the perfect accordance of the mind with the moral law is the supreme condition of the *summum bonum*. This then must be possible, as well as its object, since it is contained in the command to promote the latter. Now, the perfect accordance of the will with the moral law is holiness, a perfection of which no rational being of the sensible world is capable at any moment of his existence. Since, nevertheless, it is required as practically necessary, it can only be found in a *progress in infinitum* towards that perfect accordance, and on the

principles of pure practical reason it is necessary to assume such a practical progress as the real object of our will.

Now, this endless progress is only possible on the supposition of an endless duration of the existence and personality of the same rational being (which is called the immortality of the soul). The *summum bonum,* then, practically is only possible on the supposition of the immortality of the soul; consequently this immortality, being inseparably connected with the moral law, is a postulate of pure practical reason (by which I mean a theoretical proposition, not demonstrable as such, but which is an inseparable result of an unconditional *a priori practical* law).

This principle of the moral destination of our nature, namely, that it is only in an endless progress that we can attain perfect accordance with the moral law, is of the greatest use, not merely for the present purpose of supplementing the impotence of speculative reason, but also with respect to religion. In default of it, either the moral law is quite degraded from its holiness, being made out to be indulgent, and conformable to our convenience, or else men strain their notions of their vocation and their expectation to an unattainable goal, hoping to acquire complete holiness of will, and so they lose themselves in fantastical theosophic dreams, which wholly contradict self-knowledge. In both cases the unceasing effort to obey punctually and thoroughly a strict and inflexible command of reason, which yet is not ideal but real, is only hindered. For a rational but finite being, the only thing possible is an endless progress from the lower to higher degrees of moral perfection. From the progress he has hitherto made from the worse to the morally better, and the immutability of purpose which has thus become known to him, he may hope for a further unbroken continuance of the same, however long his existence may last, even beyond this life[1] and thus he may hope,

---

[1] One who is conscious that he has persevered through a long portion of his life up to the end in the progress to the better, and this from genuine moral motives, may well have the comforting hope, though not the certainty, that even in an

not indeed here, nor in any imaginable point of his future existence, but only in the endlessness of his duration (which God alone can survey) to be perfectly adequate to his will (without indulgence or excuse, which do not harmonize with justice).

Belief in God

In the foregoing analysis the moral law led to a practical problem, namely, that of the necessary completeness of the first and principal element of the *summum bonum,* viz. Morality: and as this can be perfectly solved only in eternity, to the postulate of *immortality.* The same law must also lead us to affirm the possibility of the second element of the *summum bonum,* viz. Happiness proportioned to that morality, and this on grounds as distinterested as before, and solely from impartial reason; that is, it must lead to the suppositition of the existence of a cause adequate to this effect; in other words, it must postulate the existence of God, as the necessary condition of the possibility of the *summum bonum.* We proceed to exhibit this connexion in a convincing manner.

Happiness is the condition of a rational being in the world with whom everything goes according to his wish and will; it rests, therefore, on the harmony of the physical nature with his whole end, and likewise with the essential determining principle of his will. But the acting rational being in the world is not the cause of the world and of nature itself. There is not the least ground, therefore, in the

existence prolonged beyond this life he will continue steadfast in these principles; and although he is never justified here in his own eyes, nor can ever hope to be so in the increased perfection of his nature, to which he looks forward, together with an increase of duties, nevertheless in this progress which, though it is directed to a goal infinitely remote, yet is in God's sight regarded as equivalent to possession, he may have a prospect of a *blessed* future; for this is the word that reason employs to designate perfect well-being independent on all contingent causes of the world, and which, like *holiness,* is an idea that can be contained only in an endless progress and its totality, and consequently is never fully attained by a creature.

moral law for a necessary connexion between morality and proportionate happiness in a being that belongs to the world as part of it, and therefore dependent on it, and which for that reason cannot by his will be a cause of this nature, nor by his own power make it thoroughly harmonize, as far as his happiness is concerned, with his practical principles. Nevertheless in the necessary pursuit of the *summum bonum,* such a connexion is postulated as necessary: we ought to endeavour to promote the *summum bonum,* which, therefore must be possible. Accordingly, the existence of a cause of all nature, distinct from nature itself, and containing the principle of this connexion, namely, of the exact harmony of happiness with morality, is also postulated.

Therefore the *summum bonum* is possible in the world only on the supposition of a Supreme Being having a causality corresponding to moral character. Now a being that is capable of acting on the conception of laws is an intelligence (a rational being), and the causality of such a being according to this conception of laws is his will; therefore, the supreme cause of nature, which must be presupposed as a condition of the *summum bonum* is a being which is the cause of nature by intelligence and will, consequently its author, that is God. It follows that the postulate of the possibility of the highest derived good (the best world) is likewise the postulate of the reality of a highest original good, that is to say, of the existence of God. Now it was seen to be a duty for us to promote the *summum bonum;* consequently it is not merely allowable, but it is a necessity connected with duty as a requisite, that we should presuppose the possibility of this *summum bonum;* and as this is possible only on condition of the existence of God, it inseparably connects the supposition of this with duty; that is, it is morally necessary to assume the existence of God.

In this manner the moral laws lead through the conception of the *summum bonum* as the object and final end of pure practical reason to religion, that is, to the recognition of all duties as divine commands, not as sanctions, that is to say, arbitrary ordinances of a foreign will and contingent in themselves, but as essential laws of every free will in itself, which, nevertheless, must be regarded as commands of the Supreme Being, because it is only from a morally perfect (holy and good) and at the same time all-powerful will, and consequently only through harmony with this will, that we can hope to attain the *summum bonum* which the moral law makes it our duty to take as the object of our endeavours. Here again, then, all remains disinterested and founded merely on duty; neither fear nor hope being made the fundamental springs, which if taken as principles would destroy the whole moral worth of actions. The moral law commands me to make the highest possible good in a world the ultimate object of all my conduct. But I cannot hope to effect this otherwise than by the harmony of my will with that of a holy

and good Author of the world; and although the conception of the *summum bonum* as a whole, in which the greatest happiness is conceived as combined in the most exact proportion with the highest degree of moral perfection (possible in creatures), includes my own happiness, yet it is not this that is the determining principle of the will which is enjoined to promote the *summum bonum,* but the moral law which, on the contrary, limits by strict conditions my unbounded desire of happiness.

Hence also morality is not properly the doctrine how we should *make* ourselves happy, but how we should become *worthy* of happiness. It is only when religion is added that there also comes in the hope of participating some day in happiness in proportion as we have endeavoured to be not unworthy of it.

Beyond Abstract Philosophy: Paul Tillich

When he was forced to leave Germany in 1933, Paul Tillich was one of the leading figures in European intellectual circles. During the past twenty-five years he has had a new and more illustrious career in the United States. "Tillich," writes the editor of a recent series of essays in his honor, "has spoken to modern man with a penetration which is perhaps unequalled by any other person."[1] This comment, while it may well be over-enthusiastic, suggests the kind of reaction that one finds among able and informed contemporary critics. For the honesty with which Tillich approaches a problem and the freshness and originality of his insights make his thinking unusually appealing and influential. With the utmost candor and the broadest vision he has examined every facet of our confused civilization, and his writing has been a source of great help to the thoughtful and perplexed of our age.

Indeed, Tillich has come nearer perhaps than anyone else in our generation to the kind of religious synthesis that Augustine achieved for his, and like Augustine, he is preeminently the apostle to the "intellectuals" of our day, to the skeptics and disillusioned who are not as a rule impressed by even the more distinguished interpreters of Christianity. In rather interesting fashion this is symbolized by Tillich's recent move from Union Theological Seminary in New York City, where he taught theological students, to the faculty of Harvard University, where he has entered with remarkable success into the life of that sophisticated university community. There is also in Tillich's thought, however, an element of imagination and an emotional depth that help make him not only a great theologian but like Augustine a great preacher as well. His sermons provide inspiration and deepened insight for many thoughtful Christians who find his philosophy largely incomprehensible.

Since coming to this country, Tillich has published several illuminating biographical sketches, each of which throws further light upon the forces at work in shaping this thought.[2] He was born in 1886 in a village in the province of Brandenburg, where his father was minister of the Prussian Territorial Church. His boyhood was spent in a nearby town, distinctly medieval in character; which was built around an old Gothic church, surrounded by an ancient wall, entered through gates with towers on them and administered from a medieval town hall. Tillich here developed a sense of spiritual kinship with the Middle Ages that involved much more than a mere mastery of historical knowledge. The medieval spirit became for him a living reality in which the past permeates and shapes the present.

---

[1] *Religion and Culture*, Walter Leibrecht, Ed., (New York, Harper and Brothers, 1959) p. 3.

[2] See *The Interpretation of History*, Part One (New York, Charles Scribner's Sons, 1936); *The Theology of Paul Tillich*, Part One (C. W. Kigley and R. W. Bretall, Eds. (New York, The Macmillan Co., 1953); and "Beyond Religious Socialism," *Christian Century*, (June 15, 1949).

It was a part of his very existence—a thing that inevitably distinguishes his outlook from those whose background and heritage are entirely American.

In 1900 Tillich moved to Berlin and at once entered into the life of a great modern city with enthusiasm, but the authoritarian structure of Prussian society before World War I and of the Lutheran Church continued even here to reinforce the medieval outlook of his early years. It required a world war and a political catastrophe in Germany to enable Tillich to break through the authoritarianism of his youth and to commit himself to fundamentally democratic social and political ideals. This commitment, though difficult and painful, was a lasting one.

In 1914 he entered the German Army as a chaplain, and his war experiences left him dissatisfied with a philosophical idealism out of touch with the hard facts of human life. At the end of the war Tillich began his academic career at the University of Berlin. After five years at Berlin he moved to Dresden as professor of philosophy of religion and social philosophy. He then went to Leipzig and later became professor of philosophy at Frankfurt University. Of his religious concern, always a primary one both then and later, Tillich writes: "As a theologian I tried to remain a philosopher, and when a philosopher to remain a theologian."[3] "Nevertheless I was and am a theologian, because the existential question of our ultimate concern and the existential answer of the Christian message are and always have been predominant in my spiritual life."[4]

During these years Tillich became increasingly interested in the relation of religion to art, to politics, to depth psychology and to sociology as well as to philosophy. He was developing the "theology of culture" with which his name later became associated and found in Berlin, Dresden, and Leipzig conditions not only favorable for this point of view but such as almost to make it inescapable. Political issues determined one's whole existence; revolution, on the one hand, and inflation, on the other, produced never ending problems. The social order of Germany was in a state of dissolution; psychoanalytic ideas were increasing in popularity and aspects of human nature that had been carefully repressed in previous generations were now frankly and freely discussed. Revolutionary art movements were also popular in Berlin, and in Dresden there was even greater emphasis upon the visual arts—painting, architecture, the dance, and the opera. All of these experiences left their mark upon the thought of Tillich. He found it impossible to develop an interpretation of religion which was not intimately associated with the vital concerns of human life. Gradually he came to see what he calls "the central proposition" of his philosophy of religion: *that as religion is the substance of culture, so culture is the expression of religion.*[5]

At Frankfort, as he describes it, he sought to make philosophy existential for the large numbers of students who were required to take work in this field. Such

---

[3] *The Interpretation of History*, p. 40.
[4] *The Theology of Paul Tillich*, p. 10.
[5] *The Interpretation of History*, p. 50.

an "existential" approach to philosophy brought him into increasing conflict with the Nazi movement, for which he never had anything but the deepest distrust. When Hitler became chancellor in 1933, Tillich was at once dismissed from his post at Frankfort; in November of that year he left Germany for the United States, and at the age of forty-seven he became a member of the faculty of Union Theological Seminary in New York. In a very short time he established himself as an outstanding figure in contemporary American theological thought. When existentialism in religion and in philosophy began to influence the thinking of this country, Tillich was among those best prepared to interpret it. As a student in Germany he had become acquainted with Kierkegaard, long before he was known in America, and his early studies of Schelling had introduced him to the existential point of view in a more appealing form. A number of his essays on existentialism, written from 1941 to 1944, are included in *Theology and Culture* (1959). In 1951 he gave the Terry Lectures at Yale, entitled *The Courage to Be,* lectures that marked another decisive step in his intellectual development.

It is not easy for the layman to grasp Tillich's thought in all its sweep and power; his books are difficult for a number of reasons. Frequent references to the culture of other centuries, to the major philosophical ideas of Western thought, and to the many theological controversies through the ages, prove perplexing rather than helpful for most American readers. His constant use of technical terms, many of which he has coined himself, provides a further difficulty. His philosophy is difficult, however, primarily because his insights are original, his suggestions are not in line with the conventional religious outlook, and even more because the revolutionary nature of his thought is both startling and at times paradoxical.

Essentially, Tillich is committed to what he terms the "Protestant principle." This means to him a vigorous support for all genuine freedom and creativity— whether in science, in art, in political life, or in theological thought. He welcomes the positive achievements of modern science, especially the depth psychology of Freud and of those who have carried further Freud's initial insights; he is aware of the recent developments in modern art and interested in exploring their larger significance; he is thoroughly familiar with modern philosophy, especially with Nietzsche and the existentialist movement. But he is convinced that a culture which is merely secular is without any ultimate foundation and orientation and is doomed, therefore, to meaninglessness and futility. As Tillich sees it, this has happened to our modern secular culture.

Our cultural predicament today would be a tragic and hopeless one, he believes, were it not for the possibility of spiritual renewal as man turns to a faith that is essentially religious. Only in such faith can he hope to escape from the confusion and despair of modern life. We must have a radical reorientation of human life to the God who is encountered in man's moments of "ultimate concern." This is a central phrase and a central concept in all Tillich's thought. Around it he builds his interpretation of religion and the discovery of meaning in human life. Such an approach is, of course, existential in point of view, and this Tillich himself recognizes clearly and specifically. With the existentialists he insists that "personal involvement" is essential for any valid religious insight. To understand Christianity we must see it through the eyes of a Christian faith. And while he does not like the term "Christian existentialism," there is no question but that this is a helpful description of his own position. As Tillich himself put it, "In religious truth the stake is one's very existence. Religious truth is existential truth, and to that extent it cannot be separated from practice. Religious truth is acted."[6]

His volume, *The Dynamics of Faith,* published in 1957 and issued in an inexpensive paperback edition the following year, contains one of the best popular statements of Tillich's general view of religion, and an especially good portrayal of the nature of faith as he interprets it. The following selection is from this volume.

---

[6] *The Interpretation of History,* p. 18.

The Nature of Faith*

What Faith Is Not

The most ordinary misinterpretation of faith is to consider it an act of knowledge that has a low degree of evidence. Something more or less probable or improbable is affirmed in spite of the insufficiency of its theoretical substantiation. This situation is very usual in daily life. If this is meant, one is speaking of *belief* rather than of faith. One believes that one's information is correct. One believes that records of past events are useful for the reconstruction of facts. One believes that a scientific theory is adequate for the understanding of a series of facts. One believes that a person will act in a specific way or that a political situation will change in a certain direction. In all these cases the belief is based on evidence sufficient to make the event probable. Sometimes, however, one believes something which has low probability or is strictly improbable, though not impossible. The causes for all these theoretical and practical beliefs are rather varied. Some things are believed because we have good though not complete evidence about them; many more things are believed because they

are stated by good authorities. This is the case whenever we accept the evidence which others accepted as sufficient for belief, even if we cannot approach the evidence directly (for example, all events of the past). Here a new element comes into the picture, namely, the trust in the authority which makes a statement probable for us. Without such trust we could not believe anything except the objects of our immediate experience. The consequence would be that our world would be infinitely smaller than it actually is. It is rational to trust in authorities which enlarge our consciousness without forcing us into submission. If we use the word "faith" for this kind of trust we can say that most of our knowledge is based on faith. But it is not appropriate to do so. We believe the authorities, we trust their judgment, though never unconditionally, but we do not have faith in them. Faith is more than trust in authorities, although trust is an element of faith. This distinction is important in view of the fact that some earlier theologians tried to prove the unconditional authority of the Biblical writers by showing their trustworthiness as witnesses. The Christian may believe the Biblical writers, but not unconditionally. He does not have faith in them. He should not even have faith in the Bible. For faith is

---

* From: *Dynamics of Faith* by Paul Tillich. Copyright 1957 by Paul Tillich. Reprinted by permission of Harper and Brothers.

more than trust in even the most sacred authority. It is participation in the subject of one's ultimate concern with one's whole being. Therefore, the term "faith" should not be used in connection with theoretical knowledge, whether it is a knowledge on the basis of immediate, prescientific or scientific evidence, or whether it is on the basis of trust in authorities who themselves are dependent on direct or indirect evidence.

The terminological inquiry has led us into the material problem itself. Faith does not affirm or deny what belongs to the prescientific or scientific knowledge of our world, whether we know it by direct experience or through the experience of others. The knowledge of our world (including ourselves as a part of the world) is a matter of inquiry by ourselves or by those in whom we trust. It is not a matter of faith. The dimension of faith is not the dimension of science, history or psychology. The acceptance of a probable hypothesis in these realms is not faith, but preliminary belief, to be tested by scholarly methods and to be changed by every new discovery. Almost all the struggles between faith and knowledge are rooted in the wrong understanding of faith as a type of knowledge which has a low degree of evidence but is supported by religious authority. It is, however, not only confusion of faith with knowledge that is responsible for the world historical conflicts between them; it is also the fact that matters of faith in the sense of ultimate concern lie hidden behind an assumedly scientific method. Whenever this happens, faith stands against faith and not against knowledge.

Knowledge of reality has never the certitude of complete evidence. The process of knowing is infinite. It never comes to an end except in a state of knowledge of the whole. But such knowledge transcends infinitely every finite mind and can be ascribed only to God. Every knowledge of reality by the human mind has the character of higher or lower probability. The certitude about a physical law, a historical fact, or a psychological structure can be so high that, for all practical purposes, it is certain. But theoretically the incomplete certitude of belief remains and can be undercut at any moment by criticism and new experience. The certitude of faith has not this character. Neither has it the character of formal evidence. The certitude of faith is "existential," meaning that the whole existence of man is involved. It has two elements: the one, which is not a risk but a certainty about one's own being, namely, on being related to something ultimate or unconditional; the other, which is a risk and involves doubt and courage, namely, the surrender to a concern which is not really ultimate and may be destructive if taken as ultimate. This is not a theoretical problem of the kind of higher or lower evidence, of probability or improbability, but it is an existential problem of "to be or not to be." It belongs to a dimension other than any theoretical judgment. Faith is not belief and it is not knowledge with a low degree of probability. Its certitude is not the uncertain certitude of a theoretical judgment.

Symbols of Faith

Man's ultimate concern must be expressed symbolically, because symbolic language alone is able to express the ultimate. . . . The language of faith is the language of symbols. If faith were what we have shown that it is not, such an assertion could not be made. But faith, understood as the state of being ultimately concerned, has no language other than symbols. When saying this I always expect the question: Only a symbol? He who asks this question shows that he has not understood the difference between signs and symbols nor the power of symbolic language, which surpasses in quality and strength the power of any nonsymbolic language. One should never say "only a symbol," but one should say "not less than a symbol." With this in mind we can now describe the different kinds of symbols of faith.

The fundamental symbol of our ultimate concern is God. It is always present in any act of faith, even if the act of faith includes the denial of God. Where there is ultimate concern, God can be denied only in the name of God. One God can deny the other one. Ultimate concern cannot deny its own character as ultimate. Therefore, it affirms what is meant by the word "God." Atheism, consequently, can only mean the attempt to remove any ultimate concern—to remain unconcerned about the meaning of one's existence. Indifference toward the ultimate question is the only imaginable form of atheism. Whether it is possible is a problem which must remain unsolved at this point. In any case, he who denies God as a matter of ultimate concern affirms God, because he affirms ultimacy in his concern. God is the fundamental symbol for what concerns us ultimately. Again it would be completely wrong to ask: So God is nothing but a symbol? Because the next question has to be: A symbol for what? And then the answer would be: For God! God is symbol for God. This means that in the notion of God we must distinguish two elements: the element of ultimacy, which is a matter of immediate experience and not symbolic in itself, and the element of concreteness, which is taken from our ordinary experience and symbolically applied to God. The man whose ultimate concern is a sacred tree has both the ultimacy of concern and the concreteness of the tree which symbolizes his relation to the ultimate. The man who adores Apollo is ultimately concerned, but not in an abstract way. His ultimate concern is symbolized in the divine figure of Apollo. The man who glorifies Jahweh, the God of the Old Testament, has both an ultimate concern and a concrete image of what concerns him ultimately. This is the meaning of the seemingly cryptic statement that God is the symbol of God. In this qualified sense God is the fundamental and universal content of faith.

It is obvious that such an understanding of the meaning of God makes the discussions about the existence or non-existence of God meaningless. It is meaningless to question the ultimacy of an ultimate concern. This element in the idea of God is in itself certain. The symbolic expression of this element varies endlessly through the whole history of mankind. Here again it would be meaningless to ask whether one or another of the figures in which an ultimate concern is sym-

bolized does "exist." If "existence" refers to something which can be found within the whole of reality, no divine being exists. The question is not this, but: which of the innumerable symbols of faith is most adequate to the meaning of faith? In other words, which symbol of ultimacy expresses the ultimate without idolatrous elements? This is the problem, and not the so-called "existence of God"—which is in itself an impossible combination of words. God as the ultimate in man's ultimate concern is more certain than any other certainty, even that of oneself. God as symbolized in a divine figure is a matter of daring faith, of courage and risk.

God is the basic symbol of faith, but not the only one. All the qualities we attribute to him, power, love, justice, are taken from finite experiences and applied symbolically to that which is beyond finitude and infinity. If faith calls God "almighty," it uses the human experience of power in order to symbolize the content of its infinite concern, but it does not describe a highest being who can do as he pleases. So it is with all the other qualities and with all the actions, past, present and future, which men attribute to God. They are symbols taken from our daily experience, and not information about what God did once upon a time or will do sometime in the future. Faith is not the belief in such stories, but it is the acceptance of symbols that express our ultimate concern in terms of divine actions.

The Truth of Faith and Scientific Truth

There is no conflict between faith in its true nature and reason in its true nature. This includes the assertion that there is no essential conflict between faith and the cognitive function of reason. Cognition in all its forms was always considered as that function of man's reason which comes most easily into conflict with faith. This was especially so when faith was defined as a lower form of knowledge and was accepted because the divine authority guaranteed its truth. We have rejected this distortion of the meaning of faith, and in doing so have removed one of the most frequent causes for the conflicts between faith and knowledge. But we must show beyond this the concrete relation of faith to the several forms of cognitive reason: the scientific, the historical and the philosophical. The truth of faith is different from the meaning of truth in each of these ways of knowledge. Nevertheless, it is truth they all try to reach, truth in the sense of the "really real" received adequately by the cognitive function of the human mind. Error takes place if man's cognitive endeavor misses the really real and takes that which is only seemingly real for real; or if it hits the really real but expresses it in a distorted way.

Science tries to describe and to explain the structures and relations in the universe, in so far as they can be tested by experiment and calculated in quantitative terms. The truth of a scientific statement is the adequacy of the description of the structural laws which determine reality, and it is the verification of this description by experimental repetitions. Every scientific truth is preliminary and subject to changes both in grasping reality and in expressing it adequately. This element of uncertainty does not diminish the truth value of a tested and verified scientific assertion. It only prevents scientific dogmatism and absolutism.

Therefore, it is a very poor method of defending the truth of faith against the truth of science, if theologians point to the preliminary character of every scientific statement in order to provide a place of retreat for the truth of faith. If tomorrow scientific progress reduced the sphere of uncertainty, faith would have to continue its retreat—an undignified and unnecessary procedure, for scientific truth and the truth of faith do not belong to the same dimension of meaning. Science has no right and no power to interfere with faith and faith has no power to interfere with science. One dimension of meaning is not able to interfere with another dimension.

If this is understood, the previous conflicts between faith and science appear in a quite different light. The conflict was actually not between faith and science but between a faith and a science each of which was not aware of its own valid dimension. When the representatives of faith impeded the beginning of modern astronomy, they were not aware that the Christian symbols, although using the Aristotelian-Ptolemaic astronomy, were not tied up with this astronomy. Only if the symbols of "God in heaven" and "man on earth" and "demons below the earth" are taken as descriptions of places, populated by divine or demonic beings can modern astronomy conflict with the Christian faith. On the other hand, if representatives of modern physics reduce the whole of reality to the mechanical movement of the smallest particles of matter, denying the really real quality of life and mind, they express a faith, objectively as well as subjectively. Subjectively science is their ultimate concern—and they are ready to sacrifice everything, including their lives, for this ultimate. Objectively, they create a monstrous symbol of this concern, namely, a universe in which everything, including their own scientific passion, is swallowed by a meaningless mechanism. In opposing this symbol of faith Christian faith is right.

Science can conflict only with science, and faith only with faith; science which remains science cannot conflict with faith which remains faith. This is true also of other spheres of scientific research, such as biology and psychology. The famous struggle between the theory of evolution and the theology of some Christian groups was not a struggle between science and faith, but between a science whose faith deprived man of his humanity and a faith whose expression was distorted by Biblical literalism. It is obvious that a theology which interprets the Biblical story of creation as a scientific description of an event which happened once upon a time interferes with the methodologically controlled scientific work; and that a theory of evolution which interprets man's descendance from older forms of life in a way that removes the infinite, qualitative difference between man and animal is faith and not science.

When faith speaks of the ultimate dimension in which man lives, and in which he can win or lose his soul, or of the ultimate meaning of his existence, it is not interfering at all with the scientific rejection of the concept of the soul. A psychology without soul cannot deny this nor can a psychology with soul confirm it. The truth of man's eternal meaning lies in a dimension other than the truth of adequate psychological concepts. There is no reason to deny to a scholar who deals with man and his predicament the right to introduce elements of faith. But if he attacks other forms of faith in the name of scientific psychology, as Freud and many of his followers do, he is confusing dimensions. In this case those who represent another kind of faith are justified in resisting these attacks. It is not always easy to distinguish the element of faith from the element of scientific hypothesis in a psychological assertion, but it is possible and often necessary.

The distinction between the truth of faith and the truth of science leads to a warning, directed to theologians, not to use recent scientific discoveries to confirm the truth of faith. Microphysics have undercut some scientific hypotheses concerning the calculability of the universe. The theory of quantum and the principle of indeterminacy have had this effect. Immediately religious writers use these insights for the confirmation of their own ideas of human freedom, divine creativity, and miracles. But there is no justification for such a procedure at all, neither from the point of view of physics nor from the point of view of religion. The physical theories referred to have no direct relation to the infinitely complex phenomenon of human freedom, and the emission of power in quantums has no direct relation to the meaning of miracles. Theology, in using physical theories in this way, confuses the dimension of science with the dimension of faith. The truth of faith cannot be confirmed by latest physical or biological or psychological discoveries—as it cannot be denied by them.

The Paradox of Faith: Reinhold Niebuhr

Reinhold Niebuhr is probably the outstanding contemporary figure in the field of religious thought that America has produced. For over thirty years he was professor of Christian Ethics at Union Theological Seminary in New York City and during this time had a remarkably wide influence not only in this country but in Europe as well. It is not by accident that he likes to call his own position "prophetic Christianity." There has been both in his life and his thought much that is reminiscent of the great Hebrew prophets of the seventh and eighth centuries B.C. Deeply conscious of the profound truth of the Christian faith, he has insisted in prophetic fashion that to be vital and meaningful religion must deal honestly and courageously with the disturbing social problems of the world about us. His interpretation of Christianity also provides an appealing synthesis of the orthodox and more liberal points of view of our own day. With surprising success he has managed to retain what is essential in each and reject what is superficial and secondary.

Niebuhr is of German extraction. His father was a German Evangelical pastor in a rural Missouri community when Reinhold was born in 1892. After attending a Lutheran college in Illinois and the Lutheran Theological Seminary in St. Louis, Niebuhr went to Yale University for further graduate study. In 1915 he was assigned by the German Evangelical Church to a small church in Detroit. During his thirteen years in this pastorate Niebuhr slowly and painfully worked out his own interpretation of the meaning of Christianity.

It was impossible for a sincere and thoughtful young pastor in Detroit to remain undisturbed by the effects of modern industrialism upon the lives of the men and women with whom he worked. Niebuhr soon reached the conclusion that the church cannot save a man's soul without doing something about the kind of life he lives. In other words, the Christian gospel became for him a social gospel. It is an essential task of the church, he came to believe, to improve the economic conditions which make it impossible for so many of its members to live decent and healthy lives. He sharply attacked the kind of pious morality that too often marks the religion of those not concerned with the world of every-day affairs; he read widely in the Marxian philosophy that the more radical labor leaders in Detroit were advocating and sought to fashion a Christian gospel capable of meeting such a challenge. As someone aptly suggested, Reinhold Niebuhr, the Christian revolutionary, was one of the by-products of the Ford automobile factories in Detroit. By the time Niebuhr left his church in Detroit to accept the post at Union Theological Seminary in New York, he was recognized as one of the ablest and most courageous Christian leaders in the country. Likewise, he was one of the few churchmen respected by both organized labor and the intellectuals. Orthodox religion has too frequently been associated with dullness, complacency, and privilege. Niebuhr did much to rescue it from so deadly an association.

Niebuhr's insight was penetrating enough to recognize the way in which modern science was challenging Christianity on both the intellectual and the ethical front: On one hand, the pure sciences have given us a picture of the universe that is thoroughly impersonal; a universe in which there is much less concern for moral ideals than religion had formerly assumed, in which indeed there seems no place and no need for the God of Christian faith. The applied sciences, at the same time, have enabled us to create an impersonal urban and industrial society in which the Christian spirit of love and brotherhood is equally impracticable and ill suited. Hence, it has become increasingly difficult for men today to believe in the God of their fathers, and more difficult, if anything, for them to treat their fellowmen as brothers, even if they want to.

Stirred by this danger, Neibuhr has done a significant job of analyzing the results of modern science on both fronts, the ethical and the intellectual. His work in ethics and politics has been particularly well known, and a number of his more influential books deal with such issues. *Moral Man and Immoral Society* (1932) is one of the most penetrating studies of the ethical implications of modern social life that has appeared in our age. It is a book that no serious student of social philosophy can afford to miss. *Christianity and Power Politics* (1940), *The Children of Light and the Children of Darkness* (1944), *The Irony of American History* (1952), and *Christian Realism and Political Problems* (1953), are among the important later studies in which Niebuhr develops and applies the point of view so provocatively stated in *Moral Man and Immoral Society.*

It is in this context that Niebuhr comes to see more clearly both the social significance of religious faith and also its essential nature. Like most thoughtful interpreters of religion since Kant, he has been acutely aware of the tension between the scientific spirit and religious faith. He sees the contradiction between the religious view of man as potentially a son of God and the more realistic scientific description of man as little more than an animal. He understands the grounds upon which the religious hope of a just society is treated by the scientific historian as in large measure an illusion. Yet he is convinced that religious faith affords a deeper insight into the true nature of man and society than scientific analysis by itself can provide. The distinctive contribution of religion to philosophic thought lies in the religious awareness of a dimension of depth in human experience, and this religious insight must be given clear and convincing statement.

In one volume after another Niebuhr has sought to work out such a statement. In *Moral Man and Immoral Society* he was willing to accept an essentially pragmatic notion of religious truth. After examining the religious view of the nature of man and of the good society, he concludes: "the truest visions of religion are illusions, which may be partially realized by being resolutely believed. For what religion believes to be true is not wholly true but ought to be true, and may become true if its truth is not doubted." A pragmatism of this sort, however, is hardly an adequate foundation for religious faith, as Niebuhr himself soon realized.

One is seldom willing to base one's life and destiny upon illusions, even though by so doing he somehow transmutes them into working truths.

It is not surprising, therefore, that when he published *An Interpretation of Christian Ethics* three years later (1935), he had adopted a more positive view of religious truth and its relation to scientific fact. Science and history, he came to see with Kant and many able contemporary scientists, are capable of dealing with reality in its surface aspects only—what Niebuhr terms its *horizontal* relationships. These the scientist analyzes, charts, and records; and the web of cause-and-effect relationships which make up the world of nature as pictured by science is the result. However, with the transcendent source of meaning in human life science is incapable of dealing. Of this transcendent reality we are immediately and inescapably aware in religious experience but this uniquely religious insight cannot be stated in rational, scientific concepts. It can only find expression Niebuhr argues, in agreement with the position taken by Paul Tillich, in symbol or myth. While such essential religious symbols or myths are not literally or scientifically true, they nonetheless possess a greater degree of ultimate truth than do the findings of science—for here we have our most revealing account of man's *vertical* relationships, his relationships to God. Hence, Niebuhr is concerned to analyze as carefully and as adequately as he can both the nature of religious myth and the insight afforded by such myths, as seen in the great myths that lie at the heart of the Hebrew-Christian faith. His discussion of this subject in *An Interpretation of Christian Ethics* and in *Beyond Tragedy* provides a desirable culmination of the point of view suggested in the philosophy of Kant and developed in somewhat different fashion by Tillich.

The Genius of Religious Myth*

I

Among the paradoxes with which St. Paul describes the character, the vicissitudes and the faith of the Christian ministry, the phrase "as deceivers yet true" is particularly intriguing. [II Corinthians 6:8] For what is true in the Christian religion can be expressed only in symbols which contain a certain degree of provisional and superficial deception. Every apologist of the Christian faith might well, therefore, make the Pauline phrase his own. We do teach the truth by deception. We are deceivers, yet true.

The necessity for the deception is given in the primary characteristic of the Christian world view. Christianity does not believe that the natural, temporal and historical world is self-derived or self-explanatory. It believes that the ground and the fulfilment of existence lie outside of existence, in an eternal and divine will. But it does not hold, as do many forms of dualism, that there is an eternal world separate and distinct from the temporal world. The relation between the temporal and the eternal is dialectical. The eternal is revealed and expressed in the temporal but not exhausted in it. God is not the sum total of finite occasions and relationships. He is their ground and they are the creation of

His will. But, on the other hand, the finite world is not merely a corrupt emanation from the ideal and eternal. Consequently the relation of time and eternity cannot be expressed in simple rational terms. It can be expressed only in symbolic terms. A rational or logical expression of the relationship invariably leads either to a pantheism in which God and the world are identified, and the temporal in its totality is equated with the eternal; or in which they are separated so that a false supernaturalism emerges, a dualism between an eternal and spiritual world without content and a temporal world without meaning or significance.

Before analysing the deceptive symbols which the Christian faith uses to express this dimension of eternity in time, it might be clarifying to recall that artists are forced to use deceptive symbols when they seek to portray two dimensions of space upon the single dimension of a flat canvas. Every picture which suggests depth and perspective draws angles not as they are but as they appear to the eye when it looks into depth. Parallel lines are not drawn as parallel lines but are made to appear as if they converged on the horizon; for so they appear to the eye when it envisages a total perspective. Only the most primitive art and the drawings made by very small children reveal the mistake of portraying things in their true proportions rather than as they are seen. The necessity of picturing things as they seem rather than as they are, in order to record on one dimension what they are in two dimensions, is a striking analogy, in the field of space, of the problem of religion in the sphere of time.

Time is a succession of events. Yet mere succession is not time. Time has reality only through a meaningful relationship of its successions. Therefore time is real only as it gives successive expressions of principles and powers which lie outside of it. Yet every . . . idea of the God who is the ground of the world must be expressed in some term taken from the world. The temporal process is like the painter's flat canvas. It is one dimension upon which two dimensions must be re-corded. This can be done only by symbols which deceive for the sake of truth.

Great art faces the problem of the two dimensions of time as well as the two dimensions of space. The portrait artist, for instance, is confronted with the necessity of picturing a character. Human personality is more than a succession of moods. The moods of a moment are held together in a unity of thought and feeling, which gives them, however seemingly capricious, a considerable degree of consistency. The problem of the artist is to portray the inner consistency of a character which is never fully expressed in any one particular mood or facial expression. This can be done only by falsifying physiognomic details. Portraiture is an art which can never be sharply distinguished from caricature. A moment of time in a personality can be made to express what transcends the moment of time only if the moment is not recorded accurately. It must be made into a symbol of something beyond itself.

This technique of art explains why art is more closely related to religion than science. Art describes the world not in terms of its exact relationships. It constantly falsifies these relationships, as analysed by science, in order to express their total meaning.

II

The Christian religion may be characterised as one which has transmuted primitive religious and artistic myths and symbols without fully rationalising them. Buddhism is much more rational than Christianity. In consequence Buddhism finds the finite and temporal world evil. Spinozism is a more rational version of God and the world than the biblical account; but it finds the world unqualifiedly good and identical with God. In the biblical account the world is good because God created it; but the world is not God. Every Christian myth, in one way or another, expresses both the meaningfulness and the incompleteness of the temporal world, both the majesty of God and his relation to the world.

We are deceivers yet true, when we say that God created the world. Creation is a mythical idea which cannot be fully rationalised. It has therefore been an offense to the philosophers who, with the scientists, have substituted the idea of causality for it. They have sought to explain each subsequent event by a previous cause. Such an explanation of the world leads the more naïve thinkers to a naturalism which regards the world as self-explanatory because every event can be derived from a previous one. The more sophisticated philosophers will at least, with Aristotle, seek for a first cause which gives an original impetus to the whole chain of causation. But such a first cause does not have a living relationship with the events of nature and history. It does not therefore account for the emergence of novelty in each new event. No new fact or event in history is an arbitrary novelty. It is always related to a previous event. But it is a great error to imagine that this relationship completely accounts for the new emergence. In both nature and history each new thing is only one of an infinite number of possibilities which might have emerged at that particular juncture. It is for this reason that, though we can trace a series of causes in retrospect, we can never predict the future with accuracy. There is a profound arbitrariness in every given fact, which rational theories of causation seek to obscure. Thus they regard a given form of animal life as rational because they can trace it historically to another form or relate it in terms of genus and species to other types of life. Yet none of these relationships, whether historical or schematic, can eliminate the profound arbitrariness of the givenness of things.

It is therefore true, to account for the meaningfulness of life in terms of the relation of every thing to a creative centre and source of meaning. But the truth of creation can be expressed only in terms which outrage reason. Involved in the idea of creation is the concept of making something out of nothing. The *Shepherd* of Hermas declares "First of all believe that God is one, who created and set in order all things and caused the universe to exist out of nothing." This was the constant reiteration of Christian belief, until in very modern times it was thought possible to substitute the idea of evolutionary causation for the idea of creation. The idea of creation out of nothing is profoundly ultra-rational; for human reason can deal only with the stuff of experience, and in experience the previous event and cause are seen, while the creative source of novelty is beyond experience.

The idea of creation relates the ground of existence to existence and is therefore mythical rather than rational. The fact that it is not a rational idea does not make it untrue or deceptive. But since it is not rational it is a temptation to deceptions. Every mythical idea contains a primitive deception and a more ultimate one. The primitive error is to regard the early form in which the myth is stated as authoritative. Thus the Christian religion is always tempted to insist that belief in creation also involves belief in an actual forming of man out of a lump of clay, or in an actual creative activity of six days. It is to this temptation that biblical literalism succumbs. But there is also a more ultimate source of error in the mythical statement of religious belief. That is to regard the relation of each fact and event in history to a Divine Creator as obviating the possibility of an organic relation to other facts and events according to a natural order. By this error, Christian theology is constantly tempted to deny the significance of the natural order, and to confuse the scientific analysis of its relationships. The error is analogous to that of certain types of art which completely falsify the natural relations of objects in order to express their ultimate significance.

We are deceivers, yet true, when we say that man fell into evil. The story of the fall of man in the Garden of Eden is a primitive myth which modern theology has been glad to disavow, for fear that modern culture might regard belief in it as a proof of the obscurantism of religion. In place of it we have substituted various accounts of the origin and the nature of evil in human life. Most of these accounts, reduced to their essentials, attribute sin to the inertia of nature, or the hypertrophy of impulses, or to the defect of reason (ignorance), and thereby either explicitly or implicitly place their trust in developed reason as the guarantor of goodness. In all of these accounts the essential point in the nature of human evil is missed, namely, that it arises from the very freedom of reason with which man is endowed. Sin is not so much a consequence of natural impulses, which in animal life do not lead to sin, as of the freedom by which man is able to throw the harmonies of nature out of joint. He disturbs the harmony of nature when he centres his life about one particular impulse (sex or the possessive impulse, for instance) or when he tries to make himself, rather than God, the centre of existence. This egoism is sin in its quintessential form. It is not a defect of creation but a defect which becomes possible because man has been endowed with a freedom not known in the rest of creation.

The idea of the fall is subject to the error of regarding the primitive myth of the garden, the apple and the serpent, as historically true. But even if this error is not committed, Christian thought is still tempted to regard the fall as an historical occurrence. The fall is not historical. It does not take place in any concrete human act. It is the presupposition of such acts. It deals with an area of human freedom which, when once expressed in terms of an act, is always historically related to a previous act or predisposition. External descriptions of human behaviour are therefore always deterministic. That is the deception into which those are betrayed who seek to avoid the errors of introspection by purely external descriptions of human behaviour. What Christianity means by the idea of the fall can only be known in introspection. The consciousness of sin and the consciousness of God are inextricably involved with each other. Only as the full dimension of human existence is measured, which includes not only the dimension of historical breadth but the dimension of transhistorical freedom, does the idea of the fall of man achieve significance and relevance.

The rationalists always assume that, since men are able to conceive of perfect standards of justice, such standards will be realised as soon as all men become intelligent enough to conceive them. They do not realise that intelligence offers no guarantee of the realisation of a standard, and that the greatest idealists, as well as the most cynical realists or the most ignorant victims of an immediate situation, fall short in their action; nor that such falling short arises not simply from the defect of the mind but from an egoistic corruption of the heart. Self intrudes itself into every ideal, when thought gives place to action. The deceptions to which the idea of the fall give rise are many; and all of them have been the basis of error at some time or other in the history of Christian theology. We are deceivers, yet true in clinging to the idea of the fall as a symbol of the origin and the nature of evil in human life.

III*

The genius of religious myth at its best is that it is trans-scientific. Its peril is to express itself in pre-scientific concepts and insist on their literal truth. . . . The mythical symbols of transcendence in profound religion are easily corrupted into scientifically untrue statements of historic fact. But the scientific description of historic sequences may be as easily corrupted into an untrue conception of total reality. It is the genius of true myth to suggest the dimension of depth in reality and to point to a realm of essence which transcends the surface of history, on which the cause-effect sequences, discovered and analyzed by science, occur. Science can only deal with this surface of nature and history, analyzing, dividing, and segregating its detailed phenomena and relating them to each other in terms of their observable sequences. It is bound to treat each new emergent in history as having its adequate cause in an antecedent event in history, thus committing the logical fallacy, *Post hoc, ergo propter hoc.*

The religious myth, on the other hand, points to the ultimate ground of existence and its ultimate fulfillment. Therefore the

---

* From: *An Interpretation of Christian Ethics* by Reinhold Niebuhr. Copyright 1935 by Harper and Brothers. Used by permission.

great religious myths deal with creation and redemption. But since myth cannot speak of the trans-historical without using symbols and events in history as its forms of expression, it invariably falsifies the facts of history, as seen by science, to state its truth. If in addition religion should insist that its mythical devices have a sacred authority which may defy the conclusions at which science arrives through its observations, religion is betrayed into deception without truth.

Philosophy is, in a sense, a mediator between science and religion. It seeks to bring the religious myth into terms of rational coherence, with all the detailed phenomena of existence which science discloses. Thus for Hegel, religion is no more than primitive philosophy in terms of crude picture-thinking, which a more advanced rationality refines. This rationalization of myth is indeed inevitable and necessary, lest religion be destroyed by undisciplined and fantastic imagery or primitive and inconsistent myth. Faith must feed on reason. (Unamuno.) But reason must also feed on faith. Every authentic religious myth contains paradoxes of the relation between the finite and the eternal which cannot be completely rationalized without destroying the genius of true religion. Metaphysics is therefore more dependent upon, and more perilous to, the truth in the original religious myth than is understood in a rationalistic and scientific culture.

It is by faith in transcendence that a profound religion is saved from complete capitulation to the culture of any age, past or present. When modern Christianity, confused by the prestige of science, the temper of a this-worldly age and the disrepute of orthodox dogmatism, sought to come to terms with current naturalism, it lost the power to penetrate into the ethical aberrations and confusions of a naturalistic culture and to correct its superficiality and false optimism.

The prophetic movement in Hebraic religion offers an interesting confirmation of the thesis that a genuine faith in transcendence is the power which lifts religion above its culture and emancipates it from sharing the fate of dying cultures. The prophets saved Hebraic religion from extinction when the Babylonian exile ended the Hebraic culture-religion with its center in the worship of the Temple. They not only saved the life of religion, but raised it to a new purity by their interpretation of the meaning of catastrophe, the redemptive power of vicarious suffering, and the possibility of a redemption which would include more than the fortunes of Israel. In somewhat the same fashion Augustine's faith disassociated Christianity from a dying Roman world, though the Greek otherworldly elements in Augustine's faith created the basis for a sacramental rather than prophetic religion of transcendence. Catholic orthodoxy survived the Graeco-Roman culture in the matrix of which it was formed, but in it Isaiah's hope for redemption at the end of history was replaced by a reference toward a realm of transcendence above history, between which and the world of nature-history a sacramental institution mediated. Thus Catholic orthodoxy robbed prophetic religion of its interest in future history and destroyed the sense of the dynamic character of mundane existence.

Only a vital Christian faith, renewing its youth in its prophetic origin, is capable of dealing adequately with the moral and social problems of our age; only such a faith can affirm the significance of temporal and mundane existence without capitulating unduly to the relativities of the temporal process. Such a faith alone can point to a source of meaning which transcends all the little universes of value and meaning which "have their day and cease to be" and yet not seek refuge in an eternal world where all history ceases to be significant. Only such a faith can outlast the death of old cultures and the birth of new civilizations, and yet deal in terms of moral responsibility with the world in which cultures and civilizations engage in struggles of death and life.

6

The Commitment
of the
Existentialist

Among contemporary philosophers the existentialists more than any other group have been concerned with the serious predicament of modern man—his loss of any real meaning or sense of enduring purpose and direction in life, and they have undertaken more successfully than other philosophers to provide a convincing answer to the search of our age for meaning and purpose. In recent years Existentialism has become a widely discussed term in this country, and a term that has much broader application than to technical philosophy alone. In literature, and even in art, as well as in religion and philosophy, the impact of existentialism is clearly apparent; and for the past two decades books, essays, and magazine articles have been appearing in increasing numbers purporting to give an explanation of this somewhat paradoxical position to the intelligent laymen. None of these, as a matter of fact, have been too successful, but the widespread interest has continued seemingly unabated. There is every indication indeed that existentialism has provided a significant expression of the spirit of our troubled age and in some profound sense touched upon the heart of modern man's predicament.

Three dimensions of existential philosophy have been distinguished by Paul Tillich: (1) the existential element in all serious thought about human life and destiny, (2) existentialism as a revolt against some aspects of industrial society and scientific thought in the nineteenth century; and (3) existentialism as a mirror of the situation in which many sensitive men and women find themselves today. In the effort to understand existentialism all three of these must be kept in mind. Tillich suggests in this connection that for many people modern art rather than philosophy may well provide a clearer portrayal of the existential point of view, and he then describes some of the specific aspects of contemporary painting that seem to him characteristically existential.[1]

In the thought of Kierkegaard and Nietzsche, the two nineteenth-century

---

[1] See "Existential Aspects of Modern Art," in *Christianity and the Existentialists*, Carl Michalson, Ed. (New York, Charles Scribner's Sons, 1956), p. 129.

figures to whom contemporary existentialism is most directly indebted, the element of revolt against certain dominant features of our modern scientific and industrial society is of primary significance. Theirs is a protest against the scientific world view in which man becomes merely a mechanical reality with no genuine individuality or creativity; against a scientific rationalism that finds no place for freedom and creativity in human life; against an age in which the individual is lost in the masses; against a democracy that involves a leveling of all men to the mediocrity of the average; against a Christianity marked by hypocrisy and pretense that has lost all genuine commitment to the faith of its founder.

One of the most illuminating treatments of this controversial subject is presented in *Irrational Man: A Study in Existential Philosophy* (1958) by William Barrett, an associate professor of philosophy at New York University and a former editor of the *Partisan Review*. Describing existentialism as "the philosophy of the atomic age," Barrett with Tillich finds portrayed in the important literature and art of our day the same sense of futility and lack of rational meaning or purpose in human life that so disturbed the existentialist philosophers, and discusses in some detail the existential point of view as seen in the work of such contemporary writers as Joyce, Kafka, Hemingway, and Faulkner as well as in modern art, especially cubism. His chapter on "The Advent of Existentialism" provides an excellent summary of the men and the forces that have contributed to the rise of existentialism as one of the dominant philosophical movements in our age. This chapter is reprinted in large part in the selection that follows.

The Advent of Existentialism*

I

The story is told (by Kierkegaard) of the absent-minded man so abstracted from his own life that he hardly knows he exists until, one fine morning, he wakes up to find himself dead. It is a story that has a special point today, since this civilization of ours has at last got its hands on weapons with which it could easily bring upon itself the fate of Kierkegaard's hero: we could wake up tomorrow morning dead—and without ever having touched the roots of our own existence. There is by this time widespread anxiety and even panic over the dangers of the atomic

age; but the public soul-searching and stock-taking rarely, if ever, go to the heart of the matter. We do not ask ourselves what the ultimate ideas behind our civilization are that have brought us into this danger; we do not search for the human face behind the bewildering array of instruments that man has forged; in a word, we do not dare to be philosophical. Uneasy as we are over the atomic age, on the crucial question of existence itself we choose to remain as absent-minded as the man in Kierkegaard's story. One reason we do so lies in the curiously remote position to which modern society has relegated philosophy, and which philosophers themselves have been content to accept.

If philosophers are really to deal with the problem of human existence—and no

* From *Irrational Man*, by William Barrett. Copyright © 1958 by William Barrett. Reprinted permission of Doubleday and Company, Inc.

other professional group in society is likely to take over the job for them—they might very well begin by asking: How does philosophy itself exist at the present time? Or, more concretely: How do philosophers exist in the modern world? Nothing very high-flown, metaphysical, or even abstract is intended by this question; and our preliminary answer to it is equally concrete and prosy. Philosophers today exist in the Academy, as members of departments of philosophy in universities, as professional teachers of a more or less theoretical subject known as philosophy. This simple observation, baldly factual and almost statistical, does not seem to take us very deeply into the abstruse problem of existence; but every effort at understanding must take off from our actual situation, the point at which we stand. "Know thyself!" is the command Socrates issued to philosophers at the beginning (or very close to it) of all Western philosophy; and contemporary philosophers might start on the journey of self-knowledge by coming to terms with the somewhat grubby and uninspiring fact of the social status of philosophy as a profession. It is in any case a fact with some interesting ambiguities.

The profession of philosophy did not always have the narrow and specialized meaning it now has. In ancient Greece it had the very opposite: instead of a specialized theoretical discipline philosophy there was a concrete way of life, a total vision of man and the cosmos in the light of which the individual's whole life was to be lived. These earliest philosophers among the Greeks were seers, poets, almost shamans—as well as the first thinkers. Even in Plato, where the thought has already become more differentiated and specialized and where the main lines of philosophy as a theoretical discipline are being laid down, the *motive* of philosophy is very different from the cool pursuit of the savant engaged in research. Philosophy is for Plato a passionate way of life; and the imperishable example of Socrates, who lived and died for the philosophic life, was the guiding line of Plato's career for five decades after his master's death. Philosophy is the soul's search for salvation, which means for Plato deliverance from the suffering and evils of the natural world. Even today the motive for an Oriental's taking up the study of philosophy is altogether different from that of a Western student: for the Oriental the only reason for bothering with philosophy is to fine release or peace from the torments and perplexities of life. Philosophy can never quite divest itself of these aboriginal claims. They are part of the past, which is never lost, lurking under the veneer of even the most sophisticatedly rational of contemporary philosophies; and even those philosophers who have altogether forsworn the great vision are called upon, particularly by the layman who may not be aware of the historical fate of specialization that has fallen upon philosophy, to give answers to the great questions.

The ancient claims of philosophy are somewhat embarrassing to the contemporary philosopher, who has to justify his existence within the sober community of professional savants and scientists. The modern university is as much an expression of the specialization of the age as is the modern factory. Moreover, the philosopher knows that everything we prize about our modern knowledge, each thing in it that represents an immense stride in certainty and power over what the past called its knowledge, is the result of specialization. Modern science was made possible by the social organization of knowledge. The philosopher today is therefore pressed, and simply by reason of his objective social role in the community, into an imitation of the scientist; he too seeks to perfect the weapons of his knowledge through specialization. Hence the extraordinary preoccupation with technique among modern philosophers, with logical and linguistic analysis, syntax and semantics; and in general with the refining away of all content for the sake of formal subtlety. The movement known as Logical Positivism, in this country (the atmosphere of humanism is probably more dominant in the European universities than here in the United States), actually trafficked upon the *guilt* philosophers felt at not being scientists;

that is, at not being researchers producing reliable knowledge in the mode of science. The natural insecurity of philosophers, which in any case lies at the core of their whole uncertain enterprise, was here aggravated beyond measure by the insistence that they transform themselves into scientists.

Specialization is the price we pay for the advancement of knowledge. A price, because the path of specialization leads away from the ordinary and concrete acts of understanding in terms of which man actually lives his day-to-day life. The philosopher who has pursued his own specialized path leading away from the urgent and the actual may claim that his situation parallels that of the scientist, that his own increasing remoteness from life merely demonstrates the inexorable law of advancing knowledge. But the cases are in fact not parallel; for out of the abstractions that only a handful of experts can understand the physicist is able to detonate a bomb that alters—and can indeed put an end to—the life of ordinary mankind. The philosopher has no such explosive effect upon the life of his time. In fact, if they were candid, philosophers today would recognize that they have less and less influence upon the minds around them. To the degree that their existence has become specialized and academic, their importance beyond the university cloisters has declined. Their disputes have become disputes among themselves; and far from gaining the enthusiastic support needed for a strong popular movement, they now have little contact with whatever general intellectual elite still remain here outside the Academy. John Dewey was the last American philosopher to have any widespread influence on non-academic life in this country.

II

Such was the general philosophic situation here when, after the Second World War, the news of Existentialism arrived. It was news, which is in itself an unusual thing for philosophy these days. True, the public interest was not altogether directed toward the philosophic matters in question. It was news from France, and therefore distin-

guished by the particular color and excitement that French intellectual life is able to generate. French existentialism was a kind of Bohemian ferment in Paris; it had, as a garnish for the philosophy, the cult its younger devotees had made of night-club hangouts, American jazz, special hairdos and style of dress. All this made news for American journalists trying to report on the life that had gone on in Paris during the war and the German Occupation. Moreover, existentialism was a literary movement as well, and its leaders—Jean-Paul Sartre, Albert Camus, Simone de Beauvoir—were brilliant and engaging writers. Nevertheless, that the American public was curious about the philosophy itself cannot altogether be denied. Perhaps the curiosity consisted in large part of wanting to know what the name, the big word, meant; nothing stirs up popular interest so much as a slogan. But there was also a genuine philosophic curiosity, however inchoate, in all this, for here was a movement that seemed to convey a message and a meaning to a good many people abroad, and Americans wanted to know about it. The desire for meaning still slumbers, though submerged, beneath the extroversion of American life.

The philosophic news from France was only a small detail in the history of the postwar years. French existentialism, as a cult, is now as dead as last year's fad. Its leaders, to be sure, are still flourishing: Sartre and Simone de Beauvoir are still phenomenally productive, though in the case of Sartre we feel that he has already made at least his penultimate statement, so that now we have his message pretty completely; Albert Camus, the most sensitive and searching of the trio, long ago split off from the group, but has continued his exploration into themes that belonged to the original existentialist preoccupations. As news and excitement, the movement is altogether dead; and yet it has left its mark on nearly all the writing and thinking of Europe of the last ten years. During the grim decade of the Cold War no intellectual movement of comparable importance appeared. Existentialism is the best in the way of a new and creative movement that these rather uninspired postwar years have been able to turn up. We have to say at least this in a spirit of cool critical assessment, even when we acknowledge all the frivolous and sensational elements that got attached to it.

The important thing, to repeat, was that here was a philosophy that was able to cross the frontier from the Academy into the world at large. This should have been a welcome sign to professional philosophers that ordinary mankind still could hunger and thirst after philosophy if what they were given to bite down on was something that seemed to have a connection with their lives. Instead, the reception given the new movement by philosophers was anything but cordial. Existentialism was rejected, often without very much scrutiny, as sensationalism or mere "psychologizing," a literary attitude, postwar despair, nihilism, or heaven knows what besides. The very themes of existentialism were something of a scandal to the detached sobriety of Anglo-American philosophy. Such matters as anxiety, death, the conflict between the bogus and the genuine self, the faceless man of the masses, the experience of the death of God are scarcely the themes of analytic philosophy. Yet they are themes of life: People do die, people do struggle all their lives between the demands of real and counterfeit selves, and we do live in an age in which neurotic anxiety has mounted out of all proportion so that even minds inclined to believe that all human problems can be solved by physical techniques begin to label "mental health" as the first of our public problems. The reaction of professional philosophers to existentialism was merely a symptom of their imprisonment in the narrowness of their own discipline. Never was the professional deformation more in evidence. The divorce of mind from life was something that had happened to philosophers simply in the pursuit of their own specialized problems. Since philosophers are only a tiny fraction of the general population, the matter would not be worth laboring were it not that this divorce of mind from life happens also

to be taking place, catastrophically, in modern civilization everywhere. It happens too, as we shall see, to be one of the central themes of existential philosophy—for which we may in time owe it no small debt.

All of this has to be said even when we do concede a certain sensational and youthfully morbid side to French existentialism. The genius of Sartre—and by this time there can scarcely be doubt that it is real genius—has an undeniably morbid side. But there is no human temperament that does not potentially reveal some truth, and Sartre's morbidity has its own unique and revelatory power. It is true also that a good deal in French existentialism was the expression of an historical mood—the shambles of defeat after the "phony war" and the experience of utter dereliction under the German Occupation. But are moods of this kind so unimportant and trifling as to be unworthy of the philosopher's consideration? Would it not in fact be a serious and appropriate task for the philosopher to elaborate what is involved in certain basic human moods? We are living in an epoch that has produced two world wars, and these wars were not merely passing incidents but characterize the age down to its marrow; surely a philosophy that has experienced these wars may be said to have some connection with the life of its time. Philosophers who dismissed existentialism as "merely a mood" or "a postwar mood" betrayed a curious blindness to the concerns of the human spirit, in taking the view that philosophic truth can be found only in those areas of experience in which human moods are *not* present.

III

Naturally enough, something very deeply American came to the surface in this initial response to existentialism. Once again the old drama of America confronting Europe was being played out. Existentialism was so definitely a European expression that its very somberness went against the grain of our native youthfulness and optimism. The new philosophy was not a peculiarly French phenomenon, but a creation of the western

European continent at the moment in history when all of its horizons—political as well as spiritual—were shrinking. The American has not yet assimilated psychologically the disappearance of his own geographical frontier, his spiritual horizon is still the limitless play of human possibilities, and as yet he has not lived through the crucial experience of human finitude. (This last is still only an abstract phrase to him.) The expression of themes like those of existentialism was bound to strike the American as a symptom of despair and defeat, and, generally, of the declining vigor of a senescent civilization. But America, spiritually speaking, is still tied to European civilization, even though the political power lines now run the other way; and these European expressions simply point out the path that America itself will have eventually to tread; when it does it will know at last what the European is talking about.

It is necessary thus to emphasize the European—rather than the specifically French —origins of existentialism, since in its crucial issues the whole meaning of European civilization (of which we in America are still both descendants and dependents) is radically put in question. Jean-Paul Sartre is not existentialism—it still seems necessary to make this point for American readers; he does not even represent, as we shall see later, the deepest impulse of this philosophy. Now that French existentialism as a popular movement (once even something of a popular nuisance) is safely dead, having left a few new reputations surviving in its wake, we can see it much more clearly for what it is—a small branch of a very much larger tree. And the roots of this larger tree reach down into the remotest depths of the Western tradition. Even in the portions of the tree more immediately visible to our contemporary eyes, we have something which is the combined product of many European thinkers, some of them operating in radically different national traditions. Sartre's immediate sources, for example, are German: *Martin Heidegger* (1889–) and *Karl Jaspers* (1883–), and for his method the great German phenomenologist, *Edmund Husserl* (1859–1938).

Heidegger and Jaspers are, strictly speaking, the creators of existential philosophy in this century: they have given it its decisive stamp, brought its problems to new and more precise expression, and in general formed the model around which the thinking of all the other existentialists revolves. Neither Heidegger nor Jaspers created their philosophies out of whole cloth; the atmosphere of German philosophy during the first part of this century had become quickened by the search for a new "philosophical anthropology"—a new interpretation of man—made necessary by the extraordinary additions to knowledge in all of the special sciences that dealt with man.

But what lifted Heidegger and Jaspers above the level of their contemporary philosophic atmosphere and impelled them to give a new voice to the intellectual consciousness of the age was their decisive relation to two older nineteenth-century thinkers: *Sören Kierkegaard* (1813–1855) and *Friedrich Nietzsche* (1844–1900). Jaspers has been the more outspoken in acknowleging this filial relationship: the philosopher, he says, who has really *experienced* the thought of Kierkegaard and Nietzsche can never again philosophize in the traditional mode of academic philosophy. Neither Kierkegaard nor Nietzsche was an academic philosopher; Nietzsche, for seven years a professor of Greek at Basel in Switzerland, did his most radical philosophizing after he had fled from the world of the university and its sober community of scholars; Kierkegaard never held an academic chair. Neither developed a system; both in fact gibed at systematizers and even the possibilities of a philosophic system; and while they proliferated in ideas that were far in advance of their time and could be spelled out only by the following century, these ideas were not the stock themes of academic philosophy. Ideas are not even the real subject matter of these philosophers—and this in itself is something of a revolution in Western philosophy: their central subject is the unique experience of the single one, the individual, who chooses to place himself on trial before the gravest question of his civilization. For both Kierkegaard and Nietzsche this gravest question is Christianity, though they were driven to opposite positions in regard to it. Kierkegaard set himself the task of determining whether Christianity can still be lived or whether a civilization still nominally Christian must finally confess spiritual bankruptcy; and all his ideas were simply sparks thrown off in the fiery process of seeking to realize the truth of Christ in his own life. Nietzsche begins with the confession of bankruptcy; God is dead, says Nitzsche, and European man if he were more honest, courageous, and had keener eyes for what went on in the depths of his own soul would know that this death has taken place there, despite the lip service still paid to the old formulae and ideals of religion. Nietzsche experimented with his own life to be able to answer the question: What next? What happens to the race when at long last it has severed the umbilical cord that bound it for millennia to the gods and a transcendent world beyond this earthly world? He placed his own life on trial in order to experience this death of God to its depths. More than thinkers, Kierkegaard and Nietzsche were witnesses— witnesses who suffered for their time what the time itself would not acknowledge as its own secret wound. No concept or system of concepts lies at the center of either of their philosophies, but rather the individual human personality itself struggling for self-realization. No wonder both are among the greatest of intuitive psychologists.

Yet modern existentialism is not of exclusively German provenance; rather it is a total European creation, perhaps the last philosophic legacy of Europe to America or whatever other civilization is now on its way to supplant Europe. The number of European thinkers of widely varying racial and national traditions who have collaborated in the fabrication of existential philosophy is much larger than the public, still somewhat bedazzled by French existentialism, imagines. The picture of French existentialism itself is not complete without the figure of *Gabriel Marcel* (1889–), Sartre's extreme opposite and trenchant critic, a devout Catholic whose philosophic sources are not German at all, but

are surprisingly enough the American idealist Josiah Royce and the French intuitionist Henri Bergson. According to the record he has left in his *Metaphysical Journal,* Marcel's existentialism developed out of purely personal experience, and perhaps that is its greatest significance for us, whatever final value his philosophic formulations may have. The intimacy and concreteness of personal feeling taught Marcel the imcompleteness of all philosophies that deal purely in intellectual abstractions.

Modern Spain has contributed two figures to existential philosophy, in *Miguel de Unamuno* (1864–1936) and *José Ortega y Gasset* (1883–1955). Unamuno, a poet first and last, wrote one of the most moving and genuine philosophic books of the whole movement; his *Tragic Sense of Life* is a work that fulfills, though in an anti-Nietzschean sense, Nietzsche's command to remain true to the earth. Unamuno had read Kierkegaard, but his thought is an expression of his own personal passion and of the Basque earth from which he sprang. Ortega, a cooler and more cosmopolitan figure, is best known in this country as the social critic of *The Revolt of the Masses.* All the basic premises of Ortega's thought derive from modern German philosophy: so far as he philosophizes, his mind is Germanic; but he was able to translate German philosophy into the language of the people, without pedantry and jargon, and particularly into the simplicity of an altogether alien language, Spanish, so that the translation itself becomes an act of creative thought. Ortega loves to hide the profundity of his thought behind the simple and casual language of a journalist or belletrist.

On the outer edge of the German tradition moves the remarkable figure of *Martin Buber* (1878–), a Jew whose culture is altogether Germanic but whose thought after many peregrinations has succeeded in rediscovering and anchoring itself profoundly to its Biblical and Hebraic inheritance. Buber is one of the few thinkers who has succeeded in the desperate modern search for roots, a fact with which his work continuously impresses us. The image of Biblical man moves like a shadow behind everything he writes, His thinking has the narrowness and concrete power, often the stubborn obstinacy, of Hebraism. At first glance his contribution would seem to be the slenderest of all the existentialists, to be summed up in the title of his most moving book, *I and Thou*. It is as if Buber had sought to recast Kierkegaard's dictum, "Purity of heart is to will one thing," into: Depth of mind is to think one thought. But this one thought—that meaning in life happens in the area between person and person in that situation of contact when one says *I* to the other's *Thou*—is worth a lifetime's digging. In any case Buber is a necessary corrective to more ambitious systematizers like Heidegger and Sartre.

IV

Thus we see that existentialism numbers among its most powerful representatives Jews, Catholics, Protestants—as well as atheists. Contrary to the first facile journalistic reactions, the seriousness of existential thought does not arise merely out of the despair of a world from which God has departed. Such a generalization was prompted largely by the identification of existential philosophy with the school of Sartre. It should appear, from the foregoing sketch, how tiny a fragment of existentialism the Sartrian school really does represent. So far as the central impulses of existential thought are concerned, it does not altogether matter, at least in one sense, in what religious sect a man finally finds his home. Nor is it mere heterogeneous lumping-together to put Catholics, Jews, Protestants, and atheists under the rubric of one philosophy. This philosophy, as a particular mode of human thought, is single even though its practitioners wind up in different religious camps. What is common, and central, to all these philosophers is that the meaning of religion, and religious faith, is recast in relation to the individual. Each has put religion itself radically in question, and it is only to be expected that the faith, or the denial of faith, that emerges in their thought should be somewhat disconcerting

to those who have followed the more public and external paths into a church. Unamuno seemed always on the verge of excommunication by the Spanish bishops; Buber is a prophet with not very much honor in his native land of Israel; and Kierkegaard fought the last battle of his life against the ordained hierarchy of the Danish Church. The atheist sect, on the other hand, sniffs the taint of heresy in Heidegger, whose thought, which he himself calls in one place a "waiting for god," has been criticized by one American philosopher as opening the back door to theology. It is evident that anyone who has passed through the depths of modern experience and strives to place religion in relation to that experience is bound to acquire the label of heretic.

Modern experience—an ambiguous enough term, to be sure, and one that will require subsequent definition—is the bond among these philosophers. The roster of names we have given is hardly complete, but surely sufficient to indicate that existentialism is not a passing fad or a mere philosophic mood of the postwar period but a major movement of human thought that lies directly in the main stream of modern history. Over the past hundred years the development of philosophy has shown a remarkable enlargement of content, a progressive orientation toward the immediate and qualitative, the existent and the actual—toward "concreteness and adequacy," to use the words that A. N. Whitehead borrowed from William James. Philosophers can no longer attempt, as the British empiricists Locke and Hume attempted, to construct human experience out of simple ideas and elementary sensations. The psychic life of man is not a mosaic of such mental atoms, and philosophers were able to cling to this belief so long only because they had put their own abstractions in place of concrete experience. Thus Whitehead himself, who as a Platonist can scarcely be lumped with the existentialists, nevertheless shares in this general existential trend within modern philosophy when he describes philosophy itself as "the critique of abstractions"—the endless effort to drag the balloon of the mind back to the earth of actual experience.

Of all the non-European philosophers, William James probably best deserves to be labeled an existentialist. Indeed, at this late date, we may very well wonder whether it would not be more accurate to call James an existentialist than a pragmatist. What remains of American pragmatism today is forced to think of him as the black sheep of the movement. Pragmatists nowadays acknowledge James's genius but are embarrassed by his extremes: by the unashamedly personal tone of his philosophizing, his willingness to give psychology the final voice over logic where the two seem in conflict, and his belief in the revelatory value of religious experience. There are pages in James that could have been written by Kierkegaard, and the Epilogue to *Varieties of Religious Experience* puts the case for the primacy of personal experience over abstraction as strongly as any of the existentialists has ever done. James's vituperation of rationalism is so passionate that latter-day pragmatists see their own residual rationalism of scientific method thereby put in question. And it is not merely a matter of tone, but of principle, that places James among the existentialists: he plumped for a world which contained contingency, discontinuity, and in which the centers of experience were irreducibly plural and personal, as against a "block" universe that could be enclosed in a single rational system.

The reader may very well ask why, in view of this broader existential trend within modern philosophy, existentialism should first have been greeted by professional philosophers in this country as an eccentric and sensational kind of tempest in a teapot. We should point out that Anglo-American philosophy is dominated by an altogether different and alien mode of thought—variously called analytic philosophy, logical positivism, or sometimes merely "scientific philosophy."

No doubt, positivism has also good claims to being the philosophy of this time: it takes as its central fact what is undoubtedly the central fact distinguishing our civilization from all others—science; but it goes on from this to take science as the ultimate ruler of human life, which it never has been and psychologically never can be. Positivist man is a curious creature who dwells in the tiny island of light composed of what he finds scientifically "meaningful," while the whole surrounding area in which ordinary men live from day to day and have their dealings with other men is consigned to the outer darkness of the "meaningless." Positivism has simply accepted the fractured being of modern man and erected a philosophy to intensify it. Existentialism, whether successfully or not, has attempted instead to gather all the elements of human reality into a total picture of man. Positivist man and existentialist man are no doubt offspring of the same parent epoch, but, somewhat as Cain and Abel were, the brothers are divided unalterably by temperament and the initial choice they make of their own being. Of course there is on the contemporary scene a more powerful claimant to philosophic mastery than either of them: Marxism. Marxist man is a creature of technics, a busy and ingenious animal, with secular religious faith in History, of which he is the chosen collaborator. Both Marxism and positivism are, intellectually speaking, relics of the nineteenth-century Enlightenment that have not yet come to terms with the shadow side of human life as grasped even by some of the nineteenth-century thinkers themselves. The Marxist and positivist picture of man, consequently, is thin and oversimplified. Existential philosophy, as a revolt against such oversimplification, attempts to grasp the image of the whole man, even where this involves bringing to consciousness all that is dark and questionable in his existence. And in just this respect it is a much more authentic expression of our own contemporary experience.

Secular or Atheistic Existentialism: Jean-Paul Sartre

Of all the men who can be classed as existentialists, two stand out prominently in this country: Sören Kierkegaard and Jean-Paul Sartre. In some way these two figures, fundamentally different in background, in outlook on life, and even in the age in which they lived, have become intimately and inextricably associated with the philosophy of existentialism in the popular mind and in a very real sense have come to represent this philosophy for most laymen.

While they have enough in common to identify them both as existentialists, their differences are also significant. Kierkegaard's point of view, of course, is deeply religious, while Sartre advocates a secular or atheistic philosophy. There are many varieties of atheism. The urbane and sophisticated atheism of Bertrand Russell is essentially a rational theory to be discussed in objective and largely impersonal fashion. The atheism of Sartre, on the other hand, is more somber and disturbing; it takes much of its mood from Friedrich Nietzsche, for whom atheism is a matter of tragic personal experience. Sartre is, to be sure, a philosopher in the French tradition, a tradition that has so often produced men who stand on the border line of philosophy and literature. Voltaire and Pascal as well as Rousseau come to mind at once as well-known examples. Like these men, Sartre is distinguished by remarkable versatility; he was known for his short stories, essays, plays, and literary criticism before he became famous as a philosopher. In temperament and point of view, however, Sartre is closer again to Nietzsche than to his French predecessors, and the source of many of his ideas can easily be seen in the philosophy of Nietzsche.

Sartre was born in Paris on June 21, 1905. He studied philosophy first in Paris and later with Husserl and Heidegger in Germany, where he was greatly influenced by both of these German philosophers. Paul Tillich indeed suggests that Sartre's greatness lies in his work as "the psychological interpreter of Heidegger," but this hardly does justice to his own unique contribution to existentialism. Returning to France, Sartre became a teacher of philosophy (at Le Havre and then in Paris) and a free-lance writer. His first novel, La Nausée, published in 1938, brought him quick recognition in literary circles, and also made clear the basic outlines of his existential philosophy. During World War II, he was captured by the Nazis and interned for some time in a German prison camp; his experiences both in the prison camp and later in the French Resistance Movement left an indelible impress upon his mind and his philosophy. In several plays and novels which appeared in the years immediately after the war, Sartre's outstanding gifts as a writer became apparent. His mastery of artistic form and literary style, and his sure grasp of the psychological problems confronting both normal and abnormal human beings in our contemporary civilization established him as one of the leading figures in French literary circles and drew a large following of all sorts of young French bohemians to the Paris cafe where he spent most of his time from morning well through the night.

Sartre's plays and short stories depict decadent men and women trapped by social injustice, war, and the spiritual decay of our civilization, as well as by their own psychological compulsions—trapped, and yet, as Sartre sees it, inescapably aware of their own responsibility for the way in which they make the decisions that confront them. His critics, not only in America but even in France, have commented upon the type of people with whom he deals and upon the coarseness and brutality that one finds in his novels and plays. Because of his popularity and influence, a hazy impression of bohemian decadence has unfortunately become associated with existentialism in the minds of the general public. But as Gabriel Marcel, who is most critical of Sartre's position on other grounds, well observes, "Sartre's philosophy is much too impressive, particularly to young people, not to be examined with the utmost seriousness and objectivity; though I admit that there is in Sartre a certain taste and propensity for scandal, this is of secondary importance, and I mention it only in passing."[1]

It was in his war experiences, and in the danger and suffering, the daring and heroism of the French Resistance movement, that Sartre found his answer to the meaning of existence. The Resistance movement came to him and to the men of his generation as a release from pettiness, boredom, and disgust into action and heroism. It was a call to decision that brought man to the very limit of his being. Here individuals who were nothing became men—made men out of themselves. —— It is necessary to emphasize experience of this kind for Americans to understand Sartre and the powerful appeal of his philosophy; in this country we have not as a people comprehended what the French lived through during the Nazi occupation, and what this war experience did to their attitudes.

In *The Republic of Silence* Sartre describes life in the French Resistance movement as he knew it at first hand from 1940 to 1945, and he strikes here a note of heroism in human life, particularly important because in so much of his writing man is distinctly unheroic in nature. Not only did he discover the heroic, he also discovered here the meaning of human freedom, and this too became one of the essential features in his existential philosophy. In their time of greatest trial the French found a final, an irreducible freedom in the ability to say "No" to the might of the Nazi occupying forces. This was an existential freedom, an ultimate and final freedom that could never be taken from a man. Sartre's view of human freedom as final and absolute, a view for which he has frequently been criticized on more theoretical grounds, is based upon this experience. It is in this vein that he writes of the life of the French Resistance:

We were never more free than during the German occupation. We had lost all our rights, beginning with the right to talk. Every day we were insulted to our faces and had to take it in silence. Under one pretext or another, as workers, Jews, or political prisoners, we were deported *en masse*. Everywhere, on

[1] *The Philosophy of Existence* (London, Harvill Press, 1948), p. 33.

billboards, in the newspapers, on the screen, we encountered the revolting and insipid picture of ourselves that our suppressors wanted us to accept. And because of all this we were free. Because the Nazi venom seeped into our thoughts, every accurate thought was a conquest. Because an all-powerful police tried to force us to hold our tongues, every word took on the value of a declaration of principles. Because we were hunted down, everyone of our gestures had the weight of a solemn commitment.

Exile, captivity, and especially death (which we usually shrink from facing at all in happier days) became for us the habitual objects of our concern. We learned that they were neither inevitable accidents, nor even constant and inevitable dangers, but they must be considered as our lot itself, our destiny, the profound source of our reality as man. At every instant we lived up to the full sense of this commonplace: "Man is mortal!" And the choice that each of us made of his life was an authentic choice because it was made face to face with death, because it could always have been expressed in concrete terms "Rather than death. . . ." And here I am not speaking of the elite among us who were real Resistants, but all Frenchmen who, at every hour of the night and day throughout four years, answered *NO*.[2]

It is not difficult to see also how Sartre was led to a deeper commitment to the philosophy of Descartes. As a young teacher of philosophy he, like every Frenchman, had turned with particular admiration to the thought of that brilliant French figure, the father of modern philosophy. Descartes had given new meaning to man's freedom—his freedom from the authority of the past, his freedom to doubt, to reject all beliefs no matter how appealing or necessary for human life, until his understanding was itself convinced without any external force or social pressure. The final and absolute authority is man's experience of his own existence. But where Descartes, as a good Christian and Catholic, is led from his own existence to the existence of God, Sartre can find no ground for this step. He is thus forced to ascribe to man himself the kind of absolute freedom that for Descartes was found in God alone. If there is no God, Sartre argues, then man must take the place of God in making of himself anything that is to be made.

Sartre's major philosophical work, *Being and Nothingness,* was published in 1943. A closely written book of over 700 pages, it took the philosophy of existentialism out of academic circles in France and made it almost overnight a topic of general conversation and dispute. Sartre's reputation as a philosopher of ability, as well as a brilliant literary figure, was established by this volume. Almost immediately with a group of disciples he started *Les Temps Modernes,* a periodical to provide expression for their literary and philosophical ideas, and in his lecture two years later on "Existentialism and Humanism" (1945), he undertook to

---

[2] *The Republic of Silence,* A. J. Liebling, Ed. (New York, Harcourt, Brace & Co., 1947), pp. 498–499. Reprinted by permission of the author and James Brown Associates, Inc.

answer a number of his critics in more popular fashion. In the English-speaking world this lecture on *Existentialism* is not only the best known statement of Sartre's philosophy, but it is also one of the widely used interpretations of existentialism. While the essay has been frequently criticized as not entirely consistent with Sartre's position as a whole nor with that of other existentialists like Heidegger or Jaspers, it is, nevertheless, one of the most direct and forthright discussions of existentialism by a major figure in the movement, and for that reason provides a valuable introduction to the subject. It may well be, as Barrett suggests in the preceding selection, that French existentialism as a cult is now dead and that we have Sartre's philosophical message pretty well complete, but his contribution has been a significant one, and it offers a desirable point at which to begin a study of existentialism.

Existentialism*

I

I should like on this occasion to defend existentialism against some charges which have been brought against it.

First, it has been charged with inviting people to remain in a kind of desperate quietism because, since no solutions are possible, we should have to consider action in this world as quite impossible. We should then end up in a philosophy of contemplation; and since contemplation is a luxury, we come in the end to a bourgeois philosophy. The communists in particular have made these charges.

On the other hand, we have been charged with dwelling on human degradation, with pointing up everywhere the sordid, shady, and slimy, and neglecting the gracious and beautiful, the bright side of human nature; for example, according to Mlle. Mercier, a Catholic critic, with forgetting the smile of the child. Both sides charge us with having ignored human solidarity, with considering man as an isolated being. The communists say that the main reason for this is that we

take pure subjectivity, the *Cartesian I think*, as our starting point; in other words, the moment in which man becomes fully aware of what it means to him to be an isolated being; as a result, we are unable to return to a state of solidarity with the men who are not ourselves, a state which we can never reach in the *cogito*.

From the Christian standpoint, we are charged with denying the reality and seriousness of human undertakings, since, if we reject God's commandments and the eternal verities, there no longer remains anything but pure caprice, with everyone permitted to do as he pleases and incapable, from his own point of view, of condemning the points of view and acts of others.

I shall try today to answer these different charges. . . . As is generally known, the basic charge against us is that we put the emphasis on the dark side of human life. Someone recently told me of a lady who, when she let slip a vulgar word in a moment of irritation, excused herself by saying, "I guess I'm becoming an existentialist." Consequently, existentialism is regarded as something ugly; that is why we are said to be naturalists; and if we are, it is rather surprising that in this day and age we cause so much more alarm and scandal than does naturalism,

* Jean-Paul Sartre, *Existentialism*, English translation by Bernhard Frechtman. (New York, The Philosophical Library, Inc., 1947). Shortened.

properly so called. The kind of person who can take in his stride such a novel as Zola's *The Earth* is disgusted as soon as he starts reading an existentialist novel; the kind of person who is resigned to the wisdom of the ages—which is pretty sad—finds us even sadder. Yet, what can be more disillusioning than saying "true charity begins at home" or "a scoundrel will always return evil for good?"

There are still people who go on mumbling these melancholy old saws, the people who say, "It's only human!" whenever a more or less repugnant act is pointed out to them, the people who glut themselves on *chansons réalistes;* these are the people who accuse existentialism of being too gloomy, and to such an extent that I wonder whether they are complaining about it, not for its pessimism, but much rather its optimism. Can it be that what really scares them in the doctrine I shall try to present here is that it leaves to man a possibility of choice? To answer this question, we must re-examine it on a strictly philosophical plane. What is meant by the term *existentialism?*

II

Most people who use the word would be rather embarrassed if they had to explain it, since, now that the word is all the rage, even the work of a musician or painter is being called existentialist. A gossip columnist in *Clartés* signs himself *The Existentialist,* so that by this time the word has been so stretched and has taken on so broad a meaning, that it no longer means anything at all. It seems that for want of an advance-guard doctrine analogous to surrealism, the kind of people who are eager for scandal and flurry turn to this philosophy which in other respects does not at all serve their purposes in this sphere.

Actually, it is the least scandalous, the most austere of doctrines. It is intended strictly for specialists and philosophers. Yet it can be defined easily. What complicates matters is that there are two kinds of existentialist; first, those who are Christian, among whom I would include Jaspers and Gabriel Marcel, both Catholic; and on the other hand the atheistic existentialists, among whom I class Heidegger, and then the French existentialists and myself. What they have in common is that they think that existence precedes essence, or, if you prefer, that subjectivity must be the starting point.

Just what does that mean? Let us consider some object that is manufactured, for example, a book or a paper-cutter: here is an object which has been made by an artisan whose inspiration came from a concept. He referred to the concept of what a paper-cutter is and likewise to a known method of production, which is part of the concept, something which is, by and large, a routine. Thus, the paper-cutter is at once an object produced in a certain way and, on the other hand, one having a specific use; and one can not postulate a man who produces a paper-cutter but does not know what it is used for. Therefore, let us say that, for the paper-cutter, essence—that is, the ensemble of both the production routines and the properties which enable it to be both produced and defined—precedes existence. Thus, the presence of the paper-cutter or book in front of me is determined. Therefore, we have here a technical view of the world whereby it can be said that production precedes existence.

When we conceive God as the Creator, He is generally thought of as a superior sort of artisan. Whatever doctrine we may be considering, whether one like that of Descartes or that of Leibnitz, we always grant that will more or less follows understanding or, at the very least, accompanies it, and that when God creates He knows exactly what He is creating. Thus, the concept of man in the mind of God is comparable to the concept of paper-cutter in the mind of the manufacturer, and, following certain techniques and a conception God produces man, just as the artisan, following a definition and a technique, makes a paper-cutter. Thus, the individual man is the realisation of a certain concept in the divine intelligence.

In the eighteenth century, the atheism of the *philosophes* discarded the idea of God, but not so much for the notion that essence precedes existence. To a certain extent, this idea is found everywhere; we find it in Diderot, in Voltaire, and even in Kant. Man has a human nature; this human nature, which is the concept of the human, is found in all men, which means that each man is a particular example of a universal concept, man. Thus, here too the essence of man precedes the historical existence that we find in nature.

Atheistic existentialism, which I represent, is more coherent. It states that if God does not exist, there is at least one being in whom existence precedes essence, a being who exists before he can be defined by a concept, and that this being is man, or, as Heidegger says, human reality. What is meant here by saying that existence precedes essence? It means that, first of all, man exists, turns up, appears on the scene, and, only afterwards, defines himself. If man, as the existentialist conceives him, is indefinable, it is because at first he is nothing. Only afterward will he be something, and he himself will have made what he will be. Thus, there is no human nature, since there is no God to conceive it. Not only is man what he conceives himself to be, but he is also what he wills himself to be after this thrust toward existence.

Man is nothing else but what he makes of himself. Such is the first principle of existentialism. It is also what is called subjectivity, the name we are labeled with when charges are brought against us. But what do we mean by this, if not that man has a greater dignity than a stone or table? For we mean that man first exists, that is, that man first of all is the being who hurls himself toward a future and who is conscious of imagining himself as being in the future. Man is at the start a plan which is aware of itself, rather than a patch of moss, a piece of garbage, or a cauliflower; nothing exists prior to this plan; there is nothing in heaven; man will be what he will have planned to be. Not what he will want to be. Because by the word "will" we generally mean a conscious decision, which is subsequent to what we have already made of ourselves. I may want to belong to a political party, write a book, get married; but all that is only a manifestation of an earlier, more spontaneous choice that is called "will." But if existence really does precede essence, man is responsible for what he is. Thus, existentialism's first move is to make every man aware of what he is and to make the full responsibility of his existence rest on him. And when we say that a man is responsible for himself, we do not only mean that he is responsible for his own individuality, but that he is responsible for all men.

The word subjectivism has two meanings, and our opponents play on the two. Subjectivism means, on the one hand, that an individual chooses and makes himself; and, on the other, that it is impossible for man to transcend human subjectivity. The second of these is the essential meaning of existentialism. When we say that man chooses his own self, we mean that every one of us does likewise; but we also mean by that that in making this choice he also chooses all men. In fact, in creating the man that we want to be, there is not a single one of our acts which does not at the same time create an image of man as we think he ought to be. To choose to be this or that is to affirm at the same time the value of what we choose, because we can never choose evil. We always choose the good, and nothing can be good for us without being good for all.

If, on the other hand, existence precedes essence, and if we grant that we exist and fashion our image at one and the same time, the image is valid for everybody and for our whole age. Thus, our responsibility is much greater than we might have supposed, because it involves all mankind. If I am a workingman and choose to join a Christian trade-union rather than be a communist, and if by being a member I want to show that the best thing for man is resignation, that the kingdom of man is not of this world, I am not only involving my own case—I want to be resigned for everyone. As a result, my action has involved all humanity. To take a more individual matter, if I want to marry, to have children; even if this marriage depends solely on my own circumstances or passion or wish, I am involving all humanity in monogamy and not merely myself. Therefore, I am responsible for myself and for everyone else. I am creating a certain image of man of my own choosing. In choosing myself, I choose man.

III

This helps us understand what the actual content is of such rather grandiloquent words as anguish, forlornness, despair. As you will see, it's all quite simple.

First, what is meant by anguish? The existentialists say at once that man is anguish. What that means is this: the man who involves himself and who realizes that he is not only the person he chooses to be, but also a law-maker who is, at the same time, choosing all mankind as well as himself, can not help escape the feeling of his total and deep responsibility. Of course, there are many people who are not anxious; but we claim that they are hiding their anxiety, that they are fleeing from it. Certainly, many people believe that when they do something, they themselves are the only ones involved, and when someone says to them, "What if everyone acted that way?" they shrug their shoulders and answer, "Everyone doesn't act that way." But really, one should always ask himself, "What would happen if everybody looked at things that way?" There is no escaping this disturbing thought except by a kind of double-dealing. A man who lies and makes excuses for himself by saying "not everybody does that," is someone with an uneasy conscience, because the act of lying implies that a universal value is conferred upon the lie.

Anguish is evident even when it conceals itself. This is the anguish that Kierkegaard called the anguish of Abraham. You know the story: an angel has ordered Abraham to sacrifice his son; if it really were an angel who has come and said, "You are Abraham, you shall sacrifice your son," everything would be all right. But everyone might first wonder, "Is it really an angel, and am I really Abraham? What proof do I have?"

There was a mad woman who had hallucinations; someone used to speak to her on the telephone and give her orders. Her doctor asked her, "Who is it who talks to you?" She answered, "He says it's God." What proof did she really have that it was God? If an angel comes to me, what proof is there that it's an angel? And if I hear voices, what proof is there that they come from heaven and not from hell, or from the subconscious, or a pathological condition? What proves that they are addressed to me? What proof is there that I have been appointed to impose my choice and my conception of man on humanity? I'll never find any proof or sign to convince me of that. If a voice addresses me, it is always for me to decide that this is the angel's voice; if I consider that such an act is a good one, it is I who will choose to say that it is good rather than bad.

Now, I'm not being singled out as an Abraham, and yet at every moment I'm obliged to perform exemplary acts. For every man, everything happens as if all mankind had its eyes fixed on him and were guiding itself by what he does. And every man ought to say to himself, "Am I really the kind of man who has the right to act in such a way that humanity might guide itself by my actions?" And if he does not say that to himself, he is masking his anguish.

There is no question here of the kind of anguish which would lead to quietism, to inaction. It is a matter of a simple sort of anguish that anybody who has had responsibilities is familiar with. For example, when a military officer takes the responsibility for an attack and sends a certain number of men to death, he chooses to do so, and in the main he alone makes the choice. Doubtless, orders come from above, but they are too broad; he interprets them, and on this interpretation depend the lives of ten or fourteen or twenty men. In making a decision he can not help having a certain anguish. All leaders know this anguish. That doesn't keep them from acting; on the contrary, it is the very condition of their action. For it implies that they envisage a number of possibilities, and when they choose one, they realize that it has value only because it is chosen. We shall see that this kind of anguish, which is the kind that existentialism describes, is explained, in addition, by a direct responsibility to the other men whom it involves. It is not a curtain separating us from action, but is part of action itself.

When we speak of forlornness, a term Heidegger was fond of, we mean only that God does not exist and that we have to face all the consequences of this. The existentialist is strongly opposed to a certain kind of secular ethics which would like to abolish God with the least possible expense. About 1880, some French teachers tried to set up a secular ethics which went something like this: God is a useless and costly hypothesis; we are discarding it; but, meanwhile, in order for there to be an ethics, a society, a civilization, it is essential that certain values be taken seriously and that they be considered as having an *a priori* existence. It must be obligatory, *a priori,* to be honest, not to lie, not to beat your wife, to have children, etc., etc. So we're going to try a little device which will make it possible to show that values exist all the same, inscribed in a heaven of ideas, though otherwise God does not exist. In other words—and this, I believe, is the tendency of everything called reformism in France— nothing will be changed if God does not exist. We shall find ourselves with the same norms of honesty, progress, and humanism, and we shall have made of God an outdated hypothesis which will peacefully die off by itself.

The existentialist, on the contrary, thinks it very distressing that God does not exist, because all possibility of finding values in a heaven of ideas disappears along with Him; there can no longer be an *a priori* Good, since there is no infinite and perfect consciousness to think it. Nowhere is it written that the Good exists, that we must be honest, that we must not lie; because the fact is we are on a plane where there are only men. Dostoievsky said, "If God didn't exist, everything would be possible." That is the very starting point of existentialism. Indeed, everything is permissible if God does not exist, and as a result man is forlorn, because neither within him nor without does he find anything to cling to. He can't start making excuses for himself.

If existence really does precede essence, there is no explaining things away by reference to a fixed and given human nature. In other words, there is no determinism, man is free, man is freedom. On the other hand, if God does not exist, we find no values or commands to turn to which legitimize our conduct. So, in the bright realm of values, we have no excuse behind us, nor justification before us. We are alone, with no excuses.

That is the idea I shall try to convey when I say that man is condemned to be free. Condemned, because he did not create himself, yet, in other respects is free; because, once thrown into the world, he is responsible for everything he does. The existentialist does not believe in the power of passion. He will never agree that a sweeping passion is a ravaging torrent which fatally leads a man to certain acts and is therefore an excuse. He thinks that man is responsible for his passion.

The existentialist does not think that man is going to help himself by finding in the world some omen by which to orient himself. Because he thinks that man will interpret the omen to suit himself. Therefore, he thinks that man, with no support and no aid, is condemned every moment to invent man. Ponge, in a very fine article, has said, "Man is the future of man." That's exactly it. But if it is taken to mean that this future is recorded in heaven, that God sees it, then it is false, because it would really no longer be a future. If it is taken to mean that, whatever a man may be, there is a future to be forged, a virgin future before him, then this remark is sound. But then we are forlorn.

To give you an example which will enable you to understand forlornness better, I shall cite the case of one of my students who came to see me under the following circumstances: his father was on bad terms with his mother, and, moreover, was inclined to be a collaborationist; his older brother had been killed in the German offensive of 1940, and the young man, with somewhat immature but generous feelings, wanted to avenge him. His mother lived alone with him, very much upset by the half-treason of her husband and the death of her older son; the boy was her only consolation.

The boy was faced with the choice of leaving for England and joining the Free French Forces—that is, leaving his mother behind—or remaining with his mother and helping her to carry on. He was fully aware that the woman lived only for him and that his going-off—and perhaps his death—would plunge her into despair. He was also aware that every act that he did for his mother's sake was a sure thing, in the sense that it was helping her to carry on, whereas every effort he made toward going off and fighting was an uncertain move which might run aground and prove completely useless; for example, on his way to England he might, while passing through Spain, be detained indefinitely in a Spanish camp; he might reach England or Algiers and be stuck in an office at a desk job. As a result, he was faced with two very different kinds of action: one, concrete, immediate, but concerning only one individual; the other concerned an incomparably vaster group, a national collectivity, but for that very reason was dubious, and might be interrupted en route. And, at the same time, he was wavering between two kinds of ethics. On the one hand, an ethics of sympathy, of personal devotion; on the other, a broader ethics, but one whose efficacy was more dubious. He had to choose between the two.

Who could help him choose? Christian doctrine? No. Christian doctrine says, "Be charitable, love your neighbor, take the more rugged path, etc., etc." But which is the more rugged path? Whom should he love as a brother? The fighting man or his mother? Which does the greater good, the vague act of fighting in a group, or the concrete one of helping a particular human being to go on living? Who can decide *a priori?* Nobody. No book of ethics can tell him. The Kantian ethics says, "Never treat any person as a means, but as an end." Very well, if I stay with my mother, I'll treat her as an end and not as a means; but by virtue of this very fact, I'm running the risk of treating the people around me who are fighting, as means; and conversely, if I go to join those who are fighting, I'll be treating them as an end, and, by doing that, I run the risk of treating my mother as a means.

If values are vague, and if they are always too broad for the concrete and specific case that we are considering, the only thing left for us is to trust our instincts. That's what this young man tried to do; and when I saw him, he said, "In the end, feeling is what counts. I ought to choose which ever pushes me in one direction. If I feel that I love my mother enough to sacrifice everything else for her—my desire for vengeance, for action, for adventure—then I'll stay with her. If, on the contrary, I feel that my love for my mother isn't enough, I'll leave."

But how is the value of a feeling determined? What gives his feeling for his mother value? Precisely the fact that he remained with her. I may say that I like so-and-so well enough to sacrifice a certain amount of money for him, but I may say so only if I've done it. I may say "I love my mother well enough to remain with her" if I have remained with her. The only way to determine the value of this affection is, precisely, to perform an act which confirms and defines it. But, since I require this affection to justify my act, I find myself caught in a vicious circle.

On the other hand, Gide has well said that a mock feeling and a true feeling are almost indistinguishable; to decide that I love my mother and will remain with her, or to remain with her by putting on an act, amount somewhat to the same thing. In other words, the feeling is formed by the acts one performs; so, I can not refer to it in order to act upon it. Which means that I can neither seek within myself the true condition which will impel me to act, nor apply to a system of ethics for concepts which will permit me to act. You will say, "At least, he did go to a teacher for advice." But if you seek advice from a priest, for example, you have chosen this priest; you already knew, more or less, just about what advice he was going to give you. In other words, choosing your adviser is involving yourself. The proof of this is that if you are a Christian, you will say, "Consult a priest." But some priests are collaborating, some are just marking time, some are resisting. Which to choose? If the young man chooses a priest who is resisting or collaborating, he has already decided on the kind of advice he's going to get. Therefore, in coming to see me he knew the answer I was going to give him, and I had only one answer to give: "You're free, choose, that is, invent." No general ethics can show you what is to be done; there are no omens in the world. The Catholics will reply, "But there are." Granted —but, in any case, I myself choose the meaning they have.

When I was a prisoner, I knew a rather remarkable young man who was a Jesuit. He had entered the Jesuit order in the following way: he had had a number of very bad breaks; in childhood, his father died, leaving him in poverty, and he was a scholarship student at a religious institution where he was constantly made to feel that he was being kept out of charity; then, he failed to get any of the honors and distinctions that children like; later on, at about eighteen, he bungled a love affair; finally, at twenty-two, he failed in military training, a childish enough matter, but it was the last straw.

This young fellow might well have felt that he had botched everything. It was a sign of something, but of what? He might have taken refuge in bitterness or despair. But he very wisely looked upon all this as a sign that he was not made for secular triumphs, and that only the triumphs of religion, holiness, and faith were open to him. He saw the hand of God in all this, and so he entered the order. Who can help seeing that he alone decided what the sign meant?

Some other interpretation might have been drawn from this series of setbacks; for example, that he might have done better to turn carpenter or revolutionist. Therefore, he is fully responsible for the interpretation. Forlornness implies that we ourselves choose our being. Forlornness and anguish go together.

IV

Actually, things will be as man will have decided they are to be. Does that mean that I should abandon myself to quietism? No. First, I should involve myself; then, act

on the old saw, "Nothing ventured, nothing gained." Nor does it mean that I shouldn't belong to a party, but rather that I shall have no illusions and shall do what I can. For example, suppose I ask myself, "Will socialization, as such, ever come about?" I know nothing about it. All I know is that I'm going to do everything in my power to bring it about. Beyond that, I can't count on anything. Quietism is the attitude of people who say, "Let others do what I can't do." The doctrine I am presenting is the very opposite of quietism, since it declares, "There is no reality except in action." Moreover, it goes further, since it adds, "Man is nothing else than his plan; he exists only to the extent that he fulfills himself; he is therefore nothing else than the ensemble of his acts, nothing else than his life."

According to this, we can understand why our doctrine horrifies certain people. Because often the only way they can bear their wretchedness is to think, "Circumstances have been against me. What I've been and done doesn't show my true worth. To be sure, I've had no great love, no great friendship, but that's because I haven't met a man or woman who was worthy. The books I've written haven't been very good because I haven't had the proper leisure. I haven't had children to devote myself to because I didn't find a man with whom I could have spent my life. So there remains within me, unused and quite viable, a host of propensities, inclinations, possibilities, that one wouldn't guess from the mere series of things I've done."

Now, for the existentialist there is really no love other than one which manifests itself in a person's being in love. There is no genius other than one which is expressed in works of art; the genius of Proust is the sum of Proust's works; the genius of Racine is his series of tragedies. Outside of that, there is nothing. Why say that Racine could have written another tragedy, when he didn't write it? A man is involved in life, leaves his impress on it, and outside of that there is nothing. To be sure, this may seem a harsh thought to someone whose life hasn't been a success. But, on the other hand, it prompts people to understand that reality alone is what counts, that dreams, expectations, and hopes warrant no more than to define a man as a disappointed dream, as miscarried hopes, as vain expectations. In other words, to define him negatively and not positively. However, when we say, "You are nothing else than your life," that does not imply that the artist will be judged solely on the basis of his works of art; a thousand other things will contribute toward summing him up. What we mean is that a man is nothing else than a series of undertakings, that he is the sum, the organization, the ensemble of the relationships which make up these undertakings.

When all is said and done, what we are accused of, at bottom, is not our pessimism, but an optimistic toughness. If people throw up to us our works of fiction in which we write about people who are soft, weak, cowardly, and sometimes even downright bad, it's not because these people are soft, weak, cowardly, or bad; because if we were to say, as Zola did, that they are that way because of heredity, the workings of environment, society, because of biological or psychological determinism, people would be reassured. They would say, "Well, that's what we're like, no one can do anything about it." But when the existentialist writes about a coward, he says that this coward is responsible for his cowardice. He's not like that because he has a cowardly heart or lung or brain; he's not like that on account of his physiological make-up; but he's like that because he has made himself a coward by his acts. There's no such thing as a cowardly constitution; there are nervous constitutions; there is poor blood, as the common people say, or strong constitutions. But the man whose blood is poor is not a coward on that account, for what makes cowardice is the act of renouncing or yielding. A constitution is not an act; the coward is defined on the basis of the acts he performs. People feel, in a vague sort of way, that this coward we're talking about is guilty of being a coward, and the thought frightens them. What people would like is that a coward or hero be born that way.

If you're born cowardly, you may set your mind perfectly at rest; there's nothing you can do about it; you'll be cowardly all your life, whatever you may do. If you're born a hero, you may set your mind just as much at rest; you'll be a hero all your life; you'll drink like a hero and eat like a hero. What the existentialist says is that the coward makes himself cowardly, that the hero makes himself heroic. There's always a possibility for the coward not to be cowardly any more and for the hero to stop being heroic. What counts is total involvement; some one particular action or set of circumstances is not total involvement.

Thus, I think we have answered a number of the charges concerning existentialism. You see that it can not be taken for a philosophy of quietism, since it defines man in terms of action; nor for a pessimistic description of man—there is no doctrine more optimistic, since man's destiny is within himself; nor for an attempt to discourage man from acting, since it tells him that the only hope is in his acting and that action is the only thing that enables a man to live. Consequently, we are dealing here with an ethics of action and involvement.

Nevertheless, on the basis of a few notions like these, we are still charged with immuring man in his private subjectivity. There again we're very much misunderstood. Subjectivity of the individual is indeed our point of departure, and this for strictly philosophic reasons. Not because we are bourgeois, but because we want a doctrine based on truth and not a lot of fine theories, full of hope but with no real basis. There can be no other truth to take off from than this: *I think; therefore, I exist.* There we have the absolute truth of consciousness becoming aware of itself. Every theory which takes man out of the moment in which he becomes aware of himself is, at its very beginning, a theory which confounds truth, for outside the Cartesian *cogito,* all views are only probable, and a doctrine of probability which is not bound to a truth dissolves into thin air. In order to describe the probable, you must have a firm hold on the true. Therefore, before there can be any truth whatsoever, there must be an absolute truth; and this one is simply and easily arrived at; it's on everyone's doorstep; it's a matter of grasping it directly.

Secondly, this theory is the only one which gives man dignity, the only one which does not reduce him to an object. The effect of all materialism is to treat all men, including the one philosophizing, as objects, that is, as an ensemble of determined reactions in no way distinguished from the ensemble of qualities and phenomena which constitute a table or a chair or a stone. We definitely wish to establish the human realm as an ensemble of values distinct from the material realm. But the subjectivity that we have thus arrived at, and which we have claimed to be truth, is not a strictly individual subjectivity, for we have demonstrated that one discovered in the *cogito* not only himself, but others as well.

The philosophies of Descartes and Kant to the contrary, through the *I think* we reach our own self in the presence of others, and the others are just as real to us as our own self. Thus, the man who becomes aware of himself through the *cogito* also perceives all others, and he perceives them as the condition of his own existence. He realizes that he can not be anything (in the sense that we say that someone is witty or nasty or jealous) unless others recognize it as such. In order to get any truth about myself, I must have contact with another person. The other is indispensable to my own existence, as well as to my knowledge about myself. This being so, in discovering my inner being I discover the other person at the same time, like a freedom placed in front of me which thinks and wills only for or against me. Hence, let us at once announce the discovery of a world which we shall call intersubjectivity; this is the world in which man decides what he is and what others are.

* * * * * *

From these few reflections it is evident that nothing is more unjust than the objections that have been raised against us. Existentialism is nothing else than an attempt to draw all the consequences of a coherent atheistic position. It isn't trying to plunge man into despair at all. But if one calls every attitude of unbelief despair, like the Christians, then the word is not being used in its original sense. Existentialism isn't so atheistic that it wears itself out showing that God doesn't exist. Rather, it declares that even if God did exist, that would change nothing. There you've got our point of view. Not that we believe that God exists, but we think that the problem of His existence is not the issue. In this sense existentialism is optimistic, a doctrine of action, and it is plain dishonesty for Christians to make no distinction between their own despair and ours and then to call us despairing.

The Prophet of Existentialism: Friedrich Nietzsche

There are many similarities between Nietzsche and Kierkegaard, the two great nineteenth-century figures to whom contemporary existentialism is most directly indebted. Both are disturbing, controversial figures who do not fit easily into any recognized mold; both were lonely men—feeling the need of human companionship but not able to find any deeply satisfying social relationships. Both were unappreciated by their contemporaries, yet were deeply conscious themselves of their own importance and of the significance of their work. Nietzsche, in particular, thought of himself as the prophet whose task it was, like John the Baptist in the New Testament, to point to the dissolution of his own world and proclaim the coming of a new day, a new age. In his greatest and most paradoxical work, *Thus Spake Zarathustra,* he makes the old Persian prophet Zarathustra (or Zoroaster) the spokesman of his own new gospel.

It is not easy to interpret Nietzsche. He cannot be understood through any one category—even that of existentialism. His philosophy has many facets, and each age sees that aspect which meets its own needs or suits its particular situation. The German Nazis, for example, found in Nietzsche an intellectually distinguished spokesman for their own attacks upon democracy and Christianity and their appeal to the will to power, and they made Nietzsche the official philosopher of Nazi Germany. No one would have been more horrified at this than Nietzsche himself; nevertheless, he did very definitely emphasize all the ideas that the Nazis took from his philosophy. Today it is the existentialists who find in Nietzsche the foundation upon which their philosophy is built, and again these ideas are all authentic aspects of his thought—more nearly representative of his strange genius, one would certainly like to believe, than the official philosophy of Nazi Germany.

Nietzsche was born in 1844 in a small village in Prussia where his father was the Lutheran minister. As a boy he was studious, well-behaved, and highly esteemed by his teachers. When he was only five years old, his father died and he was left in the care of five women—his grandmother, his mother, two aunts, and his sister. They were all good women, too good indeed to distinguish between love and indulgence. As the only male left in the house, they were devoted to young Fritz. At sixteen both in his own mind and in the minds of the women who looked after him, Nietzsche seemed clearly to be destined for the Luthern ministry. But in a year or two something began to go wrong. He was disturbed by doubt about the existence of God, lost interest in his classes, even slipped off once or twice and got quite drunk on beer. When at the age of twenty he entered the University of Bonn, he gave up religion entirely and tried desperately to enter into the social life of the institution. He joined a student corps, drank beer at noisy gatherings, and even made one pathetic attempt to fight a duel. However, beer, women and tobacco actually disgusted him. Bonn soon became unbearable, so he wrote a rather self-righteous letter of resignation and left for the University of Leipzig.

At Leipzig he picked up Schopenhauer's *World as Will and Idea* one afternoon in a bookshop and read it with increasing excitement. Fascinated by Schopenhauer, Nietzsche at twenty-one became a pessimist. It is impossible, he declared, to make sense of human life. Will—the blind striving of millions of living creatures—and not reason, really makes life what it is—cruel, stupid, futile. In such a world one can no longer believe in God. All that life has to offer a thoughtful man is resignation, renunciation. Clearly Schopenhauer helped to make Nietzsche the prophet of existentialism.

Despite this gloomy outlook on life, Nietzsche devoted himself with industry and unquestioned ability to his classes at Leipzig, becoming one of the outstanding students at the university. When in 1868 the chair of classical philology at the University of Basel in Switzerland became vacant, Nietzsche was appointed to this position, but unhappily, as a university professor, he was not a success. Teaching soon became a burden and a waste of time in his eyes. He had a neurotic dislike for mingling with people he did not know, a dislike increased, no doubt, by his fear of being ridiculed. To those who knew him casually, he seemed an oversensitive young professor, timid and just a bit peculiar. When in 1872, he published his first and only complete book, *The Birth of Tragedy Out of the Spirit of Music,* his colleagues in philology condemned it almost unanimously. Embittered Nietzsche gave himself more and more to writing; in 1879, after ten years at Basel, he retired when only thirty-four.

Twenty years of life lay ahead for him—a decade of extraordinary literary activity during which all his greatest books were written and a decade of hopeless invalidism during which he was completely broken in mind and body. His great decade was spent mostly in Italy and Switzerland, and the books he wrote were largely collections of brief essays or short comments. As the urge to creativity would seize him, he wrote furiously until exhausted; then an attack of headaches or insomnia would incapacitate him for a time. He was never able to write in an orderly systematic fashion.

Nietzsche's last years were lonely ones. He had quarreled with all his friends, and a frustrated love affair left him embittered toward all women. An early devotion to Wagner and his wife Cosima had ended in envy and recrimination. Innkeepers, servants, and a few casual acquaintances provided his only contact with his fellows. Left thus alone, he gave himself unsparingly to intensive literary effort. The intensity of this effort, his sense of being unappreciated, his loneliness, all helped bring on a mental breakdown. Disease and approaching blindness were also contributing factors. In 1889 he was placed in a hospital for the insane. For the next ten years he was cared for first by his aged mother and then by his sister Elizabeth. On August 25, 1900, Nietzsche died quietly in Wiemar where his sister had taken him.

"My time is not yet; only the day after tomorrow belongs to me," he wrote in 1888, and his faith in himself, when no one else would believe, has been amply justified. Now his memory is honored in such fashion as he himself would approve. Although frequently attacked by those who reject his views, Nietzsche is quite generally regarded today as a sensitive poet, a philosopher of unquestioned ability, and a master of German prose, whose insights in rather startling fashion anticipated the outlook of much contemporary thought.

The major themes of existentialism, for example, are all apparent in Nietzsche's philosophy. In one of his early books, entitled *Thoughts Out of Season,* he vehemently attacks the spirit of the age in which he lived. The hypocrisy and shallowness of nineteenth-century bourgeois morality was the object of his attack. The individual was no longer of importance; as a result of the influence of mass morality greatness had disappeared from human life. The progress of science and the emphasis on rationality were in large measure responsible, Nietzsche insists. The concern with "objectivity" in the study of history, for example, is merely a disguise for a cold indifference to all values, he argues. Genuine historical knowledge requires nobility of character, a profound understanding of human existence—not detachment and objectivity. Historical knowledge must be subordinated to life, the individual taught to live "unhistorically." Only then can modern scholarship get at the essential truth of history.[1]

Nothing great, nothing distinctive, can come from a society in which the individual is subordinated—in which scientific progress and material success are the great gods of mankind. This was what had happened to Europe at mid-nineteenth century, and Nietzsche saw it more clearly than his contemporaries. There was no greatness of spirit, no daring, no creativity left. Man had been all but destroyed by mankind; for this Nietzsche finds two things largely responsible—Christianity and democracy. The result will be "a flock without a shepherd, a flock in which all the sheep are equal." The spirit of the herd manifests itself in democracy, in socialism, and most of all in Christianity. Europe has been infected with the leveling spirit of mediocrity; a decadence has settled upon mankind. This is the central theme of Nietzsche's two most readable books—in which his new moral theory finds clearest statement—*Beyond Good and Evil* and *The Geneology of Morals.* In these he develops his well-known theory of the two basic types of morality: the morality of the masses, which is a slave morality, and the morality of the masters, the aristocratic morality which characterized human life in the great creative periods in the past, and to which he again is calling Europe in his own day. This is indeed for Nietzsche an "existential" morality in which man discovers his "true" self, in which the individual escapes from the rationalism and determinism of contemporary scientific naturalism and reasserts his own freedom and creativity, in which man rejects the spirit of the herd, into which the morality of the masses has cast him, and moves toward the true goal of humanity, the Superman. Nietzsche sees quite clearly, moreover, as many moralists have not, that for the feminine half of the human race, who deal with moral issues in altogether different

---

[1] *Cf.* the essay on "The Uses and Abuses of History," in *Thoughts Out of Season.*

terms, the whole history of ethics presented from the masculine point of view has very little to do with the real business of human life. Among Nietzsche's most provocative comments are those on women.

Nietzsche's existentialism finds its most revealing statement in *Thus Spake Zarathustra* (1883–1885). This is a poetic and paradoxical book full of symbols and, like all existential works, very difficult to understand. It is, moreover, a unique work of self-revelation. "All that I have thought, suffered and hoped is in it, and in such a way that my entire life appears now somehow vindicated," he wrote from Rome in May, 1883. "Behind all these simple and strange words stands my deadly seriousness and *my entire philosophy*."[2] What was happening in his own life could only be understood, Nietzsche intuitively recognized, as a personal experience of what he saw about him in the age of which he was a part. Western civilization was tearing itself loose from the moral and spiritual foundations upon which it had rested for a thousand years. Not a day goes by, Nietzsche wrote in one of his letters, that I do not lop off some comforting belief. Up to that time man had lived in the shelter and under the protection of his gods or of God. Now, as Nietzsche believed and felt more tragically than any of his contemporaries, that faith and the gods themselves were dead, and with this death went the destruction of all the moral and spiritual values that had been built upon it. He had lived through the destruction of his own Christian faith; he saw a situation about him where God was really dead for mankind, and he was keenly aware of the common fate of humanity. "Do we not now wander through an endless Nothingness?" he asks. Here was the event of greatest significance in modern life, the disturbing situation that modern man was called upon to face. Could he meet this awful challenge of tearing himself loose from his roots, of becoming adult and godless? Did he have any real idea of what it meant—of the kind of courage that it took? Here indeed was the supreme act of courage.

Nietzsche's first description of what he saw happening is found in *The Joyful Wisdom* (Section 125), where he writes movingly of the tragic discovery that God is dead. The man who has seen this is taken for a madman, and he cries out to a doomed but unheeding civilization:

Have you not heard as yet of that mad-man who on one bright forenoon lit a lantern, ran out into the market-place and cried out again and again, "I seek God! I seek God!"—Because there were standing about just at that time many who did not believe in God, the mad-man was the occasion of great merriment. Has God been lost? said one of them. Or is He hiding himself? Is He afraid of us? Has He boarded a ship? Has He emigrated? Thus they cried and laughed.

But the mad-man pierced them with his glance: "Whither has God gone?" he cried; "I am going to tell you. *We have killed Him*—you and I! We

[2] Quoted by K. F. Reinhardt, *The Existential Revolt*, (Milwaukee, Bruce Publishing Company, 1952), p. 96.

all are His murderers. But how have we accomplished this? How have we been able to empty the sea? Who gave us the sponge to wipe off the entire horizon? What were we doing when we unchained this earth from its sun? Whither does the earth move now? Whither do we ourselves move?

"Are we not groping our way in an infinite nothingness? Do we not feel the breath of the empty spaces. Has it not become colder? Is there not night and ever more night? How do we manage to console ourselves, we master-assassins? Who is going to wipe the blood off our hands? Must not we ourselves become gods to make ourselves worthy of such a deed?"[3]

The message of *Thus Spake Zarathustra* is born in this experience. Zarathustra comes to proclaim not only that God is dead, but that *man must remake himself:* the Superman is the meaning of the earth. The salvation that Nietzsche sees for mankind lies in the great aristocratic principle—in courage, strength, daring—in the Will to Power: not in the slave morality—humility, peace, kindness, mutual helpfulness—these will never rescue man from the meaninglessness of existence—but in the aristocratic morality, the will of the strong individual who in creative freedom makes his own law, his own morality—who is "Beyond Good and Evil." In this "transvaluation of all values" Nietzsche finds the only path to greatness, the only escape from the meaninglessness of a decadent European democracy, and, as a prophet in the wilderness, he calls the men of his generation to this new gospel.

---

[3] *The Joyful Wisdom,* English translation by Thomas Common. (London, George Allen and Unwin, Ltd., 1910). By permission of the publisher.

Thus Spake Zarathustra*

Prologue

1

When Zarathustra was thirty years old, he left his home and the lake of his home, and went into the mountains. There he enjoyed his spirit and his solitude, and for ten years did not weary of it. But at last his heart changed,—and rising one morning with the rosy dawn, he went before the sun, and spake thus unto it:

Thou great star! What would be thy happiness if thou hadst not those from whom thou shinest!

---

* Friedrich Nietzsche, *Thus Spake Zarathustra,* English trans. by Thomas Common. (London, George Allen & Unwin, Ltd., 1909).

For ten years hast thou climbed hither unto my cave; thou wouldst have wearied of thy light and of the journey, had it not been for me, mine eagle, and my serpent.

But we awaited thee every morning, took from thine overflow, and blessed thee for it.

Lo! I am weary of my wisdom, like the bee that hath gathered too much honey; I need hands outstretched to take it.

I would fain bestow and distribute, until the wise have once more become joyous in their folly, and the poor happy in their riches.

Therefore must I descend into the deep: as thou doest in the evening, when thou goest behind the sea, and givest light also to the nether-world, thou exuberant star!

Like thee must I go down, as men say, to whom I shall descend.

Bless me, then, thou tranquil eye, that canst behold even the greatest happiness without envy!

Bless the cup that is about to overflow, that the water may flow golden out of it, and carry everywhere the reflection of thy bliss!

Lo! This cup is again going to empty itself, and Zarathustra is again going to be a man.

Thus began Zarathustra's down-going.

2

Zarathustra went down the mountain alone, no one meeting him. When he entered the forest, however, there suddenly stood before him an old man, who had left his holy cot to seek roots. And thus spake the old man to Zarathustra:

"No stranger to me is this wanderer: many years ago passed he by. Zarathustra he was called; but he hath altered.

Then thou carriedst thine ashes into the mountains: wilt thou now carry thy fire into the valleys? Fearest thou not the incendiary's doom?

Yea, I recognise Zarathustra. Pure is his eye, and no loathing lurketh about his mouth. Goeth he not along like a dancer?

Altered is Zarathustra: a child hath Zarathustra become; an awakened one is Zarathustra: what wilt thou do in the land of the sleepers?

As in the sea hast thou lived in solitude, and it hath borne thee up. Alas, wilt thou now go ashore? Alas, wilt thou again drag thy body thyself?"

Zarathustra answered: "I love mankind."

"Why," said the saint, "did I go into the forest and the desert? Was it not because I loved men far too well?

Now I love God: men, I do not love. Man is a thing too imperfect for me. Love to man would be fatal to me.

Go not to men but stay in the forest! Go rather to the animals! Why not be like me —a bear amongst bears, a bird amongst birds?"

"And what doeth the saint in the forest?" asked Zarathustra.

The saint answered: "I make hymns and sing them; and in making hymns I laugh and weep and mumble: thus do I praise God.

With singing, weeping, laughing, and mumbling do I praise the God who is my God. But what doest thou bring us as a gift?"

When Zarathustra had heard these words, he bowed to the saint and said: "What should I have to give thee! Let me rather hurry hence lest I take aught away from thee!"—And thus they parted from one another, the old man and Zarathustra, laughing like schoolboys.

When Zarathustra was alone, however, he said to his heart: "Could it be possible! This old saint in the forest hath not yet heard of it, that *God is dead!*"

3

When Zarathustra arrived at the nearest town which adjoineth the forest, he found many people assembled in the market-place; for it had been announced that a rope-dancer would give a performance. And Zarathustra spake thus unto the people.

I teach you the Superman. Man is something that is to be surpassed. What have ye done to surpass man?

All beings hitherto have created something beyond themselves: and ye want to be the ebb of that great tide, and would rather go back to the beast than surpass man?

What is the ape to man? A laughing-stock, a thing of shame. And just the same shall man be to the Superman: a laughing-stock, a thing of shame.

Ye have made your way from the worm to man, and much within you is still worm. Once were ye apes, and even yet man is more of an ape than any of the apes.

Even the wisest among you is only a disharmony and hybrid of plant and phantom. But do I bid you become phantoms or plants?

Lo, I teach you the Superman!

The Superman is the meaning of the earth. Let your will say: The Superman shall be the meaning of the earth!

I conjure you, my brethren, remain

true to the earth, and believe not those who speak unto you of superearthly hopes! Poisoners are they, whether they know it or not.

Despisers of life are they, decaying ones and poisoned ones themselves, of whom the earth is weary: so away with them!

Once blasphemy against God was the greatest blasphemy; but God died, and therewith also those blasphemers. To blaspheme the earth is now the dreadfulest sin, and to rate the heart of the unknowable higher than the meaning of the earth!

Once the soul looked contemptuously on the body, and then that contempt was the supreme thing:—the soul wished the body meagre, ghastly, and famished. Thus it thought to escape from the body and the earth.

Oh, that soul was itself meagre, ghastly, and famished; and cruelty was the delight of that soul!

But ye, also, my brethren, tell me: What doth your body say about your soul? Is your soul not poverty and pollution and wretched self-complacency?

Verily, a polluted stream is man. One must be a sea, to receive a polluted stream without becoming impure.

Lo, I teach you the Superman: he is that sea; in him can your great contempt be submerged.

When Zarathustra had thus spoken, one of the people called out: "We have now heard enough of the rope-dancer; it is time now for us to see him!" And all the people laughed at Zarathustra. But the rope-dancer, who thought the words applied to him, began his performance.

4

Zarathustra, however, looked at the people and wondered. Then he spake thus:

Man is a rope stretched between the animal and the Superman—a rope over an abyss.

A dangerous crossing, a dangerous wayfaring, a dangerous looking-back, a dangerous trembling and halting.

What is great in man is that he is a bridge and not a goal: what is lovable in man

is that he is an over-going and a down-going.

I love those that know not how to live except as down-goers, for they are the over-goers.

I love those who do not first seek a reason beyond the stars for going down and being sacrifices, but sacrifice themselves to the earth, that the earth of the Superman may hereafter arrive.

I love him who liveth in order to know, and seeketh to know in order that the Superman may hereafter live. Thus seeketh he his own down-going.

I love him who laboureth and inventeth, that he may build the house for the Superman, and prepare for him earth, animal, and plant: for thus seeketh he his own down-going.

I love him who chasteneth his God, because he loveth his God: for he must succumb through the wrath of his God.

I love all who are like heavy drops falling one by one out of the dark cloud that lowereth over man: they herald the coming of the lightning and succumb as heralds.

Lo, I am a herald of the lightning, and a heavy drop out of the cloud: the lightning, however, is the *Superman.*—

5

When Zarathustra had spoken these words, he again looked at the people, and was silent. "There they stand," said he to his heart; "there they laugh: they understand me not; I am not the mouth for these ears.

Must one first batter their ears, that they learn to hear with their eyes? Must one clatter like kettledrums and penitential preachers? Or do they only believe the stammerer?

They have something whereof they are proud. What do they call it, that which maketh them proud? Culture, they call it; it distinguisheth them from the goatherds.

They dislike, therefore, to hear of 'contempt' of themselves. So I will appeal to their pride.

I will speak unto them of the most contemptible thing: that, however is the last man!"

And thus spake Zarathustra unto the people:

It is time for man to fix his goal. It is time for man to plant the germ of his highest hope.

Still is his soil rich enough for it. But that soil will one day be poor and exhausted, and no lofty tree will any longer be able to grow thereon.

Alas! there cometh the time when man will no longer launch the arrow of his longing beyond man—and the string of his bow will have unlearned to whizz!

I tell you: one must still have chaos in one, to give birth to a dancing star. I tell you: ye have still chaos in you.

Alas! there cometh the time when man will no longer give birth to any star. Alas! There cometh the time of the most despicable man, who can no longer despise himself.

Lo! I show you *the last man*.

"We have discovered happiness"—say the last men, and blink thereby.

They have left the regions where it is hard to live; for they need warmth. One still loveth one's neighbor and rubbeth against him; for one needeth warmth.

Turning ill and being distrustful, they consider sinful; they walk warily. He is a fool who still stumbleth over stones or men!

A little poison now and then: that maketh pleasant dreams. And much poison at last for a pleasant death.

One still worketh, for work is a pastime. But one is careful lest the pastime should hurt one.

One no longer becometh poor or rich; both are too burdensome. Who still wanteth to rule? Who still wanteth to obey? Both are too burdensome.

No shepherd, and one herd! Every one wanteth the same; every one is equal: he who hath other sentiments goeth voluntarily into the madhouse.

"Formerly all the world was insane,"—say the subtlest of them, and blink thereby.

They are clever and know all that hath happened: so there is no end to their raillery. People still fall out, but are soon reconciled—otherwise it spoileth their stomachs.

They have their little pleasures for the day, and their little pleasures for the night: but they have a regard for health.

"We have discovered happiness,"—say the last men, and blink thereby.—

And here ended the first discourse of Zarathustra, which is also called "The Prologue": for at this point the shouting and mirth of the multitude interrupted him. "Give us this last man, O Zarathustra,"—they called out—"make us into these last men! Then will we make thee a present of the Superman!" And all the people exulted and smacked their lips. Zarathustra, however, turned sad, and said to his heart.

"They understand me not: I am not the mouth for these ears.

Too long, perhaps, have I lived in the mountains; too much have I hearkened unto the brooks and trees: now do I speak unto them as unto the goatherds.

Calm is my soul, and clear, like the mountains in the morning. But they think me cold, and a mocker with terrible jests.

And now do they look at me and laugh: and while they laugh they hate me too. There is ice in their laughter."

6

Then, however, something happened which made every mouth mute and every eye fixed. In the meantime, of course, the rope-dancer had commenced his performance: he had come out at a little door, and was going along the rope which was stretched between two towers, so that it hung above the market-place and the people. When he was just midway across, the little door opened once more, and a gaudily-dressed fellow like a buffoon sprang out, and went rapidly after the first one. "Go on, halt-foot," cried his frightful voice, "go on, lazy-bones, interloper, sallow-face!—lest I tickle thee with my heel! What dost thou here between the towers? In the tower is the place for thee, thou shouldst be locked up; to one better than thyself thou blockest the way!"—And with every word he came nearer and nearer the first one. When, however, he was but a step behind, there happened the frightful thing which made every mouth mute and every eye fixed:—he uttered a yell like a devil, and jumped over the other who was in his way. The latter, however, when he thus saw his rival triumph, lost at the same time his head and his footing on the rope; he threw his pole away, and shot downwards faster than it, like an eddy of arms and legs, into the depth. The market-place and the people were like the sea, when the storm cometh on: they all flew apart and in disorder, especially where the body was about to fall.

Zarathustra, however, remained standing, and just beside him fell the body, badly injured and disfigured, but not yet dead. After a while consciousness returned to the shattered man, and he saw Zarathustra kneeling beside him.

"What art thou doing there?" said he, at last, "I knew long ago that the devil would trip me up. Now he draggeth me to hell: wilt thou prevent him?"

"On mine honour, my friend," answered Zarathustra, "there is nothing of all that whereof thou speakest: there is no devil and no hell. Thy soul will be dead even sooner than thy body: fear, therefore, nothing any more."

The man looked up distrustfully. "If thou speakest the truth," said he, "I lose nothing when I lose my life. I am not much more than an animal which hath been taught to dance by blows and scanty fare."

"Not at all," said Zarathustra, "thou hast made danger thy calling; therein there is nothing contemptible. Now thou perishest by thy calling: therefore will I bury thee with mine own hands."

When Zarathustra had said this the dying one did not reply further; but he moved his hand as if he sought the hand of Zarathustra in graitude.

7

Meanwhile the evening came on, and the market-place veiled itself in gloom. Then the people dispersed, for even curiosity and terror become fatigued. Zarathustra, however, still sat beside the dead man on the ground, absorbed in thought: so he forgot the time. But at last it became night, and a cold wind blew upon the lonely one. Then arose Zarathustra and said to his heart:

Verily, a fine catch of fish hath Zarathustra made to-day! It is not a man he hath caught, but corpse.

Sombre is human life, and as yet without meaning: a buffoon may be fateful to it.

I want to teach men the sense of their existence, which is the Superman, the lightning out of the dark cloud—man.

But still am I far from them, and my sense speaketh not unto their sense. To men I am still something between a fool and a corpse.

Gloomy is the night, gloomy are the ways of Zarathustra. Come, thou cold and stiff companion! I carry thee to the place where I shall bury thee with mine own hands.

The Prejudices of Philosophers*

1

The will to truth, which is to tempt us to many a hazardous enterprise, the famous Truthfulness of which all philosophers have

* Friedrich Nietzsche, *Beyond Good and Evil*, Ch. I. English translation by Helen Zimmern. (London, George Allen & Unwin, Ltd., 1909). By permission of the publisher. Numerical order imposed.

hitherto spoken with respect, what questions has this Will to Truth not laid before us! What strange, perplexing, questionable questions! It is already a long story; yet it seems as if it were hardly commenced. Is it any wonder if we at last grow distrustful, lose patience, and turn impatiently away? What really is this "Will to truth" in us? In fact we made a long halt at the question as to the origin of this Will—until at last we came to an absolute standstill before a yet more funda-mental question. We inquired about the value of this Will. Granted that we want the truth: *why not rather* untruth? And uncertainty? Even ignorance? The problem of the value of truth presented itself before us—or was it we who presented ourselves before the prob-lem? And could it be believed that it at last seems to us as if the problem had never been propounded before, as if we were the first to discern it, get a sight of it, and risk raising it. For there is risk in raising it, perhaps there is no greater risk.

2

The falseness of an opinion is not for us any objection to it: it is here, perhaps, that our new language sounds most strangely. The question is, how far an opinion is life-furthering, life-preserving, species-preserving, perhaps species-rearing; and we are fundamen-tally inclined to maintain that the falsest opin-ions (to which the synthetic judgments *a priori* belong) are the most indispensable to us; that without a recognition of logical fic-tions, without a comparison of reality with the purely imagined world of the absolute and im-mutable, with a constant counterfeiting of the world by means of numbers, man could not live—that the renunciation of false opinions would be a renunciation of life, a negation of life. *To recognize untruth as a condition of life:* that is certainly to impugn the traditional ideas of value in a dangerous manner, and a philosophy which ventures to do so, has thereby alone placed itself beyond good and evil.

3

That which causes philosophers to be regarded half-distrustfully and half-mockingly is not the oft-repeated discovery how innocent they are—how often and easily they make mistakes and lose their way, in short, how childish and childlike they are—but that there is not enough honest dealing with them, whereas they all raise a loud and virtuous outcry when the problem of truthfulness is even hinted at in the remotest manner. They all pose as though their real opinions had

been discovered and attained through the self-evolving of a cold, pure, divinely indifferent dialectic (in contrast to all sorts of mystics, who, fairer and foolisher, talk of "inspira-tion"); whereas, in fact, a prejudiced proposi-tion, idea, or "suggestion," which is generally their heart's desire abstracted and refined, is defended by them with arguments sought out after the event. They are all advocates who do not wish to be regarded as such, generally astute defenders, also, of their prejudices, which they dub "truths"—and very far from having the conscience which bravely ad-mits this to itself; very far from having the good taste of the courage which goes so far as to let this be understood, perhaps to warn friend or foe, or in cheerful confidence and self-ridicule.

4

It has gradually become clear to me what every great philosophy up till now has consisted of—namely, the confession of its originator, and a species of involuntary and unconscious autobiography; and moreover that the moral (or immoral) purpose in every philosophy has constituted the true vital germ out of which the entire plant has always grown. Indeed, to understand how the ab-strusest metaphysical assertions of a philos-opher have been arrived at, it is always well (and wise) to first ask oneself: "What mo-rality do they (or does he) aim at?" Accord-ingly, I do not believe that an "impulse to knowledge" is the father of philosophy; but that another impulse, here as elsewhere, has only made use of knowledge (and mistaken knowledge!) as an instrument. For every im-pulse is imperious, and as such, attempts to philosophize. To be sure, in the case of scholars, in the case of really scientific men, it may be otherwise—"Better," if you will; there may really be such a thing as "an im-pulse to knowledge," some kind of small, independent clockwork, which, when well wound up, works away industriously to that end, without the rest of the scholarly impulses taking any material part therein. The actual "interests" of the scholar, therefore, are gen-erally in quite another direction—in the family, perhaps, or in money-making, or in politics; it is, in fact, almost indifferent at what point of research his little machine is placed, and whether the hopeful young worker becomes a good philologist, a mushroom specialist, or a chemist; he is not *characterized* by becoming this or that. In the philosopher, on the contrary, there is absolutely nothing impersonal; and above all, his morality furnishes a decided and decisive testimony as to *who he is*—that is to say, in what order the deepest impulses of his nature stand to each other.

5

Psychologists should bethink themselves before putting down the instinct of self-preservation as the cardinal instinct of an organic being. A living thing seeks above all to *discharge* its strength—life itself is *Will to Power;* self-preservation is only one of the indirect and most frequent results thereof. In short, here, as everywhere else, let us beware of *superfluous* teleological principles!—one of which is the instinct of self-preservation (we owe it to Spinoza's inconsistency).

6

You desire to *live* "according to Nature"? Oh, you noble Stoics, what fraud of words!—Imagine to yourselves a being like Nature, boundlessly extravagant, boundlessly indifferent, without purpose or consideration, without pity or justice, at once fruitful and barren and uncertain: imagine to yourselves *indifference* as a power—how *could* you live in accordance with such indifference? To live —is not that just endeavoring to be otherwise than this Nature? Is not living valuing, preferring, being unjust, being limited, endeavoring to be different? And granted that your imperative, "living according to Nature," means actually the same as "living according to life"—how could you do *differently?* Why should you make a principle out of what you yourselves are, and must be? In reality, however, it is quite otherwise with you: while you pretend to read with rapture the canon of your law in Nature, you want something quite the contrary, you extraordinary stage-players and self-deluders! In your pride you

wish to dictate your morals and ideals to Nature, to Nature herself, and to incorporate them therein; you insist that it shall be Nature "according to the Stoa," and would like everything to be made after your own image, as a vast, eternal glorification and generalism of Stoicism! With all your love for truth, you have forced yourselves so long, so persistently, and with such hypnotic rigidity to see Nature *falsely,* that is to say, Stoically, that you are no longer able to see it otherwise. . . . But this is an old and everlasting story: what happened in old times with the Stoics still happens to-day, as soon as ever a philosophy begins to believe in itself. It always creates the world in its own image; it cannot do otherwise; philosophy is this tyrannical impulse itself, the most spiritual *Will to Power,* the will to "creation of the world," the will to the *causa prima.*

7

The old theological problem of "Faith" and "Knowledge," or more plainly, of instinct and reason—the question whether, in respect to the valuation of things, instinct deserves more authority than rationality, which wants to appreciate and act according to motives, according to a "Why," that is to say, in conformity to purpose and utility—it is always the old moral problem that first appeared in the person of Socrates, and had divided men's minds long before Christianity. Socrates himself, following, of course, the taste of his talent—that of a surpassing dialectician—took first the side of reason; and, in fact, what did he do all his life but laugh at the awkward incapacity of the noble Athenians, who were men of instinct, like all noble men, and could never give satisfactory answers concerning the motives of their actions? In the end, however, though silently and secretly, he laughed also at himself: with his finer conscience and introspection, he found in himself the same difficulty and incapacity. "But why"—he said to himself—"should one on that account separate oneself from the instincts! One must set them right, and the reason *also*—one must follow the instincts, but at the same time persuade the reason to support them with good arguments." This was the real *falseness* of that great and mysterious ironist; he brought his conscience up to the point that he was satisfied with a kind of self-outwitting; in fact, he perceived the irrationality in the moral judgment.

Plato, more innocent in such matters, and without the craftiness of the plebeian, wished to prove to himself, at the expenditure of all his strength—the greatest strength a philosopher had ever expended—that reason and instinct lead spontaneously to one goal, to the good, to "God"; and since Plato, all theologians and philosophers have followed the same path—which means that in matters of morality, instinct (or as Christians call it, "Faith," or as I call it, "the herd") has hitherto triumphed. Unless one should make an exception in the case of Descartes, the father of rationalism (and consequently the grandfather of the Revolution), who recognised only the authority of reason: but reason is only a tool, and Descartes was superficial.

8

Suppose that nothing else is "given" as real but our world of desires and passions, that we cannot sink or rise to any other "reality" but just that of our impulses—for thinking is only a relation of these impulses to one another:—are we not permitted to make the attempt and to ask the question whether this which is "given" does not *suffice,* by means of our counterparts, for the understanding even of the so-called mechanical (or "material") world? I do not mean as an illusion, a "semblance," a "representation" (in the Berkeleyan and Schopenhauerian sense), but as possessing the same degree of reality as our emotions themselves—as a more primitive form of the world of emotions, in

which everything still lies locked in a mighty unity, which afterwards branches off and develops itself in organic processes (naturally also, refines and debilitates)—as a kind of instinctive life in which all organic functions, including self-regulation, assimilation, nutrition, secretion, and change of matter, are still synthetically united with one another—as a *primary form* of life?—In the end, it is not only permitted to make this attempt, it is commanded by the conscience of *logical method.* Not to assume several kinds of causality, so long as the attempt to get along with a single one has not been pushed to its furtherest extent (to absurdity, if I may be allowed to say so): that is a morality of method which one may not repudiate nowadays—it follows "from its definition," as mathematicians say. The question is ultimately whether we really recognise the will as operating, whether we believe in the causality of the will; if we do so—and fundamentally our belief in this is just our belief in causality itself—we *must* make the attempt to posit hypothetically the causality of the will as the only causality.

Granted, finally, that we succeeded in explaining our entire instinctive life as the development and ramification of one fundamental form of will—namely, the Will to Power, as *my* thesis puts it; granted that all organic functions could be traced back to this Will to Power, and that the solution of the problem of generation and nutrition—it is one problem—could also be found therein: one would thus have acquired the right to define *all* active force unequivocally as *Will to Power.* The world seen from within, the world defined and designated according to its "intelligible character"—it would simply be "Will to Power," and nothing else.

The Free Spirit*

1

A new order of philosophers is appearing; I shall venture to baptize them by a name not without danger. As far as I understand them, as far as they allow themselves to be understood—for it is their nature to wish to remain something of a puzzle—these philosophers of the future might rightly, perhaps also wrongly, claim to be designated as "*tempters*." This name itself is after all only an attempt, or, if it be preferred, a temptation.

2

Will they be new friends of "truth," these coming philosophers? Very probably, for all philosophers hitherto have loved their truths. But assuredly they will not be dogmatists. It must be contrary to their pride, and also contrary to their taste, that their truth should still be truth for every one—that which has hitherto been the secret wish and ultimate purpose of all dogmatic efforts. "My opinion is *my* opinion: another person has not easily a right to it"—such a philosopher of the future will say, perhaps. One must renounce the bad taste of wishing to agree with many people. "Good" is no longer good when one's neighbour takes it into his mouth. And how could there be a "common good"! The expression contradicts itself; that which can be common is always of small value. In the end things must be as they are and have always been—the great things remain for the great, the abysses for the profound, the delicacies and thrills for the refined, and, to sum up shortly, everything rare for the rare.

3

Need I say expressly after all this that they will be free, *very* free spirits, these phi-

---

* Friedrich Nietzsche, *Beyond Good and Evil*, Ch. II. English translation by Helen Zimmern (London, George Allen & Unwin, Ltd., 1909). By permission of the publisher. Numerical order imposed.

losophers of the future—as certainly also they will not be merely free spirits, but something more, higher, greater, and fundamentally different, which does not wish to be misunderstood and mistaken? But while I say this, I feel under obligation almost as much to them as to ourselves (we free spirits who are their heralds and forerunners), to sweep away from ourselves altogether a stupid old prejudice and misunderstanding, which, like a fog, has too long made the conception of "free spirit" obscure. In every country of Europe, and the same in America, there is at present something which makes an abuse of this name; a very narrow, prepossessed, enchained class of spirits, who desire almost the opposite of what our intentions and instincts prompt—not to mention that in respect to the new philosophers who are appearing, they must still more be closed windows and bolted doors. Briefly and regrettably, they belong to the levellers, these wrongly named "free spirits"—as glib-tongued and scribe-fingered slaves of the democratic taste and its "modern ideas": all of them men without solitude, without personal solitude, blunt honest fellows to whom neither courage nor honourable conduct ought to be denied; only, they are not free, and are ludicrously superficial, especially in their innate partiality for seeing the cause of almost *all* human misery and failure in the old forms in which society has hitherto existed—a notion which happily inverts the truth entirely! What they would fain attain with all their strength, is the universal, green-meadow happiness of the herd, together with security, safety, comfort, and alleviation of life for every one; their two most frequently chanted songs and doctrines are called "Equality of Rights" and "Sympathy with all Sufferers"—and suffering itself is looked upon by them as something which must be *done away with*.

We opposite ones, however, who have opened our eye and conscience to the question how and where the plant "man" has hitherto grown most vigorously, believe that this has always taken place under the opposite conditions, that for this end the dangerousness of his situation had to be increased enormously, his inventive faculty and dissembling power (his "spirit") had to develop into subtlety and daring under long oppression and compulsion, and his Will to Life had to be increased to the unconditioned Will to Power:—we believe that severity, violence, slavery, danger in the street and in the heart, secrecy, stoicism, tempter's art and devilry of every kind,—that everything wicked, terrible, tyrannical, predatory, and serpentine in man, serves as well for the elevation of the human species as its opposite:—we do not even say enough when we only say *this much;* and in any case we find ourselves here, both with our speech and our silence, at the other extreme of all modern ideology and gregarious desirability, as their antipodes perhaps? What wonder that we "free spirits" are not exactly the most communicative spirits? that we do not wish to betray in every respect *what* a spirit can free itself from, and *where* perhaps it will then be driven?

The Meaning of Nobility*

1

Every elevation of "man" as a type has hitherto been the work of an aristocratic society and so it will always be—a society believing in a long scale of gradations of rank and differences of worth among human beings, and requiring slavery in some form or other. One must not give oneself to any humanitarian illusions about the history of the origin of an aristocratic society (that is to say, of the preliminary condition for the elevation of the type "man"): the truth is hard. Let us acknowledge unprejudicedly how every higher civilization hitherto has *originated!* Men still with a "natural" nature, barbarians in every terrible sense of the word, men of prey, still in possession of unbroken strength of will and desire for power, threw themselves upon weaker, more moral, more peaceful races (perhaps trading or cattle-rearing communities), or upon old mellow civilizations in which the final vital force was flickering out in brilliant fireworks of wit and depravity. In the beginning, the noble caste was always the barbarian caste; their superiority did not consist first of all in their physical, but in their psychical power— they were more *complete* men (which at every point also implies "more complete beasts").

2

In a tour through the many finer and coarser moralities which have hitherto prevailed or still prevail on the earth, I found certain traits recurring regularly together, and connected with one another, until finally two primary types revealed themselves to me, and a radical distinction was brought to light. There is *master-morality* and *slave-morality.* The distinctions of moral values have either originated in a ruling caste, pleasantly conscious of being different from the ruled—or among the ruled class, the slaves and dependents of all sorts.

In the first case, when it is the rulers who determine the conception "good," it is the exalted, proud disposition which is regarded as the distinguishing feature, and that which determines the order of rank. The noble type of man separates from himself the beings in whom the opposite of this exalted, proud disposition displays itself: he despises them. Let it at once be noted that in this first kind of morality the antithesis "good" and "bad" means practically the same as "noble" and "despicable";—the antithesis "good" and "evil" is of a different origin.

* Friedrich Nietzsche, *Beyond Good and Evil,* Chs. IX, VII. English translation by Helen Zimmern (London, George Allen & Unwin, Ltd., 1909). By permission of the publisher. Numerical order imposed.

The cowardly, the timid, the insignificant, and those thinking merely of narrow utility are despised; moreover, also, the distrustful with their constrained glances, the self-abasing, the dog-like kind of men who let themselves be abused, the mendicant flatterers, and above all the liars:—it is a fundamental belief of all aristocrats that the common people are untruthful. "We truthful ones"—the nobility in ancient Greece called themselves. It is obvious that everywhere the designations of moral value were at first applied to *men,* and were only derivatively and at a later period applied to *actions.*

The noble type of man regards himself as a determiner of values; he does not require to be approved of; he passes the judgment: "What is injurious to me is injurious in itself"; he knows that it is he himself only who confers honor on things; he is a creator of values. He honors whatever he recognizes in himself: such morality is self-glorification. In the foreground there is the feeling of plentitude, of power, which seeks to overflow, the happiness of high tension, the consciousness of a wealth which would fain give and bestow:—the noble man also helps the unfortunate, but not—or scarcely—out of pity, but rather from an impulse generated by the super-abundance of power. The noble man honors in himself the powerful one, him also who has power over himself, who knows how to speak and how to keep silence, who takes pleasure in subjecting himself to severity and hardness, and has reverence for all that is severe and hard. "Wotan placed a hard heart in my breast," says an old Scandinavian Saga: it is thus rightly expressed from the soul of a proud Viking. Such a type of man is even proud of not being made for sympathy; the hero of the Saga therefore adds warningly: "He who has not a hard heart when young, will never have one." The noble and brave who think thus are the furthest removed from the morality which sees precisely in sympathy, or in acting for the good of others, or in *désintéresement,* the characteristic of the moral; faith in oneself, pride in oneself, a radical enmity and irony towards "selflessness," belong as definitely to noble

morality as do a careless scorn and precaution in presence of sympathy and the "warm heart."

It is the powerful who know how to honor, it is their art, their domain for invention. The profound reverence for age and for tradition—all law rests on this double reverence—the belief and prejudice in favor of ancestors and unfavorable to newcomers, is typical in the morality of the powerful; and if, reversely, men of "modern ideas" believe almost instinctively in "progress" and the "future," and are more and more lacking in respect for old age, the ignoble origin of these "ideas" has complacently betrayed itself thereby. A morality of the ruling class, however, is more especially foreign and irritating to present-day taste in the sternness of its principle that one has duties only to one's equals; that one may act toward beings of a lower rank, toward all that is foreign, just as seems good to one, or "as the heart desires," and in any case "beyond good and evil"; it is here that sympathy and similar sentiments can have a place. The ability and obligation to exercise prolonged gratitude and prolonged revenge—both only within the circle of equals—artfulness in retaliation, *raffinement* of the idea in friendship, a certain necessity to have enemies (as outlets for the emotions of envy, quarrelsomeness, arrogance —in fact in order to be a good *friend*): all these are typical characteristics of the noble morality, which, as has been pointed out, is not the morality of "modern ideas," and is therefore at present difficult to realize, and also to unearth and disclose.

It is otherwise with the second type of morality, *slave-morality.* Supposing that the abused, the oppressed, the suffering, the unemancipated, the weary, and those uncertain of themselves, should moralize, what will be the common element in their moral estimates? Probably a pessimistic suspicion with regard to the entire situation of man will find expression, perhaps a condemnation of man, together with his situation. The slave has an unfavorable eye for the virtues of the powerful; he has a scepticism and distrust, a refinement of distrust of everything "good" that is there honored—he would fain persuade himself that the very happiness there is not genuine. On the other hand, *those* qualities which serve to alleviate the existence of sufferers are brought into prominence and flooded with light; it is here that sympathy, the kind, helping hand, the warm heart, patience, diligence, humility, and friendliness attain to honor; for here these are the most useful qualities, and almost the only means of supporting the burden of existence. Slave-morality is essentially the morality of utility.

Here is the seat of the origin of the famous antithesis "good" and "evil":—power and dangerousness are assumed to reside in the evil, a certain dreadfulness, subtlety, and strength, which do not admit of being despised. According to slave-morality, therefore, the "evil" man arouses fear; according to master-morality, it is precisely the "good" man who arouses fear and seeks to arouse it, while the bad man is regarded as the despicable being. The contrast attains its maximum when, in accordance with the logical consequences of slave-morality, a shade of depreciation—it may be slight and well-intentioned —at last attaches itself to the "good" man of this morality; because, according to the servile mode of thought, the good man must in any case be the *safe* man: he is good-natured, easily deceived, perhaps a little stupid, *un bonhomme.* Everywhere that slave-morality gains the ascendency, language shows a tendency to approximate the significations of the words "good" and "stupid."—A last fundamental difference: the desire *for freedom,* the instinct for happiness and the refinements of the feeling of liberty belong as necessarily to slave-morals and morality, as artifice and enthusiasm in reverence and devotion are the regular symptoms of an aristocratic mode of thinking and estimating.

3

To be mistaken in the fundamental problem of "man and woman," to deny here the profoundest antagonism and the necessity for an eternally hostile tension, to dream here perhaps of equal rights, equal training, equal claims and obligations: that is a typical sign of shallow-mindedness; and a thinker who has proved himself shallow at this dangerous spot—shallow in instinct!—may generally be regarded as suspicious, may, more, as betrayed, as discovered; he will probably prove too "short" for all fundamental questions of life, future as well as present, and will be unable to descend into any of the depths. On the other hand, a man who has depth of spirit as well as of desires, and has also the depth of benevolence which is capable of severity and harshness, and easily confounded with them, can only think of women as *Orientals* do: He must conceive of her as a possession, as confinable property, as a being predestined for service and accomplishing her mission therein—he must take his stand in this matter upon the immense rationality of Asia, upon the superiority of the instinct of Asia, as the Greeks did formerly; those best heirs and scholars of Asia—who, as is well known, with their increasing culture and amplitude of power, from Homer to the time of Pericles, become gradually stricter toward woman, in short, more oriental. *How* necessary, *how* logical, even *how* humanely desirable this was, let us consider for ourselves!

4

The weaker sex has in no previous age been treated with so much respect by men as at present—this belongs to the tendency and fundamental taste of democracy, in the same way as disrespectfulness to old age— what wonder is it that abuse should be immediately made of this respect? They want more, they learn to make claims, the tribute of respect is at last felt to be well-nigh galling; rivalry for rights, indeed actual strife itself, would be preferred: in a word, woman is losing modesty. And let us immediately add that she is also losing taste. She is unlearning to fear man: but the woman who "unlearns to fear" sacrifices her most womanly instincts. That woman should venture forward when the fear-inspiring quality in man—or more definitely, the *man* in man— is no longer either desired or fully developed, is reasonable enough and also intelligible enough; what is more difficult to understand is that precisely thereby—woman deteriorates.

This is what is happening nowadays: let us not deceive ourselves about it! Wherever the industrial spirit has triumphed over the military and aristocratic spirit, woman strives for the economic and legal independence of a clerk: "woman as clerkess" is inscribed on the portal of the modern society which is in course of formation. While she thus appropriates new rights, aspires to be "master," and inscribes "progress" of woman on her flags and banners, the very opposite realizes itself with terrible obviousness: *woman retrogrades.* Since the French Revolution the influence of woman in Europe has *declined* in proportion as she has increased her rights and claims; and the "emancipation of woman," in so far as it is desired and demanded by women themselves (and not only by masculine shallow-pates), thus proves to be a remarkable symptom of the increased weakening and deadening of the most womanly instincts. There is stupidity in this movement, an almost masculine stupidity, of which a well-reared woman—who is always a sensible woman—might be heartily ashamed. To lose the intuition as to the ground upon which she can most surely achieve victory; to neglect exercise in the use of her proper weapons; to let herself go before man, perhaps even "to the book," where formerly she kept herself in control and in refined, artful humility; to neutralize with her virtuous audacity man's faith in a veiled, fundamentally different ideal in woman, something eternally, necessarily feminine; to emphatically and loquaciously dissuade man from the idea that woman must be preserved, cared for, protected, and indulged, like some delicate, strangely wild, and often pleasant domestic animal; the clumsy and indignant collection of everything in the nature of servitude and bondage which the position of woman in the hitherto existing order of society has entailed and still entails (as though slavery were a counterargument, and not rather a condition of every higher culture, of every elevation of culture):—what does all this betoken, if not a disintegration of womanly instincts, a defeminizing?

That which inspires respect in woman, and often enough fear also, is her nature, which is more "natural" than that of man, her genuine, carnivora-like, cunning flexibility, her tiger claws beneath the glove, her *naiveté* in egoism, her untrainableness and innate wildness, the incomprehensibleness, extent and deviation of her desires and virtues. . . . That which, in spite of fear, excites one's sympathy for the dangerous and beautiful cat, "woman," is that she seems more afflicted, more vulnerable, more necessitous of love and more condemned to disillusionment than any other creature. Fear and sympathy: it is with these feelings that man has hitherto stood in the presence of woman, always with one foot already in tragedy, which rends while it delights.—What?—And all that is now to be at an end? And the disenchantment of woman is in progress? The tediousness of woman is slowly evolving? Oh Europe! Europe!

The Existential Christian: Sören Kierkegaard

A lonely and almost unnoticed figure in nineteenth-century Denmark who made little impression on his own age, Sören Kierkegaard (1813–1855) has become a dominant influence in our time, and his thought has shaped the development of two important twentieth-century movements: existential philosophy and the neo-orthodox or dialectical theology of Karl Barth and Emil Brunner. Something of the measure of his impact upon our age is to be seen in the translation of his forty-three esthetic, religious, and philosophical publications, first into German beginning about 1909, then into French since about 1929, and finally into English beginning in 1938. Although Kierkegaard's intense and paradoxical insights into human nature and the meaning of human life have proved strangely contemporary in spirit, he is not an easy author to read. His flashes of genius are expressed in witty anecdotes, parables, and satirical discourses. If the casual reader is not sympathetic to his point of view, he is more apt to be repelled than enlightened; if he does not choose the right starting point in his study of Kierkegaard, he is soon completely lost—and the right starting point is by no means easy to find.

Kierkegaard's own existential philosophy finds its most direct expression perhaps in two books published just before the middle of the nineteenth century—his *Concluding Unscientific Postscript* (1846), a long and difficult work, and *The Point of View for My Work as an Author* (1848), a much more personal and appealing interpretation of his thought. Although he is generally regarded as the founder of contemporary existentialism, Kierkegaard would probably not be willing to call himself an existentialist if he were alive. He was primarily concerned with attacking the conventional, superficial, and hypocritical Christianity of his age, and with his own effort to call men back to an honest and genuine Christian life. But in his portrayal of the "existential" Christian, one finds all the major ideas that have come to characterize existentialism today. For the existentialist, a man's thought cannot be separated from his life—the two are but aspects of one whole—and this is true for Kierkegaard more clearly than for most men.

Kierkegaard was the youngest of seven children. The atmosphere of his home in Copenhagen was marked by strict devotion to the orthodox Lutheran religion and by a somewhat somber and gloomy melancholy. His father, a prosperous merchant who had a marked influence on Kierkegaard, had grown up among the peasants on the Jutland Downs. When herding his sheep one day on the lonely heath, young Michael Kierkegaard was moved to curse the God of wrath who was responsible, he believed, for the misery of his young life. This act only deepened his gloom, and he never forgave himself for what he had done. Even when in later life he moved to Copenhagen and became a successful merchant, he brooded over his sin and, shortly before he died at eighty-two, he confessed this act of blasphemy to Sören, who was shaken by it "as by an earthquake." The curse of sin seemed to hang over the whole family; only the eldest son and the youngest, Sören, survived and for Sören the salvation of his soul was undoubtedly the most important concern during his early and impressionable years. He was, however, a youth of marked intellectual ability. This became apparent when at seventeen he entered the University of Copenhagen (in 1830). At first he studied theology, but soon turned to literature and philosophy, and became well acquainted with the prevailing Hegelian rationalism against which most of his own later philosophical writing was directed.

For some time at the university Kierkegaard led the life of a Bohemian intellectual; he had no financial worries and soon incurred a considerable debt for his father to pay. Although gifted and witty, his sharp satire set him apart from his fellow students so that he was never fully accepted by the university group but remained a lonely figure. Despite his superficial interest in the pleasures of social life, Kierkegaard's deeper religious concerns were always in the background. He spent some ten years at the university; in 1840 he passed his theological examinations and in 1841 preached his first sermon in a Copenhagen church. These two years also saw what was perhaps his own deepest personal and emotional experience—his falling in love with Regina Olsen, the young daughter of a prominent government official, and his decision in 1841 to break his engagement with her. This was an experience of great consequence for his literary as well as his spiritual life and marked the beginning of a decade of prolific literary activity that established Kierkegaard as one of the gifted writers in modern Europe.

Kierkegaard's reasons for breaking his engagement with Regina were quite complex and will never be fully understood: Did he consider Regina too light-hearted and happy a girl, incapable of sharing the melancholy life he envisioned for himself? There are evidences that this was the case. Was his breaking of the engagement one of the renunciations that he felt compelled to make for his own personal faith? His use of the Old Testament story of Abraham's sacrifice of Isaac, his beloved son, suggests as much. Did he come to believe that celibacy was one of the indispensable conditions of his own unordained ministry, his mission of calling the Church back to its true faith? Perhaps. In any case, he never ceased to love Regina. When she happily married another more desirable suitor a short time after seeming broken-hearted over the outcome of her engagement with him, Kierkegaard was greatly depressed. In his own words, it was Regina who made him a poet. He embarked upon a period of extraordinary literary activity, initially at least, to provide a convincing explanation for his conduct in this affair.

Kierkegaard lays great stress upon three stages in life's development, the esthetic, the ethical, and the religious, stages that reflect his own experience and his own writing. During the first two of these—the esthetic and the ethical—he wrote under suggestive and often contradictory pen names: Johannes de Silenteo, Constan Constantius, Johannes Climacus, Frater Taciturnus, and the like. His ideas were expressed in amusing anecdotes, parables, and other devices that appeal to the existentialists, all emphasizing the inability of rational and logical analysis to get at the deeper truth of experience.

✗ In the esthetic stage one cultivates an enjoyable but deceptive mood, which Kierkegaard analyzes with profound insight and artistic ability in his *Diary of The Seducer.* Detached from all moral concern a man, as so well portrayed in Mozart's *Don Giovanni,* indulges in the search for pleasure and for beauty. The esthete lives only in the present moment: he constructs for himself a world of dreams. However, as Kierkegaard skilfully shows, it is a dead-end route that leads ultimately to boredom and disgust and deprives life of all enduring meaning. Kierkegaard, however, goes further and applies this criterion to the higher esthetic experience as well. Even the poet's existence is a kind of spiritual vacuum: he is writing poetry instead of living; he occupies himself with God and truth only in his imagination instead of seeking to experience both "existentially." There is no doubt, of course, that Kierkegaard himself retained for the greater part of his life something of the esthetic, certainly something of the poet's traits. He loved irony and sarcasm and used both effectively in his writing; but the greater part of *The Point of View for My Work as an Author* is devoted to insisting that his esthetic works were a necessary preparation for his religious message.

The "existential" approach to life is limited then to the ethical and the religious levels. *To exist as a human being* means to face continuously new moral choices. The ethical man is always in the process of becoming; he is participating in existence while the esthetic man is detached, uninvolved. But the moral choices of life inevitably lead a man to tragedy and despair. An "existential" crisis occurs when man faces the despair, the "nothingness" of his ordinary existence, and sees that neither reason nor morality can rescue him from this situation. The anti-intellectualism of all modern existentialism finds its source in Kierkegaard's insistence that the paradoxical "leap" of faith alone can rescue the individual from this situation. The Christian faith, however, must be lived to be understood; it cannot be comprehended in the abstract, intellectually. Indeed, the demands of religion must always seem unreasonable and impractical—even at times immoral, by conventional standards. Kierkegaard's favorite illustration here is God's command that Abraham sacrifice his beloved son, Isaac. Only through *faith* could this deed take on its religious and existential meaning in the life of Abraham, and so enable Abram to *become* Abraham.[1] Thus where the philosophical existentialist inverts Descartes' famous "I think, therefore I am," to read "I am, therefore I think," the religious existentialist insists upon "I believe, therefore I am."

Kierkegaard's attack upon institutional Christianity grew out of this deeper insight into the true nature of the ethical and the religious. In the Denmark of his day the Lutheran Church was an established church with all the limitations that this involved. The state dominated the church; but there could never be a

---

[1] Kierkegaard's classic description of Abraham's experience is found in *Fear and Trembling.*

reconciliation, Kierkegaard insisted, between the demands of Christ and those of the state. To be a Christian one must, like Christ, be persecuted, lonely, "rejected of men." Now that everyone in Denmark was a nominal Christian, true Christianity had ceased to exist. The Church was a travesty. The young minister in Denmark was a "seeker" after clerical position and power, not after God. In characteristic and paradoxical fashion, Kierkegaard maintained that it was easier for a man to become a Christian if he was not a Christian than if he already was one. His own decision to refuse a church appointment, even after he had completed his theological course, was a logical one for him.

In 1846 Kierkegaard wrote a long review of a current novel, *The Two Ages*. The second and most interesting part of this review, entitled "The Present Age," was later published separately and provided his most direct attack upon the spirit of his age. *Do not pretend* is his message to an age filled with pretense and hypocrisy. Do not pretend to be religious if you are not. Do not pretend to be a Christian if you are not a Christian. Genuine Christianity must be related to everything a man does. Above all, it must express itself in his life, in what he is and does, not what he says or pretends to be. The existential Christian must see Christianity as a part of his very existence. Christianity's tragedy is that since all have become Christians, Christ's teachings have been watered down to a thin conventional morality, a sort of polite respectability. Christianity has been abolished in the name of the Christian Church. The militant, radical, demanding gospel of Christ no longer exists.

Kierkegaard is thus led to his famous and central doctrine that truth is subjective. This theme is developed most fully in his *Concluding Unscientific Postscript*. Man's intelligence, he insists, can never remain outside the crises and involvements of his life, nor look upon them as a spectator would look on something outside himself. The search for truth is a passionate concern, a concern with life's meaning and destiny. Each truth is intimately a part of one's existence; it is discovered in the process of living and cannot be reduced to objective scientific generalizations equally true for all men.

In 1855, after fifteen years of constant controversy with both religious leaders and literary critics, and by now almost penniless, Kierkegaard collapsed on the streets of Copenhagen and died at the age of forty-two shortly thereafter. A few years earlier in prophetic fashion he had written his own epitaph:

I have nothing further to say, but in conclusion I will let another speak, my poet, who when he comes will assign me a place among those who have suffered for the sake of an idea, and he will say:

"The martyrdom this author suffered may be briefly described thus: He suffered from being a genius in a provincial town. The standard he applied in relation to talents, industry, distinterestedness, devotedness, definition of thought, etc., was on the average far too great for his contemporaries; it raised the price on them too terribly, and reduced their price too terribly; it almost made it seem as if the provincial town and the majority in it did not possess *dominium absolutum,* but that there was a God in existence. So for a while, at the first, people entertained one another mutually with voluble discussions about how under the sun he got such extraordinary talents, why he should have independent means and at the same time be able to be so industrious—so long they disputed, that in the end it came to this: It is his pride, everything can be explained by his pride. Thereupon they went farther, from disputation to action. Since it is his pride, they said, every insidious opposition, every insolence towards him or maltreatment of him is not only permissible but is a duty to God—it is his pride that should be punished. O priceless market town! How inestimable thou art when attired in thy comical dressing-gown and in the way of becoming holy, when abandonment to every disgusting inclination of envy, rudeness, and vulgarity becomes an expression of the worship of God! But, unfortunately, even for one who is in many ways developed for eternity's class, there exists only one class, that of the temporal order, where perhaps he must remain a long while.

"Yet it is true that he found also here on earth what he sought. He himself was *that individual,* if no one else was, and he became that more and more. It was the cause of Christianity he served, his life from childhood on being marvellously fitted for such a service. Thus he carried to completion the work of reflection, the task of translating completely into terms of reflection what Christianity is, what it means to become a Christian. His purity of heart was to will only one thing. What his contemporaries complained of during his lifetime, that he would not abate the price, would not give in, this very thing is the eulogy pronounced upon him by after ages, that he did not abate the price, did not give in. But the grand enterprise he undertook did not infatuate him. Whereas as author he had dialectically a survey of the whole, he understood Christianly that the whole signified his own education in Christianity. The dialectical structure he brought to completion, of which the several parts are whole works, he could not ascribe to any man, least of all would be ascribe it to himself; if he were to ascribe it to any one, it would be to Providence, to whom it was in fact ascribed, day after day and year after year, by the author, who historically died of a mortal disease but poetically died of longing for eternity, where uninterruptedly he would have nothing else to do but to thank God."[2]

---

[2] *The Point of View* (New York, Oxford University Press, 1939), Conclusion.

The Point of View for my Work as an Author*

I

That "Christendom" is a prodigious illusion.

Everyone with some capacity for observation, who seriously considers what is called Christendom, or the conditions in a so-called Christian country, must surely be assailed by profound misgivings. What does it mean that all these thousands and thousands call themselves Christians as a matter of course? These many, many men, of whom the greater part, so far as one can judge, live in categories quite foreign to Christianity! Anyone can convince himself of it by the simplest observation. People who perhaps never once enter a church, never think about God, never mention His name except in oaths! People upon whom it has never dawned that they might have any obligation to God, people who either regard it as a maximum to be guiltless of transgressing the criminal law, or do not count even this quite necessary! Yet all these people, even those who assert that no God exists, are all of them Christians, call themselves Christians, are recognized as Christians by the State, are buried as Christians by the Church, are certified as Christians for eternity!

That at the bottom of this there must be a tremendous confusion, a frightful illusion, there surely can be no doubt. But to stir up such a question! Yes, I know the objections well. For there are those who understand what I mean, but would say with a good-natured slap on the back, "My dear fellow, you are still rather young to want to embark on such an undertaking, an undertaking which, if it is to have any success at

all, will require at least half a score of well-trained missionaries; an undertaking which means neither more nor less than proposing to reintroduce Christianity—into Christendom. No, my dear fellow, let us be men; such an undertaking is beyond your powers and mine. It is just as madly ambitious as wanting to reform the "crowd," with which no sensible person wants to mix. To start such a thing is certain ruin." Perhaps; but though ruin were certain, it is certain also that no one has learned this objection from Christianity; for when Christianity came into the world it was still more definitely "certain ruin" to start such a thing—and yet it was started. And it is certain, too, that no one learned this objection from Socrates; for he mixed with the "crowd" and wanted to reform it.

This is roughly how the case stands. Once in a while a parson causes a little hubbub from the pulpit, about there being something wrong somewhere with all these numerous Christians—but all those *to* whom he is speaking are Christians, and those he speaks *about* are not present. This is most appropriately described as a feigned emotion. Once in a while there appears a religious enthusiast; he storms against Christendom, he vociferates and makes a loud noise, denouncing almost all as not being Christians—and accomplishes nothing. He takes no heed of the fact that an illusion is not an easy thing to dispel. Supposing now it is a fact that most people, when they call themselves Christians, are under an illusion—how do they defend themselves against an enthusiast? First and foremost, they do not bother about him at all, they do not so much as look at his book, they immediately lay it aside, *ad acta;* or, if he employs the living word, they go round by another street and do not hear him. As the next step, they spirit him out of the way by carefully defining the whole concept, and settle themselves securely in their illusion; they make him a fanatic, his Chris-

* Sören Kierkegaard, *The Point of View for My Work as an Author,* English translation by Walter Lowrie (New York, Oxford University Press, 1939), Part II, Ch. I. Copyright by Harpers and Brothers. Used by permission.

tianity an exaggeration—in the end he remains the only one, or one of the few who is not seriously a Christian (for exaggeration is surely a lack of seriousness), whereas the others are all serious Christians.

No, an illusion can never be destroyed directly, and only by indirect means can it be radically removed. If it is an illusion that all are Christians—and if there is anything to be done about it, it must be done indirectly, not by one who vociferously proclaims himself an extraordinary Christian, but by one who, better instructed, is ready to declare that he is not a Christian at all. That is, one must approach from behind the person who is under an illusion. Instead of wishing to have the advantage of being oneself that rare thing, a Christian, one must let the prospective captive enjoy the advantage of being the Christian, and for one's own part have resignation enough to be the one who is far behind him—otherwise one will certainly not get the man out of his illusion, a thing which is difficult enough in any case.

If then, according to our assumption, the greater number of people in Christendom only imagine themselves to be Christians, in what categories do they live? They live in aesthetic, or at the most, in aesthetic-ethical categories.

Supposing then that a religious writer has become profoundly attentive to this illusion, Christendom, and has resolved to attack it with all the might at his disposal (with God's aid, be it noted)—what then is he to do? First and foremost, no impatience. If he becomes impatient, he will rush headlong against it and accomplish nothing. A direct attack only strengthens a person in his illusion, and at the same time embitters him. There is nothing that requires such gentle handling as an illusion, if one wishes to dispel it. If anything prompts the prospective captive to set his will in opposition, all is lost. And this is what a direct attack achieves, and it implies moreover the presumption of requiring a man to make to another person, or in his presence, an admission which he can make most profitably to himself privately.

This is what is achieved by the indirect method which, loving and serving the truth, arranges everything dialectically for the prospective captive, and then shyly withdraws (for love is always shy), so as not to witness the admission which he makes to himself alone before God—that he has lived hitherto in an illusion.

The religious writer must, therefore, first get into touch with men. That is, he must begin with aesthetic achievement. This is earnest-money. The more brilliant the achievement, the better for him. Moreover, he must be sure of himself, or (and this is the one and only security) he must relate himself to God in fear and trembling, lest the event most opposite to his intentions should come to pass, and instead of setting the others in motion, the others acquire power over him, so that he ends by being bogged in the aesthetic. Therefore he must have everything in readiness, though without impatience, with a view to bringing forward the religious promptly, as soon as he perceives that he has his readers with him, so that with the momentum gained by devotion to the aesthetic they rush headlong into contact with the religious.

Assuming that there is a prodigious illusion in the case of these many men who call themselves Christians and are regarded as Christians, the way of encountering it which is here suggested involves no condemnation or denunciation. It is a truly Christian invention, which cannot be employed without fear and trembling, or without real self-denial. The one who is disposed to help bears all the responsibility and makes all the effort. But for that reason such a line of action possesses intrinsic value. Generally speaking, a method has value only in relation to the result attained. Some one condemns and denounces, vociferates and makes a great noise—all this has no intrinsic value, though one counts upon accomplishing much by it. It is otherwise with the line of action here contemplated. Suppose that a man has dedicated himself to the use of it, suppose that he used it his whole life long—and suppose that he accomplished nothing: he has nevertheless by no means lived in vain, for his life was true self-denial.

II

That if real success is to attend the effort to bring a man to a definite position, one must first of all take pains to find HIM *where he is and begin there.*

This is the secret of the art of helping others. Anyone who has not mastered this is himself deluded when he proposes to help others. In order to help another effectively I must understand more than he—yet first of all surely I must understand what he understands. If I do not know that, my greater understanding will be of no help to him. If, however, I am disposed to plume myself on my greater understanding, it is because I am vain or proud, so that at bottom, instead of benefiting him, I want to be admired. But all true effort to help begins with self-humiliation: the helper must first humble himself under him he would help, and therewith must understand that to help does not mean to be a sovereign but to be a servant, that to help does not mean to be ambitious but to be patient, that to help means to endure for the time being the imputation that one is in the wrong and does not understand what the other understands.

Take the case of a man who is passionately angry, and let us assume that he is really in the wrong. Unless you can begin with him by making it seem as if it were he that had to instruct you, and unless you can do it in such a way that the angry man, who was too impatient to listen to a word of yours, is glad to discover in you a complaisant and attentive listener—if you cannot do that, you cannot help him at all. Or take the case of a lover who has been unhappy in love, and suppose that the way he yields to his passion is really unreasonable, impious, unchristian. In case you cannot begin with him in such a way that he finds genuine relief in talking to you about his suffering and is able to enrich his

mind with the poetical interpretations you suggest for it, notwithstanding you have no share in this passion and want to free him from it—if you cannot do that, then you cannot help him at all; he shuts himself away from you, he retires within himself—and then you only prate to him.

Be the amazed listener who sits and hears what the other finds the more delight in telling you because you listen with amazement. But above all do not forget one thing, the purpose you have in mind, the fact that it is the religious you must bring forward.

If you can do that, if you can find exactly the place where the other is and begin there, you may perhaps have the luck to lead him to the place where you are.

For to be a teacher does not mean simply to affirm that such a thing is so, or to deliver a lecture, etc. No, to be a teacher in the right sense is to be a learner. Instruction begins when you, the teacher, learn from the learner, put yourself in his place so that you may understand what he understands and in the way he understands it, in case you have not understood it before. Or if you have understood it before, you allow him to subject you to an examination so that he may be sure you know your part. This is the introduction. Then the beginning can be made in another sense. . . .

So then the religious writer, whose all-absorbing thought is how one is to become a Christian, starts off rightly in Christendom as an aesthetic writer. For a moment let it remain undetermined whether Christendom is a monstrous illusion, whether it is a vain conceit for the many to call themselves Christians; let the opposite rather be assumed. Well then, this beginning is a superfluity, counting upon a situation which does not exist—yet it does no harm. The harm is much greater, or rather the only harm is, when one who is not a Christian pretends to be one. On the other hand, when one who is a Christian gives the impression that he is not, the harm is not great. Assuming that all are Christians, this deception can at the most confirm them more and more in being such.

III

That the whole of the aesthetic work, viewed in relation to the work as a whole, is a deception—understanding this word, however, in a special sense.

From the point of view of my whole activity as an author, integrally conceived, the aesthetic work is a deception, and herein is to be found the deeper significance of the use of pseudonyms. A deception, however, is a rather ugly thing. To this I would make answer: One must not let oneself be deceived by the word "deception." One can deceive a person for the truth's sake, and (to recall old Socrates) one can deceive a person into the truth. Indeed, it is only by this means, i.e. by deceiving him, that it is possible to bring into the truth one who is in an illusion. Whoever rejects this opinion betrays the fact that he is not over-well versed in dialectics, and that is precisely what is especially needed when operating in this field. For there is an immense difference, a dialectical difference, between these two cases: the case of a man who is ignorant and is to have a piece of knowledge imparted to him, so that he is like an empty vessel which is to be filled or a blank sheet of paper upon which something is to be written; and the case of a man who is under an illusion and must first be delivered from that. Likewise there is a difference between writing on a blank sheet of paper and bringing to light by the application of a caustic fluid a text which is hidden under another text. Assuming then that a person is the victim of an illusion, and that in order to communicate the truth to him the first task, rightly understood, is to remove the illusion—if I do not begin by deceiving him, I must begin with direct communication. But direct communication presupposes that the receiver's ability to receive is undisturbed. But here such is not the case; an illusion stands in the way. That is to say, one must first of all use the caustic fluid. But this caustic means is negativity, and negativity understood in relation to the communication of the truth is precisely the same as deception.

What then does it mean, "to deceive"? It means that one does not begin *directly* with the matter one wants to communicate, but begins by accepting the other man's illusion as good money. So (to stick to the theme with which this work especially deals) one does not begin thus: I am a Christian; you are not a Christian. Nor does one begin thus: It is Christianity I am proclaiming; and you are living in purely aesthetic categories. No, one begins thus: Let us talk about aesthetics. The deception consists in the fact that one talks thus merely to get to the religious theme. But, on our assumption, the other man is under the illusion that the aesthetic is Christianity; for, he thinks, I am a Christian, and yet he lives in aesthetic categories.

Although ever so many parsons were to consider this method unjustifiable and just as many were unable to get it into their heads (in spite of the fact that they are all of them, according to their own assertion, accustomed to use the Socratic method), I for my part tranquilly adhere to Socrates. It is true, he was not a Christian; that I know, and yet I am thoroughly convinced that he has become one. But he was a dialectician, he conceived everything in terms of reflection. And the question which concerns us here is a purely dialectical one, it is the question of the use of reflection in Christendom.

What It Is to Become a Christian*

I

Objectively, what it is to become or to be a Christian is defined as follows:

1. A Christian is one who accepts the doctrine of Christianity. But if it is the *what* of this doctrine which in the last resort decides whether one is a Christian, attention is instantly turned outward, with the intent of learning down to the last detail, what then the doctrine of Christianity is, because this "what" is to decide, not merely what Christianity is, but whether I am a Christian. That same instant begins the erudite, the anxious, the timorous contradictory effort of approximation. Approximation may be protracted indefinitely, and with that the decision whereby one becomes a Christian is relegated to oblivion.

This incongruity has been remedied by the assumption that everyone in Christendom is a Christian; we are all of us what one in a way calls Christians. With this assumption things go better with the objective theories. We are all Christians. The Bible-theory has now to investigate quite objectively what Christianity is (and yet we are in fact Christians and the objective information is assumed to make us Christians, the objective information which we who are Christians now for the first time learn to know—for if we are not Christians, the road here taken will never lead us to become such). The Church theory assumes that we are Christians, but now we have to be assured in a purely objective way what Christianity is, in order that we may defend ourselves against the Turk and the Russian and the Roman yoke, and gallantly fight out the battle of Christianity so that we may make our age, as it were, a bridge to

* Sören Kierkegaard, *The Concluding Unscientific Postscript*, English translation by David Swenson. Copyright 1941 by Princeton University Press. Conclusion.

the peerless future which already is glimpsed. This is sheer aesthetics. Christianity is an existence-communication, the task is to become a Christian and continue to be one, and the most dangerous of all illusions is to be so sure of being one that one has to defend the whole of Christendom against the Turk—instead of being alert to defend our own faith against the illusion about the Turk.

2. One says, No, not every acceptance of the Christian doctrine makes one a Christian; what it principally depends upon is appropriation, that one appropriates and holds fast this doctrine quite differently from anything else, that one is ready to live in it and to die in it, to venture one's life for it, etc.

This seems as if it were something. However, the category "quite differently" is a mediocre category, and the whole formula, which makes an attempt to define more subjectively what it is to be a Christian, is neither one thing nor the other; in a way it avoids the difficulty involved in the distraction and deceit of approximation, but it lacks categorical definition. The pathos of approximation which is talked of here is that of immanence; one can just as well say that an enthusiastic lover is so related to his love: he holds fast to it and appropriates it quite differently from anything else, he is ready to live in it and die in it, he will venture everything for it. To this extent there is no difference between a lover and a Christian with respect to inwardness, and one must again recur to the *what*, which is the doctrine—and with that we again come under No. 1.

The pathos of appropriation needs to be so defined that it cannot be confused with any other pathos. The more subjective interpretation is right in insisting that it is appropriation which decides the matter, but it is wrong in its definition of appropriation, which does not distinguish it from every other immediate pathos.

That is to say, the appropriation by

which a Christian is a Christian must be so specific that it cannot be confused with anything else.

3. One defines the thing of becoming and being a Christian, not objectively by the *what* of the doctrine, nor subjectively by appropriation, not by what has gone on in the individual, but by what the individual has undergone; that he was baptized. Though one adjoins to baptism the assumption of a confession of faith, nothing decisive will be gained, but the definition will waver between accentuating the *what* (the path of approximation) and talking indefinitely about acceptance and acceptance and appropriation, etc., without any specific determination.

If, on the other hand, one were to say that he did indeed receive the Spirit in baptism and by the witness it bears together with his spirit, he knows that he was baptized—then the inference is inverted, he argues from the witness of the Spirit within him to the fact that he was baptized, not from the fact of being baptized to the possession of the Spirit. But if the inference is to be drawn in this way, baptism is quite rightly not regarded as the mark of the Christian, but inwardness is, and so here in turn there is needed a specific definition of inwardness and appropriation whereby the witness of the Spirit in the individual is distinguished from all other (universally defined) activity of spirit in man.

It is noteworthy moreover that the orthodoxy which especially has made baptism the decisive mark is continually complaining that among the baptized there are so few Christians, that almost all, except for an immortal little band, are spiritless baptized pagans—which seems to indicate that baptism cannot be the decisive factor with respect to becoming a Christian, not even according to the latter view of those who in the first form insist upon it as decisive with respect to becoming a Christian.

II

Subjectively, what it is to become a Christian is defined thus:

The decision lies in the subject. The appropriation is the paradoxical inwardness which is specifically different from all other inwardness. The thing of being a Christian is not determined by the *what* of Christianity but by the *how* of the Christian. This *how* can only correspond with one thing, the absolute paradox. There is therefore no vague talk to the effect that being a Christian is to accept, and to accept, and to accept quite differently to appropriate, to believe, to appropriate by faith quite differently (all of them purely rhetorical and fictitious definitions); but *to believe* is specifically different from all other appropriation and inwardness. *Faith is the objective uncertainty due to the repulsion of the absurd held fast in the passion of inwardness, which in this instance is intensified to the utmost degree.* This formula fits only the believer, no one else, not a lover, not an enthusiast, not a thinker, but simply and solely the believer who is related to the absolute paradox.

Faith therefore cannot be any sort of provisional function. He who, from the vantage point of a higher knowledge, would know his faith as a factor resolved in a higher idea has *eo ipso* ceased to believe. Faith *must not rest content* with unintelligibility; for precisely the relation to or the repulsion from the unintelligible, the absurd, is the expression for the passion of faith.

This definition of what it is to be a Christian prevents the erudite or anxious deliberation of approximation from enticing the individual into byways, so that he becomes erudite instead of becoming a Christian, and in most cases a smatterer instead of becoming a Christian; for the decision lies in the subject. But inwardness has again found its specific mark whereby it is differentiated from all other inwardness and is not disposed of by the chatty category "quite differently," which fits the case of every passion at the moment of passion.

The psychologist generally regards it as a sure sign that a man is beginning to give up a passion when he wishes to treat the object of it objectively. Passion and reflection are generally exclusive of one another. Becoming objective in this way is always retrogression, for passion is man's perdition, but it is his exaltation as well. In case dialectic and reflection are not used to intensify passion, it is a retrogression to become objective; and even he who is lost through passion has not lost so much as he who lost passion, for the former had the possibility.

Precisely because people in our age and in the Christendom of our time do not appear to be sufficiently aware of the dialectic of inward appropriation, or of the fact that the "how" of the individual is an expression just as precise and more decisive for what he has than is the "what" to which he appeals—for this very reason there crop up the strangest and (if one is in the humor and has the time for it) the most laughable confusions, more comic than even the confusion of paganism, because in them there was not so much at stake, and because the contradictions were not so strident.

An orthodox champion fights in defense of Christianity with the most frightful passion, he protests with the sweat of his brow and with the most concerned demeanor that he accepts Christianity pure and simple, that he will live and die in it—and he forgets that such acceptance is an all too general expression for the relation to Christianity. He does everything in Jesus' name and uses Christ's name on every occasion as a sure sign that he is a Christian and is called to fight in defense of Christendom in our age—and he has no inkling of the little ironical secret that a man, merely by describing the "how" of his inwardness, can show indirectly that he is a Christian without mentioning God's name. A man becomes converted New Year's Eve precisely at six o'clock. With that he is fully prepared. Fantastically decked out with the fact of conversion, he must now run out and proclaim Christianity—in a Christian land. Well, of course, even though we are all baptized, every man may well need to become a Christian in another sense. But here is the distinction: there is no lack of information in a Christian land, something else is lacking, and this is a something which the one man cannot directly communicate to the other. And in such fantastic categories would a converted man work for Christianity; and yet he proves (just in proportion as he is the more busy in spreading and spreading) that he himself is not a Christian. For to be a Christian is something so deeply reflected that it does not admit of the aesthetical dialectic which allows one man to be for others something he is not for himself. On the other hand, a scoffer attacks Christianity and at the same time expounds it so reliably that it is a pleasure to read him, and one who is in perplexity about finding it distinctly set forth may almost have recourse to him.

It is said to have chanced in England that a man was attacked on the highway by a robber who had made himself unrecognizable by wearing a big wig. He falls upon the traveler, seizes him by the throat and shouts, "Your purse!" He gets the purse and keeps it, but the wig he throws away. A poor man comes along the same road, puts it on and arrives at the next town where the traveler had already denounced the crime; he is arrested, is recognized by the traveler, who takes his oath that he is the man. By chance, the robber is present in the court-room, sees the misunderstanding, turns to the judge and says, "It seems to me that the traveler has regard rather to the wig than to the man," and he asks permission to make a trial. He puts on the wig, seizes the traveler by the throat, crying, "Your purse!"—and the traveler recognizes the robber and offers to swear to it—the only trouble is that already he has taken an oath.

So it is, in one way or another, with every man who has a "what" and is not attentive to the "how": he swears, he takes his oath, he runs errands, he ventures life and blood, he is executed—all on account of the wig.

Truth Is Subjectivity*

I

When the question of truth is raised in an objective manner, reflection is directed objectively to the truth, as an object to which the knower is related. Reflection is not focused upon the relationship, however, but upon the question of whether it is the truth to which the knower is related. If only the object to which he is related is the truth, the subject is accounted to be in the truth. When the question of the truth is raised subjectively, reflection is directed subjectively to the nature of the individual's relationship: if only the mode of this relationship is in the truth, the individual is in the truth, even if he should happen to be thus related to what is not true.[1] Let us take as an example the knowledge of God. Objectively, reflection is directed to the problem of whether this object is the true God; subjectively, reflection is directed to the question whether the individual is related to a something in such a manner that his relationship is in truth a God-relationship. On which side is the truth now to be found? Ah, may we not here resort to a mediation, and say: It is on neither side, but in the mediation of both? Excellently well said, provided we might have it explained how an existing individual manages to be in a state of mediation. For to be in a state of mediation is to be finished, while to exist is to become. Nor can an existing individual be in two places at the same time— he cannot be an identity of subject and object. When he is nearest to being in two places at the same time he is in passion; but passion is merely momentary, and passion is also the highest expression of subjectivity.

The existing individual who chooses to pursue the objective way enters upon the entire approximation-process by which it is proposed to bring God to light objectively. But this is in all eternity impossible, because God is a subject, and therefore exists only for subjectivity in inwardness. The existing individual who chooses the subjective way apprehends instantly the entire dialectical difficulty involved in having to use some time, perhaps a long time, in finding God objectively; and he feels this dialectical difficulty in all its painfulness, because he must use God at that very moment, since every moment is wasted in which he does not have God.[2] That very instant he has God, not by virtue of any objective deliberation but by virtue of the infinite passion of inwardness. The objective inquirer, on the other hand, is not embarrassed by such dialectical difficulties as are involved in devoting an entire period of investigation to finding God—since it is possible that the inquirer may die tomorrow; and if he lives he can scarcely regard God as something to be taken along if convenient, since God is precisely that which one takes *a tout prix,* which in the understanding of passion constitutes the true inward relationship to God.

---

* Sören Kierkegaard, *Concluding Unscientific Postscript.* English translation by David Swenson. Copyright 1941 by Princeton University Press. Book II.

[1] The reader will observe that the question here is about essential truth, or about the truth which is essentially related to existence, and that it is precisely for the sake of clarifying it as inwardness or as subjectivity that this contrast is drawn. (K)

[2] In this manner God certainly becomes a postulate, but not in the otiose manner in which this word is commonly understood. It becomes clear rather that the only way in which an existing individual comes into relation with God is when the dialectical contradiction brings his passion to the point of despair, and helps him to embrace God with the "category of despair" (faith). Then the postulate is so far from being arbitrary that it is precisely a life-necessity. It is then not so much that God is a postulate as that the existing individual's postulation of God is a necessity. (K)

It is at this point, so difficult dialectically, that the way swings off for everyone who knows what it means to think, and to think existentially; which is something very different from sitting at a desk like a fantastical being and writing about what one has never done, something very different from writing *de omnibus dubitandum,* and at the same time being as existentially credulous as the most sensuous of men. Here is where the way swings off, and the change is marked by the fact that, while objective knowledge rambles comfortably on by way of the long road of approximation without being impelled by the urge of passion, subjective knowledge counts every delay a deadly peril, and the decision so infinitely important and so instantly pressing that it is as if the opportunity had already passed unutilized.

Now when the problem is to reckon up on which side there is most truth, whether on the side of one who seeks the true God objectively, and pursues the approximate truth of the God-idea; or on the side of one who, driven by the infinite passion to God in truth (and to be at one and the same time on both sides equally is, as we have noted, not possible for an existing individual, but is merely the happy delusion of an imaginary I-am-I): the answer cannot be in doubt for anyone who has not been demoralized with the aid of science. If one who lives in the midst of Christianity goes up to the house of God, the house of the true God, with the true conception of God in his knowledge, and prays, but prays in a false spirit; and one who lives in an idolatrous community prays with the entire passion of the infinite, although his eyes rest upon the image of an idol: where is there most truth? The one prays in truth to God though he worships an idol; the other prays falsely to the true God, and hence worships in fact an idol.

II

When subjectivity is the truth, the conceptual determination of the truth must include an expression for the antithesis to objectivity, a memento of the fork in the road where the way swings off; this expression will also indicate the tension of the subjective inwardness. Here is such a definition of truth: *An objective uncertainty held fast in an appropriation-process of the most passionate inwardness is the truth,* the highest truth for an *existing individual.* At the point where the way swings off (and where this is cannot be specified objectively, since it is a matter of subjectivity) there objective knowledge is placed in abeyance. Thus the subject merely has, objectively, the uncertainty; but it is this which precisely increases the tension of that infinite passion which constitutes his inwardness. The truth is precisely the venture which chooses an objective uncertainty with the passion of the infinite. I contemplate nature in the hope of finding God, and I see omnipotence and wisdom; but I also see much else that disturbs my mind and excites anxiety. The sum of all this is an objective uncertainty. But it is for this very reason that the inwardness becomes as intense as it is, for it embraces this objective uncertainty with the entire passion of the infinite. In the case of a mathematical proposition the objectivity is given, but for this reason the truth of such a proposition is also an indifferent truth.

But the above definition of truth is an equivalent expression for faith. Without risk there is no faith. Faith is precisely the contradiction between the infinite passion of the individual's inwardness and the objective uncertainty. If I am capable of grasping God objectively, I do not believe, but precisely because I cannot do this I must believe. If I wish to preserve myself in faith, I must constantly be intent upon holding fast the objective uncertainty, so that in the objective uncertainty I am out "upon the seventy thousand fathoms of water," and yet believe.

In the principle that subjectivity, inwardness, is the truth, there is comprehended the Socratic wisdom, whose everlasting merit it was to have become aware of the essential significance of existence, of the fact that the knower is an existing individual. For this reason Socrates was in the truth by virtue of his ignorance, in the highest sense in which this was possible within paganism. To attain to an understanding of this, to comprehend that the misfortune of speculative philosophy is again and again to have forgotten that the knower is an existing individual, is in our objective age difficult enough. But to have made an advance upon Socrates, without even having understood what he understood, is at any rate not Socratic.

III

Subjectivity is the truth. By virtue of the relationship subsisting between the eternal, essential truth and the existing individual, the paradox came into being. Let us now go further, let us suppose that the eternal essential truth is itself a paradox. How does the paradox come into being? By putting the eternal essential truth into juxtaposition with existence. Hence when we posit such a conjunction within the truth itself, the truth becomes a paradox. The eternal truth has come into being in time: this is the paradox.

When the eternal truth is related to an existing individual, it becomes a paradox. When the paradox is paradoxical in itself, it repels the individual by virtue of its absurdity, and the corresponding passion of inwardness is faith. But subjectivity, inwardness, is the truth; for otherwise we have forgotten what the merit of the Socratic position is.

When Socrates believed there was a God, he held fast to the objective uncertainty with the whole passion of his inwardness, and it is precisely in this contradiction and in this risk, that faith is rooted. Now it is otherwise. Instead of the objective uncertainty, there is here a certainty, namely, that objectively it is absurd; and this absurdity, held fast in the passion of inwardness, is faith. The Socratic ignorance is like a witty jest in comparison with the earnestness of facing the absurd; and the Socratic existential inwardness is like Greek light-mindedness in comparison with the grace strenuosity of faith.

What now is the absurd? The absurd is —that the eternal truth has come into being in time, that God has come into being, has been born, has grown up, and so forth, has come into being precisely like any other individual human being, quite indistinguishable from other individuals. The absurd is precisely by its objective repulsion the measure of the intensity of faith in inwardness. Suppose a man who wishes to acquire faith; let the comedy begin. He wishes to have faith, but he wishes also to safeguard himself by means of an objective inquiry and its approximation-process. What happens? With the help of the approximation-process the absurd becomes something different: it becomes probable, it becomes increasingly probable, it becomes extremely and emphatically probable. Now he is ready to believe it, and he ventures to claim for himself that he does not believe as shoemakers and tailors and simple folk believe, but only after long deliberation. Now he is ready to believe it; and lo, now it has become precisely impossible to believe it. Anything that is almost probable, or probable, or extremely and emphatically probable, is something he can almost know, or as good as know, or extremely and emphatically almost *know*—but it is impossible to *believe.* For the absurd is the object of faith, and the only object that can be believed.

Or suppose a man who says that he has faith, but desires to make his faith clear to himself, so as to understand himself in his faith. Now the comedy begins again. The object of faith becomes almost probable, as good as probable, extremely and emphatically probable. He has completed his investigations, and he ventures to claim for himself that he does not believe as shoemakers and tailors and other simple folk believe, but that he has also understood himself in his believing. Strange understanding! On the contrary he has in fact learned something else about faith than when he believed; and he has learned that he no longer believes, since he almost knows, or as good as knows, or extremely and emphatically almost knows.

Christianity has declared itself to be the eternal essential truth which has come into being in time. It has proclaimed itself as the *Paradox,* and it has required of the individual the inwardness of faith in relation to that which is an offense to the Jews and a folly to the Greeks—and an absurdity to the understanding. It is impossible to express more strongly the fact that subjectivity is truth and that objectivity merely repels, even by virtue of the absurd. And indeed it would seem very strange that Christianity should have come into the world just to receive an explanation; as if it had been somewhat bewildered about itself, and hence had entered the world to consult that wise man, the speculative philosopher, who can help by furnishing the explanation. It is impossible to express with more intensive inwardness the principle that subjectivity is truth, than when subjectivity is in the first instance untruth, and yet subjectivity is the truth.

The Personal Dimension of Existence: Martin Buber

Probably no single small book in the literature of existential philosophy has had such influence as Martin Buber's *I and Thou*. In this volume one encounters all the major concepts of existentialism distilled to their essence and expressed in a sort of lyric poetry; and here, in his concept of the "I—Thou" relationship, we find Buber's own significant contribution to existential thought (an emphasis upon the personal dimension of existence) given its most direct and provocative statement. Many of his earlier works in German have yet to be translated but, in all, some twenty-five books have appeared in English and the increasing number of books about him bear witness to the extent of his influence.

Born in Vienna in 1878, Buber lived until he was fourteen in a predominantly Jewish area in Poland with his grandfather, Salomon Buber, a distinguished scholar of the Jewish Enlightenment. As a boy he became absorbed in the world of Biblical and rabbinic thought; he learned classic Hebrew, and at thirteen he was confirmed in the usual ceremony as a member of the Jewish religious community. Within a few years, as was so often the case among the more liberal and emancipated Jewish youth in Europe at that time, he reacted against the strict Jewish spirit of his grandfather's home and soon ceased all formal religious observances. When at eighteen he entered the University of Vienna and began to study philosophy, his interest centered not in Jewish thought but in the great Christian mystics—Jacob Boehme, Meister Eckhart and Nicolaus of Cusa. Later at the University of Berlin he came into contact with the dominant intellectual currents of the late nineteenth and early twentieth centuries.

Among the writers who influenced Buber the most in this formative period were Nietzsche, Dostoevski, and Kierkegaard. In the thought of both Nietzsche and Kierkegaard he found a strong reaction against philosophical rationalism, against the dominance of scientific naturalism, against the materialism of the age in which he lived, and a re-emphasis upon the place of creative spiritual vitality in human existence. Not only Nietzsche's philosophy, but also his style in *Thus Spake Zarathustra* had great appeal for Buber. In *I and Thou* the poetic spirit of Zarathustra reappears, although in quite different guise. Not until some years later, when Kierkegaard was rediscovered and translated into German during the first decade of the twentieth century, did Buber become familiar with the existentialism of the great Danish religious thinker. Here again he found a fresh and powerful source of intellectual stimulation. When in later years he returned to his own Jewish religious heritage, Buber became increasingly critical, however, of Kierkegaard's distinctly Christian emphasis, his highly individualistic approach to religion, and his pessimism about human nature. In the end, as a recent interpreter has well put it Buber "filtered Kierkegaard's existentialism" through his own deeper and broader Jewish loyalties.

Upon completing his work at the University of Berlin, Buber remained in

Germany where his gifts as a writer and speaker won recognition for him while he was still a young man. This early success left him dissatisfied, however, and deeply conscious of his own loneliness and "rootlessness." Although not unusual for young intellectuals, this was intensified in Buber's case because he had broken with his Jewish tradition and background and had found nothing to replace it. This sense of need led him in time to an active participation in the Zionist movement, then in its infancy. He became a leading spokesman of that branch of Zionism which saw the political state as only a part of the Jewish Renaissance and wanted the Jews to achieve wholeness in their lives by a normal, full participation in all aspects of social and cultural life. From 1916 to 1924 he was the editor of *Der Jude,* a periodical which emphasized his own broader concept of Zionism. By 1924, when he gave up the editorship of this periodical, it had become one of the most influential expressions of serious Jewish thought in Germany.

It was during this period that Buber's greatest work took shape in his mind. The first draft of *I and Thou* was completed in 1916, he tells us, but not until 1919 did he attain "decisive clarity" in his thought. In the completed work, finally published in 1923, his early enthusiasm for mysticism had become an essential aspect of a point of view definitely "existential" in outlook. The year that *I and Thou* was published Buber was appointed to the chair of Jewish philosophy at the University of Frankfort, a position which he held until the rise of the Nazis to power in 1933 forced him to resign. Then in 1938, at the age of sixty, he left Germany for Israel to accept the chair of social philosophy at the Hebrew University in Jerusalem where he played an important role in the intellectual and cultural life of Israel. His *Paths in Utopia,* written in Israel, is a mature statement of his own social philosophy, a philosophy rooted in the concrete life of the community. Upon his retirement at seventy-three from the Hebrew University, Buber visited the United States, lecturing at a number of universities and theological schools. In 1957 he returned to deliver a series of lectures at the Washington School of Psychiatry, and again in 1958 for the celebration of his eightieth birthday at Princeton University. In 1961 he was living in semi-retirement in Jerusalem.

For Buber, as for all existentialists, philosophical problems emerge only when men face questions that engage the total person, not the intellect alone. The task of philosophy is not abstract speculation but assistance to the individual in achieving an authentic selfhood by means of resolute decisions. Such a direct and deeply emotional approach to human existence has hitherto largely been the province of literature, and existential philosophers always strike a literary note. In *I and Thou* these existential elements are all apparent. Its approach to existence is one of passionate engagement and at its best its literary tone almost reaches lyric poetry. Because of the world-affirming tradition of Judaism, Buber's thought does not have the anxious preoccupation with sin, the sense of anguish and dread of Kierkegaard. His outlook is much more positive; by comparison with the typical existential pessimism about man, Buber could even be called optimistic and his fusion of existential thinking with the world-affirming spirit of Judaism is a significant philosophical achievement.

In Buber's own peculiar terminology, the attitude of detachment adopted by the scientific investigator is an "I-It" attitude. This is also the attitude of the artist who, while different from the scientist, still as novelist or painter, does not achieve the personal relation. This objective attitude is, of course, a necessary and fruitful one in many human activities, but it is not the *only* nor the most meaningful aspect of human existence. There is another and a more significant *personal* relation. "He who lives with It alone is not a man," Buber warns, for the I-It attitude can become a source of evil if the individual maintains this attitude when the personal relation is the desirable or the necessary one. It is his moving, poetic portrayal of the I-Thou relation, the personal dimension of existence, that gives Buber's existentialism its unique religious significance. As is to be expected, he always keeps close to human experience and deals with life in concrete terms. The I-Thou encounter cannot be explained, he points out: it can only be indicated. To comprehend it, one must identify it in his own experience.

Although the I-Thou encounter reveals the true meaning of human existence, we have no way of stating this meaning rationally and conceptually. For this purpose we can only make use of symbol, of myth, and of paradox. On the question of truth, Buber is quite in accord with his fellow existentialists. Truth is more a matter of moral striving than of an intellectual grasp of ideas or reality. "Human truth becomes real when one tries to translate one's relationship to truth into the reality of one's own life," he writes. "And human truth can be communicated only if one throws oneself into the process and answers for it with one's self."[1] Hence, Buber speaks of "human truth"—men *live* truth; they never express it adequately in abstract, conceptual terms.

---

[1] *Israel and the World* (New York, Schocken Books, 1948), p. 46.

I and Thou*

I

To man the world is twofold, in accordance with his twofold attitude.

The attitude of man is twofold, in accordance with the twofold nature of the primary words which he speaks.

---

* Reprinted with the permission of Charles Scribner's Sons from *I and Thou*, pp. 4–9, 11, 16–18, 33–34, 51, 53–54, 75–76, 80, 95, by Martin Buber. Copyright © 1958 Charles Scribner's Sons.

The primary words are not isolated words, but combined words.

The one primary word is the combination *I-Thou.*

The other primary word is the combination *I-It;* wherein, without a change in the primary word, one of the words *He* and *She* can replace *It.*

Hence the *I* of man is also twofold.

For the *I* of the primary word *I-Thou* is a different *I* from that of the primary word *I-It.*

* * * * * *

There is no *I* taken in itself, but only the *I* of the primary word *I-Thou* and the *I* of the primary word *I-It*.

When a man says *I*, he refers to one or other of these. The *I* to which he refers is present when he says *I*. Further, when he says *Thou* or *It*, the *I* of one of the two primary words is present.

The existence of *I* and the speaking of *I* are one and the same thing.

When a primary word is spoken, the speaker enters the word and takes his stand in it.

* * * * * *

The life of human beings is not passed in the sphere of transitive verbs alone. It does not exist in virtue of activities alone which have some *thing* for their object.

I perceive something. I am sensible of something. I imagine something. I will something. I feel something. I think something. The life of human beings does not consist of all this and the like alone.

This and the like together establish the realm of *It*.

But the realm of *Thou* has a different basis.

When *Thou* is spoken, the speaker has no thing for his object. For where there is a thing there is another thing. Every *It* is bounded by others; *It* exists only through being bounded by others. But when *Thou* is spoken, there is no thing. *Thou* has no bounds.

When *Thou* is spoken, the speaker has no *thing;* he has indeed nothing. But he takes his stand in relation.

It is said that man experiences his world. What does that mean?

Man travels over the surface of things and experiences them. He extracts knowledge about their constitution from them: he wins an experience from them. He experiences what belongs to the things.

But the world is not presented to man by experiences alone. These present him only with a word composed of *It* and *He* and *She* and *It* again.

* * * * * *

As experience, the world belongs to the primary word *I-It*.

The primary word *I-Thou* establishes the world of relation.

* * * * * *

I consider a tree.

I can look on it as a picture: stiff column in a shock of light, or splash of green shot with the delicate blue and silver of the background.

I can perceive it as movement: flowing veins on clinging, pressing pith, suck of the roots, breathing of the leaves, ceaseless commerce with earth and air—and the obscure growth itself.

I can classify it in a species and study it as a type in its structure and mode of life.

I can subdue its actual presence and form so sternly that I recognise it only as an expression of law—of the laws in accordance with which a constant opposition for forces is continually adjusted, or of those in accordance with which the component substances mingle and separate.

I can dissipate it and perpetuate it in number, in pure numerical relation.

In all this the tree remains my object, occupies space and time, and has its nature and constitution.

* * * * * *

If I face a human being as my *Thou,* and say the primary word *I-Thou* to him, he is not a thing among things, and does not consist of things.

This human being is not *He* or *She,* bounded from every other *He* and *She,* a specific point in space and time within the net of the world; nor is he a nature able to be experienced and described, a loose bundle of named qualities. But with no neighbour, and whole in himself, he is *Thou* and fills the heavens. This does not mean that nothing exists except himself. But all else lives in *his* light.

Just as the melody is not made up of notes nor the verse of words nor the statue of lines, but they must be tugged and dragged till their unity has been scattered into these many pieces, so with the man to whom I say *Thou*. I can take out from him the colour of his hair, or of his speech, or of his goodness. I must continually do this. But each time I do it he ceases to be *Thou*.

So long as the heaven of *Thou* is spread out over me the winds of causality cower at my heels, and the whirlpool of fate stays its course.

I do not experience the man to whom I say *Thou*. But I take my stand in relation to him, in the sanctity of the primary word. Only when I step out of it do I experience him once more. In the act of experience *Thou* is far away.

Even if the man to whom I say *Thou* is not aware of it in the midst of his experience, yet relation may exist. For *Thou* is more than *It* realises. No deception penetrates here; here is the cradle of the Real Life.

* * * * * *

— What, then, do we experience of *Thou?*

— Just nothing. For we do not experience it.

— What, then, do we know of *Thou?*

— Just everything. For we know nothing isolated about it any more.

* * * * * *

But this is the exalted melancholy of our fate, that every *Thou* in our world must become an *It*. It does not matter how exclusively present the *Thou* was in the direct relation. As soon as the relation has been worked out or has been permeated with a means, the *Thou* becomes an object among objects—perhaps the chief, but still one of them, fixed in its size and its limits. In the work of art realisation in one sense means loss of reality in another. Genuine contemplation is over in a short time; now the life in nature, that first unlocked itself to me in the mystery of mutual action, can again be described, taken to pieces, and classified—the meeting-point of manifold systems of laws. And love itself cannot persist in direct relation. It endures, but in interchange of actual and potential being. The

human being who was even now single and unconditioned, not something lying to hand, only present, not able to be experienced, only able to be fulfilled, has now become again a *He* or a *She,* a sum of qualities, a given quantity with a certain shape. Now I may take out from him again the colour of his hair or of his speech or of his goodness. But so long as I can do this he is no more my *Thou* and cannot yet be my *Thou* again.

Every *Thou* in the world is by its nature fated to become a thing, or continually to re-enter into the condition of things. In objective speech it would be said that every thing in the world, either before or after becoming a thing, is able to appear to an *I* as its *Thou*. But objective speech snatches only at a fringe of real life.

The *It* is the eternal chrysalis, the *Thou* the eternal butterfly—except that situations do not always follow one another in clear succession, but often there is a happening profoundly twofold, confusedly entangled.

* * * * * *

The world of *It* is set in the context of space and time.

The world of *Thou* is not set in the context of either of these.

The particular *Thou*, after the relational event has run its course, *is bound* to become an *It*.

The particular *It,* by entering the relational event, *may* become a *Thou*.

These are the two basic privileges of the world of *It*. They move man to look on the world of *It* as the world in which he has to live, and in which it is comfortable to live, as the world, indeed, which offers him all manner of incitements and excitements, activity and knowledge. In this chronicle of solid benefits the moments of the *Thou* appear as strange lyric and dramatic episodes, seductive and magical, but tearing us away to dangerous extremes, loosening the well-tried context, leaving more questions than satisfaction behind them, shattering security—in short, uncanny moments we can well dispense with. For since we are bound to leave them and go back into the "world", why not remain in it? Why not call to order what is over against us, and send it packing into the realm of objects?

In all seriousness of truth, hear this: without *It* man cannot live. But he who lives with *It* alone is not a man.

II

The unlimited reign of causality in the world of *It,* of fundamental importance for the scientific ordering of nature, does not weigh heavily on man, who is not limited to the world of *It,* but can continually leave it for the world of relation. Here *I* and *Thou* freely confront one another in mutual effect that is neither connected with nor coloured by any causality. Here man is assured of the freedom both of his being and of Being. Only he who knows relation and knows about the presence of the *Thou* is capable of decision. He who decides is free, for he has approached the Face.

Destiny and freedom are solemnly promised to one another. Only the man who makes freedom real to himself meets destiny. He who forgets all that is caused and makes decision out of the depths, who rids himself of property and raiment and naked approaches the Face, is a free man, and destiny confronts him as the counterpart of his freedom. It is not his boundary, but his fulfilment; freedom and destiny are linked together in meaning. And in this meaning destiny, with eyes a moment ago so severe now filled with light, looks out like grace itself.

No; causal necessity does not weigh heavily on the man who returns to the world of *It* bearing this spark. And, in times of healthy life, trust streams from men of spirit to all people. To all men indeed, even to the dullest, meeting—the present—has come somehow, naturally, impulsively, dimly: all men have somewhere been aware of the *Thou;* now the spirit gives them full assurance.

But in times of sickness it comes about that the world of *It,* no longer penetrated and fructified by the inflowing world of *Thou* as by living streams, but separated and stagnant, a gigantic ghost of the fens, overpowers man.

In coming to terms with a world of objects that no longer assume present being for him he succumbs to this world. Then smooth causality rises up till it is an oppressive, stifling fate.

III

The extended lines of relations meet in the eternal *Thou.*

Every particular *Thou* is a glimpse through to the eternal *Thou;* by means of every particular *Thou* the primary word addresses the eternal *Thou.* Through this mediation of the *Thou* of all beings fulfilment, and non-fulfilment, of relations comes to them: the inborn *Thou* is realised in each relation and consummated in none. It is consummated only in the direct relation with the *Thou* that by its nature cannot become *It.*

* * * * * *

Men have addressed their eternal *Thou* with many names. In singing of Him who was thus named they always had the *Thou* in mind: the first myths were hymns of praise. Then the names took refuge in the language of *It;* men were more and more strongly moved to think of and to address their eternal *Thou* as an *It.* But all God's names are hallowed, for in them He is not merely spoken about, but also spoken to.

Many men wish to reject the word God as a legitimate usage, because it is so misused. It is indeed the most heavily laden of all the words used by men. For that very reason it is the most imperishable and most indispensable. What does all mistaken talk about God's being and works (though there has been, and can be, no other talk about these) matter in comparison with the one truth that all men who have addressed God had God Himself in mind? For he who speaks the word God and really has *Thou* in mind (whatever the illusion by which he is held), addresses the true *Thou* of his life, which cannot be limited by another *Thou,* and to which he stands in a relation that gathers up and includes all others.

But when he, too, who abhors the

name, and believes himself to be godless, gives his whole being to addressing the *Thou* of his life, as a *Thou* that cannot be limited by another, he addresses God.

* * * * * *

Actually there is no such thing as seeking God, for there is nothing in which He could not be found. How foolish and hopeless would be the man who turned aside from the course of his life in order to seek God; even though he won all the wisdom of solitude and all the power of concentrated being he would miss God. Rather is it as when a man goes his way and simply wishes that it might be the way: in the strength of his wish his striving is expressed. Every rational event is a stage that affords him a glimpse into the consummating event. So in each event he does not partake, but also (for he is waiting) does partake, of the one event. Waiting, not seeking, he goes his way; hence he is composed before all things, and makes contact with them which helps them. But when he has *found,* his heart is not turned from them, though everything now meets him in the one event. He blesses every cell that sheltered him, and every cell into which he will yet turn. For this finding is not the end, but only the eternal middle, of the way.

It is a finding without seeking, a discovering of the primal, of origin. His sense of *Thou,* which cannot be satiated till he finds the endless *Thou,* had the *Thou* present to it from the beginning; the presence had only to become wholly real to him in the reality of the hallowed life of the world.

God cannot be inferred in anything—in nature, say, as its author, or in history as its master, or in the subject as the self that is thought in it. Something else is not "given" and God then elicited from it; but God is the Being that is directly, most nearly, and lastingly, over against us, that may properly only be addressed, not expressed.

* * * * * *

I know nothing of a "world" and a "life in the world" that might separate a man from God. What is thus described is actually life with an alienated world of *It,* which experiences and uses. He who truly goes out to meet the world goes out also to God. Concentration and outgoing are necessary, both in truth, at once the one and the other, which is the One.

God comprises, but is not, the universe. So, too, God comprises, but is not, my Self. In view of the inadequacy of any language about this fact, I can say *Thou* in my language as each man can in his, in view of this *I* and *Thou* live, and dialogue and spirit and language (spirit's primal act), and the Word in eternity.

Conclusion
Philosophy and
Social Action

There are two contributions that philosophy must make if it performs its function successfully in human life: (1) it must confirm the sense of meaning and purpose in a man's inner spiritual life, and (2) it must afford him some basis for meaningful social action—some social ideal to which he can give allegiance with both logical and psychological assurance. The philosophies examined in this volume have all undertaken, each in its own way, to accomplish this. The crises of our age, both spiritual and social, place heavier demands upon a man's philosophy than was true in less troubled days. Perhaps, as Barrett suggests, existentialism is the philosophy of the atomic age, but certainly the Marxian philosophy has also emerged in many ways as the dominant and compelling philosophy in an age of worldwide and too often violent revolution.

The social importance of a philosophy may be judged by the number of people who hold it, by the practices it is used to justify, or by the kind of conduct and sense of values that it produces among those who adopt it. In terms of its impact upon today's world, the Marxian Dialectical Materialism, whatever one may think of its validity, is surely one of the important social philosophies. It is probably accepted by more people, in more places, and with a more complete commitment than any other philosophy. For its more intelligent adherents, dialectical materialism is a set of doctrines which describe the fundamental character of existence both for man and for the universe, doctrines in terms of which one can formulate the laws that operate in nature as well as in human life and social activity.

An examination of the writings of those who profess to accept the Marxian position, however, reveals in their philosophy a common allegiance rather than a common meaning. Whether in the thought of Marx and Engels, or in that of Lenin, or in that of contemporary exponents of Marxism, it is not possible to find a clear-cut, objective, non-controversial presentation of dialectical materialism in philosophical terms comparable to that provided for the various philosophies discussed in this book. In part, of course, this arises from the propaganda motive that characterizes such statements, but in part it also comes from inner contradictions.

This difficulty is aptly illustrated by the writing and the spiritual pilgrimage of Sidney Hook, the ablest and best-known American philosopher to show strong attachment to the Marxian position. In his early writing Hook adopts a position that is essentially Marxian in outlook; then throughout the rest of his long career as professor of philosophy at New York University he has gradually modified this early commitment, now advocating a "democratic socialism" which is persuasively presented in *Political Power and Personal Freedom* (1959). For twenty years Hook and Max Eastman have carried on a controversy over Hook's attitude toward Marxian philosophy. Eastman's early article "The Americanization of Marx" (published in 1940 as an appendix to his *Marxism: Is it Science*), was a strong attack upon what he called "Sidney Hook's celebrated attempt to prove that Marx was not a Hegelian philosopher but an anticipator of the 'scientific pragmatism' of John Dewey." The controversy still continued unabated when Hook in 1959 (in *Political Power and Personal Freedom*) undertook to answer Eastman's later criticisms of his social philosophy. The opening paragraph of Eastman's popular attack on the validity of dialectical materialism states the heart of his position:

> Marxists profess to reject religion in favor of science, but they cherish a belief that the external universe is evolving with reliable, if not divine, necessity in exactly the direction in which they want it to go. They do not conceive themselves as struggling to build the Communist society in a world which is of its own nature indifferent to them. They conceive themselves as traveling toward that society in a world which is like a moving-stairway taking them the way they walk. Their enemies are walking the same stairway, but walking in the wrong direction. This is not a scientific, but in the most technical sense, a religious conception of the world.[1]

Eastman supports this interpretation by a detailed study of Communist thought, but the point he makes is quite apparent in an early comment (1842) on Hegelian dialectic now attributed to Engels himself: "And that faith in the omnipotence of the Idea, in the victory of eternal truth, that firm certainty that it will never waver, never depart from its path, although the whole world turn against it—there you have the foundation of the real positive philosophy, the philosophy of universal history. Just that is the supreme revelation, the revelation in which every negation of the critic becomes an affirmation. That everlasting struggle and movement of peoples and heroes, above which in the eternal world soars the Idea, only to swoop down into the thick of the fight and become the actual, self-conscious soul—there you have the source of every salvation, there the kingdom in which every one of us ought to struggle and be active at his post. . . ."[2]

---

[1] *Marxism: Is it Science* (New York, W. W. Norton and Company, 1940), p. 15.

[2] Riazanov, *Essays on the History of Marxism*, pp. 40–41. Quoted by Max Eastman, *op. cit.*, p. 62.

In *Reason, Social Myths, and Democracy* (1940), Hook has a careful and detailed examination of dialectical materialism, in which he distinguishes seven different senses in which the term "dialectic" is used by Engels, and then proceeds to point out fallacies in the Marxian treatment of dialectic in nature, in society, and in history. This is a discussion that no serious student of the subject can afford to neglect. In Hook's volume, *Political Power and Personal Freedom,* there is an enjoyable essay, entitled "Karl Marx in Limbo," designed to show that present-day Communists have altered fundamentally the central ideas in the thinking of Marx himself, and would undoubtedly be rejected by the master if he were alive. This essay, which is in essence Hook's own interpretation of Marx, is reprinted below.

* * * * * *

Karl Marx in Limbo*

It was not difficult to find the shade of Karl Marx in limbo. His spectral beard was trimmed, his monocle was gone and he seemed much more benign than his pictures show him—indeed, almost grandfatherly. Flanked by Engels and Kautsky, he was arguing a technical point with Keynes, Veblen and Schumpeter. Lenin was not in the circle. Later my guide told me he was waiting with brooding impatience for Stalin, who, although due, was still missing; there were rumors that limbo would not receive him.

Marx detached himself from his fellow shades when he learned that a visitor from earth had arrived. Instead of introducing myself as an author of several studies of his thought (I had heard that biographers and critics sometimes got an unspiritual reception when they met their subjects face to face), I announced at once that I had news for him.

"News?" he said. "I hope it's agreeable for a change. For the last twenty years or so, it has been uniformly unpleasant. Almost every new arrival prominently connected with public affairs has picked an argument with

me, as if I were responsible for what's happening on Earth."

"My news is more personal," I replied. "The Marx-Engels-Lenin Institute at Moscow is issuing a new corrected edition of your works at the command of the Central Executive Committee of the Russian Communist party."

"Corrected edition, indeed!" he remarked bitterly. "They have been correcting me by word and deed ever since 1917. Every last outrage they commit is laid at my door—even by people who should know better."

"Well," I pointed out. "Isn't it natural? You called yourself a Comunist at one time and they call themselves Communists."

"That, my dear Professor," Marx interrupted, "is known as the fallacy of the undistributed middle term, according to the logic you teach, whose laws, I gather from our cosmic news ticker, the Kremlin has just rediscovered. As well say that, because both sides in the Thirty Years War called themselves Christian, they really were in agreement with each other. Soviet Communism and mine are quite different."

"In what respect?" I inquired.

Marx's retort surprised and alarmed me a little because it indicated either that his

* From *Political Power and Personal Freedom* by Sidney Hook. Copyright 1959 by Criterion Books, Inc., New York. By permission of the publishers.

reading habits were still omnivorous or that the cosmic ticker paid attention to him. "You ought to know, since you've read the material. We called ourselves Communists in order to differentiate ourselves from sentimental socialists who had their eyes so fixed on a Utopia that they couldn't see what the necessary steps were in the process of realizing it. As you recall, when my friends and I were members of the Communist League we wrote that '*we were not among those Communists who were out destroy liberty and who wished to turn the whole world into one huge barracks or into a gigantic warehouse. There certainly were some Communists who with easy conscience refused to countenance personal liberty.*'[1] But for me personal liberty was the very oxygen of any decent society. My criticism of capitalism was based on my desire to diffuse freedom among those who were suffering from lack of it."

"But if that's true," I objected, "why have the leaders of Communist Russia canonized you and built a cult around you? Surely, to use a favorite phrase of theirs, it is no accident that—"

"It's a long story," Marx interjected, "and there *are* accidents in history even if this isn't one. The Russians were always difficult and different. More than once I had to say "*I am no Marxist.*' Bakunin, who also once called himself a Marxist, I disowned on Earth. The Communists are people of *his* kidney, and even Bakunin rages against them up here. I don't recognize the present-day Communist brood as my legitimate offspring no matter what they call themselves."

"I've heard other fathers *say* that," I replied, "but saying it is not enough to disprove parentage. Legitimate or not, they claim to be inspired by your ideas and to have built a socialist society. You may not like *how* they got there, but they *are* there, are they not?"

"By no means," Marx replied with a vehemence that seemed to make his beard-tip glow. 'A Socialist society as I always con-

ceived it is one in which '*the free development of each is the condition of the free development of all.*' That excludes the dictatorship of a party, and especially the rule of despots. A socialist society is based on equality, even if it cannot be absolute, and, in the beginning on equality of wage payments for equal working time. The Communists have substituted a new and worse system of exploitation of the workers—through piece-work, speed-up devices, and differences in earned income and living conditions greater than existed in the early days of capitalism. Why, they claim to be Marxists and socialists and yet they frankly admit that labor power is still a commodity subject to the law of value. The surplus value sweated out of them goes to their masters. . . .'"

Fearing that Marx was going to ride his ancient economic hobby horse, I interrupted. "Surely not all of it. Some of it goes into new plants, and they do have trade unions."

By this time Marx's whole beard was incandescent. "Trade unions," he burst out. "Their trade unions are worse than company unions. They are auxiliaries of the secret police whose function is to intimidate the workers into producing more. I have always taught that the working class '*regards its courage, self-confidence, independence and sense of personal dignity as more necessary than its daily bread.*' How is this possible under a regime of a ruthlessly censored press, regimented schools from kindergarten to universities, forced labor, juridical frame-ups, mass deportations and executions? No, the Soviet Union is not a socialist society."

"Nor is it a capitalist society," I added while he paused to draw a fresh breath, "since all the major instruments of production, distribution and exchange are collectivized. What kind of a social system is it then? Your theory of social development seems unable to account for it."

"This is a terminological matter," Marx declared with a touch of asperity. "The main point is that Soviet society, wherever it exists, outrages all the democratic traditions for which the socialist movement fought as well

---

[1] All italicized material is quoted from the writings of Marx.

as those of the great revolutionary movements of liberation whose heirs we always considered ourselves to be."

"Very well," I said hurriedly, "I grant your social philosophy is not theirs. But there is nothing in the notion of a completely collectivized economy which insures that *your* social philosophy will prevail rather than theirs. What I am asking you to explain, however, is the origin and development of the Soviet social system on the basis of your own theory of history. Didn't you say over and over that *'no social order ever perishes before all the productive forces for which there is room in it have developed'*? There was certainly plenty of room for the development of productive forces in Russia in 1917, even more than in the United States of 1917, which was decades ahead of Russia and which has enormously increased its productive capacities since then."

"Quite right," retorted Marx with a triumphant air. "I predicted that socialism would come first to England and the United States because those countries are ripe for it. And certainly not in a backward, undeveloped, semi-barbarous country like Russia. You see how presumptuous the Communists are in calling themselves Marxists."

I wondered why he sounded so triumphant. "I see," I exclaimed, "that the Communists are not Marxists as they claim to be and that if you came to life again in Moscow, the Grand Inquisitors of the Kremlin would probably throw you into the cellars of the Lubianka as an agent of American imperialism. But it seems even clearer to me that the Communists have refuted the central doctrine of Marxism in the name of Marxism. According to that doctrine, the mode of economic production determines political events, not conversely. But the Communists seized political power, nationalized the economy. industrialized the country, collectivized agriculture. Their culture may not be democratic, but their economy is collectivist. It is quite apparent that it was not, as you proclaimed, *'historical laws working with iron necessity toward inevitable results'* which were the driving force of events in Russia but the driv-

ing will of the Communists. Doesn't this show that men control economic forces, for good or evil, wisely or unwisely, and are not controlled by them to the extent that you taught? In other words, haven't the Communists refuted the central proposition of the theory of historical materialism?"

"Not so fast, Professor," Marx quietly replied. "If you take my words literally, you may be right. But let's look for the meaning behind the mere words. When I wrote about what was historically necessary or impossible, I assumed that there was a certain level of civilization which we could take for granted, certain basic human needs and values which would guide human action, or at least limit what human beings would do to other human beings. I was a humanist before I became a socialist, and therefore I believed it was impossible to build a socialist economy in a backward country like Russia except at a morally prohibitive cost. But if we are completely indifferent to questions of human cost and suffering, only physical and biological necessities limit our action and we are all reduced to the level of clever beasts of prey."

"Nothing can grow in a desert," he continued after a pause, "but we can make even a desert bloom like a flower garden if we are prepared to fertilize it with human corpses and water it with rivers of blood. A country which doesn't grow into socialism on the basis of an already prepared economic foundation, a tradition of skill, management, democracy and culture, will defeat the very ends in behalf of which the socialist movement came into existence."

"It is a pity," I observed, "that you didn't spend more time in elaborating on these ends. By concentrating mainly on the economic conditions of achieving them, you gave the impression that collectivism was the be-all and end-all of socialism; that, once it was achieved, all the other virtues would be added to society. The fault is not completely attributable to those of your disciples who converted a necessary condition into a sufficient one. The sentimental socialists may have ignored the means, but *you* lost sight of the ends. It seems to me that your fault is graver."

"No," said Marx, "my Hegelian teachers had convinced me that means and ends are so intertwined that they couldn't be separated. It may be I took too much for granted. But, remember, I wasn't writing textbooks or manuals or recipe books for revolutions everywhere at any time."

"Then tradition becomes an important constraining force in what men can make of man," I pointed out, "and under some conditions as decisive in influencing the direction of social change as the mode of economic production."

"I have never denied it. On the contrary, '*Men make their own history, but not just as they please. They do not choose the circumstances for themselves, but have to work on circumstances as they find them. The legacy of the dead generations weighs like a nightmare upon the brains of the living. At the very time when they seem to be creating something perfectly new, the past often creeps back.*' The Russian past could not be wiped out by any Commissar's decree; it still lives in the present. As of old, for the Russian ruler progress consists in extending the domain of their despotism. What I said at the time of the suppression of Poland by Tsarist Russia is even truer today: '*The policy of Russia is changeless. Its methods, its tactics, its maneuvers may change, but the polar star of its policy—world domination—is still a fixed star.*'"

Not wishing to discuss foreign policy in limbo, I shifted to another question.

"Well, now," I asked, "what about China. Surely here is something you didn't foresee. Do you think China can build socialism, even with the help of the Soviet Union?"

"My analysis of the Soviet Union," Marx spoke scornfully, "is even more valid for China. I predict that the attempt to introduce socialism in China will fail even more badly than it has in the Soviet Union."

"Agreed," I replied, "but what you didn't predict is that the attempt would be made! Since the consequence of the attempt, whether it fails or succeeds, is bound to give rise to momentous historical changes—in-

deed! it already has—something important about history is left unexplained."

"My main interest, as you should know," Marx patiently explained, "has always been in the Western world and the truth or falsity of my theories rests primarily upon developments there. I predicted '*the growth and centralization of large-scale industry, increasing mechanization, the concentration of capital and monopoly, the entanglement of all peoples in the net of the world market, and periodic crises of production.*' By and large, all these things have come to pass."

"Quite true," I rejoined, "but there are a number of other things you predicted which didn't come to pass. You predicted the pauperization of the working classes, the disappearance of the middle class, the atrophy of nationalism and patriotism. Large groups of workers in Western Europe, and especially in the United States, enjoy a standard of living higher than the privileged classes of some previous societies. Nationalism is as strong as ever. The middle-class has not disappeared. And the plain fact is that the workers in non-collective economies have incomparably more freedom, political power, and a greater share of what they produce than the workers in presumably collectivist economies."

"I cheerfully admit it," Marx smilingly responded, "but I believe I can take some credit for it since I taught the necessity of political action and called attention to the influence of factory legislation."

"But in addition to the predicted things which didn't happen," I objected, "there are other things which happened that you did not predict—the birth of new industries, the expansion of productive forces, the rise of fascism, the emergence of the welfare state."

"I underestimated the vitality of capitalism," said Marx, "and the extent to which the democratic process could be used to strengthen social control and responsibility. But this is a matter of detail and degree. I always argued that '*in countries like Great Britain, Holland and the United States the transition from capitalism to socialism could be effected peacefully.*' Similarly with the development of the technological revolution, I believe I was the first to recognize the impact upon society of *'conscious technical application of science to industry and agriculture.'* "

"But you claimed that technology was always a subordinate instrument to war and industry," I protested. "Yet neither you nor anyone else guessed that some day the choices we would have to make concerning its dread uses might affect the very existence of civilization as such."

"The effects of certain discoveries," he agreed, "as well as their significance, cannot always be measured by their origins. Whatever the causes of technological change in the past, unless men today think and plan better than they have in the past, they may not even survive. Limbo will become rapidly overpopulated."

I turned to ask a last question. "Do you believe the basic issue of our time is still between capitalism and socialism?"

Marx spoke deliberately. "Capitalism and socialism as they were traditionally conceived are today irrelevant abstractions in understanding social reality. Wherever free institutions exist, they have been used to make capital more socially responsible and labor more powerful and prosperous. Aside from the defense of freedom itself, the great prob-

lems arise in the West not from a quest for new forms of property but for new modes of democratic human experience which will enrich human life and multiply the possibilities of creative fulfillment. The choice is not between *either* capitalism *or* socialism but of *more* or *less* insofar as they bear upon the possibility of maximizing in each specific situation the opportunities of freedom. Socialism must today be conceived as a principle of welfare and fraternity integral to the democratization of culture on every level—economic, educational and social. It is democracy as a way of life. It relies on creative intelligence to conceive, modify or transform any or all institutions with one goal in view: the development of a community of free persons—each one different from the other and yet enjoying or respecting one another's differences."

By this time, the space ship which was to take me back to Earth had arrived, and Marx escorted me to the ectoplasmic gangplank. I told him that it was not likely that credence would be given to my report of our conversation. His last words to me were the sentence from Dante with which he completed the preface to his chief work: *"Segui il tuo corso, e lascia dir le genti—follow your own course and let people talk."*

The God that Failed: Arthur Koestler

No contemporary author has interpreted the Marxian philosophy with a greater personal sense of its meaning and appeal, and with a clearer awareness of its inner logic and ultimate outcome than Arthur Koestler. Although not a professional philosopher, Koestler was led to Marxism in his own desperate search for meaning in life. It became for him a faith that gave life purpose and direction for the seven years (1931–1938) during which he was a member of the Communist party. And since that time in half a dozen widely read books he has portrayed with marked insight the intellectual and spiritual struggles of the intelligent individual who seeks to understand and follow to its logical conclusion the Marxian philosophy and, through the work of the Communist party, to make this the dominant philosophy of our age.

In a brilliant novel, *Darkness at Noon* (1941), Koestler depicts the unsuccessful effort of a disillusioned Communist to make his philosophy consistent with the facts of experience. In *The Yogi and the Commissar* (1945) he examines the inescapable antithesis between the Marxian position and an essentially religious commitment in philosophy. In *The God That Failed* (1949), an autobiographical essay, he describes the personal experiences that first made the logic of the Marxian philosophy convincing, and then finally destroyed its hold upon him. There is no more penetrating analysis of the philosophical predicament of our age as it faces the rival claims of the Marxian position, on the one hand, and those of personal religion, on the other, than that in Koestler's essay, *The Yogi and the Commissar*. It is reprinted here in large part, as the concluding aspect of our *Search for Meaning in Life*.

Arthur Koestler was born in Budapest in 1905. His father was Hungarian, his mother Viennese. Until World War I the family was one of comfortable means, but in September 1914 their resources, like those of most other middle-class Europeans, were completely swept away. Koestler's father never recovered from this experience. In 1919 the family moved to Vienna, where they lived in straitened circumstances. During these years Koestler gained at first hand his knowledge of social tension and anxiety. When he was about twenty, he left Vienna and spent several years as a roving writer and newspaper correspondent in Palestine and the Near East. He became associated with the Ullstein chain of newspapers, which published one of the large, liberal Berlin papers. Later he moved to the Paris office of this firm and then to the home office in Berlin.

On December 31, 1931, Koestler joined the Communist party. After working for some time with the party organization in Berlin, during which time he lost his job with the Ullstein papers, he spent a year in Russia and there saw a new side of Communism. In 1936 he went to Spain as a Communist newspaper correspondent but was soon imprisoned by the Franco forces and narrowly missed being executed. A chance connection with a London newspaper brought about his unexpected release. In 1938, disillusioned by what he had learned through his experiences of Communist theory and practice, Koestler resigned from the Communist party. Living in England, he devotes himself to writing and lecturing.

Koestler's analysis of the way in which his own faith in the revolutionary Marxian philosophy developed is a revealing one. Its insights throw light upon experiences from which a man's deepest social and personal convictions derive.

A faith is not acquired by reasoning. One does not fall in love with a woman, or enter the womb of a church, as a result of logical persuasion. Reason may defend an act of faith—but only after the act has been committed, and the man committed to the act. Persuasion may play a part in a man's conversion; but only the part of bringing to its full and conscious climax a process which has been maturing in regions where no persuasion can penetrate. A faith is not acquired; it grows like a tree. Its crown points to the sky; its roots grow downward into the past and are nourished by the dark sap of the ancestral humus.

From the psychologist's point of view, there is little difference between a revolutionary and a traditionalist faith. All true faith is uncompromising, radical, purist; hence the true traditionalist is always a revolutionary zealot in conflict with pharisaian society, with the luke-warm corrupters of the creed. And vice-versa: the revolutionary's Utopia, which in appearance represents a complete break with the past, is always modeled on some image of the lost Paradise, of a legendary Golden Age. The classless Communist society, according to Marx and Engels, was to be a revival, at the end of the dialectical spiral, of the primitive Communist society which stood at its beginning. Thus all true faith involves a revolt against the believer's social environment, and the projection into the future of an ideal derived from the remote past. All Utopias are fed from mythology; the social engineer's blueprints are revised editions of the ancient text.

To the psychiatrist, both the craving for Utopia and the rebellion against the status quo are symptoms of social maladjustment. To the social reformer, both are symptoms of a healthy rational attitude. The psychiatrist is apt to forget that smooth adjustment to a deformed society creates deformed individuals. The reformer is equally apt to forget that hatred, even of the objectively hateful, does not produce that charity and justice on which a utopian society must be based.

It is also true that in the face of revolting injustice the only honorable attitude is to revolt, and to leave introspection for better times. But if we survey history and compare the lofty aims, in the name of which revolutions were started, and the sorry end to which they came, we see again and again how a polluted civilization pollutes its own revolutionary offspring.

Fitting the two half-truths—the sociologist's and the psychologist's—together, we conclude that if on the one hand oversensitivity to social injustice, and obsessional craving for Utopia are signs of neurotic maladjustment, society may, on the other hand, reach a state of decay where the neurotic rebel causes more joy in heaven than the sane executive who orders pigs to be drowned under the eyes of starving men. This in fact was the state of our civilization when, in December, 1931, at the age of twenty-six, I joined the Communist Party of Germany.[1]

[1] From the essay by Arthur Koestler in *The God That Failed,* edited by Richard Crossman. Copyright 1949 by Richard Crossman. By permission of Harper & Brothers.

The Yogi and the Commissar*

I. The Static Spectrum

I like to imagine an instrument which would enable us to break up patterns of social behaviour as the physicist breaks up a beam of rays. Looking through this sociological spectroscope we would see spread out under the diffraction grating the rainbow-coloured spectrum of all possible human attitudes to life. The whole distressing muddle would become neat, clear, and comprehensive.

On one end of the spectrum, obviously on the infra-red end, we would see the Commissar. The Commissar believes in Change from Without. He believes that all pests of humanity, including constipation and the Oedipus complex, can and will be cured by Revolution, that is, by a radical reorganization of the system of production and distribution of goods; that this end justifies the use of all means, including violence, ruse, treachery and poison; that logical reasoning is an unfailing compass and the Universe a kind of very large clockwork in which a very large number of electrons once set into motion will forever revolve in their predictable orbits; and that whosoever believes in anything else is an escapist. This end of the spectrum has the lowest frequency of vibrations and is, in a way, the coarsest component of the beam; but it conveys the maximum amount of heat.

On the other end of the spectrum,

where the waves become so short and of such high frequency that the eye no longer sees them, colourless, warmthless but all-permeating, crouches the Yogi, melting away in the ultra-violet. He has no objection to calling the universe a clockwork, but he thinks that it would be called, with about the same amount of truth, a musical-box or a fishpond. He believes that the End is unpredictable and that the Means alone count. He rejects violence under any circumstances. He believes that logical reasoning gradually loses its compass value as the mind approaches the magnetic pole of Truth or the Absolute which alone matters. He believes that nothing can be improved by exterior organization and everything by the individual effort from within; and that whosoever believes in anything else is an escapist. He believes that the debt-serviture imposed upon the peasants of India by the money lenders should be abolished not by financial legislation but by spiritual means. He believes that each individual is alone, but attached to the all-one by an invisible umbilical cord; that his creative forces, his goodness, trueness and usefulness can alone be nourished by the sap which reaches him through this cord; and that his only task during his earthly life is to avoid any action, emotion or thought which might lead to a breaking of the cord. This avoidance has to be maintained by a difficult, elaborate technique, the only kind of technique which he accepts.

Between these two extremes are spread out in a continuous sequence the spectral lines of the more sedate human attitudes. The

* Arthur Koestler, *The Yogi and the Commissar,* Copyright, 1945, by The Macmillan Company and used with their permission. Essay I.

more we approach its centre, the more does the spectrum become blurred and woolly. On the other hand, this increase of wool on the naked spectral bodies makes them look more decent, and intercourse with them more civilised. You cannot argue with a naked Commissar—he starts at once to beat his chest and next he strangles you, whether you be friend or foe, in his deadly embrace. You cannot argue with the ultra-violet skeleton either, because words mean nothing to him. You can argue with post-war planners, Fabians, Quakers, liberals and philanthropists. But the argument will lead nowhere, for the real issue remains between the Yogi and the Commissar, between the fundamental conceptions of Change from Without and Change from Within.

It is easy to say that all that is wanted is a synthesis—the synthesis between saint and revolutionary; but so far this has never been achieved. What has been achieved are various motley forms of compromise—the blurred intermediary bands of the spectrum —compromise but not synthesis. Apparently the two elements do not mix, and this may be one of the reasons why we have made such a mess of our History. The Commissar's emotional energies are fixed on the relation between individual and society, the Yogi's on the relation between the individual and the universe.

The Commissar's Dilemma. All attempts to change the nature of man by Commissar methods have so far failed, from Spartacus's Sun State through Inquisition and Reformation to Soviet Russia. This failure seems to be rooted in two disturbing phenomena. The first is the Antinomy of the Serpentine; the second the Antinomy of the Slopes.

The peak of Utopia is steep; the serpentine road which leads up to it has many tortuous curves. While you are moving up the road you never face the peak, your direction is the tangent, leading nowhere. If a great mass of people are pushing forward along the serpentine they will, according to the fatal laws of inertia, push their leader off the road and then follow him, the whole

movement flying off at the tangent into nowhere. That is what happened to most revolutionary movements, where the mass-impulse is strong and the inertia of the mass is converted into a violent centrifugal force. In the more cautious reformist movements, on the other hand, the momentum soon fades out and the ascending spiral first becomes a weary circling round and round the peak without gaining in height until it finally degenerates into a descending spiral; e.g., the Trade Unionist movement.

The second root of failure is the Antinomy of the Slopes, or of Ends and Means. Either the Means are subordinated to the End, or vice versa. Theoretically you may build up elaborate liberal or religious halfway houses; but if burdened with responsibility, and confronted with a practical decision to be taken, you have to choose one way or the other. Once you have chosen you are on the slope. If you have chosen to subordinate the Means to the End, the slope makes you slide down deeper and deeper on a moving carpet of common-sense propositions, for instance: the right of self-defence—the best defence is attack—increase of ruthlessness shortens the struggle, etc. Another well-known slope-pattern starts with the "Healer's Knife" and ends with the Moscow Purges. The fatal mechanism of this slope was already known to Pascal: Man is neither angel nor brute, and his misery is that he who would act the angel acts the brute.

The Yogi's Dilemma. The attempts to produce Change from Within on a mass-scale were equally unsuccessful. Whenever an attempt was made to organize saintliness by exterior means, the organizers were caught in the same dilemmas. The Inquisition flew off at a tangent; the Churches in the liberal era circle round and round the peak without gaining height. To subordinate the End to the Means leads to a slope as fatal as the inverse one. Gandhi's slope started with non-violence and made him gradually slide down to his present position [1942] of non-resistance to Japanese conquest: the Japanese might kill a few million Indians but some day they would get tired of it, and thus the moral integrity of India would be saved.

Obviously the prospects for the masses of common people are not brighter under this inverted Machiavellianism than under the leadership of the Commissars. One slope leads to the Inquisition and the Purges; the other to passive submission to bayoneting and raping; to villages without sewerage, septic childbeds and trachoma. The Yogi and the Commissar may call it quits.

II. The Spectrum in Motion

But they don't. Unable to form a synthesis and unsatisfied by the patched-up compromises in the medium bands of the spectrum, they attract and repel each other in rhythmical intervals. This strange minuet is one of the most exciting aspects of History which Marxism, otherwise the most serviceable guide, falls short of explaining.

Under certain historic climates mass-migrations start from one end of the spectrum to the other, general displacements from infra-red to ultra-violet or vice versa, like mighty trade winds travelling over the seas. The nineteenth century brought such a general displacement towards the Commissar or infra-red end. The present climate favours the opposite direction. Since the early 'thirties we are all travelling, more or less consciously, more or less willingly, towards the ultra-violet end.

* * * * *

In a sense spiritual life can be defined as the training for the acceptance of death; the Commissar is the human type least advanced in this training and yet by force of circumstances most advanced towards its aims. Indeed the Commissar can be defined as the human type which has completely severed relations to the subconscious. This is the more remarkable as the constant danger under which he lives—I think Lenin used the phrase "We are dead men on furlough"—is a constant temptation to communicate with those forbidden zones. In fact he is condemned to live in a permanent state of re-pressed puberty. While in a normal curriculum the great crisis of adolescence, the confrontation with the tragic and insoluble problems of existence occurs only once—a limited process, like teething—the revolutionary spends all his life in this tropical climate, and those tragic problems remain his daily bread and butter. The ordinary citizen, once the transcendental teething is over, evolves a smooth *modus vivendi* towards the absolute; the best the Commissar can hope is to find a smooth *modus moriendi*.

Yet though living in a climate of perpetual adolescence, his behaviour is as unadolescent, unecstatic and unromantic as can be imagined. One has the feeling that his subconscious has been dealt with not on the analyst's sofa but on the surgeon's table by the amputating knife. In fact one of his often recurring problems is not to give himself away by sleep-talking or other subconscious automatisms; and if he is a good Commissar he succeeds. He is a marvel of unneurotic repression: one of the most admirable achievements of the human species.

Now if life becomes impossible without pity, it is perhaps equally impossible without a grain of self-pity. The Commissar is not immune against suffering, but what he experiences is more the echo of pain than pain itself, like the aching of an amputated limb. He compels admiration, but also pity—that tender pity which the weak sometimes feel for the strong. Faced with giant figures like Blanqui, Luxemburg, Vera Figner, we can do nothing but shut up and realize what futile, frivolous dwarfs we are; yet pity remains.

That this instinct is justified becomes apparent when the Commissar faces the crisis of his life. This is a tragic and complicated process, often misunderstood. The forms it may take vary individually, but basically it is always the same; it is the revenge of the amputated organ. In a story of Gerard de Nerval's, which I remember only vaguely, a judge sentences a thief to have his hand cut off; the amputated hand then pursues the judge and finally strangles him. In the Commissar's case judge and victim are one person and the cut off organ is not a hand; it is, if we examine it closer, the Yogi's umbilical cord, his means of communication with the Absolute, with the "Oceanic Feeling," to use Freud's sober term. The Commissar lived in the conviction that it was a luxury organ, but when the crisis comes he realizes that it is not. The Man-Society connection suddenly proves to be not enough to procure psychic metabolism; the Man-Universe connection has to be re-established.

At this point one of two things might happen. Either the cut connection is re-established, and as an act of atonement the Man-Society connection is broken off; this is the classical case of the Revolutionary turning into a Mystic, the total jump from Commissar to Yogi. Or the connection is *not* re-established—then the dead cord coils up and strangles its owner. This is the equally classical case of the ex-revolutionaries whose souls died of suffocation.

Unfortunately we have as yet no scientific terminology to describe these processes, which are of vital importance for the understanding of the "subjective factor" in History. Hence the more soberly one tries to describe them the more vague imagery one has, *faute de mieux,* to use. The enormous literature of the three main contemporary schools in psychology contains not a single case history of this conversion, the revolutionary's tranformation into a cynic or mystic, whereas history, past and present, abounds in examples. Jung comes nearest to the question: his interpretation of the subconscious bears most resemblance to the "umbilical cord," but he prefers to study its effects on the most unsuitable human type, the wealthy middle-aged Babbitts. And this for good reason: were he to choose his patients among the type which inhabits the German or Russian concentration camps, his therapy would not only prove to be inadequate but he would have to introduce so many new determining factors into his system that both his terminology and his *Weltanschauung* would go to blazes. The Commissar's special displacements are *terra nova* for the psychologist.

Turning to the more muddled, intermediary bands of the spectrum we find that their reactions to the mystic current are of a revealing nature. In the pink regions the reaction first manifests itself by an intense consciousness of the Left's serial defeats, of disgust with the old parties, disgust with their worn-out leaders, with plans and promises, ideas and ideals, and most of all with one's own foolish and frustrated hopes. This pink hangover is the emotional starting point. Next comes the realization that "there must have been something basically wrong in our approach to the Masses." Next to this the discovery that on the very point where they failed— activation of the masses—fascism was horribly successful. Now the feeling which success inspires in the unsuccessful is envy. If we look at things closely we find indeed that the pink attitude to fascism is envy rather than hatred.

III. *The Pendulum*

In the critical years of the Weimar Republic, when a communist or fascist revolution seemed equally possible and the only impossibility the continuation of the worn-out regime, a certain Ernst Juenger coined the phrase of the "anti-capitalistic nostalgia of the masses." This vague but violent longing was indeed shared by groups of people of otherwise very different tendencies. Perhaps the common denominator we are looking for can best be described as an "anti-materialistic nostalgia." It is allergic to the rationalism, the shallow optimism, the ruthless logic, the arrogant self-assurance, the Promethean attitude of the nineteenth century; it is attracted by mysticism, romanticism, the irrational values, by mediaeval twilight. In short it is moving towards the very things from which the last-but-one great spectral displacement towards the infra-red has moved away. Apparently these movements have a pendular rhythm.

The swinging of this pendulum from rationalistic to romantic periods and back is not contradictory to the conception of a basic dialectic movement of history. They are like the tidal waves on a river which yet flows into the sea. One of the fatal lacunae in the Marxist interpretation of history is that it was concerned only with the course of the river, not with the waves. The mass-psychological aspect of Nazism is not describable in Marxist terms, in terms of the river's course; we need the tidal waves to account for it. On the other hand our pendulum alone is no guide to history. We must know about the river before we talk of the waves.

Perhaps it is not too hazardous to assume that these pendular changes in the mass-psychological spectrum are a process analogous to the rhythmical change of waking and sleep in the individual. The irrational or romantic periods of mass-psychology are periods of sleep and dream. The dreams are not necessarily peaceful; more often they are nightmares; but without these periodic plunges into the subconscious the vital juices would not be provided for the next wide-awake Promethean or Commissar period. Perhaps every Gothic period is followed by a Renaissance period and they are but the succession of Yoga-night and Commissar-days in the curriculum of the race. And perhaps this, our present civilization, is not dying, only sleepy.

INDEX

Index